ERISA
Text of the Law As Amended Through 1982

ERISA
Text of the Law As Amended Through 1982

Edited by

Kathleen D. Gill
Managing Editor
Pension Reporter and Employee Benefits Cases

The Bureau of National Affairs, Inc., Washington, D.C.

Copyright © 1984
The Bureau of National Affairs, Inc.
Washington, D.C. 20037

Second Printing August 1983
Third Printing May 1984

Library of Congress Cataloging in Publication Data

United States.
    ERISA: text of the law as amended through 1982.

    1. Pension trusts—Law and legislation—United States.
I. Gill, Kathleen D. II. Bureau of National Affairs
(Washington, D.C.) III. Title. IV. Title: E.R.I.S.A.
KF3512.A315G54 1983   344.73'01252
ISBN 0-87179-385-7   347.3041252   82-22789

Printed in the United States of America
International Standard Book Number: 0-87179-385-7

CONTENTS

Introduction vii

Part I   Conference Reports

Joint Explanatory Statement of the Committee of
    Conference on ERISA 1
Report of the Committee of Conference on MPPAA 111
Selected Explanatory Statements Made During House
    and Senate Floor Debate on MPPAA 114
Excerpts From the Joint Explanatory Statement of the
    Committee of Conference on ERTA 141
Excerpts From the Joint Explanatory Statement of the
    Committee of Conference on TEFRA 152

Part II   Text of ERISA

ERISA Finding List 176
Employee Retirement Income Security Act of
    1974, as Amended 182

Part III   IRC Excerpts

IRC Finding List 364
Pertinent Sections of the Internal Revenue Code 367

INTRODUCTION

The Employee Retirement Income Security Act was signed into law by President Gerald Ford September 2, 1974, after years of deliberation and intensive debate. The first major major changes in the law were enacted September 29, 1980, when President Jimmy Carter signed the Multiemployer Pension Plan Amendments Act of 1980. MPPAA also was the product of lengthy debate.

Although ERISA itself remained virtually untouched for six years, a number of changes affecting pension and benefit plans were enacted through various tax laws that amended the qualified plan provisions of the Internal Revenue Code.

In 1981, a series of savings incentives bills were introduced in Congress. Proposals were made to raise the limits on deductible contributions to individual retirement accounts and Keogh plans, encourage the adoption of employee stock ownership plans, and change the tax treatment of stock options. The retirement plan proposals and other savings incentive provisions eventually were consolidated, and in August 1981 President Ronald Reagan signed the Economic Recovery Tax Act.

Then, in May 1982, a bill was introduced in the House to reduce the contribution and benefit limits for qualified corporate plans, modify the rules for integration with Social Security, tighten the rules for loans from plans to key employees, and limit the estate tax exclusion for retirement annuities paid to beneficiaries, among other changes in the pension tax area.

Despite opposition from the pension industry, those proposals were modified and rolled into a revenue raising package introduced in an attempt to reduce budget deficits. The revenue package became the Tax Equity and Fiscal Responsibility Act of 1982, and was approved by Congress and signed by President Reagan in August of that year, only a few short months after it was first introduced.

The material that follows includes the text of conference reports and other relevant documents on ERISA (PL 93-406), MPPAA (PL 96-363), ERTA (PL 97-34), and TEFRA (PL 97-248). It also includes the text of ERISA, as amended by MPPAA and various other laws, and the text of pertinent sections of the Internal Revenue Code, as amended through January 1983, when President Reagan signed the Technical Corrections Act (PL 97-448).

Part I Conference Reports

JOINT EXPLANATORY STATEMENT OF THE COMMITTEE OF CONFERENCE ON ERISA

The managers on the part of the House and the Senate at the conference on the disagreeing votes of the two Houses on the amendments of the Senate to the bill (H.R. 2) to provide for pension reform, submit the following joint statement to the House and the Senate in explanation of the effect of the action agreed upon by the managers and recommended in the accompanying conference report:

The Senate struck out all of the House bill after the enacting clause and inserted a substitute amendment. The conference has agreed to a substitute for both the Senate amendment and the House bill. The statement following the table of contents explains the principal differences between the substitute agreed to in conference and the House and Senate bills.

I. Reporting and Disclosure (Secs. 101-111 of the Bill)

The House bill requires annual reporting of detailed financial and actuarial data and comprehensive plan descriptions to the Secretary of Labor, and disclosure of more limited data to the participants. The financial and actuarial data filed with the Secretary of Labor are required to be in the form of a conventional audited financial statement prepared by a qualified accountant and a certified actuarial statement prepared by an enrolled actuary.

The Senate bill requires submission of comparable financial and actuarial data and plan descriptions to both the Secretary of Labor and participants. Like the House bill, actuarial data is required to be certified by an enrolled actuary. Unlike the House bill, all reports were required to be submitted on forms promulgated by the Secretary. The conference substitute is described below. In general, the substitute combines the rules of both the House and Senate bill.

The conference substitute adopts the reporting format contained in both the House and Senate bills. Each plan (unless exempted) is to be required to report annually to the Secretary of Labor certain financial and actuarial data. In addition to these reports, each plan will be required to have prepared an audited financial statement and defined benefit plans must have a certified actuarial report. Special reports are also required at the time of plan terminations.

The Secretary of Labor is given the authority to prescribe forms for reports to him (other than the audited financial statement and certified actuarial report) paralleling similar authority already available to the Secretary of Treasury. The two Secretaries are to unify, to the extent feasible, the reports made to them and it is expected that all of the material subject to the form authority of either Secretary, comprising the annual reports to be made by a plan, can and should be reported on a single form.

Plans Subject to the Provisions and Exemptions

Under the conference substitute, the new reporting and disclosure requirements are to be administered by the Secretary of Labor and are to be applied to all pension and welfare plans established or maintained by an employer or employee organization engaged in, or affecting, interstate commerce. Governmental plans, certain church plans, workmen's compensation and unemployment compensation plans, plans maintained outside the United States for the benefit of persons substantially all of whom are nonresident aliens, and so-called excess benefit plans, which provide benefits in addition to those for which deductions may be taken under the tax laws, are exempted from the requirements. The Secretary of Labor also is authorized to waive and modify certain of these requirements for employee benefit plans.

1

All plans of the types subject to the reporting and disclosure provisions are to be required to file an annual report with the Secretary of Labor regardless of the number of participants involved. However, simplified reports may be authorized for plans with fewer than 100 participants.

Contents of Annual Report

The annual report generally is to include audited financial statements for both welfare plans and pension plans. With respect to welfare plans the statement is to include a statement of assets and liabilities, a statement of changes in fund balance, and a statement of changes in financial position. With respect to employee pension plans the statement is to include a statement of assets and liabilities and a statement of changes in net assets available for plan benefits, including details as to revenues and expenses and other changes aggregated by general source and application.

In the notes to the annual financial statement, the accountant is to disclose any significant changes in the plan, material lease commitments and contingent liabilities, any agreements and transactions with persons known to be parties-in-interest, information as to whether a tax ruling or determination letter has been obtained, and any other relevant matters necessary to fairly present the financial status of the plan. In addition, in he case of employee pension plans the notes should also deal with funding policy (including policy with respect to prior service costs and changes in such policies during the year). An accountant may rely on the correctness of any actuarial matter certified by any enrolled actuary if the accountant indicates his reliance on such certification.

In addition to the audited financial statement, the annual report is to include for all employee benefit plans a statement on separate schedules showing among other things, a statement of plan assets and liabilities aggregated by categories, a statement of receipts and disbursements, a schedule of all assets held for investment purposes aggregated and identified by issuer, borrower, or lessee and a schedule of each transaction involving a person known to be a party-in-interest. Also, a schedule of all loans and leases in default at the end of the year or which are classified during the year as uncollectible is to be included in the annual report.

There is also to be supplied with the annual report a schedule listing each transaction which exceeds 3 percent of the value of the fund. If some or all of the assets of a plan are held in a common or collective trust maintained by a bank or similar institution the annual report is to include the most recent annual statement of assets and liabilities of the common or collective trust. (The Secretary of Labor will have authority to prescribe for the filing of a master copy of the annual statement of this common or collective trust in order to avoid duplicative filings of this statement by plans participating in this common or collective trust.)

With respect to persons employed by the plan the annual report is to include the name and address of each fiduciary, the name of each person who receives more than minimal compensation from the plan for services rendered, along with the amount of compensation (or who performs duties which are not ministerial), the nature of the services, and the relationship to the employer or any other party in interest to the plan. Also, the reasons for any changes in trustees, accountant, actuary, investment manager, or administrator are to be provided in the annual report.

As indicated in the discussion of the funding provisions, under the conference agreement, the annual report is to include an actuarial statement for all pension plans which are subject to the funding requirements of title I. If plan benefits are purchased from, and guaranteed by, an insurance company, the annual report is to include the premiums paid, benefits paid, charges for administrative expenses, commissions and other information. The insurance carrier is to certify to the plan administrator the information needed to comply with the annual reporting requirements within 120 days after the close of the plan year, or within such other period as is prescribed by the Secretary of Labor.

The annual report for a plan is to be filed within 210 days after the close of the plan year or within such period of time as the Secretary of Labor may require in order to reduce the necessity for duplicate filing with the Internal Revenue Service. The Secretary of Labor may reject the filing of an annual report if he finds that it is incomplete or there is a material qualification in the accountant's or actuary's opinion. If a revised report is not submitted within 45 days after rejection, the Secretary may retain an accountant to perform an audit, or retain an actuary, whichever is appropriate, or bring a civil action for legal or equitable relief. The plan is to bear the costs of any expenses of an audit or actuarial report.

Accountant and Actuary Reports

Every plan is to retain on behalf of its participants an independent qualified public accountant who annually is to prepare an audited financial statement of the plan's operations. The accountant is to give an opinion as to whether the financial statements of the plan conform with generally accepted accounting principles and the statement is to be based upon an examination in accordance with generally accepted auditing standards. An accountant's opinion is not to be required for statements prepared by banks or similar institutions or an insurance carrier if the statements of the bank or insurance carrier are certified by the bank and are made part of an annual report. For purposes of this provision a qualified public accountant includes certified public accountants, licensed public accountants and any person certified by the Secretary as a qualified public accountant in accordance with regulations published by him for a person who practices in a State where there is no certification or licensing procedure for accountants. Further, to the extent a plan is not required to make an annual report to the Secretary of Labor an annual audit is not required (and an independent, qualified public accountant need not be retained). Also the Secretary of Labor may waive the requirement of an audited financial statement in cases where simplified annual reports are permitted to be filed.

Every plan subject to the funding requirements of title I must retain an enrolled actuary who is to prepare an actuarial statement on an annual basis. This statement is to show the present value of all plan liabilities for nonforfeitable pension benefits allocated by the termination priority categories. The actuary is to supply a statement to be filed with the annual report as to his opinion as to whether the actuarial statements of the plan are reasonably related to the experience of the plan and to the reasonable expectations of the plan. The actuary is to use assumptions and techniques as are necessary to form an opinion as to whether the contents of the matters upon which he reports are in the aggregate reasonably related to the experience of the plan and to reasonable expectations, and represent his best estimate of anticipated experience under the plan. The actuarial statement is not required for plans which need not file annual reports, and may be waived by the Secretary of Labor for plans for which simplified annual reports are allowed.

Reports on Termination

In addition to the annual reports which must be filed with the Secretary of Labor, special terminal reports are required to be filed for pension plans that are winding up their affairs. These terminal reports may also be required by the Secretary of Labor for welfare plans. Also in the year a plan is terminated the Secretary may require the supplementary information to be filed with the annual report.

Disclosure to Participants

Each administrator of an employee benefit plan is to furnish to each participant and to each beneficiary a summary plan description written in a manner calculated to be understood by the average plan participant or beneficiary. The summary is to include important plan provisions, names and addresses of persons responsible for plan investment or management, a description of benefits, the circumstances that may result in disqualification or ineligibility and the procedures to be followed in presenting claims for benefits under the plan.

Summary plan descriptions are to be furnished to participants within the later of 120 days after the plan is established or 90 days after an individual becomes a participant. Updated plan descriptions are also to be provided to participants every five years thereafter where there have been plan amendments in the interim; in any case, a new description is to be provided every ten years. Also, participants are to receive descriptions of material changes in a plan within 210 days after the end of any plan year in which a material change occurs. Also, the annual report and plan documents are to be available for examination by participants or beneficiaries at the principal office of the plan administrator and such other places as is necessary to provide reasonable access to these reports and documents. Thus, if the participants covered under the plan are employed in more than one geographic area, each geographic area is to have available for examination the required documents. Each participant is also to be furnished a copy within 210 days after the close of the plan year of the schedule of plan assets and liabilities and receipts and disbursements as submitted with the annual report, including any other material which is necessary to thoroughly summarize the latest annual report. Upon a written request, a plan administrator is to furnish a participant or beneficiary a complete copy of the comprehensive plan description, the latest annual report and other instruments under which the plan is established and operated. The plan administrator may charge a reasonable amount for fulfilling such a request.

Upon the request of a plan participant or beneficiary, a plan administrator is to furnish on the basis of the latest available information the total benefits accrued and the nonforfeitable pension benefit rights, if any, which have accrued. No more than one request may be made by any participant or beneficiary for this information during any one 12-month period.

A copy of the statement of the deferred vested benefits in the plan for individuals who have terminated employment during a plan year which is furnished to the Social Security Administration also is to be furnished to the individual participant.

Reports Made Public Information

The contents of the descriptions of plans and reports filed with the Secretary of Labor are to be public information and are to be available for inspection in the Department of Labor. In addition, the Secretary of Labor may use the information and data for statistical and research purposes and for the compiling and publishing of studies as he may deem appropriate. However, information with respect to a plan participant's accrued benefits and nonforfeitable pension rights is to be disclosed only to the extent that information respecting a participant's benefits for old age retirement insurance may be disclosed under the Social Security Act.

Forms to Be Provided

The Secretary of Labor may require that any information required to be filed with the Labor Department, including statements and schedules attached to the annual report, must be submitted on forms that he may prescribe. The financial statement prepared by the independent qualified accountant and the actuarial statement prepared by the enrolled actuary and the summary of the plan description are not required to be submitted on forms. However, the Secretary may prescribe the format and content of the accountant's and actuary's statements and of the summary plan description, the summary annual report, and other statements or reports required under title I to be furnished or made available to participants and beneficiaries.

Effective Dates

The conference agreement provides that the reporting and disclosure provisions generally are to take effect on January 1, 1975. However, in the case of a fiscal year plan year which begins before January 1, 1975, and ends after December 31, 1974, the Secretary of Labor may by regulation postpone the effective date until the beginning of the first plan year of the plan which begins after January 1, 1975.

II. Participation and Coverage (Secs. 201, 202, and 1011 of the Bill and Secs. 401 and 410 of the Internal Revenue Code)

The House bill provides that an employee cannot be excluded from a plan on account of age or service if the employee is at least 25 years old and has had at least one year of service, or, if he has three years of service, the employee cannot be excluded even though he is not yet 25. The 1-year service requirement (for employees 25 and older) may be extended to 3 years if the plan provides full and immediate vesting for all participants. Under the Senate amendment, an employee cannot be excluded on account of age or service if he has attained age 30 with 1 year of service.

The conference substitute is described below. In general, the substitute follows the rules of the House bill in this area with respect to technical matters.

Plans Subject to the Provisions

Under title I of the conference substitute (the labor law provisions) the new participation and coverage rules are to be enforced by the Secretary of Labor when participants bring violations to his attention or when cases come to his attention which initially were under consideration by the Secretary of Treasury on which he has previously initiated action. The rules are to apply to employee pension benefit plans of employers or employee organizations established in or affecting interstate commerce. Under this title II (the tax law provisions), the participation and coverage rules are to be administered by the Secretary of the Treasury or his delegate, and the rules apply to tax-qualified pension, profit-sharing, and stock bonus plans.[1]

Exceptions to Coverage

The participation and coverage requirements of title I (the labor law provisions) do not apply to governmental plans (including Railroad Retirement Act plans), church plans (except those electing coverage), plans maintained solely to comply with workmen's unemployment, disability, or compensation laws, plans maintained outside the United States primarily for the benefit of nonresident aliens, employee welfare plans, excess plans (which provide for benefits or contributions in excess of those allowable for tax-qualified plans), unfunded deferred compensation arrangements, plans established by labor organizations (those referred to in sec. 501(c)(5) of the Internal Revenue Code) which do not provide for employer contributions after the date of enactment, and fraternal or other plans of organizations (described in sec. 501(c)(8), 501(c)(9)) which do not receive employer contributions, or trusts described in 501(c)(18) of the Internal Revenue Code. Title I does not apply to buy-out agreements involving retiring or deceased partners (under sec. 736 of the Internal Revenue Code). In addition, title I does not apply to employer or union-sponsored individual retirement accounts (see "Employee Savings for Retirement").

The participation requirements of title II apply only to plans which qualify for certain tax deferral privileges by meeting the standards as to participation and other matters set forth in the Internal Revenue laws. However, governmental plans and

---

[1] The division of administrative responsibility between Labor and Treasury is discussed in Part XII, below "General Provisions Relating to Jurisdiction, Administration, Enforcement: Joint Pension Task Force, Etc." Except where otherwise noted, the regulations with respect to participation, vesting and funding are to be written by the Secretary of the Treasury or his delegate.

church plans which do not elect to come under the new provisions will nevertheless be treated as qualified for purposes of the tax deferral privileges for the employees, if they meet the requirements of present law. Also the rules do not apply to plans of labor organizations (described in sec. 501(c)(5)) or fraternal or other organizations (described in sec. 501(c)(8) or (9)) which do not provide for employer contributions.

Exemption for Church Plans

As indicated above, both title I and title II exempt church plans from the participation and coverage requirements of the conference substitute (although title II requires these plans to comply with present law in order to be qualified). This exemption does not apply to a plan which is primarily for the benefit of employees engaged in an unrelated trade or business, or (except as noted below) to a multiemployer plan unless all of the participating employers are churches or conventions or associations of churches (rather than merely church-related agencies). However, a multiemployer plan which was in existence on January 1, 1974, and which covers church-related agencies (such as schools and hospitals) is to be treated as a church plan for purposes of the exemption (even though it continues to cover those agencies) for plan years beginning before January 1, 1983, but not for subsequent plan years.

A church plan may make an irrevocable election to be covered under title I and title II (in a form and manner to be prescribed in regulations). A plan which makes this election is to be covered under the bill for purposes of the new participation, vesting, funding and form of benefit rules, as well as the fiduciary and disclosure rules and will also be covered under the plan termination insurance provisions.

General Rule as to Participation

Generally, under title I and title II of the conference substitute, an employee cannot be excluded from a plan on account of age or service if he is at least 25 years old and has had at least one year of service. However, if the plan provides full and immediate vesting for all participants, it may require employees to be age 25, with 3 years of service, in order to participate. As an alternative, any plan which is maintained exclusively for employees of a governmental or tax-exempt educational organization which provides full and immediate vesting for all participants may have a participation requirement of age 30, with 1 year of service.

Maximum Age Requirement

Under the conference substitute, in general, a plan may not exclude an employee because he is too old. However, because of cost factors, it was decided that in a defined benefit plan it would be appropriate to permit the exclusion of an employee who is within 5 years of attaining normal retirement age under the plan (or older) when he is first employed. (These employees would be counted as part of the employer's work force, however, for purposes of determining whether or not his plan satisfied the breadth-of-coverage requirements.) Of course, if a plan defines normal retirement age as the later of age 65, or the tenth anniversary of the employee's participation in the plan, the plan could not impose a maximum age requirement (because no employee would be within 5 years of normal retirement age when first employed). A "target benefit" plan, as defined in Treasury regulations, could also impose a maximum age requirement (even though it is not a defined benefit plan), because in many respects the pattern of costs and benefits of target benefit plans closely resembles the pattern of costs and benefits of defined benefit plans.

Year of Service Defined

Under the conference substitute, in general, for purposes of the participation requirements, the term "year of service" means a 12-month period during which the employee has worked at least 1,000 hours. This 12-month period is measured from the date when the employee enters service. Thus, the employee has fulfilled his 1,000-hour-requirement if he has 1,000 hours of work by the first anniversary date of his employment. Under the substitute, the employee (if age 25 or older) would then be admitted to the plan within 6 months of his anniversary date of employment or by the beginning of the first plan year following his first anniversary date, whichever occurred earlier. (Of course, this does not mean that an employee would have to be admitted to the plan if he were lawfully excluded for reasons other than age or service.)

The plan would not be required to admit the employee if he had "separated from the service" before the otherwise applicable admission date. In general, "separated from the service" means the employee was discharged or quit; it does not mean temporary absence due to vacation, sickness, strike, seasonal layoff, etc.

If the employee did not complete 1,000 hours of service by his first anniversary date, but is still employed, he would start over toward meeting his 1,000 hour requirement. For this purpose, the plan could provide (on a consistent basis) that the relevant 12-month period is either (a) the year between his first anniversary date and his second anniversary date, or (b) the first plan year which began after the individual was first employed. For example, assume the plan is on a calendar year basis, and that an employee begins work on July 1, 1976. Between July 1, 1976, and June 30, 1977, the employee has less than 1,000 hours of service. The plan could provide that the employee would be tested the second time for purposes of participation based on the year from July 1, 1977 through June 30, 1978, or based on the year from January 1, 1977 through December 31, 1977 (but not January 1, 1978 through December 31, 1978).

The regulations with respect to "year of service" are to be written by the Secretary of Labor for purposes of participation and vesting. The term "hour of service" will also be defined in Labor Department regulations.

For purposes of participation (and vesting), in the case of any maritime industry (as defined in Labor Department regulations), 125 days of service are to be treated as the equivalent of 1,000 hours of service, but this rule will not apply to other industries.

Seasonal and Part-time Workers

In general, the 1,000 hour standard is to apply for purposes of determining whether or not an employee may be excluded from the plan as a seasonal or part-time employee (replacing the 5-month year, 20-hour week standard now in the Internal Revenue Code). However, in the case of seasonal industries where the customary period of employment is less than 1,000 hours, the term "year of service" is to be determined in accordance with Labor Department regulations.

Breaks in Service

Under the conference substitute, a 1-year break in service occurs in any calendar year, plan year, or other consecutive 12-month period designated by the plan on a consistent basis (and not prohibited under Labor Department regulations) in which the employee has 500 hours of service or less.

The general rule is that all service with the employer (pre-break and post-break) is to be taken into account for purposes of determining whether the employee has met the participation requirements. However, if an employee has a 1-year break in service, the plan may require a 1-year waiting period before reentry, at which point the employee's pre-break and post-break service are to be aggregated, and the employee is to receive full credit for the waiting period service. For example, if the plan is on a calendar year basis, and an employee who has a 1-year break in service reenters employment on November 1, 1976, works 200 hours in 1976, and 1700 hours by November 1, 1977, the employee under this provision would be considered as reentering the plan for 1977. As a result, his pre-break and post-break service would be aggregated, and he would advance one year on the vesting schedule for 1977. He would also accrue benefits for that year. (Other rules with respect to break-in-service are explained below in connection with vesting and benefit accrual.)

In the case of a plan which has a 3-year service requirement for participation (because the plan provides 100 percent immediate vesting), the plan may provide that employees who have a 1-year break in service before completing their 3-year service requirement must start over toward fulfilling that requirement after the break in service.

Eligibility — Collective-bargaining Units, Air Pilots

Title II of the conference substitute provides that employees who are under a collective bargaining agreement can be excluded for purposes of the breadth-of-coverage requirements (coverage for 70 percent of all employees or 80 percent of all eligible employees if at least 70 percent of all employees are eligible to benefit under the plan, or coverage on a nondiscriminatory basis), if the employees are excluded from the plan and there is evidence that retirement benefits have been the subject of good-faith bargaining. However, if the union employees are covered under the plan, benefits or contributions must be provided for them on a nondiscriminatory basis.

Title II of the substitute provides another exception to the breadth-of-coverage rule. It provides that air pilots represented in accordance with the Railway Labor Act may bargain separately for tax-qualified employee plan benefits, without including other workers within the industry (but only in the case of a plan which covers no employees other than air pilots). In addition, the conferees intend that the joint congressional pension task force study group, created under this legislation, study this area to see whether a similar rule should be applied to other unions or professional groups in the future.

Nonresident Aliens

Title II of the conference substitute provides that employees who are nonresident aliens with no United States income from the employer in question are to be excluded for purposes of applying the breadth-of-coverage requirements and for purposes of applying the antidiscrimination rules (whether or not they are covered under the plan).

Predecessor Employer

Service with a predecessor employer must be counted for purposes of the plan if the successor employer continues to maintain the plan of the predecessor employer (and, of course, the successor employer cannot evade this requirement by nominally discontinuing the plan). The question of the extent to which such service must be counted in other circumstances is to be determined under regulations.

Multiemployer Plans

Under the conference substitute, service with any employer who is a member of a multiemployer plan is to be counted for purposes of the plan. The term "multiemployer plan" means a plan maintained pursuant to a collective bargaining agreement, to which more than one employer is required to contribute, and to which no one employer makes as much as 50 percent of the contributions. (This percentage test would become a 75-percent test once the plan qualifies as a multiemployer plan.) Also, the plan must provide that benefits will be payable to each participant, even though his employer subsequently ceases to make contributions under the plan. However, the plan would not be required to provide past service benefits, i.e., benefits for periods before the participant's employer entered the plan. Also, service during a period for which the employer was not a member of the plan would not be required to be counted for participation or vesting purposes.

Additional requirements relating to multiemployer plans may be prescribed in Department of Labor regulations. The conferees intend that a plan not be classified as a multiemployer plan unless it is a collectively bargained plan to which a substantial number of unaffiliated employers are required to contribute. Also, a plan is not to be classified as a multiemployer plan where there is no substantial business purpose in having a multiemployer plan (except to obtain the advantages of multiemployer plan status under this bill).

In addition to employees of employers making contributions to a multiemployer plan, under the conference substitute such a plan may cover employees of labor unions which negotiated the multiemployer plan and employees of the plan itself. For this purpose, the plan would have to satisfy the general breadth-of-coverage and nondiscrimination requirements of the Internal Revenue Code separately with respect to these union or plan employees and collectively (i.e. with respect to all groups of employees covered under the plan), but would not be required to meet the exclusive benefit rules of the tax law. Instead, the exclusive benefit rules would be applied to the beneficiaries of the multiemployer plan as a whole. (Similar treatment for union employees or plan employees would also be available in the case of a single-employer collectively bargained plan.)

H.R. 10 Plans

In general, the provisions of present law which allow a 3-year service requirement for participation (but do not allow the plan to impose an age requirement), and require 100 percent immediate vesting, would continue to govern owner-employee H.R. 10 plans (those for sole proprietors and 10 percent owners and their employees). However, certain provisions of this bill, such as the rules with respect to year of service and breaks in service are also to apply for purposes of the H.R. 10 plans.

Affiliated Employers

Title II of the conference substitute provides that in applying the breadth-of-coverage and antidiscrimination rules (as well as the vesting rules and the limitations on contributions and benefits), employees of all corporations who are members of a "controlled group of corporations" (within the meaning of sec. 1563(a) of the Internal Revenue Code of 1954) are to be treated as if they were employees of the same corporation. A comparable rule is to be provided in the case of partnerships and proprietorships which are under common control (as determined under regulations). The conferees agree with the interpretation of these provisions, as expressed in the Ways and Means Committee report (No. 93-807).

Effective Dates [2]

Under the conference substitute the changes made in the bill with respect to participation and vesting are to apply to new plans in plan years beginning after the date of enactment. For plans in existence on January 1, 1974, the general effective date of these provisions is to be plan years beginning after December 31, 1975.

The general effective date of plan years beginning after December 31, 1975 applies in the case of collectively bargained plans in the same manner as in the case of other plans. However, in order that the opening up of the contract to comply with the requirements of this bill will not require negotiations with respect to other matters, the conference substitute provides that a collective barbaining contract, in existence on January 1, 1974, which does not expire until after the general effective date for existing plans, may be reopened solely for the purpose of allowing the plan to meet the requirements of this bill, without having to be opened for any other purpose. Where it is necessary, as a result of this bill, to modify an employee benefit plan, it is the conferees' understanding that it is not an unfair labor practice under the National Labor Relations Act for a party to a collective bargaining agreement to refuse to bargain re-

---

[2] Because of the interrelationship of the effective date provisions for participation and vesting, this discussion deals with the effective dates for both.

garding matters unrelated to the modification required by this bill, provided this refusal is not otherwise an unfair labor practice. In addition, the changes required to be made in a plan are not themselves to be treated as constituting the expiration of a contract for purposes of any other provisions of this bill which depend on the date of the expiration of a contract.

Finally, the conference substitute provides that if a plan, adopted pursuant to a collective bargaining agreement in effect on January 1, 1974, contains a clause: (1) which provides supplementary benefits which are in the form of a lifetime annuity and refer to not more than one-third of the basic benefit to which the employees generally are entitled; or (2) which provides that a 25-year service employee is to be treated as a 30-year service employee, if that right is granted by a contractual agreement which is based on medical evidence as to the effects of working in an adverse environment for an extended period of time (such as workers in foundries or workers in asbestos plants), then the application of the accrued benefit provision of this bill to those benefits is to be delayed until the expiration of the collective bargaining agreement (but no later than plan years beginning after December 31, 1980). For purposes of applying the effective date rules, the conferees agree with the statement appearing in the paragraph beginning at the bottom of page 51, and in the first full paragraph on page 52 of the Ways and Means Committee report (No. 93-807). This explanation relates to situations where a collective bargaining agreement is to be treated as having terminated, and as to how the effective date rules are to be applied to a plan which includes some employees covered under one or more collective bargaining agreements, and also employees not covered under any such agreement.

An existing plan which would be entitled to a delayed participation vesting, funding, etc. provision is to be permitted to elect to have all those provisions apply sooner. Any such election is to be made under regulations, must apply with respect to all the provisions of the Act, and is to be irrevocable.

III. Vesting and Related Rules (Secs. 203-209, 1012, 1015, 1021, 1022, and 3032 of the Bill, and Secs. 401, 411, and 414 of the Internal Revenue Code.)

Under the House bill a plan was required to meet one of three minimum vesting schedules. First, a plan could provide a graded vesting standard, under which the employee must be at least 25 percent vested in his accrued benefit after 5 years of covered service, with 5 percent additional vesting for each of the next 5 years, and 10 percent additional vesting for each year thereafter (so that the employee was 100 percent vested after 15 years of service). Second, a plan could provide that each employee must be 100 percent vested after 10 years of service. Third, a plan could provide for a "rule of 45," under which each employee with 5 years or more of service would be 50 percent vested when the sum of his age and his years of service equaled 45, with 10 percent additional vesting for each year thereafter.

Under the Senate amendment, plans generally were required to comply with the first of these alternatives, the graded vesting schedule. However, plans which were already using the 10-year/100-percent vesting schedule were permitted to continue to use that method.

The conference substitute is described below.

Plans Subject to the Provisions; Exceptions from Coverage; Exemption for Church Plans

The rules in these areas are the same as the corrsponding rules discussed above under Participation and Coverage.

General Rules

Under the conference substitute [1] plans must provide full and imme-

---

[1] Unless otherwise indicated, the rules with

ERISA CONFERENCE REPORT

diate vesting in benefits derived from employee contributions.

With respect to employer contributions, the plan (except class year plans) must meet one of three alternative standards. Two of those, the 5- to 15-year graded standard and the 10-year/100-percent standard are the same as provided in the House bill (and briefly described above). The third standard under the conference substitute is a modificiation of the House-bill "rule of 45". As under the House rule, under the modified rule of 45, an employee with 5 or more years of covered service must be at least 50 percent vested when the sum of his age and years of covered service total 45, and there must be provision for at least 10 percent additional vesting for each year of covered service thereafter. Unlike the House bill, however, each employee with 10 years of covered service (regardless of his age) must be at least 50 percent vested and there must be provision for 10 percent additional vesting for each year of service thereafter.

In addition, all plans would have to meet the requirement of present law that an employee must be 100 percent vested in his accrued benefit when he attains the normal or stated retirement age (or actually retires).

Service Credited For Vesting Purposes

Generally, under the conference substitute, once an employee becomes eligible to participate in a pension plan, all his years of service with an employer (including preparticipation service, and service performed before the effective date of the Act) are to be taken into account for purposes of determining his place on the vesting schedule. However, the plan may ignore periods for which the employee declined to make mandatory contributions, and periods for which the employer did not maintain the plan or a predecessor plan, as defined in Treasury regulations (i.e., if the plan provides past service credits for purposes of benefit accrual, it must also provide past service credits for purposes of participation and vesting).

Generally, the plan may also ignore service performed before age 22; however, if a plan elects to use the rule of 45, service before age 22 may be ignored only if the employee was not a participant in the plan during the years before age 22.

The plan may also exclude part-time or seasonal service (i.e., generally years when the employee has less than 1,000 hours of service).

Also, if the employee has had a "break in service", his service performed prior to the break may be ignored to the extent permitted under the "break in service" rules (discussed below).

Service performed prior to January 1, 1971, may be ignored by the plan, unless (and until) the employee has at least 3 years of service after December 31, 1970.

Year of Service Defined

In general, under the conference substitute, the rules with respect to "year of service", seasonal and part-time employees, etc., are the same for purposes of the vesting schedule as they are for purposes of participation (i.e., generally 1,000 hours of service except for seasonal industries, where the customary work year is less than 1,000 hours). However, the relevant year for purposes of applying the vesting schedule may be any 12-month period provided under the plan (plan year, calendar year, etc.) regardless of the anniversary date of the participant's employment (even though the anniversay date is the measuring point for purposes of the participation requirements for an employee's first year).

For purposes of benefit accrual, in general, the plan may use any definition of the term "year of service" which the plan applies on a reasonable and consistent basis (subject to Department of Labor regulations). (Of course, the "year" for benefit accrual purposes cannot exceed the customary work year for the industry

_{respect to vesting appear in both title I and title II of the conference substitute. Unless otherwise indicated, the regulations with respect to vesting are to be written by the Secretary of the Treasury, or his delegate.}

involved.) However, the plan must accrue benefits for less than full time service on at least a pro rata basis. For example, if a plan requires 2,000 hours of service for a full benefit accrual (50 weeks of 40 hours each) then the plan would have to accrue at least 75 percent of a full benefit for a participant with 1,500 hours of service. Generally, a plan would not be required to accrue any benefit for years in which the participant had less than 1,000 hours of service. In the case of industries or occupations where the customary year is less than 1,000 hours (for example, the tuna fishing industry, or the winter season employees of a ski lodge), the rules with respect to benefit accrual would be determined under Department of Labor regulations. As previously indicated a special rule is provided for the maritime industries.

Breaks in Service

Under the conference substitute, a 1-year break in service occurs in any calendar year, plan year, or other consecutive 12-month period designated by the plan and applied on a consistent basis (and not prohibited under Labor Department regulations) in which the employee has no more than 500 hours of service. For example, if the plan is on a calendar year basis, and the employee works 1,000 hours in 1976, 501 hours in 1977, 501 hours in 1978, and 1,000 hours or more in 1979, the employee would not have a break in service (although the plan would not be required to accrue benefits or give vesting schedule credit for 1977 or 1978).

The rules with respect to breaks in service for vesting and benefit accrual purposes may be summarized as follows:

(1) If an employee has a 1-year break in service, the plan may require (for administrative reasons) a 1-year waiting period before his pre-break and post-break service must be aggregated under the plan. However, once the employee has completed this waiting period, he must receive credit for that year (for purposes of vesting and accrued benefit).

(2) In the case of an individual account plan (including a plan funded solely by individual insurance contracts, as well as a "target benefit plan") if any employee has a 1-year break in service, his vesting percentage in pre-break benefit accruals does not have to be increased as a result of a post-break service.

(3) Subject to rules (1) and (2), once an employee has achieved any percentage of vesting, then all of his pre-break and post-break service must be aggregated for all purposes.

(4) For all nonvested employees (and subject to rules (1) and (2)), the employee would not lose credits for pre-break service until his period of absence equaled his years of covered service. Under this "rule of parity" for example, if a nonvested employee had three years of service with the employer, and then had a break in service of 2 years, he could return, and after fulfilling his 1-year reentry requirement, he would have 4 years of covered service, because his pre-break and post-break service would be aggregated.[2]

For years beginning prior to the effective date of the vesting provisions, a plan may apply the break-in-service rules provided under the plan, as in effect from time to time. However, no plan amendment made after January 1, 1974, may provide for break-in-service rules which are less beneficial to any employee than the rules in effect under the plan on that date, unless the amendment complies with the break-in-service rules established under this bill.

The principles of some of the rules outlined above may be illustrated as follows: For example, assume a plan is on a calendar year basis, and an employee with a 1-year break in service reenters employment on November 1, 1976, works 200 hours in 1976, and 1,700 hours by November 1, 1977. In this case, the employee

---

[2] Also, in the case of a defined benefit plan, the employee would have at least 3 years of accrued benefits under the plan (2 years of accrued benefits due to his pre-break participation and 1 year of benefits accrued with respect to the 1 year reentry period).

would be eligible to reenter the plan on November 1, 1977, his pre-break and post-break service would be aggregated, he would advance one year on the vesting schedule for 1977, and he would also accrue benefits for 1977. On the other hand, if the employee reentered employment on March 1, 1976, worked 1,700 hours before December 31, 1976, and was not separated from service by March 1, 1977, he would be eligible to reenter the plan on March 1, 1977, advance one year on the vesting schedule for his 1976 service, and the plan would have to provide at least a partial benefit accrual for 1976.

Predecessor Employer

The rules concerning service with a predecessor employer are the same for purposes of vesting and benefit accrual as the rules for purposes of participation, discussed above.

Multiemployer Plans

Under the conference substitute, service with any employer, for any year in which the employer is a member of the plan, is to be counted for purposes of vesting as if all employers who are parties to the plan were a single employer.

Permitted Forfeitures of Vested Rights

Under the conference substitute, except as outlined below, an employee's rights, once vested, are not to be forfeitable for any reason. An employee's rights to benefits attributable to his own contributions may never be forfeited.

(1) The plan may provide that an employee's vested rights to benefits attributable to employer contributions may be forfeited on account of the employee's death (unless a "joint and survivor" annuity is to be provided).

(2) Also, the plan may provide that payment of benefits attributable to employer contributions may be suspended for any period in which the employee is reemployed by the same employer under whose plan the benefits are being paid (in the case of a single employer plan). In the case of a multiemployer plan, however, a suspension of benefit payments is permitted when the employee is employed in the same industry, in the same trade or craft and also in the same geographical area covered under the contract, as was the case immediately before he retired. Regulations with respect to the suspension of benefits are to be prescribed by the Department of Labor.

(3) A plan amendment may reduce an employee's vested or nonvested accrued benefit attributable to employer contributions, but only for the current year, and only if the amendment is adopted within 2½ months from the close of the plan year in question (without regard to any extensions). In the case of a multiemployer plan, the retroactive amendment may effect the current year, and the two immediately preceding years (thus, a multiemployer plan amendment adopted by December 31, 1978, could effect plan benefits for 1976, if the plan was on a calendar year). However, no plan amendment which reduces accrued benefits is permitted unless the Secretary of Labor has 90 days prior notice of the proposed amendment, and approves it (or fails to disapprove it). No such approval is to be granted, except to prevent substantial economic hardship, including a serious danger that the plan will be terminated unless the amendment is allowed. In addition, it must be found that the economic hardship cannot be overcome by means of a funding variance. Subject to these rules, no plan amendment may retroactively reduce the accrued benefit of any participant (whether or not that benefit is vested).

(4) A plan may provide that an employee's rights to benefits from employer contributions may be forfeited where the employee is less than 50 percent vested in these benefits and withdraws all or any part of his own mandatory contributions to the plan. However, the plan must also provide a "buy back" rule, i.e., that the employee's forfeited benefits will be fully restored if the employee repays the withdrawn contributions

(with interest of 5-percent per annum, compounded annually) to the plan.

In the case of a plan which does not provide for mandatory contributions after the date of enactment, the plan may provide, in this case, that the employee will forfeit a proportionate part of his pre-date-of-enactment accrued benefits derived from employer contributions even if he is 50 percent or more vested in these benefits. Also, the plan is not required to have a "buy back" clause with respect to the withdrawal of pre-enactment contributions. Additional regulations in this area are to be prescribed by the Secretary of the Treasury, or his delegate.

(5) A plan may provide for the "cash out" of an employee's accrued benefit. In other words, the plan may pay out, in a lump sum, the entire value of an employee's vested accrued benefit. (However, portability is available to the employee because other provisions of the bill permit the employees to reinvest in an individual retirement account on a tax-sheltered basis.) If the plan does make such a cash-out, then the plan would not be required to vest the employee in his accrued benefits which are not vested at the time he separates from the service, if the employee is later reemployed. (However, the employee's pre-break service would have to be taken into account for all other purposes, subject to the break-in-service rules, e.g., for purposes of his place on the vesting schedule.)

A cash-out could be made from the plan without the employee's consent only if the payment (a) was made due to the termination of the employee's participation in the plan, (b) constituted the value of the employee's entire interest in the plan, and (c) did not exceed an amount (to be prescribed in regulations by the Secretary of the Treasury or his delegate), based on the reasonable administrative needs of the plan, and, in any event, not in excess of $1,750 (with respect to the value of the benefit attributable to the employer's contributions). Despite the foregoing provision, generally, the conferees prefer that all amounts contributed for retirement purposes be retained and used for those purposes. Thus, a plan could provide for no cash-out, or the employee's collective bargaining unit might wish to bargain for such a provision.

A higher cash-out could be made with the employee's consent. However, even these voluntary cash-outs could only be made if the employee terminated his participation in the plan, or under other circumstances to be prescribed in regulations.

Moreover, the plan must provide, in all cases (except where a distribution equal to the value of the full accrued benefit is made), that all accrued benefits must be fully restored (except to the extent provided under the break-in-service rules) if the employee repays the amount of the cash-out, with interest. Repayment of an involuntary cash-out would have to be allowed under the plan at any time after the employee reentered employment under the plan, and repayment of voluntary cash-outs would have to be allowed under circumstances to be prescribed in regulations. However, an individual account plan would not be required to permit repayment after the employee had a one year break in service.

Accrued Benefit

Under the conference substitute, the term "accrued benefit" refers to pension or retirement benefits. The term does not apply to ancillary benefits, such as payment of medical expenses (or insurance premiums for such expenses), or disability benefits which do not exceed the normal retirement benefit payable at age 65 to an employee with comparable service under the plan, or to life insurance benefits payable as a lump sum.

Also, the accrued benefit does not include the value of the right to receive early retirement benefits, or the value of social security supplements or other benefits under the plan which are not continued for any employee after he has attained normal retirement age. However, an accrued benefit may not be reduced on account of increasing age or service (except to the extent of social security supplements or their equivalents).

In the case of a plan other than a defined benefit plan, the accrued benefit is to be the balance in the employee's individual account.

In the case of a defined benefit plan, the accrued benefit is to be determined under the plan, subject to certain requirements. In general, the accrued benefit is to be defined in terms of the benefit payable at normal retirement age. Normal retirement age generally is to be the age specified under the plan. However, it may not be later than age 65 or the tenth anniversary of the time the participant commenced participation, whichever last occurs. No actuarial adjustment of the accrued benefit would be required, however, if an employee voluntarily postponed his own retirement. For example, if the plan provided a benefit of $400 a month payable at age 65, this same $400 a month benefit (with no upward adjustment) could also be paid by the plan to an individual who voluntarily retired at age 68.

Each defined benefit plan is to be required to satisfy one of three accrued benefit tests (which limit the extent of "back-loading" permitted under the plan).

The three percent test.—Under this alternative each participant must accrue, for each year of participation, at least 3 percent of the benefit which is payable under the plan to a participant who begins participation at the earliest possible entry age and serves continuously until age 65, or normal retirement age under the plan, whichever is earlier. This test is to be applied on a cumulative basis (i.e., any amount of "front loading" is permitted). Also, in the case of a plan amendment, the test would be cumulative. For example, assume that a plan provided a flat benefit of $200 a month payable at age 65 during the first 10 years of an individual's participation, then amended to provide a flat benefit of $400 a month; the participant's accrued benefit at the end of his 11th year of participation would equal $132 (3 percent of $400, times 11 years of service.)

In addition, if a plan elects this alternative, and if the plan provides a given benefit to a person who is employed when he attains retirement age, who has a given amount of service, then any employee who has that amount of service, even though he leaves before retirement age, would be entitled to this same benefit when he reaches retirement age. For example, if the plan is based on compensation and provides a 40 percent of salary benefit for an employee who served at least 20 years and is still employed at age 65, then the plan must provide that an employee who served 20 years from age 35 to age 55 would be entitled to that same 40 percent of compensation benefit (beginning at normal retirement age or age 65).

$133\frac{1}{3}$ percent test.—Under this alternative, the plan is to qualify if the accrual rate for any participant for any later year is not more than $133\frac{1}{3}$ percent of his accrual rate for the current year. Thus, (unlike the House bill) the conference substitute permits an unlimited amount of "front loading" under this test. The accrual rate can be based on either a dollar or percentage rate. In applying these rules, a plan amendment in effect for the current year is to be treated as though it were in effect for all plan years. (For example, if a plan provides a one percent rate of accrual for all participants in 1976, and is amended to provide a 2 percent rate of accrual for all participants in 1977, the plan will meet this test, even though 2 is more than $1\frac{1}{3}$ times 1). Also, if the plan has a scheduled increase in the rate of accruals, which will not be in effect for any participant until future years, this scheduled increase will not be taken into account for purposes of the backloading rules until it actually takes effect. Also, in applying the $133\frac{1}{3}$ percent test, social security benefits and all other factors used to compute benefits under the

plan will be treated as remaining constant, at current year levels, for all future years.

Pro rata rule.—As a third alternative, the conference substitute contains a modified version of the rule contained in the Senate amendment. Under this test, for purposes of determining the accrued benefit, the retirement benefit is to be computed as though the employee continued to earn the same rate of compensation annually that he had earned during the years which would have been taken into account under the plan (but not in excess of 10), had the employee retired on the date in question. This amount is then to be multiplied by a fraction, the numerator of which is the employee's total years of active participation in the plan up to the date when the computation is being made, and the denominator of which is the total number of years of active participation he would have had if he continued his employment until normal retirement age. This test is cumulative in the sense that unlimited front loading is permitted. For purposes of this test, social security benefits and all other relevant factors used to compute benefits shall be treated as remaining constant at current year levels for all future years. Also for purposes of this rule the term "normal retirement age" would be defined as set forth above, and the test would apply only to the benefit payable at, or after, normal retirement age (i.e., it would not take account of subsidized early retirement (to the extent such a benefit does not exceed the benefit payable at normal retirement age) and social security supplements.) [3]

---

[3] For example, assume a social security offset plan providing a benefit equal to 2 percent of high-3 years compensation per year of service with the employer, minus 30 percent of the primary social security benefit, with a normal retirement age of 65. Assuming also an employee who began employment at age 25, and terminated employment at age 45, 100 percent vested, with high-3 years pay of $19,000, $20,000, and $21,000. At the time the employee separates from service the primary social security benefit payable to him at age 65 (under the social security law as an effect when he terminates) would be $6,000 if he continued to work with the employer at his same annual rate of compensation

A plan is not to be treated as failing to meet the tests solely because the accrual of benefits under the plan does not become effective until the employee has two continuous years of service, measured from the anniversary date of employment.

In the case of a plan funded exclusively through the purchase of insurance contracts, the accrued benefit is to be the cash surrender value of the contract (determined as though the funding requirements with respect to the plan had been fully satisfied).

In the case of a variable annuity plan, the accrued benefit is to be determined in accordance with regulations to be prescribed by the Secretary of the Treasury or his delegate.

Benefits Accrued in the Past

Generally, the vesting rules of the conference substitute are to apply to all accrued benefits, including those which accrued before the effective date of the provisions (subject, however, to the break-in-service rules discussed above). However, many plans now in existence have no accrued benefit formula for the past, thus making it impossible in these cases to determine what the employee is vested in. To deal with this situation, the conference substitute provides that the accrued benefit under a plan for years prior to the effective

---

until normal retirement age. His accrued benefit under the plan would equal $7,100. (If the employee had remained in service until age 65, he would have 40 years service, times 2 percent per year (80 percent), times $20,000 average high-3 years compensation ($16,000), minus 30 percent of the $6,000 primary social security benefit payable to the employee at age 65 under then current law ($16,000 minus $1,800 equals $14,200) times 20/40ths (20 years of service over 40 total years from age 25 to age 65) equals $7,100.)

In the case of a plan amendment, the rule would work as follows. Assume an individual begins participation at age 25 in a plan which provides 1 percent of high-three-years pay during his first 10 years of service. In the 11th year the plan amends to provide 2 percent of pay for all future years of service. The employee separates from service at the end of the 11th year (and is 100 percent vested). His accrued benefit would equal 19.25 percent of average high-three-years pay (10 years of participation) times 1 percent per year. 30 (years of projected participation) times 2 percent per year, times 11/40ths (11 years of participation over 40 total years between age 25 and age 65)).

date of the vesting provisions for any participant is to be not less than the greater of (1) the accrued benefit under the provisions of the plan (as in effect from time to time), or (2) an accrued benefit which is not less than one-half of the benefit which would have accrued under one of the three back-loading tests described above.

The plan may choose which of the 3 standards it wishes to apply for the past (subject to the antidiscrimination rules); however, the same standard must be applied to all the plan's participants on a consistent basis. The plan is not required to choose, for the past, the same test which it applies in the future.

Changes in Vesting Schedule

The conference substitute provides that if, at any time in the future, the plan changes its vesting schedule, the vesting percentage for each participant in his accrued benefit accumulated to the date when the plan amendment is adopted (or the date the amendment becomes effective, if later) cannot be reduced as a result of the amendment. In addition, as a further protection for long service employees, any participant with at least 5 years of service may elect to remain under the pre-amendment vesting schedule with respect to all of his benefits accrued both before and after the plan amendment.

Allocations Between Employee and Employer Contributions

The House bill and the Senate amendment are quite similar in the rules they apply in allocating contributions between those made by the employee and the employer and the conference substitute follows the House bill as to technical matters in the case of this provision. In addition, the substitute makes a clarifying amendment which provides (in the case of a defined benefit plan), that the accrued benefit attributable to employee contributions can never be less than the sum of those contributions (computed without interest). This assures that the employee will at least be vested in his own contributions to the plan, on a dollar-for-dollar basis. (Thus, for example, in the case of an individual insurance contract, employer contributions to the plan must at least absorb the load factor, but, of course, payment of the load factor by the employer would not cause the plan to be treated as a plan which was not funded solely through the purchase of insurance contracts.

Discrimination

Under the conference substitute the rules of the House bill are adopted with respect to the relationship of the minimum vesting standards of the bill to the antidiscrimination rules of present law (sec. 401(a)(4) of the Internal Revenue Code). In general, a plan which meets the vesting requirements provided in this substitute is not to be considered as discriminatory, insofar as its vesting provisions are concerned, unless there is a pattern of abuse under the plan (such as the firing of employees before their accrued benefits vest) or there has been (or there is reason to believe there will be) an accrual of benefits or forfeitures tending to discriminate in favor of employees who are officers, shareholders or who are highly compensated.

In the past, however, the law in this area has been administered on a case-by-case basis, without uniform results in fact situations of a similar nature. As a result, except in cases where actual misuse of the plan occurs in operation, the Internal Revenue Service is directed not to require a vesting schedule more stringent than 40 percent vesting after 4 years of employment with 5 percent additional vesting for each of the next 2 years, and 10 percent additional vesting for each of the following five years. Also, this more rapid vesting would generally not be required except in a case where the rate of likely turnover for officers, shareholders, or highly compensated employees was substantially less (perhaps as much as 50 percent less) than the rate of likely turnover for rank-and-file employees. Of course, where there is a pattern of firing employees to avoid vesting, the limitations described above would not apply. Also, it generally is not intended that any plan (or successor plan of a now existing plan) which is presently under a more rapid vesting schedule should be permitted to cut back its vesting schedule as a result of this statement.

In addition, the conferees have directed the joint pension task force study group to examine problems of the interrelationship of the vesting and the antidiscrimination rules carefully. The conferees also expect the Treasury or the Internal Revenue Service to supply information with respect to patterns of benefit loss for different categories of plans (as designated by the task force) under the minimum vesting schedules prescribed under this legislation, and such other information as the task force study group may require. In other words, the experimental rules outlined above (40 percent vesting after 4 years, etc.) are intended to apply only until the responsible congressional committees can review the situation after receiving the report of the task force study group.

Moreover, the conferees intend that the antidiscrimination rules of present law in areas other than the vesting schedule are not to be changed. Thus, the present antidiscrimination rules with respect to coverage, and with respect to contributions and benefits are to remain in effect. Also, the antidiscrimination rules may be applied with respect to benefit accruals.

The conference substitute contains a technical rule to be applied in the case of target benefit plans (and other defined contribution plans), which provides that regulations may establish reasonable earnings assumptions and other factors for these plans in order to prevent discrimination.

Plan Termination

Under the conference substitute, as under present law, all accrued benefits in a qualified pension plan must become fully vested (in accordance with the rules of the bill concerning allocation of assets upon plan termination and to the extent then funded) in the event of a plan termination, or the complete discontinuance of contributions under the pension plan. Under the substitute, this rule is no longer to apply to cases where employers have not made contributions to plans covered under the funding requirements of the bill, because the bill reaches this problem by imposing an excise tax on underfunding. However, the rule of full immediate vesting is still to apply in the case of a termination, or partial termination of a plan, and in the case of the discontinuance of contributions to plans which are not subject to the new funding requirements (e.g., profit-sharing plans, church plans, and government plans). Also, the substitute contains a provision to make clear that the vesting requirements under the bill are not intended to operate to overturn rules which require that, in the event of plan termination, the benefits under the plan are not to be distributed in a manner that discriminates in favor of officers, shareholders, or highly compensated employees.

Class Year Plans

Under the substitute, the minimum vesting requirements are satisfied in the case of a class year plan if the plan provides for 100 percent vesting of the benefits derived from employer contributions within 5 years after the end of the plan year for which the contributions were made. Also, under this substitute, forfeitures with respect to employer contributions would be permitted on a class-year-by-class-year basis, for any year for which the employee withdraws his own mandatory contributions to the plan, if he is less than 50 percent vested with respect to that year. For purposes of these rules, withdrawals will be applied to the earliest year for which the employee has made contributions which have not yet been withdrawn.

Recordkeeping Requirements

Under the conference substitute, in the case of a single employer plan, the employee, once each year, is to be entitled to request his plan administrator to furnish a statement as to his vesting and accrued benefit status. A similar statement is to be supplied automatically when a vested employee terminates his coverage under the plan. In the case of multiemployer plans, the recordkeeping and information supplying duties are to be performed by the plan administrator and, to the maximum extent practicable (in light of their different circumstances), multiemployer plans are to meet the same standards in this area as single employer plans (in accordance with regulations to be prescribed by the Secretary of Labor or his delegate).

Variations

Under the conference substitute, a variation is to be available with respect to the vesting schedule (for benefits attributable to employer contributions) and the accrued benefit rules for plans in existence on January 1, 1974. Under this procedure, a variation is to be allowed only if it is found by the Secretary of Labor that application of the rules of the bill would increase the cost of the plan to such an extent that there would be a substantial danger that the plan would be terminated, or that there would be a substantial reduction in benefits provided under the plan, or in the compensation of the employees. Also, it would have to be determined that the application of the vesting schedule requirements, or accrued benefit requirements, or discontinuance of the plan, would be adverse to the interest of the plan participants as a whole. Finally, it would have to be determined that the hardship described above could not be sufficiently mitigated by the granting of a funding variance.

The variation with respect to benefit accruals is not to apply for any year except years (not in excess of 7) during which the variation is in effect. (For example, there could be no variation with respect to the rules for benefits accrued in the past.)

No plan may receive a vesting variation unless application is made (in accordance with regulations to be prescribed by the Secretary of Labor or his delegate) within two years after the date of enactment of this bill. The variation would be granted for an initial period not to exceed 4 years. Plans can receive one additional variation (for a period not to exceed 3 years), but application for the additional variation would have to be made at least one year prior to the expiration of the initial variation period.

During the period when a variation is in effect, there can be no plan amendment which has the effect of increasing plan liabilities because of benefit increases, changes in accruals, or changes in the rate of vesting, except to a de minimis extent (in accordance with regulations to be prescribed by the Secretary of Labor).

Amounts Designated as Employee Contributions

To clarify present law, the substitute provides that amounts contributed to a qualified plan in taxable years beginning after December 31, 1973, are to be treated as employee contributions if they are designated as employee contributions under the plan. This rule does not apply, however, to government "pick-up" plans, where the contribution is paid by the government, with no withholding from the employee's salary, and these amounts would be treated as employer contributions no matter how designated under the plan.

Joint and Survivor Annuities

Under the conference substitute, when a plan provides for a retirement benefit in the form of an annuity, and the participant has been married for the one-year period ending on the annuity starting date, the plan must provide for a joint and survivor annuity. The survivor annuity must be not less than half of the annuity payable to the participant during the joint lives of the participant and his spouse.

In the case of an employee who retires, or who attains the normal retirement age, the joint and survivor provision is to apply unless the employee elected otherwise.

In the case of an employee who is eligible to retire prior to the normal retirement age under the plan, and who does not retire, the joint and survivor provisions need not be applicable under the plan, unless the employee made an affirmative election. Moreover, the plan need not make this option available until the employee is within 10 years of normal retirement age. (Of course, a plan may provide that a joint and survivor annuity is to be the only form of benefit payable under the plan, and in this case, no election need be provided.)

These rules should help to avoid the situation where an employee who had not yet retired might have his own retirement benefit reduced as a result of inaction on his part and should also help to prevent adverse selection as against the plan.

The employee is to be afforded a reasonable opportunity, in accordance with regulations, to exercise his election out of, (or, before normal retirement age, possibly into) the joint and survivor provision before the annuity starting date (or before he becomes eligible for early retirement). The employee is to be supplied with a written explanation of the joint and survivor provision, explained in layman's language, as well as the practical (dollar and cents) effect on him (and his or her spouse) of making an election either to take or not to take the provision. At the same time, regulations in this area should take cognizance of the practical difficulties which certain industries (particularly those having multiemployer plans) may have in contacting all of their participants.

To prevent adverse selection the plan may provide that any election, or revocation of an election, is not to become effective if the participant dies within some period of time (not in excess of two years) of the election or revocation (except in the case of accidental death where the accident which causes death occurs after the election).

Also, the conferees agree with the statements in the Ways and Means Committee report (No. 93-807) to the effect that the bill does not require the plan to "subsidize" the joint and survivor feature (although the plan is permitted to do so) and that plans may make reasonable actuarial adjustments to take account of the possibility that total costs of the plan otherwise might be increased because of adverse selection.

Alienation

Under the conference substitute, a plan must provide that benefits under the plan may not be assigned or alienated. However, the plan may provide that after a benefit is in pay status, there may be a voluntary revocable assignment (not to exceed 10 percent of any benefit payment) by an employee which is not for purposes of defraying the administrative costs of the plan. For purposes of this rule, a garnishment or levy is not to be considered a voluntary assignment. Vested benefits may be used as collateral for reasonable loans from a plan, where the fiduciary requirements of the law are not violated.[4]

Social Security Benefits of Terminated Participants

The conference substitute codifies the current administrative practice which provides that qualified plans may not use increases in social security benefits or wage base levels to reduce employee plan benefits that are already in pay status. A similar protection is also extended against reductions in plan benefits where social security benefit levels (or wage base levels) are increased after the individuals concerned are separated from service prior to retirement. This requirement also applies to plans covered under title I (even if the plan is not qualified). A similar principle will apply in the case of an individual receiving disability benefits under social security and also under an employer plan.

---

[4] This rule will not apply to irrevocable assignments made before the date of enactment and the plan provision required under this rule need not be adopted prior to January 1, 1976 (so long as the plan complies with the substance of this rule after enactment).

Integration with Social Security

As discussed above, title I and title II of the conference substitute provide that plans may not use increases in social security benefit levels to decrease plan benefits in the case of retirees, or individuals who separate from service prior to retirement. The conference substitute also provides (consistent with the Ways and Means Committee report) for a two-year study, by the Congress, of the issues involved in the integration of private pension plans with social security.

Consequently, the substitute provides, in effect, that until July 1, 1976, pension plans may not increase their level of integration by taking into account changes in the social security wage base, or in social security benefit levels after 1971. Thus, in general, plans may integrate in accordance with Rev. Rul. 71-446, 1971-2 C.B. 187. (For example, an excess plan would integrate in accordance with section 3 of that ruling, and the tables set forth therein.) Of course, plans which do not satisfy the integration requirements as to form, but do in operation satisfy the requirements of Rev. Rul. 771-446, will be permitted to integrate under the conference substitute.

Certain plans, which are currently integrated above 1971 levels, are permitted to retain their current levels of integration (as in effect on June 27, 1974), but would not be permitted an increase. (For example, a unit benefit excess plan which now provides 1 percent of pay in excess of $11,000 per year of future service could remain at this level, but could not change to take account of a wage base higher than $11,000.)

To prevent undue hardship, in the case of plans which are automatically keyed to changes in the social security wage base or benefit levels (for example, a unit benefit excess plan now at the $13,200 wage base in effect on June 27, 1974), the plan is not required to amend until June 30, 1975, but any such amendment must be retroactive to January 1, 1975, and must provide that the plan does not take account of any changes in the social security wage base or in social security benefit levels which may occur after June 27, 1974.

For purposes of the rules with respect to retirees, or other individuals who have separated from service, any change in the plan after June 30, 1976, which takes account of the increases in the social security wage base or benefit levels which are temporarily frozen under these provisions, may not be used to reduce plan benefits otherwise payable to individuals who retire, or separate from service, between June 27, 1974 and June 30, 1976.

Payment of Benefits

Under the conference substitute, a plan is generally required to commence benefit payments (unless the participant otherwise elects) not later than the 60th day after the close of the plan year in which the latest of the following events occurs:

(1) the participant attains age 65 (or any earlier normal retirement age specified under the plan),

(2) ten years have elapsed from the time the participant commenced participation in the plan, or

(3) the participant terminates his service with the employer.

Also, if the plan permits an employee who has not separated from service to receive a subsidized early retirement benefit if he meets certain age and service requirements, the plan must also permit an employee who fulfills the service requirement, but separates from service before he meets the age requirement, to receive benefit payments, on an actuarially reduced basis, when the separated employee meets the age requirement. For example, if the plan provides a benefit of $100 a month at age 65, or at age 55 for employees with 30 years of service who are still employed on their 55th birthday, then an employee who separates from service at age 50 with 30 years service, would have the right to draw down an actuarially reduced benefit (perhaps $50 a month) at age 55. The actuarial adjustments are to be made in accordance with regulations to be prescribed by the Secretary of the Treasury, or his delegate.

Comparability of Plans Having Different Vesting Provisions Under the Antidiscrimination Rules

The conference substitute provides that highly mobile employees, such as engineers, are permitted to trade off high benefits which might be available under one retirement plan of their employer for their right to participate in another plan with lower benefits, but more rapid vesting.

Protection of Pension Rights Under Government Contracts

Under the conference substitute, the Secretary of Labor is to undertake a study of steps which can be taken to ensure that professional, scientific, technical, and other personnel employed under Federal contracts are protected against loss of their pensions resulting from job transfers or loss of employment. The Secretary of Labor is to report to Congress on this subject within two years after the date of enactment of the bill and is, if feasible, to develop recommendations for Federal procurement regulations to safeguard pension rights in the situations in question within one year after filing his report. These regulations are to become effective unless either House of Congress adopts a resolution of disapproval within 120 days after the proposed regulations are submitted to the Congress. Any such disapproval is to be referred to the Labor Committee of the relevant House.

Effective Dates

The effective dates of the provisions with respect to participation and vesting are discussed above under "Participation and Coverage."

IV. Funding (Secs. 301-306, 1013, and 1014 of the Bill and Secs. 412, 413, and 4971 of the Internal Revenue Code)

The House bill would provide new minimum funding standards for plans of employers (or employee organizations) in interstate commerce (title I) and for tax-qualified plans (title II). Under the House version of the bill, the new minimum funding standard would require that currently-created costs be funded currently, and that costs attributable to already existing liabilities, past service liabilities created under plan amendments, and experience losses be amortized over stated periods of time. The House funding standards generally are based on accrued liabilities and not only on vested liabilities. However, if the funding requirements are higher under a second general standard which is based on "vested" liabilities, this standard would apply in lieu of the other rules. Where the funding requirements would create financial hardship, and certain standards are met, the Secretary of the Treasury or Secretary of Labor could permit variances in meeting the funding requirements.

The Senate amendment is basically similar to the House bill, but differs somewhat with respect to some of the periods of time allowed for amortizing past service cost and with respect to several technical provisions. Also, the Senate amendment does not include a second general funding standard based upon "vested" liabilities.

Generally, the conference substitute follows the House bill with respect to amortization periods and with respect to technical aspects, but modifies the House bill in other respects.

General Rule as to Funding

The conference substitute establishes new minimum funding requirements for plans of employers and unions in or affecting interstate commerce (title I) and qualified plans (title II) so these plans will accumulate sufficient assets within a reasonable time to pay benefits to covered employees when they retire. Of course, contributions generally may be greater than these minimum requirements if the employer so desires. (However, there may be limits on the ability to currently deduct these larger contributions, under the tax laws.) The new requirements generally are not to apply to profit-sharing or stock bonus plans, governmental plans, certain church plans, plans with no employer contributions, and certain insured plans. Under the tax provisions, once a plan or trust has been tax qualified, the minimum funding requirements will apply, and they are to continue to apply to the plan or trust, even if it later loses its qualified status. If a plan loses its qualified status, the deduction rules for nonqualified plans are to apply even though the minimum funding standard continues to apply to the plan.

Generally, under the new funding requirements, the minimum amount that an employer is to contribute annually to a defined benefit pension plan includes the normal costs of the plan plus amortization of past service liabilities, experience losses, etc. Except as described below (under "Variances — alternative funding methods"), minimum amortization payments required by the conference substitute are calculated on a level payment basis — including interest and principal — over stated periods of time and are based on all accrued liabilities. Generally, initial past service liabilities and past service liabilities arising under plan amendments are to be amortized over no more than 30 years (40 years for the unfunded past service liabilities on the effective date of these new funding rules, in the case of existing plans), and experience gains and losses are to be amortized over no more than 15 years. However, generally experience gains and losses need not be calculated more often than every three years. With respect to multiemployer plans, past service liabilities generally may be amortized over no more than 40 years, and experience losses over no more than 20 years. Following the Senate amendment, the conference substitute does not include a second general minimum funding standard based only on "vested" liabilities.

If an employer would otherwise incur substantial business hardship, and if application of the minimum funding requirements would be adverse to plan participants in the aggregate, the Internal Revenue Service may waive the requirement of current payment of part or all of a year's contributions of normal costs, and amounts needed to amortize past service liabilities and experience losses. This waiver is to be available for single employer and multiemployer plans. The amount waived (plus interest) is to be amortized not less rapidly than ratably (including interest) over 15 years, and no more than 5 waivers may be granted for any 15 consecutive years. Also, the Secretary of Labor may extend the amortization period for amortization of past service costs up to an additional 10 years, on a showing of economic hardship.

For money purchase pension plans, the minimum amount that an employer is to annually contribute to the plan generally is the amount that must be contributed for the year under the plan formula. For purposes of this rule, a plan (for example, a so-called Taft-Hartley plan) which provides an agreed level of benefits and a specified level of contributions during the contract period is not to be considered a money purchase plan if the employer or his representative participated in the determination of the benefits. On the other hand, a "target benefit plan" is to be treated as a money purchase plan for purposes of the minimum funding rules.

Under the new funding rules, generally each covered plan is to maintain a new account called a "funding standard account." This account is to aid both the taxpayer-employer and the Government in administering the minimum funding rules. The account also is used to assure that a taxpayer who has funded more than the minimum amount required is properly credited for that excess and for the interest earned on the excess. Similarly, where a taxpayer has paid too little, the account is to assist in enforcing the minimum funding standard, and to assure that the taxpayer is charged with interest on the amount of underfunding.

Each year the funding standard account is to be charged with the liabilities which must be paid to meet the minimum funding standard. Also, each year the funding standard account is to be credited with contributions under the plan and with any other decrease in liabilities (such as amortized experience gains). If the plan meets the minimum funding requirements as of the end of each year, the funding standard account will show a zero balance (or a positive balance, if the employer has contributed more than the minimum required). If the minimum contributions have not been made, the funding standard account will show a deficiency (called an "accumulated funding deficiency"). If there is an accumulated funding deficiency, an excise tax is to be imposed on the employer who is responsible for making contributions to the plan. Also, the responsible employer may be subject to civil action in the courts on failure to meet the minimum funding standards.

The differences between the House bill and the conference substitute are described below.

Additional Funding Standard

The conference substitute, following the Senate amendment, does not include an additional funding standard which would require a contribution of the first year's payment under a 20-year amortization schedule of unfunded vested liabilities.

Reasonable Actuarial Assumptions

The conference substitute combines the rules relating to actuarial assumptions of the House bill and of the Senate amendment and requires that, for purposes of the minimum funding standard, all plan costs, liabilities, rates of interest, and other factors under the plan are to be determined on the basis of actuarial assumptions and methods which, in the aggregate, are reasonable. Actuarial assumptions are to take into account the experience of the plan and reasonable expectations. These assumptions are expected to take into consideration past experience as well as other relevant factors.

In addition, under the conference substitute, the actuarial assumptions in combination are to offer the actuary's best estimate of anticipated experience under the plan. The conferees intend that under this provision a single set of actuarial assumptions will be required for all purposes (e.g., for the minimum funding standard, reporting to the Department of Labor and to participants and beneficiaries, financial reporting to stockholders, etc.).

Treatment of Certain Changes as Experience Gains or Losses

The House bill does not indicate how funding is to be provided where there is a change in liabilities arising from changes in actuarial assumptions used. The Senate amendment would include such changes in liabilities as experience gains or losses. Under the conference substitute, changes in plan liabilities resulting from changes in actuarial assumptions are to be amortized over a 30-year period.

Definition of Experience Gain or Loss

Under the conference substitute (following title II of the House bill and the Senate amendment) experience gain or loss is the difference between the anticipated experience of the plan and the actual experience.

The conferees understand that certain plans are maintained pursuant to collectively bargained agreements which provide for a predetermined level of contributions over a period longer than 12 months, such as a specified dollar amount per hour of covered service by an employee or a specified dollar amount per ton of coal mined. It is intended that, for the funding requirements to be workable in these cases, employers generally must be allowed to base their contributions on the bargained and agreed upon basis during the period to which the collective bargaining agreement relates (but generally for not more than three years). Under such a plan, if the actuarial assumptions were reasonable and the actuarial calculations were correct as of the beginning of the term of the agreement, and the agreed upon contributions were made when required during the term of the agreement, it is intended that there would be no deficiency in the funding standard account for the term of the collectively bargained agreement (limited as indicated above). This would be the case even if the amount of contributions were less than what was reasonably expected at the beginning of the term of the agreement (for example, because the hours worked or the tons of coal mined were less than reasonably anticipated). In this case, it is expected that any difference between the reasonably anticipated contributions and actual contributions would be treated as an experience loss which could be made up under the next agreement by adjustment of the contribution rate (or by adjustment of the level of benefits).

Change in Funding Method or Plan Year

The conference substitute (following the House bill and Senate amendment) provides that a change in a plan's funding method (or plan year) can be used to determine plan costs and liabilities only if the change is approved by the administering Secretary. (Note that this requirement of prior approval does not apply to use of the alternative minimum funding standard, described below.) The conferees intend that a change in funding method or plan year also is to be reported to the Pension Benefit Guaranty Corporation in order that the Corporation may be fully apprised of events which may adversely affect the funding status of a plan.

Full Funding Limitation

Both the House bill and the Senate amendment include special provisions establishing the minimum amount to be funded where the difference between plan liabilities and plan assets is smaller than the amount otherwise required to be contributed under the minimum funding requirement for the year. Generally, these provisions are substantially the same; the conference substitute follows the House bill in the technical aspects. However, the conferees wish to clarify statements in the House report with respect to the time at which plan liabilities and plan assets are to be valued for purposes of determining the full funding standard. Generally, the conferees intend that assets and liabilities are to be valued at the usual time used by the plan for such valuations, if done on a consistent basis and in accordance with regulations.

Retroactive Plan Amendments

The House bill generally would allow limited amendments of plans which retroactively decrease plan benefits (without the approval of the Secretary of Labor), and also would allow other plan amendments which retroactively decrease plan benefits, with the approval of the Secretary of Labor. The Senate amendment included no similar provisions.

The conference substitute generally allows limited retroactive plan amendments, but only with the approval of the Secretary of Labor.

Under the conference substitute, plan amendments that reduce plan benefits may be made after the close of the plan year, and yet apply to that year if they are made within 2½ months after the end of the plan year. However, since a single plan year is not a workable standard for multiemployer plans, with respect to multiemployer plans, an amendment may be made under the conference substitute within 2 years of the close of the plan year.

To protect participants, amendments made under this provision are not to decrease vested benefits of any participant determined as of the time the amendment is adopted. In addition, such a retroactive amendment cannot reduce the accrued benefit (whether or not vested) of any participant determined as of the beginning of the first plan year to which the amendment applies. Moreover, such an amendment is not to retroactively reduce the accrued benefit of any participant, unless there would otherwise be an accumulated funding deficiency for all or part of the plan year in question, the funding deficiency could not be avoided through the implementation of any other reasonably available alternative (including amortization of experience losses or a waiver of the funding requirement), and the funding deficiency was not primarily attributable to the failure by employers to discharge contractual obligations to make contributions under the plan (e.g., failing to contribute a required amount per hour of work of plan participants).

Under the conference substitute, the plan administrator is to notify the Secretary of Labor of any amendment which retroactively decreases plan liabilities, before the amendment goes into effect. The amendment can then go into effect only if the Secretary has approved it, or if the Secretary does not disapprove it within 90 days after notice is filed. It is expected that within the 90-day period the Secretary may notify the plan of a tentative disapproval, if he needs more information or more time before making a final determination. The Secretary of Labor is not to approve any retroactive amendment unless he determines that it meets the requirements discussed above and determines that it is necessary because of substantial business hardship.

Three-Year Determination of Gains And Losses

Under the House bill, experience gains and losses would be determined every three years (more frequently in particular cases as required by regulations). Under the Senate amendment, an annual determination of gains and losses and an annual valuation of liabilities would be required.

The conference substitute follows the rules of the House bill. The conferees intend that regulations may be issued to require a determination of gains and losses and valuation of a plan's liabilities more frequently than every three years with respect to situations where there is a need for more frequent review. For example, the regulations might provide that a determination of experience gains and losses would be made more frequently than every three years by plans which have sustained substantial experience gains or losses for several periods in succession.

Year-By-Year Waivers

Title II of the House bill and the Senate amendment both provide that the Secretary of the Treasury may waive all or part of the minimum funding requirement for a plan year if an employer is unable to satisfy this requirement without incurring substantial business hardship.

The conference substitute follows the House bill with respect to the technical aspects and with respect to the number of variances that may be granted in any consecutive period of years. In addition, under the conference substitute, it is made clear that this waiver is to be available for employers contributing to a multiemployer plan. For multiemployer plans, the Secretary of Treasury may waive part or all of the funding requirements if at least 10 percent of the employers contributing to the plan demonstrate that they would experience substantial business hardship without the waiver, and if applying the minimum funding standard would be adverse to the interests of plan participants as a whole.

Variances—Extension of Amortization Periods

The House bill would allow the Secretary of Labor to extend the amortization periods for funding past service liabilities or experience gains and losses of plans for an additional ten years, in cases of substantial business hardship. (Under the labor provisions of the House bill, this would be available for all plans under the general variance provision; under the tax provisions this would be available only for multiemployer plans.) A similar provision is included under the Senate amendment.

Under the conference substitute, the Secretary of Labor may extend the amortization period for unfunded past service liabilities and experience gains and losses for both mult'employer and single employer plans. These periods may be extended up to an additional ten years where there would otherwise be a substantial risk that the plan might be terminated or a substantial risk that pension benefit levels or employee compensation might be limited. Additionally, to grant an extension of time the Secretary must find that (1) the extension would carry out the purposes of the Act, (2) the extension would provide adequate protection for participants and beneficiaries, and (3) not granting the extension would be adverse to the interests of plan participants and beneficiaries as a whole.

Variances — Alternative Funding Methods

Title I of the House bill provides that the Secretary of Labor may prescribe an alternative minimum funding method for multiemployer or single employer plans in certain cases of hardship. The Senate amendment does not include any similar provision. The conference substitute does not include a general provision allowing the Secretary of Labor to prescribe an alternative minimum funding method. However, the substitute provides an alternative method for a multiemployer plan to satisfy the minimum requirements for funding past service liabilities existing as of 12 months after the first date on which the minimum funding standards apply to the plan. This alternative method may be used only by multiemployer plans which were in existence on January 1, 1974, if (on that date) the contributions under the plan were based on a percentage of pay.

Under this alternative, an eligible plan may elect to fund, over the relevant amortization period, the applicable past service liabilities with contributions that are a level annual percentage of the aggregate pay of all participants under the plan (instead of funding these liabilities with level dollar payments) over the appropriate amortization period. The minimum amount to be paid under this alternative is the interest (at the rate otherwise used by the plan in determining its liabilities) on initial past service liabilities and past service liabilites created by plan amendment. Also, this interest assumption, by itself, must be a reasonable rate; and the assumption with respect to aggregate pay must, by itself, be a reasonable assumption. This is necessary because these two assumptions have a key role, individually, in determining the amount that will be contributed to a plan under this alternative amortization method.

Limit on Increase in Benefits During Variance

The House bill provides that while a variance is in effect the plan cannot be amended to increase liabilities by an increase in benefits, a change in the accrual of benefits, or a change in the rate of vesting. A similar limitation is included in the Senate amendment.

The conference substitute generally follows the House bill in its technical aspects and limits plan amendments which increase liabilities where there has been a year-by-year waiver, or an extension of time to amortize past service costs or experience gains and losses. This limitation is to apply until the waived amount has been fully amortized or until the extension of time for amortization is no longer in effect. Also, under the conference substitute, benefits may not be increased if there has been a plan amendment which retroactively decreased plan benefits within the preceding 12 months (24 months in the case of multiemployer plans). However, the conference substitute makes it clear that reasonable, *de minimis* increases in plan liabilities are to be allowed, under regulations of the Secretary of Labor. (It is expected that the regulations will indicate the types of plan amendments considered *de minimis* for this purpose.) Also, amendments are to be allowed even though they increase plan liabilities if they are required as a condition of tax qualification. Further, amendments which merely repeal (in whole or in part) a previous retroactive decrease in benefits are to be allowed.

Alternative Minimum Funding Standard

Under title II of the House bill, the same funding method and assumptions would be used for determining the minimum amount that must be contributed to a plan and for determining the maximum amount for which a current tax deduction is available. The Senate amendment does not include a similar requirement.

The conference substitute generally follows the rules of the House bill in requiring the funding method used by a plan to be the same for purposes of determining the minimum amount to be contributed and the maximum deduction for contributions. However, the conference substitute also would allow the use of an alternative minimum funding standard in order that there may be some leeway between the minimum required contributions and the maximum deductible contributions.

Under the alternative funding standard, generally the minimum amount to be contributed to a plan is (1) the excess (if any) of the value of accrued benefits over the value of plan assets, plus (2) normal cost. Under this standard, plan assets are to be annually valued at fair market value and plan liabilities are to be valued on the same basis as the Pension Benefit Guaranty Corporation would have computed them if the plan terminated. These valuation methods are used because this minimum funding standard is similar to a "termination test" funding standard. When the financial status of a plan is examined on a termination basis, it is considered appropriate to use fair market valuations rather than valuations which tend to spread out fluctuations in value. In addition, under this standard normal cost is to be the lesser of normal cost as determined under the method used by the plan or normal cost under the unit credit method.

The alternative standard generally is to be available only for plans using funding methods which provide contributions which are no less than the contributions required under the entry age normal method. In this case, plan participants and beneficiaries will have the protection of a relatively faster build-up of plan assets in the early years of the plan than under, e.g., the unit credit method.

On electing to use the alternative method, a plan must maintain an alterminate funding standard account. The account will be charged with normal costs plus the excess of accrued benefits over assets (but not less than zero), and will be credited with contributions. There is to be no carryover of contributions over the minimum required from one year to another, because this amount automatically will become part of the next year's calculation in determining whether liabilities are greater than assets (that is, excess contributions will become part of plan assets for purposes of the next year's calculation). On the other hand, any shortfall of contributions less than the amount required will be carried over from year to year (with interest added) and an excise tax will be payable on these amounts (or on the funding deficiency as shown by the basic funding standard account, if smaller).

A plan that chooses to use the alternative funding method is to maintain both an alternative funding standard account and the basic funding standard account. The basic funding standard account will be charged and credited under the usual rules, but an excise tax generally will not be owed on any "deficiency" shown in that basic account. A plan making this choice is required to maintain both accounts because the minimum funding requirement will be the minimum required contribution under either account, whichever is the lesser.

The requirement under the alternative method could become higher than under the basic method if there was a substantial decrease in the market value of the assets, or if there was a substantial increase in plan liabilities (as through a plan amendment). If the minimum required contributions are lower under the basic standard than under the alternative standard, it is expected that the plan will switch back to the basic funding method.

If a plan switches back from the alternate funding standard to the basic funding standard, generally there is to be a 5-year amortization of the excess of charges over credits that have built up in the basic funding standard account over the years in which the alternative funding standard has been used. This will give the employer a reasonable period of time to fund the amounts that otherwise would have been contributed under the basic funding method, but were not contributed while the alternative funding method was being used. However, to the extent that excess charges (over contributions) have been previously built up in the alternate funding standard account, these are not to be amortized over 5 years, but instead are to be contributed immediately if the excise tax on underfunding is to be avoided. When an employer switches back from the alternative funding standard to the basic funding standard, the employer ceases to maintain the alternate minimum funding standard account. If the employer in some subsequent year returns to the alternate standard, a new account with a zero balance is to be established.

Timing of Contributions

The conference substitute clarifies the intent of both the House bill and the Senate amendment, that contributions made after the close of a plan year may relate back to that plan year for purposes of the minimum funding standards. Under the conference substitute, the contribution may relate back to the plan year if it is made within 2½ months after the close of that plan year, plus any extension granted by the Internal Revenue Service up to an additional 6 months (for a maximum of 8½ months after the end of the year).

Coverage and Exemptions from Coverage

Under title I of the House bill, pension plans of employers in interstate commerce and pension plans of employee organizations with members in interstate commerce generally are covered by the minimum funding rules. Under title II, the new minimum funding rules apply to plans which are, or have been determined to be, tax-qualified. The Senate amendment is substantially the same as title II of the House bill, and in addition reaches substantially the same result as title I of the House bill by generally requiring all plans in interstate commerce to qualify under the tax laws. The conference substitute follows the House bill.

Under the conference substitute, government plans, including plans financed by contributions required under the Railroad Retirement Act, are to be exempt from the new funding requirement but they must meet the requirements of present law (sec. 401(a)(7) of the Internal Revenue Code). The conferees intend that no changes are to be made in the application of the present funding requirements of the Internal Revenue Code to government plans. Although present law establishes a "safe haven rule" for payment of normal cost plus interest on past service costs, it is not intended that this safe haven rule become a requirement for government plans, but that (as under present Regs. § 1.401-6(c)(1)) the determination on whether a plan has terminated is to be made on "all the facts and circumstances in the particular case." Thus, it is intended that there be no change in the application of present law to government plans.

The conference substitute exempts church plans from the new funding requirement if they meet the requirements of present law. However, church plans which elect to be covered under the participation, vesting, and termination insurance provisions are also to be covered by the new funding requirements.

The conference substitute excludes

from the minimum funding rules plans established and maintained outside the United States if they are primarily for the benefit of persons substantially all of whom are nonresident aliens. This is specifically provided in the title I provisions, while under title II, such plans would have no need to seek tax deferral qualification.

The conference substitute excludes from the minimum funding rules of title I unfunded plans maintained by the employer primarily to provide deferred compensation for select management or highly compensated employees (under title II, such plans do not seek tax qualification). The conferees intend that this exemption is to include "consultant contracts" for retired management employees. Additionally, the substitute exempts from the funding rules plans adopted by a partnership exclusively for the benefit of a partner pursuant to section 736 of the Internal Revenue Code.

Under the conference substitute, plans which have not provided for employer contributions at any time after the date of enactment are to be exempt from the minimum funding rules (i.e., plans of unions funded exclusively by contributions of the union members).

An exemption is also provided for profit-sharing and stock bonus plans; however, money purchase pension plans and other individual account plans generally are not excluded from the minimum funding rules.

It is intended that plans generally are to be considered money purchase pension plans which meet the "definitely determinable" standard where the employer's contributions are fixed by the plan, even if the employer's obligation to contribute for any individual employee may vary based on the amount contributed to the plan in any year by the employee. For example, it is expected that a matching plan which provides that an employer will annually contribute up to 6 percent of an employee's salary, but that this contribution will be no more than the employee's own (nondeductible) contribution, will meet the "definitely determinable" criteria. In this case, the employer's contributions are set by the plan, will not vary with profits, and cannot be varied by the employer's action (other than by a plan amendment). (Of course, the plan must meet the nondiscrimination and other requirements of the Code to be qualified.)

Plans funded exclusively by the purchase of certain qualified level premium individual insurance contracts also are not to be subject to the minimum funding requirements. Additionally, the conference substitute makes it clear that where, instead of buying a series of such individual contracts, the employer holds a group insurance contract under which each employee's plan benefit is funded in the same manner as if individual contracts were purchased, the situation is to be treated the same as where there are individual insurance contracts. This generally will be available where the employer's premium is based on the sum of the level premiums attributable to each employee, where an employee's accrued benefit at any point in time is comparable to what would be provided under an individual contract, and as otherwise determined by regulations.

Supplemental unfunded plans which provide benefits in excess of limitations on contributions and benefits under the Internal Revenue Code and plans which are for the highly paid are to be excluded from the new funding standard. In addition, plans established by fraternal societies or other organizations described in section 501(c) (8) or (9) of the Internal Revenue Code are to be exempt if no employer contributions are made to the plan. Also, trusts which are part of plans described in section 501(c)(18) of the Code are to be exempt from the funding standards of title I (the standards of title II do not apply because those plans are not qualified plans).

With respect to the civil enforcement of the funding requirements see "Labor and Tax Administration and Enforcement," *"Labor Department"* (Part VII, below). The excise tax provisions on underfunding in the conference substitute are the same as those in the House bill. However, before sending a notice of deficiency with respect to the first level (and second level) tax, the Internal Revenue Service is to notify the Secretary of Labor and provide him reasonable opportunity to obtain a correction of the funding deficiency, or to comment on the imposition of these taxes. The Service will be able to waive (or abate) the second level, but not the first level, tax upon a correction of underfunding that is obtained by the Secretary of Labor.

Maximum Deduction Limitation

The substitute generally provides that deductions are to be allowed to the extent of contributions required to meet the minimum funding standards. In addition, the present "5 percent" method allowing deductions of not in excess of 5 percent of the annual compensation of covered employees is repealed. Also, the "normal cost" method allowing deductions for normal cost, plus 10 percent of unfunded past service cost, is to be amended to allow deductions for contributions of normal cost, plus amortization over 10 years. Further, deductible limits are to be determined under the funding method and actuarial assumptions used for the minimum funding rules.

Generally, under the substitute, the maximum deduction is to be limited to the required contribution where a plan is subject to the full funding limitation. However, a special election is available under the substitute with regard to deductions if a plan becomes fully funded as a result of an amendment that decreases plan liabilities (benefits payable under the plan). This election is available only with respect to plan amendments that are negotiated through the collective bargaining process. Under this election, the maximum amount deductible generally will be normal cost under the plan less the amount needed to amortize over 10 years (principal plus interest) the decrease in plan liabilities as a result of the plan amendment. However, if a plan is fully funded without regard to the collectively bargained decrease in liabilities, no deduction is to be allowed. If a plan elects this provision, the amounts deductible in future years for contributions to the plan will be decreased (pursuant to regulations) by the amount required for a 10-year amortization of the collectively bargained decrease in liabilities.

A special rule is provided with respect to plans of regulated public utilities doing business in 40 States and furnishing certain telephone or other communications services which are rate regulated. (This rule also applies to plans of other companies which are members of a controlled group that includes such a public utility doing business in 40 States.) Under this provision, if the Secretary of the Treasury finds that the plan is a collectively bargained plan, the rules described above for deductions where there have been decreases in liabilities on account of plan amendments would apply to decreases in plan liabilities as a result of an increase in benefits under Title II of the Social Security Act.

Effective Dates

In the case of new plans, the funding provisions are to apply to the first full plan year beginning after the date of enactment of the bill. For example, if a plan was established on October 1, 1974, but its plan year is a calendar year, the new provisions are to apply to the plan year beginning January 1, 1975.

Generally, in the case of plans existing on January 1, 1974, the new funding provisions are to become applicable for plan years beginning after December 31, 1975. In the case of collectively bargained plans (both single employer and multiemployer plans) existing on January 1, 1974, the effective date would be delayed until the termination of the contract existing on January 1, 1974, but not later than plan years beginning after December 31, 1980. Where an employer has plans which involve both collective bargaining unit employees and other employees, the effective dates applicable to collective bargained plans are to govern if (on January 1, 1974) at least 25 percent of the plan participants are members of the employee unit covered by the collectively bargained agreement. (This is described more fully in connection with the effective dates for participation.)

Where a qualified plan does not meet the funding requirements of existing law because of vesting or participation requirements made applicable by the substitute and where the funding requirements of the conference substitute do not become applicable until a later time than the vesting or participation requirements, then to the extent that failure to meet the funding requirements of existing law is attributable to these new vesting or participation requirements, no plan is to be disqualified in this interim period on the grounds of underfunding.

The effective date for the rules with respect to maximum deduction limits is the same as the effective date for the funding rules generally.

V. Fiduciary Responsibility (Secs. 401-414 and 2003 of the Bill and Sec. 4975 of the Internal Revenue Code

House Bill and Senate Amendment

The House bill generally includes rules governing the responsibility of plan fiduciaries only in the labor provisions of the bill (title I). The labor provisions establish rules governing the basic responsibilities of plan fiduciaries, the structure of plan administration, and also establish certain transactions as "prohibited transactions." (Present law under the Internal Revenue Code has similar prohibited transaction rules, which were unchanged by the House bill.)

Under the House bill, all plan fiduciaries must act, with respect to the plan, in accordance with a "prudent man" rule. In addition, plan fiduciaries generally must diversify plan investments (with certain exceptions for profit-sharing plans, etc., that invest in employer securities) and must act for the exclusive benefit of the plan participants and beneficiaries. The House bill also provides that all plans must be in writing, that plan assets generally are to be held in trust, and that trustees generally are to have the exclusive authority to manage and control plan assets. However, asset management in certain circumstances may be delegated to qualified investment managers. The bill also provides that plan trustees may allocate their responsibilities if the plan so provides and that in this event generally only the persons to whom responsibilities have been allocated would be liable for a surcharge.

Under the House bill, fiduciaries generally are prohibited from dealing on behalf of a plan with persons known to be parties-in-interest unless the dealings are for adequate consideration. Also, the bill generally prohibits fiduciaries from dealing with plan assets for their own accounts, receiving consideration from other parties dealing with the plan in a transaction involving the plan, or acting in a transaction involving the plan on behalf of a person who is adverse to the plan.

Under the House bill, a fiduciary is to be personally liable for losses to the plan resulting from violations of the fiduciary responsibility rules.

The Senate amendment includes rules governing fiduciary responsibility in both the labor and tax provisions. The labor provisions of the amendment, as in the case of the House bill, deal with the basic responsibility of fiduciaries, plan administrators, and structure; also and these provisions would establish certain transactions as prohibited transactions. Fiduciaries (and parties-in-interest) are to be personally liable under the labor provisions for losses sustained by a plan that result from a violation of these rules. The tax provisions of the amendment also establish prohibited transaction rules (which are nearly identical to the rules in the labor provisions) which are to be enforced through an excise tax on parties-in-interest.

The Senate amendment rules governing the basic responsibilties of plan fiduciaries (e.g., acting with prudence and for the exclusive benefit of participants and beneficiaries) are similar to the rules of the House bill.

With respect to plan administration, the amendment does not require plan assets generally to be held in trust nor does it require that assets be administered by trustees. The amendment would, however, deem plan assets to be held in trust. Also, the Senate amendment does not include provisions similar to those of the House bill with respect to allocation of responsibilities among trustees.

Under both the labor and tax provisions of the Senate amendment, plan fiduciaries generally are prohibited from engaging in specified transactions with parties-in-interest whether or not these transactions are for adequate consideration. However, the amendment provides for administrative variances from these prohibitions if certain conditions are met, and also would provide statutory exemptions for, e.g., paying reasonable compensation to parties-to-interest for services rendered to the plan which are necessary for the plan's operation. The amendment also would prohibit a fiduciary from dealing with the plan assets on his own account, receiving consideration from other parties dealing with the plan, and acting on behalf of a person adverse to the plan.

Fiduciary Responsibility Rules, in General

The conference substitute establishes rules governing the conduct of plan fiduciaries under the labor laws (title I) and also establishes rules governing the conduct of disqualified persons (who are generally the same people as "parties in interest" under the labor provisions) with respect to the plan under the tax laws (title II). This division corresponds to the basic difference in focus of the two departments. The labor law provisions apply rules and remedies similar to those under traditional trust law to govern the conduct of fiduciaries. The tax law provisions apply an excise tax on disqualified persons who violate the new prohibited transaction rules; this is similar to the approach taken under the present rules against self-dealing that apply to private foundations.

The labor provisions deal with the structure of plan administration, provide general standards of conduct for fiduciaries, and make certain specific transactions "prohibited transactions" which plan fiduciaries are not to engage in. The tax provisions include only the prohibited transaction rules and apply only to disqualified persons, not fiduciaries (unless the fiduciary is otherwise a disqualified person and the transaction involved him, or the fiduciary benefited from the transaction). To the maximum extent possible, the prohibited transaction rules are identical in the labor and tax provisions, so they will apply in the same manner to the same transaction. (However, there are some differences, such as not prohibiting under the tax law an act to which the tax sanction cannot appropriately apply.)

Coverage of the Labor Provisions

The labor fiduciary responsibility rules generally apply to all employee benefit plans (both retirement plans and welfare plans) in or affecting interstate commerce. The usual exceptions for government plans, church plans (which do not elect to have the participation, vesting, funding, and insurance rules apply), workmen's compensation plans, and nonresident alien plans apply here as well as to the other parts of the labor provisions. In addition, the labor fiduciary rules do not apply to an unfunded plan primarily devoted to providing deferred compensation for a select group of management or highly compensated employees. For example, if a "phantom stock" or "shadow stock" plan were to be established solely for the officers of a corporation, it would not be covered by the labor fiduciary rules. Also, a deferred compensation arrangement solely for retiring partners (under sec. 736 of the Internal Revenue Code) is to be exempt from the fiduciary responsibility rules. Additionally, the fiduciary responsibility rules do not apply to a so-called excess benefit plan which is unfunded.

Since mutual funds are regulated by the Investment Company Act of 1940 and, since (under the Internal Revenue Code) mutual funds must be broadly held, it is not considered necessary to apply the fiduciary rules to mutual funds merely because plans invest in their shares. Therefore, the substitute provides that the mere investment by a plan in the shares of a mutual fund is not to be sufficient to cause the assets of the fund to be considered the assets of the plan. (However, a plan's assets will include the shares of a mutual fund held by the plan.)

The substitute also provides that a mutual fund is not to be considered a fiduciary or a party-in-interest merely because a plan invests in its shares, except that the mutual fund may be a fiduciary or party-in-interest if it acts in connection with a plan covering the employees of the investment company, the investment adviser, or its principal underwriter.

An insurance company also is not considered to hold plan assets if a plan purchases an insurance policy from it, to the extent that the policy provides payments guaranteed by the company. If the policy guarantees basic payments but other payments may vary with, e.g., investment performance, then the variable part of the policy and assets attributed thereto are not to be considered as guaranteed, and are to be considered as plan assets subject to the fiduciary rules. (However, such assets need not be held in trust under the fiduciary responsibility rule.)

Additionally, it is understood that assets placed in a separate account managed by an insurance company are separately managed and the insurance company's payments generally are based on the investment performance of these particular assets. Consequently, insurance companies are to be responsible under the general fiduciary rules with respect to assets held under separate account contracts, and the assets of these contracts are to be considered as plan assets (but need not be held in trust). However, to the extent that insurance companies place some of their own funds in these separate accounts to provide for contingencies, this separate account "surplus" is not to be subject to the fiduciary responsibility rules.

These rules are to apply with respect to insurance policies issued by an insurance company, or by an insurance service or insurance organization. The conferees understand that some companies that provide, e.g., health insurance, are not technically considered as "insurance companies." It is intended that these companies are to be included within the terms "insurance service or insurance organization."

Structure of Plan Administration

Establishment of plan.—Under the labor provisions of the conference substitute, every covered employee benefit plan (both retirement and welfare plan) is to be established and maintained in writing. A written plan is to be required in order that every employee may, on examining the plan documents, determine exactly what his rights and obligations are under the plan. Also, a written plan is required so the employees may know who is responsible for operating the plan. Therefore, the plan document is to provide for the "named fiduciaries" who have authority to control and manage the plan operations and administration. A named fiduciary may be a person whose name actually appears in the document, or may be a person who holds an office specified in the document, such as the company president. A named fiduciary also may be a person who is identified by the employer or union, under a procedure set out in the document. For example, the plan may provide that the employer's board of directors is to choose the person who manages or controls the plan. In addition, a named fiduciary may be a person identified by the employers and union acting jointly. For example, the members of a joint board of trustees of a Taft-Hartley plan would usually be named fiduciaries.

Plan contents.—Under the labor provisions of the substitute, each plan is to provide a procedure for establishing a funding policy and method to carry out the plan objectives. This procedure is to enable the plan fiduciaries to determine the plan's short- and long-run financial needs and communicate these requirements to the appropriate persons. For example, with a retirement plan it is expected that under this procedure the persons who manage the plan will determine whether the plan has a short-run need for liquidity, (e.g., to pay benefits) or whether liquidity is a long-run goal and investment growth is a more current need. This in turn is to be communicated to the persons responsible for investments, so that investment policy can be appropriately coordinated with plan needs. Also, the plan documents are to set out the basis for contributions to and payments from the plan. Thus, the plan is to specify what part (if any) of contributions are to come from employees and what part from employers. Also, it is to specify the basis on which payments are to be made to participants and beneficiaries.

It is customary for those who manage and control the plan to allocate their responsibilities and, within limits, designate others to carry out the daily management of the plan. The conference substitute establishes special rules which will enable fiduciaries to continue to allocate and delegate their responsibilities. However, allocation or delegation is to be allowed only if the plan provides for it (or provides procedures for it) in accordance with the terms of the substitute, as discussed below.

Each plan also is to provide a procedure for amendments and for identifying who can amend the plan. Additionally, following common practice, a plan may provide that a person may serve in more than one fiduciary capacity under the plan, including service both as administrator and trustee. As described below, the plan may also provide for the hiring of investment (and other) advisers and investment managers.

Establishment of trust.—The labor provisions of the substitute generally provide that all plan assets are to be held in trust by trustees and also provide that the trustees are to manage and control the plan assets. Also, the plan trustees are to be appointed in the plan or trust documents or appointed by a named fiduciary. However, in order that persons who act as trustees recognize their special responsibilities with respect to plan assets, trustees are to accept appointment before they act in this capacity.

If the plan provides that the trustees are subject to the direction of named fiduciaries, then the trustees are not to have the exclusive management and control over the plan assets, but generally are to follow the directions of the named fiduciary. Therefore, if the plan sponsor wants an investment committee to direct plan investments, he may provide for such an arrangement in the plan. In addition, since investment decisions are basic to plan operations, members of such an investment committee are to be named fiduciaries. (For example, the plan could provide that the investment committee is to consist of the persons who serve as the president, vice-president for finance, and comptroller of the employer.) If the plan so provides, the trustee who is directed by an investment committee is to follow that committee's directions unless it is clear on their face that the actions to be taken under those directions would be prohibited by the fiduciary responsibility rules of the bill or would be contrary to the terms of the plan or trust.

In addition (as discussed below), to the extent that the management of plan assets is delegated to a special category of persons called "investment managers", the trustee is not to have exclusive discretion to manage and control the plan assets, nor would the trustee be liable for any act of such investment manager.

A trust is not to be required in the

case of plan assets which consist of insurance (including annuity) contracts or policies issued by an insurance company qualified to do business in a State (or the District of Columbia). The same exemption will apply to the new section 403(b) custodial account arrangement involving investment in mutual funds, since these are treated as amounts contributed for an annuity contract under the tax law. Although these contracts need not be held in trust, nevertheless, the person who holds the contract is to be a fiduciary and is to act in accordance with the fiduciary rules of the substitute with respect to these contracts. For example, this person is to prudently take and keep exclusive control of the contracts, and is to use prudent care and skill to preserve this property.

To the extent that plan assets are held by an insurance company they need not be held in trust. However, to the extent the substitute treats assets held by an insurance company as "plan assets", the insurance company is to be treated as a fiduciary with respect to the plan, and is to meet the fiduciary standards of the conference substitute.

The labor provisions of the substitute also provide that the assets of H.R. 10 plans (plans for the self-employed and their employees) and individual retirement accounts need not be held in trust to the extent they are held in custodial accounts qualified under the Internal Revenue Code. It is recognized that the substitute generally amends the Internal Revenue Code to make use of custodial accounts more available for all plans, and that this is expected to decrease the cost of asset administration for many plans. Custodial accounts also may be used by all plans under the labor provisions. However, a plan (which is not exempt from the trust requirements) that uses a custodial account also will have to have a trustee (who can be the plan administrator or sponsor). The plan trustee will have the responsibility for investment decisions with regard to the assets and the custodian will (as under present practice) merely retain custody of these assets. Since the plan sponsor could be the trustee, the costs of plan administration will remain as low as with the present custodial account arrangements, but the plan also would have a responsible person in charge of investment decisions.

A trust also is not to be required for a plan not subject to the participation, vesting and funding provisions of title I, and the plan termination insurance provisions, to the extent provided by the Secretary of Labor.

Liability for breach of co-fiduciary responsibility, in general.—Under the labor provisions of the conference substitute, a fiduciary of a plan is to be liable for the breach of fiduciary responsibility by another fiduciary of the plan if he knowingly participates in a breach of duty committed by the other fiduciary. Under this rule, the fiduciary must know the other person is a fiduciary with respect to the plan, must know that he participated in the act that constituted a breach, and must know that it was a breach. For example, A and B are co-trustees, and the terms of the trust provide that they are not to invest in, *e.g.,* commodity futures. If A suggests to B that B invest part of the plan assets in commodity futures, and if B does so, A, as well as B, is to be liable for the breach.

In addition, a fiduciary is to be liable for the breach of fiduciary responsibility by another fiduciary of the plan, if he knowingly undertakes to conceal a breach committed by the other. For the first fiduciary to be liable, he must know that the other is a fiduciary with regard to the plan, must know of the act, and must know that it is a breach. For example, A and B are co-trustees, and B invests in commodity futures in violation of the trust instrument. If B tells his co-trustee A of this investment, A would be liable with B for breach of fiduciary responsibility if he concealed this investment.

Also, if a fiduciary knows that another fiduciary of the plan has committed a breach, and the first fiduciary knows that this is a breach, the first fiduciary must take reasonable steps under the circumstances to remedy the breach. In the second example above, if A has the authority to do so, and if it is prudent under the circumstances, A may be required to dispose of the commodity futures acquired by B. Alternatively, the most appropriate steps in the circumstances may be to notify the plan sponsor of the breach, or to proceed to an appropriate Federal court for instructions, or bring the matter to the attention of the Secretary of Labor. The proper remedy is to be determined by the facts and circumstances of the particular case, and it may be affected by the relationship of the fiduciary to the plan and to the co-fiduciary, the duties and responsibilities of the fiduciary in question, and the nature of the breach.

A fiduciary also is to be liable for the loss caused by the breach of fiduciary responsibility by another fiduciary of the plan if he enables the other fiduciary to commit a breach through his failure to exercise prudence (or otherwise comply with the basic fiduciary rules of the bill) in carrying out his specific responsibilities. For example, A and B are co-trustees and are to jointly manage the plan assets. A improperly allows B to have the sole custody of the plan assets and makes no inquiry as to his conduct. B is thereby enabled to sell the property and to embezzle the proceeds. A is to be liable for a breach of fiduciary responsibility.

Allocation of duties of co-trustees.—Under the conference substitute, if the plan assets are held by co-trustees, then each trustee has the duty to manage and control those assets. For example, shares of stock held in trust by several trustees generally should be registered in the name of all the trustees, or in the name of the trust. In addition, each trustee is to use reasonable care to prevent his co-trustee from committing a breach of fiduciary duty.

Although generally each trustee must manage and control the plan assets, nevertheless, under the substitute specific duties and responsibilities with respect to the management of plan assets may be allocated among co-trustees by the trust instrument. For example, the trust instrument may provide that trustee A is to manage and control one-half of the plan assets, and trustee B is to manage and control the other half of the plan assets.

Also, the trust instrument may provide that specific duties may be allocated by agreement among the co-trustees. In this case, however, the conferees intend that the trust instrument is to specifically delineate the duties that may be allocated by agreement of the co-trustees and is to specify a procedure for such allocation. Also, the trustees must act prudently in implementing such an allocation procedure.

If duties are allocated among co-trustees in accordance with the substitute, a trustee to whom duties have not been allocated is not to be liable for any loss that arises from acts or omissions of the co-trustee to whom such responsibilities have been allocated.

However, a co-trustee will be liable notwithstanding allocation if he individually fails to comply with the other fiduciary standards. For example, a co-trustee would be liable on account of his own acts if he did not act in accordance with the prudent man standard and thereby caused the plan to suffer a loss. In addition, the general rules of co-fiduciary liability are to apply. Therefore, for example, if a trustee had knowledge of a breach by a co-trustee, he would be liable unless he made reasonable efforts to remedy the breach.

Under the substitute, it is made clear that if plan assets are held in separate trusts a trustee of one trust is not responsible as a co-trustee of the other trust.

The conferees understand that under certain circumstances, trustees (and other fiduciaries) in discharging their responsibilities in accordance with the prudent man rule will hire agents to perform ministerial acts. In this case, the liability of the trustees (and other fiduciaries) for acts of their agents is to be established in accordance with the prudent man rule.

Allocation and delegation of duties other than the management of plan assets.—The substitute also provides for the allocation and delegation by fiduciaries of duties that do not involve the management and control of plan assets.[1] However, in order that participants and beneficiaries, etc., may readily determine who is responsible for managing a plan, the substitute generally provides that only "named fiduciaries" will be able to allocate or delegate their responsibilities.

Under the substitute, if the plan so provides, named co-fiduciaries may allocate their specific responsibilities among themselves, and named fiduciaries may delegate all or part of their duties (which do not involve asset management) to others. The substitute also provides that upon proper allocation or delegation fiduciaries will not be liable for the acts or omissions of the persons to whom duties have been allocated or delegated.

Allocation or delegation (and the consequent elimination of liability) can only occur under specific circumstances. The plan must specifically allow such allocation or delegation, and the plan must expressly provide a procedure for it. For example, the plan may provide that delegation may occur only with respect to specified duties, and only on the approval of the plan sponsor or on the approval of the joint board of trustees of a Taft-Hartley plan. Also, in implementing the procedures of the plan, plan fiduciaries must act prudently and in the interests of participants and beneficiaries. The fiduciaries also must act in this manner in choosing the person to whom they allocate or delegate their duties. Additionally, they must act in this manner in continuing the allocation or delegation of their duties.

---

[1] For example, these rules would govern the allocation or delegation of duties with respect to payment of benefits.

In order to act prudently in retaining a person to whom duties have been delegated, it is expected that the fiduciary will periodically review this person's performance. Depending upon the circumstances, this requirement may be satisfied by formal periodic review (which may be by all the named fiduciaries who have participated in the delegation or by a specially designated review committee), or it may be met through day-to-day contact and evaluation, or in other appropriate ways. Since effective review requires that a person's services can be terminated, it may be necessary to enter into arrangements which the fiduciary can promptly terminate (within the limits of the circumstances).

Even though a named fiduciary has properly delegated his duties in accordance with the substitute, he may still be liable for the acts of a co-fiduciary if he breaches the general rules of co-fiduciary liability by, *e.g.*, knowingly concealing a breach of a co-fiduciary.

Investment managers, investment committees, etc.—Under the substitute, if the plan so provides, a person who is a named fiduciary with respect to the control or management of plan assets may appoint a qualified investment manager to manage all or part of the plan assets. (However, in choosing an investment manager, the named fiduciary must act prudently and in the interests of participants and beneficiaries, and also must act in this manner in continuing the use of an investment manager.) In this case, the plan trustee would no longer have responsibility for managing the assets controlled by the qualified investment manager, and the trustee would not be liable for the acts or omissions of the investment manager. Also, as long as the named fiduciary had chosen and retained the investment manager prudentially, the named fiduciary would not be liable for the acts or omissions of the manager. Under the substitute, a qualified investment manager may be an investment adviser registered under the Investment Advisers Act of 1940, a bank (as defined in that Act), or an insurance company qualified to perform investment management services under State law in more than one State. To be qualified, the investment manager also must acknowledge in writing that he is a plan fiduciary.

As described above *(Establishment of trust)* the plan may also provide that the trustee is to be subject to the direction of named fiduciaries with respect to investment decisions. In this case, if the trustee properly follows the instructions of the named fiduciaries, the trustee generally is not to be liable for losses which arise out of following these instructions. (The named fiduciaries, however, would be subject to the usual fiduciary responsibility rules and would be subject to liability on breach of these rules.)

In addition, a plan may provide that named fiduciaries (or fiduciaries to whom duties have been properly delegated) may employ investment and other advisers. However, a fiduciary cannot be relieved of his own responsibilities merely because he follows the advice of such a person. (Also, investment advisers would be fiduciaries under the substitute.)

Basic Fiduciary Rules

Prudent man standard.—The substitute requires that each fiduciary of a plan act with the care, skill, prudence, and diligence under the circumstances then prevailing that a prudent man acting in a like capacity and familiar with such matters would use in conducting an enterprise of like character and with like aims. The conferees expect that the courts will interpret this prudent man rule (and the other fiduciary standards) bearing in mind the special nature and purpose of employee benefit plans.

Under the Internal Revenue Code, qualified retirement plans must be for the exclusive benefit of the employees and their beneficiaries. Following this requirement, the Internal Revenue Service has developed general rules that govern the investment of plan assets, including a requirement that cost must not exceed fair market value at the time of purchase, there must be a fair return commensurate with the prevailing rate, sufficient liquidity must be maintained to permit distributions, and the safeguards and diversity that a prudent investor would adhere to must be present. The conferees intend that to the extent that a fiduciary meets the prudent man rule of the labor provisions, he will be deemed to meet these aspects of the exclusive benefit requirements under the Internal Revenue Code.

Under the conference substitute, plan fiduciaries also must act in accordance with plan documents and instruments to the extent that they are consistent with the requirements established in the bill.

Exclusive benefit for employees.— Under the conference substitute each fiduciary of a plan must act solely in the interests of the plan's participants and beneficiaries and exclusively to provide benefits to these participants and beneficiaries (or to pay reasonable plan administrative costs).

Since the assets of the employee benefit plan are to be held for the exclusive benefit of participants and beneficiaries, plan assets generally are not to inure to the benefit of the employer. However, the conference substitute allows an employer's contributions to be returned to him in certain limited situations.

An employer's contributions can be returned within one year after they are made to the plan, if made as a mistake of fact. (For example, an employer may have made an arithmetical error in calculating the amounts that were to be contributed to the plan.) Also, if an employer contributes to a plan on the condition that the plan is tax-qualified or on the condition that a current tax deduction is allowed for the contribution, and it is later determined that the plan is not qualified (or the deduction is not allowed), the contribution can be returned if the plan provides for it. In this case, the contribution can be returned within one year after the disallowance of qualification or deduction. With regard to a disallowance of deductions, contributions can be returned only to the extent of the amount for which a deduction is denied. (For example, if $100 is contributed on the condition it is deductible and $20 is later determined not to be deductible, only $20 could be returned, and not $100). Also with respect to qualification, contributions can be returned on the denial of initial or of continuing qualification (in the case of contributions made after *e.g.*, a plan amendment).

An employer's contributions under an H.R. 10 plan also can be returned to the employer to the extent permitted to avoid payment of an excise tax on excess contributions.

Under the labor (but not the tax) provisions of the substitute, the transfer or distribution of the assets of a welfare plan on termination of the plan is to be in accordance with the terms of the plan except as otherwise prescribed by regulations of the Secretary of Labor. It is intended that the Secretary of Labor would allow the terms of the plan (or in the case of a plan subject to collective bargaining, the collective bargaining agreement) to govern such distribution or transfer of assets except to the extent that implementation of the plan or agreement would unduly impair the accrued benefits of the plan participants or would not be in the best interests of the plan participants. Where such distribution or transfer is incidental to the merger of one multiemployer plan with another, it is expected that the Secretary of Labor would disallow the distribution or transfer only where the merger would reasonably be expected to jeopardize the ability of the plan to meet its obligations or would otherwise not be in the best interests of the plan participants.

Also, under the labor (but not the tax) provisions of the substitute, on termination of a pension plan to which the plan termination insurance provisions do not apply, the assets of the plan are to be allocated in accordance with the provisions under the plan termination insurance title of the Act governing such allocation (as if the plan were covered by termination insurance), except as otherwise provided in regulations prescribed by the Secretary of Labor. It is intended that regulations by the Secretary of Labor in this case would be similar to the regulations governing the distribution of assets on termination of a welfare plan as described above.

Diversification requirement. — The substitute requires fiduciaries to diversify plan assets to minimize the risk of large losses, unless under the circumstances it is clearly prudent not to do so. It is not intended that a more stringent standard of prudence be established with the use of the term "clearly prudent." Instead, by using this term it is intended that in an action for plan losses based on breach of the diversification requirement, the plaintiff's initial burden will be to demonstrate that there has been a failure to diversify. The defendant then is to have the burden of demonstrating that this failure to diversify was prudent. The substitute places these relative burdens on the parties in this matter, because the basic policy is to require diversification, and if diversification on its face does not exist, then the burden of justifying failure to follow this general policy should be on the fiduciary who engages in this conduct.

The degree of investment concentration that would violate this requirement to diversify cannot be stated as a fixed percentage, because a prudent fiduciary must consider the facts and circumstances of each case. The factors to be considered include (1) the purposes of the plan; (2) the amount of the plan assets; (3) financial and industrial conditions; (4) the type of investment, whether mortgages, bonds or shares of stock or otherwise; (5) distribution as to geographical location; (6) distribution as to industries; (7) the dates of maturity.

A fiduciary usually should not invest the whole or an unreasonably large proportion of the trust property in a single security. Ordinarily the fiduciary should not invest the whole or an unduly large proportion of the trust property in one type of security or in various types of securities dependent upon the success of one enterprise or upon conditions in one locality, since the effect is to increase the risk of large losses. Thus, although the fiduciary may be authorized to invest in industrial stocks, he should not invest a disproportionate amount of the plan assets in the shares of corporations engaged in a particular industry. If he is investing in mortgages on real property he should not invest a disproportionate amount of the trust in mortgages in a particular district or on a particular class of property so that a decline in property values in that district or of that class might cause a large loss.

The assets of many pension plans are managed by one or more investment managers. For example, one investment manager, A, may be responsible for 10 percent of the assets of a plan and instructed by the named fiduciary or trustee to invest solely in bonds; another investment manager, B, may be responsible for a different 10 percent of the assets of the same plan and instructed to invest solely in equities. Such arrangements often result in investment returns which are quite favorable to the plan, its participants, and its beneficiaries. In these circumstances, A would invest solely in bonds in accordance with his instructions and would diversify the bond investments in accordance with the diversification standard, the prudent man standard, and all other provisions applicable to A as a fiduciary. Similarly, B would invest solely in equities in accordance with his instructions and these standards. Neither A nor B would incur any liability for diversifying assets subject to their management in accordance with their instructions.

The conferees intend that, in general, whether the plan assets are sufficiently diversified is to be determined by examining the ultimate investment of the plan assets. For example, the conferees understand that for efficiency and economy plans may invest all their assets in a single bank or other pooled investment fund, but that the pooled fund itself could have diversified investments. It is intended that, in this case, the diversification rule is to be applied to the plan by examining the diversification of the investments in the pooled fund. The same is true with respect to investments in a mutual fund. Also, generally a plan may be invested wholly in insurance or annuity contracts without violating the diversification rules, since generally an insurance company's assets are to be invested in a diversified manner.

(With respect to special rules regarding diversification of assets and investment in employer securities, etc., by certain individual account plans, see "Employer securities and employer real property," below.)

Certain individual account plans.— Under the substitute, a special rule is provided for individual account plans where the participant is permitted to, and in fact does, exercise independent control over the assets in his individual account. In this case, the individual is not to be regarded as a fiduciary and other persons who are fiduciaries with respect to the plan are not to be liable for any loss that results from the exercise and control by the participant or beneficiary. Therefore, if the participant instructs the plan trustee to invest the full balance of his account in, e.g., a single stock, the trustee is not to be liable for any loss because of a failure to diversify or because the investment does not meet the prudent man standards. However, the investment must not contradict the terms of the plan, and if the plan on its face prohibits such investments, the trustee could not follow the instructions and avoid liability.

The conferees recognize that there may be difficulties in determining whether the participant in fact exercises independent control over his account. Consequently, whether participants and beneficiaries exercise independent control is to be determined pursuant to regulations prescribed by the Secretary of Labor. The conferees expect that the regulations will provide more stringent standards with respect to determining whether there is an independent exercise of control where the investments may inure to the direct or indirect benefit of the plan sponsor since, in this case participants might be subject to pressure with respect to investment decisions. (Because of the difficulty of ensuring that there is independence of choice in an employer established individual retirement account, it is expected that the regulations will generally provide that sufficient independent control will not exist with respect to the acquisition of employer securities by participants and beneficiaries under this type of plan.) In addition, the conferees expect that the regulations generally will require that for there to be independent control by participants, a broad range of investments must be available to the individual participants and beneficiaries.

Transfer of assets outside of the United States.—In order to prevent "runaway assets," the labor provisions of the substitute generally prohibit a fiduciary from transferring or maintaining the indicia of ownership of any plan assets outside the jurisdiction of the district courts of the United States. However, such a transaction may be permitted under regulations issued by the Secretary of Labor.

It is recognized that investment in securities of foreign companies and governments have been and may well continue to be in the best interests of plan participants in appropriate circumstances and with proper safeguards, and that the physical transfer of securities back and forth overseas may involve unduly high cost and impose unreasonable limitations on the investment of plan funds in such securities. The basic objective of the requirement that the indicia of ownership remain within the jurisdiction of a United States District Court is to preclude frustration of adequate fiduciary supervision and remedies for breach of trust. However, the risk of misappropriation of plan assets or their removal beyond the effective process of an American court is minimal where the assets are under the management or control of a bank, trust company or similar institution which is subject to adequate regulation and examination by State or Federal supervisory agencies. Such an institution would be responsive to legal process and to the traditional principles of fiduciary responsibility under trust law. Accordingly, it is contemplated that the Secretary of Labor will, as a general rule, grant an exemption to such institutions meeting standards that would assure the safety of plan assets. It is further contemplated that the Secretary will issue temporary regulations authorizing institutions with a history of investing pension funds in foreign securities as a matter of policy to continue to do so pending formal action on an application for exemption.

Prohibited Transactions

In general.—The conference substitute prohibits plan fiduciaries and parties-in-interest from engaging in a number of specific transactions. Prohibited transaction rules are included both in the labor and tax provisions of the substitute. Under the labor provisions (title I), the fiduciary is the main focus of the prohibited transaction rules. This corresponds to the traditional focus of trust law and of civil enforcement of fiduciary responsibilities through the courts. On the other hand, the tax provisions (title II) focus on the disqualified person. This corresponds to the present prohibited transaction provisions relating to private foundations.[2]

The prohibited transactions, and exceptions therefrom, are nearly identical in the labor and tax provisions. However, the labor and tax provisions differ somewhat in establishing liability for violation of prohibited transactions. Under the labor provisions, a fiduciary will only be liable if he

---

[2] Generally, the substitute defines a prohibited transaction as the same type of transaction that constitutes prohibited self-dealings with respect to private foundations, with differences that are appropriate in the employee benefit area. As with the private foundation rules, under the substitute, both direct and indirect dealings of the proscribed type are prohibited.

knew or should have known that he engaged in a prohibited transaction. Such a knowledge requirement is not included in the tax provisions. This distinction conforms to the distinction in present law in the private foundation provisions (where a foundation's manager generally is subject to a tax on self-dealing if he acted with knowledge, but a disqualified person is subject to tax without proof of knowledge).

Under the labor provisions a fiduciary will be liable for losses to a plan from a prohibited transaction in which he engaged if he would have known the transaction involving the particular party-in-interest was prohibited if he had acted as a prudent man. The type of investigation that will be needed to satisfy the test of prudence will depend upon the particular facts and circumstances of the case. In the case of a significant transaction, generally for a fiduciary to be prudent he must make a thorough investigation of the other party's relationship to the plan to determine if he is a party-in-interest. In the case of a normal and insubstantial day-to-day transaction, it may be sufficient to check the identity of the other party against a roster of parties-in-interest that is periodically updated.

In general, it is expected that a transaction will not be a prohibited transaction (under either the labor or tax provisions) if the transaction is an ordinary "blind" purchase or sale of securities through an exchange where neither buyer nor seller (nor the agent of either) knows the identity of the other party involved. In this case, there is no reason to impose a sanction on a fiduciary (or party-in-interest) merely because, by chance, the other party turns out to be a party-in-interest (or plan).

The labor prohibitions affect "parties-in-interest", and the tax prohibitions affect "disqualified persons." The two terms are substantially the same in most respects, but the labor term includes a somewhat broader range of persons, as described below.

Coverage.—The prohibited transaction rules under the labor provisions apply to all plans to which the general labor fiduciary rules apply, as described above. The tax law prohibited transaction rules apply to all qualified retirement plans (under secs. 401, 403(a), and 405(a) of the Internal Revenue Code) and to all qualified individual retirement accounts, individual retirement annuities, and individual retirement bonds (under secs. 408 and 409 of the Code). In addition, the tax law rules are to continue to apply even if the plan, etc., should later lose its tax qualification.

The tax law prohibited transaction provisions follow the labor provisions with respect to whether the assets of an insurance company or mutual fund are to be considered the assets of a plan. Also, the tax provisions exclude from the new prohibited transaction rules government plans, and church plans which have not elected coverage under the new participation, vesting, funding and insurance provisions. (The latter plans, if they are qualified plans, will be subject to present law.)

Party-in-interest transactions. — Under the substitute, the direct or indirect sale, exchange, or leasing of any property between the plan and a party-in-interest [3] (with exceptions subsequently noted) is a prohibited transaction. Under this rule, the transaction is prohibited whether or not the property involved is owned by the plan or party-in-interest, and the prohibited transaction includes sales, etc., from the party-in-interest to the plan, and also from the plan to the party-in-interest. Also, following the private foundation rules of the tax law, a transfer of property by a party-in-interest to a plan is treated as a sale or exchange if the property is subject to a mortgage or a similar lien which the party-in-interest placed on the property within 10 years prior to the transfer to the plan or if the plan assumes a mortgage or similar lien placed on

---
[3] Hereafter, the term "party-in-interest" will include the term "disqualified person" unless otherwise indicated.

the property by a party in interest within 10 years prior to the transfer. This rule prevents circumvention of the prohibition on sale by mortgaging the property before transfer to the plan.

The conference substitute also generally prohibits the direct or indirect lending of money or other extension of credit between a plan and parties-in-interest. For example, a prohibited transaction generally will occur if a loan to a plan is guaranteed by a party-in-interest, unless it comes within the special exemption for employee stock ownership plans.

It is intended that prohibited loans include the acquisition by the plan of a debt instrument (such as a bond or note) which is an obligation of a party-in-interest. (However, the transition rules described below establish special rules for certain debt instruments held by a plan before July 1, 1974.) Similarly, it is intended that it would be a prohibited transaction (in effect a loan by the plan to the employer) if the employer funds his contributions to the plan with his own debt obligations.

With certain exceptions described below, the direct or indirect furnishing of goods or services or facilities between a plan and a party-in-interest also is prohibited. This would apply, for example, to the furnishing of personal living quarters to a party-in-interest.

The substitute prohibits the direct or indirect transfer of any plan income or assets to or for the benefit of a party-in-interest. It also prohibits the use of plan income or assets by or for the benefit of any party-in-interest. As in other situations, this prohibited transaction may occur even though there has not been a transfer of money or property between the plan and a party-in-interest. For example, securities purchases or sales by a plan to manipulate the price of the security to the advantage of a party-in-interest constitutes a use by or for the benefit of a party-in-interest of any assets of the plan.

The labor provisions and the tax provisions differ slightly on the wording with respect to this latter prohibition. The labor provision prohibits such use of the plan's "assets", and the tax provision prohibits use of the plan's "income or assets". (This same difference appears with respect to other prohibited transactions, as well.) The conferees intend that the labor and tax provisions are to be interpreted in the same way and both are to apply to income and assets. The different wordings are used merely because of different usages in the labor and tax laws. In addition, even though the term "income" is used in the tax law, it is intended that this is not to imply in any way that investment in growth assets (which may provide little current income) is to be prohibited where such investment would otherwise meet the prudent man and other rules of the substitute.

Since the substitute prohibits both direct and indirect transactions, it is expected that where a mutual fund, *e.g.*, acquires property from a party-in-interest as part of the arrangement under which the plan invests or retains its investment in the mutual fund, this is to be a prohibited transaction.

Employer securities and employer real property.—The labor provisions also generally prohibit the direct or indirect acquisition by the plan (or holding by the plan) of securities of the employer or real property leased to the employer, except if otherwise allowed. This prohibition (and the exceptions to it) is described in detail below.

Additional prohibitions.—The substitute generally prohibits a fiduciary from dealing with the income or assets of a plan in his own interest or for his own account. However, this does not prohibit the fiduciary from dealings where he has an account in the plan and the dealings apply to all plan accounts without discrimination.

The substitute also prohibits a fiduciary from receiving consideration for his own personal account from any party dealing with the plan in connection with the transaction involving the income or assets of the plan. This prevents, *e.g.*, "kickbacks", to a fiduciary.

In addition, the labor provisions (but not the tax provisions) prohibit a fiduciary from acting in any transaction involving the plan on behalf of a person (or representing a party) whose interests are adverse to the interests of the plan or of its participants or beneficiaries. This prevents a fiduciary from being put in a position where he has dual loyalties, and, therefore, he cannot act exclusively for the benefit of a plan's participants and beneficiaries. (This prohibition is not included in the tax provisions, because of the difficulty in determining an appropriate measure for an excise tax.)

Administrative exemptions or variances.—The conferees recognize that some transactions which are prohibited (and for which there are no statutory exemptions) nevertheless should be allowed in order not to disrupt the established business practices of financial institutions which often perform fiduciary functions in connection with these plans consistent with adequate safeguards to protect employee benefit plans. For example, while brokerage houses generally would be prohibited from providing, either directly or through affiliates, both discretionary investment management and brokerage services to the same plan, the conferees expect that the Secretary of Labor and Secretary of the Treasury would grant a variance with respect to these services (and other services traditionally rendered by such institutions), provided that they can show that such a variance will be administratively feasible and that the type of transaction for which an exemption is sought is in the interest of and protective of the rights of plan participants and beneficiaries. Thus, variances might be granted to brokers or their affiliates to act as investment managers if the Secretary determines that such arrangements are in the interests of plan participants and beneficiaries and that satisfactory safeguards are provided, including *e.g.*, such protections as the monitoring of the investment manager's decisions by a person with appropriate investment experience as specified by the Secretaries, who is not affiliated with the broker. The conferees did not grant a statutory exemption to brokers for this type of multiple service because of the difficulty of establishing precise statutory standards for protecting against potential abuses. The conferees note that the general issue of institutional investment management by brokers is under consideration in separate legislation, and expect that any action taken by the Secretaries on requests for variances under this Act will be consistent with the outcome of such legislation.

In addition, the conferees recognize that some individual transactions between a plan and a party-in-interest may provide substantial independent safeguards for the plan participants and beneficiaries and may provide substantial benefit to the community as a whole, so that the transaction should be allowed under a variance. For example, it is understood that the pension plan of a major corporation with its principal office in Dayton, Ohio, has become committed to invest in a joint venture that will own an office building in a downtown redevelopment area in Dayton. This building is to be a key element of the redevelopment project The joint venture will lease a portion of this building to the employer that established and maintained this pension plan. Under the general rules, this would be a prohibited indirect lease between the plan and a party-in-interest. However, it is understood that the transaction has substantial safeguards that ensure that the transaction will inure to the benefit of the plan participants and beneficiaries. For example there are other major investors in the joint venture at this time so the joint venture will seek an adequate rate of return. Additionally, it is understood that the building has another major tenant and the terms of the lease for this tenant and for the employer are substantially identical. Furthermore, it is understood that the rental under these leases is generally higher than the rental for similar space now available in the area. Also, the City of Dayton will have a major investment in the land (and in a superstructure), so that the City will have an independent financial interest in ensuring that the transaction is financially sound.

Under this transaction, each party in the joint venture is to share in profits and losses in proportion to its capital contribution. Therefore, this is not a "tax shelter" transaction with an attempted shift of early period losses away from a tax-exempt entity to taxable entities. Also, it is understood that while the joint venture will borrow to finance the acquisition of the building, neither the joint venture nor the plan (nor any other joint venturer) is to be "personally liable" on the mortgage debt. Therefore, if the transaction were to fail, the plan's liability would be limited to the funds advanced to the joint venture.

It is expected that in this situation, because of the substantial safeguards for the plan and its participants and beneficiaries, because of the lack of "tax abuse" aspects, because the transaction became binding before the conferees' decisions were announced, and because of the importance of the project to the entire community of Dayton, Ohio, that the Secretary of the Treasury and Secretary of Labor will grant a variance to the transaction for its whole term.

Under the substitute, variances may be conditional or unconditional and may exempt a transaction from all or part of the prohibited transaction rules. In addition, variances may be for a particular transaction or for a class of transactions, and may be allowed pursuant to rulings or regulations. A variance from the prohibited transaction rules is to have no effect with respect to the basic fiduciary responsibility rules requiring prudent action, diversification of investments, actions exclusively for the benefit of participants and beneficiaries, etc. (This is the case with respect to all statutory exemptions from the prohibited transaction rules as well.)

Under the substitute, the Secretary of Labor and the Secretary of the Treasury each must establish a procedure for allowing variances, but neither the Secretary of Labor nor the Secretary of the Treasury is to be required to grant a variance. Variances are to be granted only when each Secretary separately determines that the transaction in question is an appropriate case for a variance. Thus, for example, the Secretary of Labor may refuse to grant a variance if the transaction would constitute an abuse of the labor laws, even though the Secretary of the Treasury may be willing to grant a variance in the particular situation. Similarly, the Secretary of the Treasury may, for example, refuse to grant a variance if the transaction would constitute a tax abuse even though the Secretary of Labor may be willing to grant a variance in the same situation.

In addition, variances are not to be allowed unless each Secretary finds that the transaction is in the interests of the plan and its participants and beneficiaries, that it does not present administrative problems, and that adequate safeguards are provided for participants and beneficiaries.

Although the Secretary of Labor and the Secretary of the Treasury are to separately determine whether a variance is to be provided, they are to coordinate their activities. It is expected that the Secretaries of Labor and Treasury will develop an administrative procedure to allow one application for a variance and that the two departments will coordinate their activities with respect to this single application to prevent unneeded delays and duplication of effort by the applicant.

Before allowing a variance, adequate notice (including publication in the Federal Register) is to be given interested persons, who are to have an opportunity to present their views. In the case of a variance from the prohibitions against a fiduciary dealing with plan assets for his own account, acting on behalf of an adverse party to the plan, or receiving consideration for his personal account, there is to be a hearing and a determination on the record that the conditions required for granting a variance are met. (However, the Secretary of the Treasury may accept the record of a Department of Labor hearing, if he wishes, and make his determination with respect to the variance on the facts presented in that record.)

Exemption for loans to participants and beneficiaries.—Following current practice, the substitute does not prohibit a loan by a plan to a participant or beneficiary in certain circumstances. To be permitted, such loans must be made in accord with specific provisions in the plan governing such loans. In addition, a reasonable interest rate must be charged and the loan must be adequately secured. Such loans must be made available to all participants on a reasonably equivalent basis. Consequently, the plan could not unreasonably discriminate between applicants on the basis of, e.g., age or sex; but the plan could make distinctions on the basis of, e.g., credit worthiness or financial need. Also, such loans cannot be made available to highly-compensated employees in an amount greater than the amount available to other employees. The conferees intend that this will allow a plan to lend the same percentage of a person's vested benefits to participants with both large and small amounts of accrued vested benefits. (However, the percentage is to be consistent with the requirements of adequate security.) The conferees also intend that a plan may provide that the same dollar amounts may be loaned to participants and beneficiaries without regard to the amount of their vested benefits if adequate security is otherwise provided. For example, a plan could provide for loans to participants and beneficiaries in an amount up to, *e.g.*, $30,000 to buy a house (even if the $30,000 is greater than the amount of the participant's or beneficiary's vested benefits) if the loan is adequately secured by, *e.g.*, a first mortgage on the house.

Exemption for services, etc.—The substitute allows a party-in-interest to furnish to a plan office space, legal services, accounting services, or other similar services necessary for the establishment or operation of the plan, if no more than reasonable compensation is paid for these services, etc. It is expected that such arrangements will allow the plan to terminate the services, etc., on a reasonably short notice under the circumstances so the plan will not become locked into an arrangement that may become disadvantageous. It is also expected that the compensation arrangements will allow for changes so the plan will not be locked into a disadvantageous price.

The substitute also specifically allows the plan to pay a fiduciary or other party-in-interest reasonable compensation (or reimbursement of expenses) for services rendered to the plan if the services are reasonable and necessary. However, to prevent double payment, this does not apply with regard to a fiduciary who is receiving full-time pay from an employer or association of employers (with employees covered by the plan) or from a union (with members covered by the plan), except for the reimbursement of expenses properly and actually incurred and not otherwise reimbursed.

The substitute also makes it clear that a party-in-interest may serve as a fiduciary in addition to being an officer, employee, agent or other representative of a party-in-interest.

Exemption for loans to employee stock ownership plans.—Under the substitute, certain loans or extensions of credit from a party-in-interest to an employee stock ownership plan are not to be prohibited. The conferees understand that it is common practice for these plans to purchase the employer's stock from major shareholders (or from the employer). The proceeds to pay for the purchase often are obtained by the plan from an unrelated lender with a guarantee of repayment by the shareholder. In this case, the substitute does not prohibit the party-in-interest from guaranteeing the loan (or from providing his assets as collateral for the loan). In addition, the conferees understand that it is common practice for a party-in-interest to sell his stock in the employer to these plans and take back a purchase money note from the plan. The substitute also does not prohibit such a loan if the only collateral given by the plan for the loan consists of qualifying employer's securities.

These exceptions to the prohibited transaction rules are to be allowed if the transaction is for the benefit of the plan participants and beneficiaries (and, not, e.g., primarily to benefit the party-in-interest who is selling the stock), and if the interest rate charged on the loan to the plan remains at not more than a reasonable interest rate.

Although these transactions normally are for the benefit of plan participants and beneficiaries, the conferees recognize that there may be potential problems. For example, the interest rate should not be too high and the purchase price of the stock from the party-in-interest should not be too high, so that plan assets might be drained off. Also, the terms of the note between the party-in-interest and the plan should not allow the party-in-interest to call the note at his convenience, which might put undue financial strain on the plan. Because of such potential problems, the conferees intend that all aspects of these transactions will be subject to special scrutiny by the Department of Labor and Internal Revenue Service to ensure that they are primarily for the benefit of plan participants and beneficiaries.

This exception from the prohibited transaction rules is to be available only for employee stock ownership plans and not for other plans. The conferees understand that the basic element common to all employee stock ownership plans is that they are qualified stock bonus plans designed to invest primarily in qualifying securities of the employer whose employees are covered by the plan. In addition it is understood that a qualified money purchase pension plan designed to invest primarily in such securities of the employer may be coupled with such a qualified stock bonus plan (and that a profit-sharing plan sometimes may be used). Furthermore, it is understood that a frequent characteristic of some employee stock ownership plans is that they leverage their purchase of qualifying employer securities as a way to achieve transfers in the ownership of corporate stock and other capital requirements of a corporation and that such a plan is designed to build equity ownership of shares of the employer corporation for its employees in a nondiscriminatory manner.

The conferees intend that the exemption from the prohibited transaction rules with respect to loans to employee stock ownership plans is to apply only in the case of loans (and guarantees) used to leverage the purchase of qualifying employer securities (and related business interests).

Exemption for bank deposits.—In certain cases the prohibited transaction rules of the substitute do not prevent a bank or similar institution (e.g., a savings and loan association or credit union) which is a plan fiduciary from investing all or part of the plan's assets in deposits with the bank, etc., if the deposits bear a reasonable interest rate. This exemption is allowed if the plan covers only employees of the bank, etc., or employees of its affiliates. In this case, it would be contrary to normal business practice for a bank to invest its plan assets in another bank.

A deposit with a bank, etc., fiduciary also is not prohibited if it is expressly authorized by the plan or is specifically authorized by a fiduciary (other than the bank or an affiliate of the bank) who is expressly empowered by the plan to direct that this investment be made. In this case, there is no conflict of interest involving the bank fiduciary upon a deposit with the bank, etc.

This exception, as all other exceptions to the prohibited transaction rules, is not to affect the applicability of the prudent man, diversification, etc., rules. However, it is expected that generally these rules will not be violated if all plan assets in an individual account plan are invested in a federally-insured account, so long as the investments are fully insured. (If an individual's account balance is greater than the amount covered by Federal insurance, this will not violate the prudence and diversification requirements if the individual participant or beneficiary has control over his account and determines, for himself, that the assets should be so invested.)

Exemptions for purchase of insurance.—The substitute does not prohibit a plan from purchasing life insurance, health insurance, or annuities from the employer that maintains the plan if the employer is an insurer qualified to do businses in a State (or the District of Columbia). In this case, it would be contrary to normal business practice to require the plan of an insurance company to purchase its insurance from another insurance company. This exemption is available only if no more than adequate consideration is paid for the insurance by the plan.

This exemption also applies to the purchase of life insurance, health insurance, and annuities from an insurer that is wholly-owned, directly or indirectly, by the employer establishing the plan (or is wholly owned by a party-in-interest with respect to the employer establishing a plan). This rule applies if the total premiums and annuity considerations written by all such wholly-owned insurers for life insurance, health insurance, and annuity premiums purchased by all employers which are parties-in-interest and their plans are not more than 5 percent of the total premiums and annuity considerations written for all lines of insurance by these insurers. (In computing this 5 percent figure, all premiums and annuity considerations written by an insurance company for a plan which it maintains are to be excluded from both the numerator and the denominator of the fraction.) This exception also is allowed only if no more than adequate consideration is paid for the insurance.

The conferees understand that for some purposes, certain insurance contracts may be considered as securities. However, the substitute provides that insurance contracts are not to be considered as "employer securities" to the extent that the exception described above from the prohibited transaction requirements would apply to the purchase of insurance contracts by a plan. (Otherwise, the rules with respect to employer securities might, as a practical matter, prevent this exemption from operating as it is intended.)

Exemption for ancillary bank services.—Unless otherwise specifically allowed by statutory or administrative exemption, generally a fiduciary is not to be able to provide "multiple services" to a plan. (However, the prohibition against providing multiple services is not to apply to parties-in-interest, who are not fiduciaries.) This rule was adopted because of the potential problems inherent in situations where persons who can act on behalf of a plan also are in a position to personally benefit at the expense of the plan in exercising that authority. However, as indicated above, it is expected that administrative exemptions will be established for sound commercial and financial practices where there are adequate safeguards. Also, the substitute provides some limited statutory exemptions from the general rule.

Under the substitute, a bank or similar financial institution (such as a savings and loan association or credit union) which is supervised by Federal or State authorities, is not prohibited from providing multiple ancillary services in certain limited circumstances. First, no more than reasonable compensation can be charged by the bank, etc., for these services. Also the bank, etc., must have established adequate internal safeguards to assure that its provision of ancillary services is in accord with sound banking and financial practice, as determined by Federal and State banking authorities. In addition, the bank's action must be in accordance with binding specific guidelines issued by the bank that will prevent the bank from providing ancillary services in an unreasonable or excessive manner or in a manner that would be inconsistent with the best interests of the plan's participants and beneficiaries. Such guidelines are to be subject to, and not inconsistent with, coordinated regulations of the Secretaries of Labor and Treasury, which are to be issued after consultation with State and Federal banking authorities. The bank's guidelines must be reported to the Department of Labor and Internal Revenue Service, and must be reported to each plan to which multiple services are provided. Of course, if the bank does not follow the guidelines, the exemption will not be available.

Placing plan funds in noninterest bearing checking accounts is an example of the type of an ancillary service that might be provided by a bank that is a plan fiduciary. However, a number of short-term investment vehicles have been developed recently so that such cash balances should be kept to the very minimum necessary for the current operations of the plan. Therefore, it is expected that adequate guidelines and procedures to prevent unreasonable cash balances will require the bank to invest plan funds in such vehicles to the maximum extent feasible. Also, in determining whether a plan pays more than reasonable compensation for its checking account services, the interest available on an alternate use of the funds is to be considered. It is also expected that proper procedures and guidelines will keep to a minimum the amount of discretion on the part of the bank, etc., in determining the amount of cash balances. The conferees intend that such limitation of discretion is to be included in guidelines that govern other ancillary services that may be provided by banks, etc.

Exemption for conversion of securities.—Under the substitute a plan may hold or acquire certain employer securities. Since some of these securities may be convertible (*e.g.*, from bonds to stock) the substitute would not prohibit such a conversion to the extent provided in regulations if the plan receives at least fair market value under the conversion. It is expected that a conversion will be permitted if all the securities of the class held by the plan are subject to the same terms and such terms were determined in an arm's-length transaction, so that conversions cannot be tailored to apply only to a particular plan. Similarly, it is intended that a conversion generally will not be permitted if all but an insignificant percentage of unrelated holders of such securities do not exercise such conversion privileges. Also, it is intended that any acquisition of employer securities pursuant to a conversion privilege must be within the limits established by the general rule governing the acquisition and holding of employer securities, discussed below.

Exemption for certain pooled investment funds.—The conferees understand that it is common practice for banks, trust companies and insurance companies to maintain pooled investment funds for plans. If the bank, etc., is the plan trustee and invests the plan assets in its pooled fund (rather than managing the assets individually) this would be considered a purchase of investment units in the fund and would be prohibited under the general rules. However, since generally the net effect of pooling plan assets is to achieve more efficient investment management, in certain circumstances the substitute allows the purchase and sale of interests in a pooled fund maintained by a bank, etc., which is a plan fiduciary.

To be allowed, no more than reasonable compensation may be paid by the plan in the purchase (or sale) and no more than reasonable compensation may be paid by the plan for investment management by the pooled fund. In addition, it generally is inappropriate for the bank, etc., to make the decisions with respect to investment in a pooled fund because of a potential conflict of interest. Therefore, this exception is allowed only if the transaction is specifically permitted by the plan or if a plan fiduciary (other than the bank, etc., or its affiliates) who has authority to manage and control the plan assets specifically permits such investment.

Banks, etc., that operate such pooled investment funds are, of course, plan fiduciaries. As fiduciaries they must act, e.g., for the exclusive benefit of participants and beneficiaries. Therefore, a bank, etc., cannot use pooled funds as a place to dump unwanted investments which were initially made on its own (or another's) behalf.

Exemptions for owner-employees, etc.—The substitute retains the prohibited transaction rules (but not the disqualification sanction) of present law (sec. 503(g) of the Internal Revenue Code) with respect to owner-employees. Consequently, under the substitute the exceptions from the prohibited transaction rules described above generally will not apply with respect to sales, loans, payments for services, etc., between a plan and an owner-employee with regard to that plan. Also, since shareholder employees of subchapter S corporations are generally treated as owner-employees, the same limitations apply with respect to shareholder-employees. Additionally, these limitations apply to participants and beneficiaries of (and employers who establish and maintain) individual retirement accounts, individual retirement annuities, and individual retirement bonds, since these persons generally have the same type of control with respect to a plan as do owner-employees.

Exemptions for distribution of plan assets.—It is not a prohibited transaction for a plan to distribute its assets in accordance with the provisions of the plan and in the case of a pension plan if the distribution is in accord with the allocation of assets rules under the termination insurance provisions of the substitute.

Also, a distribution of assets from a welfare (or pension) plan, as described above in "basic fiduciary rules", is exempt from the labor provisions as to prohibited transactions.

Employer Securities and Employer Real Property

Eligibile individual account plans.—The labor provisions of the substitute generally limit the acquisition and holding by a plan of employer securities and of employer real property (combined) to 10 percent of plan assets. (Employer securities are securities issued by an employer with employees covered by the plan or its affiliates. Employer real property is real property which is leased by a plan to an employer (or its affiliates) with employees covered by the plan.)

However, a special rule is provided for individual account plans which are profit-sharing plans, stock bonus plans, employee stock ownership plans, or thrift or savings plans, since these plans commonly provide for substantial investments in employer securities or real property. Also, money purchase plans which were in existence on the date of enactment, and which invested primarily in employer securities on that date are to be treated the same way as profit-sharing, etc., plans. (However, employer-established individual retirement accounts are not to be eligible individual account plans.)

In recognition of the special purpose of these individual account plans, the 10 percent limitation with respect to the acquisition or holding of employer securities or employer real property does not apply to such plans if they explicitly provide for greater investment in these assets. In addition, the diversification requirements of the substitute and any diversification principle that may develop in the application of the prudent man rule is not to restrict investments by eligible individual account plans in qualifying employer securities or qualifying employer real property.

These exceptions apply only if the plan explicitly provides for the relevant amount of acquisition or holding of qualifying employer securities or qualifying real property. For example, if a profit-sharing plan is to be able to invest half of its assets in qualifying employer securities, the plan must specifically provide that up to 50 percent of plan assets may be invested. In this way, the persons responsible for asset management, as well as participants and beneficiaries, will clearly know the extent to which the plan can acquire and hold these assets. Plans in existence on the date of enactment will have one year from January 1, 1975, to be amended to comply with this requirement. If the plan does not comply within one year (but, e.g., complies 2 years after January 1, 1975), then during the interim period, the plan will be subject to the 10 percent rule as well as the diversification requirement. This means, generally, that the plan will not be able to acquire any additional employer securities or employer real property during this period (and preparation should be made for divestiture of half of the excess of employer securities and real property by January 1, 1980.)

Under the substitute, only "qualifying" employer securities may be acquired and held by individual account plans under the rules described above. Stock of the employer will constitute qualifying securities. Also, certain debt will be qualifying employer securities if it is traded on a national securities exchange or has a price otherwise established by independent persons, and if the plan holds no more than a quarter of the issue and independent persons hold at least one-half of the issue. (Qualifying employer debt securities essentially are debt securities that meet the present rules of section 503(e) of the Internal Revenue Code.)

Also, under the substitute only "qualifying" employer real property may be acquired and held by eligible account plans under the rules described above. Real property which is leased to an employer is qualifying employer real property if a substantial number of the parcels are distributed geographically and if each parcel of real property and the improvements on it are suitable (or adaptable without excessive cost) for more than one use.[4] For example, the plan might acquire and lease to the employer multipurpose buildings which are located in different geographical areas. It is intended that the geographic dispersion be sufficient so that adverse economic conditions peculiar to one area would not significantly affect the economic status of the plan as a whole. All of the qualifying real property may be leased to one lessee, which may be the employer or an affiliate of the employer.

To the extent that an eligible individual account plan can acquire qualifying employer securities, it may acquire these securities from parties-in-interest if the acquisition is for adequate consideration and no commission is charged in the transaction. (The conferees intend that if a purchase is made from an underwriter who assumes the risks of market fluctuations after the award date, the underwriter's margin is not to be regarded as a "commission.") A similar exception from the prohibited transaction rules (in both the labor and tax provisions) is available for the acquisition from an employer of qualifying employer real property, the leasing of such property to the employer (or its affiliate) and the sale of such real property back to the employer on termination of the lease for adequate consideration. However, real property is not qualifying employer real property unless it is leased to the employer. Therefore, except for qualifying leasebacks, a plan generally is prohibited from acquiring real property from the employer.

Other plans.—Under the substitute, a plan other than an eligible individual account plan cannot acquire any employer securities or real property if immediately after doing so the plan

---

[4] Qualifying employer real property includes the real property and related personal property.

would hold more than 10 percent of the fair market value of its assets in employer securities of real property. The acquisition rules apply not only to the purchase of employer securities, etc., but also to acquisition in other ways such as by exercise of warrants or by acquisition on default of a loan where the stock was made security for the loan. Also, these plans (as eligible individual account plans) are not to acquire any employer securities or employer real property other than qualifying employer securities or qualifying employer real property.

In addition, if a plan holds more than 10 percent of the fair market value of its assets in employer securities and real property on January 1, 1975, it is to dispose of enough of these assets to bring its holdings of employer securities, etc. to no more than 10 percent of plan assets on or before December 31, 1984.

In general, the 10 percent holding rule will be met on the first date after January 1, 1975 (and on or before December 31, 1984) that a plan holds no more than 10 percent of the fair market value of its assets in employer securities or employer real property. Thus, if a plan on January 1, 1975, holds qualifying employer securities and qualifying employer real property worth $200,000 and has total assets worth $1,000,000, the plan must bring its employer securities, etc., down to 10 percent of plan assets. If, e.g., there is a substantial market rise in the value of the plan's other assets in the year 1976, so all plan assets are now worth $2,000,000, but employer securities are still worth $200,000, then the holding requirement has been met and from that time on, only the acquisition rule will affect the plan. (Under the acquisition rule, the plan could not acquire any more qualifying employer securities in 1976, since immediately after the acquisition more than 10 percent of plan assets would be invested in employer securities.) Also, if the fair market value of other plan assets decrease to $1,500,000 in 1977, so the plan has $200,000 of employer securities and $1,500,000 total assets, the plan will not violate the holding (or acquisition) rules, since it met the holding rules in 1976.

Under the substitute, a plan is not required to dispose of more qualifying employer securities than would bring its holdings down to 10 percent of the fair market value of assets on the date of enactment. Thus, if a plan had $200,000 of employer securities and $1,000,000 total assets on date of enactment, it would satisfy the 10 percent holding rule when it had employer securities of $100,000, even if its total assets had dropped to $900,000.

The substitute allows a special election for calculating the 10 percent holding rule (but not the 10 percent acquisition rule). Under this election, the 10 percent holding rule is met if on or before December 31, 1984, the value of employer securities which are held on January 1, 1975, is no greater than 10 percent of the fair market value of plan assets on January 1, 1975, plus employer contributions to the plan made after December 31, 1974, and prior to January 1, 1985. For this purpose, employer contributions are to be included only to the extent of the growth in the value of plan assets (other than employer securities) from January 1, 1975, through December 31, 1984. Election to make this provision applicable must be made prior to January 1, 1976, and the election is irrevocable once it is made. For purposes of this rule, employer securities held on January 1, 1975, are to include employer securities the ownership of which is derived solely from the employer securities held on January 1, 1975, or from the exercise of rights derived from such ownership under regulations to be prescribed by the Secretary of Labor. This election is to be available only for a plan which holds no employer real property, and does not acquire employer real property until after December 31, 1984.

A plan must be half-way toward meeting the 10-percent rule by

December 31, 1979. The maximum percentage of assets that a plan may have in employer securities and employer real property on that date is to be established by regulations (which are to be issued by December 31, 1976). Generally, it is expected that the regulations will provide that the maximum percentage of assets that a plan may have in employer securities and real property on (or before) December 31, 1979, is to be determined by adding 10 percent to half of the percentage of employer securities, etc., held by the plan on January 1, 1975 in excess of 10 percent. For example, if 15 percent of the plan's assets are in employer securities on January 1, 1975, generally it is expected that the plan must have reduced its percentage of employer securities to 12½ percent on or before December 31, 1979. (That is, $10 + \frac{(15-10)}{2} = 12\frac{1}{2}$.)

If securities are qualifying employer securities they generally can be acquired or held notwithstanding the prohibited transaction rules, if acquisition is for adequate consideration and no commission is charged and if acquisition is allowed by the employer securities rules. However (except as noted above for eligible individual account plans), acquisition and holding of these assets must also meet the rules of prudence, diversification, etc. Therefore, if the diversification and prudence rules require that less than 10 percent of plan assets are to be held in employer securities and employer real property, the lower limit is to govern. Furthermore, the exclusive benefit rule also may apply. Thus, while a plan may be able to acquire employer securities or real property under the employer securities rules, the acquisition must be for the exclusive benefit of participants and beneficiaries. Consequently, if the real property is acquired primarily to finance the employer, this would not meet the exclusive benefit requirements.

Generally these rules apply only to the holding (or acquiring) of qualified employer securities or qualified employer real property. Under the general prohibited transaction rules, a plan is not to hold (or acquire) any other employer securities or employer real property (since this would be a prohibited loan or lease, respectively). Of course, the general transition rules discussed below will apply to employer securities or real property held on July 1, 1974.

Civil Liability

Fiduciaries.—Under the labor provisions (but not the tax provisions) of the substitute, a fiduciary who breaches the fiduciary requirements of the bill is to be personally liable for any losses to the plan resulting from this breach. Such a fiduciary is also to be liable for restoring to the plan any profits which he has made through the use of any plan asset. In addition, such a fiduciary is to be subject to other appropriate relief (including removal) as ordered by a court. The place and manner of bringing civil actions against a fiduciary is described below.

Generally, a plan fiduciary is not to be liable for any breach of fiduciary duty if it occurred before he became a fiduciary or after he was no longer a fiduciary.

Party-in-interest. — A party-in-interest who engages in a prohibited transaction with respect to a plan that is not qualified (at the time of the transaction) under the Internal Revenue Code may be subject to a civil penalty of up to 5 percent of the amount involved in the transaction. If the transaction is not corrected after notice from the Secretary of Labor, the penalty may be up to 100 percent of the transaction.

Exculpatory provisions and liability insurance.—Under the substitute, exculpatory provisions which relieve a fiduciary from liability for breach of the fiduciary responsibility rules are to be void and of no effect. (However, this is not to affect the fiduciary's ability to allocate or delegate his responsibilities, as described above.)

The substitute also provides, however, that a plan may purchase insurance for itself and for its fiduciaries to cover liability or loss resulting from their acts or omissions if the insurance permits recourse by the insurer against the fiduciaries in case of a breach of fiduciary responsibility. Also, under the substitute, a fiduciary may purchase insurance to cover his own liability, and an employer or union may purchase liability insurance for plan fiduciaries (and these policies need not provide for recourse).

Excise Tax on Prohibited Transactions

In general.—As indicated above, the substitute establishes an excise tax on disqualified persons who participate in specific prohibited transactions respecting a pension plan. The tax applies with respect to a plan which has qualified after the effective date of the prohibited transaction provisions (or has been determined to qualify by the Secretary of the Treasury under section 401, 403(a), or 405(a) of the Code) and with respect to a qualified individual retirement account, bond or annuity (under sections 408 or 409). The prohibited transaction rules and excise tax sanctions are to continue to apply even if the plan, etc., should later lose its tax qualification.

This excise tax generally follows the same procedures as the tax on self-dealing enacted in 1969 Tax Reform Act with respect to private foundations. The tax is at two levels: initially, disqualified persons who participate in a prohibited transaction are to be subject to a tax of 5 percent of the amount involved in the transaction per year. A second tax of 100 percent is imposed if the transaction is not corrected after notice from the Internal Revenue Service that the 5-percent tax is due.

Following present law with respect to private foundations, under the substitute where a fiduciary participates in a prohibited transaction in a capacity other than that, or in addition to that, of a fiduciary, he is to be treated as other disqualified persons and subject to tax. Otherwise, a fiduciary is not to be subject to the excise tax.

The first-level tax is owed for each taxable year (or part of a year) in the period that begins with the date when the prohibited transaction occurs and ends on the earlier of the date of collection or the date of mailing of a deficiency notice for the first-level tax (under section 6212 of the Internal Revenue Code). The first-level tax is imposed automatically without regard to whether the violation was inadvertent.

If more than one person is liable for the excise tax as a result of a particular prohibited transaction, they all are to be jointly and severally liable. For example, if the prohibited transaction involves $100,000, all disqualified persons who participated in the transaction will be jointly and severally liable for the first-level tax of $5,000 (per year in the taxable period) and also jointly and severally liable for the second-level tax of $100,000.

The excise tax on a prohibited transaction is dependent upon the amount involved in the transaction. The substitute provides that the amount involved is the greater of the fair market value of the property (including money) given or received in a transaction. However, with regard to services which are necessary to the operation of the plan and which generally may be paid for if the compensation is not excessive, the amount involved generally is the excess compensation. For the first-level tax, the amount involved in a prohibited transaction is valued as of the date of the transaction. However, for the second-level tax, the amount involved is valued at the highest fair market value during the correction period. The higher valuation is used for the second-level tax so the person subject to tax will not delay returning the amount involved to the trust in order to earn income with this amount.

A prohibited transaction may be corrected to avoid a second-level tax at any time before the 90th day after the Internal Revenue Service mails a notice of deficiency with respect to the second-level tax. However, the 90-day period may be extended by any period within which a deficiency cannot be assessed (because of petitions to the Tax Court), and may also be extended for a period which the Internal Revenue Service determines is both reasonable and necessary to correct the prohibited transaction.

To correct a prohibited transaction, the transaction must be undone to the extent possible, but in any case the final position of the plan must be no worse than it would have been if the disqualified person were acting under the highest fiduciary standards. The higher valuation to be used in computing any second-level tax that might be applicable is also the valuation to be used in correcting the transaction. In other words, correction requires that the plan receive the benefit of whatever bargain turns out to have been involved in the transaction.

Before sending a notice of deficiency with respect to the first level and second level taxes, the Internal Revenue Service is to notify the Secretary of Labor and provide him a reasonable opportunity to obtain a correction of the prohibited transaction or to comment on the imposition of these taxes. However, the Service will be able to waive (or abate) only the second level tax (and not the first level tax) upon a correction that is obtained by the Secretary of Labor.

Voluntary retroactive application.— Under present law, if a prohibited transaction occurs, a plan (and trust) loses its exemption from taxation. If a trust is disqualified because of an act of the trustee and the employer, then the income tax imposed on the trust may be paid out of funds otherwise available to provide employees' retirement benefits and the sanction may then fall on innocent employees. To correct this problem in the future, the substitute eliminates disqualification and instead would impose an excise tax sanction for a violation of the prohibited transaction provisions.

The substitute also makes the excise tax sanction available—on a wholly voluntary basis—instead of the disqualification sanction in the case of plans which have engaged in prohibited transactions in (open) years before the effective date of the new prohibited transactions. Therefore, if a disqualified person with respect to a plan elects to be subject to and pays the excise tax, the plan and trust are not to be disqualified. For purposes of this application of the excise tax, the prohibited transactions are to be defined by present section 503(b) or (g) of the Code and the amount involved is to be the amount that would be determined under new section 4975 of the Code. Since the tax is to be wholly voluntary, the joint and several liability provisions of new section 4975 are not to apply (unless there is an election by several disqualified persons to this effect). Also, the first-level tax that is to be paid under this provision will be owed for taxable periods calculated under new section 4975. Thus, if the prohibited transaction (under present section 503) occurred in 1972 and is corrected in 1974, the first-level tax will be owed for 1972, 1973, and 1974. As under new section 4975, the second-level tax will be owed only if the transaction is not corrected within the time allowed by that section.

Since this is to be a relief provision, no liability is to be imposed under the labor provisions of the substitute on a person who may be a plan fiduciary after January 1, 1975, if he fails to pay the tax and the plan is disqualified. Consequently, any decision to pay or not to pay this optional tax is to be deemed to have been made before January 1, 1975, and, therefore, to be made before the substitute would establish any duties on plan fiduciaries.

Definitions

The substitute defines "fiduciary" as any person who exercises any discretionary authority or control respecting management of a plan, exercises any authority or control respecting the management or disposition of its assets or has any discretionary authority or responsibility in the administration of the plan. Under this definition, fiduciaries include officers and directors of a plan, members of a plan's investment committee and persons who select these individuals. Consequently, the definition includes persons who have authority and responsibility with respect to the matter in question, regardless of their formal title. The term "fiduciary" also includes any person who renders investment advice for a fee and includes persons to whom "discretionary" duties have been delegated by named fiduciaries.

While the ordinary functions of consultants and advisers to employee benefit plans (other than investment advisers) may not be considered as fiduciary functions, it must be recognized that there will be situations where such consultants and advisers may because of their special expertise, in effect, be exercising discretionary authority or control with respect to the management or administration of such plan or some authority or control regarding its assets. In such cases, they are to be regarded as having assumed fiduciary obligations within the meaning of the applicable definition.

The labor definition of a "party-in-interest" includes the following general categories. (1) Plan administrators, officers, fiduciaries, trustees, custodians, counsel and employees. (2) Persons providing services to a plan. (3) The employer, its employees, officers, directors, or 10-percent shareholders. (4) Controlling or controlled parties or parties under common control (and their employees, officers, directors, or 10-percent shareholders). (Under the substitute, "control" is generally defined at 50-percent ownership. However, the Secretary of Labor and Secretary of Treasury may, by regulation, reduce this percentage.) (5) Employee organizations with members covered by the plan, its employees, its officers and directors and its affiliates (6) Certain relatives and partners of parties-in-interest are also treated as parties-in-interest.

Under the tax provisions, the same general categories of persons are disqualified persons, with some differences. Although fiduciaries are disqualified persons under the tax provisions, they are to be subject to the excise tax only if they act in a prohibited transaction in a capacity other than that of a fiduciary. Also, only highly-compensated employees are to be treated as disqualified persons, not all employees of an employer, etc.

Prohibition Against Certain Persons Holding Office

The labor provisions of the substitute prohibit a person who is convicted of certain specified crimes from serving as a plan administrator, fiduciary, officer, trustee, custodian, counsel, agent, employee or consultant of a plan for five years after conviction or five years after the end of imprisonment, whichever is later. However, such a person may serve as an administrator, etc., of a plan if his citizenship rights have been fully restored or if the United States Board of Parole determines that his service would not be contrary to the purposes of the labor provisions of the substitute.

Corporations and partnerships are not to be barred from acting as plan administrators, etc., without a determination from the Board of Parole that such service would be inconsistent with the labor provisions of the substitute.

No one is to knowingly permit another to serve as a plan administrator, etc., in violation of this provision. Those who violate this provision may be fined up to $10,000 and also may be imprisoned for up to one year. This provision is to apply to crimes committed before the date of enactment.

Bonding

The labor provisions of the substitute generally require every fiduciary of an employee benefit plan (and every person who handles funds or other property of a plan) to be bonded. This provision generally is identical to present section 13 of the Welfare and Pension Plans Disclosure Act and it is intended that the construction given to the bonding requirements before enactment of the substitute would continue. Generally, the amount of the bond is to be not less than 10 percent of the funds handled and not less than $1,000 (nor more than $500,000, except as otherwise required by the 10 percent rule or as prescribed by the Secretary of Labor). The substitute would not require a bond if plan benefits are paid only from the general assets of a union or employer. A bond also is not to be required for a domestic trust or insurance corporation subject to State or Federal supervision or examination if it has capital and surplus combined in excess of $1 million (or such other higher amount determined by the Secretary of Labor). However, a special rule is provided for banks or other financial institutions exercising trust powers if their deposits are not insured by the Federal Deposit Insurance Corporation. In this case a bond will not be required if the corporation meets bonding (or similar requirements) of State law which the Secretary of Labor determines are at least equivalent to bonding requirements imposed on banks under Federal law.

It is expected that regulations to be prescribed by the Secretary of Labor under this provision would include procedures for exempting plans where other bonding arrangements of the employer, employee organization, investment manager or other fiduciaries or the overall financial condition of the plan or the fiduciaries meet specified standards deemed adequate to protect the interests of the beneficiaries and participants, including bonds subject to a reasonable maximum for professional investment managers supervising large aggregations of clients' funds.

Effective Date and Transition Rules

Generally, the new fiduciary responsibility rules are to take effect on January 1, 1975. However, with respect to any plan which is covered by plan termination insurance and which terminates before January 1, 1975, the fiduciary rules are to take effect on the date of enactment of the bill.

Under the labor provisions, the Secretary of Labor may postpone until January 1, 1976, the effective date with respect to the requirements for establishing a plan and establishing a trust, the rules regarding liability for breach by a co-fiduciary (other than the rules allowing delegation of asset management functions to an investment manager) and the rules prohibiting exculpatory clauses. The Secretary of Labor may allow such a delay only for plans in existence on the date of enactment and only if he determines (on application of the plan) that the delay is (1) necessary to amend the plan instrument, and (2) not adverse to the plan participants and beneficiaries.

To prevent undue hardship, the substitute also provides transition rules for situations where employee benefit plans are now engaging in activities which do not violate current law, but would be prohibited transactions under the substitute.

One of the transition rules permits the leading or joint use of property involving a plan and a party in interest under a binding contract in effect on July 1, 1974 (or pursuant to renewals of the contract), to continue for 10 years beyond that date until June 30, 1984. For this transition rule to apply, the lease or joint use must remain at least as favorable to the plan as an arm's-length transaction with an unrelated party and must not otherwise be a prohibited transaction under present law. A similar 10-year transition rule applies to loans or other extensions of credit under a binding contract in effect on July 1, 1974 (and renewals thereof), where the loan remains as favorable as an arm's-length transaction with an unrelated party and is not prohibited under present law.

The substitute allows a plan to sell property, at arm's-length terms, to a party in interest where the property is now under a lease or joint use which qualifies for the 10-year transition rule described above. Sales of this type must occur before July 1, 1984. This transition rule is provided because it appears that such leases are not uncommon and in such cases often a party in interest is the best available buyer.

The substitute allows a fiduciary to provide multiple services to a plan until June 30, 1977, if he ordinarily and customarily furnishes services on June 30, 1974. Under this provision, such a fiduciary would not be limited to providing these services to plans which he served on that date, but he could take on new customers after that date. Under the substitute, multiple services also can be provided until June 30, 1977, if they were being provided under a binding contract in effect on July 1, 1974 (or under renewals of such a contract). It is intended that under this provision fiduciaries can continue to provide such services for the next three years in order that they might continue their business during the pendency of and application for a variance from the prohibited transaction rules. However, these services can only be provided under the transition rules if the price is at least an arm's-length price during the whole transition period and if they would not constitute a prohibited transaction under current section 503 of the Internal Revenue Code.

The substitute permits a plan to dispose of excess employer securities or employer real property owned by the plan on June 30, 1974, and at all times thereafter to a party-in-interest if the holding of such property would violate the rules governing holding of employer securities and real property, and if the sale, etc., is at fair market value.

VI. LABOR AND TAX ADMINISTRATION AND ENFORCEMENT (SECS. 501-516 AND 1041-1052 OF THE BILL AND SECS. 7476 AND 7802 OF THE INTERNAL REVENUE CODE)

Labor Department

Criminal penalty.—Under the bill as passed by the House, any person who willfully violates any of the provisions in title I of the Act, makes any statement in any report required to be filed or to be kept under that title knowing that it is false or misleading in any material fact, or forges or counterfeits or passes as true any document knowing it was forged or counterfeit for the purpose of influencing the acts of the Secretary of Labor is guilty of a crime which is punishable by a fine of up to $10,000 and 5 years of imprisonment, or both. If the act is committed by someone other than an individual the fine may be up to $200,000.

The bill as passed by the Senate did not contain comparable provisions but did provide for a fine of up to $1,000 and 6 months imprisonment, or both, for willful violation of the disclosure provisions.

Under the conference agreement, any person who willfully violates any provisions in title I of the bill relating to reporting and disclosure may be fined not more than $5,000 or imprisoned for not more than 1 year, or both, except that in the case of a violation by a person other than an individual the fine may not exceed $100,000. The conference agreement retains present criminal provisions of Title 18, U.S.C. relating to false statements, bribery, kickbacks, embezzlement, etc., in connection with employee benefit plans.

Civil penalty for failure to disclose.—Under the bill as passed by the House, if a plan administrator fails or refuses to furnish a participant or a beneficiary with a copy of the latest annual report (or such other information that is required to be furnished under the Act) within 30 days after a request for it, the administrator may be personally liable to the participant or beneficiary for up to $50 a day from the date of the failure and a court, in its discretion, may grant such other relief as it deems proper. The bill as passed by the Senate contains no comparable provision but relies upon the existing provisions of law to impose liability on the plan administrator. Under the conference agreement the administrator may be personally liable to the participant or beneficiary for up to $100 per day from the date of the failure and the court may in its discretion order such other relief as it deems proper.

Civil actions by participants and beneficiaries.—In addition, under the bill as passed by both the House and Senate, civil action may be brought by a participant or beneficiary to recover benefits due under the plan, to clarify rights to receive future benefits under the plan, and for relief from breach of fiduciary responsibility.

Under the conference agreement, civil actions may be brought by a participant or beneficiary to recover benefits due under the plan, to clarify rights to receive future benefits under the plan, and for relief from breach of fiduciary responsibility. The U.S. district courts are to have exclusive jurisdiction with respect to actions involving breach of fiduciary responsibility as well as exclusive jurisdiction over other actions to enforce or clarify benefit rights provided under title I. However, with respect to suits to enforce benefit rights under the plan or to recover benefits under the plan which do not involve application of the title I provisions, they may be brought not only in U.S. district courts but also in State courts of competent jurisdiction. All such actions in Federal or State courts are to be regarded as arising under the laws of the United States in similar fashion to those brought under section 301 of the Labor-Management Relations Act of 1947. The U.S. district courts are to have jurisdiction of these actions without regard to the amount in controversy and without regard to the citizenship of the parties.

In any action brought by a participant or beneficiary, the court may allow reasonable attorney's fees or costs to either party. An action in the U.S. district court may be brought in the district where the plan is administered or where the breach of fiduciary duty took place, or where a defendant resides or may be found. Process may be served in any other district where a defendant resides or may be found. If a participant or beneficiary brings an action in Federal court to enforce rights under title I, he is to provide a copy of the complaint to the Secretary of Labor and the Secretary of Treasury by certified mail. A copy is not required to be provided in any action which is solely for the purpose of recovering benefits under the plan. The Secretary of Labor or the Secretary of Treasury, or both, are to have the right to intervene in any action at their discretion.

Civil actions by the Secretary of Labor.—Under the bill as passed by the House, the Secretary of Labor may bring suit for breach of fiduciary responsibility and to enjoin any act or practice which violates the provisions of title I of the Act. The Secretary of Labor may also intervene in actions brought under the Act by participants and beneficiaries.

Under the bill as passed by the Senate, the Secretary of Labor may petition the court for an order requiring the return of assets transferred from a retirement fund, requiring the payment of benefits to a participant or beneficiaries, restraining conduct violating the fiduciary rules, and granting such other appropriate relief including the removal of a fiduciary. The Secretary is also authorized to bring suit when he believes that an employee benefit fund is being or has been administered in violation of the Act or the governing documents of the retirement fund. In addition, the bill as passed by the Senate authorizes the Secretary of Labor to intervene at his discretion in actions brought under the Act by participants or beneficiaries.

The conference agreement generally conforms to the provisions as passed by the House. The Secretary of Labor may bring an action for breach of a fiduciary duty or to enjoin any act or practice which violates the provision of title I of the Act or to obtain any other appropriate relief to enforce any provision of that title. In the case of a transaction by a party in interest with respect to a plan which is not qualified under the Internal Revenue Code, the Secretary of Labor may assess a civil penalty not to exceed 5 percent of the amount of the transaction. If not corrected, an additional penalty of not more than 100 percent of the transaction may be imposed.

In the case of any plan which has been found by the Internal Revenue Service to be a qualified employee benefit plan under the Internal Revenue Code (or with respect to any plan which has a pending application for a determination to be so qualified), the Secretary of Labor is not to bring an action for equitable relief with respect to a violation of the participation, vesting and funding standards of title I unless he is requested to do so either by the Secretary of the Treasury or by one or more participants, beneficiaries, or fiduciaries of the plan.

Benefit claim procedure.—The bill as passed by the House contains no provisions providing for procedures for resolving disputes between the plan administrator and participants or beneficiaries. Under the bill as passed by the Senate each pension plan is required to establish a procedure for a review of disputes between the plan administrator and participants or beneficiaries and afford an opportunity for arbitration of any dispute. Under the conference agreement every employee benefit plan is required to provide adequate notice in writing to any participant or beneficiary whose claim for benefits under the plan has been denied, setting forth the specific reasons for denial written in a manner calculated to be understood by the participant. In addition, the plan administrator is required to afford a reasonable opportunity to any participant or beneficiary whose claim for benefits has been denied for a full and fair review of this decision by the plan administrator.

Investigatory authority.—Under the bill as passed by the House, the Secretary of Labor, where he has reasonable cause to believe that violations of the provisions of this bill have been committed, may enter places, inspect accounts and question persons to the extent he deems necessary in order to determine whether any provision of title I has been or is about to be violated. The Secretary is authorized to request the filing of supporting schedules of information and to publish and report on any investigation to interested persons or government officials.

Under the bill as passed by the Senate, the Secretary may enter premises and inspect records and accounts but he may make no more than one examination of books and records per year unless he has reasonable cause to believe that there was a violation of title I. The bill as passed by the Senate also authorizes the Secretary to require the filing of supporting schedules of information. The Secretary of Labor is further authorized to make arrangements with the Secretary of Treasury to prevent duplication of effort regarding investigation of violations relating to fiduciaries.

Under the conference agreement, the Secretary of Labor is to have the power in order to determine whether there have been violations or there are about to be violations of any provision of title I to make an investigation. In connection with the investigation, he may require the submission of reports, books and records, and the filing of supporting data, but no plan may be required to submit such books, records or supporting data more than once annually unless the Secretary has reasonable cause to believe there may exist a violation under title I. The Secretary also may enter places and inspect records and accounts and question those persons he deems necessary to enable him to determine the facts relative to the investigation if he has reasonable cause to believe there may exist a violation under title I. The Secretary is authorized to make available to persons covered by the plan and to any department or agency of the United States information concerning any matter which has been the subject of the investigation.

Subpoena power.—Under the bill as passed by the House, the Secretary of Labor is given the same powers of subpoena as are given to the Federal Trade Commission. The bill as passed by the Senate contains the same provisions as that passed by the House and in addition provides that the Secretary of Labor may delegate his auditing and investigation functions with respect to insured banks acting as fiduciaries to appropriate Federal banking agencies. The conference agreement adopts the provisions of the bill as passed by the Senate.

Appropriations authorized, etc.—Under the bill as passed by the House and the Senate, there is authorized appropriations of such sums as may be necessary to enable the Secretary of Labor to carry out his functions and duties under the bill. In addition, under the bill as passed by the Senate, the Secretary of Labor is authorized to increase the number of supergrade positions in the Department of Labor. Under the conference agreement the Secretary of Labor is authorized to add one additional position in the GS-18 level in the Department of Labor and to place 20 additional positions in the GS-16 and 17 level in the Department of Labor.

Service of process.—Under the bill as passed by the House, subpoena or other legal process of a court upon a trustee or plan administrator constitutes service on the plan. In addition, a plan may sue or be sued as an entity. The bill as passed by the Senate does not contain comparable provisions. The conference agreement basically adopts the provisions as passed by the House but provides that where a plan does not designate in its plan description an individual as agent for service of legal process, service upon the Secretary of Labor is to constitute adequate service. In that case the Secretary upon receipt of service of process is to notify the administrator or any trustee of the pending action within 15 days after he is served.

Enforcement of judgment. — The bill as passed by the House provides that a money judgment under title I of the Act against the plan is to be enforceable only against the plan as an entity and not against any other person unless that person's liability is established in his individual capacity. The bill as passed by the Senate did not contain a comparable provision. Under the conference agreement the House provisions are adopted.

Government representation.—Both the House bill and the Senate amendment provide for the Secretary of Labor to be represented by attorneys appointed by him in civil actions arising under the Act, except for litigation before the Supreme Court and the Court of Claims. The conference agreement adds the qualification that "all such litigation shall be subject to the direction and control of the Attorney General." The new language was added in order to make clear that even though litigation is conducted by Labor Department attorneys, there is to be authority in the Attorney General to resolve those situations where two or more agencies of the Federal government have varying positions with respect to issues in litigation and, in such situations, to assure that the government takes uniform positions before the courts. In addition, the Attorney General is to have authority concerning the presentation to the courts of the government's position with respect to such issues of general importance as the constitutionality of Federal laws. Under the conference agreement, it is intended that in civil litigation involving the Secretary of Labor under this bill, the Secretary, in the normal course, will be represented in court by the Solicitor of Labor and his attorneys, with appropriate arrangements being made between the Secretary of Labor and the Attorney General with respect to the active involvement of the Justice Department in the types of situations discussed above.

Reports to Congress.—Under the bill as passed by the House, the Secretary of Labor is to report annually to the

Congress regarding the administration of title I. This report is to include an explanation of the variances granted, a status report on any plan operating with a variance and its progress in achieving compliance with the Act, the projected date for terminating the variance and information, and recommendations for further legislation in connection with matters covered by title I. Under the conference agreement, the provisions of the bill as passed by the House generally are adopted.

Cooperation between agencies.—Under the bill as passed by both the House and the Senate, the Secretary of Labor is authorized to cooperate with other agencies and make agreements for mutual assistance. In addition, under the bill as passed by the House, the Attorney General is authorized to receive from the Secretary of Labor for appropriate action evidence which has been developed that warrants consideration for criminal prosecution under Federal law. Under the conference agreement, the provisions for cooperation of other agencies including the authorization for the Attorney General to receive matters relating to criminal prosecution is adopted.

Administrative matters.—Under the bill as passed by the House, the Administrative Procedure Act is applicable to the provisions of title I. In addition, no employee of the Department of Labor is to administer or enforce title I with respect to any employee organization of which he is a member or employer organization in which he has an interest. The bill as passed by the Senate does not add any comparable provisions. Under the conference agreement, the provisions of the bill as passed by the House are adopted.

Interference with rights.—Under the bill as passed by both the House and the Senate, it is unlawful to interfere with the attainment of any rights to which a participant or beneficiary may become entitled or to coercively interfere through the use of fraud, force, or violence with any participant or beneficiary for the purpose of preventing him from exercising any right to which he is or may become entitled to under the plan or title I. The penalties and degrees of proof for violations of the provisions are somewhat different. Under the conference agreement, the participant or beneficiary may bring a civil action against any person who interferes with his rights which are protected under the Act. In addition, any person who willfully uses fraud, force, violence or threats to restrain, coerce or intimidate any participant or beneficiary for purposes of interfering with the participant's or beneficiary's rights under the plan or title I of the Act is to be fined $10,000 or imprisoned for not more than 1 year, or both.

Advisory Council.—Under the bill as passed by both the House and the Senate, there is established an Advisory Council on Employee Welfare and Pension Benefit Plans. Under the conference agreement, the Council is to consist of 15 members appointed by the Secretary of Labor. Not more than 8 members are to be of the same political party. The Council is to be made up of members who are to be representatives of employee organizations and employers, and members from the fields of insurance, corporate trusts, actuarial counseling, investment counseling, investment management, and accounting, and from the general public. Members are generally to serve for terms of 3 years, are to advise the Secretary of Labor with respect to the carrying out of his functions under the bill and are to submit to the Secretary recommendations as to the administration of the provisions of the bill.

Tax Court Declaratory Judgment Proceedings

Both the House bill and the Senate amendment provide a procedure for obtaining a declaratory judgment with respect to the tax-qualified status of an employee benefit plan. Under both the House and Senate versions of the bill, jurisdiction to issue a declaratory judgment is given to the

United States Tax Court. This remedy is available only if the Internal Revenue Service has issued a determination as to the status of the plan which is adverse to the party petitioning in the Tax Court, or has failed to issue a determination but the petitioner has exhausted his administrative remedies inside the Internal Revenue Service.

The differences between the bill as passed by both the House and the Senate are technical in nature. For example, the Senate amendment provides that the burden of proof is to be on the petitioner (the employer, plan administrator, or employee) as to those grounds set forth in the Internal Revenue Service determination; the burden of proof is to be on the Service as to any other grounds that the Service relies upon in the court proceeding (e.g., if the Service does not issue a determination as to the plan, then the Service is to have the burden of proof as to every ground as to which it relies). On the other hand, the House bill does not make specific provisions for burden of proof.

Under the conference agreement, the House provision is accepted with a number of amendments. The Pension Benefit Guaranty Corporation is permitted to be a petitioner, on the same basis as other petitioners. Employees are permitted to be petitioners if they qualify as interested parties under Treasury regulations and have exhausted their administrative remedies. It is contemplated that only those employees who are entitled to petition the Secretary of Labor under section 3001 of this Act are to be treated as interested parties. It is contemplated that the question as to who bears the burden of proof will be determined by the Tax Court under its existing rule-making authority. Under the existing Tax Court rules the taxpayer has the burden of proof as to matters in the notice of deficiency. As to matters raised by the Service at the time of the Tax Court hearing, the Service has the burden. It is expected that rules similar to these will be adopted by the Tax Court.

Under the House bill, the declaratory judgment provisions are to take effect on January 1, 1978. The bill as passed by the Senate provides that the declaratory judgment provisions are to take effect on January 1, 1975.

Both the House and Senate bills authorize the assignment of the declaratory judgment proceedings provided in this bill to be heard by commissioners of the Tax Court. They also authorize a commissioner to enter a decision of the court in these proceedings. The conference substitute provides for this same procedure, but in doing so the conferees wish to make clear that it is not intended that this be construed as indicating that all of these proceedings should be heard by commissioners and decisions entered by them rather than by the judges of the court. Instead, it is intended to provide more flexibility to the Tax Court in the use of commissioners in these types of cases. It is anticipated, for example, that if the volume of these cases should be large, that the Tax Court will expedite the resolution of these cases by authorizing commissioners to hear and enter decisions in cases where similar issues have already been heard and decided by the judges of the court or in other cases where, in the discretion of the court, it is appropriate for the commissioners to hear and decide cases.

Under the conference agreement, the declaratory judgment provisions are to take effect with respect to petitions filed more than one year after the date of enactment.

Administering Office in Internal Revenue Service

Under the bill as passed by both the House and the Senate, there is established an Office of Employee Plans and Exempt Organizations, in the Internal Revenue Service, headed by an Assistant Commissioner of Internal Revenue, to administer the tax provisions with regard to employee benefit plans and other exempt organizations.

The House bill does not provide a compensation schedule for the employees of the new Office of Employee

Plans and Exempt Organizations. The bill as passed by the House authorizes appropriations for this office in the amount of $20 million for fiscal year 1974 and $70 million for each fiscal year thereafter. However, the bill as passed by the House neither imposes nor earmarks any specific revenue source for this authorization of appropriations.

The bill as passed by the Senate provides for the Assistant Commissioner in charge of this office to be classified as GS-18 and that this is to be in addition to the number of positions at that level otherwise authorized for the Internal Revenue Service. Also the bill as passed by the Senate authorizes for the Service an additional 20 positions at the level of GA-17 and 16. The Senate amendment authorizes appropriations for each of the fiscal years 1974, 1975, and 1976 in the amount of $35 million plus one-half of the revenue of the private foundation investment income tax (under section 4940 of the Code). For each fiscal year thereafter the bill as passed by the Senate authorizes appropriations of amounts equal to the collections of a new excise tax on employee benefit plans ($1 per participant per plan per calendar year, beginning with 1974) plus one-half of the private foundation investment income tax collections.

The conference agreement accepts the Senate provision authorizing the Assistant Commissioner Office of Employee Plans and Exempt Organizations to be classified as a GS-18 and providing to the Service an additional 20 positions in the level of GS-16 and 17. However, the conference agreement does not accept the Senate provision authorizing a new tax on employee benefit plans of $1 per participant. In place of the authorization of the new excise tax on participants, the conference provides a permanent authorization for fiscal year 1975 and for each fiscal year thereafter of an amount equal to the revenues from the private foundation investment income taxes if the rate of such tax was 2 percent plus an amount equal to that 2-percentage-point figure or $30,000,000, whichever is the larger.

Under the House bill, the provisions regarding the new office are to take effect 90 days after the date of enactment. Under the bill as passed by the Senate, no specified effective date is provided. The conference agreement accepts the House provision.

VII. CONTRIBUTIONS ON BEHALF OF SELF-EMPLOYED INDIVIDUALS AND SHAREHOLDER-EMPLOYEES (SEC. 2001 OF THE BILL AND SECS. 401, 404, 1379, AND 4972 OF THE CODE)

Under the House bill the maximum limitations on deductions for self-employed individuals would be increased from 10 percent of their self-employment income, not to exceed $2,500, up to 15 percent of their self-employment income, not to exceed $7,500. In any event, a minimum of $750 would be deductible by self-employed individuals, without regard to the percentage limitations. The Senate amendment, although containing a number of technical differences, is generally similar to the House bill in this area.

The conference substitute is described below. Generally, the substitute in this case follows the House bill with respect to technical matters.

Specific Contribution Limits on Proprietorships, Partnerships, or Subchapter S Corporations

The conference substitute increases the maximum deductible contribution on behalf of self-employed persons to the lesser of 15 percent of earned income or $7,500. The same change is made as to excludable contributions on behalf of subchapter S corporation shareholder-employees. In applying the percentage limitation, not more than $100,000 of earned income may be taken into account. Self-employed persons (but not shareholder-employees) are permitted to set aside up to $750 a year out of earned income, without regard to the percentage limitation.

Defined Benefit Limits For Proprietorships, Partnerships, and Subchapter S Corporations

The substitute authorizes Treasury regulations to allow self-employed persons and shareholder-employees in effect to translate the 15-percent/$7,500 limitations on contributions into approximately equivalent limitations on benefits which individuals can receive under a defined benefit plan. In this respect, the substitute contains a table (based on certain interest and mortality rates) which will serve as a guideline for regulations. The Treasury Department may, by regulations, modify this table from time to time for years beginning after December 31, 1977, to take account of changes in interest and mortality rates which occur after 1973.

The conference substitute also contains technical rules to prevent an individual from obtaining unintended high benefit accruals late in his career merely by establishing a "token plan" early in his career.

A plan which covers owner-employees is not permitted to use the defined benefit provisions unless it provides benefits for all participants on a nonintegrated basis (i.e., without taking social security benefits into account).

Excess Contributions

Present law provides that excess contributions to an H.R. 10-plan on behalf of an owner-employer must be repaid from the plan and provides, in the case of a willful excess contribution, that the owner-employee is barred from participating in a qualified plan for 5 years. The conference substitute repeals these provisions and, in lieu thereof, the substitute imposes an excise tax of 6 percent on excess contributions to plans for the self-employed. The tax is payable by the employer who maintains the plan.

In the case of a defined contribution plan (for example, a money purchase pension plan) excess contributions include amounts contributed for the self-employed person in excess of the 15-percent/$7,500 limitations. (However, the tax would never exceed 6% of the assets of the account). In the case of a defined benefit plan, the tax is imposed where the plan is fully funded at the close of the employer's taxable year, and is imposed on the amount that has not been deductible for the taxable year or any prior taxable year. Also, in the case of either type of plan, excess contributions include voluntary contributions by owner-employees in excess of the allowable amount of such contributions.

The tax applies for the year in which the excess contribution is made and for every subsequent year that the excess contribution is outstanding. The excess contribution may be eliminated (so as to stop the running of the tax) in one of two ways—either by repayment of the excess contribution from the plan (which would reduce or eliminate the tax for subsequent years), or by a carryover of the excess payment and applying it against the amount allowable in the next year (or a subsequent year).

In the case of a defined benefit plan, the repayment would have to be made to the employer. In the case of a defined contribution plan, the repayment could be made either to the employer or to the employee (but, as under present law, a distribution could generally not be made to the employee from a money purchase plan until he attained retirement age). An excess voluntary contribution would be repaid to the owner-employee who made it. Of course, any distribution made to eliminate an excess contribution would not be in violation of the exclusive benefit rules of present law, or the fiduciary standards imposed under this bill.

The excess contribution could also be eliminated through means of a carryover. For example, if contributions of $10,000 were made to a plan (where voluntary contributions were not permitted) on behalf of a self-employed person (who was entitled to the full $7,500 deduction) the $2,500 excess contribution could be purged in the next year if the contribution made on behalf of the individual in that year were limited to $5,000. In this case, the 6-percent tax would be imposed, but only once, because the excess contribution had been eliminated in the second year. Also in the second year the individual would be entitled to a deduction of $7,500 ($5,000 of contributions in that year, plus the $2,500 carryover). Of course, there would be no tax on underfunding under these circumstances even if the plan were a money purchase plan, the terms of which required a $7,500 contribution for the individual in the second year.

Premature Distributions

The conference substitute increases the tax on premature distributions to 10 percent of the amount of the premature distribution (instead of 10 percent of the marginal regular tax on the premature distribution, as under present law).

Withdrawing of Voluntary Contributions by Owner-Employees

The conference substitute allows an owner-employee to withdraw his own voluntary contributions to an H.R. 10-plan before retirement without penalty. It also contains a technical amendment which repeals the "stacking" rules of section 72(m)(1) (i.e., the rules which determine the order in which different categories of income are deemed to be distributed). The conferees intend that distributions from an H.R. 10-plan to an owner-employee be treated first as repayments of any excess contributions made on his behalf, and second as withdrawals of voluntary contributions.

Effective Dates

In general, the amendments with respect to H.R. 10-plans are to apply to taxable years beginning after December 31, 1973. The rule with respect to the $100,000 contribution base limitation is to apply to taxable years beginning after December 31, 1975, or, if earlier, the first year in which contributions under the plan exceed the deductible contribution limits of present law. The rules facilitating the use of defined benefit plans for the self-employed are to apply to taxable years beginning after December 31, 1975. The rules with respect to excess contributions are to apply to contributions made in taxable years beginning after December 31, 1975, and the rules with respect to premature distributions are to apply to distributions made in taxable years beginning after December 31, 1975. The rule permitting withdrawal of voluntary contributions by owner-employees is to apply to taxable years ending after the date of enactment.

VIII. TAX DEDUCTIONS FOR INDIVIDUAL RETIREMENT ACCOUNTS (SEC. 2002 OF THE BILL AND SECS. 219, 408, 409, 4973, 4974, AND 6693 OF THE INTERNAL REVENUE CODE)

Under the House bill, individuals not covered by qualified or government pension plans (or sec. 403(b) annuity contracts) would be permitted to take a deduction of up to 20 percent of their earned income, not to exceed $1,500, for retirement savings. This amount could be set aside in a special trusteed or custodial account with a bank, savings and loan, or credit union, used to purchase an annuity contract, or invested in qualified retirement bonds. This amount could not be drawn down without penalty before age 59½ (except in case of death or disability) and payment of benefits from the account would have to begin by age 70½. An individual could establish the account himself, or, alternatively, an employer or labor union could maintain accounts of this type for employees or members.

The provisions of the Senate amendment are similar in most respects. However, under the Senate amendment the allowable deduction could not exceed 15 percent of earned income, not to exceed $1,500. Moreover, under the Senate amendment, the assets of the account could be invested in life insurance contracts. Also, there is no provision in the Senate amendment for union-sponsored accounts.

The rules of the conference substitute are described below. In general it follows the House bill, except that the conference substitute accepts the Senate limitation of 15 percent—$1,500.

Deductions for Contributions to IRA's

Under the conference substitute, the maximum annual deduction is to be $1,500, or 15 percent of compensation, whichever is less. Consequently, the percentage limitation for contributions to individual retirement accounts is the same as the percentage limitation for contributions to H.R. 10 plans (although the H.R. 10 plan has a $7,500 limitation on the amount which may be set aside in order to provide an incentive for the self-employed to establish qualified plans which will also benefit their employees).

This deduction is to be available to any individual who is not an active participant in a qualified or government plan, or a section 403(b) contract (available to employees of certain types of tax-exempt organizations) and is to be available whether or not the taxpayer itemizes his other deductions. The individual may himself make payments into such an account or this may be done by his employer or his union. If both husband and wife are eligible, each can make contributions to his or her own individual retirement account.

The conferees agree with the statement appearing in the report of the House Committee on Ways and Means (No. 93-807) that if an employee is given the option to elect not to be covered by a qualified, etc., plan and he so elects, generally he will not be treated as being an active participant in the plan for purposes of the retirement savings deduction. The conferees also agree with the statement in this report that where an employee who elects out of a qualified plan can elect later to become an active participant in it and can receive benefits for all prior years (for which he elected out) upon payment of, e.g., all mandatory contributions plus interest for prior periods, the employee is to be treated as being an active participant in the plan for the prior years with respect to which he pays the required amount and accrues benefits.

Requirements for an IRA

Under the conference substitute, the assets of an individual retirement account may be invested in a trusteed or custodial account with a bank, savings and loan, or credit union, or in an annuity contract, or a qualified retirement bond.

In addition, the substitute allows a retirement savings deduction for amounts paid under certain life insurance endowment contracts (which will be treated as individual retirement annuities) to the extent the amounts paid are properly allocable to retirement savings. However, only the retirement saving element in the contract, and not the part of the premium used to purchase life insurance, is to be deductible. For example, if a premium of $1,000 were paid under a qualified endowment contract, and $200 of this amount were allocable (under regulations) to the cost of the life insurance element, and $800 to the retirement savings aspect of the contract, then $800 would be allowed as a retirement savings deduction (if the individual were eligible for a deduction of this amount).

Under the conference substitute, the total amounts payable under qualified endowment contracts cannot be greater than $1,500 per year. However, an individual may contribute (and deduct) the difference between his maximum allowable retirement savings deduction and the retirement savings element under an endowment contract through another funding medium (such as a trusteed bank account). Under the conference substitute the insurance companies are to provide (before the close of the year) every individual who has purchased a qualified endowment contract with a statement as to the portion of the premiums which is deductible and the portion which is not deductible, as well as any other information required under regulations. A similar statement must be furnished to the Internal Revenue Service.

Insurance contracts are restricted to endowment contracts in order to provide a substantial savings element. The endowment contract also must be issued by a life insurance company qualified to sell insurance in the jurisdiction where the contract is sold (and may include no insurance element other than life insurance). In addition, the contract must mature no later than the taxable year in which the individual attains age 70½. The conferees intend that for an endowment contract to qualify, the premiums payable under the contract (for any given maturity value) are not to increase over the life of the contract, the cash surrender value of the contract at the maturity date is to be not less than the death benefit payable under the contract at any time, and the death benefit at some point during the life of the contract must exceed the greater of the cash value or the sum of the premiums paid under the contract.

Distributions from qualified endowment contracts are to be taxable as ordinary income to the extent allocable to retirement savings, and are to be taxed as life insurance proceeds to the extent allocable to life insurance. When a contract has matured, the full value of the contract will constitute retirement savings, and all amounts payable under a matured contract are to be taxed as ordinary income to the recipient (whether or not he is the individual who made contributions to the account and whether or not that individual is alive at the time the payments are made from the account).

Under the conference substitute, the assets of an individual retirement account may not be commingled with other property, except in a common trust fund or investment fund (i.e., a group trust), solely for the purposes of diversifying investments, under rules similar to those established in Rev. Rul. 56-267, 1956-1 C.B. 206. Also, following Rev. Rul. 56-267, the conferees intend that, solely for purposes of diversification of investments, the assets of qualified individual retirement accounts may be pooled with the assets of qualified section 401(a) trusts, without adversely affecting the tax-qualification of either the individual retirement accounts or the section 401(a) trusts. The conferees intend that the group trust itself will be entitled to exemption from tax under the Internal Revenue Code in accordance with the rules of Rev. Rul. 56-267.

The conferees intend that this legislation with respect to individual retirement accounts is not to limit in any way the application of the Federal securities laws to individual retirement accounts or the application to them of the laws relating to common trusts or investment funds maintained by any institution. As a result, the Securities and Exchange Commission will have the authority to act on the issues arising with respect to individual retirement accounts independently of this legislation.

The conferees understand that the Internal Revenue Service anticipates developing a prototype individual retirement account which would include a full disclosure of all the material elements governing the retirement savings deduction. This prototype plan would qualify under the requirements for an individual retirement account. Other plans would be required to seek prior approval from the Internal Revenue Service and the conferees expect that one of the requirements for approval would be a disclosure statement of all the material elements governing the retirement savings deductions. The conferees also expect the Internal Revenue Service to develop a pamphlet which sets forth the restrictions and limitations with regard to the individual retirement accounts, including, for example, the penalties for premature distributions, the fact that the account is not eligible for estate and gift tax advantages or the lump-sum distribution rules that qualified plans are entitled to. It is the hope of the conferees that such pamphlet would receive wide distribution so that individuals would be fully informed on the restrictions and limitations of such an account. Also, in accordance with regulations to be prescribed by the Secretary of Treasury or his delegate, there is to be disclosure of such matters as load factors for insurance contracts and earnings factors for individual retirement accounts. These required disclosures are to be made in layman's language, and civil penalties are imposed under the substitute for failure to adequately disclose.

Requirements for an IRA Annuity

Under the conference substitute, retirement savings may also be invested in annuity contracts. This may be an individual annuity contract, or a joint and survivor contract for the benefit of the individual and his spouse. The annual premium for the contract is not to exceed $1,500, and the contract is to be nontransferable and is not to be used as security for a loan. Also, distributions from the account must begin by the end of the year in which the individual attains age 70½.

Employer and Union-Sponsored IRA's

Under the substitute, employers and labor unions (and other employee associations) are to be able to establish individual retirement accounts for their employees or members. There is no requirement that the accounts must be established on a nondiscriminatory basis (since any employee not covered under an employer-sponsored account could establish his own account) but, of course, if the employer also maintains a qualified plan, he cannot satisfy the coverage requirements with respect to that plan by taking into account the fact that employees not covered under the plan are covered by individual retirement accounts. Even if the contributions are made by the employer, these amounts constitute income to the employee, and are subject to FICA and FUTA taxes. However, employer contributions are not to be subject to withholding for income tax purposes if it is reasonable for the employer to believe that the employee will be entitled to receive a deduction for the contribution.

Taxation of Distributions—In General

Generally, the individual is to have a zero basis in his individual retirement account and the proceeds are to be fully taxable when distributed. These distributions are not to be eligible for capital gains treatment, or the special averaging rules applicable to lump-sum distributions from qualified plans (although the general averaging rules of sec. 1301 are to be available). Also, the amounts in individual retirement accounts are not to be excluded from tax for purposes of estate and gift tax.

Premature Distributions

In the event of a premature distribution (or deemed distribution) from the account before the individual attains age 59½, the individual's tax on this amount is to be increased by 10 percent of the total distribution (except in the case of death or disability, or distributions of excess contributions made within the time for filing the individual's tax return for the year in which the excess contributions occur).

If an individual borrows money from an individual account (or from a group trust in which the account assets were invested) the entire account of the individual is disqualified, earnings on the account are no longer tax-exempt, and the participant is then to be taxed as if he had received a distribution of the fair market value of all the assets in his account. (If he borrows money, using his interest in the account as security, the portion used as security is to be treated as a distribution.) A similar result (i.e., deemed distribution of the entire account) would follow if the individual borrowed money from the insurance company issuing an annuity or endowment contract, or otherwise used the contract as security for a loan. Clearly, if the assets of the account were invested in such a way as to provide for the direct and immediate benefit of the participant (for example, if the account were used for a downpayment on the house where he lived) then the entire account would be deemed to be distributed. Of course, in the case of any deemed distribution from an individual retirement account, the amount of the distribution would not be includible in income a second time in a later year when the amount was actually distributed. (Questions of the order in which income is distributed where only part of the account is disqualified are to be determined under regulations.)

An individual may invest directly in an endowment contract but does not receive a deduction for the part of the premium which is allocable to life insurance protection. Thus, where the assets of an individual retirement account are invested in a qualifying endowment contract for the participant, this transaction is to be treated as an automatic rollover by the account, and only the amount of the assets which are allocable to the purchase of life insurance protection under the endowment contract are to be deemed to be distributed to the participant. This amount would be includible in income by the participant, but would not be subject to the 10 percent tax on premature distributions.

Application of Prohibited Transaction and Other Taxes to IRA's

Generally, an individual retirement account is to be exempt from Federal tax, but the unrelated business income of the account, if any, is to be subject to tax (under sec. 511).

Under the House bill, individual retirement accounts generally would be subject to the prohibited transaction rules of present law. However, with respect to prohibited transactions, the conference substitute (generally following the Senate amendment) replaces present law with an excise tax on prohibited transactions (instead of using disqualification as a sanction) and changes the existing prohibited transaction rules. Consequently, the conference substitute applies the new prohibited transaction rules applicable to an owner-employee (e.g., no borrowing from the account is permitted) to individual retirement accounts, with respect to transactions involving the employer or union sponsor of the account, or other parties in interest.

However, if an individual participant engages in an unauthorized transaction with his individual retirement account then, as indicated previously, the sanction, in general, is disqualification of the account. In this case the assets of the account are to be deemed to be distributed, and the appropriate taxes, including the 10 percent additional tax on premature distributions, are to apply. However, the individual is not to be subject to the prohibited transaction excise taxes (of sec. 4975).

Thus, where there is a union or employer-sponsored account, and there is an individual retirement account trust covering more than one employee, only the employee who engages in the prohibited transaction is to be subject to disqualification of his separate account. However, if the employer (or union) sponsoring the account is the party engaging in a prohibited transaction, then the employer (or other party) will be liable for the excise tax, but the individual participants will not.

Excess Contributions

In general, where contributions in excess of the deductible limits are made to an individual retirement account, no deduction is allowed for the excess amount, and this amount will be subject to a 6 percent tax for the year in which it is made, and each year thereafter, until there is no excess. The distribution is not to be includible in income if the excess is distributed to the individual on or before the due date for filing the employee's tax return for the year in question (including extensions). If the distribution occurs after that date, however, the distribution is to constitute taxable income to the employee (because his basis in his account is always zero) and will also give rise to a 10-percent additional tax if the distribution occurs before the employee is 59½.

The excess contribution may be removed by a distribution, or by underutilizing the allowable deduction limits for a later year. For example, if an employee contributed $3,000 in one year, and nothing the second year, then a 6 percent tax on $1,500 would be imposed only once (assuming the employee was entitled to a full $1,500 contribution for both years). (Similarly, if the participant withdrew the $1,500 excess contribution in the year in which the contribution was made, the 6 percent excise tax would be imposed only for that year.) Also (to prevent undue hardship resulting from bad investment experience), the tax may never exceed 6 percent of the assets in the account (but a decline in the asset value of the account does not remove the excess contribution and the 6 percent tax will be imposed until the excess contribution has been distributed or eliminated by underutilization of allowable contributions in a subsequent year).

A similar tax is to be imposed on excess contributions for section 403(b) plan investments in mutual fund stock (which are permitted under the conference substitute). (Section 403(b) allows deductions of up to 20 percent of salary, without regard to discrimination requirements, in the case of employees of educational and certain other types of exempt organizations.) However, the 6 percent tax is not imposed on section 403(b) annuity contracts, since earnings on annuity contracts are not taxable until distributed, even when the annuities are purchased outside the scope of a qualified plan.

No retirement savings deduction is to be allowed for contributions made during or after the year in which the individual attains age 70½, and contributions of an individual after attaining this age are to be treated as excess contributions.

Excise Tax on Excess Accumulations

Under the conference substitute, distribution of the assets of an individual retirement account must begin by the year in which the participant attains age 70½, and must be distributed no less rapidly than ratably over his lifetime (or the lives of the participant and his spouse). To enforce this requirement, the substitute imposes an excise tax of 50 percent on the amount, if any, by which the amount of the distributions from the account fail to equal the minimum distribution required for the year in order to satisfy the age 70½ payout requirements.

Tax-Free Rollovers To Facilitate Pension Transfers

To facilitate portability of pensions —or their transfer with the employee as he changes jobs—the conference substitute provides that money or property may be distributed from a tax-qualified plan or from an individual retirement account to the plan participant, on a tax-free basis, if the same money or property is reinvested by the participant within 60 days in a qualifying individual retirement account.

In the case of distributions from a qualified plan, the distribution must be a lump-sum distribution (see Part X, Lump-Sum distributions) to qualify as a tax-free rollover.

Amounts received from a qualified plan may also be transferred to another qualified plan through the medium of an individual retirement account (with the consent of the individual's new employer) but in this case the conduit retirement account must consist of nothing but assets transferred from a qualified plan (and the earnings on this amount) to prevent a situation where retirement savings might indirectly obtain tax advantages not intended. (These qualified plan distributions may also be reinvested directly in the qualified plan of the individual's new employer on a tax-free basis, if the reinvestment occurs within 60 days after the individual receives the distribution.) However, an individual may have one individual retirement account for transferred savings from a qualified plan and another which represents a normal individual account set aside. For similar reasons, if the individual retirement account contains assets transferred from an H.R. 10 plan, on behalf of a self-employed person, no rollover is permitted from that retirement account to a qualified corporate plan.

Also, in the case of rollovers from a qualified plan, the amount contributed to the individual retirement account is to be the amount received, less the amount contributed to the plan by the individual as an employee contribution. (This is because the employee must always have a zero basis in his individual retirement account.)

Under the committee substitute, rollovers are permitted to and from qualifying investments in individual retirement bonds (discussed below) on the same basis as investments in other types of individual retirement accounts and annuities. At age 70½, the individual must cash in his bonds (since the proceeds of the bonds will be deemed to be distributed in full) but the assets may be rolled over into an investment which will satisfy the age 70½ payment requirements.

Tax-free rollovers between individual retirement accounts may occur only once every three years.

Qualified Retirement Bonds

Deductible employee savings may be invested in a special retirement bond to be issued by the Federal Government. Generally, the rules governing retirement bonds are closely comparable to the rules governing other forms of qualifying individual retirement savings. Thus, the bonds may be cashed prior to age 59½, but, except in the case of a rollover, the individual is generally to be subject to a 10 percent penalty tax (unless the bonds are cashed due to death or disability). However, the bond may be redeemed within 12 months of its purchase without penalty (and without payment of interest) and in this case the individual is not to be entitled to a deduction for the contribution.

The bonds are to cease to bear interest when the individual attains age 70½, and the proceeds of the bonds are to be deemed to be distributed in that year (whether or not the bonds are actually cashed in). However, as discussed above, the individual may roll the proceeds over into another qualifying form of individual retirement investment.

Other Rules

The conference substitute provides that the proceeds of individual retirement accounts, etc., are to constitute retirement income for purposes of the retirement income credit. The substitute also includes the provisions of the Senate amendment that if a retirement account or annuity is transferred pursuant to a divorce settlement, the transfer is not to be taxable.

Effective Dates

The deduction for retirement savings is to be available for taxable years beginning after December 31, 1974. The tax-free rollover of assets between qualified plans applies to transfers after the date of enactment.

IX. OVERALL LIMITATIONS ON CONTRIBUTIONS AND BENEFITS

(Sec. 2004 of the Bill and Secs. 401, 403 and 415 of the Internal Revenue Code)

Under the House bill, in general, in the case of defined benefit plans, the pension which may be paid from a qualified plan with respect to any individual may not exceed 100 percent of his compensation in his high three years of employment or $75,000, whichever is the lesser. In the case of defined contribution plans, the annual additions to an individual's account may not exceed the lesser of $25,000, or 25 percent of his compensation. (Both the $75,000 amount and the $25,000 amount referred to above are subject to cost-of-living allowances.) If an employee is under both a defined benefit plan and a defined contribution plan then the sum of (1) the percentage utilization of the maximum limit under the defined benefit plan, and (2) the percentage utilization of the maximum limit under the defined contribution plan, cannot exceed 140 percent.

Under the Senate amendment, benefits under a defined benefit plan are limited to 75 percent of the participant's high-three-consecutive-years of compensation, taking into account no more than $100,000 of compensation per year. A closely comparable limitation is provided for defined contribution plans, so that deductible contributions may not exceed amounts sufficient to fund a pension for the employee equal to 75 percent of his average high-three-years of compensation (not in excess of the first $100,000 in any one year). Where an employer had both a defined benefit plan and a defined contribution plan, the maximum benefit payable under the defined benefit plan would have to be reduced in proportion to the amount of the benefit which was funded through the defined contribution plan.

The conference substitute closely follows the provisions of the House bill. The detailed provisions of the conference substitute are discussed below.

Coverage of Limitations

The conference substitute imposes an overall limitation (described below) on the contributions and benefits which are allowable under qualified pension, profit-sharing, and stock bonus plans and annuities (including H.R. 10-plans in cases where the overall limits are lower than the H.R. 10-plan limits). The overall limitation also applies to annuity contracts or mutual fund arrangements for employees of educational, charitable, etc., organizations or of public schools (i.e., sec. 403(b) annuities), as well as individual retirement accounts, annuities and retirement bonds.

Application to Defined Benefit Plans

Under the conference substitute, in general, the highest annual benefit which can be paid (in the form of a straight-life annuity) out of a defined benefit plan to a participant is not to exceed the lesser of (a) $75,000, or (b) 100 percent of the participant's average compensation in his high-three-years of employment. (Both of these ceilings are to be adjusted to reflect cost-of-living increases.)

In the event of retirement before age 55, the $75,000 ceiling (but not the 100 percent ceiling) is to be scaled down on an actuarial basis (but not below $10,000). In general, there is no required scale down for preretirement ancillary benefits (such as medical, death and disability), but there would have to be an adjustment for post-retirement ancillary benefits, such as term-certain annuities, post-retirement death benefits, or a guaranteed payment for a period of years.

If a benefit were paid in the form of a joint and survivor annuity for the benefit of the participant and his spouse, the value of this feature would not be taken into account unless the survivor benefit were greater than the joint benefit.

Upward adjustments in the benefit schedule would be permitted to reflect any employee contributions to the plan, including rollover contributions from another qualified plan or from an individual retirement account.

Also the substitute would provide a de minimis rule, which would allow a qualified plan to pay an annual retirement benefit of up to $10,000 per annum, notwithstanding the 100-percent limitation, or the required adjustment for certain ancillary benefits, to any employee who had not participated in a qualified defined contribution plan of the employer.

As a further adjustment to the rules described above, the maximum allowable defined benefit would have to be scaled down proportionately for an employee with less than 10 years of service.

Application to Defined Contribution Plans

In the case of a defined contribution plan, the annual additions for the year are not to exceed the lesser of $25,000 (subject to an annual cost-of-living increase) or 25 percent of the participant's compensation from the employer. The term "annual additions" means the sum of (a) the employer's contributions, (b) the lesser of (i) one-half of all the employee's contributions, or (ii) the employee's contributions in excess of 6 percent of his compensation, and (c) any forfeitures which are added to the employee's account. Annual additions do not include rollovers from a qualified plan or individual retirement account. If forfeitures for a particular year could cause the plan not to meet these requirements with respect to a particular employee, these forfeitures must be reallocated to other participants in the plan (i.e., they may not be held in a suspense account), but regulations are to provide for the situation where none of the employees in the plan are eligible to receive forfeitures.

For purposes of the overall limitation, target benefit plans (i.e., plans where the employer establishes a target benefit for his employees, but where the employee's actual pension is based on the amount in his individual account) are to be treated as defined contribution plans. If the plan is a hybrid, i.e., part target benefit and part defined benefit, the plan will be treated as a defined contribution plan, for purposes of those rules, to the extent that benefits under the plan are based on the individual account of the participant. In the case of other plans which have characteristics both of a defined benefit plan and a defined contribution plan (such as a defined contribution plan with a guaranteed benefit, or certain variable annuity plans) the Secretary or his delegate may prescribe regulations applying the limitations to the defined benefit of the plan, and the part of the plan in which benefits are based on individual account balances.

Application of Limitation to Combinations of Plans

Under the substitute, where an employer has two or more plans, the overall ceiling is to be computed, in general, by aggregating similar plans (defined contribution or defined benefit) to determine if the limitation for that type of plan has been met on an overall basis (i.e., for purposes of this test a 1.0 fraction is used). If an employer maintains a defined benefit plan and a defined contribution plan, each plan would be subject to the limit appropriate to that type of plan ($75,000 or 100 percent benefits for the defined benefit plan, $25,000 or 25 percent contributions for the defined contribution plan); in addition, the two plans must be combined in computing the overall limitation.

To achieve this purpose, the substitute establishes a formula (to be applied each year to each employee) under which a defined benefit plan fraction for the year is added to a defined contribution plan fraction. Each fraction indicates what portion the participant has used of the maximum permitted limit for the kind of plan involved. If the sum of these fractions exceeds 1.4 then one or more of the plans will be disqualified.

The order in which plans are to be disqualified is to be determined under regulations. The regulations are to provide that no terminated plan may be disqualified until all other plans of the employer have been disqualified. However (unlike the House bill), the substitute does not require that plans having the fewest number of participants must be disqualified before plans having more participants because, in some cases, such a rigid rule might result in lower qualified plan benefits for the employees viewed as a whole.

Plans of all corporations, partnerships, or proprietorships which are under common control must be aggregated (using a 50-percent common control test).

Application of Limitations to Section 403(b) Annuities for Teachers or Employees of Tax-Exempt Organizations

In general, section 403(b) annuities are to be treated as defined contribution plans for purposes of the limitations. Thus, such plans would be subject to the 25 percent/$25,000 limitations which apply to other defined contribution plans, and also are to be subject to the limitations of present law under section 403(b) (20 percent of includable contributions, times years of service, minus all tax excludable contributions by the employer for annuities for prior taxable years).

However, under present law, certain categories of employees covered under section 403(b), such as teachers, typically have a pattern of low contributions in the early stages of their careers, with relatively high "catch-up" contributions made late in their careers. (Often section 403(b) plans operate on a salary-reduction basis.) In order to make allowance, for this problem, the conference substitute provides teachers, hospital employees, and employees of home health care institutions (which are tax-exempt and which the Secretary of Health, Education and Welfare has classified as a home health agency for purposes of medicare) with a choice of three alternative rules which permit a significant amount of "catch up." The individual may elect the alternative he wishes to use (in a time and manner to be prescribed in regulations) and the election, once made, is to be irrevocable.

Under the first alternative (which may be used only once) at the time an employee separates from service he may use the catch-up rules of section 403(b) for the 10-year period ending on the date of his separation, without regard to the 25-percent limitation of section 415 (in other words, his exclusion allowance would equal 20 percent of current compensation, times 10, minus employer contributions already made for annuities for the 10-year period). The $25,000 limitation would apply, however.

Under the second alternative, which could be used each year by the employee, catch-up contributions otherwise permitted under section 403(b), could equal the lesser of 25 percent of current compensation plus $4,000, or his exclusion allowance computed under section 403(b), but the deductible amount under this alternative could never exceed $15,000 for any one year.

For purposes of the overall limitations (sec. 415) in applying either of these two alternatives, the employee is not to be required to combine contributions to a 403(b) contract (which the participant would be deemed to control) with contributions by his employer to a qualified plan which he does not control (for example, a State wide plan for teachers). (Of course, the combination rules under section 403(b) of present law would not be changed.)

Under the third alternative, however, the employee would be permitted to come under the overall limitation (sec. 415) for all purposes (and the exclusion allowance of sec. 403(b) would not apply). This would mean that the employee would be covered under the overall limitation rules on combination plans, including the 1.4 fraction. For purposes of the combination rules both the employer and the employee would be deemed to have control of the 403(b) contract, but such a contract (which is to be treated as a defined contribution plan) could be combined with a State wide defined benefit plan, and benefits under the two plans, considered together, could equal 1.4 times the amount which could be provided under either plan when viewed separately.

If contributions to provide a section 403(b) annuity exceed the allowable limitations, the excess amounts must be included in income by the employee. Also, the employee's exclusion allowance under section 403(b) is to be reduced by the amount of the excess contribution (even though it was not excludable from the employee's income). If amounts are contributed for the purchase of mutual fund stock (which is permitted under another provision of the conference substitute), these amounts are to be subject to the 6 percent tax on over-funding until the excess is eliminated (see discussion above on individual retirement accounts). This tax is not imposed on contributions for annuity contracts, since earnings on these contracts are not taxed to the individual (until distributed) even when the annuity is not covered under section 403(b).

Treatment of Benefits or Contributions Over the Limitations

The House bill provided that benefits or contributions in addition to those allowable under qualified plans may be paid or accrued under a qualified plan, if the contributions by the employer for the additional benefits were not deductible until they were includable in income by the employee.

The Senate amendment provided, in effect, that no retirement benefits could be paid, except from a qualified plan.

To avoid technical difficulties, the conference substitute omits both provisions. The conferees intend that, for tax purposes, additional benefits may not be paid from a qualified plan. However, for purposes other than tax law, a qualified plan and a plan providing additional benefits may be treated as one plan by the employer.

Applications of Limitation Where Records Not Available

Under the conference substitute, the Treasury is authorized to prescribe reasonable assumptions which may be used by the employer in cases where the facts needed to compute the overall limitation are not known.

Application of Limitation to Existing Cases

The conference substitute contains a provision which provides that an individual who is an active plan participant on or before October 2, 1973, may receive a pension equal to the lesser of (a) 100 percent of his annual compensation on that date (or on the date he separated from service with the employer), or (b) the benefit payable under the terms of the plan as in effect on that date (assuming no later change in compensation). If the regular rules of the (sec. 415) provision result in a higher limit (due to pre-retirement cost-of-living-increases, for example) than that allowable under this transition provision, the individual is to be entitled to the higher limitation. If an individual covered under this feature is also covered under a defined contribution plan, contributions may continue to be made to the defined contribution plan, to the extent that prior contributions to this plan (or other plans of the same employer), plus the defined benefit available under this feature (which may exceed 1.0 for these purposes), do not exceed the 1.4 fraction. In the case of a participant who separated from the service of the employer prior to October 2, 1973, the benefit allowed under this feature cannot exceed the individual's vested benefit on the date when he separated from service.

Aggregate Deduction Limits in the Case of Profit-Sharing and Pension Plans, Etc.

The conference substitute provides that carryover deductions of excess contributions in a combination pension and profit-sharing plan may not exceed 25 percent of aggregate compensation for any year (present law allows 30 percent). Also, the carryover of unused aggregate contribution limitations to a profit-sharing plan for any year is not to exceed 25 percent (compared to 30 percent under present law).

Timing of Contributions

Under the substitute, contributions by cash basis taxpayers which are made by the time for filing the tax return for the year in question may be treated as paid in the year in question.

Effective Dates

The new rules with respect to limitations on corporate plans are to apply to years beginning after December 31, 1975. (For purposes of this provision the term "year" is to be defined in regulations.) In applying the limitations, contributions or accruals which occur before the effective date must, of course, be taken into account. For example, an employee with an accrued benefit of $60,000 on December 31, 1975, could accrue an additional benefit of $15,000 after that date (for a total benefit of $75,000) assuming that this was not in excess of the 100-percent limitation.

X. LUMP-SUM DISTRIBUTIONS (SEC. 2005 OF THE BILL AND SEC. 402(e) OF THE CODE)

General Rule

Both the House bill and the Senate amendment treat the post-1973 taxable portion of a lump-sum distribution from a qualified pension, profit-sharing or stock bonus plan as ordinary income taxed under an averaging device which treats it as if it were received evenly over a period of years. Under the House bill, this special averaging treatment provides the treatment which would be applicable if the amount were spread over a period of 10 years, while the Senate amendment provides the treatment which would be applicable if it were spread over 15 years. Both the House and Senate versions treat the portion of the payment attributable to the pre-1974 period as long-term capital gain.

The conference substitute accepts the 10-year averaging period provided under the House bill. Both the House bill and the Senate amendment compute the ordinary income portion under the same general type of averaging device and this same general procedure is used in the conference substitute. The ordinary income portion is to be computed without regard to the taxpayer's other income (i.e., in effect it is taxed entirely separately as if this were the only income received by the individual). The tax rate schedule to be used in this separate-treatment approach is the schedule provided in the Code for unmarried individuals (whether or not the taxpayer is married). If the plan participant has service both before 1974 and after 1973, the amount attributed to the post-1973 service is the total taxable distribution times a fraction, the numerator of which is calendar years of active participation after 1973 and the denominator of which is total years of active participation. It is understood that the Treasury Department will provide regulations for allocating fractions of years for plan participants who have both pre-1974 and post-1973 value in lump-sum distributions.

The taxable portion of a distribution is to be the portion of the distribution attributable to employer contributions and to income earned on the account. The portion of the distribution representing the employee's contributions remains nontaxable.

Definition of a Lump-Sum Distribution

The House bill would change the requirements used in determining what qualifies as a lump-sum distribution. The Senate amendment makes no changes in the existing rules on this subject. The conferees have accepted the new House rules.

Under existing law, a distribution generally is treated as a lump-sum distribution if it clears the employee's balance in a single trust, even though there are other trusts in that plan and even though the employee receiving the distribution is a participant in several plans maintained by the same employer. The conference substitute retains the requirement that an employee's entire account be distributed. For this purpose, however, all trusts which are part of a plan are to be treated as a single trust. Furthermore, for this purpose all plans of a given category (the categories are pension plans, profit-sharing plans, and stock bonus plans) maintained by an employer are to be treated as a single plan.

The conference substitute also follows the House bill in permitting a distribution to an employee (common-law definition of employee) after he attains age 59½ to be treated as a lump-sum distribution entitled to the special averaging and partial capital gain treatment, even though the recipient has not left his employment. Under present law, the age 59½ rule applies only to self-employed persons.

This change from existing law is a part of the effort to eliminate to the extent feasible the distinctions between taxation of lump-sum distributions to regular employees and to the self-employed, as discussed below.

Multiple Lump-Sum Distributions in One Taxable Year

The House bill requires that a taxpayer who wishes to use the special averaging and capital gains treatment described above for one lump-sum distribution must use that treatment for the aggregate of the lump-sum distributions he receives in the same taxable year. The Senate amendment and existing law contain no comparable provision. The conference substitute accepts the House rule.

Aggregation of Distributions Over Six Years

Both the House bill and the Senate amendment require that the lump-sum distributions received by an individual during a taxable year be aggregated with all lump-sum distributions to that recipient during his five prior taxable years, but only for purposes of determining the tax brackets in which the income is to be taxed. However, the House bill limits this five-year "lookback" rule to lump-sum distributions made after 1973. No similar provision is contained in the Senate amendment.

The conferees accepted this rule enunciated in both the House and Senate versions and also accepted the House bill restriction limiting the lookback aggregation to distributions made after 1973.

Treatment of Distributions of Annuity Contracts

Both the House bill and the Senate amendment provide that a distribution of an annuity contract is to remain nontaxable, but must be included in the six-year aggregation computation described above in order to determine the tax bracket rates on a taxable lump-sum distribution. The House bill provides the annuity contract is to be included in the aggregation computation at its fair market value, while the Senate amendment fixes the value as the cash surrender value as of the time of the distribution.

The conference substitute, as in both the House and Senate versions, includes an annuity contract distribution within the aggregation computation, but continues to treat the annuity contract distribution itself as nontaxable.

The conference substitute provides that the value of an annuity contract for the purposes of the aggregation rule referred to above is to be its current actuarial value. Normally this will be sufficiently close to the cash surrender value of the annuity so that, under Treasury regulations, the cash surrender value (disregarding any loan on the policy) would be treated as the "current actuarial value." However, if the cash surrender value is artificially reduced, Treasury regulations may provide for a simplified method of determining the cash surrender value the annuity would normally carry. It the annuity contract has no cash surrender value, its current actuarial value is to be the present value of the payments anticipated under the annuity contract, computed with regard to the life expectancy of the recipient (and the life expectancy of the recipient's spouse, unless the recipient elects not to take the annuity as a joint and survivor annuity). The present value of these anticipated payments is to be determined under tables to be issued by the Treasury Department.

Recipients Eligible for Lump-Sum Distributions

The House bill provides that the only recipients of lump-sum distributions who may elect the special averaging treatment are individuals, estates, and trusts. The Senate amendment (and present law) place no restrictions on who may use the special averaging treatment. The conference substitute generally accepts the restrictions of the House bill, but with modifications in the case of lump sum distributions to trusts.

Under the conference substitute, a

lump-sum distribution may be made to multiple trusts, but, if this occurs, the tax paid on account of the distribution is to be the tax payable as if the entire distribution were made to one recipient, with the tax liability apportioned among the multiple trusts in accordance with the relative amounts received by each.

In cases of distributions to individuals and estates (in which instances an entire lump-sum distribution must be made to one recipient) the recipient is to make an election as to whether to claim the special averaging treatment. (The personal representative of the employee is to make the election if distributions are made to multiple trusts). This election is of significance because, as discussed below, only one election may be made with respect to an employee who has attained age 59½.

As under the House bill, the conference substitute provides that an employee must generally be regarded as the recipient, for purposes of the requirement of aggregation of all lump-sum distributions in a period of six taxable years, even if he or she causes the distribution to be made to a trust, if the employee retains such an interest in the trust as would require his taxation as the substantial owner of the trust under the present tax rules, even if the grantor of the trust is technically the employer of plan.[1]

In the House bill, a trust would be allowed to elect the special averaging treatment only if (1) the use of the trust would not affect the includibility of the distribution in the employee's gross estate, and (2) the trust would be sole recipient of the entire balance to the credit of the employee. These provisions were not adopted by the conferees.

As indicated above, attainment of age 59½ is made a criterion of eligibility for a regular employee (as well as for self-employed person, as under present law) for the special averaging lump-sum treatment under the conference substitute. It was not considered necessary, however, to specify that a beneficiary is entitled to the special averaging and partial capital gain treatment for a distribution on account of the death of an employee *after* his retirement (as well as before).[2]

Number of Elections

The House bill allows the special averaging treatment to be elected freely until the employee attains age 59½, after which time only one election may be made with respect to that employee. The Senate amendment does not have an election procedure. As is the case under present law, the Senate version makes the treatment mandatory for lump-sum distributions and does not limit the number of times this special treatment may be used.

The conferees followed the House bill in allowing only one election with respect to an employee after he has attained age 59½. Thus, if an employee has made one election after attaining age 59½, he may not thereafter obtain the special averaging treatment for another distribution. As under present law, however, an employee, or his beneficiary, who is barred from the special averaging treatment by an earlier election may nevertheless gain the partial capital gain treatment for pre-1974 value if the distribution is made on account of the employee's death or separation from service. In addition, such an employee who receives a distribution because of attaining age 59½ may also receive the partial capital gains treatment although he is barred from the special averaging for the ordinary income portion.

A recipient who elects this special averaging treatment may still elect the usual income averaging provided under sec. 1301.[3] A taxpayer who surren-

---

[1] If the lump-sum distribution is made to a recipient other than a trust during employee's lifetime, it is intended that the usual assignment-of-income and constructive receipt rules are to apply to determine whether the employee is to be liable for the tax upon the distribution.

[2] Thus, no change in present law is intended by the deletion of references to this in sections 402(a)(2) and 403(a)(2)(A)(iii) of the code.

[3] H. Rept. 93-807, p. 150, which indicates that a common-law employee who uses the

ders an annuity may use the normal 5-year income averaging and also may use the special averaging for lump-sum distributions.

Lump-sum Distributions to the Self-employed

Under the House bill, the same 10-year ordinary income averaging may be elected for distributions on account of plan participation by self-employed persons as may be elected on account of the participation of regular employees. (Under present law, lump-sum distributions to self-employed persons are taxed under special 5-year averaging provisions.) There is no comparable Senate provision.

The conferees accepted the House provision eliminating the distinction of treatment between regular employees and the self-employed in this respect. If they elect the special averaging treatment, self-employed persons are also entitled to capital gain taxation on the pre-1974 value of their lump-sum distributions.

Computation of Tax in Lump-sum Distribution

It is recognized that the computation of tax due on a lump-sum distribution with an annuity lump-sum distribution, as reflected in the reports of the House Ways and Means Committee and the Senate Finance Committee, is incorrect in that it subtracts the entire minimum distribution allowance from the amount of the annuity, instead of subtracting only that portion of the minimum distribution allowance that is proportionate to the amount of the annuity distribution as compared with the total distribution. This incorrectly in-

---

special averaging provided under present law may nevertheless also use the regular five-year income averaging for his other income and capital gain, is incorrect. Under the conference substitute, however, both types of income averaging may be used concurrently by both regular employees and the self-employed.

creases the tax on the taxable distribution because it minimizes the tax attributable to the annuity distribution. The less the tax attributable to the annuity distribution, the larger is the tax attributable to the taxable distribution.

The correct computation is as follows:

First example.—On December 31, 1975, A terminates his services and receives a lump sum distribution of $65,000 from a qualified plan. The distribution includes employer securities with a fair market value of $25,000 and a basis of $10,000. A has been participating in the plan since January 1, 1966. The plan is noncontributory. A is married; both A and his wife are 50. Their only other income is A's salary of $15,000 and his salary from a second job ($5,000). Their itemized deductions are $3,000. Their average base period income (for purposes of regular income averaging) from the preceding four years (1971 through 1974) is $14,000.

The tax on the portion of the distribution which is not treated as a long-term capital gain is computed as follows:

Net distribution ($65,000 total distribution less $15,000 unrealized appreciation on employer securities	$50,000
Less: Minimum distribution allowance: 50 percent of first $20,000	$10,000
Reduced by: 20 percent of net distributions in excess of $20,000	6,000
	4,000
Distribution less allowance	46,000

The tax on 1/10th of the distribution less allowance computed from the tax rate schedule for single taxpayers is $816.00.

Multiply this amount by 10: $8,160.00.

Then, multiply by the fraction,

$$\frac{\text{Years of participation in plan after 1973}}{\text{Total years of participation}} = \frac{2}{10} = 0.2$$

which yields $1,632.00.

Thus, the tax on the ordinary income portion of the distribution is $1,632.00.

The amount of the distribution taxed as a long-term capital gain is the amount of the net distribution multiplied by the fraction,

$$\frac{\text{Years of participation before 1974}}{\text{Total years of participation}} = \frac{8}{10} = 0.8$$

Net distribution	$50,000
Capital gains element	40,000

The capital gains element is taxed along with other income (exclusive of the ordinary income element) in the normal way. The tax on the taxable income of $35,500 ($15,000 salary from first job, plus $5,000 from second job, plus $40,000 capital gains element of lump-sum distribution, less $20,000 capital gains exclusion, less $3,000 itemized deductions, less two $750 personal exemptions) is calculated using the tax rate schedule for married taxpayers filing joint returns. In this case the alternative tax on capital gains is not available, but the regular-five-year income averaging provisions are:

Ordinary tax	$10,130.00
Tax—Using regular income averaging [1]	8,828.00

Selecting the tax computation method which yields the smallest amount of tax, A uses the regular five-year income averaging method and has a tax of $8,828.00.

Finally, A combines the tax on the capital gains portion of the distribution and his salary, with the tax on the ordinary income portion of the distribution:

Tax on salary and capital gains portion of distribution	$ 8,828.00
Tax on ordinary income portion of distribution	1,632.00
Total 1975 income tax	10,460.00

A's basis in the employer securities is $10,000.

Second example.—On December 31, 1976, A receives a distribution from a qualified plan with respect to his second job. In this case the distribution is a nontransferable annuity contract, the value of which is $6,000; and a cash distribution of $4,000 financed solely by the employer. A had participated in the plan since January 1, 1967. Mr. and Mrs. A's only other income in 1976 is A's salary of $25,000 and interest of $3,000 on the $40,000 cash received in the prior lump-sum distribution. They have itemized deductions of $2,100. Mr. and Mrs. A's 1976 tax is computed as follows:

First, compute the tax on the portion of the distribution which is not treated as a long-term capital gain and which is taxed separately.

Step 1:

1976 cash distribution	4,000
1976 annuity contract	6,000
Prior year net distribution	50,000
Total	60,000
Less: Minimum distribution allowance: 50 percent of first $20,000	$10,000
Reduced by: 20 percent of net distribution in excess of $20,000	8,000
Total	2,000
	58,000

Ten times the tax on one-tenth of $58,000 (from the rate schedule for single taxpayer) is $10,680.

Step 2:

1976 annuity	$6,000
Minimum distribution allowance from step 1	$2,000
Portion of minimum distribution allowance attributable to annuity distribution	
$\frac{\$6,000}{60,000} \times -2,000 = \$200$	200
Remainder	5,800

[1] As indicated above, average base period income is $14,000.

Ten times the tax on one-tenth of $5,800 (from the rate schedule for single taxpayers) is $820.

Step 3:
$$\$10,680 - \$820 = \$9,860$$

Step 4:
Determine ordinary income and capital gains elements of A's distribution and his prior year distribution. The ordinary income element of A's latest distribution is determined by multiplying the cash distribution of $4,000 by:

$$\frac{\text{Years of participation in plan after 1973}}{\text{Total years of participation}} = 3/10 = 0.3$$

$$\left\{\frac{\$1,200 + \$10,000}{\$4,000 + \$50,000}\right\} \times \$9,860 = \$2,045.04$$

Thus, A's ordinary income element is $1,200. $10,000 of Mr. A's prior distribution of $50,000 was ordinary income.

Thus, the tax on the ordinary income element is the fraction of the tax from Step No. 3 which the ordinary income elements of the 1976 and prior year distributions bear to the entire distributions.

Step 5:

The tax on the ordinary income element of A's 1975 distribution from their 1975 income tax income return was $1,632.00. Subtracting that from the tax calculated in Step No. 4 yields the tax on the ordinary income element of A's latest distribution:

$$\$2,045.04 - \$1,632.00 = \$413.04$$

Second, compute the tax on all other income, including the capital gains portion of the distribution.

Step 6:

In Step No. 4, the ordinary income element of the distribution was calculated as $1,200. Therefore, the long-term capital gains element is:

$$\$4,000.00 - \$1,200 = \$2,800.00$$

Step 7:

The capital gains element is taxed along with other income in the regular manner.

Capital gains element	$ 2,800
Less: 50 percent of net long-term capital gain	1,400
Total	1,400
Salary	25,000
Interest	3,000
Adjusted gross income	29,400
Less: Itemized deductions	2,100
Less: Personal exemptions (2 × $750)	1,500
Taxable income	25,800

The tax on $25,800 is calculated using the tax rate schedule for married taxpayers filing joint returns. In this case, neither the alternative tax on capital gains nor the regular five-year income averaging provision is available.

Ordinary tax $6,308.00

Third, A combines the tax on the capital gains portion of the distribution and his other income, with the tax on the ordinary income portion of the distribution.

Step 8:

Tax on capital gains portion of distribution and on other income	$6,308.00
Tax on ordinary income portion of distribution	413.04
Total 1976 income tax	6,721.04

If in the examples above, A has attained age 59½, he may elect to treat only one of the distributions as a lump-sum distribution qualifying for ten-year averaging. In computing the tax liability on the distribution which he elects to qualify for ten-year averaging, A will not aggregate any distribution (except in the case of a distribution of an annuity contract) made after attaining age 59½ which is not treated as a lump-sum distribution for purposes of the ten-year averaging.

XI. SALARY REDUCTION AND CASH OR DEFERRED PROFIT-SHARING PLANS (SEC. 2006 OF THE BILL)

Under present law, in general, an employee's contributions to a qualified retirement plan maintained by his employer are not tax deductible. In the case of a salary reduction plan, or a cash or deferred profit-sharing plan, however, the Internal Revenue Service has permitted employees to exclude from income certain amounts contributed by their employers to the plan, even where the source of these amounts is the employee's agreement to take salary or bonus reductions, or forego salary increases.

On December 6, 1972, the Service issued proposed regulations which would have changed this result in the case of salary reduction plans, and which called into question the continued viability of the treatment of cash and deferred profit-sharing plans.

In order to allow time for congressional study of these areas, the conference substitute provides for a temporary freeze of the status quo. Thus, contributions to plans in existence on June 27, 1974, are to be governed under the law as it was applied prior to January 1, 1972. This treatment is to continue at least through December 31, 1976, or (if later) until regulations are issued in final form in this area, which would change the pre-1972 administration of the law. These regulations, if issued, are not to be retroactive for purposes of the social security taxes or the Federal withholding taxes, and are not to be retroactive prior to January 1, 1977, for Federal income tax purposes.

In the case of plans not in existence on June 27, 1974, contributions made on a salary reduction basis, or made, at the employee's option, a cash or deferred profit-sharing plan, are to be treated as employee contributions (until January 1, 1977, or until new regulations are prescribed in this area). This will prevent a situation where a new plan might begin in reliance on pre-1972 law while Congress has not yet determined what the law should be in the future.

Generally a plan will be treated as having been established on June 27, 1974, if the plan had been reduced to writing and had been adopted and approved by the directors on or before that date, even if contributions had not yet been made to the plan on a salary reduction basis.[1] New participants may, of course, be added to an existing plan in the normal course of business.

Also to be covered under these principles are so-called cafeteria plans, under which the employees may have a choice between certain fringe benefits, some of which would constitute taxable income to the employee, whereas other forms of benefit might not. Thus, existing cafeteria plans also are to be governed under pre-1972 law until at least January 1, 1977. However, in the case of new plans, the value of any benefits selected under a cafeteria plan are to be includable in income until at least January 1, 1977 (or, if later, until new regulations in this area have been promulgated). In general, the same rules to be applied in determining whether or not a salary reduction plan was in existence on June 27, 1974, are also to be applied to cafeteria plans. Of course, minor plan amendments (such as changing the plan to allow cash payments to cover cases of breakage, i.e., where two alternative benefits available under the cafeteria plan do not have exactly the same value) would not cause an existing plan to be classified as a new plan for purposes of these rules.

The conferees agree with the statements in the Ways and Means Committee report (No. 93-807) to the effect that there should be no inferences drawn from this action as to

---

[1] Where shareholder approval is required for formal adoption of the plan, such shareholder approval must also have occurred by June 27, 1974.

whether or not the pre-1972 application of the law is, or is not, correct, or as to whether new regulations in this area should, or should not, be issued, or as to what these regulations, if any, should provide.

XII. GENERAL PROVISIONS RELATING TO JURISDICTION, ADMINISTRATION, ENFORCEMENT; JOINT PENSION TASK FORCE, ETC. (SEC. 3001-3004, 3021-3022, 3031, 3041-3043 OF THE BILL)

General Provisions Relating to Jurisdiction, Administration and Enforcement

Under the bill and amendment as passed by the House and the Senate jurisdiction with respect to the requirements for plans seeking tax benefits under the Internal Revenue Code is basically with the Internal Revenue Service. In addition, the bill and amendment as passed by the House and the Senate provides jurisdiction to the Secretary of Labor to enforce standards for plans which do not seek special tax benefits under the Internal Revenue Code, and to enforce certain standards as they apply to tax-qualified plans.

Under the conference substitute, procedures are established which will provide a significant and appropriate role in the enforcement of the participation, vesting, and funding standards to both the Department of Labor and the Internal Revenue Service (with respect to plans which seek qualification under the Internal Revenue Code) without a duplication of effort on the part of the two departments. In addition to the specific areas of the conference substitute where areas of jurisdiction are delegated to one department or the other, the conference substitute provides general guidelines for the coordination of administration and enforcement.

The administration of qualified plans is separated into two stages: first, the stage when the plan seeks from the Internal Revenue Service initial qualification of entitlement to special tax benefits under the Internal Revenue Code; second, the operational stage with respect to the continued eligibility of the plan for the special tax benefits.

Initial stage jurisdiction.—In determining whether a pension, profit-sharing, or stock bonus plan or a trust which is a part of such a plan, is initially entitled to the special tax benefits provided under the tax law, the Secretary of the Treasury is to require that the person applying for the initial qualification of the plan is to provide, in addition to any materials and information which would generally be necessary for the administration of the tax laws, such other forms and information as may reasonably be made available at the time of the determination as the Secretary of Labor may require. The Secretary of the Treasury is also to require that the applicant for a determination provide evidence that any employee who is an interested party with respect to the plan has been notified of the request for a determination. Also the Secretary of the Treasury is to notify the Secretary of Labor and the Pension Benefit Guaranty Corporation when he receives an application for a determination as to the tax status of a plan.

The Secretary of the Treasury when he makes a determination with respect to a plan or trust is to notify the Secretary of Labor of his determination and furnish to the Secretary of Labor the forms and information submitted for the Secretary of Labor. For this purpose a determination includes a determination that a plan is, or is not, qualified for the special tax benefits under the Internal Revenue Code. The Secretary of the Treasury is also to notify the Secretary of Labor if a request for a determination is withdrawn.

Under the conference substitute, the Secretary of the Treasury is to afford the Secretary of Labor an opportunity to comment on the initial determination in any case involving the participation or vesting standards in which the Secretary of Labor requests such an opportunity. It is expected that the two departments will set up procedures implementing this procedure in a manner which affords the Secretary of Labor an ample opportunity to comment but which does not cause undue delay in the granting of initial determinations. A request by the Secretary of Labor to comment upon an application for an initial determination is to be made only upon the request (in writing) of the Pension Benefit Guaranty Corporation or on the request of 10 employees (or 10 percent of the employees if lesser) who would be viewed as interested parties under the plan. A copy of the request submitted to the Secretary of Labor is to be transmitted by him to the Secretary of the Treasury within 5 business days of its receipt.

If the Secretary of Labor does not submit comments on behalf of such groups of employees within 30 days after receiving a petition from the necessary number of interested employees, the Secretary of the Treasury is to afford these interested employees a reasonable opportunity to comment upon the initial request for a determination. The above procedure for enabling employees to comment upon an application for a determination is not the exclusive means by which employees may participate in the determination proceedings. Employees may of course proceed on their own through the declaratory judgment provisions which are provided in the bill. The Pension Benefit Guaranty Corporation and the Secretary of Labor (upon petition by the required number of employees) may intervene in any declaratory judgment proceedings in the Tax Court whether the proceedings are brought on behalf of the employer or interested employees. In addition, the Pension Benefit Guaranty Corporation is to be entitled to bring a suit for a declaratory judgment under rules to be prescribed by the Tax Court.

If a plan is qualified by the Secretary of the Treasury, the plan is to be treated as meeting the initial requirements of the Secretary of Labor with respect to participation and vesting.

The above outlined procedures apply not only to the initial qualification of a plan which seeks the special tax benefits provided under the Internal Revenue Code but apply to a request for an IRS determination with respect to any amendment to the terms of a plan or a trust which seeks a favorable determination from the Internal Revenue Service.

Operational stage jurisdiction. — The conference substitute also provides procedures for the exercise of the respective jurisdictional authority of the departments with respect to plans qualified for special tax treatment under the Internal Revenue Code during their operation. The Secretary of the Treasury in carrying out the administration of the Internal Revenue Code with respect to any plan or trust is to examine the plan to determine whether the plan satisfies the requirements relating to minimum participation standards and minimum vesting standards (in secs. 410(a) and 411 of the Code).

The Secretary of the Treasury is to notify the Secretary of Labor before commencing any proceedings to determine whether the plan or trust is in compliance with the minimum vesting and participation standards. While the notice need not be made prior to the time the Internal Revenue Service begins an audit or a review of a plan to verify that the minimum standards have been satisfied, it is expected that if in the course of a review or audit doubts or questions are raised by the Internal Revenue Service as to whether the plan has met the minimum standards, the Secretary of the Treasury is to notify the Secretary of Labor. Notification is to be made prior to the time the Internal Revenue Service issues a 30-day letter of an intention to disqualify the plan or trust. Except in cases of jeopardy the Secretary of the Treasury is not to issue a determination that the trust or plan does not satisfy the minimum standards until the expiration of a period of 60 days after the date on which he notifies the Secretary of Labor. This period of time is provided for the Secretary of Labor so that, if he chooses to do so, he may examine the plan to determine whether he should begin to take any action to compel compliance under those portions of the participation and vesting provisions of the bill in which he has jurisdiction or to coordinate any action he may be required to take by reason of a complaint from a participant or beneficiary. This 60-day period may be extended by the Secretary of the Treasury if he determines that an extension of this period would enable the Secretary of Labor to obtain compliance with the requirements of the law during this extended period. In order to assist the Secretary of Labor in deciding whether he should seek compliance with the requirements of the law the Secretary of the Treasury is to provide the Secretary of Labor with copies of any notices which he issues to the plan administrator with respect to the minimum participation and vesting standards.

The Secretary of the Treasury in administering the provisions relating to taxes on the failure to meet minimum funding standards (sec. 4971 of the Internal Revenue Code) is to notify the Secretary of Labor before imposing any tax on an employer. In addition, prior to the imposition of the tax, in other than jeopardy situations, the Secretary of the Treasury is to afford the Secretary of Labor an opportunity to comment on the appropriateness of imposing the tax. After consultation with the Secretary of Labor, the Secretary of the Treasury may in appropriate cases waive or abate the 100 percent excise tax on failure to satisfy the minimum funding standards. In order to coordinate their respective responsibilities under the funding standards, it is anticipated that both Secretaries will consult with each other as is needed with respect to the provisions relating to minimum funding standards, both those provided in the Internal Revenue Code and the funding standards provided by title I. As part of this coordination, at the request of the Secretary of Labor or the Pension Benefit Guaranty Corporation, the Internal Revenue Service is to initiate an immediate investigation with respect to any liability for the tax on failure to meet the minimum funding standards.

If the Secretary of Labor or the Pension Benefit Guaranty Corporation seek compliance on any case involving the construction or application of the minimum participation, vesting or funding standards, a reasonable opportunity is to be afforded to the Secretary of the Treasury to review and comment upon any proposed pleadings or briefs before they are filed. Of course, the Secretary of Labor need not obtain the approval of the Secretary of the Treasury and the Secretary of the Treasury may intervene and file his own pleadings or briefs in any case.

The Secretary of the Treasury in carrying out the provisions relating to tax on prohibited transactions (sec. 4975 of the Internal Revenue Code) is to inform the Secretary of Labor before imposing the tax under that section. In addition, the Secretary of Labor is to be afforded an opportunity, in other than jeopardy situations to comment on the appropriateness of imposing the tax. After consultation with the Secretary of Labor, the Secretary of the Treasury may in appropriate cases waive or abate the 100 percent excise tax on failure to correct a self-dealing violation. It also is anticipated that both Secretaries will consult as is needed with respect to the provisions relating to prohibited transactions (including the exemptions which may be provided therefrom) in order to coordinate the rules applicable under these standards. To best coordinate these rules the two Secretaries may want to set up a board to review and coordinate these rules. As part of this coordination, the Internal Revenue Service at the request of the Secretary of Labor or the Pension Benefit Guaranty Corporation is to initiate an immediate investigation with respect to the liability of any person for the tax on prohibited transactions.

Issuance of regulations—Under the conference substitute the Department of the Treasury is to prescribe the necessary regulations under the general provisions relating to participation, vesting, and funding except where specific authority is given to the Secretary of Labor to prescribe the regulations. For example, the Secretary of Labor is to prescribe regulations defining what constitutes a year of service for purposes of the participation and vesting standards of the Act. Regulations which are prescribed by the Treasury or Labor Departments in those areas in which jurisdiction is assigned to them are to be binding upon the other department (unless provided otherwise by the bill). Where the final authorization to prescribe regulations under a provision is provided to one department or the other, it is expected that the two departments will consult and coordinate closely with each other in prescribing the necessary regulations which need to be issued under the various provisions of the bill.

Under the conference substitute whenever in the bill the Secretary of the Treasury and the Secretary of Labor are required to carry out provisions relating to the same subject matter, they are to consult with each other in the developing of rules, regulations, practices and forms to the extent possible for the efficient administration of the provisions in order to reduce to the maximum extent practical, duplication of effort, conflicting requirements and the burden of compliance (including the annual reports which must be filed by the plan administrators). The two Secretaries may make arrangements or agreements for cooperation and mutual assistance in the performance of the functions they have under the bill as they find practicable and consistent with the law. The maximum coordination is expected in those areas where one agency has the authority to prescribe regulations and also, of course, where the regulations are to be a cooperative effort of both agencies.

Joint Task Force and Studies

Under the bill, as passed by the House, the Secretary of Labor is to undertake studies relating to private pension plans, including the cost impact of the bill on pension plans, the role of pension plans in providing economic security, the operation of pension plans, and methods of encouraging the growth of the private pension system. In addition, the Committee on Education and Labor and the Committee on Ways and Means are to undertake studies of retirement plans financed or maintained by the United States, or by State and local governments. This study is to include consideration of the adequacy of the participation, vesting, and fiduciary standards, as well as financing and funding methods. In studying whether the funding standards of the bill should be imposed on government plans the study is to take into account the taxing power of the governmental unit maintaining the plan. The two committees are to report the results of the governmental study to the House of Representatives by December 31, 1976.

Under the bill as passed by the Senate, the Secretary of Labor is authorized to undertake the studies relating to employee benefit plans which are generally similar to the studies provided for in the bill as passed by the House. However, the bill as passed by the Senate authorizes the Secretary of Treasury to undertake the study of governmental plans and report to the Committee on Finance and the Committee on Ways and Means by December 31, 1976.

Under the conference substitute the staffs of the Committee on Ways and Means and the Committee on Education and Labor of the House, the Joint Committee on Internal Revenue Taxation, and the Committee on Finance and the Committee on Labor and Public Welfare of the Senate are to carry out duties assigned to the Joint Pension Task Force. By agreement among the Chairmen of these committees, the Joint Pension Task Force is to be furnished with office space, clerical personnel, actuarial and other consultants, and the supplies and equipment which are necessary for the Task Force to carry out its duties. The Joint Pension Task Force is authorized to engage in specified studies and make a report to the abovementioned committees within 24 months after the date of enactment of the bill. In addition, the Joint Pension Task Force is to study any other matter which any of the committees referred to above may refer to it.

The Joint Pension Task Force is specifically authorized to engage in four studies. First, it is to study and review the three vesting alternatives in the bill to determine the extent of discrimination, if any, among employees in various age groups resulting from the application of these provisions. (The results of this study are to be reported only to the tax committees.) Second, it is to study the means of providing for the portability of pension rights among different pension plans. Third, it is to study the appropriate treatment under the termination insurance provisions of the Act for plans established and maintained by small employers. Fourth, it is to study the effects and desirability of the pre-emption of State law provisions of the bill. In addition elsewhere in this statement it is indicated that the Joint Pension Task Force is to study the effect of the rules in this bill limiting the extent to which antidiscrimination rules may be enforced through additional requirements as to early vesting and the effect on benefits and costs of integrating social security benefits with the benefits payable under retirement plans.

The substitute agreed to by the conferees also provides for a congressional study of retirement plans established and maintained, or financed, by the Government of the United States, by any State (including the District of Columbia), or any political subdivision thereof. The study is to include an analysis of the adequacy of existing levels of participation, vesting, and financing arrangements; existing fiduciary standards; and the unique circumstances affecting mobility of government employees and individuals employed under Federal procurement contracts. In considering whether plans are adequately financed consideration shall be given to the necessity for minimum funding standards as well as the taxing power of the government maintaining the plan. This study is to be submitted not later than December 31, 1976, by the Committee on Education and Labor and the Committee on Ways and Means to the House of Representatives and by the Committee on Finance and the Committee on Labor and Public Welfare to the Senate.

Enrollment of Actuaries

Standards.—The House bill requires that reasonable standards and qualifications are to be established for enrolling actuaries to practice, and specifies the standards that are to be applied for enrolling actuaries to practice. Under the Senate amendment, reasonable standards and qualifications are to be established for enrollment to practice, but the standards to be used are to be determined in regulations.

The conference substitute largely follows the provisions of the House bill. With respect to persons applying for enrollment before January 1, 1976, the substitute provides that the standards and qualifications are to include a requirement for "responsible actuarial experience relating to pension plans," and deletes the requirement for experience in the "administration" of pension plans. This change is intended only to clarify the application of the standards before January 1, 1976, so that persons who apply for enrollment before that date have responsible actuarial experience (and not only administrative experience) relating to pension plans. With respect to persons who perform actuarial services for smaller and simpler plans, the conferees anticipate that, to the extent feasible, the standards for enrollment will make it possible to use standard actuarial tables and standard earnings assumptions whether or not the actuary's training includes the highest level of actuarial skills. The limited number of persons with a high level of actuarial skills makes it desirable that the standards acceptable for persons examining smaller and simpler plans need not be as restrictive as in the case of those examining the larger plans.

The conference substitute also provides that actuaries may be enrolled on a temporary basis for a limited period. This makes it clear that actuaries can be enrolled almost immediately after enactment of the bill in order that enrolled actuaries will be available to help plans meet the requirements of the new law. The conferees intend that such temporary enrollment is not to be in lieu of any special enrollment standards for persons who apply for enrollment before January 1, 1976, but is only to allow immediate enrollment before the final standards are established.

Procedures.—The House bill provides for separate enrollment of actuaries by the Department of Labor (title I) and the Internal Revenue Service (title II). However, the House bill also provides that standards for enrollment after January 1, 1976, are to be established by joint regulations. The Senate amendment provides for enrollment only before the Internal Revenue Service.

Under the conference substitute, a single standard for enrollment is achieved by directing the Secretary of Labor and the Secretary of Treasury to establish a joint board which will set standards for enrollment and enroll actuaries to practice before the Department of Labor and Internal Revenue Service. In order that enrollment might begin as soon as possible, it is provided than an interim joint board is to be established no later than the last day of the first month following the date of enactment.

The joint board also is to administer the standards for disenrollment of actuaries and is to write the regulations on enrollment (to be approved by the two Secretaries or their delegates). As under the House bill, an actuary can be disenrolled only after notice and hearing, and if there is a finding that he does not comply with the governing rules or regulations, or is shown not to be competent in actuarial matters.

Reports.—Both the House bill and the Senate amendment provide that actuarial reports are to be made separately to the Department of Labor and the Internal Revenue Service. The conference substitute largely follows the provisions of the House bill in the technical aspects. In keeping with the general principle of eliminating, to the maximum extent feasible, duplication of effort in reporting, the conference substitute also requires the Secretaries of Labor and Treasury to take such steps as may be necessary to assure coordination, to the maximum extent feasible, between the actuarial reports they file with the Secretary of Labor and the Internal Revenue Service.

XIII. PLAN TERMINATION INSURANCE (SECS. 4001-4082 OF THE BILL)

Administering Corporation and Its Organization

Both the House bill and the Senate amendment call for a public corporation named the Pension Benefit Guaranty Corporation to administer the plan termination provisions within (or with) the Department of Labor. The Secretary of Labor would be the chairman of a three-man board of directors. Under the House bill, the other two directors would be other officers or employees of the Department of Labor, while under the Senate amendment, the Secretaries of Commerce and of the Treasury would be the other directors.

The conferees decided, following the Senate amendment, to place the corporation within the Department of Labor under a board consisting of the Secretaries of Labor, Commerce, and the Treasury, with the Secretary of Labor to be chairman of the board. The corporation is to be "within" the Department of Labor in that it is to be quartered there and it is to receive such housekeeping services as it may request from the Labor Department. The board of directors is to establish policy, while the chairman is to be responsible for the overall supervision of the corporation's personnel, organization, and budget practices. The corporation's personnel will be appropriately classified in the usual categories, and they are to be nonpolitical. The conferees contemplate that the corporation may make contractual arrangements for the performance of some of its functions by other agencies, and, in particular, it is anticipated that it may arrange for such functions as recordkeeping to be performed by the Department of Labor insofar as those activities are analogous to the regular duties of the Labor Department. Generally, the other functions of the corporation are to be performed by its own employees, as well as by private parties contracting to perform special duties.

During the temporary start-up period following the date of enactment, the corporation may, in its discretion, make arrangements for performance of any of its functions by other agencies, and, in particular, the Department of Labor.

The conferees also established a seven-man Advisory Committee to advise the corporation on such issues as the investment of funds, appointment of trustees for terminating plans, whether plans should be liquidated immediately through purchase of annuities or continued in operation under a trustee, and on other problems with regard to which the corporation requests advice. The seven members are to be appointed by the President upon the recommendation of the board of directors. Employee organizations and employers are each to have two representatives on the Advisory Committee, with the general public to have three. The President is to designate one of the appointees as chairman.

The Advisory Committee members are to serve staggered, three-year terms, and are to meet at least six times a year. The members may select employees for the Advisory Committee, but its employees, as well as those of the corporation, are to be appointed in accordance with Civil Service regulations.

Portability Assistance

The Pension Benefit Guaranty Corporation is to provide advice and assistance, upon request, to individuals regarding establishing individual retirement accounts or other forms of deductible individual retirement savings, and also regarding the desirability, in particular cases, of transferring an employee's interest in a qualified plan to a form of individual retirement savings upon that employee's separation from service.

Investments, Borrowing Authority, and Tax Exemption

Both the House and the Senate versions authorize the corporation to borrow up to $100 million from the Federal Treasury. The conferees expect the program, ultimately, to be self-financing.

The Senate amendment exempts the corporation from Federal taxation (except for social security and unemployment taxes) and from State and local taxation (except that the corporation's real and tangible personal property, other than cash and securities, may be taxed to the same extent according to value as other such property is taxed).

The conferees accepted both the borrowing authority and the tax exemption.

The assets in the corporation's funds representing collections of premiums may be invested in obligations issued or guaranteed by the United States. The assets representing terminated plans in the process of liquidation are to be invested by the trustees of the liquidating plans consistently with investment policies suggested to the corporation by the Advisory Committee.

Premiums

In the establishment of premium rates for plan termination insurance the House bases its rate on a combination of a plan's unfunded insured benefits and its total (whether or not funded) insured benefits. The Senate amendment, on the other hand, initially provides a premium of $1 per year per plan participant. In addition, the Senate amendment provides for collection of the premiums as a tax (therefore by the Internal Revenue Service), while the House bill does not make use of the tax collection procedure but instead the corporation is to bill and collect the premiums from the plans charging interest on unpaid premiums past due.

The conferees decided to require the corporation to establish separate uniform premium rates for single-employer and for multiemployer plans for retirement benefits. Single-employer plans are to pay $1 per plan participant during the first full plan year following enactment (and a prorated amount for any part of a plan year preceding that first full plan year). Multiemployer plans are to pay 50 cents per plan participant during these periods.

For the first fractional part of a year (after enactment) and the first full plan year after the date of enactment, premiums are to be paid within 30 days after the beginning of the period of coverage. The corporation may follow this or another system thereafter.

In the case of participants in multiemployer plans, no participant is to be counted more than once in computing the per capita ($1 or 50 cents per person) premium. Thus, if, during the course of a plan year, an employee leaves one employer in the multiemployer plan to work for another employer in the plan, the plan need nevertheless pay only one 50-cent premium on account of his participation.

The corporation is directed to establish by regulation appropriate procedures for determining the amount of the premium where there are practical problems such as rapid turnover of participants during a plan year.

During the second full plan year, both single-employer and multi-employer plans may elect to pay a premium determined under the formula of the House bill but not less than one-half of what they would have to pay under the per capita rates. (This rate base for multi-employer plans continues until 1978.) One-half of the premium referred to above is to be determined according to the plan's unfunded insured benefits (but with the premium not to exceed 0.1 percent of unfunded vested benefits for single-employer plans and .025 percent for multiemployer plans). The other half of the premium is to be based on the total insured benefits. In this case the premium is to be fixed at a uniform rate (determined separately for single-employer and multi-employer plans) which is calculated by the corporation to produce the same total yearly revenue as is produced by the premiums on unfunded insured benefits.

In subsequent years the corporation may set premiums using the per capita rate base, the unfunded insured benefits rate base, or the total insured benefits rate base, or any combination of these (subject to the rate limitations above described). If the corporation should want to combine any two or more of these three rate bases, it is to design the bases to produce approximately equal amounts of aggregate premium revenue yearly from each.

The corporation may exceed the rate limitations, produce unequal amounts of aggregate premium income from the different rate bases, or use other rate bases, but only as to plan years beginning after Congress approves these revisions through a special procedure set forth in the conference substitute.

The conferees also decided that the corporation should establish by regulations equitable methods of valuing a plan's assets and benefits for the purpose of setting premium rates.

The basic enforcement mechanism is to be a civil action brought by the corporation for the collection of unpaid premiums past due. There is to be a civil penalty of up to 100 percent of the amount of unpaid premiums to be assessed after 60 days following the due date of the premiums, but application of this penalty may be postponed in cases in which payment of the premiums entails hardship to the plan. The plan is to be liable for both the premiums for coverage of benefits and for any penalty assessed for failure to pay premiums. Besides the penalty, the corporation may also charge interest (at the rate imposed at the time under section 6601(a) of the Internal Revenue Code, or its successor, upon tax underpayments) for unpaid premiums that are past due. Additionally, a court, in any action brought to enforce the insurance provisions, including an action to collect unpaid premiums, may award the corporation all or any part of its costs of litigation.

The corporation may elect to insure nonbasic benefits in covered plans and do this through separate funds. If it does so, uniform premium rates are to be established by the corporation for the risk insured in each category. The term "nonbasic benefits" may include both what are sometimes called ancillary benefits and what are sometimes called supplemental benefits.

As to basic retirement benefits, coverage is to continue although premiums are not paid when due.

As explained subsequently, the corporation is also to provide insurance protection for employer liability upon the termination of plans. In this case the corporation is free to determine the rates in a manner it determines as appropriate. These premiums are to be set at rates sufficient to fund the contingent liability covered. This coverage is not to remain in effect if premiums due are unpaid. For coverage of employer liability, the corporation is to provide regulations to set the appropriate period for which the premiums (which are to be paid by the employer) should be paid. Employers electing this coverage may give notice of their election prior to the coverage period, and the five-year waiting period during which the premiums must be paid before contingent employer liability is covered is to begin with that notification.

Establishment of Pension Benefit Guaranty Funds

Under the House bill, separate trust funds were to be established for single-employer plans and for multiemployer plans. In addition, the corporation would be given the option to establish other trust funds, including a fund for employers paying the optional extra premium for coverage against employer liability. The corporation was to have the discretion to grant coverage against this contingent employer liability for employers in single-employer plans. (There was to be no employer liability for employers in multiemployer plans.) Although premium rates were to be established separately to reflect experience and corporation costs for single-employer plans and multiemployer plans, only one trust fund was specifically provided under the Senate amendment. However, authority was granted to establish funds for insurance of contingent employer liability and insurance of other classes of benefits.

Under the conference substitute, four separate revolving funds are specifically established. They are for the basic retirement benefits of single-employer and multiemployer plans and for such nonbasic benefits of single employer and multiemployer plans that the corporation chooses to insure. It is intended that separate accounts will be maintained in the two basic retirement funds for employer liability payments and for premiums paid for employer liability coverage.

The resources of each fund are not to be used to pay the losses or expenses of another fund, and the funds may draw upon the general funds of the Treasury only to the extent of their borrowing authority. The funds are to be self-sufficient and are not to be a charge on the Federal budget.

Among the receipts to be included in each fund are the appropriate portions of premiums, penalties, interest, and other charges; employer liability payments; amounts borrowed from the Treasury; and interest earned by fund assets.

Disbursements are to be made from each fund for payments of insured benefits (including employer contingent liability coverage), repayment to the Treasury of borrowed amounts, operational and administrative expenses, and payments for assets being purchased under certain circumstances from a plan being terminated.

Plans Covered

The House bill required mandatory

coverage of all plans to which the funding standards of the bill would apply, except that no plan having less than 25 participants (of whom at least 10 must have vested benefits) during any five consecutive years, or any plan with assets covering less than 10 percent of the value of the plan's insured benefits, would be covered. The Senate amendment required mandatory coverage of all qualified plans except money purchase pension plans, profit-sharing plans, stock bonus plans, governmental plans, church plans (other than those electing to be covered), and certain fraternal association plans.

Subject to specific exceptions, the conference substitute requires mandatory coverage of employee pension benefit plans that either affect interstate commerce (and, in the case of nonqualified plans, have for five years met the standards for qualified plans) or that are qualified under the Internal Revenue Code, the so-called 403 (b) plans of certain educational and other tax-exempt organizations, and some so-called H.R. 10 plans for the self-employed and their employees. Covered plans must pay the appropriate premium for coverage. As to whether any particular benefit receives insurance coverage, see "Benefits guaranteed," below.

A plan once determined to be a qualified plan by the Internal Revenue Service is a covered plan even if the determination is subsequently deemed erroneous. However, once a qualified plan loses its qualification, benefits thereafter accruing are not insured.

Plans specifically excluded from coverage are:

(1) individual account plans (such as money-purchase pension plans, profit-sharing plans, thrift and savings plans, and stock bonus plans),

(2) governmental plans (including plans set up under the Railroad Retirement Act of 1935 or 1937),

(3) a church plan which has not volunteered for coverage, is not for employees in an unrelated trade or business, and is not a multiemployer plan in which one or more of the employers are not churches or a convention or association of churches,

(4) plans established by fraternal societies or other organizations described in section 501(c)(8), (9), or (18) of the Internal Revenue Code which receive no employer contributions and which cover only members (not employees),

(5) a plan that has not after the date of enactment provided for employer contributions,

(6) nonqualified deferred compensation plans established for a select group of management or highly compensated employees,

(7) a plan outside the United States for nonresident aliens,

(8) a plan primarily for a limited group of highly paid employees, where the benefits to be paid (or contributions received) are in excess of the limitations set forth in section 415 of the Internal Revenue Code (as added by the conference substitute),

(9) a qualified plan established exclusively for "substantial owners" (defined below),

(10) a plan of an international organization exempt from tax under the International Organizations Immunities Act.

(11) a plan maintained only to comply with workmen's compensation, unemployment compensation, or disability insurance laws,

(12) a plan established and maintained by a labor organization described in section 501(c)(5) of the Internal Revenue Code that does not after the date of enactment provide for employer contributions,

(13) a plan which is a defined benefit plan to the extent it is treated as an individual account plan under section 3(35)(B) of the Act, or

(14) a plan established and maintained by one or more professional service employers that has from the date of enactment not had more than 25 active participants. Once one of these plans has more than 25 active participants, it remains covered although the number of such employees drops to 25 or less.)

Benefits Guaranteed

The House bill would provide coverage for benefits required to be vested under the bill's minimum vesting standards (up to the insurance limitations) if the plan providing the benefit had been covered for more than five years prior to the termination. The corporation could elect to cover (subject to certain conditions) nonbasic benefits if both the plans providing them and the plan provisions providing the particular benefits had been in existence for more than five years prior to the termination, or if the plans providing the coverage were tax-qualified. The Senate amendment provided coverage for benefits vested under the plan up to the insurance limitations and without regard to whether they exceeded the vesting required under the bill. The benefits, however, had to have been provided by plan provisions in effect at least three years prior to the termination.

Under the conference substitute, vested retirement benefits guaranteed by the plan (other than benefits vesting only because of the termination) are to be covered to the extent of the insurance limitations except to the extent indicated below. (Nonbasic benefits the corporation had chosen to guarantee are also to be covered. These nonbasic benefits may include that part of annuities in excess of $750 monthly, medical benefits, etc. This coverage is not necessarily to be subject to the phase-in rule limiting coverage of basic retirement benefits.)

One of the principal limitations on the coverage is that it is to be phased in at the rate of 20 percent per year until the plan or benefit is fully covered after it has been in effect for five years. (For this purpose, the period of existence of a successor plan covering substantially the same employees and providing substantially the same benefits is to be added to the period of existence of its predecessor plan in determining how long a benefit has been in effect.)

In determining how long a plan or amendment has been in effect for purposes of the phase-in schedule, the first year following the end of the plan year in which the plan or amendment first becomes effective constitutes the first year (after which 20 percent of the benefit is covered).

The phase-in rule applies to all benefits provided by qualified plans from the date the benefit was provided. In the case of nonqualified plans that affect commerce, the phase-in rule applies only to benefit increases since the original plan benefits must have been in existence for five years when the plan is first covered (after at least five years of meeting all the standards applicable to qualified plans).

In the case of a plan not covered the day after enactment, the five-year phase-in rule is to commence only when the plan is covered.

The benefit coverage of "substantial owners" is not to be phased in. Resultingly, the benefits of substantial owners may be covered only after their plans have been in effect for 5 years, but at that time their benefits may be covered entirely (up to the basic insurance limitation).

In the case of a termination after the date of enactment (after December 31, 1977, in the case of a termination of a multiemployer plan), the phase-in rule is not to apply unless the corporation finds substantial evidence that the plan was terminated for a reasonable business purpose and not for the purpose of obtaining the payment of benefits by the corporation under the bill. For example, if guaranteed benefits had been increased by one or more amendments made during the 5 years before the termination (or if the plan was created during those 5 years), and the employer's financial condition at the time of termination had not deteriorated significantly from his employer's financial condition immediately after the amendment, then no part of the benefit increase attributable to the amendment is to be insured.

If such a termination was for any purpose other than a reasonable business purpose (whether or not the primary purpose) of obtaining insurance benefits, benefits established or increased during the five years prior to termination are to receive no coverage. For the purpose of this provision, a termination to avoid the liability or responsibility imposed under Title IV on an employer is to be considered a termination for a purpose other than a reasonable business purpose.

Guarantee of benefits is not to extend to benefits accrued after the Secretary of the Treasury or his delegate issues a notice of determination that any trust in the plan is no longer tax-qualified (unless the determination is later held erroneous) or after a plan amendment is adopted that causes the Secretary or his delegate to issue a notice of determination that any trust in the plan is not tax-qualified (unless the determination is later held erroneous or unless the amendment is retroactively revoked to comply with the amendment).

Insurance Limitations

The House bill limited insurance benefits to the actuarial equivalent of an annuity, beginning at age 65, of $20 per month per year of credited service, regardless of the number of plans in which the employee had been a participant. This maximum amount would be adjusted according to changes in all employees' average wages. No insurance at all would be paid to a "substantial owner," which is defined as a person who owns a sole proprietorship, more than five percent of a partnership, or five percent of either the entire stock or the voting stock of a corporation.

The Senate amendment would have restricted insurance benefits to the actuarial equivalent of the lesser of 50 percent of average wages during the five years preceding termination or $750 monthly. This maximum was to be adjusted in accordance with changes in the social security contribution and benefit base. The insurance maximum was thus set without regard to the number of plans in which the employee had been a participant, and the insured benefits of an "owner-employee" in the plan during the year of termination or any of the preceding three years were to be reduced by his pro rata share of the accumulated funding deficiency requiring the insurance payments.

In general, the conferees followed the outline of the Senate amendment. However, the limitation is set as the actuarial equivalent of the lesser of 100 percent of the employee's wages during his highest-paid five consecutive years (without regard to temporary absences from participation during that period), or $750 monthly. This amount is adjusted to reflect changes in the social security and benefit base.

In computing the limitation, the guarantee of nonbasic benefits is to be disregarded. In other words, employees are entitled to receive insurance payments for nonbasic benefits although those insured benefits, together with the payment of guaranteed retirement benefits, exceeds the maximum limitation.

The maximum benefit for an "owner-employee" as to each benefit or benefit increase is also limited by a fraction representing the number of years in the 30 years (the period for amortizing an unfunded past service liability for single-employer plans created after January 1, 1974) preceding termination in which the owner-employee was an active plan participant. An owner-employee is defined as a person owning 10 percent of an enterprise, whether a corporation or a partnership, or a sole proprietorship, at any time in the five years preceding the termination.

Employer's Contingent Liability Coverage

The House bill authorized the corporation to insure employers against the contingent liability that could arise against employers to reimburse the corporation for its losses caused by coverage of those employers' terminated plans. The amount of premiums charged for this coverage was to be based upon the actual and projected costs of this coverage. (Since there was to be no employer contingent liability for employers in multicmployer plans, there was no provision for coverage of such employers.)

The Senate amendment mandated the corporation to offer contingent liability coverage that was to be applicable to all electing plans (including both single-employer and multi-employer plans) if the extra premium for the coverage had been paid for each of the five plan years immediately preceding the plan year of the termination. The coverage was not to be granted, however, if the employer remained in the same or in a similar business. The premiums were to be calculated by the corporation at a rate sufficient to fund any contingent liability coverage payments.

Under the conference substitute, coverage of contingent employer liability is mandatory for single and multiemployer plans, but the corporation is instructed to attempt with private insurers to devise within a 36-month period a system under which risks are equitably distributed by the corporation and the private insurers with respect to classes of employers insured by each. The corporation may thereafter require all employers to obtain coverage from the private insurers, the corporation, or both, depending upon the system devised. The corporation is to fix the premiums at a rate sufficient to fund any payment by the corporation required by the coverage. Private insurers are left free to fix the rates of their own premiums, and other terms and conditions of insurance, but the corporation may level any charge upon employers obtaining private insurance that may be necessary to assure that the costs to all employers are reasonable and equitable and to assure the liquidity and adequacy of the corporation's funds used for this purpose. The corporation may not make any coverage payment with respect to contingent liability until the insurance has been in effect, and the premiums have been paid, for more than five years.

The corporation may set the premium levels and collect the premiums (in arrears) for this coverage during any time up to, but not later than, three years after the date of enactment. An employer may then pay premiums for the period since the date of enactment, and this period is to be counted toward completion of the five-year payment of premiums requirement. Once obtained, coverage is to be prospective only, not retroactive.

In making arrangements with private insurers, the corporation is also to consider using private industry guarantees, indemnities, or letters of credit as an alternative or supplement to private insurance.

Termination By Plan Administrator

The House bill requires an employer or employee organization planning to terminate a plan to first notify the corporation. The Senate amendment requires a 90-day notification period that may be extended by agreement. A notification by the corporation during one of these periods that the plan assets are insufficient is to cause a termination by the corporation under the provisions for a termination by the corporation. If, in the course of an authorized voluntary termination, a plan administrator determines that the plan assets are insufficient, he is required to so notify the corporation, which is then to terminate the plan under the regular proceedings for a termination by the corporation.

The Senate amendment also provides that a change from an insured plan into a money purchase plan, a profit-sharing plan, or a stock bonus plan (none of which may be covered) is to be treated as a voluntary termination (for which authorization from the corporation must first be obtained).

Under the conference substitute, the plan administrator must file notice with the corporation at least 10 days before the date of the proposed termination, and he may pay no benefit under termination procedures of the plan for 90 days after the proposed termination date, unless, in the interim, he receives a notice of determination from the corporation that the plan assets are sufficient to discharge the plan obligations as they fall due. The plan administrator or the corporation is authorized to petition the court for appointment of a trustee to manage the plan under the same procedure by which a trustee may be appointed in the case of an involuntary termination, if the best interest of the participants and beneficiaries would be served by the appointment. In other respects the conferees accepted the substance of the Senate amendment.

A plan termination in the sense that benefits stop accruing (as provided in section 411(d)(3) of the Internal Revenue Code) is not to be termination under the insurance provisions so long as the employer continues to meet the funding standards provided by the substitute.

Date of Termination

The termination date of a plan is to be determined by the plan administrator or the corporation, depending upon which terminates the plan and also depending upon whether this date is agreed to by the other party. If there is not agreement between the corporation and the plan administrator, the termination date is to be established by the court. However, in the case of terminations of plans which occur before the date of enactment, the date of termination is to be set by the corporation on the basis of the date on which benefits ceased to accrue or on any other appropriate basis.

Termination by Pension Benefit Guaranty Corporation

Under the House bill, the Secretary of Labor may terminate a plan, after a hearing, (a) if he determines that the plan failed to meet the minimum funding standards, the plan is unable to pay benefits when due, or failure to terminate will cause long-run loss to the corporation, or (b) if the employer or an appropriate employee organization applies to him for authority to terminate. In terminating a plan, the Secretary of Labor must distribute the plan's assets in accordance with the priority schedule contained in the bill. He is permitted to distribute the assets without ending the plan or without appointing a receiver, and also he may order the plan's continuation under a receiver until all benefit liabilities are satisfied. At any time, however, he may wind up the plan (after a hearing) with a distribution of remaining assets.

Under the Senate amendment, the corporation may institute termination proceedings for the causes listed in the House bill or if a distribution in excess of $10,000 is made to an owner-employee (other than on account of death or disability) if, after the distribution, there are unfunded vested liabilities.

Under the conference substitute, the corporation may institute termination proceedings in court if it finds that:

(1) minimum funding standards have not been met,

(2) the plan is unable to pay benefits when due,

(3) a distribution is made to an owner-employee of $10,000 in any 24-month period if not paid by reason of death and if, after the distribution, there are unfunded vested liabilities, or

(4) the possible long-run liability to the corporation with respect to the plan may reasonably be expected to increase unreasonably if the plan is not terminated.

In seeking a termination the corporation is to apply to the appropriate United States District Court, with notice to the plan, for appointment of a trustee to administer the plan pending issuance of a termination decree. Unless cause is shown within three days thereafter why a trustee should not be appointed, the appointment is to be made and the trustee is to administer the plan until the corporation decides whether the plan should be terminated. The court may appoint the trustee from a list furnished to the court by the corporation, or it may appoint the existing plan administrator or the corporation itself. Even without the appointment of a trustee, however, the corporation may, with notice to the plan, apply for a termination decree.

If it grants the decree, the court is to order the trustee (after first appointing a trustee, if none has yet been appointed) to terminate the plan.

A trustee with the discretion to commence the final liquidation of the trust must first give the corporation at least 10 days' notice. If the corporation should oppose the trustee's proposal, the court is to resolve the dispute.

In the case of small plans, the corporation may prescribe a simplified procedure and may pool assets of small plans so long as the rights of the participants and employers (including the right to a court decree of termination) are preserved. Furthermore, the corporation may agree with any plan administrator to designate a trustee who, without court appointment, is to have the usual powers of trustees appointed by the court.

If the application for a trustee is rejected by the court, the trustee is to transfer all assets and records of the plan back to the plan administrator within three days. If the corporation fails to apply within 30 days after appointment of the trustee for a termination decree, the trustee is to transfer the assets and records back to the plan administrator. This 30-day period may be extended by agreement or court order.

The corporation may file for termination despite the pendency in any court of bankruptcy, mortgage foreclosure, or equity receivership proceeding, or any proceeding to reorganize, conserve, or liquidate such plan or its property, or any proceeding to enforce a lien against property of the plan. The court may also stay any of these proceedings. In the termination proceedings, the court is to have the exclusive jurisdiction of the plan and its assets with powers of a court in bankruptcy and of a court in a Chapter X proceeding.

The compensation of the trustee is to be approved by the corporation, and, in the case of a trustee appointed by the court, with the consent of the court. Trustees are authorized to employ professional assistance in accordance with regulations to be issued by the corporation.

Reportable Events

Under the House bill, certain events indicating possible danger of plan termination must be reported by the plan administrator to the corporation. These events are:

(a) a tax disqualification;

(b) a benefit decrease by plan amendment;

(c) a decrease in active participants to 80 percent of the number at the beginning of the plan year, or 75 percent of the number at the beginning of the previous plan year;

(d) an IRS determination that there has been a plan termination or partial termination for tax purposes;

(e) a failure to meet the minimum funding standards;

(f) inability to pay benefits when due;

(g) a distribution of $10,000 or more in a 24-month period to a "substantial owner," if the plan has unfunded nonforfeitable benefits after the distribution (unless the distribution was made on account of death);

(h) filing of a report preliminary to a merger, consolidation, transfer of assets or liabilities, or a distribution in excess of $25,000 to a participant in any plan year, or the granting by the Secretary of Labor of a hearing in regard to a variation on the bill's standards; or

(i) the occurrence of any other event which the corporation determines may be indicative of a need to terminate the plan.

The Senate amendment is essentially the same as the House bill points through (f). As to point (g), the Senate amendment requires reporting of any distribution of $10,000 or more to an owner-employee (unless the distribution is made on account of death or disability), if the distribution increases or creates unfunded vested liabilities. The Senate amendment does not include provisions corresponding to points (h) and (i) of the House bill.

The Senate amendment provisions requiring the Secretary of Treasury to report certain occurrences to the corporation are essentially the same as those of the House bill. There are no corresponding provisions regarding the Secretary of Labor.

The Conference substitute requires the plan administrator to inform the corporation with respect to the same listing of reportable events as listed in the House bill. However, the corporation is authorized to waive the requirement and to require any of the events referred to above to be included in the annual report made by the plan. In addition, any employer in a covered plan who knows, or has reason to know, that a reportable event has occurred is immediately to notify the plan administrator of this event.

Management Functions

Under the House bill, the Secretary of Labor is given authority to transfer funds of terminated plans to the corporation for investment and for payment of benefits, as well as to obtain outside financial counsel and to take any other consistent action to assure equitable payments to participants and beneficiaries. The Senate amendment provides that investments of funds of terminated plans are to be handled by the court-appointed trustees.

Under the conference substitute, the trustee is to take over general management of the assets. The Advisory Committee is to make timely recommendations to the corporation regarding investment policy relating to funds of terminated plans and on whether terminating plans, at the time, should be operated as liquidating trusts or liquidated (with the proceeds used to purchase annuities for the participants and beneficiaries). The corporation is to make recommendations to trustees of terminated plans regarding investments and is to direct each trustee whether to operate his plan as a wasting trust or to liquidate it and purchase annuities. If the trustee disagrees with the directive of the corporation, he is authorized to apply to the court for a resolution of the dispute.

Allocation of Assets at Termination

Under the House bill, priorities are provided for distribution of assets upon termination of a plan. In general, net assets (assets less expenses and less those assets irrevocably allocated to individual accounts at least 2 years before termination) are allocated in the following order:
 (a) employee contributions,
 (b) vested benefits of employees already receiving benefits or entitled to choose early retirement (except for disability),
 (c) other vested benefits,
 (d) other accrued benefits,
 (e) interest on employee contributions,
 (f) remaining liabilities proposed in the plan for payment upon termination, and
 (g) pro rata to each person entitled to receive a distribution on account of priorities (a) through (f).

The Senate amendment requires that plan assets be distributed according to the following priorities:
 (a) voluntary employee contributions,
 (b) mandatory employee contributions,
 (c) benefits in pay status at least 3 years (at the benefit level existing 3 years before termination),
 (d) other insured benefits.

Both the House bill and the Senate amendment also have other provisions regarding allocation within a priority category when the remaining assets are insufficient to satisfy all the benefits in that category, regarding benefits in more than one priority category, and regarding similar related problems.

Under the conference substitute, assets are to be allocated among plan benefits in the levels of priorities stated below:
 (1) Voluntary employee contributions,
 (2) Mandatory employee contributions,
 (3) Equally among individuals in the following two subcategories:
 (i) in the case of benefits in pay status three years prior to termination (at the lowest pay level in that period and at the lowest benefit level under the plan during the five years prior to termination) and
 (ii) in the case of benefits which would have been in pay status three years prior to termination had the participant been retired (and had his

benefits commenced then, at the lowest benefit level under the plan during the five years prior to termination),

(4) All other guaranteed benefits up to the insurance limitations (but irrespective of the limitation to one $750 monthly benefit regardless of the number of plans in which the employee participated) and (on an equal level of priority) benefits that would be so guaranteed except for the special limitation on coverage of a "substantial owner,"

(5) All other (meaning uninsured) vested benefits, and

(6) All other benefits under the plan.

The plan may, under regulations, establish subclasses and categories within these six classes.

Employer Liability

Both the House bill and the Senate amendment required employer liability for insurance payments made by the corporation because of terminations of the employers' plans. The House bill set a limit on employer liability of 50 percent of the employer's net worth, as compared with 30 percent under the Senate amendment. In addition, the House bill did not impose any liability in the case of multiemployer plans.

As previously discussed, both the House bill and the Senate amendment authorized the corporation to insure employers against employer liability, under different sets of conditions.

Under the conference substitute, employer liability is required for employers in both single-employer and multiemployer plans. The employer liability is limited to 30 percent of net worth, with net worth valued as of a date chosen by the corporation, but not more than 120 days prior to the termination.

Net worth is to be computed without taking the contingent employer liability into the calculation. It is determined on the basis chosen by the corporation to reflect best the operating value of the employer, and it is to be increased by any transfers made by the employer prior to the termination that the corporation finds improper.

In determining the employer who may be liable for insurance coverage losses of the corporation, all trades or businesses (whether or not incorporated) under common control are to be treated as a single employer. Trades or businesses under common control may, for this purpose, include partnerships and proprietorships as well as corporations.

If, as a result of the cessation of operations at any facility, more than 20 percent of the participants in a plan are separated from their employment, the employer is to be treated as an employer in a terminating plan that is maintained by more than one employer. Furthermore, in the case of withdrawals of employers in multiemployer plans resulting in substantial reductions of contributions, the corporation may treat the withdrawal as constituting a termination with respect to employees of such employers.

In determining the amount of the corporation's liability, the amount of employer liability (but not the employer's net worth), the application of the lien arising out of employer liability, the appropriate allocation of assets in the event of a termination, the value of the plan's assets, the amount of benefits payable with respect to each participant, the amount of benefits guaranteed with respect to each participant, the present value of the aggregate amount of benefits potentially payable by the corporation, and the fair market value of the plan's assets, the date of determination is to be the date of termination.

In determining the fair market value of a plan's assets, unrealized gain is to be taken into account.

Lien for Employer Liability

The House bill provides for the imposition of a lien upon all property and rights in property belonging to an employer who is liable to the corporation as a result of a plan termination. Under this provision, the lien would arise if payment were not made after demand for payment was made by the corporation and would be in the amount of the liability including interest. Further, the lien would not be valid against the general Federal tax lien.

The Senate amendment provided that the lien would also be inferior to the special estate and gift tax lien imposed under the Internal Revenue Code and, if arising from an obligation incurred by the employer prior to termination of the plan, a lien or other security interest which is perfected not later than 30 days after termination. The amendment further modifies the House bill by authorizing the corporation to subordinate the lien under certain circumstances.

The conference substitute in general follows the lien imposition provisions of both bills but provides (1) additional rules relating to the period during which the lien will be in existence; (2) that the priority of the lien is to be determined in the same manner as under the Federal tax lien rules to minimize circular priority problems; (3) rules relating to the civil action to foreclose the lien, including the period during which an action must be commenced; and (4) authority for the corporation to release or subordinate the lien under certain circumstances.

More specifically, the revised and added provisions may be explained as follows:

(1) The conference substitute adopts the lien priority rules of the Internal Revenue Code. Generally, these rules provide protection against the lien for a purchaser, holder of a security interest, mechanic's lienor, or judgment lien creditor if any such person's title or interest is acquired or perfected before notice of the lien is filed. Protection is also provided for certain other interests even if acquired or perfected after notice of the lien is filed. Generally, if the purchaser or creditor does not have actual notice or knowledge of the lien, this status is provided for a purchaser or a holder of a security interest in a security (stocks, bonds, negotiable instruments, etc.), a purchaser of a motor vehicle, a purchaser of certain household goods or personal effects in a casual sale for less than $250, an insurer which makes a loan secured by a policy issued by it, and a financial institution which makes a passbook loan secured by an account with the institution. This status is also provided for certain retail purchases, possessory liens, real property tax assessments, liens for repairs to a residence, and attorney's liens.

Protection against the lien is also provided with respect to certain advances which are made, after notice of the lien is filed, pursuant to a commercial transaction financing agreement, a real property construction or improvement financing agreement, or an obligatory disbursement agreement.

In the case of bankruptcy or insolvency proceedings, the lien is to be treated in the same manner as a tax due and owing to the United States.

The conference substitute provides that, for purposes of determining the priority between a Federal tax lien and the employer liability lien, each is to be treated as a judgment lien arising when notice of that lien is filed. The effect of this is to adopt a "first to file" priority rule with respect to the employer liability lien and the Federal tax lien imposed under section 6321 of the Internal Revenue Code.

(2) The conference substitute provides that the corporation may bring a civil action in a district court of the United States to enforce the employer liability lien or to subject any property belonging to an employer to the payment of the employer's liability to the corporation. Generally, this action must be commenced within 6 years after the date upon which the plan is terminated or prior to the expiration of any period for collection agreed upon in writing by the corporation and the employer before the expiration of the 6-year period.

(3) The conference substitute provides for both the release and subordination of the lien. The lien may be released or subordinated if the corporation determines, with the con-

sent of the board of directors, that release or subordination of the lien would not adversely affect the collection of liability to the corporation. Under these conditions, the corporation may issue a certificate of release or subordination of the lien with respect to the employer's property or any part thereof.

Recapture of Plan Payments

The House bill contains no provision for the recovery shortly prior to termination of payments to participants that might be deemed excessive. Under the Senate amendment, certain payments of a terminated plan affecting interstate commerce made during a three-year period prior to termination may be recovered. Payments made on account of death or disability were not to be subject to recovery, and the corporation was authorized to waive recovery of certain amounts when the recovery would have caused substantial hardship.

In the case of a distribution to an owner-employee that exceeds $10,000 and creates or increases unfunded vested liabilities, the three-year lookback period would not begin until the corporation is informed of the distribution (which is a reportable event under both the Senate amendment and the conference substitute).

Under the conference substitute, the trustee may recover all payments to a participant in excess of $10,000 (or the amount he would have received as a monthly benefit under a lifetime annuity commencing at age 65, if greater) made during any twelve-month period within the three years prior to termination.

As under the Senate amendment, the conference substitute provides that there is to be no recovery of payments for after death or death or disability, that the three-year period is not to end, in the case of a distribution to a substantial owner (after which the plan has unfunded vested liabilities), until the corporation is notified of the distribution, and that the corporation is authorized to waive any recovery that would cause substantial economic hardship.

Restoration of Plans

Neither the House bill nor the Senate amendment had any specific provision that procedures against a plan in the termination phase might be abandoned by the corporation if the employer and plan enjoyed a favorable reversal of business trends, or if some other factor made termination no longer advisable.

Under the conference substitute, the corporation may cease any termination activities and do what it can to restore the plan to its former status. As a result, a terminated plan being operated by a trustee as a wasting trust may be restored if, during the period of its operation by the trustee, experience gains or increased funding make it sufficiently solvent. The corporation may, when appropriate, transfer to the employer or plan administrator part or all of the remaining assets and liabilities.

Liability of Substantial Employer for Withdrawal

Since employers in multiemployer plans were not liable for the corporation's losses under the House bill, that bill contained no provision regulating the withdrawal of a substantial employer from a multiemployer plan.

Under the Senate amendment, the plan administrator was to inform the corporation of the withdrawal of a substantial owner (as defined). The corporation could then either require payment into escrow of the substantial owner's potential liability or require deposit of a bond in the amount of 150 percent of the liability. If the plan terminated within five years, the payment or bond was to be forfeited. The corporation could, in the case of a withdrawal causing a significant reduction in plan contributions, require allocation between participants no longer in the plan because of the withdrawal and the remaining participants. The portion of the fund allocable to the departed participants would be treated as a termination. The corporation could waive all these procedures if there were an indemnity agreement between the remaining employers in the plan sufficient to satisfy all plan liabilities.

Under the conference substitute, the plan administrator is required to notify the corporation within 60 days after the withdrawal of a substantial employer from a plan under which more than one employer makes contributions.

The corporation may require the substantial owner either to pay the potential liability (as determined by the corporation) into escrow or to post a bond in 150 percent of the amount of the liability. The liability is normally to be determined as the substantial employer's share (with the substantial employer's share computed according to that employer's proportion of the total employer contributions to the plan within the past five years) of the total plan liability that would have existed if the plan had terminated when the substantial owner withdrew. However, the corporation is also authorized to determine the liability according to any other equitable basis prescribed by it in regulations.

If the plan terminates within five years, the payment or bond is forfeited for the benefit of the plan, but the employer may be refunded any amount not needed to meet the plan's liabilities. If there is no termination, the payment or bond is to be returned to the substantial employer or cancelled.

As alternatives to the bond or escrow payments requirement, the corporation may, if the withdrawal causes a significant reduction in the amount of plan contributions, require the plan fund to be allocated between those participants no longer under the plan because of the withdrawal and those participants still covered. That portion of the fund allocable to participants no longer in the plan is to be treated as a termination, while the remainder is to be a new plan.

The corporation is entitled to waive the use of either of these procedures if there is an indemnity agreement between all the other employers in the plan sufficient to satisfy all plan liabilities.

Liability of Employers on Termination of Plan Maintained by More Than One Employer

The House bill did not provide employer liability for employers in multiemployer plans. Under the Senate amendment, the employer liability on termination of a multiemployer plan was to be allocated among the employers who had contributed to the plan during the five years before termination, in proportion to their contributions. The 30-percent of net worth limit on employer liability was to be applied separately to each employer.

Under the conference substitute, the general rule of the Senate amendment is accepted with the three modifications:

1. This particular computation of employer liability is to apply to all plans having more than one employer making contributions at the time of the termination, or at any time within the five plan years preceding the date of termination.

2. The allocation is not to be in accordance with actual contributions made by employers during the last five plan years ending prior to the termination, but according to the amounts required to be contributed by each employer during that period.

3. The corporation is authorized to determine the liability of each employer on any other equitable basis prescribed in the corporation's regulations.

This regulatory authority extends in two directions. That is, the corporation is authorized to permit other equitable methods of allocation to be used by the employers in the plan, where such other method of allocation would not increase the likelihood that the entire plan would terminate. Also, the corporation is authorized to require the use of other equitable methods where allocation in proportion to contributions would produce inequitable results. For example, the corporation is authorized to require a different allocation basis if the employers in a plan have agreed on a contribution formula that would have the effect of shifting employer liability from those employers that had net assets to those employers that had little or no net assets.

In this regard, it should be noted that the affiliated employer rules are to apply in this area. That is, if one member of an affiliated group has employer liability, then that liability is to extend to the entire affiliated group. Also, the 30-percent-of-net-assets limit is to apply with respect to the net assets of the entire group.

Effective Dates

The House bill applied the provisions on premiums and benefits to plan years beginning after June 1, 1974, for single-employer plans. In the case of a multiemployer plan involving a collective bargaining agreement covering more than 25 percent of the total participants, these provisions applied to plan years beginning after the earlier of December 31, 1980, or the date on which the last such agreement relating to that plan terminated (without regard to extensions made after the date of enactment of the bill). Provisions other than those regarding premiums and benefits payable were to take effect on the date of enactment of the bill.

The Senate amendment required premiums to be collectible with respect to plan years beginning after December 31, 1973. The provisions regarding terminations and corporation and employer liability applied to plan years beginning after December 31, 1976, unless the corporation determined it had sufficient funds to cover earlier terminations. The remaining provisions were to take effect as of the date of enactment of the bill.

Under the conference substitute, benefits payable by single-employer plans are covered with respect to plans terminated after June 30, 1974, provided the usual requirements for coverage are met. Employers do not, however, incur contingent liability coverage for plans terminating between June 30, 1974, and the date of enactment.

These plans are not covered, however, unless they send the Secretary of Labor a notice received by him not later than 10 days after enactment. If reasonable cause is shown for failure to meet this requirement, notice can be received as late as October 31, 1974.

The opportunity to give notice as late as October 31, 1974 (where good cause is shown), is not intended to apply to situations where the failure to give timely notice was the result of inconvenience or inadvertence. In determining where there is reasonable cause shown for not having given notice within the 10-day period, it is intended that the showing be by clear and convincing evidence that it was not reasonably possible to have given the notice within the time allowed.

With respect to mutliemployer plans, benefits generally are not covered for plans terminating before January 1, 1978. However, the corporation may, in its discretion, cover the benefits of multiemployer plans that had been maintained for five years prior to a termination after the date of enactment, if the corporation determines that this coverage will not jeopardize the coverage of multiemployer plans terminating after December 31, 1977.

Notwithstanding the usual requirements for coverage (discussed above with respect to coverage of plans and coverage of benefits), the corporation may exercise its discretion to cover multiemployer plans which terminate after the date of enactment and before January 1, 1978, if these plans were maintained for five years prior to termination and if the plans—

(A) have been in substantial compliance with the funding requirements for a qualified plan with respect to the employees and former employees in those employment units on the basis of which the participating employers have contributed to the plan for the preceding five years, and

(B) if the participating employers and employee organization or organizations had no reasonable recourse other than termination.

Where in exercise of its discretion to cover benefits of multiemployer plans that have been in substantial compliance with the funding requirements and had no reasonable alternative to termination, or in exercise of its discretion to cover any multiemployer plan terminating before January 1, 1978, the corporation is to notify the Committee on Education and Labor and the Committee on Ways and Means of the House of Representatives, and the Committee on Labor and Public Welfare and the Committee on Finance of the Senate.

If the corporation decides to exercise its discretion with respect to a multiemployer plan, the corporation—

(A) may establish requirements for the continuation of payments which commenced before January 2, 1974, with respect to retired paritcipants under the plan,

(B) may not make payments with respect to any participant who, on January 1, 1974, was receiving payment of retirement benefits, in excess of the amounts and rates payable with respect to that participant on that date,

(C) may not make payments which are derived, directly or indirectly, from amounts borrowed from the Treasury, and

(D) is to review from time to time these discretionary payments and reduce or terminate them to the extent necessary to allow the corporation to guarantee benefits of multiemployer plans terminating after December 31, 1977, without increasing premium rates.

The premiums for both single-employer and multiemployer plans are to be payable for fractional years beginning with the date of enactment.

If the Pension Benefit Guaranty Corporation finds that a plan (other than a multiemployer plan) has terminated after June 30, 1974, and before the date of enactment (and therefore would be eligible for coverage of benefits under the plan termination insurance provisions, but the employer would not be subject to employer liability under those provisions) then the guarantee of benefits is not to apply unless the corporation finds substantial evidence that the plan was terminated for a reasonable business purpose and not for the purpose of obtaining the payment of benefits by the corporation under this bill or of avoiding employer liability.

Temporary Authority for Initial Period

Under the conference substitute, the corporation may appoint a receiver during the first 270 days after enactment for a plan if (1) the corporation receives notice that a plan is to be terminated, or (2) the corporation determines the plan should be terminated. Within 20 days after the appointment, the corporation must apply to the court for a decree approving the appointment.

If the court rejects the application or the corporation fails to apply within the 20 days, the plan assets are to be transferred back to the plan administrator within three days.

As an alternative to this procedure, the corporation may request the plan administrator to apply to the district court for the appointment of a receiver until the plan can be terminated.

The receiver is to determine whether the plan assets are sufficient to discharge the plan obligations. If the receiver's determination is approved by the corporation and the **court,** the receiver is to terminate the plan in accordance with the insurance provisions.

The corporation is also to have special temporary powers during the first 270 days after enactment to—

(1) contract for printing without regard to the provisions of chapter 5 of title 44, United States Code,

(2) waive any notice,

(3) extend the 90-day termination notice period (during which the plan administrator who has filed a notice of termination may not terminate the plan unless he receives a notice of sufficiency of plan assets from the corporation) for an additional 90-day period without the agreement of

the plan administrator or approval of the court, and

(4) waive or reduce contingent employer liability for plan terminations, the requirements respecting withdrawals of substantial owners from plans, and the requirements respecting the liability of employers on termination of plans maintained by more than one employer if this appears necessary to avoid unreasonable hardship for an employer who was unable, as a practical matter, to continue its plan.

XIV. ADDITIONAL ITEMS

Preemption of State Laws (Sec. 514 of the Bill)

Under the substitute, the provisions of title I are to supersede all State laws that relate to any employee benefit plan that is established by an employer engaged in or affecting interstate commerce or by an employee organization that represents employees engaged in or affecting interstate commerce. (However, following title I generally, preemption will not apply to government plans, church plans not electing under the vesting, etc., provisions, workmen's compensation plans, non-U.S. plans primarily for nonresident aliens, and so-called "excess benefit plans.")

The preemption provision will take effect on January 1, 1975, except that preemption with respect to plan termination insurance will take effect on the date of enactment of this bill. However, it will not affect any causes of action that have arisen before January 1, 1975, and it will not affect any act or omission which occurred before that date. In addition, the preemption provisions will not apply to any criminal law of general application of a State.

The preemption provisions of title I are not to exempt any person from any State law that regulates insurance, banking or securities. However, the substitute generally provides that an employee benefit plan is not to be considered as an insurance company, bank, trust company, or investment company (and is not to be considered as engaged in the business of insurance or banking) for purposes of any State law that regulates insurance companies, insurance contracts, banks, trust companies, or investment companies. This rule does not apply to a plan which is established primarily to provide death benefits; such plans, of course, may be regulated under the State insurance, etc., laws.

The substitute provides that the congressional Pension Task Force is to study this provision and report back to the labor committees of the Congress on the results of its study. It is expected that the Pension Task Force will consult closely with State insurance, etc., authorities in the course of this study.

Collectively Bargained Plans. (Sec. 1014 of the Bill and Sec. 413 of the Internal Revenue Code)

The tax provisions of the substitute provide, in the case of collectively bargained plans, that the vesting requirements are to be applied as if all employers who are parties to the plan are a single employer. Generally the substitute provides similar rules with respect to the application of the participation, discrimination, exclusive benefits, etc. requirements so that the collectively bargained plan generally will be looked to as a unit to see if these requirements are satisfied, rather than testing the requirements on an employer-by-employer basis.

In addition, the tax provisions of the substitute generally provide that, for purposes of these rules, employees of labor unions and of a collectively bargained plan are to be treated as employees of an employer which is a party to the collective bargaining agreement. However, this rule is to apply only if the union, etc. as an employer additionally meets the nondiscrimination and coverage requirements of the tax laws.

The conferees understand that the rules of the substitute are the same as the rules of present law, and it is intended that the substitute merely confirm the rules of present law.

Puerto Rican Plans (Sec. 1022 of the Bill)

Under the conference substitute, a

trust which is part of a pension, profit-sharing, or stock bonus plan which is exempt from income taxes under the laws of Puerto Rico, and which is exclusively for the benefit of participants who are Puerto Rican residents, is to be treated as a tax-exempt domestic trust for years after 1973. (Such plans would be subject to title I of the bill but would be exempt from the requirements of title II.)

A plan may elect (in a time and manner to be prescribed in regulations) to be subject to the requirements of a tax-exempt domestic trust for all purposes (including title II). In this case, a Puerto Rican trust which meets the qualification requirements of U.S. tax law may cover U.S. mainland employees of the employer, as well as his Puerto Rican employees. In the case of a trust making this election, the income source rules of subchapter N will apply to trust distributions to the extent provided in regulations. An election, once made, will be irrevocable, and will apply for plan years beginning after the date of the election.

Remedial Retroactive Plan Amendments (Sec. 1024 of the Bill and Sec. 401(b) of the Internal Revenue Code)

Under the substitute, retroactive plan amendments which correct a plan that does not meet the requirements for tax qualification are allowed to cure a new plan or to cure an amendment to an existing plan. Such retroactive changes can be made within the time for filing the employer's tax return for the year in which the plan was put into effect or in which the amendment was adopted (or such later time as is designated by the Secretary of the Treasury).

Mergers And Transfers of Plan Assets (Sec. 1021 of the Bill)

Under the bill as passed by the House, a plan must provide protection to participants in the case of a merger of the plan with another plan or the transfer of assets or liabilities from a plan. The value of benefits to the participant and the extent to which the benefits have been funded is to be protected by comparing what the participant's benefit would be if the plan had terminated immediately before the merger and what the participant's benefits would be under the merged plan had the merged plan been terminated just after the merger. The postmerger termination benefit may not be less than the premerger termination benefit. Further, a plan could not make a lump-sum distribution to a participant or beneficiary if the distribution exceeded the premerger termination benefit. Further, no merger or transfer of assets or liabilities could occur without an actuarial statement indicating compliance with the requirements being filed with the Secretary of the Treasury at least 30 days before the merger or distribution. The bill as passed by the Senate did not contain comparable provisions.

Under the conference agreement, a trust is not to constitute a qualified tax-exempt trust under the tax law, and also is not to satisfy the requirements of title I, unless it provides that in the case of any merger or consolidation of a plan, or any transfer of assets or liabilities of a plan, to any other plan each participant in the plan would receive post merger termination benefits which are equal to or greater than the premerger termination benefits. In the case of multiemployer plans these rules are to apply only to the extent that the Pension Benefit Guaranty Corporation determines that these rules are necessary for the participant's protection. These rules are to apply to mergers or transfers made after the date of enactment of the bill, but the plan provision to this effect does not have to be adopted prior to January 1, 1976.

Registration With Social Security (Secs. 1031 and 1032 of the Bill and Secs. 6057, 6058, 6652, and 6691 of the Internal Revenue Code)

The substitute generally follows the House bill with respect to registration with Social Security. However, the House bill includes requirements for registration under both the labor and tax provisions. Under the substitute, the registration procedure is included only in the tax provisions, but this procedure applies to all plans to which the vesting standards of the labor provisions apply. In addition, under the substitute the labor provisions as well as the tax provisions require the plan administrator to furnish each person an individual statement giving him the information reported to the government; this is included so the individual may enforce his rights to receive this statement by civil action in the courts.

Under the substitute, each plan which is covered by the vesting requirements of the labor provisions is to file with the Internal Revenue Service an annual statement regarding individuals who have terminated employment in the year in question and who have a right to a deferred vested benefit in the plan. Also, the plan administrator is to furnish each person an individual statement giving him the same information which is reported to the Government.

The Social Security Administration is to maintain records of the retirement plans in which individuals have vested benefits, and is to provide this information to participants and beneficiaries on their request and also on their application for Social Security benefits.

The provisions governing registration with Social Security are to apply to a multiemployer plan to the extent provided in regulations.

The provisions requiring registration with Social Security are to apply to plan years beginning after December 31, 1975, except that reports need not be made by Social Security for 3 years after that date.

Rules for Certain Negotiated Plans (Sec. 2007 of the Bill and Sec. 404 (c) of the Internal Revenue Code)

Under the bill as passed by the House, special rules were provided for welfare and benefit plans established before 1954 as a result of an agreement between a union and the government during a period of government operation of the major part of the productive facilities of the industry in which the employer is engaged. The special provisions enable these types of plans to establish two separate trusts—one for the payment of welfare benefits and a second for the payment of retirement benefits. In order to facilitate the restructuring of a welfare and pension plan into two separate plans the bill as passed by the House provides special rules for self-employed individuals who were treated as participants under the plan. The bill as passed by the Senate did not contain provisions pertaining to this matter. The conference substitute accepts the House provision without amendment.

Tax Treatment of Survivor Benefit Plans of the Uniformed Services (Sec 2008 of the Bill and Sec. 122 of the Internal Revenue Code)

The Senate amendment included a provision designed to continue the same tax treatment for servicemen and former servicemen of the United States under the Survivor Benefit Plan (recently enacted in P.L. 92-245) as formerly was available for them under the Retired Serviceman's Family Protection Plan in the case of annuities for surviving spouses or certain child beneficiaries. Under the present tax law, a member or former member of the uniformed services of the United States who receives a reduced amount of retired or retainer pay because of his election to contribute to the program for survivor annuity benefits is not required to include in his gross income the amount of this reduction in his pay. However, the law governing these annuities has recently been changed by the new Survivor Benefit Plan to provide that survivor annuity benefits apply unless the retired serviceman elects not to participate. The amendment conforms the existing tax treatment to this change in the election requirements under the new Survivor Benefit Plan. Thus, where a serviceman (or former serviceman) does not elect out of the new Survivor Benefit Plan and as a result receives reduced retired pay, the amount of the reduction is not taxed to him. Similar conforming amendments are also made to other provisions of the tax laws.

The conference substitute includes this entire provision from the Senate amendment.

Russell Long,
Harrison Williams,
Jennings Randolph,
Gaylord Nelson,
Lloyd Bentsen,

J. K. Javits,
Richard Schweiker,
Wallace Bennett,
Carl T. Curtis,

Managers of the Part of the Senate

Carl D. Perkins,
Frank Thompson,
John H. Dent,
Phillip Burton,

Albert H. Quie,
John N. Erlenborn,
Ronald Sarasin,

Managers on the Part of the House as to Title I of the House Bill.

Al Ullman,
James A. Burke of Massachusetts,
Martha W. Griffiths,
Dan Rostenkowski,

H. T. Schneebeli,
Harold R. Collier,
Joel Broyhill of Virginia

Managers on the Part of the House as to Title II of the House Bill.

REPORT OF THE COMMITTEE OF CONFERENCE ON MPPAA

Conference Report
(H. Rept. No. 96-1343)

The committee of conference on the disagreeing votes of the two Houses on the amendments of the Senate to the amendment of the House to the amendment of the Senate to the bill (H.R. 3904) to amend the Employee Retirement Income Security Act of 1974 and the Internal Revenue Code of 1954 to improve retirement income security under private multiemployer pension plans by strengthening the funding requirements for those plans, to authorize plan preservation measures for financially troubled multiemployer pension plans, and to revise the manner in which the pension plan termination insurance provisions apply to multiemployer plans, and for other purposes, having met, after full and free conference, have agreed to recommend and do recommend to their respective Houses as follows:

Amendments numbered 2 and 3: That the Senate recede from its amendments numbered 2 and 3 to the House amendment to the Senate amendment.

Amendment numbered 1: That the House recede from its disagreement to the amendment of the Senate numbered 1 to the House amendment to the Senate amendment and agree to the same with an amendment as follows: In lieu of the matter proposed to be inserted by the Senate amendment insert the following:

Sec. 414. Treatment of Certain Retirement Benefits.

(a) **General Rule.**—Paragraph (15) of section 3304(a) of the Internal Revenue Code of 1954 (relating to requirements for approval of State laws) is amended by striking out the semicolon at the end thereof and inserting in lieu thereof the following: "except that—

"(A) the requirements of this paragraph shall apply to any pension, retirement or retired pay, annuity, or other similar periodic payment only if—

"(i) such pension, retirement or retired pay, annuity, or similar payment is under a plan maintained (or contributed to) by a base period employer or chargeable employer (as determined under applicable law), and

"(ii) in the case of such a payment not made under the Social Security Act or the Railroad Retirement Act of 1974 (or the corresponding provisions of prior law), services performed for such employer by the individual after the beginning of the base period (or remuneration for such services) affect eligibility for, or increase the amount of, such pension, retirement or retired pay, annuity, or similar payment, and

"(B) the State law may provide for limitations on the amount of any such a reduction to take into account contributions made by the individual for the pension, retirement or retired pay, annuity, or other similar periodic payment;".

(b) **Effective Date.**—The amendment made by subsection (a) shall apply to certifications of States for 1981 and subsequent years.

And the Senate agrees to the same.

For Senate amendment No. 1:
    AL ULLMAN,
    JAMES C. CORMAN,
    CHARLES RANGEL,
    WILLIAM M. BRODHEAD,
    BARBER B. CONABLE,
    BILL FRENZEL,

For Senate amendments Nos. 2 and 3:
    CARL D. PERKINS,
    FRANK THOMPSON, JR.,
    JOHN BRADEMAS,
    WILLIAM CLAY,
    JOHN ASHBROOK,
    JOHN N. ERLENBORN,
Managers on the Part of the House.

    HARRISON A. WILLIAMS,
    JENNINGS RANDOLPH,
    HOWARD M. METZENBAUM,
    DICK SCHWEIKER,
    JACOB K. JAVITS,

RUSSELL B. LONG,
SPARK M. MATSUNAGA,
DAVID L. BOREN,
ROBERT DOLE,
JOHN H. CHAFFEE,
Managers on the Part of the Senate.

Joint Explanatory Statement of the Committee of Conference

The managers on the part of the House and the Senate at the conference on the disagreeing votes of the two Houses on the amendments of the Senate to the amendment of the House to the amendment of the Senate to the bill (H.R. 3904) to amend the Employee Retirement Income Security Act of 1974 and the Internal Revenue Code of 1954 to improve retirement income security under private multiemployer pension plans by strengthening the funding requirements for those plans, to authorize plan preservation measures for financially troubled multiemployer pension plans, and to revise the manner in which the pension plan termination insurance provisions apply to multiemployer plans, and for other purposes, submit the following joint statement to the House and the Senate in explanation of the effect of the action agreed upon by the managers and recommended in the accompanying conference report:

Treatment of Certain Retirement Benefits

The House amendment to the Senate amendment to the bill provides that the pension offset requirement of existing unemployment law would only apply to a pension which is paid under a plan maintained or contributed to by a base period employer and which is increased by reason of services performed after the beginning of the base period. The House amendment also provides that the pension offset requirement would not apply in the case of social security benefits and railroad retirement benefits. The House amendment also authorizes the State to make limitations in the amount of the pension offset to take into account contributions made by the individual for the retirement benefit.

The Senate amendment numbered 1 to the House amendment to the Senate amendment to the bill provides that the pension offset requirement of existing law would only apply to pensions paid under plans maintained or contributed to by base period or chargeable employers. The Senate amendment also allows States to make limitations to take into account employee contributions identical to that contained in the House amendment.

The conference agreement generally follows the Senate amendment.

Preemption

The House amendment to the Senate amendment to the bill provides no exemption from the preemption provision of section 514 of the Employee Retirement Income Security Act of 1974 ("ERISA").

The Senate amendments numbered 2 and 3 to the House amendment to the Senate amendment to the bill provide an exemption from section 514(a) of ERISA for the Hawaii Prepaid Health Care Law as in effect on January 1, 1979, and require a study by the Secretary of Labor on the feasibility of extending the exemption to other State health care laws. The Secretary of Labor is to report to the Congress on the study within two years after the date of enactment.

The Senate recedes to the House position. In adopting the House position, the Conferees do not imply a position as to the effect of section 514 of ERISA on the Hawaii Prepaid Health Care Law or other similar State laws, or as to correctness of any court decisions in this area.

For Senate amendment No. 1:
AL ULLMAN,
JAMES C. CORMAN,
CHARLES RANGEL,
WILLIAM M. BRODHEAD,
BARBER B. CONABLE,
BILL FRENZEL,

For Senate amendments Nos. 2 and 3:
CARL D. PERKINS,
FRANK THOMPSON, JR.,
JOHN BRADEMAS,
WILLIAM CLAY,

JOHN ASHBROOK,
JOHN N. ERLENBORN,
Managers on the Part of the House.

HARRISON A. WILLIAMS,
JENNINGS RANDOLPH,
HOWARD M. METZENBAUM,
DICK SCHWEIKER,

JACOB K. JAVITS,
RUSSELL B. LONG,
SPARK M. MATSUNAGA,
DAVID L. BOREN,
ROBERT DOLE,
JOHN H. CHAFEE,
Managers on the Part of the Senate.

*SELECTED EXPLANATORY STATEMENTS MADE DURING HOUSE AND SENATE FLOOR DEBATE ON MPPAA

I. Senate debate, July 29, 1980—Statements by Sens. Harrison A. Williams, Jr. (D-NJ) and Jacob K. Javits (R-NY)

Mr. Williams: Mr. President, the legislation we are about to consider, the Multiemployer Pension Plan Amendments Act of 1980, enjoys extremely broad support. The legislation was jointly referred to the Labor and Human Resources Committee and the Finance Committee, and in each committee the vote to report the bill favorably was unanimous. In the Labor and Human Resources Committee, those voting in favor of reporting the bill, in addition to myself, included Senators RANDOLPH, PELL, KENNEDY, CRANSTON, RIEGLE, METZENBAUM, SCHWEIKER, JAVITS, HATCH, and HUMPHREY.

The bills approved by the Finance Committee and our committee were fundamentally the same.

Following the markups in our committees, we and our staffs worked together to resolve the differences between our two bills. The Labor and Human Resources Committee and the Finance Committee have now coalesced around a compromise bill, and we offer that bill jointly for consideration by the Senate.

Before discussing the pressing need for this legislation and its key provisions, I want to mention the contributions of those Members who have been so helpful in bringing this measure to fruition.

I pay special tribute to Senator JAVITS, whose dedication to the objective of pension reform and creative approach to solving problems has had a major impact on this legislation. Senator SCHWEIKER also played a vital role in producing a fair and workable bill.

Great credit is also due Senator LONG and his colleagues on the Finance Committee, especially Senator BENTSEN.

The Employee Retirement Income Security Act of 1974, known as ERISA, established a program to guarantee the payment of pension benefits under private pension plans. The Pension Benefit Guaranty Corporation was created to administer this program. When Congress passed ERISA, it deferred mandatory insurance coverage of multiemployer pension plans because we felt that not enough was known about the plans to design a fair and workable guarantee program.

The PBGC was given discretionary authority to guarantee benefits under multiemployer plans so that it could accumulate experience and expertise in dealing with multiemployer plans. However, the PBGC's experience in the past 5 years indicates that the provisions of current laws relating to multiemployer plans are not workable. Current law creates an incentive for employers to withdraw from multiemployer plans, shifting the burden of funding the plans to other employers or the PBGC.

Multiemployer plans usually cover employees working in an industry in a specific geographic area. Such plans are advantageous to employees because, unlike most single employer plans, employees retain pension credit when moving from one participating employer to another.

In addition, they usually provide benefits to employees even though their employer withdraws from the plan.

However, the decline of the industry covered by a plan can pose a serious threat to the solvency of multiemployer plans. Industry decline, whether caused by technological change,

---

* [*Editor's Note:* The conference report on MPPAA was a brief statement that offered nothing in the way of explanation or legislative history. For that reason, several senators and representatives made statements during floor debate on the bill to explain the intent of Congress and to provide some legislative history.]

foreign competition, or changes in patterns of consumption, can cause the insolvency of a multiemployer plan just as it can cause the insolvency of employers that contribute to the plan.

There is a common belief that multiemployer plans are in serious financial trouble because the plan trustees have acted irresponsibly, or have promised excessively high benefits. This is simply not true. The PBGC made an in-depth study of multiemployer plans in 1978 and the results are instructive. The truth is that financially troubled plans do not offer high benefits—they usually offer very low benefits. Further, these troubled plans have usually not granted any benefit increases in the recent past. For example, there is one plan which offers a retirement benefit of only $30 a month—which can hardly be called excessive. Unfortunately, employment in the industry has decreased so much that employers who contribute to the plan must pay $2,500 per year for each active employee.

I think this case illustrates the nature and extent of the problems facing multiemployer plans in declining industries. Nobody is trying to avoid responsibility for funding benefits or plotting how to dump their plans onto the PBGC. The trustees have held the line on benefits, the employers are shouldering an enormous financial burden, and active workers see a large portion of the compensation package directed to a pension plan that promises very low benefits. But the parties' efforts are not enough to solve these problems.

We passed ERISA in order to encourage the growth and maintenance of private pension plans. Six years of experience demonstrates that the provisions of current law encourage plan termination. For example, employers who withdraw from a multiemployer plan more than 5 years before the plan terminates, escape any liability for unfunded benefits. But employers who remain with plans are forced to pay not only for the benefits of their own employees, but also for the retirees who worked for employers who withdrew. Obviously, the present system encourages employers to abandon a weak plan at the first sign that the industry is in trouble.

In order to carry out the policy of protecting the interests of participants and beneficiaries and encouraging the growth and maintenance of multiemployer plans, the bill makes some important changes in current law. Unavoidable insolvency will be the only insurable event, rather than plan termination. Plan termination will still be possible, but employers must continue to fund the plan.

In addition, in order to remove incentives for employers to withdraw from multiemployer plans, the bill imposes withdrawal liability on withdrawing employers. There are special withdrawal provisions that address the specific problems of plans in the construction industry and the entertainment industry.

The bill includes a presumptive rule for determining the share of a plan's unfunded liabilities that is allocated to a withdrawn employer, but allows a plan, within limits, to adopt a different rule. The committees have also provided rules which will insure that plans treat all employers in an even-handed fashion.

In order to balance the needs of employers and the plan, this compromise bill limits the liability of employers that are bankrupt or undergoing liquidation. Also, the compromise provides a special "deductible" rule that benefits employers whose withdrawal liability is relatively small.

As a final relief measure, the bill provides a 20-year cap on employer withdrawal liability payments. However, relief measures are not available when all the employers have abandoned the plan in a "mass withdrawal."

As I have stated, the committees wish to promote the financial health of all multiemployer plans. The bill generally requires multiemployer plans to fund benefit increases over 30 years. These are the same requirements that apply to single-employer plans. Also, the bill identifies plans that are headed for financial trouble and places them in "reorganization." These plans must satisfy tougher funding requirements designed to keep the plan solvent.

Of course, the committees realize that increased funding requirements can burden the employers. A special provision phases-in the stricter funding rules, and plans with large numbers of retirees are given a special credit against funding requirements.

All of these elements of this legislation—faster funding of benefits, a process of "reorganization" for financially troubled plans, withdrawal liability for employers that leave plans, and the change of the insurable event from plan termination to plan insolvency—are essential to the success of the program. However, the most important aspect of this legislation is that it provides a substantial guarantee of the pension benefits of American workers covered by multiemployer plans. I emphasize in this regard that the premium payments that support this guarantee are raised entirely from the pension plans that benefit from the program. No general revenues are used to finance the program.

Mr. President, the provisions of current law will automatically go into effect in the very near future, and mandatory coverage under current law will seriously injure the stability of the multiemployer pension plan system. It is therefore imperative that we enact this long overdue reform legislation before this threat becomes reality. The 8 million workers covered under multiemployer plans are entitled to an effective, workable pension insurance system.

Mr. President, Mr. JAVITS, whom I mentioned earlier, has been certainly one of the most creative forces here and one of the most productive forces behind ERISA and our response to this situation that involves multiemployer plans. It is a pleasure to work with the Senator on these plans.

Mr. Javits: Mr. President, I reciprocate exactly as Senator WILLIAMS said, that our original creative partnership brought ERISA into being. I think succeeding generations will show it to be a blessing to millions upon millions of workers. It now covers some 30 million workers and the plan assets involved are estimated at close to $300 billion—a colossal investment fund. I thank him for the cooperation which he has now extended over all of these years—about 6 years, taking into consideration this bill.

I also express my appreciation to Senator BENTSEN of Texas and Senator NELSON of Wisconsin for their distinguished and invaluable cooperation as members of the Committee on Finance in respect of their jurisdiction, which is also embodied in this bill as it originally was passed and as it now comes before the Senate.

I thank Senator LONG for two things, his cooperation and participation as chairman of the Committee on Finance, and Senator DOLE for comparable cooperation as ranking member. I also thank both of them for having expressed a certain confidence in us whom I have already named to work out the finite details of this highly complex legislation.

Mr. President, also, because our staffs are so important and I would rather do this at the beginning than at the end, I express my appreciation for the work of Senator WILLIAMS' staff, Steve Sacher and Gary Ford, and of my staff, Peter Turza, and our labor counsel, Don Zimmerman, now also having an assistant in David Dunn.

We now come to the Senate, Mr. President, with a single ERISA bill, jointly approved by the Senate Labor and Human Resources Committee, chaired by Senator WILLIAMS, and by the Senate Finance Committee, chaired by Senator LONG. In connection with members of that committee, I also express my appreciation to Senator SCHWEIKER, who took my place as ranking member of the Senate Labor and Human Resources Committee, for his cooperation in bringing out this bill and for his confidence in Senator WILLIAMS and myself in respect thereof.

The bill before us, the Multiemployer Pension Plan Amendments Act, was approved by the Senate Labor Committee on March 24 and June 27 of this year and by the Committee on Finance on June 12 and July 24, and is the product of almost 3 years of hard work and close interaction among the administration, the Congress, and numerous interested groups from the private sector.

When, with Senator WILLIAMS, I developed ERISA, enacted by Congress in 1974, we realized that there was some uncertainty about the impact of title IV of the original bill, which dealt with plan termination on multiemployer plans. Because we realized what a difficult problem that was, where the liability upon a whole group of employers could, for reasons often beyond the control of any one of those employers, be imposed upon others of the employers in a multiemployer plan, and realized that certain types of business had to have multiemployer plans—a very striking example, of course, being the building industry—we deferred the mandatory insurance coverage for this type of plan—to wit, the effective date of such coverage—until January 1, 1978. During the interim period, the Pension Benefit Guaranty Corporation (PBGC) was to use its discretion to cover terminations that occurred prior to that date.

On August 4, 1977, I announced that I had information that a number of multiemployer plans intended to terminate on or about January 1, 1978, thereby shifting possibly hundreds of millions of dollars of liability to the PBGC insurance system. On that day, I introduced S. 2019 which would have postponed the mandatory coverage date for 1 year until January 1, 1979. The legislation which was eventually enacted in late 1977 (Public Law 95-214) delayed the effective date until July 1, 1979 (see Oversight of ERISA, 1977: Hearings on S. 2125 before the Subcommittee on Labor of the Senate Human Resources Committee, 95th Cong., 1st sess. (1977)). It also directed the PBGC to prepare a comprehensive study of multiemployer plan termination insurance by July 1, 1978.

The PBGC engaged in a full-scale reappraisal of title IV's applicability to multiemployer plans and after extensive discussions and interaction with interested parties across the country, issued a report on July 1, 1978 containing new ideas and options for redesigning the multiemployer plan termination insurance program. On that date, the PBGC also released a status report on contingent employer liability insurance.

On February 27, 1979, the PBGC issued legislative policy recommendations for consideration by the Congress. These recommendations were later embodied in Senate legislative text on May 3, 1979, when, at the request of the administration, Senators WILLIAMS, LONG, and I introduced S. 1076 (H.R. 3904). Hearings on this administration bill were held by the Senate Labor Committee on June 26 and 27, 1979 (see Multiemployer Pension Plan Amendments Act of 1979: Hearings on S. 1076 before the Senate Committee on Labor and Human Resources, 96th Cong., 1st sess. (1979)). In order to give the Congress additional time to study and shape the legislation, H.R. 3915 was enacted to delay the mandatory coverage date from July 1, 1979 to May 1, 1980. Two additional delay bills were subsequently enacted.

Then began our effort to deal with the problem which I have already described.

We had a first text of what we are now trying to do on May 3, 1979, when Senator WILLIAMS, Senator LONG, and I introduced S. 1076, which is the precursor of the bill which is before us today.

Subsequently, there were extensions of the time within which insurance would be applicable up to and including July 31, 1980, hence the urgency of our consideration of this measure becomes significant.

Now, it has been properly said that this is a very complicated bill and, indeed, the subject of pensions and pension law, as well as pension agreements, is extremely complicated. But that should not make us shrink from undertaking the responsibility of dealing with it, and we have not backed away from it.

But we have sought to have a consensus of the administration, of the Congress, both Houses, and of private interests affected by employers or employees.

Therefore, the organizations which we have brought into agreement on this legislation become a very significant part of commending this legislation to the Senate.

In other words, the quality of those organizations, their capacities for judging what is just and unjust, and their constituencies, all are critical in an evaluation by Senators as to the passage of this legislation.

I am very pleased to say that that consensus has been very well arrived at.

The amendments which the Senate Labor Committee and the Senate Finance Committee have agreed upon are essentially the original administration bill with the addition of a number of improvements which the committees thought necessary. Both the administration's bill and the Senate committees' bill reflect the extensive input of many diverse organizations in the private sector.

Groups which have had a significant impact on and generally support the plan termination insurance amendments include the National Coordinating Committee for Multiemployer Plans, the National Construction Employers Council, the United Food and Commercial Workers International Union, the Western Conference of Teamsters Pension Trust Fund, the United Mine Workers of America, the Food Marketing Institute, the Bituminous Coal Operators Association, and the AFL-CIO.

In addition to the foregoing groups, other organizations which have had an impact on S. 1076 include the American Association of Retired Persons, the Graphic Arts Supplemental Retirement and Disabilities Fund, and the Associated General Contractors of America. The general plan termination insurance principles of the bill are supported by the ERISA Industry Committee, the American Bankers Association, the American Council on Life Insurance, the National Association of Manufacturers, and the U.S. Chamber of Commerce.

S. 1076 is necessarily a complex bill, both substantively and politically, and in order to develop a consensus in support of the legislation, it was necessary to make compromises. I doubt that any one group that had an impact on this legislation is pleased with all of it. Personally, I have reservations about certain provisions of the bill, but I believe that as the Nation needs this legislation, it should be enacted, and I commend it to the Senate.

The establishment and implementation of plan termination insurance, which we championed in the 1974 ERISA legislation, was and still is the right thing to do. Its purpose is to assure that working men and women receive the pensions for which they worked over a long span of years even if their plan terminates. All of us know about the disappointment and hardships endured when thousands who lost their jobs, or who were fired, or were the subject of other exigencies, lost all or much of their pensions.

Indeed, the most striking horror story is that of Studebaker Motors, which closed its doors before ERISA's passage. The plan termination insurance is, of course, the key to the fact that the promise of a pension benefit will be kept.

If the plan (and the employer or related industry) is hit by hard times, the PBGC insurance system will be there to guarantee that plan participants and beneficiaries receive what they earned—their pension benefits.

Now, the multiemployer plan is the other side of the coin from the single employer plan.

It appears that the single-employer plan termination insurance program is working quite well. I think, however, there is general agreement that ERISA's present scheme for multiemployer plan termination insurance is not doing well and that it must be redesigned. Unlike some who have proposed in one way or another, to abolish multiemployer termination insurance, I am firmly committed to protecting workers and retirees covered by pension plans through the pension insurance system. I believe that we must try our best, in the face of limited resources and large unfunded liabilities, to develop an insurance system that will be as protective and yet as fair as our social system can carry. I believe that the bill approved by the Senate Labor Committee and the Senate Finance Committee is such an effort to do the best we can under difficult circumstances.

Two basic purposes of the bill are to protect participants and beneficiaries in multiemployer plans and to eliminate problems that impede the maintenance and growth of such plans. To carry out these purposes, the bill contains a number of provisions of general applicability to multiemployer plans.

For example, the bill would require 30-year, rather than the present 40-year amortization of certain unfunded past service liabilities. It would also speed up the present 20-year amortization of net experience gains or losses to 15 years. These faster funding requirements, which are the present norms for single-employer plans, will help assure that plan assets are sufficient to cover emerging liabilities.

Under the bill, an employer who withdraws from a multiemployer plan would be liable to the plan for a proportionate share of the unamortized amount of the plan's unfunded vested benefits. In the absence of effective withdrawal liability, an employer could withdraw from a plan leaving unfunded benefit obligations for his employees which must be paid by the remaining employers in the plan. If the plan, or related industry in which it is located, is experiencing or in the foreseeable future will experience financial difficulty, the absence of effective withdrawal liability would encourage a "last man out" mentality, with employers withdrawing from plans to avoid possible plans termination liability.

So we provide, as a very important element of this bill, certain definitions of withdrawal; and in particular industries, those definitions are especially designed to deal with the problems of the industry.

A withdrawal would generally occur when an employer permanently ceases to have an obligation to contribute under the plan or permanently ceases all covered operations under the plan. A special definition of withdrawal is provided for certain employees in the building and construction industry as well as in certain segments of the entertainment industry, where we believe there is a comparable situation. In such industries, a withdrawal occurs if an employer ceases to have an obligation to contribute under the plan and the employer continues to perform work in the jurisdiction of the collective bargaining agreement of the type for which contributions were previously required.

This special definition is justified on the grounds that in both industries an employer's leaving the plan jurisdiction or going out of business does not typically reduce the contribution base. An employer would reduce the contribution base if it continued the same kind of work in the bargaining agreement's jurisdiction without having an obligation to contribute to the plan.

The bill would also provide another special definition of withdrawal, under certain circumstances, for employers in the trucking industry.

I will not go into the details of that, because they are fully set forth in the bill and in the general description of the bill which is contained in detail in the RECORD of Thursday last, July 24. I invite Members, in the interest of their constituents, and to advise their constituents effectively, to acquaint themselves with these details.

S. 1076 also imposes liability for an employer's partial withdrawal from a plan in two circumstances. The first is where, as a result of a decline in an employer's covered operations, the number of the employer's contribution base units has for 3 consecutive plan years declined by at least 70 percent from previous levels.

The second circumstance is where there is a partial cessation of the employer's contribution obligation. At the request of labor and management in the retail food industry, a stricter partial withdrawal rule with abatement protections is permitted for that industry.

To impose withdrawal liability in an equitable and feasible manner, the bill contains a number of "employer relief" provisions. To help small employers, the bill provides a mandatory de minimis rule under which a plan must provide that the employer's liability is reduced by a computed amount.

In addition, a discretionary de minimis rule permits a plan to provide for the reduction of employer liability by an amount larger than that required under the mandatory rule. The bill establishes certain objective criteria for permitting an employer who engages in a bona fide, arm's-length sale of assets to an unrelated party to be relieved of his liability.

In order to encourage new employers to join multiemployer plans, a "free look" rule is provided under which a new employer who does not contribute for more than 6 consecutive plan years may leave a plan without incurring liability when several conditions are satisfied.

The bill imposes a periodic payment cap on the amount of withdrawal liability of 20 annual payments of an amount determined on the basis of the employer's contributions over the 5 years preceding the withdrawal. Additionally, liability limitations are provided as follows: First, the liability of an insolvent employer undergoing liquidation or dissolution would be limited to the sum of 50 percent of the liability plus that portion of 50 percent of the liability which does not exceed the liquidation or dissolution value; second, the liability of an individual (sole proprietor or partner) would not reach personal assets exempt under bankruptcy law; and third, where all or substantially all of an employer's assets are transferred in a bona fide sale in an arm's-length transaction to an unrelated party, the liability would not exceed, where the liquidation or dissolution value of the employer does not exceed $2 million, the greater of first, 30 percent of the liquidation or dissolution value or second, the liability attributable to the employer's employees.

For sales in which the liquidation value exceeds $2 million, the 30-percent limitation would be incrementally increased as in a tax table so that it would reach 80 percent for a liquidation value exceeding $10 million. Any dispute over an employer's withdrawal liability must be resolved through arbitration.

The bill provides for two types of withdrawal liability—related funds in which a multiemployer may voluntarily participate. The first is a PBGC fund to reimburse plans for withdrawal liability that is uncollectible because an employer is involved in bankruptcy or insolvency proceedings. The second is a reinsurance fund which may be established by plan sponsors to relieve employers of portions of withdrawal liability that would have been paid by other employers had it not been forgiven, by the 20-year periodic payment cap, de minimus rule, and so forth, or which are unattributable, uncollectible, or attributable to the employer. The bill also permits the establishment of a third type of reinsurance fund in which employers in the construction industry may participate.

The effective date for the imposition of withdrawal liability is April 29, 1980. The committees decided in part to move up the date from February 27, 1979, the date contained in earlier versions of the bill, because the original purpose of a retroactive effective date—namely, to avoid encouragement of employer withdrawals while the bill was being considered—has been achieved. It should also be noted that the April 29 effective date is the product of strong political pressures by certain withdrawing employers who were caught by the earlier date. I realize that permitting these employers to avoid liability only increases the burdens of those employers remaining with the plans in question, but it appears necessary to accept the April 29 date in order to enact the bill before the August 1 deadline for action.

That somewhat increases the burdens of those employers who remain; but it appears necessary to accept this April 29, 1980, date in order to enact the bill before the August 1 deadline for action, which we now face; and it applies, of course, only within the particular multiemployer plans to which it relates.

The bill also contains provisions dealing with mergers and transfers of assets and liabilities as well as with plan partitions. In those cases where an employer withdrew from a multiemployer plan prior to the effective date of withdrawal liability, the PBGC would continue to have its partition authority under ERISA section 4063(d) and its authority to guarantee benefits under the terminated plan under the full ERISA section 4022 single-employer plan guarantee.

For multiemployer plans experiencing financial difficulty, the bill provides mandatory reorganization under which plans are required to meet a special faster funding requirement called the minimum contribution requirement (MCR). Employers who remain with a plan in reorganization are protected from too rapid increases in funding under the MCR through an overburden credit and a safe harbor provision. The overburden credit, which is applied to reduce a plan's accumulated funding deficiency, is available to plans with more retirees than active participants for a plan year. I am pleased to note that the permissive reduction of certain recently granted benefits by plans in reorganization has been deleted in the compromise bill.

If, despite reorganization, a plan becomes unable to meet benefit payments, those payments would have to be suspended until they are supportable by employer contributions and other plan assets. If such an insolvent plan is unable to pay benefits at the levels guaranteed under the bill, the PBGC would make up the difference through financial assistance insolvency insurance.

The level of guarantee provided by the bill has been a subject of much debate. The original administration proposal was to guarantee 100 percent of the first $5 of pension accrual per month per year of service and 60 percent of the next $15 per month per year of service. The original proposal at the March 24 Senate Labor Committee markup of S. 1076 was 100 percent of the first $5 and 75 percent of the next $15. The 75 percent figure would be reduced to 65 percent for those plans which did not meet certain minimal pre-ERISA funding requirements.

At the markup, I opposed both the administration and the committee proposals and offered an amendment to raise the guarantee to 100 percent of the first $5 and 85 percent of the next $15. The 85 percent would be reduced to 80 percent for those plans which did not meet certain nominal pre-ERISA funding requirements.

My efforts to raise the guarantee were supported by the American Association of Retired Persons, the United Food and Commercial Workers International Union, and the United Mine Workers of America. With the assistance of the Senator from Rhode Island (Mr. PELL) a compromise guarantee was approved which was 100 percent of the first $5 and 80 percent of the next $15, with certain modifications in meeting special situations.

For those plans not meeting the specific pre-ERISA funding requirements, the 80-percent figure would be reduced to 70 percent. As with all compromises I was not fully satisfied with the 80-70 percent figure we settled on, but it was better than the original proposal. Subsequently, in order to get a joint bill to the Senate floor, it was unfortunately necessary to reduce the guarantee to 100 percent of the first $5 and 75 percent/65 percent of the next $15. This guarantee reduction was ameliorated somewhat by the elimination of the permissive authority of plans in reorganization to eliminate certain accrued benefits.

Even though I believe that the bill's provisions on lower guarantee levels are too severe, I believe they are the best that are possible of agreement. I urge my Senate colleagues and affected workers and retirees to join in opposing proposals for guarantees lower than the Senate committee's guarantee level, as already approved by the House of Representatives.

I should add that the bill requires the PBGC to propose a feasible supplemental guarantee program for that portion of a participant's benefit that is not guaranteed because of the partial guarantee of the accrual rate in excess of $5.

In order to pay for the proposed termination insurance program, the bill would raise the present premium of 50 cents per participant per year to $2.60 over 9 years. The PBGC would be required to increase the premium automatically if it projects that for any year its assets are less than twice what it paid out in the preceding year. The PBGC would have discretion to accelerate the premium if the board of directors determines that increased premium income is necessary to provide assistance to plans which are receiving assistance and to plans the board finds are reasonably likely to require assistance.

The premium in S. 1076 is less than the premium permitted in the Senate Labor Committee bill which could have risen to $3.40 in the 10th year. Without actual experience under a mandatory program, it is not possible to say with assurance what the premium should be. I believe that the premium settled on in the joint bill is on the low side, but only experience will tell what the appropriate premium level should be.

The bill also contains a number of proposals based upon certain provisions of S. 209, the Williams-Javits ERISA Improvements Act of 1979. These proposals treat delinquent contributions, return of mistaken contributions, the preemption of the Hawaii prepaid health care law, and severance pay and supplemental retirement income arrangements. The bill also contains proposals on church plans and program oversight. As to the church pension plans, I might say that I am not too happy about those as it exempts also those who work for schools and similar institutions which are church-related but, nonetheless, if we want a bill there were some things we had to give and that was one of them and I was very unhappy with it.

S. 1076 represents years of hard work and debate by interested parties across the country and four committees of Congress. There may be areas where the legislation can be improved, but I believe that is the best that can be produced at this time. The question is when and in order to improve it in areas A and B would there be grave deficiencies created in areas C and D?

Multiemployer plan insurance protection in my judgment is a vital element of ERISA's basic objectives affecting over 8 million plan participants. The time has come while we still remain among the many diverse interests in balance to adopt these amendments and to enact them into law, and I am satisfied that it is best to do that to insure a pension guarantee program which provides mandatory benefit guarantees to the millions of workers who are affected.

Mr. President, that completes my statement.

II. House debate, August 25, 1980— Statements by Reps. Frank Thompson, Jr. (D-NJ) and John N. Erlenborn (R-Ill)

Mr. Thompson: Mr. Speaker, my amendment, in its broad outlines, does the following:

It deletes the crippling nongermane amendments. It restores certain House provisions of H.R. 3904. Some of these are essential to better protect the interests of retirees of our inflation ravaged society. Other provisions reflect compromises between the majority and minority members of both committees. Finally certain provisions inserted by the other body at the 11th hour, required technical changes to make them workable.

For example, we have worked with the Senator who offered the amendment on the Senate floor to modify an important provision to preserve 100 percent guarantees for benefits of current retirees and older workers nearing retirement, so that the provision does indeed provide the protection it was intended to give without bankrupting the PBGC.

As my distinguished colleague, the chairman of the Ways and Means Committee will explain in further detail, we have also amended the bill so that it protects workers who are receiving social security benefits and have been forced back into the labor market by the high cost of surviving in this economy.

Mr. Speaker, this legislation probably affects more individuals and more economic interests than any other piece of legislation we have considered. For that reason it reflects an extraordinary degree of compromise, a balancing of the competing economic interests of younger and older workers, corporations and unions, small businesses and larger businesses. My amendment preserves that balance.

I urge my colleagues support of the amendment.

Mr. Speaker, I would also like to take this time to further clarify the meaning of certain provisions of the bill, including those with respect to which some of my distinguished colleagues have had questions.

The withdrawal liability provisions of the bill are essential to the creation of a statutory structure that fosters plan stability and growth. That is a basic purpose of this legislation, because plan stability and growth are critical to protecting the interests of plan participants and beneficiaries, whose interests it is our primary intent to protect through the provisions of this bill.

Mr. Speaker, the bill provides that transactions undertaken to evade or avoid withdrawal liability may not be used as a method of escaping withdrawal liability that would otherwise be imposed. It is intended that the plan sponsor, the arbitrator, and the courts follow the substance rather than the form of such transactions in determining, assessing, and collecting withdrawal liability. This rule is to apply when evasion of liability is a principal purpose of a transaction, whether or not the transaction has other purposes as well. It is, of course, intended that the rules relating to the determination of withdrawal liability should be applied in a manner consistent with the controlled group concept.

Furthermore, we intend that the term "employer" be construed in a manner consistent with the bill and its purposes. We intend that employers not be able to evade or avoid withdrawal liability through changes in identity, form or control, or through transactions which are less than bona fide and arms length. Hence, for example, a building and construction industry employer—or for that matter any employer contributing to a plan—will not be able to evade withdrawal liability by going out of business and resuming business under a different identity.

A further example of our intention that, consistent with the purposes of the bill, the courts and arbitrators look behind mere form or labels is in the context of a labor dispute. An employer is not considered to have withdrawn solely because it suspends contributions during a labor dispute. A temporary suspension of contributions during a strike or lockout would not be a permanent cessation of an obligation to contribute within the meaning of section 4203. However, consistent with the purposes of the bill, if the facts and circumstances of a particular situation indicate that contributions have ceased permanently—for example, all employees covered under the plan have been permanently replaced or the facility has been closed—the fact that the cessation of any contribution obligation was precipitated by a labor dispute does not mean that no withdrawal has taken place.

We also wish to make it clear that the statutory imposition of withdrawal liability is not intended to restrict the parties' freedom to agree to additional or supplemental measures to protect a plan from the consequences of an employer's withdrawal. For example, a plan may agree to accept an employee group with past-service credit only if the employer of such group guarantees that the existing liabilities assumed by the plan will be fully funded even if the cost would be greater than the employer's statutory liability. Of course, employers can also agree by contract to waive limitations on their statutory withdrawal liability.

Moreover, a plan may adopt rules for terms and conditions not set forth in the bill relating to the satisfaction of an employer's withdrawal liability, provided that such rules are consistent with the bill and are not contrary to any regulations promulgated by the corporation. Plan rules adopted under this section might, for example, require the posting of adequate security, or set forth other rules to facilitate collection.

Section 4224(a) authorizes plans, acting under PBGC regulations, to provide an alternative method for payment of withdrawal liability. It is expected that plan trustees will need to make practical collection decisions which are consistent with their fiduciary duties and characteristic of a responsible creditor concerned with maximizing the total ultimate recovery at supportable costs. Thus, for example, where it is prudent and in the participants' interest, plan trustees may decide to settle a withdrawal liability dispute for less than the full amount claimed, to cooperate with an employer's other creditors in a contractual or court-supervised renegotiation of the employer's indebtedness, or even to forego the assessment of further collection of liability where it is apparent from the circumstances that the costs involved would exceed the amount likely to be recovered.

We also note that the prohibited transaction rules of ERISA—other than those relating to self-dealing—do not apply to any action required or permitted under the provisions of the bill relating to withdrawal liability. Thus, actions taken under the bill's withdrawal provisions are generally exempt from the proscriptions of ERISA section 406(a). However, plan fiduciaries continue to be subject to the general standards for fiduciary conduct set forth in other provisions of ERISA.

Section 4225 of the bill imposes specified limitations on withdrawal liability in certain circumstances. Generally, the existence of these circumstances is peculiarly within the knowledge of the withdrawing employer. It is therefore intended that, in the absence of clear showings by the withdrawing employer as to the applicability and extent of the limitations, a plan may assume that the limitations do not apply.

Because delinquencies of employers in making required contributions are also a serious problem for many multiemployer plans, we wish to make clear the public policy in this area, which this bill is intended to further. Failure of employers to make promised contributions in a timely fashion imposes a variety of costs on plans. While contributions remain unpaid, the plan loses the benefit of investment income that could have been earned if the past due amounts had been received and invested on time. Moreover, additional administrative costs are incurred in detecting and collecting delinquencies. Attorneys' fees and other legal costs arise in connection with collection efforts.

These costs detract from the ability of plans to formulate or meet funding standards and adversely affect the financial health of plans. Participants and beneficiaries of plans as well as employers who honor their obligation to contribute in a timely fashion bear the heavy cost of delinquencies in the form of lower benefits and higher contribution rates. Moreover, in the context of this legislation, uncollected delinquencies can add to the unfunded liability for all employers.

Recourse available under current law for collecting delinquent contributions is insufficient and unnecessarily cumbersome and costly. Some simple collection actions brought by plan trustees have been converted into lengthly, costly, and complex litigation concerning claims and defenses unrelated to the employer's promise and the plans' entitlement to the contributions. This should not be the case. Federal pension law must permit trustees of plans to recover delinquent contributions efficaciously, and without regard to issues which might arise under labor-management relations law—other than 29 U.S.C. 186. Sound national pension policy demands that employers who enter into agreements providing for pension contributions not be permitted to repudiate their pension promises.

In this regard we endorse judicial decisions such as *Lewis* v. *Benedict Coal Corp.*, 361 U.S. 459 (1960) ; *Lewis* v. *Mill Ridge Coals, Inc.*, 298 F.2d 552 (6th Cir., 1962) ; and *Huge* v. *Long Hauling Company, Inc.*, 590 F.2d 457 (3rd Cir., 1978). Cases such as *Western Washington Laborers-Employers Health and Security Trust Fund* v. *McDowell,* ___ F. Supp. ___, 103 LRRM 2219 (W.D. Wash., 1979) and *Washington Area Carpenters Welfare Fund, et al.* v. *Overhead Door Company*, C.A. No. 79-0097, USDC D.C., April 22, 1980, are considered to have been incorrectly decided and this legislation is intended to clarify the law in this respect by providing a direct, unambiguous ERISA cause of action to a plan against a delinquent employer.

These same principles apply to a plan's claim for employer withdrawal liability assessed in accordance with this legislature.

The public policy of this legislation to foster the preservation of the private multiemployer plan system necessitates that provision be made to discourage delinquencies and simplify delinquency collection. The bill imposes a Federal statutory duty to contribute on employers that are already obligated to make contributions to multiemployer plans. A plan sponsor that prevails in any action to collect delinquent contributions will be entitled to recover the delinquent contributions, court costs, attorney's fees, interest on the contributions owed and liquidated damages. The intent of this section is to promote the prompt payment of contributions and assist plans in recovering the costs incurred in connection with delinquencies.

It is intended that the specific provisions of this section concerning interest and liquidated damages are not limitations on the amounts otherwise set forth in collective bargaining agreements or plan documents; they constitute a minimum, not a maximum. For example, we understand that there are multiemployer plans which currently provide, in the event of employer contribution delinquency, for the payment of interest and liquidated damages which are in excess of the provisions of this section. Such practice will not be affected by the provisions of this section which directs a court to award unpaid contributions, interest, liquidated damages, reasonable attorney's fees, and costs as well as where the plan does not sufficiently address such items.

Under the provisions of the bill, in addition to any other consequences that flow from a default in paying withdrawal liability, a failure to make withdrawal liability payments within the time prescribed is to be treated in the same manner as a delinquent contribution to the plan. Thus, the court must award the plan not only the liability that is in default, plus interest, but also liquidated damages and attorneys' fees. Of course, the imposition of withdrawal liability does not, of itself, relieve an employer of any other liability it may owe a plan; that is, for breach of an obligation set forth in a collective bargaining agreement. The liability enforcement provisions do not affect a plan's recourse for satisfaction of such other debts.

The committees intend that the role of the arbitrator under this Act will be similar to that of a judge applying applicable law to the facts presented, and not a mediator attempting to reconcile competing interests. In arbitration proceedings under various labor laws, issues are often compromised, in part so as to avoid damaging ongoing relationships between management and labor. Unlike proceedings of that type, the proceeding contemplated by the committees is intended to resolve disputes, to the extent possible, in favor of one of the parties rather than in favor of compromise. It would be inappropriate, for example, for an arbitrator to reduce the plan's determination of an employer's withdrawal liability merely because compromise is a customary form of resolving disputes. Such a compromise could be made, in this context, only at the expense of the other employers participating in the plan.

My distinguished colleagues from New York and California, respectively, Representative WEISS and Representative CORMAN, have asked me to clarify the meaning of the provision defining withdrawal in an entertainment industry plan because it differs from the provision which originally passed the House. The rule was modified in the Senate so that it would be operative immediately upon enactment, and a special provision added with respect to application of the rule to the motion picture industry. Entertainment ventures are often temporary projects which offer employment only for the duration of a production that, by its nature, is not established as a permanent enterprise. Certain elements of the industry might suffer serious disruption if withdrawal liability were imposed, for example, when a Broadway show closes or a musical group concludes a limited engagement. Because such events are not likely to harm the affected plans, section 4201(b)(3) provides that, for employers that contribute to an entertainment industry plan for entertainment work that is performed primarily on a temporary or project-by-project basis, withdrawal occurs only if the employer's contribution obligation ceases with respect to that project, but the employer continues the same type of work in the plan's jurisdiction, or resumes such work within 5 years, without an obligation to contribute. In certain entertainment businesses, some of the employees work for an employer on a continuing basis—for example providing technical or craft services for successive projects—while other personnel are employed only for discrete projects. Where the employment covered under a particular entertainment industry plan is continuous rather than project based, the general withdrawal rule would apply. On the other hand, even though an entertainment industry employer's business is continuous, such as an advertising agency that produces television commercials, the special withdrawal rule would apply with respect to work performed on a project basis. Moreover, the special rule applies even though the project may be of an extended duration.

The purpose and scope of the rule has not changed even though the language was modified by the other body to make it operative immediately upon enactment. With the exception of the production of motion pictures, if a plan covers both stable employment and stable employers, the special withdrawal rule still applies to employment that is of a temporary or project-by-project nature covered under the same plan. This is obviously the case, since virtually all plans in the entertainment industry cover some stable employers, and the special rule would have no application at all if it did not cover project-by-project employment under such a plan.

With respect to the motion picture industry, however, it is expected that under the PBGC's regulations the entertainment industry exception in the bill will not apply to employers in a plan which covers stable employers in the motion picture industry. The joint Senate explanatory statement included in the CONGRESSIONAL RECORD does not correctly reflect this limitation on the exception, which applies only to the motion picture industry, as of course the language of the bill itself indicates. The purpose of the Senate amendment with respect to that industry is to ensure that the motion picture industry employers are not able to avoid all liability by reason of their mode of operations through multiple corporations, limited partnerships, and the like, so that employers do not unload their responsibilities onto the PBGC or other members of the industry in an unfair way.

In addition to the special definition of withdrawal for the entertainment industry, the bill provides a similar though not precisely the same definition of withdrawal for the building and construction industry. As has already been stated, this special rule is necessary because in both industries the cessation of an employer's operations covered under the plan or an employer's going out of business does not ordinarily have the same significance for the funding of the plan as in most other industries.

One of the principal characteristics of these industries which led to the development of the special definition is the limited duration of an employer's participation in the plan and the extreme fluctuations in the covered employment of a particular employer. Frequently, such an employer will enter into a plan's jurisdiction only long enough to complete the construction of one building or for the run of one Broadway play. Therefore, the intermittent entry and withdrawal from plans by those employers is the norm rather than the exception. It is also important to note that such short-term participation often results in an employer's leaving a greater amount of assets with the plan than liabilities because, for example, of the temporary employment increase in a plan's geographical jurisdiction. Moreover, even when an employer in one of these industries has a long-sustained attachment to a plan, its work is generally of a project-by-project nature and therefore subject to extremes of activity or inactivity. For example, a local building contractor may have a long attachment to a plan, but work consisting of a series of contracts, each of temporary duration.

The bill authorizes the PBGC to extend this special definition of withdrawal to similar industries if the characteristics that would make the use of such rules appropriate are clearly shown and such use would not pose a significant risk to the system. In exercising that authority, it is our intention that, in addition to considering the effects of withdrawals on the plan's contribution base, an important element in the corporation's analysis as to whether it will extend the special rules to a requesting industry will be the project-by-project or temporary nature of the employer's participation in the plan, and the existence or non-existence of a consistent pattern of entry and withdrawal by various employers.

The bill also contains a special withdrawal liability rule for certain trucking industry plans where substantially all of the contributions are made by employers primarily engaged in the long and short haul trucking industry, the household goods moving industry or the public warehousing industry. The phrase "substantially all" appears in several provisions of the tax laws—including the industrial development bond and the private foundation rules—where the Internal Revenue Service has interpreted the phrase to mean at least 85 percent. It is our intent that, as used in this special trucking industry withdrawal liability rule, the substantially all requirement would only be satisfied where at least 85 percent of the contributions to the plan are made by employers who are primarily engaged in the specified industries.

I would also like to clarify the meaning of one of the partial withdrawal liability tests—that described by proposed ERISA section 4205(b)(2)(A)(i) which is contained in section 104 of the bill—about which there may be some confusion. This provision describes a partial withdrawal in a case where the employer permanently ceases to have an obligation to contribute under one or more but fewer than all collective bargaining agreements under which the employer has been obligated to contribute to the plan but continues to perform the same type work under the collective bargaining agreement for which contributions were previously required or where the employer transfers the same type work to another geographical location. Examples of these two situations are where an employer bargains out of making contributions to a plan that the employer was previously required to make under a collective bargaining agreement that is otherwise in effect with respect to other requirements, or where an employer's collective bargaining obligation has ceased altogether but the employer continues to perform work of the same type which was previously covered by the agreement and for which contributions were required without the obligation to contribute to that plan, or where work that was undertaken at one geographic location for which contributions to a plan were made is transferred by the employer to another of his plants at a different geographic location where contributions to a plan for the work performed are not required.

It is important to emphasize and to understand that in no case do these rules impose liability on an employer for merely ceasing or terminating an operation; rather, they address only situations where work of the same type is continued by the employer but for which contributions to a plan which were required are no longer required.

The bill also provides a special partial withdrawal rule for the construction industry. Under the bill which originally passed the House, partial withdrawal occurs only where an employer continues its obligation to contribute for only a token amount of the work it does that is of the type and in the area that would otherwise be covered work. The Senate substitute contains a construction industry partial withdrawal rule which is essentially identical to the House rule but for the use of the term "insubstantial" in lieu of "token." The House accepts the Senate version of the rule which better reflects the purpose of the rule. Consistent with the special construction industry withdrawal rule, the construction industry partial withdrawal rule does not define a partial withdrawal in terms of a mere decline in covered work, but rather in terms of the performance by a contributing employer of work of the type that would be covered by the plan within the same geographic area of the collective bargaining agreement without obligation to contribute for such work. A partial withdrawal occurs only when an employer has substantially shifted its work mix in the jurisdiction so that only an insubstantial portion of such work in the jurisdiction is covered by the plan. For example, an employer would be deemed to have partially withdrawn if the number of contribution base units with respect to which the employer is required to contribute declines by 70 percent and such base units then constitute only 30 percent of the employer's work of the type in the jurisdiction. On the other hand, an employer who is required to contribute for all of its work of the type in the jurisdiction would not incur a partial withdrawal if the number of its contribution base units declines by 70 percent because it would still be contributing for 100 percent of its work of the type in the jurisdiction.

The bill contains a number of provisions intended to ease administrative burdens on plans. For example, the corporation is authorized to prescribe regulations setting forth permitted adjustments to denominators used in any fraction for allocating unfunded vested benefits, provided the adjustment would: First, be consistent with the purposes of title IV of ERISA; and second, be appropriate to ease administrative burdens of plan sponsors in making their calculations. It is intended that prior to issuance of such regulations, and in accordance with section 405 of the bill, plans may adopt reasonable rules consistent with the standards described above.

One of the alternative allocation methods involves attribution of the unfunded vested benefits earned through service with the withdrawn employer, plus a proportional share of liabilities that are not attributable to current contributors—the direct attribution method. In attributing unfunded vested benefits to a particular employer, secondary determinations will need to be resolved under plan rules. For example, although the original employers may still be contributing to the plan, complete records of service prior to establishment of the plan may not be available, and it thus may not be clear what preestablishment service is attributable to what employers. One way in which plan rules might resolve that problem would be to attribute preestablishment creditable time to employers in proportion to the attribution of the participants' service after the plan was set up. Plan rules will also be needed to clarify the attribution of creditable nonwork periods such as military service, and to define attribution where a participant has covered employment under the plan with more than one employer during a year. The corporation is authorized to issue regulations to prevent any abuse in this area.

The corporation is authorized to prescribe by regulation standard approaches for alternative methods for allocating unfunded vested benefits to employers. It is intended that the corporation shall prescribe regulations providing that any one of the alternative methods set forth in the bill for the allocation of unfunded vested benefits may be used by a plan which uses the direct attribution method in allocating unattributable liabilities to employers contributing under the plan. It is also intended that, consistent with section 405, prior to the issuance of such regulations, a plan which uses the direct attribution method may use any one of the bill's alternative methods for allocating unattributable benefits, provided that all employers are treated uniformly and use of such method by the plan is consistent with the purposes of title IV of ERISA.

The bill provides that a plan may use its own actuarial assumptions to value unfunded vested benefits for withdrawal liability purposes, or assumptions prescribed in PBGC regulations. The assumptions set forth in these regulations are expected to include assumptions appropriate for termination situations where, for example, the age at which participants are assumed to retire may differ from the retirement age assumed for continuing employees. It is intended that the regulations prescribe a set of assumptions that could be used when a plan adopts the attributable method of allocating unfunded vested benefits, as well as assumptions that may be used generally. Of course, the corporation's regulations may prescribe ranges of applicable assumptions, to enable plans to use a PBGC-prescribed approach adapted to the plans' own experience.

A plan that does not use PBGC assumptions must use assumptions that are reasonable in the aggregate. Under the bill's plan reorganization provisions, many plans will be computing the value of their unfunded vested benefits, subject to Treasury Department standards and oversight. Rather than performing a separate calculation, plans will be able to use those same figures for withdrawal liability purposes if the computation was satisfactory for purposes of the reorganization provisions. Similarly, it is intended that a plan be permitted to base its withdrawal liability determination on the value of vested benefits reported on the schedule B attached to the plan's annual report, provided the schedule B figure was computed appropriately.

Section 307 expands the information to be included in the annual report of the plan, pursuant to section 103(d) of the law. The plan's enrolled actuary, in the course of doing his valuation, may become aware of events and trends that may have a materially adverse impact on the plan. Moreover, the actuary may observe a trend but choose actuarial assumptions on the basis that the trend will not continue if it is reasonable to do so; for example, an assumption that recent declines in the plan's contribution base will not continue. So that interested persons may have fuller understanding of a plan's position and its possible future, section 307 would require the annual report to include disclosure on these aspects to the best of the actuary's knowledge.

I wish to respond to a question on indemnification of trustees of a withdrawal liability payment fund under section 4223 of the bill posed by my distinguished colleague, Mr. GIBBONS. If an employee or official of an employer contributing to a member fund, or an employee or official of a union which represents employees participating in a member fund, is selected as trustee of the withdrawal liability fund, it is intended that such trustee may receive the same sort of indemnity or indemnification insurance which the employer or the union could provide for this person were the person serving as a trustee of a multiemployer plan.

The bill reduces the level of benefits guaranteed participants in multiemployer plans because we have concluded that the present guarantee levels create an incentive to plan termination which in the long run is inimical to the interests of plan participants and beneficiaries. Because we believe that the withdrawal liability provisions of the bill may create resistance to benefit improvements, particularly for retirees, we believe it is necessary to provide flexibility for plans to adjust recent benefit increases to mitigate any chilling effect the bill will have on employer willingness to agree to such increases. Such flexibility is in the interests of plan participants and beneficiaries.

The bill makes clear that in the case of plans terminating or requiring financial assistance from PBGC after enactment, PBGC's guarantees will extend not only to nonforfeitable benefits provided under the terms of the plan, but also to those nonforfeitable benefits to which participants are entitled under the requirements of title I of ERISA. This will protect participants in those instances, which still exist, where a plan has never been amended to conform to the requirements of title I. Despite the failure to amend such plans, their participants have been entitled to the benefits mandated by title I since those requirements became applicable, and they should be protected by PBGC's guarantees just as if those provisions have been written into their plan on their effective date. PBGC's regulations may provide a practicable basis for determining guaranteed benefits in those cases where plans would have an option with respect to title I compliance—such as a choice among vesting schedules—but failed to adopt amendments exercising that option.

The bill sets two different guarantee levels—65 percent of the accrual rate in excess of $5 versus 75 percent of the accrual rate in excess of $5—application of which depends on the funding status of a plan before the funding standards of ERISA were imposed on the plan. It is intended that such test apply only to a plan which provided only pension benefits during the 10 year testing period described in the bill. Application of the test to a plan which provided both pension and welfare benefits would be inappropriate and it is intended that the higher guarantee level providing 75 percent of the accrual rate in excess of the first $5—but not in excess of $15—apply to such a plan.

The bill provides for a supplemental guarantee program. It is intended that the supplemental guarantee program offer several levels of additional, optional guarantees. It is intended that the supplemental program offer one level of additional guarantees that, in conjunction with the statutory guarantees, would make the benefit guarantees in a participating multiemployer plan equivalent to the statutory guarantees for single employer plans. In addition, the supplemental guarantee program should offer at least one alternative level of additional guarantees, providing, for example, a 90-percent guarantee for yearly benefit accruals in excess of $5.

In determining the accrual rate for purposes of calculating guarantee levels, the accrual rate is determined by dividing the participant's (or beneficiary's) benefit that is: First, described in section 4022A(a); second, eligible for the corporation's guarantee under section 4022A(b); third, no greater than the monthly benefit payable under the plan at normal retirement age in life annuity form; and fourth, determined without regard to any reduction under Code section 411(a)(3)(E), by the number of years and fractional years of service credited to the participant under the plan for benefit accrual purposes, including credited preplan service, whether or not it has been disregarded under Code section 411(a)(3)(E).

Of course, the corporation may interpret these terms in a manner suitable to particular situations. For example, when a plan gives benefit credit for no more than a maximum number of years, only the years credited by the plan should be treated as years of participation for this purpose.

Although this bill has added important new responsibilities for plan trustees, particularly under the reorganization provisions, this legislation simply reaffirms the present law, that these plan trustees as fiduciaries have sole responsibility to the participants and beneficiaries of the plan. A recent Court of Appeals decision, Amax Coal Company against NLRB which was wrongly decided apparently suggests that the trustees are collective bargaining agents for the parties who appoint them. That is an erroneous interpretation of both ERISA and federal labor law and does not reflect congressional intent.

The bill changes the definition of a multiemployer plan by deleting the test relating to proportionate employer contributions and the test relating to continuity of benefits in the event of a cessation of employer contributions. Under the new definition some plans will be considered multiemployer plans that previously would not have been defined as such. My distinguished colleague from New York, Representative PEYSER, has asked that I clarify that this change is not intended to have a retroactive impact on a plan that prior to this legislation paid single employer premiums to PBGC and did not qualify as a multiemployer plan despite the fact that more than one employer made contributions, because they authorized the reduction of benefits as to those employees whose employer ceased participation in the plan. The impact of this change in the definition of a multiemployer plan is intended to be prospective only.

Since ERISA, we have had time to examine the multiemployer plan universe more closely and now feel that

SELECTED STATEMENTS ON MPPAA

broadening the scope of the definition of a multiemployer plan will result in greater consistency. It is clear, however, that this change is not intended to have any retroactive effect.

With respect to the termination of a plan under section 4041A(a)(1), I want to make it clear that, except as provided in section 412(c)(8) of the Internal Revenue Code of 1954, as amended, an amendment terminating a multiemployer plan under this paragraph may not retroactively deprive participants of service credit earned prior to adoption of such an amendment.

Mr. Speaker, it has been brought to our attention that with respect to a large multiemployer plan covering the coal mining industry, agreements have been effective among the plan, the employers, and the union since December 1977, to transfer assets and liabilities to single employer plans established by certain employers who formerly were obligated to contribute to the multiemployer plan. In some instances the actual physical transfer of assets has not yet been accomplished, pending IRS approval. It is not our intention that the transfer of assets provisions of the bill apply retroactively to those transactions, which were legally consummated before the effective date of the bill.

Finally, the distinguished gentleman from Texas, Representative FROST, has asked me to clarify the effect of ERISA's preemption provision on a state law requiring that health insurance contracts written in that state must provide covered persons the option to choose the specialist of their choice or must provide that the services of a particular specialist must be covered by the insurance contract if that patient chooses to go to that specialist. It is clear that ERISA does not preempt such a law, which does not require that particular benefits be provided and therefore does not cause any cost-creating State law conflicts that preemption was intended to prevent. For example, a State law requiring that podiatrist or optometrist services be covered by health insurance contracts if a person chooses to have a particular service performed by a podiatrist or an optometrist, is not preempted.

Mr. Speaker, I respectfully urge my colleagues to support this amendment.

* * *

Mr. Speaker, I yield, for debate purposes only, 15 minutes to the gentleman from Illinois (Mr. ERLENBORN).

(Mr. ERLENBORN asked and was given permission to revise and extend his remarks.)

Mr. Erlenborn: Mr. Speaker, I thank the gentleman from New Jersey (Mr. Thompson) for yielding this time to me.

Mr. Speaker, today we consider H.R. 3904 and write what is, hopefully, the last chapter in the continuing saga of this Multiemployer Pension Plan Amendments Act of 1980.

Before I explain some of the provisions of H.R. 3904 in more detail, I would like for the following points to be clearly understood.

The multiemployer bill has been caught up in jurisdictional and parliamentary maneuvers for too long and must now be enacted without further delay. I do want the record to show, however, my support for the three nongermane amendments added by the Senate—that is, the Boren OSHA amendment, the Wallop MSHA amendment, and the Schweiker EEO-affirmative action amendment. I would have preferred that the House disagree with the Senate amendments and request a conference. The rejection by the Rules Committee of this option and the adoption of a closed rule represents an undesirable end run around the regular procedures of this body. At the very least the House should have been afforded an opportunity to vote on each of the three nongermane amendments.

Second, I would like to point out that the legislative game of chicken which the Senate has forced this body into has placed the entire multiemployer program in a state of jeopardy. Present law went into effect on August 1 with respect to mandatory termination insurance coverage for multiemployer plans as a result of the objection to a further extension of the effective date by those in this body who have led the opposition to the Senate nongermane amendments.

If even one plan of major dimension, say with $200 to $500 million in funded liabilities, were to utilize this window period to take advantage of the higher benefit guarantees and lower employer liability provisions under present law, then premiums would have to skyrocket from the current level of $0.50 per participant per year to $10 or $20 or more. This development would split the current business-labor coalition in support of H.R. 3904 into a million pieces. For this reason, I urge the House to adopt this legislation today. For the same reason, I urge the Senate to accept the bill as amended and send it to the President for his signature. This is not a matter that can wait another few weeks or even a few days, but should be disposed of by the Congress promptly.

Third, I would like to state my general support of the amendments made to H.R. 3904 by the manager of the legislation, Mr. THOMPSON. I support the amendments and the bill in hopes that the program will be successful in continuing the private pension coverage for the 7 to 8 million working men and women who now participate in multiemployer plans. The continued coverage of such persons and their eligibility for future pensions must be assured, if we are to place an increasing reliance on private pensions to help relieve the strains of our overburdened social security system. I will be candid in stating, however, that I will have to reassess my support for this legislation, if the Senate does not accept the bill we pass today but proceeds to further liberalize the more tightly drawn House provisions which better insure the self-financing nature of the program.

With regard to the concept of termination insurance and H.R. 3904 as a whole, I must concede to holding to my earlier reservations when plan termination insurance was first proposed under ERISA. The plan termination insurance provisions under present law, and to a lesser degree the provisions of H.R. 3904, infringe on the freedom of the collective bargaining process to permit the balancing of benefits and contribution income.

To elaborate, under a multiemployer plan before ERISA an employer's legal obligation was limited to making contributions to the plan at a negotiated rate set forth in the collective-bargaining agreement maintaining the plan. Benefits were then set by the joint board of trustees based on the expected level of contributions and plan investment income. Benefits could be adjusted up or down to meet the financial circumstances of the plan. In other words, such plans did not operate as defined benefit plans which fix only benefits, but they operated as defined contribution plans which fix contribution rates and adjust the benefit levels as necessary. ERISA changed all that by asserting that such plans be treated as defined benefit plans, by removing the ability of such plans to adjust benefits downward, and by making employers liable for plan benefits rather than just their negotiated contributions.

This decision by the Congress to upset the legal structure of multiemployer plans by calling them "defined benefit plans" was upheld in 1978 by the 9th circuit court decision Connolly against PBGC. I take no particular satisfaction in relating that the PBGC used the arguments I made in the 1974 House debate in opposition to termination insurance in order to persuade the court that Congress did indeed intend to force multiemployer plans into the defined benefit mold.

Before title IV of ERISA was thrust upon multiemployer plans, there was little or no evidence of pension losses which would warrant the complex and intrusive regulatory scheme we see created in H.R. 3904. Unfortunately, we failed in 1974 to heed two important principles expressed in what we might call Murphy's maxim and Luce's law. If you recall, Murphy's maxim states that "if it ain't broke, don't fix it," and Luce's law reminds us that "no good deed goes unpunished."

Now that H.R. 3904 is about to "fix" multiemployer plans by subjecting them to the monstrosity of multiple agency administration and regulation, we in the Congress ought to remain vigilant in our oversight function to minimize regulatory problems and to fine-tune the law where necessary. The bill could have been better balanced and made more affordable. In committee and in the previous consideration of H.R. 3904 in the House, I suggested several amendments which would help keep H.R. 3904 from becoming just another reflection of "Billings' law" which states: "Live within your income, even if you have to borrow to do so."

I restate these recommendations at this point in order to emphasize their usefulness in the event future program experience dictates their adoption.

First, the bill recognizes the need to strengthen the funding of multiemployer plans and requires 30-year rather than 40-year amortization of unfunded liabilities. I believe it necessary that we further shorten the funding period to 20 years with respect to future increases in past service liabilities for both single and multiemployer plans. One need only look at the $1 billion plus unfunded liability of the Chrysler Corp. plans—which have been historically funded over 30 years—and realize that 30-year funding is inadequate, if the termination insurance system is to survive in the event a major plan collapses. In the long run, adequate funding is the only answer to reducing the risk and exposure of the termination insurance system.

Second, gratuitous past service benefits for active participants which are related to years of service with an employer before the employer joined with a multiemployer plan should be excluded from the benefit guarantee. These benefits can create large unfunded liabilities and actually precipitate a plan's decline into insolvency. At a minimum, in order to prevent abuse, such gratuitous past service benefits should not be guaranteed for plans in reorganization or nearing insolvency. A modification of this rule would be to exclude the guarantee of such benefits only for groups entering a plan in the future.

Third, for benefits payable before age 65 the guarantee should be adjusted by some percentage of an actuarial reduction factor; for example, 3 percent per year. We should not be encouraging overly generous subsidized early retirement benefits by insuring them at the same level as for age 65 normal retirement. It should be noted that both the single employer plan guarantee program and social security adjust benefit levels below age 65.

Fourth, the guarantee of future increases in pre-ERISA accrued benefits should be scaled-back; for example, by grading in the guarantee of such benefits over 10 years. This would encourage plans to fund for any future benefit increases they wish to make which are related to pre-ERISA service.

These adjustments to the benefit guarantees that I have suggested are necessary lest we create the very chaos and scramble to the exit for PBGC handouts that this legislation purports to avoid. However, I am still somewhat wary that the bill may not create enough disincentive for plans to terminate where employers withdraw en masse and avoid further obligation through changes in corporate or other business structure. The incentive ought to be for employers to stick with the plan and to fund all of the employees' vested accrued benefits rather than have them cut back to guaranteed levels. Therefore, the following suggestions are given to reduce or even eliminate the future chance of plan termination:

Fifth, benefit guarantees related only to mass withdrawal plan terminations should contain higher coinsurance factors. For example, monthly benefit guarantees ought to be 90 or 95 percent, rather than 100 percent, of the first $5 times years of service, plus 50 percent, rather than 60 to 70 percent, of the next $15 times years of service. The level of these guarantees should be put in the perspective of the individual's total retirement income including social security. Consider the case of a 30-year career employee retiring at age 65 at a low level of earned income, say the minimum wage. Social security plus a $5 times years of service monthly pension—$150 per month—provides 98 percent of the employee's preretirement net after tax income. By insuring 95 percent rather than 100 percent of the first $5 times years of service pension, the employee's combined social security and pension income still replaces 96.5 percent rather than 98 percent of preretirement net income. Surely such reduced guarantee levels are modest, especially when considering they may make the triggering of mass withdrawal terminations and subsequent benefit reductions unlikely.

Sixth, mass withdrawal terminations would also be made less attractive if the unions and employers could not turn around, right after a termination, and establish a new tax qualified pension plan—and perhaps even give past service credit for guaranteed and/or nonguaranteed benefit. I take note that the bill H.R. 12335 which was introduced in the 95th Congress addressed this issue in part. It is possible that with the introduction of this one provision, all mass withdrawal terminations might be avoided.

The above suggestions were offered to improve the structure of the title IV program so as to avoid making financing from general revenues inevitable. A number of the amendments offered by the manager of H.R. 3904, Mr. THOMPSON, can also be characterized as strengthening the stated policy of the bill "to provide a financially self-sufficient program for the guarantee of employee benefits under multiemployer plans."

The first amendment to the Senate passed bill fitting this description is the provision—section 4022A(f)—to permit the program to better balance premium costs and guarantee levels in the event premiums prove less than adequate or more than adequate to finance the initial guarantee levels. The second amendment adding section 4244A restores the meaning of the concept of plan reorganization as initially suggested by the PGBC by permitting troubled plans to better balance benefits and expected contributions. A third provision amending section 4022A(g) restores the House-passed rule requiring plans to have a 15- to 1-ratio of plan assets to annual benefit payments before they are eligible for the supplemental program; the PBGC may modify this requirement but only in the extreme case where a soundly funded plan is likely to achieve a 15- to 1-ratio at a later date, or where the 15- to 1-ratio is not indicative of sound funding or a small probability of termination or insolvency.

Several other provisions of the bill need elucidation due to their esoteric actuarial import. The addition of the phrase "at the election of the plan sponsor" to section 4241(b)(4)(A)(i)(II) is intended to continue to require the plan to use the latest actuarial valuation up to the adjustment date but to permit the use of an actuarial valuation at a date later than the adjustment date only "at the election of the plan sponsor."

One other actuarial concept, that of "unfunded vested benefits," needs clarifications as it relates to the determination of employer withdrawal liability and the minimum contribution requirement. In H.R. 3904, "unfunded vested benefits" is defined as the excess of the value of nonforfeitable benefits under a plan, as defined under title IV, over the value of the assets of the plan.

Generally it is expected that the actuarial assumptions and methods employed in the calculation of the value of nonforfeitable benefits will follow the practice illustrated in interpretation 1 of the recommendation A(6) found on pages 369-371 of the 1979 Yearbook of the American Academy of Actuaries. It is also expected that such values will be included on schedule B of the ERISA annual report form 5500—relating to the items, present value of vested benefits.

In conclusion, Mr. Speaker, I suggest we adopt as a motto for H.R. 3904 the statement attributed to Macaulay that, "the smallest actual good is better than the most magnificent promise of impossibilities."

**III. Senate debate, August 26, 1980—
Statements by Sens. Harrison A.
Williams, Jr. (D-NJ) and
Jacob K. Javits (R-NY)**

Mr. Williams: Mr. President, last month we amended and approved, by a vote of 85 to 1, H.R. 3904, the Multiemployer Pension Plan Amendments Act of 1980. However, over objections by Senator JAVITS, myself, and others, the Senate included amendments to such unrelated laws as the Occupational Safety and Health Act, the Mine Safety and Health Act, and the Civil Rights Act of 1964. Earlier this week, the House of Representatives deleted these nongermane amendments, made several germane changes, and passed the bill, as amended, for a second time. The Senate must now pass on the most recent House version of the bill.

Our decisions today will likely determine the fate of this legislation. So I ask my colleagues to weigh its merits carefully. I ask that this great institution not deny 8 million Americans, working and retired, the protections that this bill affords.

Four committees of the Congress have considered this legislation, and four have approved it. Both business and labor have scrutinized its every word, and both support it. Uniformly, those groups who would be affected by this measure, those who would be protected by it, and those who must pay for it, support its enactment.

We have worked for 2 years, and drawn on 6 years of practical experience, in fashioning this legislation. We have assured sounder funding of multiemployer plans. We have more equitably allocated the burden of paying for pension benefits in these plans. And we have, most importantly, provided substantial benefit protection for the 8 million workers covered by these plans.

Mr. President, it is time to act. On August 1, a law which everyone agrees is unfair, unworkable and potentially enormously expensive, took effect because the Senate added nongermane amendments that paralyzed the House in its deliberations on this matter.

Only now—a month later—has a fragile compromise been struck in the House that allows us one more opportunity to enact this legislation.

We should delay no more. I ask my colleagues not to again ensnare this legislation in a tangle of unrelated matters.

It is clear that the House feels that substantive and fundamental changes to essential worker protection programs such as the mine safety and health program, and our Nation's equal employment opportunity programs should not be made in an ill-considered manner, in connection with pension legislation.

I believe that there is wisdom in the action which has been taken by the House, and I believe that in view of the necessity of enacting this pension legislation, the Senate should accede to that action.

The effects of those nongermane amendments are, as we are coming to understand them, profound. For example, the amendment offered by the Senator from Oklahoma, relating to the Occupational Safety and Health Act, would exempt 2.4 million workplaces from safety inspections under OSHA.

These workplaces employ 9 million workers. This was not a mere codification of the existing appropriation rider. The current appropriation rider exempts 800,000 fewer workplaces, and denies protection to 3.8 million fewer workers than does the amendment of the Senator from Oklahoma.

I believe, as I have always believed, that such profound changes in statutory programs should be adopted by the Congress only after thorough study by the legislative committee. It is only as a result of such study that we can fully appreciate the effects of our actions. The House of Representatives apparently shares that belief, and it would not accept this amendment. I would urge my colleagues to accept the wisdom of the House's position.

The same can be said for the amendment offered by the Senator from Wyoming, as modified by the Senators from Georgia and Florida.

That amendment would transfer from the jurisdiction of the Mine Safety and Health Administration the mines that so far this year are responsible for 66 percent of all the mining fatalities which did not occur in coal mines. And that amendment would transfer those mines to an agency which is truly unequipped to deal with the safety and health problems at those very hazardous operations. OSHA has no experience in mine safety, it has no standards, and it would no doubt take years for OSHA to develop applicable standards. It has limited resources, and could not devote enough of these resources to the hazardous mines.

The House of Representatives was just unwilling to agree to such dramatic changes to the programs of two Federal agencies without a clear understanding of the need and a clear idea of what the effects of this change would be on workers.

With respect to both of these amendments, I certainly do not believe that by agreeing to the House's refusal to accept these amendments, we are saying that that is the end of the matter. It is not. These are clearly matters for continuing scrutiny by both the Senate and the House of Representatives.

But by agreeing now to the House's refusal to accept these nongermane amendments, we are rededicating ourselves to the careful and thoughtful examination of important programs through the proper legislative procedure. We are rededicating ourselves to the proposition that the Congress of the United States will not rush to ill-considered conclusions.

In addition to striking these nongermane amendments, the House made several changes in the pension provisions of the bill. Although I, of course, much preferred the Senate bill in these areas, I am prepared to accept most of the changes that have been made by the House.

I would like to summarize these changes briefly for my colleagues:

First. The Senate version of the bill provided that the Hawaii prepaid health care law would not be preempted by section 514(a) of the Employee Retirement Income Security Act of 1974. It also required the Secretary of Labor to conduct a study of the feasibility of extending this exemption to other State health care laws.

The House deleted this provision.

Second. The Senate version of the bill did not allow the benefit guarantee level to be reduced except by Congress.

The House has amended this provision so that, if premiums prove inadequate to support the guarantee level, the guarantee level will decrease automatically to the point at which it can be supported by premiums. In sum, the House version does not require the Congress to act in order for guarantees to be decreased.

Third. The House added to the Senate bill a provision that was in the earlier House version. This provision would authorize the trustees of a multiemployer plan that is in serious financial difficulty to reduce or eliminate benefit increases that have been in effect for less than 5 years.

The Senate version of the bill did not grant plan trustees this authority.

Fourth. The Senate bill provided for compulsory arbitration of disputes over an employer's withdrawal liability. The plan was to have met its burden of proof in the arbitration with respect to the plan's unfunded vested benefits if certain standards were satisfied, and the arbitrator's findings of fact were to be presumed correct—subject to rebuttal—in any subsequent court proceeding.

The House amended this provision to provide that any plan determination would be rebuttably presumed to be correct in any proceeding—whether before an arbitrator or a court.

Fifth. Both the Senate and House versions of the bill allow an employer that withdraws from a multiemployer plan to pay withdrawal liability in annual installments in accordance with a payment schedule determined by the plan. Under the Senate bill, the amount of an employer's annual payment was based on the employer's highest contribution base units and rates in 2 of the previous 5 years.

The House changed the manner in which the two amounts are determined. The House bill focuses on the 3 plan years in the last 10 during which the employer's contribution base units and rates were greatest.

Sixth. Both the Senate and the House versions of the bill direct the PBGC to establish by regulation a supplemental guarantee program for multiemployer plans. This program will insure benefits that exceed the guarantee levels established in the bills.

As passed by the Senate, H.R. 3904 provided that the PBGC would establish terms and conditions that a plan must satisfy in order to qualify for supplemental coverage. The House added specific requirements for coverage, including a requirement that, generally, a plan's assets equal or exceed 15 times the plan's annual benefit payments.

Seventh. Both the Senate and the House bills contain a "safe harbor" funding provision for plans in reorganization. This safe harbor has the effect of limiting the increase in required employer contributions for plans in reorganization.

Under the Senate bill, a plan in reorganization could increase benefits for either past or future service and still get the benefit of the safe harbor rule; but employers would be required to contribute amounts necessary to fund the normal cost of the increase.

The House amendment provides that if a plan in reorganization increases benefits for past service, the employers lose the protection of the safe harbor rule.

Eighth. The Senate version of the bill authorized a special reinsurance fund for employers in the building and construction industry.

The House deleted this provision.

Ninth. The Senate version of the bill granted the General Accounting Office access to the records of plans, employers and unions on their study of the program.

The House bill limits access to plan records only.

Tenth. The House modified the Senate provision regarding unemployment compensation to assure that unemployment compensation is not reduced as a result of increases in social security or railroad retirement benefits, and made certain other changes in this area.

Eleventh. As approved by the Senate, H.R. 3904 provided that if a participant is retired or within 36 months of his normal date of retirement on July 29, 1980, the participant's benefit would be fully rather than partially, guaranteed.

Twelfth. As approved by the Senate, H.R. 3904 provided a mandatory de minimis deductible of the lesser of $100,000 or 0.75 percent of the plan's total unfunded vested benefits. The House reduced the dollar amount in this formula to $50,000.

Mr. President, the amendment that I have offered simply would strike the unemployment compensation pension-offset provisions adopted by the House and insert in their place the pension-offset provision adopted by the Senate as an amendment to the pending legislation on July 29.

The amendment would limit the pension offset to those persons who are receiving pension or retirement income from an employer for whom they worked during their unemployment compensation base period or an employer who is chargeable for unemployment compensation benefits under the State law.

The amendment also would authorize the States to limit the amount of the pension offset to take into account employee contributions to the pension or retirement plan from which they are receiving benefits.

Under the amendment, this change in the current requirements of law would apply to certifications of State unemployment compensation programs by the Secretary of Labor for 1981 and subsequent years.

Mr. President, the changes made by this amendment are not entirely satisfactory to me.

They do reduce the harmful effects of the unfair and punitive pension-offset requirement of current law. Fewer retirees will suffer the reduction of the unemployment benefits to which they have a right. Some will suffer smaller reductions in those benefits than under current law.

But the inequities are not eliminated— or even reduced to an acceptable minimum—by the provisions of this bill as it now stands. Many of those problems would be solved by the language that came over to us from the House earlier today—language that we find it necessary to remove for the time being so as not to endanger or further delay enactment of this urgently needed legislation in the midst of complex impediments posed by the

Congressional Budget Act and its procedures.

With the language in H.R. 3904 as we are now about to vote final passage, there remains the unacceptable discrimination against older workers whose retirement income derives from pensions or annuities. For these workers, unemployment benefits frequently will be reduced by some or all of the amount of their retirement benefits, but there is no such offset for those who have retired on the proceeds of regular savings, life insurance, real estate holdings, or investments in securities.

H.R. 3904 now provides that the States "may" take account of employee contributions to the pension fund, but it should flatly so require. To deny an involuntarily unemployed older worker full entitlement to unemployment compensation benefits, reducing them by the amount of the claimant's own contributions to a pension fund, is one of the inequities of current law that probably will remain in some States. The most glaring case in point involves individuals who were self-employed during their regular working years and established a Keogh plan retirement account entirely with their own funds. After retirement, and after being laid off from a job that may have been necessary for survival, they find that their own financial resources, saved over the years, are being used to reduce their unemployment benefits. This kind of treatment should be flatly prohibited, which the bill does not do.

Some unemployed workers still will have their unemployment benefits reduced, even if the employer who funded their pension is not the same employer who is charged for the unemployment benefits. In other cases, social security recipients will continue to lose unemployment benefits to the extent of half or somewhat less of their social security payments.

Mr. President, H.R. 3904 is one of the most important and urgently needed bills with which I have been involved in many years. Since we are operating under a severe time restriction for enactment of the ERISA provisions of this bill, I am constrained not to press further at this time for improvement of the pension-offset provisions in the bill, although they represent half or less of a loaf of relief for retired Americans who must work to survive.

I remain convinced, however, that the remaining inequities in the pension-offset as modified by this bill— and they are numerous—must be dealt with promptly. I also believe that outright repeal of the pension-offset provision is the only solution.

Therefore, I shall work diligently with Senator JAVITS and the other cosponsors of S. 3012, our bill to repeal this provision altogether, for its enactment at the earliest possible time. I would welcome the support of all Senators in this endeavor.

Let me repeat what I said earlier. I believe that, with respect to the ERISA provisions, the Senate bill was a better bill, that it afforded greater protection for participants and beneficiaries, and for employers as well. I especially dislike the House provision under which guarantee levels can be reduced without congressional action.

But, taken as a whole, the bill before us is a sound bill. It will greatly improve the lot of America's retirees. And, most importantly, I believe that the time has come for conciliation, and for action.

This unemployment offset amendment, Mr. President, was originally offered by the Senator from Rhode Island (Mr. CHAFEE) and the Senator from New Jersey (Mr. BRADLEY). My understanding is that it will be favorably received when this measure is returned to the House.

Mr. Javits: Mr. President, we come to the Senate floor today with H.R. 3904 as amended by the House of Representatives in response to the Senate amendments passed on July 29, 1980. Despite my opposition to certain changes made by the House, I am recommending to the Senate that it accept the latest House version and consider but two amendments.

As Senator WILLIAMS and I reported to the Senate on August 6, 1980, the failure of the House to respond to the Senate bill before August 1, 1980, resulted in ERISA's present termination insurance going into effect. While I know of no multiemployer plans which have terminated since August 1—in part, I believe, because of uncertainty about congressional intentions—a potentially dangerous situation persists.

There are at least five plans I know about for which it is economically advantageous to terminate under the present rules, particularly the 30 percent of net worth limitation on employer liability and the 100 percent guarantee of vested benefits. If these five plans with gross termination liabilities totaling $11 billion terminated, and we assume collection of employer liability similar to what the Pension Benefit Guaranty Corporation (PBGC) has experienced to date, the net liability which could be shifted to the PBGC by these five plans alone is $800 million.

In light of the present law, annual 50-cent premium per participant and the fact that the PBGC has already committed virtually all of its funds to plans covered during the discretionary period, the PBGC, even with its $100 million borrowing authority from the Treasury, would have insufficient resources to pay the potential guaranteed benefits under these plans.

The bill approved by the House makes the following changes in the Senate-passed bill:

The Wallop amendment which would transfer regulatory authority of stone, sand, and gravel, clay and phosphate surface mining from the Mine Safety and Health Administration to the Occupational Safety and Health Administration was deleted.

The Boren amendment which would grant a permanent blanket exemption for certain small businesses from the enforcement provisions of the Occupational Safety and Health Act was dropped.

The Schweiker amendment which would exempt Government contractors with five or fewer employees from the affirmative action requirements of any equal employment opportunity Executive order was dropped.

The Chafee-Bradley amendment which would, among other things, require the reduction of unemployment compensation benefits by the amount of a pension benefit only if the pension comes from the last employer, was expanded so that payments under either the Social Security Act or the Railroad Retirement Act cannot be used to reduce unemployment insurance benefits.

The Wallop amendment to expand the de minimis rule on employer withdrawal liability was dropped.

The Domenici amendment which would apply the present 100-percent guarantee to the benefits of the participants in multiemployer plans who were in pay status as of July 29, 1980 or who are within 3 years of normal retirement and are vested was made inapplicable to participation in plans that are terminated as a result of all employers withdrawing from the plan.

The Bentsen-Long amendment to facilitate a program by the South Bend Lathe Co. to pay lost pension benefits to its employees was left intact.

The Cranston amendment giving the PBGC regulatory authority to modify the motion picture element of the entertainment industry withdrawal liability rule was kept.

In addition, the House made the following changes to the ERISA bill:

The provision saving the Hawaii prepaid health care law from ERISA preemption was deleted.

A provision that benefit guarantees automatically be reduced if the Congress does not approve a PBGC request for increased premiums was added.

An amendment to require that a plan electing supplemental guarantee coverage meet a 15 to 1 assets to benefit ratio test was added.

A provision permitting a plan in reorganization to reduce or eliminate benefits not in effect for 5 years was added.

The provision requiring arbitration of disputes over withdrawal liability was dropped, and a requirement that a plan's withdrawal liability determinations be presumed correct was added.

The Senate safe harbor provision for funding under the minimum contribution requirement was replaced by a rule that if a plan in reorganization increases benefits for past service, the employers lose the protection of the safe harbor rule.

The Senate provision on the annual amount payable under the 20-year cap on withdrawal liability would be changed so that it would be computed in relation to the 3 years during which an employer's contribution base units were the highest out of the 10 years preceding a withdrawal.

The Senate provision authorizing a special insurance fund for employers in the building and construction industry was deleted even though certain related Tax Code provisions were maintained.

The Senate provision granting the General Accounting Office access to records of plans, employers, and unions for a GAO study of the insurance program was limited to plan records only.

Mr. President, I am pleased with the changes the House made dealing with unemployment insurance and the providing of a full guarantee for certain participants in or near pay status. The House's elimination of the unemployment insurance offset regarding social security and railroad retirement benefits is a significant step toward the full elimination of the retirement income offset as provided in my bill, S. 3012. Unfortunately, in order to get this bill through the Senate, it appears necessary to replace the House provision with the more limited, original Senate provision. I am also of the view that the House's delegation of the OSHA, MSHA, and affirmative action Senate amendments was desirable.

I am greatly troubled by the House changes which would disadvantage participants and beneficiaries of employee benefit plans. Among these, I would include the adding of the automatic guarantee reduction provision, the asset-benefit test for supplemental guarantee coverage, and the permissive authority of plans to eliminate certain recently guaranteed benefits. These provisions are a step backward from the policy of protecting plan participants and beneficiaries. Ordinarily, I would oppose these provisions and others in the House bill, but under the present time pressures for passage of this measure, I am willing to accept these changes in order to pass a bill today. The House's deletion of the Hawaii preemption exemption would also disadvantage participants and beneficiaries, and the Senate may wish to consider restoring the exemption provided in the original Senate bill for the limited situation.

I recommend to my colleagues that they vote for passage of the bill before us even though they may dislike certain aspects of what the House has done to the Senate bill. If we do not act today, the consequences in the months and years ahead may be most unfortunate.

EXCERPTS FROM THE JOINT EXPLANATORY STATEMENT OF THE COMMITTEE OF CONFERENCE ON ERTA

* * *

G. Corporate Rate Reduction and Other Business Provisions

* * *

37. Incentive stock options

House bill.—Under present law, the taxation of stock options granted by an employer to an employee as compensation is governed by section 83. The value of the option constitutes ordinary income to the employee when granted only if the option itself has a readily ascertainable fair market value at that time. If the option does not have a readily ascertainable value when granted, it does not constitute ordinary income at that time. Instead, when the option is exercised, the difference between the value of the stock at exercise and the option price constitutes ordinary income to the employee. Ordinary income on grant or on exercise of a stock option is treated as personal service income and, hence, generally is taxed at a maximum rate of 50 percent.

An employer who grants a stock option generally is allowed a business expense deduction equal to the amount includible in the employee's income in its corresponding taxable year (sec. 83(h)).

The bill reinstitutes "restricted stock options," under which there is no tax consequences when a restricted stock option is granted or when the option is exercised, and the employee is generally taxed at capital gains rates when the stock received on exercise of the option is sold. Similarly, no business expense deduction will be allowed to the employer with respect to a restricted stock option.

To receive restricted stock option treatment, the bill provides that the employee must not dispose of the stock within two years after the option is granted, and must hold the stock itself for at least one year. If all requirements other than these holding period rules are met, the tax will be imposed on sale of the stock, but gain will be treated as ordinary income rather than capital gain, and the employer will be allowed a deduction at that time.

In addition, at the time the option is exercised, the option holder must be an employee either of the company granting the option, a parent or subsidiary of that corporation, or a corporation (or parent or subsidiary of that corporation) which has assumed the option of another corporation as a result of a corporate reorganization, liquidation, etc., or must have been such an employee within three months of the date of exercise (twelve months if the employee is disabled (within the meaning of section 105(d))). This requirement and the holding period requirements are waived in the case of the death of the employee.

For an option to qualify as a "restricted stock option," terms of the option itself must meet the following conditions:

1. The option must by its terms be exercisable within ten years of the date it is granted.

2. The option price must equal or exceed 85 percent of the fair market value of the stock at the time the option is granted.

3. The option by its terms must be nontransferable other than at death and must be exercisable during the employee's lifetime only by the employee.

4. The employee must not, immediately before the option is granted, own stock representing more than ten percent of the voting power or value of all classes of stock of the employer corporation or its parent or subsidiary. However, the stock ownership limitation will be waived if the option price is at least 110 percent of the fair market value (at the time the option is granted) of the stock subject to the option and the option by its terms is not exercisable more than five years from the date it is granted.

5. In the case of a corporation whose stock is tradable on a stock exchange or any over-the-counter market, under the terms of the plan, the aggregate fair market value of the stock (determined at the time of grant of the option) for which any employee may be granted restricted stock options in any calendar year may not exceed $75,000. Only $150,000 of prior options can be exercised.

6. The option by its terms is not exercisable while there is outstanding any restricted stock option which was granted to the employee at an earlier time. For this purpose, an option which has not been exercised in full is outstanding for the period which under its initial terms it could have been exercised. Thus, the cancellation of an earlier option will not enable a subsequent option to be exercised any sooner. Also, for this purpose an option is considered to retain its original date of grant even if the terms of the option or the plan are later amended to qualify the option as a restricted stock option.

The bill provides that stock acquired on exercise of the option may be paid for with stock of the corporation (or its parent or subsidiary) granting the option.

The difference between the option price and the fair market value of the stock at the exercise of the option will not be an item of tax preference.

The bill will apply to options granted after May 21, 1976, and exercised after December 31, 1980. However, in the case of an option which was granted on or before January 1, 1981, and which was not a qualified option, the corporation granting the option may elect (within six months after enactment of the bill) to have the option not be treated as a restricted stock option.

In the case of an option granted after May 21, 1976, and outstanding on the date of enactment, the option terms (or the terms of the plan under which the option was granted) may be changed, to conform to the restricted stock option rules, within one year of the date of enactment of the bill, without the change giving rise to a new option requiring the setting of an option price based on a later valuation rate.

All such changes relate back to the time of granting the original option. For example, if the option price of a ten-year option granted in 1978 is increased during the one year after date of enactment to 85 percent (110 percent, if applicable) of the fair market value of the stock on the date the option was granted in 1978, the price requirement will be met. Likewise, if the term of an option held by a 10-percent shareholder is shortened to five years from the date the option was granted, the 10-percent stock ownership limitation will not apply.

Any restricted stock option must meet the requirements of new section 424(b) (5), limiting the amount of options which may be granted to an employee to $75,000 per year (determined at time of grant). In the case of options outstanding on date of enactment granted under a plan (or plans) providing for the granting of more than $75,000 of options per year, the employer may amend the plan to specify that only certain options under the plan (up to $75,000 granted per year) will be treated as restricted stock options.

Senate amendment.—The amendment provides for "incentive stock options," which will be taxed in a manner similar to the tax treatment previously applied to restricted and qualified stock options. That is, there will be no tax consequences when an incentive stock option is granted or when the option is exercised, and the employee will be taxed at capital gains rates when the stock received on exercise of the option is sold. Similarly, no business expense deduction will be allowed to the employer with respect to an incentive stock option.

The term "incentive stock option" means an option granted to an individual, for any reason connected with his or her employment, by the employer corporation or by a parent or subsidiary corporation of the employer corporation, to purchase stock of any of such corporations.

To receive incentive stock option treatment, the amendment provides that the employee must not dispose of the stock within two years after the option is granted, and must hold the stock itself for at least one year. If all requirements other than these holding period rules are met, the tax will be imposed on sale of the stock, but gain will be treated as ordinary income rather than capital gain, and the employer will be allowed a deduction at that time.

In addition, for the entire time from the date of granting the option until three months before the date of exercise, the option holder must be an employee either of the company granting the option, a parent or subsidiary of that corporation, or a corporation (or parent or subsidiary of that corporation) which has assumed the option of another corporation as a result of a corporate reorganization, liquidation, etc. This requirement and the holding period requirements are waived in the case of the death of the employee.

For an option to qualify as an "incentive stock option," terms of the option itself must meet the following conditions:

1. The option must be granted under a plan specifying the number of shares of stock to be issued and the employees or class of employees to receive the options. This plan must be approved by the stockholders of the corporation within 12 months before or after the plan is adopted.

2. The option must be granted within ten years of the date the plan is adopted or the date the plan is approved by the stockholders, whichever is earlier.

3. The option must by its terms be exercisable only within 20 years of the date it is granted.

4. The option price must equal or exceed the fair market value of the stock at the time the option is granted. This requirement will be deemed satisfied if there has been a good faith attempt to value the stock accurately, even if the option price is less than the stock value.

5. The option by its terms must be nontransferable other than at death and must be exercisable during the employee's lifetime only by the employee.

6. The employee must not, immediately before the option is granted, own stock representing more than ten percent of the voting power or value of all classes of stock of the employer corporation or its parent or subsidiary. However, the stock ownership limitation will be waived if the option price is at least 110 percent of the fair market value (at the time the option is granted) of the stock subject to the option and the option by its terms is not exercisable more than five years from the date it is granted.

7. The option by its terms is not to be exercisable while there is outstanding any incentive stock option which was granted to the employee at an earlier time. For this purpose, an option which has not been exercised in full is outstanding for the period which under its initial terms it could have been exercised. Thus, the cancellation of an earlier option will not enable a subsequent option to be exercised any sooner. Also, for this purpose an option is considered to retain its original date of grant even if the terms of the option or the plan are later amended to qualify the option as an incentive stock option.

The amendment provides that stock acquired on exercise of the option may be paid for with stock of the corporation granting the option.

The difference between the option price and the fair market value of the stock at the exercise of the option will not be an item of tax preference.

Also, under the amendment, any option which was a qualified stock option or restricted stock option under prior law will become an incentive stock option, if it was not exercised before January 1, 1981, and if it otherwise satisfies requirements for incentive stock options. Such an option will not be subject to the minimum tax.

An option will not be disqualified because of the inclusion of any condition not inconsistent with the qualification requirements, nor because the corporation may make a cash payment to the employee at the time of exercise.

The amendment generally applies to options exercised or granted after December 31, 1980, or outstanding on such date. However, in the case of an option which was granted on or before December 31, 1980, the corporation granting the option must elect to have the option treated as an incentive stock option. Only $50,000 of stock may be purchased with restricted options granted in any year prior to 1981, and only $250,000 of stock from such options could be purchased in the aggregate.

In the case of an option granted before 1982, the modification or deletion of any stock appreciation right or right to receive cash payments to permit the option to qualify as an incentive stock option can be made within one year of the enactment of the bill without the modification being treated as the grant of a new option.

In addition, the terms of a stock option plan or an option issued before 1982 can be modified to conform to the incentive stock option rules within one year of the date of enactment of the bill, without the modification being considered as giving rise to a new option requiring a new option price.

Conference agreement.—The agreement generally follows the Senate amendment except—
(1) the term of the option may not exceed 10 years from the date of grant,
(2) a disabled employee has 12 months after leaving employment to exercise the option,
(3) the amendment clarifies that additional cash or other property may be transferred to the employee at the time the option is exercised, so long as such property is subject to inclusion in income under the provisions of section 83,
(4) the managers wish to clarify that alternative rights may be granted, so long as no alternative options to purchase stock are granted which cause the option to violate the terms of section 422A(b), and
(5) in the case of options granted after 1980, the terms of the plan must limit the amount of aggregate fair market value of the stock (determined at the time of the grant of the option) for which any employee may be granted incentive stock options in any calendar year to not more than $100,000 plus the carryover amount. The carryover amount from any year is one-half of the amount by which $100,000 exceeds the value (at time of grant) of the stock for which incentive stock options were granted in such prior year. Amounts may be carried over 3 years. Options granted in any year use up the $100,000 current year limitation first and then the carryover from earliest year.

The agreement will apply to options granted after January 1, 1976, and exercised after December 31, 1980, or outstanding on such later date.

However, in the case of options granted before January 1, 1981, an option is an incentive stock option only if the employer elects such treatment for an option. The aggregate value (determined at time of grant) of stock for which any employee may be granted incentive stock options prior to 1981 shall not exceed $50,000 per calendar year and $200,000 in the aggregate.

In the case of an option granted after January 1, 1976, and outstanding on the date of enactment, the option terms (or the terms of the plan under which the option was granted or shareholder approval) may be changed, to conform to the incentive stock option rules, within one year of the date of enactment, without the change giving rise to a new option requiring the setting of an option price based on a later valuation date.

All such changes relate back to the time of granting the original option. For example, if the option price of a ten-year option granted in 1978 is increased during the one year after date of enactment to 100 percent (110 percent, if applicable) of the fair market value of the stock on the date the option was granted in 1978, the price requirement will be met. Likewise, if the term of an option held by a 10-percent shareholder is shortened to five years from the date the option was granted, the 10-percent stock ownership limitation will not apply.

* * *

H. Savings Incentives Provisions

40. Self-employed retirement savings (Keogh plans)

House bill.—The deduction limit for employer contributions to a defined contribution Keogh plan, to a defined contribution plan maintained by a subchapter S corporation, or to a simplified employee pension (SEP) is increased from $7,500 to $15,000. The 15-percent limit on contributions is not changed. To provide a similar increase in the level of benefits permitted under a defined benefit Keogh or subchapter S corporation plan, the compensation taken into account in determining permitted annual benefit accruals is increased from $50,000 to $100,000.

The bill also increases the amount of compensation which may be taken into account to determine contributions to a Keogh plan, to a subchapter S plan, or to a SEP. Under the bill, the includible compensation limit is increased from $100,000 to $200,000. However, if annual compensation in excess of $100,000 is taken into account, the rate of employer contributions for a plan participant who is a common-law employee cannot be less than the equivalent of 7½ percent of that participant's compensation.

The House bill also extends to all partners the present-law rule under which a loan from a Keogh plan to an owner-employee or his use of an interest in the plan as security for a loan is treated as a distribution.

In addition, the House bill permits (1) the penalty-free correction of an excess contribution to a Keogh plan if the excess is withdrawn before the return filing due date and (2) early withdrawals from a terminated Keogh plan by an owner-employee without regard to the 5-year ban on Keogh plan contributions for the owner-employee.

Senate amendment.—The Senate amendment generally follows the House bill except that it contains no provision relating to excess contributions to Keogh plans or distributions made on account of the termination of a Keogh plan.

Conference agreement.—The conference agreement follows the House bill.

41. Individual retirement accounts

House bill.—In the case of an individual who is not an active participant in an employer-sponsored plan, the annual contribution limit is raised from the lesser of $1,500 or 15 percent of compensation to the lesser of $2,000 or 100 percent of compensation. The limit for a spousal IRA is increased from $1,750 to $2,250, and the present-law requirement that contributions under a spousal IRA be equally divided between the spouses is deleted.

In the case of an employee who is an active participant in a plan, a deduction is allowed for contributions to an IRA or for voluntary contributions to the plan. The voluntary contributions and earnings thereon under a plan are subject to IRA-type rules, except that (1) distributions starting at age 70½ are not mandated and (2) rollovers may be made to an IRA with regard to the present law rule limiting rollovers to one per year.

Under the House bill, benefits under a qualified plan (including deductible employee contributions and earnings thereon) are taxed only when paid to the employee or a beneficiary and are not taxed if merely made available. Of course, as under present law, if benefits are paid with respect to an employee to a creditor of the employee, a child of the employee, etc., the benefits paid would be treated as if paid to the employee.

Under present law, individuals generally may self-direct IRA investments or investments under an account in a qualified plan. Under the House bill, amounts invested in collectibles (antiques, art, gems, stamps, etc.) under an IRA or a self-directed account in a qualified plan are treated as distributions for income tax purposes.

Under the House bill, the proceeds of a redeemed U.S. retirement bond which is distributed under a qualified bond purchase plan may be rolled over, tax-free, to an IRA. U.S. retirement bonds purchased for an employee may be redeemed only after the employee attains age 59½, dies or becomes disabled. Also, the bill clarifies the treatment of IRA retirement bonds acquired in a tax-free rollover.

Senate amendment.—The Senate amendment is generally the same as the House bill, except that (1) active plan participants are allowed a deduction for contributions to an IRA or for qualified voluntary contributions to a plan limited annually to the lesser of $1,500 ($1,625 for a spousal IRA) or 100 percent of compensation for the year, and (2) a surviving or divorced spouse may deduct at least $1,125 annually for life for contributions to a spousal IRA established by the individual's former spouse at least 5 years before the death or divorce.

In addition, the Senate amendment does not include provisions relating to investments in collectibles under IRAs or self-directed accounts in qualified plans or to rollovers of the redemption proceeds of U.S. retirement bonds. Also, voluntary contributions and earnings thereon are taxed only if paid, but other plan benefits are taxed if paid or made available.

The Senate amendment requires that Treasury provide the Congress (before June 30, 1982) a study of the tax incentives for individual retirement savings.

Conference agreement.—The conference agreement follows the House bill, except that a divorced spouse is allowed a deduction for contributions to a spousal IRA established by the individual's former spouse at least 5 years before the divorce if the former spouse contributed to the IRA under the spousal IRA rules for at least three of the five years preceding the divorce. If these requirements are met, the limit on the divorced spouse's IRA contributions for a year is not less than the lesser of (1) $1,125, or (2) the sum of the divorced spouse's compensation and alimony includible in gross income.

* * *

44. Employee stock ownership plans (ESOPs)

House bill.—No provision.

Senate amendment.—The Senate amendment accelerates the termination of the present law investment-based tax credit for ESOP contributions by one year, so that it expires at the end of 1982, and replaces it with a payroll-based tax credit. The payroll-based credit (which is not available if contributions allocated to officers, shareholders (more than 10 percent), and employees whose compensation exceeds $83,000 (adjusted for inflation) exceed specified limits) is limited to one-half of one percent of aggregate employee compensation in calendar year 1983, three-quarters of one-percent in 1984, and one percent in 1985 and subsequent years.

The amendment generally increases from 15 percent of aggregate employee compensation to 25 percent of such compensation the deduction allowed the employer for contributions to an ESOP where the contributions are applied by the plan to make principal payments on a loan incurred to purchase employer stock. An unlimited deduction is allowed the employer for contributions applied to pay interest on the loan.

The Senate amendment also provides that (1) contributions applied to pay loan interest, and (2) forfeitures of fully leveraged ESOP stock are disregarded for purposes of the present law limit on contributions to any participant's account (generally, for 1981, the lesser of $41,500 or 25 percent of compensation). This rule applies only if contributions allocated to officers, shareholders (more than 10 percent) and employees whose compensation exceeds $83,000, do not exceed specified limits.

Distributions from a tax credit ESOP which are made on account of the sale of corporate assets or the disposition of a subsidiary are permitted without regard to the present law rule which generally precludes distributions of employer securities for at least 84 months. The Senate amendment also changes the cash distribution and put-option rules to reflect certain State laws and corporate charter restrictions which prevent compliance with present law rules. In addition, the Senate amendment repeals (for all but tax credit ESOPs) the present law rule requiring that employees be entitled to direct voting of employer securities allocated under a defined contribution plan of a closely held corporation.

The non-tax rules of ERISA are also amended to supersede State securities laws to permit Continental Airlines to establish and maintain an ESOP, to issue previously authorized stock to an ESOP, to permit the company to guarantee a loan to the ESOP, and to permit the ESOP to distribute company stock to employees and beneficiaries.

Conference agreement.—The conference agreement generally follows the Senate amendment except that the new payroll-based tax credit for contributions to a tax credit ESOP is allowed only for wages paid in calendar years 1983 through 1987. The credit is limited for 1983 and 1984 to one-half of one percent of compensation paid to employees under the plan and to three-quarters of one percent of such compensation for 1985, 1986, and 1987. The tax credit expires on December 31, 1987.

In addition, the present-law rule requiring that an employee must be entitled to vote stock allocated to his account under a defined contribution plan is deleted with respect to profit-sharing plans for securities acquired after 1979, but is still applicable to all other defined contribution plans.

The conference agreement does not include the Senate provision which supersedes State securities laws with respect to Continental Airlines.

45. Dividend reinvestment plans

House bill.—Under present law (sec. 305(a)), a pro rata stock distribution is not taxable to a shareholder at the time he or she receives it, but it is taxable only when the taxpayer sells or otherwise disposes of the shares received as a distribution. Any gain on the sale generally is treated as a long-term capital gain if the underlying shares (on which the distribution was declared) were held for more than one year. Stock distributions which are not pro rata, including stock distributions received pursuant to a shareholder's option to receive either stock or cash, are taxable at fair market value when the shares are initially received.

Under the House bill, a domestic public utility corporation may establish a plan under which shareholders who choose to receive a dividend in the form of common stock rather than cash or other property may elect to exclude up to $1,500 per year ($3,000 in the case of a joint return) of the stock dividends from income.

To qualify, the stock must be newly issued common stock, designated by the board of directors of the corporation to qualify for this purpose. The number of shares to be distributed to any shareholder must be determined by reference to a value which is not less than 95 percent (and not more than 105 percent) of the stock's value during the period immediately before the distribution date.

Generally, stock will not qualify where the corporation has repurchased any of its stock within one year before or after the distribution date (or any member of the same affiliated group of corporations has purchased common stock of any other member of such group). However, if the corporation establishes a business purpose for the purchase not inconsistent with the purpose of the dividend reinvestment provision to aid in the raising of new capital, the purchase will not disqualify any dividend otherwise eligible for exclusion.

Stock received as a qualified dividend will have a zero basis, so that when the stock is later sold the full amount of the sales proceeds will be taxable. In general, proceeds from the sale of such stock will be taxed as capital gains. However, where the stock is sold within one year after distribution, any gain will be treated as ordinary income. In addition, if shares of stock of the distributing corporation are sold by the taxpayer any time after the record date for the dividend and before a date one year after the dividend distribution date, the sale will be treated as a sale of the qualified dividend stock. These rules are designed to prevent the immediate resale of stock without the recognition of ordinary income which would have resulted in the case of a taxable dividend.

Under the House bill, the earnings and profits of the distributing corporation will not be reduced by reason of the distribution of qualified stock, whether or not the shareholder elects to exclude the dividend from income.

Only individual shareholders are eligible for the exclusion. Corporations, trusts, estates, non-resident aliens, and persons holding at least 5 percent of the voting power or value of stock in the corporation (using the attribution rules of section 318) are not eligible to exclude any dividends under this provision.

A public utility is qualified if during the 10 years prior to its taxable year in which the dividend is paid, at least 60 percent of the cost of the depreciable property the corporation acquired for the members of an affiliated group (in which the public utility is a member) was public utility recovery property (within the meaning of new sec. 168A). For periods before 1981, the determination of whether property would have been public utility recovery property shall be made as if section 168A had been in effect.

Senate amendment.—No provision.

Conference agreement.—The conference agreement generally follows the House bill. The exclusion from income applies to dividends up to $750 a year ($1,500 on a joint return), and the exclusion will be allowed for dividends distributed in calendar years 1982 through 1985.

46. Qualified group legal services plans

House bill.—No provision.

Senate amendment.—Employer contributions to, and benefits provided under, a qualified group legal services plan are excluded from an employee's income. This income exclusion expires December 31, 1981.

Under the Senate amendment, the income exclusion for qualified group legal services plans is extended through December 31, 1984.

Conference agreement.—The conference agreement follows the Senate amendment.

* * *

K. Administrative Provisions

* * *

69. Penalty for failure to file information returns

House bill.—Present law requires taxpayers to file a variety of information returns with the Secretary. Generally, such returns relate to payments to, and transactions with, other persons. The penalty for failure to file most information returns is $1 per return, subject to a maximum of $1,000 for any calendar year (Code sec. 6652 (b)). Present law generally does not require a taxpayer who must file an information return to furnish a copy to the person to whom the payment relates. However, such a requirement is imposed as to some information returns (Code sec. 6678).

The bill generally requires that information returns be furnished to the person to whom the payments on the return relate.

The bill also increases the penalty for failure to file most information returns with the Secretary. The increased penalty is $10 for each return, subject to a maximum penalty of $25,000 for any calendar year. Because the obligation to furnish a statement and the requirement to file an information return are different obligations, a taxpayer could be subject to both the information and statement penalties.

The bill retains the $1 penalty of present law for failure to file information returns with respect to certain payments aggregating less than $10.

The provision is effective as to returns and statements required to be furnished after December 31, 1981.

Senate amendment.—No provision.

Conference agreement.—The conference agreement follows the House bill.

* * *

78. Railroad retirement taxes

House bill.—The House bill has the following provisions:

Tier II taxes.—Under present law (code section 3221), there is imposed on railroad employers a tax of 9.5 percent of compensation paid in a calendar month, subject to a maximum limitation. Currently, the annual taxable compensation base is $22,200; however, in no case does the tax apply to any amount paid in a month in excess of one-twelfth of the annual limitation ($1,850 in 1981). The annual (and monthly) limitation on taxable compensation for the purposes of section 3221 is indexed pursuant to section 230(c) and (d) of the Social Security Act. The rate of tax under section 3221 applies to employers only.

The House bill will, pursuant to a negotiated agreement between railway management and labor, provide for adjustments in the financing of the tier-II pension component. The tax on employers under section 3221 will be increased from 9.5 to 11.75 percent, an increase of 2.25 points. In addition, the provision will provide for a new tax of 2 percent on the compensation of employees (as defined in section 3221).

Advance transfers to the railroad retirement account.—Generally, under the railroad retirement and social security interchange, for a given fiscal year there is computed the amount of social security taxes that would have been collected if railroad employment had been covered directly by social security. This amount is netted against the amount of benefits social security would have paid to railroad beneficiaries based on railroad and nonrailroad earnings during that period. Where social security benefits that would have been paid exceed social security taxes that would have been due, the excess, plus an allowance for interest and administrative expenses, is transferred from the social security trust funds to the Railroad Retirement Account. The financial interchange amount for a given fiscal year is determined and transferred no later than June of the year following the close of the preceding fiscal year.

The House bill provides advanced, limited transfers to the Railroad Retirement Account from the general fund in amounts necessary to make monthly benefit payments. In no case will the amounts outstanding at any time for any fiscal year under this authority exceed the estimated interchange transfer for that fiscal year. The Board will pay the prevailing rate of interest currently being paid on short-term instruments of the Department of the Treasury on amounts transferred under this authority. The borrowing authority will be effective upon enactment.

Payments of employee taxes by railroad employers.—Under present law (code section 3221(e)(1)(iii)), payments made by railroad employers of railroad employee taxes under section 3211 without deduction from the remuneration of the employee are excluded from the definition of compensation for the purposes of the Railroad Retirement Tax Act (RRTA). Until 1981, a similar provision was included in the Federal Insurance Contributions Act (code section 3121(a)(6) and section 209(f) of the Social Security Act). The exclusion of such payment from the definition of wages for FICA tax and social security benefit computation purposes was eliminated by section 1141(a)(1) of Public Law 96-499, the Omnibus Reconciliation Act of 1980.

The House bill provides that payments by an employer of employee railroad payroll taxes, without deduction from the employee's remuneration, will be included in taxable compensation for RRTA purposes. This change will conform the provisions of the Railroad Retirement Tax Act to the corresponding provisions of the recently amended Federal Insurance Contributions Act. The changes made by this provision will be effective with respect to compensation paid for services rendered after September 30, 1981.

Definition of compensation.—Under present law, there is imposed on employers a tax on so much of compensation paid in any calendar month by such employer for services rendered by an employee. It is unclear whether the intent of the law is to tax compensation when paid or when earned. The House bill provides that compensation that is paid in one calendar month but that would be payable in a prior or subsequent taxable month but for the fact that the prescribed date of payment would fall on a Saturday, Sunday, or legal holiday will be deemed to have been paid in such prior or subsequent taxable month. The bill thus makes clear the treatment for RRTA purposes of compensation "bunched" in any month for services rendered in the preceding month.

The House bill also provides that, in the absence of evidence to the contrary (e.g., the statutory presumption curing "bunching" of compensation problems in certain months, as clarified by the immediately preceding provision), payments by railroad employers shall be presumed to be compensation for services rendered as an employee in the period for which the payment is made, an employee receiving retroactive wage payments (such as lump sum retroactive wage payments and crew consists payments) will be deemed under the provision to be compensation paid in the period for which the payment is made unless the employee requests in writing (pursuant to existing provisions in sec. 3231(e)(2)) that such compensation was earned in a period other than the period in which it was paid.

This provision generally applies to taxable years ending on or after the date of enactment. It also applies in taxable years ending before enactment for which the period for assessment, collection, or claim for credit or refund of taxes has not expired.

Senate amendment.—No provision.

Conference agreement.—The conference agreement follows the House bill with several modifications. The conference agreement does not include the House bill provision dealing with advance transfers to the railroad retirement account. Under the conference agreement, the provision that clarifies the definition of compensation is effective for taxable years beginning after December 31, 1981. It is the specific intent of the conferees that no inference be drawn from this clarification for taxable years beginning after 1981 as to Congressional intent with respect to prior legislation concerning the definition of compensation for the purposes of administrative or judicial proceedings.

L. Miscellaneous Provisions

* * *

80. Fringe benefit regulations

House bill.—Prior to June 1, 1981, the Treasury was prohibited from issuing final regulations, under Code section 61, relating to the income tax treatment of fringe benefits. The House bill extends this prohibition until May 31, 1983.

Senate amendment.—The Senate amendment is the same as the House bill except that the prohibition is extended until December 31, 1983.

Conference agreement.—The conference agreement follows the House bill and the Senate amendment, and extends the prohibition until December 31, 1983.

* * *

105. Separate report on social security trust funds

House bill.—No provision.

Senate amendment.—Reports on the receipts, outlays, surplus or deficit, and reserve balance of each of the 3 social security trust funds are included in the President's annual budget submission in January in a separate section of the budget. The information is brought up to date in sections within the context of the (July 15) mid-session budget review. In addition, the Board of Trustees publishes an annual report on the financial status of the trust funds and includes in the report its current estimates of the short-run and long-run actuarial balances of each trust fund.

The amendment requires the President, in the annual budget message and mid-session review, to include a separate statement which contains a summary of his requests for new budget authority, and estimates of outlays, revenues, and surplus or deficit of the Federal Old-Age and Survivors Insurance, Federal Disability Insurance, and Federal Hospital Insurance trust funds. The separate statement will show the revenues, outlays, and surplus or deficit estimates for the trust funds, will describe the economic assumptions that were used in making the estimates for the trust funds and the relationship to economic assumptions made for other parts of the budget, will indicate the financial prospects of the trust funds, and will present a comparative summary of the 3 trust funds with all the other portions of the unified budget. This report will be in addition to the usual budget submission which includes the budget estimates for the trust funds within the unified budget estimates.

Conference agreement.—The conference agreement follows the House bill.

* * *

109. Interfund borrowing among social security trust funds

House bill.—No provision.

Senate amendment.—The Senate amendment includes a resolution that it is the Sense of the Senate that the Senate Finance Committee report a bill to the Senate by November 15, 1981, which would authorize interfund borrowing among the social security trust funds, or other such measures as may be required.

Conference agreement.—The conference agreement follows the House bill.

* * *

EXCERPTS FROM THE JOINT EXPLANATORY STATEMENT OF THE COMMITTEE OF CONFERENCE ON TEFRA

The managers on the part of the House and the Senate at the conference on the disagreeing votes of the two Houses on the amendments of the Senate to the bill (H.R. 4961) to make miscellaneous changes in the tax laws, and for other purposes, submit the following joint statement to the House and the Senate in explanation of the effect of the action agreed upon by the managers and recommended in the accompanying conference report:

The Senate amendment to the text of the bill struck out all of the House bill after the enacting clause and inserted a substitute text.

The House recedes from its disagreement to the amendment of the Senate with an amendment which is a substitute for the House bill and the Senate amendment. The differences between the House bill, the Senate amendment, and the substitute agreed to in conference are noted below, except for clerical corrections, conforming changes made necessary by agreements reached by the conferees, and minor drafting and clarifying changes.

Title I—Provisions Relating to Savings in Health and Income Security Programs

Subtitle A—Medicare

1. **One month delay in entitlement to medicare benefits**

Senate amendment
The Senate amendment defers eligibility for parts A and B of medicare until the first day of the month following the month in which an individual attains age 65.

The provision would be effective with respect to individuals reaching age 65 after August 1982.

House bill
No provision.

Conference agreement
The conference agreement does not include the Senate amendment.

2. **Medicare payments secondary for older workers choosing to remain covered under group health plans**

Senate amendment
The Senate provision amends the Federal Age Discrimination in Employment Act (ADEA) to require employers to offer their employees age 65 through 69 and their dependents the same health benefits as are offered to their younger employees. The provision makes medicare the secondary payor for such employees (and their spouses) age 65 through 69. The provision would not apply to employers with less than 20 employees.

Medicare's payment for any item or service furnished to an employee (or his or her spouse) would be reduced where the combined payment under medicare and the employer's health benefits plan would otherwise exceed an amount equal to: (1) for items or services reimbursed on a cost or cost-related basis, their reasonable cost; or, (2) for items reimbursed on a charge basis, the higher of the reasonable charge (or other amount payable under medicare, without regard to the program deductibles or coinsurance) or the amount payable under the employer group plan (without regard to deductibles or coinsurance imposed under that plan). In no case would medicare pay more than medicare would have paid in the absence of any employer plan coverage. This provision would be effective January 1, 1983.

House bill
No provision.

Conference agreement

The conference agreement includes the Senate amendment. It is the intent of the conferees that an employee will have the option of rejecting the plan offered by the employer, thereby, retaining medicare as primary coverage. It is the understanding of the conferees that the Secretary of Labor will promulgate regulations to prevent employers from offering a group health insurance plan or option which is designed to circumvent this provision in an attempt to induce employees to reject the employer general health benefit plan offered to other employees under the age of 65.

* * *

Titles II and III—Revenue Measures and Tax Payer Compliance

* * *

C. Compliance Provisions

* * *

2. Other compliance provisions

* * *

w. Withholding on pensions, annuities, and certain deferred income

Present law

Under present law, income tax generally is not required to be withheld on pension or annuity payments. However, a recipient may elect to have tax withheld on annuity payments.

House bill

No provision.

Senate amendment

The Senate amendment provides that payors generally will be required to withhold tax from all designated distributions (the taxable part of payments made from or under a pension, profit-sharing, stock bonus, or annuity plan, a deferred compensation plan where the payments are not otherwise considered wages, an IRA, or a commercial annuity contract (whether or not the contract was purchased under an employer's plan for employees)). A partial surrender of an annuity contract and certain loans from employee plans and IRAs will also be considered a distribution subject to withholding. The withholding rate is determined by the nature of the distribution. Tax will be withheld on periodic payments in excess of $5,400, under the wage withholding tables. Tax on certain total distributions will be withheld under a schedule designed to reflect the special tax treatment accorded to lump sum distributions, and tax on other non-periodic distributions will be withheld at a flat 10-percent rate. Withholding will be required with respect to payments made after December 31, 1982, unless the recipient elects not to have tax withheld.

In general, a recipient may elect (for any reason) not to have tax withheld, except that a recipient of a total distribution may elect out only to the extent that the distribution is rolled over to another eligible retirement plan. An election is generally effective for the distribution for which the election is made, except that an election with respect to periodic payments is generally effective for a calendar year. Thus, an election not to have tax withheld from periodic payments must be renewed annually.

In addition, the amendment generally requires that payors notify recipients of the withholding rules and their rights to elect out. With respect to periodic payments, notice must be provided (1) no earlier than 6 months and not later than 2 months before making the first payment, and (2) annually, within the third quarter of the calendar year. With respect to other payments, notice must be provided no later than the time of distribution.

Conference agreement

The conference agreement generally follows the Senate amendment except that (1) a recipient may elect (for any reason) not to have tax withheld from any distribution (including total distributions which are not rolled over to another eligible retirement plan); (2) an election with respect to a periodic payment is effective until revoked, although a payor would still be required to provide annual notice of a participant's right to make, renew, or revoke an election, and (3) a payor of a periodic payment is required to provide initial notice of a recipient's right to make, renew, or revoke an election no earlier than six months before and no later than the date of the first payment. It is expected that the notice will also advise recipients that penalties may be incurred under the estimated tax payment rules if the payments of estimated tax are not adequate and sufficient tax is not withheld from any designated distributions.

As under the Senate amendment, tax would generally be withheld on periodic payments pursuant to the recipient's withholding certificate. For example, a married recipient whose spouse is not a wage earner would not be subject to tax on periodic distributions payable at an annual rate of up to $7,400 if both the wage earner and his spouse were at least age 65 and a withholding certificate were filed. If no certificate is filed, the amount withheld will be determined by treating the payee as a married individual claiming three withholding exemptions. Thus, in effect, there would be no withholding on pensions payable at an annual rate of $5,400 or less.

Annuity payments and other distributions under the Civil Service Retirement System are subject to the income tax withholding rules. The conferees intend that the cost of administering the withholding rules will be borne by the Civil Service Retirement System.

The conferees recognize the difficulty some payors may have in immediately complying with the new withholding requirements for annuity payments. Accordingly, the civil and criminal penalties for failure to withhold tax will not apply to any failure before July 1, 1983, if the payor made a good faith effort to withhold, and actually withholds from any subsequent 1983 payments sufficient amounts to satisfy the pre-1983 requirements. No relief is provided for any failure to timely pay over any amounts that are in fact withheld. Also, the Secretary is authorized, on a case-by-case basis, to exempt payors from any obligation to withhold with respect to pre-July 1983 payments if the payor has attempted to comply in good faith, has a plan to assure its ability to comply by July 1, 1983, and cannot comply on January 1, 1983, without undue hardship. If such a waiver of the withholding obligations is granted, the payor will not be required to make up the withholding obligation out of post-June 1983 payments.

x. Pension reporting requirements

Present law

Under present law, distributions under a tax-qualified plan or annuity contract are required to be reported only if the amount includible in income totals $600 or more for the calendar year. Distributions from an IRA are required to be reported without regard to the amount of the distributions. Penalties generally apply to any person failing to file a required report.

House bill
No provision.

Senate amendment

The Senate amendment provides for reporting of necessary information by employers and plan administrators of plans from which designated distributions can be made and issuers of insurance or annuity contracts from which designated distributions can be made. The form and manner of reporting will be determined under forms or regulations prescribed by the Secretary of the Treasury. These reports are to be made to the Secretary, to the participants and beneficiaries, and to such other persons as the Secretary may prescribe. As under present law, penalties apply to any person failing to file any required report.

The provision is effective for calendar years beginning after December 31, 1982.

Conference agreement
The conference agreement generally follows the Senate amendment. In addition, the conference agreement makes it clear that an exchange of insurance contracts under which any designated distribution may be made (including a section 1035 tax-free exchange) is intended to be a reportable event even though no designated distribution occurs in the particular transaction. Thus, to insure proper reporting of any designated distributions under the new contract, it is anticipated that, under regulations to be issued by the Secretary, the issuer of the contract to be exchanged will be required to provide information to the policyholder, the issuer of the new contract, and such other persons as the Secretary may require.

y. Pension recordkeeping requirements

Present law
Under present law, no separate penalty is imposed for failure to maintain a data base sufficient to provide required reports.

House bill
No provision.

Senate amendment
The Senate amendment imposes a new penalty if the data base needed for reports is not maintained whether or not reports are due for the period during which the recordkeeping failure occurs. No penalty is imposed for a failure to meet the recordkeeping rules when the failure is due to reasonable cause and not willful neglect. Also, no penalty is imposed for a recordkeeping failure that is due to a prior failure with respect to which the penalty has already been imposed, or which occurred before 1983, if all reasonable efforts have been made to correct the prior failure. The recordkeeping penalties are effective on January 1, 1985.

Conference agreement
The conference agreement follows the Senate amendment.

z. Partial rollovers of IRAs

Present law
Under present law, distributions from qualified pension, etc., plans and IRAs are eligible for tax-free rollover treatment. However, inconsistent rules apply. For example, distributions from an IRA are eligible for tax-free rollover treatment only if the entire amount of the distribution is rolled over to another eligible retirement plan, while distributions from qualified plans are eligible for tax-free rollover treatment to the extent of any amount so transferred.

House bill
No provision.

Senate amendment
Under the Senate amendment, distributions from IRAs are eligible for tax-free rollover treatment to the extent that the distribution is rolled over to another eligible retirement plan. The provision applies to IRA distributions made after December 31, 1982.

Conference agreement
The conference agreement follows the Senate amendment.

* * *

D. Pension Provisions

1. Overall limits on contributions, benefits, and exclusions

Present law
Present law limits 1982 contributions on behalf of an employee to a qualified profit-sharing or other defined contribution plan to the lesser of 25 percent of compensation or $45,475. Annual benefits payable under a qualified defined benefit pension plan are limited to the lesser of 100 percent of compensation or $136,425 for life, beginning at age 55. The limits (set at $25,000 and $75,000 in 1974) are automatically adjusted for cost-of-living increases.

If an employee participates in a defined contribution plan and a defined benefit plan maintained by the same employer, the fraction of the separate limits used by each plan is computed and the sum of the fractions is subject to an overall limit of 1.4 (i.e., 140 percent of the otherwise applicable separate limits).

House bill
No provision.

Senate amendment

The Senate amendment makes several changes to the overall limits on contributions and benefits for an employee under a tax-qualified pension, etc., plan. The amendment (1) reduces the dollar limit for annual additions to profit-sharing plans and other defined contribution plans from $45,475 to $30,000; (2) reduces the dollar limit for annual benefits under defined benefit pension plans from $136,425 to $90,000, and requires that an interest rate assumption of at least 5 percent be used to determine whether alternative benefit forms (e.g., lump sum distributions) are within the annual benefit limit; (3) suspends cost-of-living adjustments to the dollar limits until 1986, at which time the limits will be adjusted for post-1984 cost-of-living increases (as measured by the social security benefit index), and provides that employers cannot deduct contributions to fund anticipated cost-of-living increases, (4) requires that the dollar limit ($90,000 for 1983) be actuarially reduced (using an interest rate assumption of at least 5 percent) if benefits commence before age 62 (increased from age 55); and (5) reduces the aggregate limit for an individual who participates in a defined contribution plan and a defined benefit plan of the same employer from 1.4 (140 percent of the otherwise applicable separate dollar or percentage limit) to the lesser of 1.25, as applied only to the dollar limits, or 1.4, as applied under present law.

In general, these provisions will apply to plan years beginning after December 31, 1982, except that plan amendments are required with respect to plan years beginning after December 31, 1983.

Conference agreement

The conference agreement generally follows the Senate amendment except that the dollar limit for benefits under a defined benefit plan commencing before age 62 is to be actuarially reduced (using an interest rate of not less than the greater of 5 percent or the rate specified in the plan)[1] to the equivalent of the dollar limit for benefits commencing at age 62 (age 55 where the $75,000 minimum applies). Thus, the dollar limit is not less than $75,000 at age 55 or later. For ages below 55 the limit is not less than the actual equivalent of a $75,000 annual benefit commencing at age 55. Also, for benefits commencing after age 65 the dollar limit is increased (using an interest rate not exceeding the lesser of 5 percent or the rate specified in the plan) to the equivalent of the benefit limit as applied to benefits commencing at age 65. In no event, however, could future cost-of-living increases in the dollar limit be assumed in determining actuarial equivalence.

The conference agreement revises the transition rule relating to cases where the sum of the defined benefit plan and defined contribution plan fractions exceeds 1.25 (as applied to the dollar limits). Under the provision, the Secretary of the Treasury is to prescribe regulations under which the defined contribution plan fraction (as determined for the last year ending before January 1, 1983) is reduced, so that the sum of the fractions does not exceed the aggregate limit under the conference agreement.

The conference agreement clarifies present law by providing that the employer's deduction limit for the year under a defined benefit plan may not be based on benefits in excess of the dollar limit applicable for the year (without regard to anticipated cost-of-living increases). Deductions may be based on benefits which take into account anticipated salary increases, subject to limitation described in the preceding sentence.

The conference agreement also places a $100,000 aggregate limit on the estate tax exclusion for certain retirement benefits under qualified pension, etc., plan, tax-sheltered annuities, individual retirement accounts (IRA's) and certain military retirement plans. The limit applies with respect to decedents dying after December 31, 1982.

---

[1] Rev. Rul. 79-90 1979-1CB 156, requires that a plan specify the actuarial assumptions used by the plan to determine benefit equivalence.

2. Loans from retirement plans

Present law

A qualified pension, etc., plan or a tax-sheltered annuity program generally is permitted to make reasonable loans to participants other than owner-employees under an H.R. 10 plan or shareholder-employees under a subchapter S corporation plan. If a self-employed individual borrows from an H.R. 10 plan or if an individual borrows from an IRA, the loan is treated as a distribution, subject to the usual income tax rules.

House bill

No provision.

Senate amendment

The Senate amendment generally provides that a loan received by a participant under a qualified plan or a tax-sheltered annuity program is treated as a distribution to the extent that the participant's outstanding loan balance under all plans in which the participant participates exceeds $10,000. A higher limit (not to exceed $50,000) is permitted if the loan proceeds are applied towards the purchase, reconstruction, etc., of a personal residence. Loan amounts treated as distributions generally are subject to the usual income tax and withholding rules for plan distributions.

The amendment applies to loans made after July 1, 1982. Loans made before that date are not affected except to the extent that the loan is renegotiated, revised, or extended. A loan is treated as received if the proceeds are paid to or on behalf of a participant or beneficiary or if the loan is extended, etc. The amendment changes the tax treatment of loans but does not change the rules of the Employee Retirement Income Security Act of 1974 limiting the availability of loans.

Conference agreement

In general

The conference agreement follows the Senate amendment except that a loan from a tax-qualified plan, or, government plan, or tax sheltered annuity which is to be repaid within 5 years is treated as a distribution only to the extent that the amount of the loan, when added to the outstanding loan balance with respect to the employee under all plans of the employer, exceeds the lesser of (1) $50,000, or (2) one-half of the present value of the employee's nonforfeitable accrued benefit under such plans, but not less than $10,000. For this purpose, plans of separate employers which generally are treated as a single employer under the pension, etc., plan rules (sec. 414) are treated as plans of a single employer.

A loan made with respect to an employee under a qualified plan, etc., which is not required to be repaid within 5 years, is treated as a distribution. For this purpose, the period within which a loan is required to be repaid is determined at the time the loan is made. If a repayment period of less than 5 years is subsequently extended beyond 5 years, it is intended that the balance payable under the loan at the time of the extension is to be treated as distributed at the time of the extension. In addition, if payments under a loan with a repayment period of less than 5 years are not in fact made, so that an amount remains payable at the end of 5 years, the amount remaining payable is treated as if distributed at the end of the 5-year period. A loan which is treated as a distribution on account of a repayment period of more than 5 years will not be treated as other than a distribution merely because it is repaid within 5 years (whether by reason of a renegotiation of the payment period or otherwise). Of course, a loan to a beneficiary which is treated as a distribution is included in the income of the participant, if the participant is alive at the time the loan is treated as a distribution.

The conference agreement provides an exception to the 5-year repayment rule to the extent that a loan made with respect to a plan participant is applied toward acquiring, constructing, or substantially rehabilitating any house, apartment, condominium, or mobile home (not used on a transient basis) which is used or is to be used within a reasonable time as the principal residence of the participant or a member of the participant's family.

The determination as to whether a dwelling is to be used as a principal residence of the participant or dependent is to be determined at the time the loan is entered into.

Certain mortgage loans

Under the conference agreement, investments (including investments in residential mortgages) which are made in the ordinary course of an investment program will not be considered as loans, if the amount of the mortgage loan does not exceed the fair market value of the property purchased with the loan proceeds. An investment program exists, for example, when trustees determine that a specific percentage or amount of plan assets will be invested in residential mortgages under specified conditions. However, mortgage loans made as a result of the direction of investments of an individual account will not be considered as made under an investment program and no loan which benefits an officer, director, or owner or his beneficiaries will be treated as an investment. In addition, the agreement makes no changes to the present-law prohibited transaction rules and fiduciary standards for qualified pension, etc., plans and does not restrict the rules of present law under which certain loans are treated as distributions.

Effective dates

The conference agreement applies to loans made after August 13, 1982.

Amounts outstanding on August 13, 1982, under a loan which is renegotiated, extended, revised, or renewed after such date will not be treated as made on the date of the renegotiation, etc., to the extent such amounts are required to be, and are repaid on or before August 13, 1983. Thus, such amounts will continue to be treated as amounts outstanding with respect to the participant on August 13, 1982.

The conferees intend that a scheduled change in the interest rate charged on a loan balance (e.g., a variable rate contract) will not be treated as a revision or renegotiation of the loan.

3. Parity under the qualified plan rules for corporate and noncorporate employers; group-term life insurance

Present law

Under present law, plans which benefit self-employed individuals, owner-employees, or shareholder-employees of subchapter S corporations are subject to additional, more restrictive, qualification requirements designed to limit benefits for such individuals and provide additional protections for rank-and-file employees.

House bill
No provision.

Senate amendment

The Senate amendment increases the dollar limits applicable to defined contribution H.R. 10 plans, plans of subchapter S corporations, and SEPs, from $15,000 in 1982 to $20,000 in 1983, $25,000 in 1984, and $30,000 in 1985. The 15-percent of earned income limit is not changed. To provide a similar increase in the level of benefits permitted under a defined benefit H.R. 10 plan or subchapter S corporation plan, the compensation taken into account in determining permitted annual benefit accruals is increased from $100,000 to $133,000 in 1983, $167,000 in 1984 and $200,000 in 1985.

Beginning in 1986, the bill adjusts the limits for post-1984 cost-of-living increases.

Conference agreement

In general

The conference agreement generally eliminates distinctions in the tax law between qualified pension, etc., plans of corporations and those of self-employed individuals (H.R. 10 plans). The agreement (1) repeals certain of the special rules, for H.R. 10 plans, (2) extends other of the special rules to all qualified plans, including those maintained by corporate employers, and (3) generally applies the remainder of the special rules, with appropriate modifications, only to those plans (whether maintained by a corporate or noncorporate employer) which primarily benefit the employer's key employees (top-heavy plans). The top-heavy plan rules are provided in addition to the usual rules for plan qualification.

The special rules for H.R. 10 plans which are repealed include those which (1) set lower limits on contributions and benefits for self-employed individuals, (2) prevent certain H.R. 10 plans from limiting coverage to a fair cross section of employees, and (3) prohibit integration with social security.

The special rules for H.R. 10 plans which are extended to all qualified plans are certain of those rules relating to (1) distributions made to the employee or to the employee's beneficiaries after the employee's death, and (2) integration of a defined contribution plan with social security.

The special rules for H.R. 10 plans which generally are extended (with modifications) to plans of corporate and noncorporate employers which primarily benefit key employees (top-heavy plans) include those rules relating to (1) includible compensation, (2) vesting (alternative schedules are provided) and (3) distributions. The rules for a top-heavy plan also require that such a plan provide a non-key employee a nonintegrated minimum benefit or a nonintegrated minimum contribution, and in some cases reduce the aggregate limit on contributions and benefits for a key employee who is covered by more than one plan of an employer.

These provisions apply for years beginning after December 31, 1983.

Repeal of rules for H.R. 10 plans

● *Deductible contributions and permitted benefit accruals*

The conference agreement generally repeals the special deduction limits (sec. 404(e)(1), (2), and (4)) for contributions on behalf of a self-employed individual under an H.R. 10 plan. Conforming amendments are made with respect to simplified employee pensions and plans of subchapter S corporations.

In addition, the conference agreement repeals the special qualification rules for a defined benefit plan which covers a self-employed individual or a shareholder-employee of a subchapter S corporation (sec. 401(j)). Thus, defined benefit plans which cover a self-employed individual or a shareholder-employee of a subchapter S corporation will be subject to the rules applicable to other defined benefit plans.

● *Earned income*

For purposes of the pension rules, the conference agreement revises the definition of earned income of a self-employed individual so that the amount of earned income corresponds to the amount of compensation of a common-law employee. Under the agreement, earned income is computed after taking into account amounts contributed by the employer to a qualified plan to the extent a deduction is allowed for the contributions. Also, in this regard, no change is made to the present-law rule (sec. 401(d)(11)) for owner-employees which has the effect of limiting the earned income which may be taken into account from the trade or business with respect to which the plan is established.

In addition, no change is made to the present-law rules under which no deduction is allowed for contributions to an H.R. 10 plan on behalf of a self-employed individual to the extent that the contributions are allocable to the purchase of incidental life, health, or accident insurance (sec. 404(e)(3)), and under which a self-employed individual generally is denied a basis in amounts applied under an H.R. 10 plan to purchase life insurance protection for the individual (sec. 72(m)(2)).

● *Coverage*

The agreement repeals the additional qualification requirement under which an H.R. 10 plan benefiting an owner-employee generally is required to benefit all employees who have completed at least three years of service with the employer (sec. 401(d)(3)(A)).

The agreement retains the special rules for H.R. 10 plans under which all employees of all unincorporated trades or businesses controlled by an owner-employee (or owner-employees) are treated as if employed by a single trade or business for purposes of the nondiscrimination rules (sec. 401(a)(9) and (10)).

●*Employee contributions*
The agreement repeals the special rules precluding employer contributions on behalf of an owner-employee under an H.R. 10 plan in excess of the deduction limit (sec. 401(d)(5)), and those rules limiting or precluding mandatory or voluntary employee contributions by an owner-employee (sec. 4972). The agreement also repeals the six-percent excise tax on excess contributions made on behalf of an owner-employee.

●*Miscellaneous restrictions*
The following special H.R. 10 plan rules are also repealed:
(1) the requirement that a profit-sharing plan provide a definite contribution formula for employees who are not owner-employees (sec. 401(d)(2)(B));
(2) the requirement that an owner-employee must consent to participate (sec. 401(d)(4)(A));
(3) the requirement that the plan trustee be a bank or other approved financial institution (sec. 401(d)(1));
(4) the prohibition against contributions on behalf of an owner-employee for the five taxable years following an early withdrawal by the owner-employee (sec. 401(d)(5)(C)); and
(5) the denial of the $5,000 income exclusion for death benefits paid with respect to a self-employed individual under the plan (sec. 101(b)).
Nothing in the agreement requires that an H.R. 10 plan delete these provisions. For example, an employer may prefer that an H.R. 10 plan continue to provide that an owner-employee must consent to participate, thereby permitting an owner-employee to elect against plan participation.

Extension of certain H.R. 10 rules to all plans

●*Required distributions*
The agreement extends to all qualified plans the requirement that payment of a participant's benefits must commence not later than (1) the taxable year in which the participant attains age 70½, or (2) if later, the year in which the participant retires (sec. 401(a)(9)).

In addition, if a participant dies before the entire interest is distributed, the entire remaining interest generally must be distributed to the participant's beneficiary or beneficiaries within 5 years. However, this rule does not apply if the distribution has commenced to the participant and is payable over a period which does not exceed the joint life expectancy of the participant and the participant's spouse. A conforming change is made to the IRA distribution rules.

●*Integration with social security*
The bill extends to all qualified defined contribution plans a rule under which the tax rate applicable to employers for old age, survivors, and disability insurance (OASDI) under social security is the maximum rate at which employer contributions can be reduced under plans that are integrated with social security. This provision is designed to decrease the extent of integration in defined contribution plans without increasing the extent of integration in any plan.

For 1982, the employer's tax rate with respect to OASDI benefits under social security is 5.4 percent, and the taxable wage base is the first $32,400 of an employee's pay. Thus, if the provisions were applicable for 1982, a profit-sharing plan could provide contributions of 5.4 percent of 1982 pay in excess of $32,400 and no contributions for 1982 with respect to the first $32,400 of pay. Similarly, if a plan provided for 1982 contributions of 10 percent of pay in excess of $32,400, it would integrate only if it provided for 1982 contributions of at least 4.6 percent (10% minus 5.4%) with respect to the first $32,400 of pay. The same rules apply to a self-employed individual.

The wage base and tax rates which apply for any plan year are the wage base and tax rates in effect on the first day of the plan year.

The remaining present-law rules which restrict integration with social security under an H.R. 10 defined contribution which benefits an owner-employer are repealed.

Additional qualification requirements for top-heavy plans

● *In general*

Under the agreement, additional qualification requirements are provided for plans which primarily benefit an employer's key employees (top-heavy plans). These additional requirements (1) limit the amount of a participant's compensation which may be taken into account, (2) provide greater portability of benefits for plan participants who are non-key employees, (3) provide minimum nonintegrated contributions or benefits for plan participants who are non-key employees, and (4) reduce the aggregate limit on contributions and benefits for certain key employees. Further, additional restrictions are placed on distributions to key employees.

● *Top-heavy plans*

Under the agreement, a defined benefit plan is a top-heavy plan for a plan year if, as of the determination date, (1) the present value of the accumulated accrued benefits for participants who are key employees for the plan year exceeds sixty percent of the present value of the accumulated accrued benefits for all employees under the plan, or (2) the plan is part of a top-heavy group. A defined contribution plan is a top-heavy plan for a plan year if, as of the determination date, (1) the sum of the account balances of participants who are key employees for the plan year exceeds sixty percent of the sum of the account balances of all employees under the plan, or (2) the plan is a part of a top-heavy group. Under these rules, a simplified employee pension is considered a defined contribution plan, and at the election of the employer, the account balance of any employee covered by a simplified employee pension is deemed to be the sum of the employer contributions made on the employee's behalf.

The determination date for any plan year generally is the last day of the preceding plan year. However, in the case of the first plan year, the determination date is the last day of that year. Further, to the extent provided in regulations, the determination date may be determined on the basis of a year other than a plan year.

● *Top-heavy groups*

The agreement also provides rules under which two or more plans of a single employer are aggregated to determine whether the plans, as a group, are top-heavy. The aggregation group must include (1) any plan which covers a key employee, and (2) any plan upon which a plan covering a key employee depends for qualification under the Code's coverage or antidiscrimination rules (secs. 401(a)(4) and 410). In addition, in testing for top-heaviness, an employer may elect to expand the aggregation group to take into account any other plan maintained by the employer, if such expanded aggregation group continues to satisfy the coverage and antidiscrimination rules.

An aggregation group is a top-heavy group if, as of the determination date, the sum of (1) the present values of the accumulated accrued benefits for key employees under any defined benefit plans included in the group, and (2) the sum of the account balances of key employees under any defined contribution plans included in the group, exceeds 60 percent of the same amount determined for all participants under all plans included in the group. If an aggregation group is a top-heavy group, each plan required to be included in the group is a top-heavy plan. Of course, no plan included in the aggregation group at the election of the employer is subject to the top-heavy plan rules on account of such election.

The top-heavy group rules apply to all plans of related employers which are treated as a single employer (sec. 414).

● *Additional rules*

For purposes of determining the present value of accumulated accrued benefits under a defined benefit plan and the sum of the account balances under a defined contribution plan, benefits derived from both employer contributions and employee contributions generally are taken into account. However, accumulated deductible employee contributions under a plan are to be disregarded. In addition, to insure relative stability and to preclude distortions under the top-heavy plan computation, the present value of the accrued benefit of a participant in a defined benefit plan or the account balance of a participant in a defined contribution plan generally includes any amount distributed with respect to the participant under the plan within the five-year period ending on the determination date.

A rollover contribution (or similar transfer) made after December 31, 1983, generally is not taken into account under the transferee plan for purposes of the top-heavy plan computation. The conferees intend that this rule will not apply if the contribution (or transfer) is made incident to a merger or consolidation of two or more plans or the division of a single plan into two or more plans. In addition, the conferees intend that this rule will not apply to rollover contributions (or transfers) between plans of the same employer, including plans of related employers which are treated as a single employer (sec. 414). Of course, in any case in which a rollover contribution (or transfer) is required to be taken into account under the transferee plan, the amount distributed by the transferor plan is not also taken into account under the transferor plan.

If an employee ceases to be treated as a key employee, the employee's accrued benefit under a defined benefit plan or the employee's account balance under a defined contribution plan is disregarded under the top-heavy plan computation for any plan year following the last plan year for which the employee was treated as a key employee.

● *Key employees*

Key employees generally include employees who (1) are officers (but in no event will officers of any employer include more than 50 employees or, if lesser, the greater of 3 employees or 10 percent of all employees),[1] (2) are one of the 10 employees owning the largest interests in the employer (there are not 10 employees owning greater interests than the employee), (3) own more than a five-percent interest in the employer, or (4) own more than a one-percent interest in the employer and have annual compensation from the employer in excess of $150,000. An employee is considered an officer, or as owning an interest in the employer, if the employee was an officer, or owned such an interest, at any time during the plan year or the four preceding plan years. In the case of an employer which has more officers than are required to be counted as key employees, the officers to be taken into account are the officers with the highest compensation.

Under the agreement, an employee is considered as owning more than a five-percent interest in a corporate employer if the employee owns more than five percent of the employer's outstanding stock or stock possessing five percent of the total combined voting power of all stock of the employer. An employee is also treated as owning stock owned by certain members of the employee's family or, in certain cases, by partnerships, estates, trusts, or corporations in which the employee has an interest (sec. 318). The same rules apply to determine whether an individual owner is a one-percent owner.

In the case of an employer which is not a corporation, ownership will be determined in accordance with regulations prescribed by the Secretary. The conferees intend that these regulations be based on principles similar to the principles of section 318. In addition, to determine whether a self-employed individual who is a one-per-

---

[1] As under present law, the determination as to whether an employee is an officer is to be determined upon the basis of all the facts and circumstances, including, for example, the source of the employee's authority, the term for which elected or appointed, and the nature and extent of the employee's duties. As generally accepted in connection with corporations, the term "officer" means an administrative executive who is in regular and continued service. It implies continuity of service and excludes those employed for a special and single transaction, or those with only nominal administrative duties. Thus, for example, all the employees of a bank who have the title of vice president or assistant vice president would not automatically be considered to be officers. See, for example, Rev. Rul. 80-314, 1980-2 C.B. 152.

cent owner, is a key employee, compensation means earned income from the trade or business with respect to which the plan is maintained.

● *Qualification rules*

These additional rules for top-heavy plans are tax-qualification requirements. Thus, a top-heavy plan is a qualified plan, and a trust forming part of a top-heavy plan is a qualified trust only if the additional requirements are met. Except as the Secretary of the Treasury may provide by regulations, a plan (whether or not top-heavy in fact) will constitute a qualified plan only if the plan includes provisions which will automatically take effect if the plan becomes a top-heavy plan and which meet the additional qualification requirements for top-heavy plans.

● *Includible compensation*

For any plan year for which a plan is a top-heavy plan, only the first $200,000 of an employee's compensation may be taken into account in determining contributions or benefits under the plan. Beginning in 1986, this $200,000 limit will be adjusted under the same rules used to adjust the overall limits on contributions and benefits. For a self-employed individual, compensation means earned income as redefined by the conference agreement.

● *Vesting*

For any plan year for which a plan is a top-heavy plan, an employee's right to the accrued benefit derived from employer contributions must become nonforfeitable (sec. 411(a)) under a vesting schedule which satisfies one of two alternative schedules provided by the agreement. These vesting schedules apply to all accrued benefits, whether or not the accrued benefits are required by the top-heavy plan rules.

A plan will satisfy the first alternative vesting schedule (three-year full vesting) if an employee who has at least three years of service with the employer or employers maintaining the plan has a nonforfeitable right to 100 percent of his accrued benefit derived from employer contributions. As under present law, a plan which provides three-year, 100 percent vesting will satisfy the participation requirements if the plan provides that an employee who is at least 25 years old, with three years of service, is eligible to participate.

A plan will satisfy the second alternative vesting schedule (six-year graded vesting) if an employee has a nonforfeitable right to at least 20 percent of the accrued benefit derived from employer contributions at the end of two years of service, 40 percent at the end of three years of service, 60 percent at the end of four years of service, 80 percent at the end of five years of service with the employer, and 100 percent at the end of six years of service with the employer.

For purposes of determining service under these vesting schedules, the present-law rules (sec. 411) relating to years of service, breaks in service, and certain permitted forfeitures etc., apply. Accordingly, all years of service with the employer generally are to be taken into account, including years of service completed prior to enactment and service during periods for which a plan is not a top-heavy plan.

● *Minimum nonintegrated benefit for non-key employees*

In addition, a qualified pension, etc., plan which is a top-heavy plan must provide a minimum benefit or contribution for each non-key employee who is a participant in the plan.

Under the conference agreement, any individual excluded from coverage under a defined benefit or defined contribution plan because of compensation below a specified amount, or any individual considered to be a participant for purposes of the coverage requirements (sec. 410) must be provided the applicable minimum contribution or benefit.

For a plan year for which a defined benefit plan is a top-heavy plan, each plan participant who is not a key employee for the year generally must accrue a benefit which, when expressed as an annual retirement benefit, is not less than two percent of the employee's average annual compensation from the employer during the employee's testing period, multiplied by the employee's years of service with the employer. However, an employee's minimum benefit is not required to exceed 20 percent of such average annual compensation. All years of an employee's service otherwise required to be taken into account under the plan generally are required to be taken into account under the minimum benefit rules, except a year of service (1) ending before the date of enactment, or (2) within which ends a plan year for which the plan is not a top-heavy plan.

For purposes of the minimum benefit rules, only benefits derived from employer contributions (other than amounts employees have elected to defer (e.g. under a salary reduction cash or deferred arrangement)) to the plan are taken into account, and an employee's social security benefits are disregarded. Thus, the required minimum benefit for an employee may not be eliminated or reduced on account of the employee's social security benefits attributable to contributions by the employer (i.e., the minimum benefit is a "nonintegrated" benefit).

The term annual retirement benefit is defined as a benefit payable annually in the form of a life annuity (with no ancillary benefits) beginning at the normal retirement age. An employee's testing period is the period of the employee's consecutive years of service (not exceeding five) during which the employee had the greatest aggregate compensation from the employer. However, a year of service (and compensation paid to the employee during such year) need not be included in the employee's testing period if it ends before the date of enactment or begins within or after the last plan year for which the plan is a top-heavy plan.

● *Minimum nonintegrated contribution for non-key employees*

For a plan year for which a defined contribution plan is a top-heavy plan, the employer generally must contribute on behalf of each plan participant who is not a key employee for the year an amount not less than three percent of the participant's compensation. However, if the employer's contribution rate for each participant who is a key employee for the plan year is less than three percent, the required minimum contribution rate for each non-key employee generally is limited to not more than the highest contribution rate for any key employee. For example, if, under a profit-sharing plan, no amount is contributed by the employer for any key employee, then under this limitation no contribution is required under the minimum contribution rules for any non-key employee. Under the minimum contribution rules, reallocated forfeitures are taken into account as employer contributions.

However, the limitation to the rate of contributions for key employees does not apply with respect to a defined contribution plan upon which a defined benefit plan depends for qualification under the Code's coverage or antidiscrimination rules, if the defined benefit plan benefits a key employee (or if a plan which benefits a key employee also depends upon the defined benefit plan). Under such circumstances, the required minimum contribution rate for a non-key employee is in every case three percent even if the contribution rate on behalf of a key employee is less than 3 percent. For purposes of the limitation, as well as for purposes of the minimum contribution rules generally, all defined contribution plans of the employer are considered a single plan.

To determine the contribution rate for an employee (including a key employee), the employer contributions and reallocated forfeitures on behalf of the employee for the year are divided by the employee's total compensation (or, with respect to a self-employed individual, the individual's earned income) from the employer for the year, not to exceed $200,000. Amounts paid by the employer for the year to provide social security benefits for the employer are disregarded. Thus, the required minimum contribution for a non-key employee may not be eliminated or reduced on account of benefits attributable to taxes paid by the employer under social security (i.e., the minimum contribution is a "nonintegrated" contribution). Similarly, the employer contribution rate for a key employee is determined without regard to employer contributions under social security. For example, if a plan is integrated with social security by providing key employees with employer contributions equal to 5 percent of compensation in excess of $32,400, the contribution rate for an employee whose total compensation is $50,000 is 1.76 percent ((0.05 × $17,600) ÷ $50,000).

● *No duplication of minimum benefits for non-key employees under a top-heavy group*

If a non-key employee participates in both a defined benefit plan and a defined contribution plan maintained by an employer, the employer is not required by this section to provide the non-key employee with both the minimum benefit and the minimum contribution.

Rules are also provided to preclude inappropriate omissions or required duplication of minimum benefits or contributions. It is anticipated that these rules would preclude an employee who is covered under more than one plan from receiving lower benefits or contributions than that employee would receive if covered under one plan. Similarly, larger total benefits should not be required merely because an employee is covered under more than one plan (except as required where the limit of 1.0 is exceeded by a top-heavy plan). For example, if an employee participates in a top-heavy money purchase pension plan that provides an annual nonintegrated contribution rate of 5 percent of compensation and a defined benefit plan that provides an annual benefit of 1 percent of pay, the employer would not be required to provide an additional 1-percent benefit for non-key employees participating in the defined benefit plan.

Of course, contributions to either plan on behalf of the non-key employee may otherwise be required (for example, by reason of the nondiscrimination rules). In any case in which separate plans are required to be considered together for purposes of the coverage or nondiscrimination rules, the required minimum benefit or minimum contribution may of course be taken into account. However, two plans are not necessarily comparable merely because one plan provides the required minimum benefit while the other provides the required minimum contribution. Similarly, the fact that two plans both provide the required minimum benefit, or that two plans both provide the required minimum contribution, does not insure that the two plans, as a whole, are comparable.

● *Aggregate limit on contributions and benefits for key employees*

The agreement includes additional rules with respect to the aggregate limit on benefits and contributions (sec. 415(e)) for a key employee who participates in both a defined benefit plan and a defined contribution plan which are included in a top-heavy group. Unless certain requirements are met, for any year for which the plans are included in the top-heavy group, the aggregate limit for the key employee is the lesser of 1.0 (as applied only to the dollar limits) or 1.4 (as determined under present law). However, the aggregate limit is increased to the lesser of 1.25 (as applied only to the dollar limits) or 1.4 (as under present law) if the plans of the employer in which the key employee participates (1) meet the requirements of the concentration test, and (2) provide either an extra minimum benefit (in the case of the defined benefit plan) or an extra minimum contribution (in the case of the defined contribution plan) for non-key employees participating in the plans. The extra contribution or benefit is in addition to the minimum contribution or benefit required for all top-heavy plans.

The concentration test is generally satisfied with respect to a key employee for a year if, as of the last determination date before the first day of such year, the sum of (1) the present value of the accumulated accrued benefits for key employees under the defined benefit plans of the employer in which the key employee participates, and (2) the sum of the account balances of key employees under the defined contribution plans of the employer in which the key employee participates is not greater than 90 percent of the same amount determined for all participants under the plans.

For purposes of this computation, the rules for determining whether two or more plans constitute a top-heavy group apply.

The requirement for an extra minimum benefit for non-key employees is satisfied for a year if, for the plan year ending with or within such year, each non-key employee who is a participant in a defined benefit plan of the employer in which the key employee is a participant accrues an extra benefit which, when expressed as an annual retirement benefit, is not less than the lesser of (1) one percent of the employee's average annual compensation, multiplied by the employee's years of service with the employer, or (2) 10 percent of such average annual compensation. This extra minimum benefit generally is determined in the same manner as the minimum benefit required under the rules for a top-heavy defined benefit plan. However, for purposes of the extra minimum benefit, a year of service is required to be taken into account only if (1) such year of service includes the last day of a plan year for which the plan is a top-heavy plan (or included in a top-heavy group), and (2) such plan year ends with or within a year for which the aggregate limit of the key employee exceeds 1.0 (as applied to the dollar limits).

The requirement for an extra minimum contribution is satisfied with respect to a key employee for a year if, for the plan year ending with or within such year, the employer contributes on behalf of each non-key employee who is a participant in a defined contribution plan in which the key employee is a participant an extra amount not less than the amount equal to one percent of the employee's compensation for the year. Accordingly, the extra minimum contribution generally is determined under the rules for top-heavy defined contribution plans.

In some cases, the aggregate of a key employee's accrued benefit under an employer's defined benefit plans and annual additions under the employer's defined contribution plans may exceed 1.0 (as applied to the dollar limits) at the time the key employee becomes subject to an aggregate limit of 1.0. In such a case, the key employee is permitted no further benefit accruals under the defined benefit plans and no additional employer contributions under the defined contribution plans until (1) the aggregate of the key employee's accrued benefits and annual additions is less than 1.0 (as applied to the dollar limits), or (2) the aggregate limit for the key employee is increased to 1.25 (as applied to the dollar limits) under the bill. Of course, in no event are further benefit accruals permitted if the aggregate of the employee's accrued benefit and annual additions exceeds 1.25 (as applied to the dollar limit) or 1.4 (as applied under present law).

● *Distributions to key employees*

The agreement also provides new rules for distributions from top-heavy plans to key employees. If a distribution is made to a key employee before he attains age 59½, an additional income tax is imposed equal to 10 percent of the amount includible in income, unless the distribution is made on account of death or disability.

In addition, a top-heavy plan must provide that distributions to a key employee will commence no later than the taxable year in which the key employee attains age 70½, whether or not he separates from service in that year. As under present law, the required distributions must be made in such a manner that more than 50 percent of the total benefits for the employee are payable to the employee over the employee's life expectancy (or the joint life expectancy of the employee and the employee's spouse).

Organizations performing management functions

The conference agreement expands the class of employers which, under the present-law rules for affiliated service groups (sec. 414(m)), are to be treated as a single employer for purposes of certain of the tax-law rules for qualified pension, etc., plans (including the rules for top-heavy plans), cafeteria or medical reimbursement plans, or simplified employer pensions (SEPs). Under the provision, if an organization's principal business is performing, on a regular and continuing basis, management functions for another organization, the person performing the functions and the organization for whom the functions are performed are treated as a single employer.

Under the provision, any person related to the organization performing the management functions is also included in the group which is treated as a single employer. An organization related to the organization for whom the functions are performed is included in the group under the management function rules, if the management functions are also performed, on a regular and continuing basis, for such related organization. However, the provision does not change present law under which aggregation of employers is otherwise required.

For purposes of the provision, the term "organization" includes an individual, corporation, partnership, etc. Whether organizations are related is determined under present law (sec. 103(b)(6)(C).

The conferees intend that the provision is to apply only where the management functions performed by one person for another are functions historically performed by employees, including partners or sole proprietors in the case of an unincorporated trades and businesses. For this purpose, the present-law rules relating to affiliated service organizations and to services historically performed by employees in the case of an affiliated service organization are to apply.

Employee leasing

The conference agreement also provides that, for purposes of certain of the tax-law rules for qualified pension, etc., plans (including the rules for top-heavy plans) and SEPs, an individual (a leased employee) who performs services for another person (the recipient) may be treated as the recipient's employee where the services are performed pursuant to an agreement between the recipient and a third person (the leasing organization) who is otherwise treated as the individual's employer. Under the provision, the individual is to be treated as the recipient's employee only if the individual has performed services for the recipient (or for the recipient and persons related to the recipient) on a substantially full-time basis for a period of at least 12 months, and the services are of a type historically performed by employees in the recipient's business field. For this purpose, the present-law rules relating to services historically performed by employees in the case of an affiliated service organization are to apply.

The employee leasing rules do not apply where services in a particular business field historically have been performed by one person for another. For example, some prepaid health care service programs organized on a group practice basis involve two or three components: the health plan, a separate medical group that provides or arranges physicians' services to the health plan members, and often a related hospital. The hospital and the medical group each may employ its own staff (nurses, technicians, etc.), but both sets of employees may be jointly managed. Alternatively, the staff that supports the medical group may be employed by the health plan. These forms of operation are well established in the group practice prepaid health care field. The conferees intend that the "historically performed" exception is to apply in these cases (whether the form of operation is currently in effect or put into effect for existing components of an established group practice prepaid health care service program or for the components of a new program) if the health plan, the hospital, and the medical group provide substantially similar, though not necessarily exactly equivalent retirement benefits through tax qualified plans to salaried non-union employees and partners.

For purposes of determining whether a pension, etc., plan or a SEP maintained by the recipient satisfies the applicable tax-law requirements, the leased employee is treated as the recipient's employee for periods after the close of the 12-month period described in the preceding paragraph. However, the leased employee's years of service for the recipient are determined by taking into account the entire period for which the leased employee performed services for the recipient (or for a related person).

Under the provision, contributions or benefits for the leased employee which are provided by the leasing organization under a qualified plan or a SEP maintained by the leasing organization are to be treated as if provided by the recipient to the extent such contributions or benefits are attributable to services performed by the leased employee for the recipient.

Under the provision, an individual who otherwise would be treated as a recipient's employee will not be treated as such an employee, if certain requirements are met with respect to contributions and benefits provided for the individual under a qualified money purchase pension plan maintained by the leasing organization. Such a plan qualifies if it provides that (1) an individual is a plan participant on the first day on which the individual becomes an employee of an employer maintaining the plan, (2) each employee's rights to or derived from employer contributions under the plan are nonforfeitable (sec. 411 (a)) at the time the contributions are made, and (3) amounts are to be contributed by the employer on behalf of an employee at a rate not less than 7½ percent of the employee's compensation for the year (the 7½ percent contribution is not to be reduced by integration with social security).

For purposes of the provision, the term person includes individuals and organizations (corporations, partnerships, etc.). Whether persons are related persons is determined under present law (sec. 103(b)(6)(C)).

The provision authorizes the Secretary of the Treasury to prescribe regulations under which a leased employee will not be treated as the recipient's employee, notwithstanding that the provision may otherwise apply. Under the conference agreement, the Secretary is to prescribe such regulations where it is determined that to treat a leased employee as the recipient's employee is not appropriate, taking into account the purposes underlying those qualified plan rules with respect to which the provision applies.

Certain corporations performing personal services

Under the conference agreement, if a corporation, the principal activity of which is the performance of personal services substantially all of which are performed by employee-owners for or on behalf of another corporation, partnership, or entity (including related parties), is availed of for the principal purpose of evasion or avoidance of Federal income tax by securing for any employee-owner significant tax benefits which would not otherwise be available, then the Secretary may allocate all income, as well as such deductions, credits, exclusions, etc., as may be allowable, between or among the corporation and employee-owners involved. For this purpose, an employee-owner is defined as any employee who owns (after application of the attribution rules under section 318) more than 10 percent of the outstanding stock of the corporation. The conferees intend that the provisions overturn the results reached in cases like *Keller* v. *Commissioner*, 77 TC 1014 (1981), where the corporation served no meaningful business purpose other than to secure tax benefits which would not otherwise be available.

The provision applies to taxable years beginning after December 31, 1982.

Disincorporation relief

The conferees understand that a number of personal service corporations may wish to liquidate when the parity provisions of the conference agreement take effect. Therefore, a transitional rule is provided under which personal service corporations may, during 1983 or 1984, complete a one-month liquidation under section 333 of the Code without the risk that the corporation would incur tax on its unrealized receivables. Of course, the income represented by unrealized receivables will retain its character as ordinary income and will be fully recognized by the distributee shareholder upon subsequent collection or other disposition.

Group-term life insurance

The conference agreement also provides that the income exclusion for employer-provided group term life insurance (sec. 79) will apply with respect to a key employee only if the life insurance is provided under a program of the employer which does not discriminate in favor of key employees as to (1) eligibility to participate, or (2) the life insurance benefits provided under the plan.

A program of an employer providing group-term life insurance for employees generally will not be considered to discriminate in favor of key employees as to eligibility to participate if (1) the program benefits at least 70 percent of all employees, (2) at least 85 percent of all participating employees are not key employees, or (3) the program benefits employees who qualify under a classification set up by the employer and found by the Secretary of the Treasury not to discriminate in favor of key employees. Alternatively, a program of an employer providing group-term life insurance which is provided under a cafeteria plan (sec. 125) will not be considered to discriminate in favor of key employees as to eligibility to participate if the eligibility rules for cafeteria plans are satisfied. For purposes of the provision's rules relating to eligibility to participate, employees of certain related employers would generally be treated as if employed by a single employer. However, the following employees could be excluded from consideration: (1) those who have not completed 3 years of service with the employer, (2) part-time and seasonal employees, and (3) nonresident aliens who receive no U.S. source income from the employer. For this purpose, part-time employees are those whose customary employment is for not more than 20 hours in any one week, and seasonal employees are those whose customary employment is for not more than 5 months in any calendar year. In addition, employees not covered by the program but covered by a collective bargaining agreement need not be taken into account if group-term life insurance was the subject of good faith bargaining between the employer and employee representatives.

A program of an employer providing group-term life insurance for employees will not be considered to discriminate in favor of key employees as to the benefits provided, if the program does not discriminate in favor of such employees with regard to the type and amount of the benefits. For this purpose, group-term life insurance benefits will not be considered to discriminate merely because the amount of life insurance provided employees bears a uniform relationship to compensation. Of course, the requirement that group-term life insurance benefits be nondiscriminatory can be satisfied where, under the facts and circumstances, no discrimination in favor of key employees occurs. For example, the requirement would be satisfied when the life insurance benefits are a level dollar amount which is the same for all covered employees.

The conferees intend that the Secretary of the Treasury is to revise the tables for computing the amount includible in an employee's gross income on account of employer-provided group-term life insurance. The conferees further intend that the tables be periodically revised to reflect current group-term life insurance costs.

Effective dates

The agreement's provisions relating to parity between corporate and noncorporate employers, top-heavy plans, organizations performing management functions, employee leasing, and group-term life insurance apply to years beginning after December 31, 1983.

The provisions relating to certain corporations performing personal services applies to taxable years beginning after December 31, 1982.

4. Retirement savings for church employees

Present law

Under present law, public schools and certain tax-exempt organizations (including churches) may contribute to a tax-sheltered annuity contract for an employee. Annual contributions excluded from an employee's income are limited to 20 percent of the employee's compensation multiplied by the number of the employee's years of service with the employer, reduced by amounts already contributed by the employer. Employer contributions to a tax-sheltered annuity are also subject to the overall limit on annual additions to tax-favored retirement savings arrangements. Special one-time elections increase the overall limit for a year to allow contributions in that year that are permitted under the exclusion allowance on account of prior years of service. The elections are not available to most church employees.

House bill
No provision.

Senate amendment
The Senate amendment revises the present-law tax-sheltered annuity rules as they apply to church employees by (1) providing a minimum exclusion allowance equal to the lesser of $3,000 or 100 percent of compensation for employees with adjusted gross income of $17,000 or less; (2) providing that all years of service with organizations that are part of a particular church are treated as years with one employer; (3) extending to all church employees the special catchup elections to increase the annual contribution limit; (4) providing an additional election for church employees which increases the contribution limit by up to $10,000 for any year, subject to a $40,000 lifetime cap; (5) permitting churches to maintain segregated defined contribution retirement savings programs pursuant to the tax-sheltered annuity rules; and (6) providing a special retroactive correction period for church plans.

These changes apply to taxable years beginning after December 31, 1981, except that the provision permitting retroactive amendments applies after July 1, 1982.

Conference agreement
The conference agreement follows the Senate amendment with regard to permitted contributions for church employees under the exclusion allowance and annual contribution limit for tax-sheltered annuities.

The conference agreement also follows the Senate amendment by allowing a church which maintains a tax-sheltered annuity, retirement income account, or pension plan, a retroactive amendment period if the annuity, account or plan, is required to be amended by reason of any law, or any regulation, ruling or other action under the tax laws. During the correction period, the annuity, account, or plan would be treated as satisfying the applicable tax-law requirement. To qualify for this treatment, the required amendment or other modification generally must be made not later than at the next earliest church convention. However, the Secretary of the Treasury may prescribe an alternative time period within which the required amendment is to be made. In this regard, the Secretary is to take into account that church governing bodies typically meet at lengthy intervals. Of course, in no event is the permitted correction period for a church to be less than that allowed under present law (sec. 401(b)).

The conference agreement also follows the Senate amendment by providing that the tax rules for tax-sheltered annuities are to apply to church-maintained retirement income accounts that are defined contribution plans (sec. 414(i)). However, the conference agreement further provides that a church-maintained retirement income program in existence on August 13, 1982 will not be considered as failing to satisfy the requirements for a tax-sheltered annuity (sec. 403(b)) merely because the program is a defined benefit plan (sec. 414(j)). For this purpose, a church-maintained retirement income program is considered to be in existence on August 13, 1982, notwithstanding that after that date the program is amended, otherwise modified, or extended to benefit other employees. In addition, if a church-maintained retirement income program which is otherwise a defined benefit plan provides a benefit which is based, in part, on the balance of a separate account of an employee, the conferees intend that the separate account can qualify as a defined contribution plan for purposes of the rules relating to retirement income accounts.

The conferees intend that the assets of a retirement income account for the benefit of an employee or his beneficiaries may be commingled in a common fund made up of such accounts. However, that part of the common fund which equitably belongs to any account must be separately accounted for (i.e., it must be possible at all times to determine the account's interest in the fund), and cannot be used for, or diverted to, any purposes other than the exclusive benefit of such employee and beneficiaries. Provided those requirements are met, the assets of a retirement income account also may be commingled with the assets of a tax-qualified plan without adversely affecting the status of the account or the qualification of the plan.

The conferees also intend that the assets of a church plan (sec. 414(e)) may be commingled in a common fund with other amounts devoted exclusively to church purposes (for example, a fund maintained by a church pension board) if that part of the fund which equitably belongs to the plan is separately accounted for and cannot be used for or diverted to purposes other than for the exclusive benefit of employees and their beneficiaries. Of course, the reasonable costs of administering a retirement income account (including an account which is a part of a common fund) may be charged against the account. Such costs include the reasonable costs of administering a retirement income program of which the account is a part, including costs associated with informing employees and employers of the availability of the program.

5. State judicial retirement plans

Present law

Under present law, State or local government employees may defer compensation under an eligible State deferred compensation plan, subject to prescribed annual limits. If a plan of a State or local government is not an eligible plan, amounts under the plan are includible in an employee's income when there is no substantial risk of forfeiture.

House bill
No provision.

Senate amendment

The Senate amendment provides that participants in a qualified State judicial plan are not required to include benefits in gross income merely because there is no substantial risk that the benefits will be forfeited. The plan must be a mandatory retirement plan for State judges under which each contributes the same percentage of income and receives a retirement benefit based upon compensation paid to judges holding similar positions. The plan must have been continuously in existence since December 31, 1978, and must meet certain additional requirements. The provision applies to taxable years beginning after December 31, 1978.

Conference agreement

The conference agreement follows the Senate amendment.

6. Contribution for disabled employees

Present law

Under present law, contributions to a tax-qualified profit-sharing or other defined contributions to a tax-qualified profit-sharing or other defined contribution plan generally may not be made for an employee after the employee separates from the service of the employer.

House bill
No provision.

Senate amendment

The Senate amendment permits an employer to continue deductible contributions to a profit-sharing or other defined contribution plan for an employee (other than an officer, owner, or highly compensated individual) who is permanently and totally disabled provided that the contributions are nonforfeitable when made. For this purpose, a disabled employee's compensation is deemed equal to his annualized compensation prior to his becoming disabled. The provision applies to years beginning after December 31, 1981.

Conference agreement
The conference agreement follows the Senate amendment.

7. Participation in group trusts by governmental plans

Present law
Under present law, a group trust is exempt from tax only if each of the participating trusts is a qualified trust forming a part of a qualified pension, etc., plan or an IRA.

House bill
No provision.

Senate amendment
The Senate amendment provides that the tax-exempt status of a group trust will not be adversely affected merely because a participating trust is part of a governmental plan without regard to whether the governmental trust is a qualified plan. The provision applies to taxable years beginning after December 31, 1981.

Conference agreement
The conference agreement modifies the Senate amendment generally to permit all governmental retirement plans to participate in a tax-exempt group trust. Under the conference agreement, the tax-exempt status of a group trust will not be adversely affected merely because the trust accepts monies from (a) a retirement plan of a State or local government, whether or not the plan is a qualified plan and whether or not the assets are held in trust, or (b) any State or local governmental monies intended for use in satisfying an obligation of such State or local government to provide a retirement benefit under a governmental plan. Of course, any group trust in which a plan of a private employer participates will remain subject to the present-law rules relating to unrelated business taxable income (sec. 511 et seq.), notwithstanding that the trust includes a governmental plan.

E. Insurance Provisions

* * *

3. Life insurance reserves and contract liabilities

Present law
Present law permits taxpayers to revalue life insurance reserves computed on a preliminary term basis to a net level premium basis. Under an approximate revaluation method, reserves for other than term insurance are generally increased by $21 per $1,000 insurance in force, less 2.1 percent of reserves under such contracts. Also, in computing reserves for certain contracts, taxpayers may reflect the future liability for interest (which may be guaranteed for more than one year) in excess of the assumed rate for such contracts.

Under present law, life insurance companies are deemed to allocate investment yield to pension contracts on the basis of the current earnings rate whether or not that rate exceeds the rate guaranteed under the contract. However, if the guaranteed rate of interest exceeds the current earnings rate, a taxpayer can allocate investment yield at the actual rate rather than the current earnings rate by removing life contingencies from the contracts.

For purposes of qualifying as a life insurance company for tax purposes, present law requires that more than 50 percent of a company's total reserves must consist of life insurance reserves. The Internal Revenue Service has several pending ruling requests concerning the reserve treatment of funds held under certain pension contracts that do not involve life contingencies (i.e., that do not contain permanent annuity purchase rate guarantees).

House bill
No provision.

Senate amendment
The Senate amendment revises the approximate revaluation formula for preliminary term reserves by reducing the revaluation from $21 to $19 per $1,000 of other than term insurance in force, for business written after March 31, 1982. In addition, no reserve deductions will be allowed for excess interest guaranteed beyond the close of a taxable year.

The Senate amendment provides that, beginning July 1, 1983, the policy or contract liability for group pension contracts, for purposes of determining the excludable policyholder share of investment yield, is limited to the amount of interest actually credited to the contracts. The intention is to eliminate the so-called "double-dip" available under present law with respect to these contracts.

Finally, the Senate amendment provides that, for any taxable year ending before January 1, 1985, life insurance company status for a company will not be changed by treating reserves for group pension contracts without permanent annuity purchase rate guarantees as not being insurance reserves.

The reduction for revaluing preliminary term reserves is effective for taxable years beginning after 1981 and before January 1, 1985, but only for business written after March 31, 1982. The limitation on computing reserves for guaranteed interest is effective for guarantees made after July 1, 1982, and before January 1, 1985. The limitation on interest credited to group pension contracts applies to periods beginning after July 1, 1983 and before January 1, 1985. The provision dealing with the status of a company as a life insurance company applies to taxable years ending before January 1, 1985.

Conference agreement

Generally, the conference agreement follows the Senate amendment. However, the reduction in the approximate revaluation formula for preliminary term reserves is made permanent rather than applying only for the 2-year period.

A transitional rule is provided for the rules disallowing excess interest guaranteed beyond the close of a taxable year for certain situations when the establishment of such reserves for taxable years beginning before January 1, 1982, did not result in any Federal income tax benefits. In these cases, the amount of such reserves may be recomputed by a taxpayer as of the beginning of the first taxable year beginning after December 31, 1981, to reflect the amount that would have been determined as of the close of the previous taxable year if the new limitation had been in effect. This recomputation would be taken into account for purposes of determining any increase or decrease in reserves for taxable years beginning after December 31, 1981. However, taxpayers taking advantage of this transition rule must compute such reserves in accordance with the new rule notwithstanding the fact that the interest rate guarantees were made prior to July 1, 1982.

Except for the permanent change relating to the revaluation of preliminary term reserves, the other provisions relating to life insurance reserves and contract liabilities will apply only during a period (1982-1983) rather than a 3-year period. The provisions relating to the allocation of investment yield to group pension contracts will apply as of January 1, 1983 (rather than July 1, 1983) during the 2-year period.

* * *

7. Amounts received under annuity contracts

Present law

Under present law, taxation of interest or other current earnings on a policyholder's investment in an annuity contract generally is deferred until annuity payments are received or amounts characterized as income are withdrawn. Amounts paid out before the annuity starting date are first a return of capital and are taxable (as ordinary income) only after investment in the contract is recovered. There is no tax penalty for withdrawals or surrenders before the annuity starting date or before a certain age.

House bill

No provision.

Senate amendment

The Senate amendment provides that amounts received before the annuity starting date will be treated first as withdrawals of income earned on investments to the extent of such income, the remainder being treated as a return of capital. Likewise, loans under the contract, or amounts received upon assignment or pledging of the contract, will be treated as amounts received under the contract. These provisions apply as of July 1, 1982, but do not apply to income amounts allocable to investments made before July 2, 1982, to endowment or life insurance contracts (except to the extent prescribed in regulations), or to contracts purchased under qualified pension plans.

In addition, the Senate amendment imposes a penalty on certain distributions from an annuity contract. The penalty will be equal to 10 percent of the amount includible in income, to the extent the amount is allocable to an investment made within 10 years of the receipt. However, the penalty will not apply to a distribution that is (1) made on or after the policyholder reaches age 59½; (2) made to a beneficiary on or after death of the policyholder; (3) attributable to the policyholder becoming disabled; (4) a payment under an annuity for life or at least 5 years; (5) from a qualified pension plan; or (6) allocable to an investment before July 2, 1982.

The penalty only applies to distributions made after December 31, 1982.

Conference agreement
The conference agreement generally follows the Senate amendment, but reduces the amount of the penalty to 5 percent and changes the effective date for the provisions to August 13, 1982 (except that the penalty still applies to distributions made after December 31, 1982).

Also under the conference agreement, a replacement contract obtained in a tax-free exchange of contracts succeeds to the status of the surrendered contract for purposes of the new provisions. Such exchanges are subject to the new provisions in this Act for information reporting on pension plans and commercial annuity contracts.

* * *

F. Employment Tax Provisions

* * *

3. Extension of Social Security hospital insurance taxes and Medicare coverage to Federal employees

Present law
Federal employees generally are not subject to social security hospital insurance taxes nor does their employment qualify them for Medicare coverage.

House bill
No provision.

Senate amendment
Federal employment would become subject to the hospital insurance portion of the FICA tax, effective January 1, 1983, and the newly covered Federal employment would be used in determining eligibility for protection under medicare part A (hospital insurance). A transitional provision would provide credit for additional hospital insurance quarters of coverage for certain Federal employees who have attained age 57 by 1983, and who otherwise would not qualify for medicare protection even though they have made hospital insurance tax contributions based on their Federal employment.

Conference agreement
The conference agreement follows the Senate amendment, with several clarifying and other changes, as follows: All Federal employment currently excluded from FICA taxes would be covered, except for certain services performed by penal inmates, medical interns and student nurses, and temporary emergency employment; hospital insurance quarters of coverage would be earned and credited in the same way as for other covered employment (i.e., specified amounts of covered earnings in a year would result in specified numbers of quarters of coverage); and the transitional provision, which would apply to Federal employees who perform service during and before January 1983, would give such employees credit toward medicare eligibility (up to the minimum amount required) for past Federal employment. Employees of States and localities, including the District of Columbia, would continue to be exempt from FICA taxes.

The conference agreement permits individuals who have worked for the Federal Government to obtain medicare benefits if they file and meet the insured status and other disability eligibility requirements of the social security disability cash benefits program, even though no such cash benefits would otherwise be payable. The medicare application would be treated as an application for disability benefits (for purposes of determining eligibility to medicare).

The Secretary of Health and Human Services and the Director of the Office of Personnel Management are required fully to inform Federal employees (particularly those who might be or become eligible for medicare benefits because of a disability) of the terms and conditions of medicare eligibility.

* * *

Part II Text of ERISA
ERISA Finding List

ERISA Sections

Section
1. Short title and table of contents 182

Title 1—Protection of Employee Benefit Rights
Subtitle A—General Provisions

2. Findings and declaration of policy 185
3. Definitions 186
4. Coverage 193

Subtitle B—Regulatory Provisions

Part 1—Reporting and Disclosure

101. Duty of disclosure and reporting 194
102. Plan description and summary plan description 194
103. Annual reports 195
104. Filing with Secretary and furnishing information to participants 200
105. Reporting of participant's benefit rights 203
106. Reports made public information 203
107. Retention of records 203
108. Reliance on administrative interpretations 203
109. Forms 204
110. Alternative methods of compliance 204
111. Repeal and effective date 204

Part 2—Participation and Vesting

201. Coverage 205
202. Minimum participation standards 206
203. Minimum vesting standards 207
204. Benefit accrual requirements 211
205. Joint and survivor annuity requirement 216
206. Other provisions relating to form and payment of benefits 217
207. Temporary variances from certain vesting requirements 218
208. Mergers and consolidations of plans or transfers of plan assets 218
209. Recordkeeping and reporting requirements 219
210. Plans maintained by more than one employer, predecessor plans, and employer groups 219
211. Effective dates 220

ERISA FINDING LIST

Section

Part 3—Funding

301.	Coverage	221
302.	Minimum funding standards	222
303.	Variance from minimum funding standard	226
304.	Extension of amortization periods	227
305.	Alternative minimum funding standard	227
306.	Effective dates	228

Part 4—Fiduciary Responsibility

401.	Coverage	228
402.	Establishment of plan	229
403.	Establishment of trust	229
404.	Fiduciary duties	231
405.	Liability for breach by co-fiduciary	232
406.	Prohibited transactions	233
407.	10 percent limitation with respect to acquisition and holding of employer securities and employer real property by certain plans	233
408.	Exemptions from prohibited transactions	236
409.	Liability for breach of fiduciary duty	239
410.	Exculpatory provisions; insurance	239
411.	Prohibition against certain persons holding certain positions	240
412.	Bonding	241
413.	Limitation on actions	242
414.	Effective date	242

Part 5—Administration and Enforcement

501.	Criminal penalties	243
502.	Civil enforcement	243
503.	Claims procedure	246
504.	Investigative authority	246
505.	Regulations	246
506.	Other agencies and departments	246
507.	Administration	247
508.	Appropriations	247
509.	Separability provisions	247
510.	Interference with rights protected under Act	247
511.	Coercive interference	247
512.	Advisory council	248
513.	Research, studies, and annual report	249
514.	Effect on other laws	249

Title II—Amendments to the Internal Revenue Code Relating to Retirement Plans

1001.	Amendment of Internal Revenue Code of 1954	251

Section

Subtitle A—Participation, Vesting, Funding, Administration, etc.

Part 1—Participation, Vesting and Funding

1012.	Minimum vesting standards	251
1013.	Minimum funding standards	252
1016.	Conforming and clerical amendments	252
1017.	Effective dates and transitional rules	255

Part 2—Certain Other Provisions Relating to Qualified Retirement Plans

1022.	Miscellaneous provisions	257
1024.	Effective dates	259

Part 3—Registration and Information

1031.	Registration and information	259
1032.	Duties of Secretary of Health, Education, and Welfare	261
1033.	Reports by actuaries	261
1034.	Effective dates	262

Part 4—Declaratory Judgments Relating to Qualification of Certain Retirement Plans

1041.	Tax Court procedure	263

Part 5—Internal Revenue Service

1051.	Establishment of Office	264
1052.	Authorization of appropriations	265

Subtitle B—Other Amendments to the Internal Revenue Code Relating to Retirement Plans

2001.	Contributions on behalf of self-employed individuals and shareholder-employees	265
2002.	Deduction for retirement savings	265
2003.	Prohibited transactions	267
2004.	Limitations on benefits and contributions	269
2005.	Taxation of certain lump sum distributions	269
2006.	Salary reduction regulations	270
2007.	Rules for certain negotiated plans	272
2008.	Certain Armed Forces survivor annuities	272

Title III—Jurisdiction, Administration, Enforcement; Joint Pension Task Force, Etc.

Subtitle A—Jurisdiction, Administration and Enforcement

3001.	Procedures in connection with the issuance of certain determination letters by the Secretary of the Treasury	273
3002.	Procedures with respect to continued compliance with requirements relating to participation, vesting, and funding standards	274

Section

3003.	Procedures in connection with prohibited transactions	276
3004.	Coordination between the Department of the Treasury and the Department of Labor	276

Subtitle B—Joint Pension Task Force; Studies
Part 1—Joint Pension Task Force

3021.	Establishment	277
3022.	Duties	277

Part 2—Other Studies

3031.	Congressional study	277
3032.	Protection for employees under federal procurement, construction, and research contracts and grants	278

Subtitle C—Enrollment of Actuaries

3041.	Establishment of Joint Board for the Enrollment of Actuaries	280
3042.	Enrollment by Joint Board	280
3043.	Amendment of Internal Revenue Code	280

Title IV—Plan Termination Insurance
Subtitle A—Pension Benefit Guaranty Corporation

4001.	Definitions	281
4002.	Pension Benefit Guaranty Corporation	282
4003.	Investigatory authority; cooperation with other agencies; civil actions	285
4004.	Temporary authority for initial period	286
4005.	Establishment of pension benefit guaranty funds	287
4006.	Premium rates	289
4007.	Payment of premiums	292
4008.	Report by the corporation	293
4009.	Portability assistance	293

Subtitle B—Coverage

4021.	Plans covered	294
4022.	Single-employer plan benefits guaranteed	295
4022A.	Multiemployer plan benefits guaranteed	297
4022B.	Aggregate limit on benefits guaranteed	302
4023.	Plan fiduciaries	302

Subtitle C—Terminations

4041.	Termination of single-employer plans	302
4041A.	Termination of multiemployer plans	303
4042.	Termination by corporation	304
4043.	Reportable events	308

Section

4044.	Allocation of assets	309
4045.	Recapture of certain payments	310
4046.	Reports to trustee	311
4047.	Restoration of plans	311
4048.	Date of termination	312

Subtitle D—Liability

4061.	Amounts payable by the corporation	312
4062.	Liability of employer	312
4063.	Liability of substantial employer for withdrawal	313
4064.	Liability of employers on termination of plan maintained by more than one employer	315
4065.	Annual report of plan administrator	315
4066.	Annual notification to substantial employers	315
4067.	Recovery of employer liability for plan termination	316
4068.	Lien for liability of employer	316

Subtitle E—Special Provisions for Multiemployer Plans

Part 1—Employer withdrawals

4201.	Withdrawal liability established	317
4202.	Determination and collection of liability; notification of employer	317
4203.	Complete withdrawal	317
4204.	Sale of assets	319
4205.	Partial withdrawals	320
4206.	Adjustment for partial withdrawal	322
4207.	Reduction or waiver of complete withdrawal liability	324
4208.	Reduction of partial withdrawal liability	324
4209.	De minimis rule	325
4210.	No withdrawal liability for certain temporary contribution obligation periods	326
4211.	Methods for computing withdrawal liability	326
4212.	Obligation to contribute; special rules	332
4213.	Actuarial assumptions, etc.	332
4214.	Application of plan amendments	332
4215.	Plan notification to corporation of potentially significant withdrawals	333
4216.	Special rules for section 404(c) plans	333
4217.	Application of part in case of certain pre-1980 withdrawals	334
4218.	Withdrawal not to occur merely because of change in business form or suspension of contributions during labor dispute	334

ERISA FINDING LIST 181

Section

4219.	Notice, collection, etc., of withdrawal liability	334
4220.	Approval of amendments	337
4221.	Resolution of disputes	337
4222.	Reimbursements for uncollectible withdrawal liability	338
4223.	Withdrawal liability payment fund	338
4224.	Alternative method of withdrawal liability payments	340
4225.	Limitation on withdrawal liability	340

Part 2—Merger or Transfer of Plan Assets or Liabilities

4231.	Mergers and transfers between multiemployer plans	341
4232.	Transfers between a multiemployer plan and a single-employer plan	342
4233.	Partition	343
4234.	Asset transfer rules	344
4235.	Transfers pursuant to change in bargaining representative	344

Part 3—Reorganization; Minimum Contribution Requirements for Multiemployer Plans

4241.	Reorganization status	346
4242.	Notice of reorganization and funding requirements	348
4243.	Minimum contribution requirement	348
4244.	Overburden credit against minimum contribution requirement	351
4244A.	Adjustments in accrued benefits	352
4245.	Insolvent plans	354

Part 4—Financial Assistance

4261.	Financial assistance	356

Part 5—Benefits After Termination

4281.	Benefits under certain terminated plans	356

Part 6—Enforcement

4301.	Civil actions	357
4302.	Penalty for failure to provide notice	358
4303.	Election of plan status	358

Subtitle F—Transition Rules and Effective Dates

4401.	Amendment to Internal Revenue Code of 1954	358
4402.	Effective date; special rules	359

*EMPLOYEE RETIREMENT INCOME SECURITY ACT OF 1974, AS AMENDED

SHORT TITLE AND TABLE OF CONTENTS

Section 1. This Act may be cited as the "Employee Retirement Income Security Act of 1974."

Table of Contents

Section
1. Short title and table of contents.

Title I—Protection of Employee Benefit Rights

Subtitle A—General Provisions
2. Findings and declaration of policy.
3. Definitions.
4. Coverage.

Subtitle B—Regulatory Provisions

Part 1—Reporting and Disclosure
101. Duty of disclosure and reporting.
102. Plan description and summary plan description.
103. Annual reports.
104. Filing with Secretary and furnishing information to participants
105. Reporting of participant's benefit rights.
106. Reports made public information.
107. Retention of records.
108. Reliance on administrative interpretations.
109. Forms.
110. Alternative methods of compliance.
111. Repeal and effective date.

Part 2—Participation and Vesting
201. Coverage.
202. Minimum participation standards.

Section
203. Minimum vesting standards.
204. Benefit accrual requirements.
205. Joint and survivor annuity requirement.
206. Other provisions relating to form and payment of benefits.
207. Temporary variances from certain vesting requirements.
208. Mergers and consolidations of plans or transfers of plan assets.
209. Recordkeeping and reporting requirements.
210. Plans maintained by more than one employer, predecessor plans, and employer groups.
211. Effective dates.

Part 3—Funding
301. Coverage.
302. Minimum funding standards.
303. Variance from minimum funding standard.
304. Extension of amortization periods.
305. Alternative minimum funding standard.
306. Effective dates.

Part 4—Fiduciary Responsibility
401. Coverage.
402. Establishment of plan.
403. Establishment of trust.
404. Fiduciary duties.
405. Liability for breach by co-fiduciary.
406. Prohibited transactions.
407. 10 percent limitation with respect to acquisition and holding of employer securities and employer real property by certain plans.
408. Exemptions from prohibited transactions.

* [*Editor's Note:* This is the text of ERISA, as amended by various public laws, including PL 95-598, which dealt with bankruptcy proceedings, and PL 96-364, the Multiemployer Pension Plan Amendments Act of 1980 (MPPAA). The text of sections of the Internal Revenue Code that were amended by ERISA, MPPAA, and various tax laws (including PL 97-34, the Economic Recovery Tax Act of 1981, and PL 97-248, the Tax Equity and Fiscal Responsibility Act of 1982) follows the text of ERISA.

Except as otherwise provided in PL 96-364 and in subsection (b) below:

(a) if the way in which any amendments under PL 96-364 will apply to a particular circumstance is to be set forth in regulations, any reasonable action during the period before such regulations take effect shall be treated as complying with such regulations for such period.

(b) Subsection (a) shall not apply to any action which violates any instruction issued, or temporary rule prescribed, by the agency having jurisdiction, but only if such instruction or rule was published, or furnished to the party taking the action, before such action was taken.]

Section
409. Liability for breach of fiduciary duty.
410. Exculpatory provisions; insurance.
411. Prohibition against certain persons holding certain positions
412. Bonding.
413. Limitation on actions.
414. Effective date.

Part 5—Administration and Enforcement
501. Criminal penalties.
502. Civil enforcement.
503. Claims procedure.
504. Investigative authority.
505. Regulations.
506. Other agencies and departments.
507. Administration
508. Appropriations.
509. Separability provisions.
510. Interference with rights protected under Act.
511. Coercive interference.
512. Advisory Council.
513. Research, studies, and annual report.
514. Effect on other laws.

Title II—Amendments to the Internal Revenue Code Relating to Retirement Plans

[Excerpts]

Section
1001. Amendment of Internal Revenue Code of 1954.

Subtitle A—Participation, Vesting, Funding, Administration, etc.

Part 1—Participation, Vesting, and Funding
* * *
Section
1012. Minimum vesting standards.
1013. Minimum funding standards.
* * *
1016. Conforming and clerical amendments.
1017. Effective dates and transitional rules.

Part 2—Certain Other Provisions Relating to Qualified Retirement Plans
* * *
1022. Miscellaneous provisions.
* * *
1024. Effective dates.

Part 3—Registration and Information
1031. Registration and information.
1032. Duties of Secretary of Health, Education, and Welfare.
1033. Reports by actuaries.
1034. Effective dates.

Part 4—Declaratory Judgments Relating to Qualification of Certain Retirement Plans
1041. Tax Court procedure.

Part 5—Internal Revenue Service
1051. Establishment of Office.
1052. Authorization of appropriations.

Subtitle B—Other Amendments to the Internal Revenue Code Relating to Retirement Plans
2001. Contributions on behalf of self-employed individuals and shareholder-employees.
2002. Deduction for retirement savings.
2003. Prohibited transactions.
2004. Limitations on benefits and contributions.
2005. Taxation of certain lump sum distributions.
2006. Salary reduction regulations.
2007. Rules for certain negotiated plans.
2008. Certain armed forces survivor annuities.

Title III—Jurisdiction, Administration, Enforcement; Joint Pension Task Force, Etc.

Subtitle A—Jurisdiction, Administration, and Enforcement
Section
3001. Procedures in connection with the issuance of certain determination letters by the Secretary of the Treasury.
3002. Procedures with respect to continued compliance with requirements relating to participation, vesting, and funding standards.
3003. Procedures in connection with prohibited transactions.
3004. Coordination between the Department of the Treasury and the Department of Labor.

Subtitle B—Joint Pension Task Force; Studies

Part 1—Joint Pension Task Force
Section
3021. Establishment.
3022. Duties.

Part 2—Other Studies
3031. Congressional study.
3032. Protection for employees under Federal procurement, construction, and research contracts and grants.

Subtitle C—Enrollment of Actuaries
3041. Establishment of Joint Board for the enrollment of actuaries.
3042. Enrollment by Joint Board.
3043. Amendment of Internal Revenue Code.

Sec. 1

Title IV—Plan Termination Insurance

Subtitle A—Pension Benefit Guaranty Corporation

Section
4001. Definitions.
4002. Pension Benefit Guaranty Corporation.
4003. Investigatory authority; cooperation with other agencies; civil actions.
4004. Temporary authority for initial period.
4005. Establishment of pension benefit guaranty funds.
4006. Premium rates.
4007. Payment of premiums.
4008. Report by the corporation.
4009. Portability assistance.

Subtitle B—Coverage

4021. Plans covered.
4022. Single-employer plan benefits guaranteed.
4022A. Multiemployer plan benefits guaranteed.
4022B. Aggregate limit on benefits guaranteed.
4023. Plan fiduciaries.

Subtitle C—Terminations

4041. Termination of single-employer plans.
4041A. Termination of multiemployer plans.
4042. Termination by corporation.
4043. Reportable events.
4044. Allocation of assets.
4045. Recapture of certain payments.
4046. Reports to trustee.
4047. Restoration of plans.
4048. Date of termination.

Subtitle D—Liability

4061. Amounts payable by the corporation.
4062. Liability of employer.
4063. Liability of substantial employer for withdrawal.
4064. Liability of employers on termination of plan maintained by more than one employer.
4065. Annual report of plan administrator.
4066. Annual notification to substantial employers.
4067. Recovery of employer liability for plan termination.
4068. Lien for liability of employer.

Subtitle E—Special Provisions for Multiemployer Plans

Part 1—Employer Withdrawals

4201. Withdrawal liability established.
4202. Determination and collection of liability; notification of employer.
4203. Complete withdrawal.
4204. Sale of assets.
4205. Partial withdrawals.
4206. Adjustment for partial withdrawal.
4207. Reduction or waiver of complete withdrawal liability.
4208. Reduction or abatement of partial withdrawal liability.
4209. De minimis rule.
4210. No withdrawal liability for certain temporary contribution obligation periods.
4211. Methods for computing withdrawal liability.
4212. Obligation to contribute; special rules.
4213. Actuarial assumptions, etc.
4214. Application of plan amendments.
4215. Plan notification to corporation of potentially significant withdrawals.
4216. Special rules for section 404(c) plans.
4217. Application of part in case of certain pre-1980 withdrawals.
4218. Withdrawal not to occur merely because of change in business form or suspension of contributions during labor dispute.
4219. Notice, collection, etc., of withdrawal liability.
4220. Approval of amendments.
4221. Resolution of disputes.
4222. Reimbursements for uncollectible withdrawal liability.
4223. Withdrawal liability payment fund.
4224. Alternative method of withdrawal liability payments.
4225. Limitation on withdrawal liability.

Part 2—Merger or Transfer of Plan Assets or Liabilities

4231. Mergers and transfers between multiemployer plans.
4232. Transfers between a multiemployer plan and a single-employer plan.
4233. Partition.
4234. Asset transfer rules.
4235. Transfers pursuant to change in bargaining representative.

Part 3—Reorganization; Minimum Contribution Requirement for Multiemployer Plans

4241. Reorganization status.

Sec. 1

4242. Notice of reorganization and funding requirements.
4243. Minimum contribution requirement.
4244. Overburden credit against minimum contribution requirement.
4244A. Adjustment in accrued benefits.
4245. Insolvent plans.

Part 4—Financial Assistance
4261. Financial assistance.

Part 5—Benefits After Termination
4281. Benefits under certain terminated plans.

Part 6—Enforcement
4301. Civil actions.
4302. Penalty for failure to provide notice.
4303. Election of plan status.

Subtitle F—Transition Rules and Effective Dates
4401. Amendment to Internal Revenue Code of 1954.
4402. Transition rules and effective dates.

Title I—Protection of Employee Benefit Rights

Subtitle A—General Provisions

FINDINGS AND DECLARATION OF POLICY

Sec. 2. (a) The Congress finds that the growth in size, scope, and numbers of employee benefit plans in recent years has been rapid and substantial; that the operational scope and economic impact of such plans is increasingly interstate; that the continued well-being and security of millions of employees and their dependents are directly affected by these plans; that they are affected with a national public interest; that they have become an important factor affecting the stability of employment and the successful development of industrial relations; that they have become an important factor in commerce because of the interstate character of their activities, and of the activities of their participants, and the employers, employee organizations, and other entities by which they are established or maintained; that a large volume of the activities of such plans is carried on by means of the mails and instrumentalities of interstate commerce; that owing to the lack of employee information and adequate safeguards concerning their operation, it is desirable in the interests of employees and their beneficiaries, and to provide for the general welfare and the free flow of commerce, that disclosure be made and safeguards be provided with respect to the establishment, operation, and administration of such plans; that they substantially affect the revenues of the United States because they are afforded preferential Federal tax treatment; that despite the enormous growth in such plans many employees with long years of employment are losing anticipated retirement benefits owing to the lack of vesting provisions in such plans; that owing to the inadequacy of current minimum standards, the soundness and stability of plans with respect to adequate funds to pay promised benefits may be endangered; that owing to the termination of plans before requisite funds have been accumulated, employees and their beneficiaries have been deprived of anticipated benefits; and that it is therefore desirable in the interests of employees and their beneficiaries, for the protection of the revenue of the United States, and to provide for the free flow of commerce, that minimum standards be provided assuring the equitable character of such plans and their financial soundness.

(b) It is hereby declared to be the policy of this Act to protect interstate commerce and the interests of participants in employee benefit plans and their beneficiaries, by requiring the disclosure and reporting to participants and beneficiaries of financial and other information with respect thereto, by establishing standards of

Sec. 2 (b)

conduct, responsibility, and obligation for fiduciaries of employee benefit plans, and by providing for appropriate remedies, sanctions, and ready access to the Federal courts.

(c) It is hereby further declared to be the policy of this Act to protect interstate commerce, the Federal taxing power, and the interests of participants in private pension plans and their beneficiaries by improving the equitable character and the soundness of such plans by requiring them to vest the accrued benefits of employees with significant periods of service, to meet minimum standards of funding, and by requiring plan termination insurance.

DEFINITIONS

Sec. 3. For purposes of this title:

(1) The terms "employee welfare benefit plan" and "welfare plan" mean any plan, fund, or program which was heretofore or is hereafter established or maintained by an employer or by an employee organization, or by both, to the extent that such plan, fund, or program was established or is maintained for the purpose of providing for its participants or their beneficiaries, through the purchase of insurance or otherwise, (A) medical, surgical, or hospital care or benefits, or benefits in the event of sickness, accident, disability, death or unemployment, or vacation benefits, apprenticeship or other training programs, or day care centers, scholarship funds, or prepaid legal services, or (B) any benefit described in section 302(c) of the Labor Management Relations Act, 1947 (other than pensions on retirement or death, and insurance to provide such pensions).

(2) (A) Except as provided in subparagraph (B), the terms "employee pension benefit plan" and "pension plan" mean any plan, fund, or program which was heretofore or is hereafter established or maintained by an employer or by an employee organization, or by both, to the extent that by its express terms or as a result of surrounding circumstances such plan, fund, or program—

(i) provides retirement income to employees, or

(ii) results in a deferral of income by employees for periods extending to the termination of covered employment or beyond, regardless of the method of calculating the contributions made to the plan, the method of calculating the benefits under the plan or the method of distributing benefits from the plan.

(B) The Secretary may by regulation prescribe rules consistent with the standards and purposes of this Act providing one or more exempt categories under which—

(i) severance pay arrangements, and

(ii) supplemental retirement income payments, under which the pension benefits of retirees or their beneficiaries are supplemented to take into account some portion or all of the increases in the cost of living (as determined by the Secretary of Labor) since retirement,

shall, for purposes of this title, be treated as welfare plans rather than pension plans. In the case of any arrangement or payment a principal effect of which is the evasion of the standards or purposes of this Act applicable to pension plans, such arrangement or payment shall be treated as a pension plan.

(3) The term "employee benefit plan" or "plan" means an employee welfare benefit plan or an employee pension benefit plan or a plan which is both an employee welfare benefit plan and an employee pension benefit plan.

(4) The term "employee organization" means any labor union or any organization of any kind, or any agency or employee representation committee, association, group, or plan, in which employees participate and which exists for the purpose, in whole or in part, of dealing with employers concerning an employee benefit plan, or other matters incidental to employment relationships; or any employees'

Sec. 2 (c)

beneficiary association organized for the purpose in whole or in part, of establishing such a plan.

(5) The term "employer" means any person acting directly as an employer, or indirectly in the interest of an employer, in relation to an employee benefit plan; and includes a group or association of employers acting for an employer in such capacity.

(6) The term "employee" means any individual employed by an employer.

(7) The term "participant" means any employee or former employee of an employer, or any member or former member of an employee organization, who is or may become eligible to receive a benefit of any type from an employee benefit plan which covers employees of such employer or members of such organization, or whose beneficiaries may be eligible to receive any such benefit.

(8) The term "beneficiary" means a person designated by a participant, or by the terms of an employee benefit plan, who is or may become entitled to a benefit thereunder.

(9) The term "person" means an individual, partnership, joint venture, corporation, mutual company, joint-stock company, trust, estate, unincorporated organization, association, or employee organization.

(10) The term "State" includes any State of the United States, the District of Columbia, Puerto Rico, the Virgin Islands, American Samoa, Guam, Wake Island, and the Canal Zone. The term "United States" when used in the geographic sense means the States and the Outer Continental Shelf lands defined in the Outer Continental Shelf Lands Act (43 U.S.C. 1331-1343).

(11) The term "commerce" means trade, traffic, commerce, transportation, or communication between any State and any place outside thereof.

(12) The term "industry or activity affecting commerce" means any activity, business, or industry in commerce or in which a labor dispute would hinder or obstruct commerce or the free flow of commerce, and includes any activity or industry "affecting commerce" within the meaning of the Labor Management Relations Act, 1947, or the Railway Labor Act.

(13) The term "Secretary" means the Secretary of Labor.

(14) The term "party in interest" means, as to an employee benefit plan—

(A) any fiduciary (including, but not limited to, any administrator, officer, trustee, or custodian), counsel, or employee of such employee benefit plan;

(B) a person providing services to such plan;

(C) an employer any of whose employees are covered by such plan;

(D) an employee organization any of whose members are covered by such plan;

(E) an owner, direct or indirect, of 50 percent or more of—

(i) the combined voting power of all classes of stock entitled to vote or the total value of shares of all classes of stock of a corporation,

(ii) the capital interest or the profits interest of a partnership, or

(iii) the beneficial interest of a trust or unincorporated enterprise,

which is an employer or an employee organization described in subparagraph (C) or (D);

(F) a relative (as defined in paragraph (15) of any individual described in subparagraph (A), (B), (C), or (E);

(G) a corporation, partnership, or trust or estate of which (or in which) 50 percent or more of—

(i) the combined voting power of all classes of stock entitled to vote or the total value of shares of all classes of stock of such corporation,

(ii) the capital interest or profits interest of such partnership, or

(iii) the beneficial interest of such trust or estate,

is owned directly or indirectly, or held

by persons described in subparagraph (A), (B), (C), (D), or (E);

(H) an employee, officer, director (or an individual having powers or responsibilities similar to those of officers or directors), or a 10 percent or more shareholder directly or indirectly, of a person described in subparagraph (B), (C), (D), (E), or (G), or of the employee benefit plan; or

(I) a 10 percent or more (directly of indirectly in capital or profits) partner or joint venturer of a person described in subparagraph (B), (C), (D), (E), or (G).

The Secretary, after consultation and coordination with the Secretary of the Treasury, may by regulation prescribe a percentage lower than 50 percent for subparagraph (E) and (G) and lower than 10 percent for subparagraph (H) or (I). The Secretary may prescribe regulations for determining the ownership (direct or indirect) of profits and beneficial interests, and the manner in which indirect stockholdings are taken into account.

Any person who is a party in interest with respect to a plan to which a trust described in section 501(c)(22) of the Internal Revenue Code of 1954 is permitted to make payments under section 4223 shall be treated as a party in interest with respect to such trust.

(15) The term "relative" means a spouse, ancestor, lineal descendant, or spouse of a lineal descendant.

(16)(A) The term "administrator" means—

(i) the person specifically so designated by the terms of the instrument under which the plan is operated;

(ii) if an administrator is not so designated, the plan sponsor; or

(iii) in the case of a plan for which an administrator is not designated and a plan sponsor cannot be identified, such other person as the Secretary may by regulation prescribe.

(B) The term "plan sponsor" means (i) the employer in the case of an employee benefit plan established or maintained by a single employer, (ii) the employee organization in the case of a plan established or maintained by an employee organization, or (iii) in the case of a plan established or maintained by two or more employers or jointly by one or more employers and one or more employee organizations, the association, committee, joint board of trustees, or other similar group of representatives of the parties who establish or maintain the plan.

(17) The term "separate account" means an account established or maintained by an insurance company under which income, gains, and losses, whether or not realized, from assets allocated to such account, are, in accordance with the applicable contract, credited to or charged against such account without regard to other income, gains, or losses of the insurance company.

(18) The term "adequate consideration" when used in part 4 of subtitle B means (A) in the case of a security for which there is a generally recognized market, either (i) the price of the security prevailing on a national securities exchange which is registered under section 6 of the Securities Exchange Act of 1934, or (ii) if the security is not traded on such a national securities exchange, a price not less favorable to the plan than the offering price for the security as established by the current bid and asked prices quoted by persons independent of the issuer and of any party in interest; and (B) in the case of an asset other than a security for which there is a generally recognized market, the fair market value of the asset as determined in good faith by the trustee or named fiduciary pursuant to the terms of the plan and in accordance with regulations promulgated by the Secretary.

(19) The term "nonforfeitable" when used with respect to a pension benefit or right means a claim obtained by a participant or his bene-

Sec. 3 (14) (H)

ficiary to that part of an immediate or deferred benefit under a pension plan which arises from the participant's service, which is unconditional, and which is legally enforceable against the plan. For purposes of this paragraph, a right to an accrued benefit derived from employer contributions shall not be treated as forfeitable merely because the plan contains a provision described in section 203(a)(3).

(20) The term "security" has the same meaning as such term has under section 2(1) of the Securities Act of 1933 (15 U.S.C. 77b(1)).

(21)(A) Except as otherwise provided in subparagraph (B), a person is a fiduciary with respect to a plan to the extent (i) he exercises any discretionary authority or discretionary control respecting management of such plan or exercises any authority or control respecting management or disposition of its assets, (ii) he renders investment advice for a fee or other compensation, direct or indirect, with respect to any moneys or other property of such plan, or has any authority or responsibility to do so, or (iii) he has any discretionary authority or discretionary responsibility in the administration of such plan. Such term includes any person designated under section 405(c)(1)(B).

(B) If any money or other property of an employee benefit plan is invested in securities issued by an investment company registered under the Investment Company Act of 1940, such investment shall not by itself cause such investment company or such investment company's investment adviser or principal underwriter to be deemed to be a fiduciary or a party in interest as those terms are defined in this title, except insofar as such investment company or its investment adviser or principal underwriter acts in connection with an employee benefit plan covering employees of the investment company, the investment adviser, or its principal underwriter. Nothing contained in this subparagraph shall limit the duties imposed on such investment company, investment adviser, or principal underwriter by any other law.

(22) The term "normal retirement benefit" means the greater of the early retirement benefit under the plan, or the benefit under the plan commencing at normal retirement age. The normal retirement benefit shall be determined without regard to—

(A) medical benefits, and

(B) disability benefits not in excess of the qualified disability benefit.

For purposes of this paragraph, a qualified disability benefit is a disability benefit provided by a plan which does not exceed the benefit which would be provided for the participant if he separated from the service at normal retirement age. For purposes of this paragraph, the early retirement benefit under a plan shall be determined without regard to any benefit under the plan which the Secretary of the Treasury finds to be a benefit described in section 204(b)(1)(G).

(23) The term "accrued benefit" means—

(A) in the case of a defined benefit plan, the individual's accrued benefit determined under the plan and, except as provided in section 204(c)(3), expressed in the form of an annual benefit commencing at normal retirement age, or

(B) in the case of a plan which is an individual account plan, the balance of the individual's account.

(24) The term "normal retirement age" means the earlier of—

(A) the time a plan participant attains normal retirement age under the plan, or

(b) the later of—

(i) the time a plan participant attains age 65, or

(ii) the 10th anniversary of the time a plan participant commenced participation in the plan.

Sec. 3 (24)

(25) The term "vested liabilities" means the present value of the immediate or deferred benefits available at normal retirement age for participants and their beneficiaries which are nonforfeitable.

(26) The term "current value" means fair market value where available and otherwise the fair value as determined in good faith by a trustee or a named fiduciary (as defined in section 402(a)(2)) pursuant to the terms of the plan and in accordance with regulations of the Secretary, assuming an orderly liquidation at the time of such determination.

(27) The term "present value", with respect to a liability, means the value adjusted to reflect anticipated events. Such adjustments shall conform to such regulations as the Secretary of the Treasury may prescribe.

(28) The term "normal service cost" or "normal cost" means the annual cost of future pension benefits and administrative expenses assigned, under an actuarial cost method, to years subsequent to a particular valuation date of a pension plan. The Secretary of the Treasury may prescribe regulations to carry out this paragraph.

(29) The term "accrued liability" means the excess of the present value, as of a particular valuation date of a pension plan, of the projected future benefits cost and administrative expenses for all plan participants and beneficiaries over the present value of future contributions for the normal cost of all applicable plan participants and beneficiaries. The Secretary of the Treasury may prescribe regulations to carry out this paragraph.

(30) The term "unfunded accrued liability" means the excess of the accrued liability, under an actuarial cost method which so provides, over the present value of the assets of a pension plan. The Secretary of the Treasury may prescribe regulations to carry out this paragraph.

(31) The term "advance funding actuarial cost method" or "actuarial cost method" means a recognized actuarial technique utilized for establishing the amount and incidence of the annual actuarial cost of pension plan benefits and expenses. Acceptable actuarial cost methods shall include the accrued benefit cost method (unit credit method), the entry age normal cost method, the individual level premium cost method, the aggregate cost method, the attained age normal cost method, and the frozen initial liability cost method. The terminal funding cost method and the current funding (pay-as-you-go) cost method are not acceptable actuarial cost methods. The Secretary of the Treasury shall issue regulations to further define acceptable actuarial cost methods.

(32) The term "governmental plan" means a plan established or maintained for its employees by the Government of the United States, by the government of any State or political subdivision thereof, or by any agency or instrumentality of any of the foregoing. The term "governmental plan" also includes any plan to which the Railroad Retirement Act of 1935 or 1937 applies, and which is financed by contributions required under that Act and any plan of an international organization which is exempt from taxation under the provisions of the International Organizations Immunities Act (59 Stat. 669).

(33) (A) The term "church plan" means a plan established and maintained (to the extent required in clause (ii) of subparagraph (B)) for its employees (or their beneficiaries) by a church or by a convention or association of churches which is exempt from tax under section 501 of the Internal Revenue Code of 1954.

(B) The term "church plan" does not include a plan—

(i) which is established and maintained primarily for the benefit of employees (or their beneficiaries) of such church or convention or association of churches who are employed in connection with one or more unrelated trades or businesses (within the meaning of section 513 of the Internal Revenue Code of 1954), or

Sec. 3 (25)

(ii) if less than substantially all of the individuals included in the plan are individuals described in subparagraph (A) or in clause (ii) of subparagraph (C) (or their beneficiaries).

(C) For purposes of this paragraph—

(i) A plan established and maintained for its employees (or their beneficiaries) by a church or by a convention or association of churches includes a plan maintained by an organization, whether a civil law corporation or otherwise, the principal purpose or function of which is the administration or funding of a plan or program for the provision of retirement benefits or welfare benefits, or both, for the employees of a church or a convention or association of churches, if such organization is controlled by or associated with a church or a convention or association of churches.

(ii) The term employee of a church or a convention or association of churches includes—

(I) a duly ordained, commissioned, or licensed minister of a church in the exercise of his ministry, regardless of the source of his compensation;

(II) an employee of an organization, whether a civil law corporation or otherwise, which is exempt from tax under section 501 of the Internal Revenue Code of 1954 and which is controlled by or associated with a church or a convention or association of churches; and

(III) an individual described in clause (v).

(iii) A church or a convention or association of churches which is exempt from tax under section 501 of the Internal Revenue Code of 1954 shall be deemed the employer of any individual included as an employee under clause (ii).

(iv) An organization, whether a civil law corporation or otherwise, is associated with a church or a convention or association of churches if it shares common religious bonds and convictions with that church or convention or association of churches.

(v) If an employee who is included in a church plan separates from the service of a church or a convention or association of churches or an organization, whether a civil law corporation or otherwise, which is exempt from tax under section 501 of the Internal Revenue Code of 1954 and which is controlled by or associated with a church or a convention or association of churches, the church plan shall not fail to meet the requirements of this paragraph merely because the plan—

(I) retains the employee's accrued benefit or account for the payment of benefits to the employee or his beneficiaries pursuant to the terms of the plan; or

(II) receives contributions on the employee's behalf after the employee's separation from such service, but only for a period of 5 years after such separation, unless the employee is disabled (within the meaning of the disability provisions of the church plan or, if there are no such provisions in the church plan, within the meaning of section 72(m)(7) of the Internal Revenue Code of 1954) at the time of such separation from service.

(D) (i) If a plan established and maintained for its employees (or their beneficiaries) by a church or by a convention or association of churches which is exempt from tax under section 501 of the Internal Revenue Code of 1954 fails to meet one or more of the requirements of this paragraph and corrects its failure to meet such requirements within the correction period, the plan shall be deemed to meet the requirements of this paragraph for the year in which the correction was made and for all prior years.

(ii) If a correction is not made within the correction period, the plan shall be deemed not to meet the requirements of this paragraph beginning with the date on which the earliest failure to meet one or more of such requirements occurred.

(iii) For purposes of this subparagraph, the term "correction period" means—

(I) the period ending 270 days after the date of mailing by the Secretary of a notice of default with respect to the plan's failure to meet one or more of the requirements of this paragraph; or

(II) any period set by a court of competent jurisdiction after a final determination that the plan fails to meet such requirements, or, if the court does not specify such period, any reasonable period determined by the Secretary on the basis of all the facts and circumstances, but in any event not less than 270 days after the determination has become final; or

(III) any additional period which the Secretary determines is reasonable or necessary for the correction of the default, whichever has the latest ending date.

(34) the term "individual account plan" or "defined contribution plan" means a pension plan which provides for an individual account for each participant and for benefits based solely upon the amount contributed to the participant's account, and any income, expenses, gains, and losses, and any forfeitures of accounts of other participants which may be allocated to such participant's account.

(35) The term "defined benefit plan" means a pension plan other than an individual account plan; except that a pension plan which is not an individual account plan and which provides a benefit derived from employer contributions which is based partly on the balance of the separate account of a participant—

(A) for the purposes of section 202, shall be treated as an individual account plan, and

(B) for the purposes of paragraph (23) of this section and section 204, shall be treated as an individual account plan to the extent benefits are based upon the separate account of a participant and as a defined benefit plan with respect to the remaining portion of benefits under the plan.

(36) The term "excess benefit plan" means a plan maintained by an employer solely for the purpose of providing benefits for certain employees in excess of the limitations on contributions and benefits imposed by section 415 of the Internal Revenue Code of 1954 on plans to which that section applies, without regard to whether the plan is funded. To the extent that a separable part of a plan (as determined by the Secretary of Labor) maintained by an employer is maintained for such purpose, that part shall be treated as a separate plan which is an excess benefit plan.

(37)(A) The term "multiemployer plan" means a plan—

(i) to which more than one employer is required to contribute,

(ii) which is maintained pursuant to one or more collective bargaining agreements between one or more employee organizations and more than one employer, and

(iii) which satisfies such other requirements as the Secretary may prescribe by regulation.

(B) For purposes of this paragraph, all trades or businesses (whether or not incorporated) which are under common control within the meaning of section 4001(c)(1) are considered a single employer.

(C) Notwithstanding subparagraph (A), a plan is a multiemployer plan on and after its termination date if the plan was a multiemployer plan under this paragraph for the plan year preceding its termination date.

(D) For purposes of this title, notwithstanding the preceding provisions of this paragraph, for any plan year which began before the date of the enactment of the Multiemployer Pension Plan Amendments Act of 1980, the term "multiemployer plan" means a plan described in section 3(37) of this Act as in effect immediately before such date.

(E) Within one year after the date of the enactment of the Multiemployer Pension Plan Amendments Act of 1980, a multiemployer plan may irrevocably elect, pursuant to procedures established by the corporation and subject to the provisions of sections 4403 (b) and (c), that the plan shall not be treated as a multiemployer plan for all purposes under this Act or the Internal Revenue Code of 1954 if for each of the last 3 plan years ending prior to the effective date of the Multiemployer Pension Plan Amendments Act of 1980—

(i) the plan was not a multiemployer plan because the plan was not a plan described in section 3(37)(A)(iii) of this Act and section 414(f)(1)(C) of the Internal Revenue Code of 1954 (as such provisions were in effect on the day before the date of the enactment of the Multiemployer Pension Plan Amendments Act of 1980); and

(ii) the plan had been identified as a plan that was not a multiemployer plan in substantially all its filings with the corporation, the Secretary of Labor and the Secretary of the Treasury.

(38) The term "investment manager" means any fiduciary (other than a trustee or named fiduciary, as defined in section 402(a)(2))—

(A) who has the power to manage, acquire, or dispose of any asset of a plan;

(B) who is (i) registered as an investment adviser under the Investment Advisers Act of 1940; (ii) is a bank, as defined in that Act; or (iii) is an insurance company qualified to perform services described in subparagraph (A) under the laws of more than one State; and

(C) has acknowledged in writing that he is a fiduciary with respect to the plan.

(39) The terms "plan year" and "fiscal year of the plan" mean with respect to a plan, calendar, policy, or fiscal year on which the records of the plan are kept.

(40) (A) The term "multiple employer welfare arrangement" means an employee welfare benefit plan, or any other arrangement (other than an employee welfare benefit plan), which is established or maintained for the purpose of offering or providing any benefit described in paragraph (1) to the employees of two or more employers (including one or more self-employed individuals), or to their beneficiaries, except that such term does not include any such plan or other arrangement which is established or maintained—

(i) under or pursuant to one or more agreements which the Secretary finds to be collective bargaining agreements, or

(ii) by a rural electric cooperative.

(B) For purposes of this paragraph—

(i) two or more trades or businesses, whether or not incorporated, shall be deemed a single employer if such trades or businesses are within the same control group,

(ii) the term "control group" means a group of trades or businesses under common control,

(iii) the determination of whether a trade or business is under "common control" with another trade or business shall be determined under regulations of the Secretary applying principles similar to the principles applied in determining whether employees of two or more trades or businesses are treated as employed by a single employer under section 4001(b), except that, for purposes of this paragraph, common control shall not be based on an interest of less than 25 percent, and

(iv) the term "rural electric cooperative" means—

(I) any organization which is exempt from tax under section 501(a) of the Internal Revenue Code of 1954 and which is engaged primarily in providing electric service on a mutual or cooperative basis, and

(II) any organization described in paragraph (4) or (6) of section 501(c) of the Internal Revenue Code of 1954 which is exempt from tax under section 501(a) of such Code and at least 80 percent of the members of which are organizations described in subclause (I).

COVERAGE

Sec. 4. (a) Except as provided in subsection (b) and in sections 201, 301, and 401, this title shall apply to any employee benefit plan if it is established or maintained—

(1) by any employer engaged in commerce or in any industry or activity affecting commerce; or

(2) by any employee organization or organizations representing employees engaged in commerce or in any industry or activity affecting commerce; or

(3) by both.

(b) The provisions of this title shall not apply to any employee benefit plan if—

(1) such plan is a governmental plan (as defined in section 3(32));

(2) such plan is a church plan (as defined in section 3(33)) with respect to which no election has been made under section 410(d) of the Internal Revenue Code of 1954;

(3) such plan is maintained solely for the purpose of complying with applicable workmen's compensation laws or unemployment compensation or disability insurance laws;

(4) such plan is maintained outside of the United States primarily for the benefit of persons substantially all of whom are nonresident aliens; or

(5) such plan is an excess benefit plan (as defined in section 3(36)) and is unfunded.

Subtitle B—Regulatory Provisions

Part I—Reporting and Disclosure

DUTY OF DISCLOSURE AND REPORTING

Sec. 101. (a) The administrator of each employee benefit plan shall cause to be furnished in accordance with section 104(b) to each participant covered under the plan and to each beneficiary who is receiving benefits under the plan—

(1) a summary plan description described in section 102(a)(1); and

(2) the information described in sections 104(b)(3) and 105(a) and (c).

(b) The administrator shall, in accordance with section 104(a), file with the Secretary—

(1) the summary plan description described in section 102(a)(1);

(2) a plan description containing the matter required in section 102(b);

(3) modifications and changes referred to in section 102(a)(2);

(4) the annual report containing the information required by section 103; and

(5) terminal and supplementary reports as required by subsection (c) of this section.

(c)(1) Each administrator of an employee pension benefit plan which is winding up its affairs (without regard to the number of participants remaining in the plan) shall, in accordance with regulations prescribed by the Secretary, file such terminal reports as the Secretary may consider necessary. A copy of such report shall also be filed with the Pension Benefit Guaranty Corporation.

(2) The Secretary may require terminal reports to be filed with regard to any employee welfare benefit plan which is winding up its affairs in accordance with regulations promulgated by the Secretary.

(3) The Secretary may require that a plan described in paragraph (1) or (2) file a supplementary or terminal report with the annual report in the year such plan is terminated and that a copy of such supplementary or terminal report in the case of a plan described in paragraph (1) be also filed with the Pension Benefit Guaranty Corporation.

(d) Cross Reference.—

For regulations relating to coordination of reports to the Secretaries of Labor and the Treasury, see section 3004.

PLAN DESCRIPTION AND SUMMARY PLAN DESCRIPTION

Sec. 102. (a)(1) A summary plan description of any employee benefit plan shall be furnished to participants and beneficiaries as provided in section 104(b). The summary plan description shall include the informa-

Sec. 101

tion described in subsection (b), shall be written in a manner calculated to be understood by the average plan participant, and shall be sufficiently accurate and comprehensive to reasonably apprise such participants and beneficiaries of their rights and obligations under the plan. A summary of any material modification in the terms of the plan and any change in the information required under subsection (b) shall be written in a manner calculated to be understood by the average plan participant and shall be furnished in accordance with section 104(b)(1).

(2) A plan description (containing the information required by subsection (b)) of any employee benefit plan shall be prepared on forms prescribed by the Secretary, and shall be filed with the Secretary as required by section 104(a)(1). Any material modification in the terms of the plan and any change in the information described in subsection (b) shall be filed in accordance with section 104(a)(1)(D).

(b) The plan description and summary plan description shall contain the following information: The name and type of administration of the plan; the name and address of the person designated as agent for the service of legal process, if such person is not the administrator; the name and address of the administrator; names, titles and addresses of any trustee or trustees (if they are persons different from the administrator); a description of the relevant provisions of any applicable collective bargaining agreement; the plan's requirements respecting eligibility for participation and benefits; a description of the provisions providing for nonforfeitable pension benefits; circumstances which may result in disqualification, ineligibility, or denial or loss of benefits; the source of financing of the plan and the identity of any organization through which benefits are provided; the date of the end of the plan year and whether the records of the plan are kept on a calendar, policy, or fiscal year basis;

the procedures to be followed in presenting claims for benefits under the plan and the remedies available under the plan for the redress of claims which are denied in whole or in part (including procedures required under section 503 of this Act).

ANNUAL REPORTS

Sec. 103. (a)(1)(A) An annual report shall be published with respect to every employee benefit plan to which this part applies. Such report shall be filed with the Secretary in accordance with section 104(a), and shall be made available and furnished to participants in accordance with section 104(b).

(B) The annual report shall include the information described in subsections (b) and (c) and where applicable subsections (d) and (e) and shall also include—

(i) a financial statement and opinion, as required by paragraph (3) of this subsection, and

(ii) an actuarial statement and opinion, as required by paragraph (4) of this subsection.

(2) If some or all of the information necessary to enable the administrator to comply with the requirements of this title is maintained by—

(A) an insurance carrier or other organization which provides some or all of the benefits under the plan, or holds assets of the plan in a separate account,

(B) a bank or similar institution which holds some or all of the assets of the plan in a common or collective trust or a separate trust, or custodial account, or

(C) a plan sponsor as defined in section 3(16)(B),

such carrier, organization, bank, institution, or plan sponsor shall transmit and certify the accuracy of such information to the administrator within 120 days after the end of the plan year (or such other date as may be prescribed under regulations of the Secretary).

Sec. 103 (a) (2)

(3)(A) Except as provided in subparagraph (C), the administrator of an employee benefit plan shall engage, on behalf of all plan participants, an independent qualified public accountant, who shall conduct such an examination of any financial statements of the plan, and of other books and records of the plan, as the accountant may deem necessary to enable the accountant to form an opinion as to whether the financial statements and schedules required to be included in the annual report by subsection (b) of this section are presented fairly in conformity with generally accepted accounting principles applied on a basis consistent with that of the preceding year. Such examination shall be conducted in accordance with generally accepted auditing standards, and shall involve such tests of the books and records of the plan as are considered necessary by the independent qualified public accountant. The independent qualified public accountant shall also offer his opinion as to whether the separate schedules specified in subsection (b)(3) of this section and the summary material required under section 104(b)(3) present fairly, and in all material respects the information contained therein when considered in conjunction with the financial statements taken as a whole. The opinion by the independent qualified public accountant shall be made a part of the annual report. In a case where a plan is not required to file an annual report, the requirements of this paragraph shall not apply. In a case where by reason of section 104(a)(2) a plan is required only to file a simplified annual report, the Secretary may waive the requirements of this paragraph.

(B) In offering his opinion under this section the accountant may rely on the correctness of any actuarial matter certified to by an enrolled actuary, if he so states his reliance.

(C) The opinion required by subparagraph (A) need not be expressed as to any statements required by subsection (b)(3)(G) prepared by a bank or similar institution or insurance carrier regulated and supervised and subject to periodic examination by a State or Federal agency if such statements are certified by the bank, similar institution, or insurance carrier as accurate and are made a part of the annual report.

(D) For purposes of this title, the term "qualified public accountant" means—

(i) a person who is a certified public accountant, certified by a regulatory authority of a State;

(ii) a person who is a licensed public accountant, licensed by a regulatory authority of a state; or

(iii) a person certified by the Secretary as a qualified public accountant in accordance with regulations published by him for a person who practices in States where there is no certification or licensing procedure for accountants.

(4)(A) The administrator of an employee pension benefit plan subject to the reporting requirement of subsection (d) of this section shall engage, on behalf of all plan participants, an enrolled actuary who shall be responsible for the preparation of the materials comprising the actuarial statement required under subsection (d) of this section. In a case where a plan is not required to file an annual report, the requirement of this paragraph shall not apply, and, in a case where by reason of section 104(a)(2), a plan is required only to file a simplified report, the Secretary may waive the requirement of this paragraph.

(B) The enrolled actuary shall utilize such assumptions and techniques as are necessary to enable him to form an opinion as to whether the contents of the matters reported under subsection (d) of this section—

(i) are in the aggregate reasonably related to the experience of the plan and to reasonable expectations; and

(ii) represent his best estimate of anticipated experience under the plan.

The opinion by the enrolled actuary shall be made with respect to, and shall be made a part of, each annual report.

(C) For purposes of this title, the term "enrolled actuary" means an actuary enrolled under subtitle C of title III of this Act.

(D) In making a certification under this section the enrolled actuary may rely on the correctness of any accounting matter under section 103 (b) as to which any qualified public accountant has expressed an opinion, if he so states his reliance.

(b) An annual report under this section shall include a financial statement containing the following information:

(1) With respect to an employee welfare benefit plan: a statement of assets and liabilities; a statement of changes in fund balance; and a statement of changes in financial position. In the notes to financial statements, disclosures concerning the following items shall be considered by the accountant: a description of the plan including any significant changes in the plan made during the period and the impact of such changes on benefits; a description of material lease commitments, other commitments, and contingent liabilities; a description of agreements and transactions with persons known to be parties in interest; a general description of priorities upon termination of the plan; information concerning whether or not a tax ruling or determination letter has been obtained; and any other matters necessary to fully and fairly present the financial statements of the plan.

(2) With respect to an employee pension benefit plan: a statement of assets and liabilities, and a statement of changes in net assets available for plan benefits which shall include details of revenues and expenses and other changes aggregated by general source and application. In the notes to financial statements, disclosures concerning the following items shall be considered by the accountant: a description of the plan including any significant changes in the plan made during the period and the impact of such changes on benefits; the funding policy (including policy with respect to prior service cost), and any changes in such policies during the year; a description of any significant changes in plan benefits made during the period; a description of material lease commitments, other commitments, and contingent liabilities; a description of agreements and transactions with persons known to be parties in interest; a general description of priorities upon termination of the plan; information concerning whether or not a tax ruling or determination letter has been obtained; and any other matters necessary to fully and fairly present the financial statements of such pension plan.

(3) With respect to all employee benefit plans, the statement required under paragraph (1) or (2) shall have attached the following information in separate schedules:

(A) a statement of the assets and liabilities of the plan aggregated by categories and valued at their current value, and the same data displayed in comparative form for the end of the previous fiscal year of the plan;

(B) a statement of receipts and disbursements during the preceding twelve-month period aggregated by general sources and applications;

(C) a schedule of all assets held for investment purposes aggregated and identified by issuer, borrower, or lessor, or similiar party to the transaction (including a notation as to whether such party is known to be a party in interest), maturity date, rate of interest, collateral, par or maturity value, cost, and current value;

(D) a schedule of each transaction involving a person known to be party in interest, the identity of such party in interest and his relationship or that of any other party in interest to the plan, a description of each asset to which the transaction relates; the purchase or selling price in case of a sale or purchase, the rental in case of a lease, or the interest rate and maturity date in case of a loan; expenses incurred in connection with the transaction; the cost of the asset, the current value of the asset, and the net gain (or loss) on each transaction;

(E) a schedule of all loans or fixed income obligations which were in default as of the close of the plan's fiscal year or were classified during the year as uncollectable and the following information with respect to each loan on such schedule (including a notation as to whether parties involved are known to be parties in interest): the original principal amount of the loan, the amount of principal and interest received during the reporting year, the unpaid balance, the identity and address of the obligor, a detailed description of the loan (including date of making and maturity, interest rate, the type and value of collateral, and other material terms), the amount of principal and interest overdue (if any) and an explanation thereof;

(F) a list of all leases which were in default or were classified during the year as uncollectable; and the following information with respect to each lease on such schedule (including a notation as to whether parties involved are known to be parties in interest): the type of property leased (and, in the case of fixed assets such as land, buildings, leasehold, and so forth, the location of the property), the identity of the lessor or lessee from or to whom the plan is leasing, the relationship of such lessors and lessees, if any, to the plan, the employer, employee organization, or any other party in interest, the terms of the lease regarding rent, taxes, insurance, repairs, expenses, and renewal options; the date the leased property was purchased and its cost, the date the property was leased and its approximate value at such date, the gross rental receipts during the reporting period, expenses paid for the leased property during the reporting period, the net receipts from the lease, the amounts in arrears, and a statement as to what steps have been taken to collect amounts due or otherwise remedy the default;

(G) if some or all of the assets of a plan or plans are held in a common or collective trust maintained by a bank or similar institution or in a separate account maintained by an insurance carrier or a separate trust maintained by a bank as trustee, the report shall include the most recent annual statement of assets and liabilities of such common or collective trust, and in the case of a separate account or a separate trust, such other information as is required by the administrator in order to comply with this subsection; and

(H) a schedule of each reportable transaction, the name of each party to the transaction (except that, in the case of an acquisition or sale of a security on the market, the report need not identify the person from whom the security was acquired or to whom it was sold) and a description of each asset to which the transaction applies; the purchase or selling price in case of a sale or purchase, the rental in case of a lease, or the interest rate and maturity date in case of a loan; expenses incurred in connection with the transaction; the cost of the asset, the current value of the asset, and the net gain (or loss) on each transaction. For purposes of the preceding sentence, the term "reportable transaction" means a transaction to which the plan is a party if such transaction is—

(i) a transaction involving an amount in excess of 3 percent of the current value of the assets of the plan;

(ii) any transaction (other than a transaction respecting a security) which is part of a series of transactions with or in conjunction with a person in a plan year, if the aggregate amount of such transactions exceeds 3 percent of the current value of the assets of the plan;

(iii) a transaction which is part of a series of transactions respecting one

Sec. 103 (b) (3) (E)

or more securities of the same issuer, if the aggregate amount of such transactions in the plan year exceeds 3 percent of the current value of the assets of the plan; or

(iv) a transaction with or in conjunction with a person respecting a security, if any other transaction with or in conjunction with such person in the plan year respecting a security is required to be reported by reason of clause (i).

(4) The Secretary may, by regulation, relieve any plan from filing a copy of a statement of assets and liabilities (or other information) described in paragraph (3) (g) if such statement and other information is filed with the Secretary by the bank or insurance carrier which maintains the common or collective trust or separate account.

(c) The administrator shall furnish as a part of a report under this section the following information:

(1) The number of employees covered by the plan.

(2) The name and address of each fiduciary.

(3) Except in the case of a person whose compensation is minimal (determined under regulations of the Secretary) and who performs solely ministerial duties (determined under such regulations), the name of each person (including but not limited to, any consultant, broker, trustee, accountant, insurance carrier, actuary, administrator, investment manager, or custodian who rendered services to the plan or who had transactions with the plan) who received directly or indirectly compensation from the plan during the preceding year for services rendered to the plan or its participants, the amount of such compensation, the nature of his services to the plan or its participants, his relationship to the employer of the employees covered by the plan, or the employee organization, and any other office, position, or employment he holds with any party in interest.

(4) An explanation of the reason for any change in appointment of trustee, accountant, insurance carrier, enrolled actuary, administrator, investment manager, or custodian.

(5) Such financial and actuarial information including but not limited to the material described in subsections (b) and (d) of this section as the Secretary may find necessary or appropriate.

(d) With respect to an employee pension benefit plan (other than (A) a profit sharing, savings, or other plan, which is an individual account plan, (B) a plan described in section 301(b), or (C) a plan described both in section 4021(b) and in paragraph (1), (2), (3), (4), (5), (6), or (7) of section 301(a)) an annual report under this section for a plan year shall include a complete actuarial statement applicable to the plan year which shall include the following:

(1) The date of the plan year, and the date of the actuarial valuation applicable to the plan year for which the report is filed.

(2) The date and amount of the contribution (or contributions) received by the plan for the plan year for which the report is filed and contributions for prior plan years not previously reported.

(3) The following information applicable to the plan year for which the report is filed: the normal costs, the accrued liabilities, an identification of benefits not included in the calculation; a statement of the other facts and actuarial assumptions and methods used to determine costs, and a justification for any change in actuarial assumptions or cost methods; and the minimum contribution required under section 302.

(4) The number of participants and beneficiaries, both retired and nonretired, covered by the plan.

(5) The current value of the assets accumulated in the plan, and the present value of the assets of the plan used by the actuary in any computation of the amount of contributions to the plan required under section 302 and a statement explaining

Sec. 103 (d)

the basis of such valuation of present value of assets.

(6) The present value of all of the plan's liabilities for nonforfeitable pension benefits allocated by the termination priority categories as set forth in section 4044 of this Act, and the actuarial assumptions used in these computations. The Secretary shall establish regulations defining (for purposes of this section) "termination priority categories" and acceptable methods, including approximate methods, for allocating the plan's liabilities to such termination priority categories.

(7) A certification of the contribution necessary to reduce the accumulated funding deficiency to zero.

(8) A statement by the enrolled actuary—

(A) that to the best of his knowledge the report is complete and accurate, and

(B) the requirements of section 302 (c)(3) (relating to reasonable actuarial assumptions and methods) have been compiled with.

(9) A copy of the opinion required by subsection (a)(4).

(10) A statement by the actuary which discloses—

(A) any event which the actuary has not taken into account, and

(B) any trend which, for purposes of the actuarial assumptions used, was not assumed to continue in the future, but only if, to the best of the actuary's knowledge, such event or trend may require a material increase in plan costs or required contribution rates.

(11) Such other information regarding the plan as the Secretary may by regulation require.

(12) Such other information as may be necessary to fully and fairly disclose the actuarial position of the plan. Such actuary shall make an actuarial valuation of the plan for every third plan year, unless he determines that a more frequent valuation is necessary to support his opinion under subsection (a)(4) of this section.

(e) If some or all of the benefits under the plan are purchased from and guaranteed by an insurance company, insurance service, or other similar organization, a report under this section shall include a statement from such insurance company, service, or other similar organization covering the plan year and enumerating—

(1) the premium rate or subscription charge and the total premium or subscription charges paid to each such carrier, insurance service, or other similar organization and the approximate number of persons covered by each class of such benefits; and

(2) the total amount of premiums received, the approximate number of persons covered by each class of benefits, and the total claims paid by such company, service, or other organization; dividends or retroactive rate adjustments, commissions, and administrative service or other fees or other specific acquisition costs paid by such company, service, or other organization; any amounts held to provide benefits after retirement; the remainder of such premiums; and the names and addresses of the brokers, agents, or other persons to whom commissions or fees were paid, the amount paid to each, and for what purpose. If any such company, service, or other organization does not maintain separate experience records covering the specific groups it serves, the report shall include in lieu of the information required by the foregoing provisions of this paragraph (A) a statement as to the basis of its premium rate or subscription charge, the total amount of premiums or subscription charges received from the plan, and a copy of the financial report of the company, service, or other organization and (B) if such company, service, or organization incurs specific costs in connection with the acquisition or retention of any particular plan or plans, a detailed statement of such costs.

FILING WITH SECRETARY AND FURNISHING INFORMATION TO PARTICIPANTS

Sec. 104. (a)(1) The administrator of any employee benefit plan subject to this part shall file with the Secretary—

(A) the annual report for a plan year within 210 days after the close of such year (or within such time as may be required by regulations promulgated by the Secretary in order to reduce duplicative filing);

(B) the plan description within 120 days after such plan becomes subject to this part and an updated plan description, no more frequently than once every 5 years, as the Secretary may require;

(C) a copy of the summary plan description at the time such summary plan description is required to be furnished to participants and beneficiaries pursuant to subsection (b)(1)(B) of this section; and

(D) modifications and changes referred to in section 102(a)(2) within 60 days after such modification or change is adopted or occurs, as the case may be.

The Secretary shall make copies of such plan descriptions, summary plan descriptions, and annual reports available for inspection in the public document room of the Department of Labor. The administrator shall also furnish to the Secretary, upon request, any documents relating to the employee benefit plan, including but not limited to the bargaining agreement, trust agreement, contract, or other instrument under which the plan is established or operated.

(2)(A) With respect to annual reports required to be filed with the Secretary under this part, he may by regulation prescribe simplified annual reports for any pension plan which covers less than 100 participants. In addition, and without limiting the foregoing sentence, the Secretary may waive or modify the requirements of section 103(d)(6) in such cases or categories of cases as to which he finds that (i) the interests of the plan participants are not harmed thereby and (ii) the expense of compliance with the specific requirements of section 103(d)(6) is not justified by the needs of the participants, the Pension Benefit Guaranty Corporation, and the Department of Labor for some portion or all of the information otherwise required under section 103(d)(6).

(B) Nothing contained in this paragraph shall preclude the Secretary from requiring any information or data from any such plan to which this part applies where he finds such data or information is necessary to carry out the purposes of this title nor shall the Secretary be precluded from revoking provisions for simplified reports for any such plan if he finds it necessary to do so in order to carry out the objectives of this title

(3) The Secretary may by regulation exempt any welfare benefit plan from all or part of the reporting and disclosure requirements of this title, or may provide for simplified reporting and disclosure if he finds that such requirements are inappropriate as applied to welfare benefit plans.

(4) The Secretary may reject any filing under this section—

(A) if he determines that such filing is incomplete for purposes of this part; or

(B) if he determines that there is any material qualification by an accountant or actuary contained in an opinion submitted pursuant to section 103(a)(3)(A) or section 103(a)(4)(B).

(5) If the Secretary rejects a filing of a report under paragraph (4) and if a revised filing satisfactory to the Secretary is not submitted within 45 days after the Secretary makes his determination under paragraph (4) to reject the filing, and if the Secretary deems it in the best interest of the participants, he may take any one or more of the following actions—

(A) retain an independent qualified public accountant (as defined in section 103(a)(3)(D)) on behalf of the participants to perform an audit,

(B) retain an enrolled actuary (as defined in section 103(a)(4)(C) of this Act) on behalf of the plan participants, to prepare an actuarial statement,

Sec. 104 (a) (5)

(C) bring a civil action for such legal or equitable relief as may be appropriate to enforce the provisions of this part, or

(D) take any other action authorized by this title.

The administrator shall permit such accountant or actuary to inspect whatever books and records of the plan are necessary for such audit. The plan shall be liable to the Secretary for the expenses for such audit or report, and the Secretary may bring an action against the plan in any court of competent jurisdiction to recover such expenses.

(b) Publication of the summary plan descriptions and annual reports shall be made to participants and beneficiaries of the particular plan as follows:

(1) The administrator shall furnish to each participant, and each beneficiary receiving benefits under the plan, a copy of the summary, plan description, and all modifications and changes referred to in section 102(a)(1)—

(A) within 90 days after he becomes a participant, or (in the case of a beneficiary) within 90 days after he first receives benefits, or

(B) if later, within 120 days after the plan becomes subject to this part. The administrator shall furnish to each participant, and each beneficiary receiving benefits under the plan, every fifth year after the plan becomes subject to this part an updated summary plan description described in section 102 which integrates all plan amendments made within such five-year period, except that in a case where no amendments have been made to a plan during such five-year period this sentence shall not apply. Notwithstanding the foregoing, the administrator shall furnish to each participant, and to each beneficiary receiving benefits, under the plan, the summary plan description described in section 102 every tenth year after the plan becomes subject to this part. If there is a modification or change described in section 102(a)(1), a summary description of such modification or change shall be furnished not later than 210 days after the end of the plan year in which the change is adopted to each participant, and to each beneficiary who is receiving benefits under the plan.

(2) The administrator shall make copies of the plan description and the latest annual report and the bargaining agreement, trust agreement, contract, or other instruments under which the plan was established or is operated available for examination by any plan participant or beneficiary in the principal office of the administrator and in such other places as may be necessary to make available all pertinent information to all participants (including such places as the Secretary may prescribe by regulations).

(3) Within 210 days after the close of the fiscal year of the plan, the administrator shall furnish to each participant, and to each beneficiary receiving benefits under the plan, a copy of the statements and schedules, for such fiscal year, described in subparagraphs (A) and (B) of section 103(b)(3) and such other material as is necessary to fairly summarize the latest annual report.

(4) The administrator shall, upon written request of any participant or beneficiary, furnish a copy of the latest updated summary plan description, plan description, and the latest annual report, any terminal report, the bargaining agreement, trust agreement, contract, or other instruments under which the plan is established or operated. The administrator may make a reasonable charge to cover the cost of furnishing such complete copies. The Secretary may by regulation prescribe the maximum amount which will constitute a reasonable charge under the preceding sentence.

(c) The Secretary may by regulation require that the administrator of any employee benefit plan furnish to each participant and to each beneficiary receiving benefits under the

Sec. 104 (b)

plan a statement of the rights of participants and beneficiaries under this title.

(d) Cross Reference—

For regulations respecting coordination of reports to the Secretaries of Labor and the Treasury, see section 3004.

REPORTING OF PARTICIPANT'S BENEFIT RIGHTS

Sec. 105. (a) Each administrator of an employee pension benefit plan shall furnish to any plan participant or beneficiary who so requests in writing, a statement indicating, on the basis of the latest available information—

(1) the total benefits accrued, and

(2) the nonforfeitable pension benefits, if any, which have accrued, or the earliest date on which benefits will become nonforfeitable.

(b) In no case shall a participant or beneficiary be entitled under this section to receive more than one report described in subsection (a) during any one 12 month period.

(c) Each administrator required to register under section 6057 of the Internal Revenue Code of 1954 shall, before the expiration of the time prescribed for such registration, furnish to each participant described in subsection (a)(2)(C) of such section, an individual statement setting forth the information with repect to such participant required to be contained in the registration statement required by section 6057(a)(2) of such Code.

(d) Subsection (a) of this section shall apply to a plan to which more than one unaffiliated employer is required to contribute only to the extent provided in regulations prescribed by the Secretary in coordination with the Secretary of the Treasury.

REPORTS MADE PUBLIC INFORMATION

Sec. 106. (a) Except as provided in subsection (b), the contents of the descriptions, annual reports, statements, and other documents filed with the Secretary pursuant to this part shall be public information and the Secretary shall make any such information and data available for inspection in the public document room of the Department of Labor. The Secretary may use the information and data for statistical and research purposes, and compile and publish such studies, analyses, reports, and surveys based thereon as he may deem appropriate.

(b) Information described in section 105 (a) and 105(c) with respect to a participant may be disclosed only to the extent that information respecting that participant's benefits under title II of the Social Security Act may be disclosed under such Act.

RETENTION OF RECORDS

Sec. 107. Every person subject to a requirement to file any description or report or to certify any information therefor under this title or who would be subject to such a requirement but for an exemption or simplified reporting requirement under section 104(a)(2) or (3) of this title shall maintain records on the matters of which disclosure is required which will provide in sufficient detail the necessary basic information and data from which the documents thus required may be verified, explained, or clarified, and checked for accuracy and completeness, and shall include vouchers, worksheets, receipts, and applicable resolutions, and shall keep such records available for examination for a period of not less than six years after the filing date of the documents based on the information which they contain, or six years after the date on which such documents would have been filed but for an exemption or simplified reporting requirement under section 104(a)(2) or (3).

RELIANCE ON ADMINISTRATIVE INTERPRETATIONS

Sec. 108. In any criminal proceeding under section 501 based on any act or omission in alleged violation of this part or section 412, no person shall be subject to any liability or punishment for or on account of the failure of such person to (1) comply with this part or section 412, if he pleads and proves that the act or omission complained of was in good faith, in conformity with, and in reliance on any regulation or written ruling of the Secretary, or (2) publish and file any information required by any provision of this part if he pleads and proves that he published and filed such information in good faith, and in conformity with any regulation or written ruling of the Secretary issued under this part regarding the filing of such reports. Such a defense, if established, shall be a bar to the action or proceeding, notwithstanding that (A) after such act or omission, such interpretation or opinion is modified or rescinded or is determined by judicial authority to be invalid or of no legal effect, or (B) after publishing or filing the plan description, annual reports, and other reports required by this title, such publication or filing is determined by judicial authority not to be in conformity with the requirements of this part.

FORMS

Sec. 109. (a) Except as provided in subsection (b) of this section, the Secretary may require that any information required under this title to be submitted to him, including but not limited to the information required to be filed by the administrator pursuant to section 103(b)(3) and (c), must be submitted on such forms as he may prescribe.

(b) The financial statement and opinion required to be prepared by an independent qualified public accountant pursuant to section 103(a)(3)(A), the actuarial statement required to be prepared by an enrolled actuary pursuant to section 103(a)(4)(A) and the summary plan description required by section 102(a) shall not be required to be submitted on forms.

(c) The Secretary may prescribe the format and content of the summary plan description, the summary of the annual report described in section 104(b)(3) and any other report, statements or documents (other than the bargaining agreement, trust agreement, contract, or other instrument under which the plan is established or operated), which are required to be furnished or made available to plan participants and beneficiaries receiving benefits under the plan.

ALTERNATIVE METHODS OF COMPLIANCE

Sec. 110. (a) The Secretary on his own motion or after having received the petition of an administrator may prescribe an alternative method for satisfying any requirement of this part with respect to any pension plan, or class of pension plans, to subject to such requirement if he determines—

(1) that the use of such alternative method is consistent with the purposes of this title and that it provides adequate disclosure to the participants and beneficiaries in the plan, and adequate reporting to the Secretary,

(2) that the application of such requirement of this part would—

(A) increase the costs to the plan, or

(B) impose unreasonable administrative burdens with respect to the operation of the plan, having regard to the particular characteristics of the plan or the type of plan involved; and

(3) that the application of this part would be adverse to the interests of plan participants in the aggregate.

(b) An alternative method may be prescribed under subsection (a) by regulation or otherwise. If an alternative method is prescribed other than by regulation, the Secretary shall provide notice and an opportunity for interested persons to present their views, and shall publish in the Federal Register the provisions of such alternative method.

REPEAL AND EFFECTIVE DATE

Sec. 111. (a)(1) The Welfare and Pension Plans Disclosure Act is repealed except that such Act shall continue to apply to any conduct and events which occurred before the effective date of this part.

(2)(A) Section 664 of title 18, United States Code, is amended by striking out "any such plan subject to the provisions of the Welfare and Pension Plans Disclosure Act" and inserting in lieu thereof "any employee benefit plan subject to any provision of title I of the Employee Retirement Income Security Act of 1974"

(B)(i) Section 1027 of such title 18 is amended by striking out "Welfare and Pension Plans Disclosure Act" and inserting in lieu thereof "title I of the Employee Retirement Income Security Act of 1974", and by striking out "Act" each place it appears and inserting in lieu thereof "title".

(ii) The heading for such section is amended by striking out "WELFARE AND PENSION PLANS DISCLOSURE ACT" and inserting in lieu thereof "EMPLOYEE RETIREMENT INCOME SECURITY ACT OF 1974".

(iii) The table of sections of chapter 47 of such title 18 is amended by striking out "Welfare and Pension Plans Disclosure Act" in the item relating to section 1027 and inserting in lieu thereof "Employee Retirement Income Security Act of 1974".

(C) Section 1954 of such title 18 is amended by striking out "any plan subject to the provisions of the Welfare and Pension Plans Disclosure Act as amended" and inserting in lieu thereof "any employee welfare benefit plan or employee pension benefit plan, respectively, subject to any provision of title I of the Employee Retirement Income Security Act of 1974"; and by striking out "sections 3(3) and 5 (b)(1) and (2) of the Welfare and Pension Plans Disclosure Act, as amended" and inserting in lieu thereof "sections 3(4) and (3)(16) of the Employee Retirement Income Security Act of 1974".

(D) Section 211 of the Labor-Management Reporting and Disclosure Act of 1959 (29 U.S.C. 441) is amended by striking out "Welfare and Pension Plans Disclosure Act" and inserting in lieu thereof "Employee Retirement Income Security Act of 1974".

(b)(1) Except as provided in paragraph (2), this part (including the amendments and repeals made by subsection (a)) shall take effect on January 1, 1975.

(2) In the case of a plan which has a plan year which begins before January 1, 1975, and ends after December 31, 1974, the Secretary may postpone by regulation the effective date of the repeal of any provision of the Welfare and Pension Plans Disclosure Act (and of any amendment made by subsection (a)(2)) and the effective date of any provision of this part, until the beginning of the first plan year of such plan which begins after January 1, 1975.

(c) The provisions of this title authorizing the Secretary to promulgate regulations shall take effect on the date of enactment of this Act.

Part 2—Participation and Vesting

COVERAGE

Sec. 201. This part shall apply to any employee benefit plan described in section 4(a) (and not exempted under Section 4(b)) other than—

(1) an employee welfare benefit plan;

(2) a plan which is unfunded and is maintained by an employer primarily for the purpose of providing deferred compensation for a select group of management or highly compensated employees;

(3)(A) a plan established and maintained by a society, order, or association described in section 501(c)(8) or (9) of the Internal Revenue Code of 1954, if no part of the contributions to or under such plan are made by employers of participants in such plan, or

(B) a trust described in section 501(c)(18) of such Code;

(4) a plan which is established and maintained by a labor organization described in section 501(c)(5) of the Internal Revenue Code of 1954 and

which does not at any time after the date of enactment of this Act provide for employer contributions;

(5) any agreement providing payments to a retired partner or a deceased partner's successor in interest, as described in section 736 of the Internal Revenue Code of 1954;

(6) an individual retirement account or annuity described in section 408 of the Internal Revenue Code of 1954, or a retirement bond described in section 409 of such Code; or

(7) an excess benefit plan.

(8) Any plan, fund or program under which an employer, all of whose stock is directly or indirectly owned by employees, former employees or their beneficiaries, proposes through an unfunded arrangement to compensate retired employees for benefits which were forfeited by such employees under a pension plan maintained by a former employer prior to the date such pension plan became subject to this Act.

MINIMUM PARTICIPATION STANDARDS

Sec. 202. (a)(1)(A) No pension plan may require, as a condition of participation in the plan, that an employee complete a period of service with the employer or employers maintaining the plan extending beyond the later of the following dates—

(i) the date on which the employee attains the age of 25; or

(ii) the date on which he completes 1 year of service.

(B)(i) In the case of any plan which provides that after not more than 3 years of service each participant has a right to 100 percent of his accrued benefit under the plan which is nonforfeitable at the time such benefit accrues, clause (ii) of subparagraph (A) shall be applied by substituting "3 years of service" for "1 year of service".

(ii) In the case of any plan maintained exclusively for employees of an educational institution (as defined in section 170(b)(1)(A)(ii) of the Internal Revenue Code of 1954) by an employer which is exempt from tax under section 501(a) of such Code, which provides that each participant having at least 1 year of service has a right to 100 percent of his accrued benefit under the plan which is nonforfeitable at the time such benefit accrues, clause (i) of subparagraph (A) shall be applied by substituting "30" for "25". This clause shall not apply to any plan to which clause (i) applies.

(2) No pension plan may exclude from participation (on the basis of age) employees who have attained a specified age, unless—

(A) the plan is a—

(i) defined benefit plan, or

(ii) target benefit plan (as defined under regulations prescribed by the Secretary of the Treasury), and

(B) such employees begin employment with the employer after they have attained a specified age which is not more than 5 years before the normal retirement age under the plan.

(3)(A) For purposes of this section, the term "year of service" means a 12-month period during which the employee has not less than 1,000 hours of service. For purposes of this paragraph, computation of any 12-month period shall be made with reference to the date on which the employee's employment commenced, except that, in accordance with regulations prescribed by the Secretary, such computation may be made by reference to the first day of a plan year in the case of an employee who does not complete 1,000 hours of service during the 12-month period beginning on the date his employment commenced.

(B) In the case of any seasonal industry where the customary period of employment is less than 1,000 hours during a calendar year, the term "year of service" shall be such period as may be determined under regulations prescribed by the Secretary.

(C) For purposes of this section, the term "hour of service" means a time of service determined under regulations prescribed by the Secretary.

Sec. 202 (a) (1)

TEXT OF ERISA

(D) For purposes of this section, in the case of any maritime industry, 125 days of service shall be treated as 1,000 hours of service. The Secretary may prescribe regulations to carry out the purposes of this subparagraph.

(4) A plan shall be treated as not meeting the requirements of paragraph (1) unless it provides that any employee who has satisfied the minimum age and service requirements specified in such paragraph, and who is otherwise entitled to participate in the plan, commences participation in the plan no later than the earlier of—

(A) the first day of the first plan year beginning after the date on which such employee satisfied such requirements, or

(B) the date 6 months after the date on which he satisfied such requirements,

unless such employee was separated from the service before the date referred to in subparagraph (A) or (B), whichever is applicable.

(b)(1) Except as otherwise provided in paragraphs (2), (3), and (4), all years of service with the employer or employers maintaining the plan shall be taken into account in computing the period of service for purposes of subsection (a)(1).

(2) In the case of any employee who has any 1-year break in service (as defined in section 203(b)(3)(A)) under the plan to which the service requirements of clause (i) of subsection (a)(1)(B) apply, if such employee has not satisfied such requirements, service before such break shall not be required to be taken into account.

(3) In computing an employee's period of service for purposes of subsection (a)(1) in the case of any participant who has any 1-year break in service (as defined in section 203(b)(3)(A)), service before such break shall not be required to be taken into account under the plan until he has completed a year of service (as defined in subsection (a)(3)) after his return.

(4) In the case of an employee who does not have any nonforfeitable right to an accrued benefit derived from employer contributions, years of service with the employer or employers maintaining the plan before a break in service shall not be required to be taken into account in computing the period of service for purposes of subsection (a)(1) if the number of consecutive 1-year breaks in service equals or exceeds the aggregate number of such years of service before such break. Such aggregate number of years of service before such break shall be deemed not to include any years of service not required to be taken into account under this paragraph by reason of any prior break in service.

MINIMUM VESTING STANDARDS

Sec. 203. (a) Each pension plan shall provide that an employee's right to his normal retirement benefit is nonforfeitable upon the attainment of normal retirement age and in addition shall satisfy the requirements of paragraphs (1) and (2) of this subsection.

(1) A plan satisfies the requirements of this paragraph if an employee's rights in his accrued benefit derived from his own contributions are nonforfeitable.

(2) A plan satisfies the requirements of this paragraph if it satisfies the requirements of subparagraph (A), (B), or (C).

(A) A plan satisfies the requirements of this subparagraph if an employee who has at least 10 years of service has a nonforfeitable right to 100 percent of his accrued benefit derived from employer contributions.

(B) A plan satisfies the requirements of this subparagraph if an employee who has completed at least 5 years of service has a nonforfeitable right to a percentage of his accrued

Sec. 203 (a) (2)

benefit derived from employer contributions which percentage is not less than the percentage determined under the following table:

Years of service:	Nonforfeitable percentage
5	25
6	30
7	35
8	40
9	45
10	50
11	60
12	70
13	80
14	90
15 or more	100

(C) (i) A plan satisfies the requirements of this subparagraph if a participant who is not separated from the service, who has completed at least 5 years of service, and with respect to whom the sum of his age and years of service equals or exceeds 45, has a nonforfeitable right to a percentage of his accrued benefit derived from employer contributions determined under the following table:

If years of service equal or exceed—	and sum of age and service equals or exceeds—	then the nonforfeitable percentage is—
5	45	50
6	47	60
7	49	70
8	51	80
9	53	90
10	55	100

(ii) Notwithstanding clause (i), a plan shall not be treated as satisfying the requirements of this subparagraph unless any participant who has completed at least 10 years of service has a nonforfeitable right to not less than 50 percent of his accrued benefit derived from employer contributions and to not less than an additional 10 percent for each additional year of service thereafter.

(3)(A) A right to an accrued benefit derived from employer contributions shall not be treated as forfeitable solely because the plan provides that it is not payable if the participant dies (except in the case of a survivor annuity which is payable as provided in section 205).

(B) A right to an accrued benefit derived from employer contributions shall not be treated as forfeitable solely because the plan provides that the payment of benefits is suspended for such period as the employee is employed, subsequent to the commencement of payment of such benefits—

(i) in the case of a plan other than a multiemployer plan, by an employer who maintains the plan under which such benefits were being paid; and

(ii) in the case of a multiemployer plan, in the same industry, in the same trade or craft, and the same geographic area covered by the plan, as when such benefits commenced.

The Secretary shall prescribe such regulations as may be necessary to carry out the purposes of this subparagraph, including regulations with respect to the meaning of the term "employed".

(C) A right to an accrued benefit derived from employer contributions shall not be treated as forfeitable solely because plan amendments may be given retroactive application as provided in section 302(c)(8).

(D)(i) A right to an accrued benefit derived from employer contributions shall not be treated as forfeitable solely because the plan provides that, in the case of a participant who does not have a nonforfeitable right to at least 50 percent of his accrued benefit derived from employer contributions, such accrued benefit may be forfeited on account of the withdrawal by the participant of any amount attributable to the benefit derived from mandatory contributions (as defined in the last sentence of section 204(c)(2)(C)) made by such participant.

(ii) Clause (i) shall not apply to a plan unless the plan provides that any accrued benefit forfeited under

Sec. 203 (a) (3)

a plan provision described in such clause shall be restored upon repayment by the participant of the full amount of the withdrawal described in such clause plus, in the case of a defined benefit plan, interest. Such interest shall be computed on such amount at the rate determined for purposes of section 204(c)(2)(C) (if such subsection applies) on the date of such repayment (computed annually from the date of such withdrawal). In the case of a defined contribution plan the plan provision required under this clause may provide that such repayment must be made before the participant has any 1-year break in service commencing after the withdrawal.

(iii) In the case of accrued benefits derived from employer contributions which accrued before the date of the enactment of this Act, a right to such accrued benefit derived from employer contributions shall not be treated as forfeitable solely because the plan provides that an amount of such accrued benefit may be forfeited on account of the withdrawal by the participant of an amount attributable to the benefit derived from mandatory contributions, made by such participant before the date of the enactment of this Act if such amount forfeited is proportional to such amount withdrawn. This clause shall not apply to any plan to which any mandatory contribution is made after the date of the enactment of this Act. The Secretary of the Treasury shall prescribe such regulations as may be necessary to carry out the purposes of this clause.

(iv) For purposes of this subparagraph, in the case of any class-year plan, a withdrawal of employee contributions shall be treated as a withdrawal of such contributions on a plan year by plan year basis in succeeding order of time.

(v) Cross Reference.—

For nonforfeitability where the employee has a nonforfeitable right to at least 50 percent of his accrued benefit, see section 206(c).

(E)(i) A right to an accrued benefit derived from employer contributions under a multiemployer plan shall not be treated as forfeitable solely because the plan provides that benefits accrued as a result of service with the participant's employer before the employer had an obligation to contribute under the plan may not be payable if the employer ceases contributions to the multiemployer plan.

(ii) A participant's right to an accrued benefit derived from employer contributions under a multiemployer plan shall not be treated as forfeitable solely because—

(I) the plan is amended to reduce benefits under section 4244A or 4281, or

(II) benefit payments under the plan may be suspended under section 4245 or 4281.

(b)(1) In computing the period of service under the plan for purposes of determining the nonforfeitable percentage under subsection (a)(2), all of an employee's years of service with the employer or employers maintaining the plan shall be taken into account, except that the following may be disregarded:

(A) years of service before age 22, except that in the case of a plan which does not satisfy subparagraph (A) or (B) of subsection (a)(2), the plan may not disregard any such year of service during which the employee was a participant;

(B) years of service during a period for which the employee declined to contribute to a plan requiring employee contributions;

(C) years of service with an employer during any period for which the employer did not maintain the plan or a predecessor plan, defined by the Secretary of the Treasury;

(D) service not required to be taken into account under paragraph (3);

(E) years of service before January 1, 1971, unless the employee has had

Sec. 203 (b) (1)

at least 3 years of service after December 31, 1970; and

(F) years of service before this part first applies to the plan if such service would have been disregarded under the rules of the plan with regard to breaks in service, as in effect on the applicable date.

(G) in the case of a multiemployer plan, years of service—
(i) with an employer after—
(I) a complete withdrawal of such employer from the plan (within the meaning of section 4203), or
(II) to the extent permitted by regulations prescribed by the Secretary of the Treasury, a partial withdrawal described in section 4205(b)(2)(A)(i) in connection with the decertification of the collective bargaining representative; and
(ii) with any employer under the plan after the termination date of the plan under section 4048.

(2)(A) For purposes of this section, except as provided in subparagraph (C), the term "year of service" means a calendar year, plan year, or other 12-consecutive-month period designated by the plan (and not prohibited under regulations prescribed by the Secretary) during which the participant has completed 1,000 hours of service.

(B) For purposes of this section, the term "hour of service" has the meaning provided by section 202(a)(3)(C).

(C) In the case of any seasonal industry where the customary period of employment is less than 1,000 hours during a calendar year, the term "year of service" shall be such period as determined under regulations of the Secretary.

(D) For purposes of this section, in the case of any maritime industry, 125 days of service shall be treated as 1,000 hours of service. The Secretary may prescribe regulations to carry out the purposes of this subparagraph.

(3)(A) For purposes of this paragraph, the term "1-year break in service" means a calendar year, plan year, or other 12-consecutive-month period designated by the plan (and not prohibited under regulations prescribed by the Secretary) during which the participant has not completed more than 500 hours of service.

(B) For purposes of paragraph (1), in the case of any employee who has any 1-year break in service, years of service before such break shall not be required to be taken into account until he has completed a year of service after his return.

(C) For purposes of paragraph (1), in the case of any participant in an individual account plan or an insured defined benefit plan which satisfies the requirements of subsection 204(b)(1)(F) who has any 1-year break in service, years of service after such break shall not be required to be taken into account for purposes of determining the nonforfeitable percentage of his accrued benefit derived from employer contributions which accrued before such break.

(D) For purposes of paragraph (1), in the case of a participant who, under the plan, does not have any nonforfeitable right to an accrued benefit derived from employer contributions, years of service before any 1-year break in service shall not be required to be taken into account if the number of consecutive 1-year breaks in service equals or exceeds the aggregate number of such years of service prior to such break. Such aggregate number of years of service before such break shall be deemed not to include any years of service not required to be taken into account under this subparagraph by reason of any prior break in service.

(4) Cross References.—

(A) **For definitions of "accrued benefit" and "normal retirement age", see sections 3(23) and (24).**

Sec. 203 (b) (2)

(B) For effect of certain cash out distributions, see section 204(d)(1).

(c)(1)(A) A plan amendment changing any vesting schedule under the plan shall be treated as not satisfying the requirements of subsection (a)(2) if the nonforfeitable percentage of the accrued benefit derived from employer contributions (determined as of the later of the date such amendment is adopted, or the date such amendment becomes effective) of any employee who is a participant in the plan is less than such nonforfeitable percentage computed under the plan without regard to such amendment.

(B) A plan amendment changing any vesting schedule under the plan shall be treated as not satisfying the requirements of subsection (a)(2) unless each participant having not less than 5 years of service is permitted to elect, within a reasonable period after adoption of such amendment, to have his nonforfeitable percentage computed under the plan without regard to such amendment.

(2) Subsection (a) shall not apply to benefits which may not be provided for designated employees in the event of early termination of the plan under provisions of the plan adopted pursuant to regulations prescribed by the Secretary of the Treasury to preclude the discrimination prohibited by section 401(a)(4) of the Internal Revenue Code of 1954.

(3) The requirements of subsection (a)(2) shall be deemed to be satisfied in the case of a class year plan if such plan provides that 100 percent of each employee's right to or derived from the contributions of the employer on his behalf with respect to any plan year are nonforfeitable not later than the end of the 5th plan year following the plan year for which such contributions were made. For purposes of this part, the term "class year plan" means a profit sharing, stock bonus, or money purchase plan which provides for the separate nonforfeitability of employees' rights to or derived from the contributions for each plan year.

(d) A pension plan may allow for nonforfeitable benefits after a lesser period and in greater amounts than are required by this part.

BENEFIT ACCRUAL REQUIREMENTS

Sec. 204. (a) Each pension plan shall satisfy the requirements of subsection (b)(2), and in the case of a defined benefit plan shall also satisfy the requirements of subsection (b)(1).

(b)(1)(A) A defined benefit plan satisfies the requirements of this paragraph if the accrued benefit to which each participant is entitled upon his separation from the service is not less than—

(i) 3 percent of the normal retirement benefit to which he would be entitled at the normal retirement age if he commenced participation at the earliest possible entry age under the plan and served continuously until the earlier of age 65 or the normal retirement age specified under the plan, multiplied by

(ii) the number of years (not in excess of $33\frac{1}{3}$) of his participation in the plan.

In the case of a plan providing retirement benefits based on compensation during any period, the normal retirement benefit to which a participant would be entitled shall be determined as if he continued to earn annually the average rate of compensation which he earned during consecutive years of service, not in excess of 10, for which his compensation was the highest. For purposes of this subparagraph, social security benefits and all other relevant factors used to compute benefits shall be treated as remaining constant as of the current year for all years after such current year.

(B) A defined benefit plan satisfies the requirements of this paragraph for a particular plan year if under the plan the accrued benefit payable

Sec. 204 (b) (1)

at the normal retirement age is equal to the normal retirement benefit and the annual rate at which any individual who is or could be a participant can accrue the retirement benefits payable at normal retirement age under the plan for any later plan year is not more than 133⅓ percent of the annual rate at which he can accrue benefits for any plan year beginning on or after such particular plan year and before such later plan year. For purposes of this subparagraph—

(i) any amendment to the plan which is in effect for the current year shall be treated as in effect for all other plan years;

(ii) any change in an accrual rate which does not apply to any individual who is or could be a participant in the current year shall be disregarded;

(iii) the fact that benefits under the plan may be payable to certain employees before normal retirement age shall be disregarded; and

(iv) social security benefits and all other relevant factors used to compute benefits shall be treated as remaining constant as of the current year for all years after the current year.

(C) A defined benefit plan satisfies the requirements of this paragraph if the accrued benefit to which any participant is entitled upon his separation from the service is not less than a fraction of the annual benefit commencing at normal retirement age to which he would be entitled under the plan as in effect on the date of his separation if he continued to earn annually until normal retirement age the same rate of compensation upon which his normal retirement benefit would be computed under the plan, determined as if he had attained normal retirement age on the date any such determination is made (but taking into account no more than the 10 years of service immediately preceding his separation from service). Such fraction shall be a fraction, not exceeding 1, the numerator of which is the total number of his years of participation in the plan (as of the date of his separation from the service) and the denominator of which is the total number of years he would have participated in the plan if he separated from the service at the normal retirement age. For purposes of this subparagraph, social security benefits and all other relevant factors used to compute benefits shall be treated as remaining constant as of the current year for all years after such current year.

(D) Subparagraphs (A), (B), and (C) shall not apply with respect to years of participation before the first plan year to which this section applies but a defined benefit plan satisfies the requirements of this subparagraph with respect to such years of participation only if the accrued benefit of any participant with respect to such years of participation is not less than the greater of—

(i) his accrued benefit determined under the plan, as in effect from time to time prior to the date of the enactment of this Act, or

(ii) an accrued benefit which is not less than one-half of the accrued benefit to which such participant would have been entitled if subparagraph (A), (B), or (C) applied with respect to such years of participation.

(E) Notwithstanding subparagraphs (A), (B), and (C) of this paragraph, a plan shall not be treated as not satisfying the requirements of this paragraph solely because the accrual of benefits under the plan does not become effective until the employee has two continuous years of service. For purposes of this subparagraph, the term "years of service" has the meaning provided by section 202 (a)(3)(A).

(F) Notwithstanding subparagraphs (A), (B), and (C), a defined benefit plan satisfies the requirements of this paragraph if such plan—

(i) is funded exclusively by the purchase of insurance contracts, and

(ii) satisfies the requirements of paragraphs (2) and (3) of section 301(b) (relating to certain insurance contract plans),

but only if an employee's accrued benefit as of any applicable date is not less than the cash surrender value his insurance contracts would have on such applicable date if the requirements of paragraphs (4), (5), and (6) of section 301(b) were satisfied.

(G) Notwithstanding the preceding subparagraphs, a defined benefit plan shall be treated as not satisfying the requirements of this paragraph if the participant's accrued benefit is reduced on account of any increase in his age or service. The preceding sentence shall not apply to benefits under the plan commencing before benefits payable under title II of the Social Security Act which benefits under the plan—

(i) do not exceed social security benefits, and

(ii) terminate when such social security benefits commence.

(2) A plan satisfies the requirements of this paragraph if—

(A) in the case of a defined benefit plan, the plan requires separate accounting for the portion of each employee's accrued benefit derived from any voluntary employee contributions permitted under the plan; and

(B) in the case of any plan which is not a defined benefit plan, the plan requires separate accounting for each employee's accrued benefit.

(3)(A) For purposes of determining an employee's accrued benefit, the term "year of participation" means a period of service (beginning at the earliest date on which the employee is a participant in the plan and which is included in a period of service required to be taken into account under section 202(b)) as determined under regulations prescribed by the Secretary which provide for the calculation of such period on any reasonable and consistent basis.

(B) For purposes of this paragraph, except as provided in subparagraph (C), in the case of any employee whose customary employment is less than full time, the calculation of such employee's service on any basis which provides less than a ratable portion of the accrued benefit to which he would be entitled under the plan if his customary employment were full time shall not be treated as made on a reasonable and consistent basis.

(C) For purposes of this paragraph, in the case of any employee whose service is less than 1,000 hours during any calendar year, plan year or other 12-consecutive-month period designated by the plan (and not prohibited under regulations prescribed by the Secretary) the calculation of his period of service shall not be treated as not made on a reasonable and consistent basis merely because such service is not taken into account.

(D) In the case of any seasonal industry where the customary period of employment is less than 1,000 hours during a calendar year, the term "year of participation" shall be such period as determined under regulations prescribed by the Secretary.

(E) For purposes of this subsection in the case of any maritime industry, 125 days of service shall be treated as a year of participation. The Secretary may prescribe regulations to carry out the purposes of this subparagraph.

(c)(1) For purposes of this section and section 203 an employee's accrued benefit derived from employer contributions as of any applicable date is the excess (if any) of the accrued benefit for such employee as of such applicable date over the accrued benefit derived from contributions made by such employee as of such date.

(2)(A) In the case of a plan other than a defined benefit plan, the accrued benefit derived from contribu-

Sec. 204 (c) (2)

tions made by an employee as of any applicable date is—

(i) except as provided in clause (ii), the balance of the employee's separate account consisting only of his contributions and the income, expenses, gains, and losses attributable thereto, or

(ii) if a separate account is not maintained with respect to an employee's contributions under such a plan, the amount which bears the same ratio to his total accrued benefit as the total amount of the employee's contributions (less withdrawals) bears to the sum of such contributions and the contributions made on his behalf by the employer (less withdrawals).

(B)(i) In the case of a defined benefit plan providing an annual benefit in the form of a single life annuity (without ancillary benefits) commencing at normal retirement age, the accrued benefit derived from contributions made by an employee as of any applicable date is the annual benefit equal to the employee's accumulated contributions multiplied by the appropriate conversion factor.

(ii) For purposes of clause (i), the term "appropriate conversion factor" means the factor necessary to convert an amount equal to the accumulated contributions to a single life annuity (without ancillary benefits) commencing at normal retirement age and shall be 10 percent for a normal retirement age of 65 years. For other normal retirement ages the conversion factor shall be determined in accordance with regulations prescribed by the Secretary of the Treasury or his delegate.

(C) For purposes of this subsection, the term "accumulated contributions" means the total of—

(i) all mandatory contributions made by the employee,

(ii) interest (if any) under the plan to the end of the last plan year to which section 203(a)(2) does not apply (by reason of the applicable effective date), and

(iii) interest on the sum of the amounts determined under clauses (i) and (ii) compounded annually at the rate of 5 percent per annum from the beginning of the first plan year to which section 203(a)(2) applies (by reason of the applicable effective date) to the date upon which the employee would attain normal retirement age.

For purposes of this subparagraph, the term "mandatory contributions" means amounts contributed to the plan by the employee which are required as a condition of employment, as a condition of participation in such plan, or as a condition of obtaining benefits under the plan attributable to employer contributions.

(D) The Secretary of the Treasury is authorized to adjust by regulation the conversion factor described in subparagraph (B), the rate of interest described in clause (iii) of subparagraph (C), or both, from time to time as he may deem necessary. The rate of interest shall bear the relationship to 5 percent which the Secretary of the Treasury determines to be comparable to the relationship which the long-term money rates and investment yields for the last period of 10 calendar years ending at least 12 months before the beginning of the plan year bear to the long-term money rates and investment yields for the 10-calendar year period 1964 through 1973. No such adjustment shall be effective for a plan year beginning before the expiration of 1 year after such adjustment is determined and published.

(E) The accrued benefit derived from employee contributions shall not exceed the greater of—

(i) the employee's accrued benefit under the plan, or

(ii) the accrued benefit derived from employee contributions determined as though the amounts calculated under clauses (ii) and (iii) of subparagraph (C) were zero.

Sec. 204 (c) (2)

(3) For purposes of this section, in the case of any defined benefit plan, if an employee's accrued benefit is to be determined as an amount other than an annual benefit commencing at normal retirement age, or if the accrued benefit derived from contributions made by an employee is to be determined with respect to a benefit other than an annual benefit in the form of a single life annuity (without ancillary benefits) commencing at normal retirement age, the employee's accrued benefit, or the accrued benefits derived from contributions made by an employee, as the case may be, shall be the actuarial equivalent of such benefit or amount determined under paragraph (1) or (2).

(4) In the case of a defined benefit plan which permits voluntary employee contributions, the portion of an employee's accrued benefit derived from such contributions shall be treated as an accrued benefit derived from employee contributions under a plan other than a defined benefit plan.

(d) Notwithstanding section 203(b)(1), for purposes of determining the employee's accrued benefit under the plan, the plan may disregard service performed by the employee with respect to which he has received—

(1) a distribution of the present value of his entire nonforfeitable benefit if such distribution was in an amount (not more than $1,750) permitted under regulations prescribed by the Secretary of the Treasury, or

(2) a distribution of the present value of his nonforfeitable benefit attributable to such service which he elected to receive.

Paragraph (1) shall apply only if such distribution was made on termination of the employee's participation in the plan. Paragraph (2) shall apply only if such distribution was made on termination of the employee's participation in the plan or under such other circumstances as may be provided under regulations prescribed by the Secretary of the Treasury.

(e) For purposes of determining the employee's accrued benefit, the plan shall not disregard service as provided in subsection (d) unless the plan provides an opportunity for the participant to repay the full amount of a distribution described in subsection (d) with, in the case of a defined benefit plan, interest at the rate determined for purposes of subsection (c)(2)(C) and provides that upon such repayment the employee's accrued benefit shall be recomputed by taking into account service so disregarded. This subsection shall apply only in the case of a participant who—

(1) received such a distribution in any plan year to which this section applies, which distribution was less than the present value of his accrued benefit,

(2) resumes employment covered under the plan, and

(3) repays the full amount of such distribution with, in the case of a defined benefit plan, interest at the rate determined for purposes of subsection (c)(2)(C).

In the case of a defined contribution plan, the plan provision required under this subsection may provide that such repayment must be made before the participant has any 1-year break in service commencing after such withdrawal.

(f) For the purposes of this part, an employer shall be treated as maintaining a plan if any employee of such employer accrues benefits under such plan by reason of service with such employer.

(g) The accrued benefit of a participant under a plan may not be decreased by an amendment of the plan, other than an amendment described in section 302(c)(8).

(h) Cross Reference.—

For special rules relating to class year plans and plan provisions

Sec. 204 (h)

adopted to preclude discrimination, see sections 203(c)(2) and (3).

JOINT AND SURVIVOR ANNUITY REQUIREMENT

Sec. 205. (a) If a pension plan provides for the payment of benefits in the form of an annuity, such plan shall provide for the payment of annuity benefits in a form having the effect of a qualified joint and survivor annuity.

(b) In the case of a plan which provides for the payment of benefits before the normal retirement age as defined in section 3(24), the plan is not required to provide for the payment of annuity benefits in a form having the effect of a qualified joint and survivor annuity during the period beginning on the date on which the employee enters into the plan as a participant and ending on the later of—

(1) the date the employee reaches the earliest retirement age, or

(2) the first day of the 120th month beginning before the date on which the employee reaches normal retirement age.

(c)(1) A plan described in subsection (b) does not meet the requirements of subsection (a) unless, under the plan, a participant has a reasonable period in which he may elect the qualified joint and survivor annuity form with respect to the peri d beginning on the date on which the period described in subsection (b) ends and ending on the date on which he reaches normal retirement age if he continues his employment during that period.

(2) A plan does not meet the requirements of this subsection unless, in the case of such election, the payments under the survivor annuity are not less than the payments which would have been made under the joint annuity to which the participant would have been entitled if he had made an election under this subsection immediately prior to his retirement and if his retirement had occurred on the date immediately preceding the date of his death and within the period within which an election can be made.

(d) A plan shall not be treated as not satisfying the requirements of this section solely because the spouse of the participant is not entitled to receive a survivor annuity (whether or not an election has been made under subsection (c)) unless the participant and his spouse have been married throughout the 1-year period ending on the date of such participant's death.

(e) A plan shall not be treated as satisfying the requirements of this section unless, under the plan, each participant has a reasonable period (as prescribed by the Secretary of the Treasury by regulations) before the annuity starting date during which he may elect in writing (after having received a written explanation of the terms and conditions of the joint and survivor annuity and the effect of an election under this subsection) not to take such joint and survivor annuity.

(f) A plan shall not be treated as not satisfying the requirements of this section solely because, under the plan there is a provision that any election under subsection (c) or (e), and any revocation of any such election, does not become effective (or ceases to be effective) if the participant dies within a period (not in excess of 2 years) beginning on the date of such election or revocation, as the case may be. The preceding sentence does not apply unless the plan provision described in the preceding sentence also provides that such an election or revocation will be given effect in any case in which—

(1) the participant dies from accidental causes,

(2) a failure to give effect to the election or revocation would deprive the participant's survivor of a survivor annuity, and

(3) such election or revocation is made before such accident occurred.

Sec. 205(a)

(g) For purposes of this section:

(1) The term "annuity starting date" means the first day of the first period for which an amount is received as an annuity (whether by reason of retirement or by reason of disability).

(2) The term "earliest retirement age" means the earliest date on which, under the plan, the participant could elect to receive retirement benefits.

(3) The term "qualified joint and survivor annuity" means an annuity for the life of the participant with a survivor annuity for the life of his spouse which is not less than one-half of, or greater than, the amount of the annuity payable during the joint lives of the participant and his spouse and which is the actuarial equivalent of a single annuity for the life of the participant.

(h) For the purposes of this section, a plan may take into account in any equitable fashion (as determined by the Secretary of the Treasury) any increased costs resulting from providing joint and survivor annuity benefits under an election made under subsection (c).

(i) This section shall apply only if—

(1) the annuity starting date did not occur before the effective date of this section, and

(2) the participant was an active participant in the plan on or after such effective date.

OTHER PROVISIONS RELATING TO FORM AND PAYMENT OF BENEFITS

Sec. 206. (a) Each pension plan shall provide that unless the participant otherwise elects, the payment of benefits under the plan to the participant shall begin not later than the 60th day after the latest of the close of the plan year in which—

(1) the date on which the participant attains the earlier of age 65 or the normal retirement age specified under the plan,

(2) occurs the 10th anniversary of the year in which the participant commenced participation in the plan, or

(3) the participant terminates his service with the employer.

In the case of a plan which provides for the payment of an early retirement benefit, such plan shall provide that a participant who satisfied the service requirements for such early retirement benefit, but separated from the service (with any nonforfeitable right to an accrued benefit) before satisfying the age requirement for such early retirement benefit, is entitled upon satisfaction of such age requirement to receive a benefit not less than the benefit to which he would be entitled at the normal retirement age, actuarially reduced under regulations prescribed by the Secretary of the Treasury.

(b) If—

(1) a participant or beneficiary is receiving benefits under a pension plan, or

(2) a participant is separated from the service and has nonforfeitable rights to benefits,

a plan may not decrease benefits of such a participant by reason of any increase in the benefit levels payable under title II of the Social Security Act or the Railroad Retirement Act of 1937, or any increase in the wage base under such title II, if such increase takes place after the date of the enactment of this Act or (if later) the earlier of the date of first entitlement of such benefits or the date of such separation.

(c) No pension plan may provide that any part of a participant's accrued benefit derived from employer contributions (whether or not otherwise nonforfeitable) is forfeitable solely because of withdrawal by such participant of any amount attributable to the benefit derived from contributions made by such participant. The preceding sentence shall not apply (1) to the accrued benefit of any participant unless, at the time of such withdrawal, such participant has a nonforfeitable right to at least 50 percent of such accrued benefit, or (2) to the extent that an accrued benefit is permitted to be forfeited in accordance with section 203(a)(3)(D)(iii).

(d)(1) Each pension plan shall provide that benefits provided under the plan may not be assigned or alienated.

(2) For the purposes of paragraph (1) of this subsection, there shall not be taken into account any voluntary and revocable assignment of not to exceed 10 percent of any benefit payment, or of any irrevocable assignment or alienation of benefits executed before the date of enactment of this Act. The preceding sentence shall not apply to any assignment or alienation made for the purposes of defraying plan administration costs. For purposes of this paragraph a loan made to a participant or beneficiary shall not be treated as an assignment or alienation if such loan is secured by the participant's accrued nonforfeitable benefit and is exempt from the tax imposed by section 4975 of the Internal Revenue Code of 1954 (relating to tax on prohibited transactions) by reason of section 4975(d)(2) of such code.

TEMPORARY VARIANCES FROM CERTAIN VESTING REQUIREMENTS

Sec. 207. In the case of any plan maintained on January 1, 1974, if, not later than 2 years after the date of enactment of this Act, the administrator petitions the Secretary, the Secretary may prescribe an alternate method which shall be treated as satisfying the requirements of section 203(a)(2) or 204(b)(1) (other than subparagraph (D) thereof or both for a period of not more than 4 years. The Secretary may prescribe such alternate method only when he finds that—

(1) the application of such requirements would increase the costs of the plan to such an extent that there would result a substantial risk to the voluntary continuation of the plan or a substantial curtailment of benefit levels or the levels of employees' compensation,

(2) the application of such requirements or discontinuance of the plan would be adverse to the interests of plan participants in the aggregate, and

(3) a waiver or extension of time granted under section 303 or 304 of this Act would be inadequate.

In the case of any plan with respect to which an alternate method has been prescribed under the preceding provisions of this subsection for a period of not more than 4 years, if, not later than 1 year before the expiration of such period, the administrator petitions the Secretary for an extension of such alternate method, and the Secretary makes the findings required by the preceding sentence, such alternate method may be extended for not more than 3 years.

MERGERS AND CONSOLIDATIONS OF PLANS OR TRANSFERS OF PLAN ASSETS

Sec. 208. A pension plan may not merge or consolidate with, or transfer its assets or liabilities to, any other plan after the date of the enactment of this Act, unless each participant in the plan would (if the plan then terminated) receive a benefit immediately after the merger, consolidation, or transfer which is equal to or greater than the benefit he would have been entitled to receive immediately before the merger, consolidation, or transfer (if the plan had then terminated). The preceding sentence shall not apply to any transaction to the extent that participants either before or after the transaction are covered under a multiemployer plan to which title IV of this Act applies.

TEXT OF ERISA

RECORDKEEPING AND REPORTING REQUIREMENTS

Sec. 209. (a)(1) Except as provided by paragraph (2) every employer shall, in accordance with regulations prescribed by the Secretary, maintain records with respect to each of his employees sufficient to determine the benefits due or which may become due to such employees. The plan administrator shall make a report, in such manner and at such time as may be provided in regulations prescribed by the Secretary, to each employee who is a participant under the plan and who—

(A) requests such report, in such manner and at such time as may be provided in such regulations,

(B) terminates his service with the employer, or

(C) has a 1-year break in service (as defined in section 203(b)(3)(A)). The employer shall furnish to the plan administrator the information necessary for the administrator to make the reports required by the preceding sentence. Not more than one report shall be required under subparagraph (A) in any 12-month period. Not more than one report shall be required under subparagraph (C) with respect to consecutive 1-year breaks in service. The report required under this paragraph shall be sufficient to inform the employee of his accrued benefits under the plan and the percentage of such benefits which are nonforfeitable under the plan.

(2) If more than one employer adopts a plan, each such employer shall, in accordance with regulations prescribed by the Secretary of Labor, furnish to the plan administrator the information necessary for the administrator to maintain the records and make the reports required by paragraph (1). Such administrator shall maintain the records and, to the extent provided under regulations prescribed by the Secretary, make the reports, required by paragraph (1).

(b) If any person who is required, under subsection (a), to furnish information or maintain records for any plan year fails to comply with such requirement, he shall pay to the Secretary a civil penalty of $10 for each employee with respect to whom such failure occurs, unless it is shown that such failure is due to reasonable cause.

PLANS MAINTAINED BY MORE THAN ONE EMPLOYER, PREDECESSOR PLANS, AND EMPLOYER GROUPS

Sec. 210. (a) Notwithstanding any other provision of this part or part 3, the following provisions of this subsection shall apply to a plan maintained by more than one employer:

(1) Section 202 of this subsection shall be applied as if all employees of each of the employers were employed by a single employer.

(2) Section 203 and 204 shall be applied as if all such employers constituted a single employer, except that the application of any rules with respect to breaks in service shall be made under regulations prescribed by the Secretary.

(3) The minimum funding standard provided by section 302 shall be determined as if all participants in the plan were employed by a single employer.

(b) For purposes of this part and part 3—

(1) in any case in which the employer maintains a plan of a predecessor employer, service for such predecessor shall be treated as service for the employer, and

(2) in any case in which the employer maintains a plan which is not the plan maintained by a predecessor employer, service for such predecessor shall, to the extent provided in regulations prescribed by the Secretary of the Treasury, be treated as service for the employer.

(c) For purposes of sections 202, 203, and 204, all employees of all corporations which are members of a controlled group of corporations

Sec. 210 (c)

(within the meaning of section 1563 (a) of the Internal Revenue Code of 1954, determined without regard to section 1563(a)(4) and (e)(3)(C) of such code) shall be treated as employed by a single employer. With respect to a plan adopted by more than one such corporation, the minimum funding standard of section 302 shall be determined as if all such employers were a single employer, and allocated to each employer in accordance with regulations prescribed by the Secretary of the Treasury.

(d) For purposes of sections 202, 203, and 204, under regulations prescribed by the Secretary of the Treasury, all employees of trades or businesses (whether or not incorporated) which are under common control shall be treated as employed by a single employer. The regulations prescribed under this subsection shall be based on principles similar to the principles which apply in the case of subsection (c).

EFFECTIVE DATES

Sec. 211. (a) Except as otherwise provided in this section, this part shall apply in the case of plan years beginning after the date of the enactment of this Act.

(b)(1) Except as otherwise provided in subsection (d), sections 205, 206(d), and 208 shall apply with respect to plan years beginning after December 31, 1975.

(2) Except as otherwise provided in subsections (c) and (d) in the case of a plan in existence on January 1, 1974, this part shall apply in the case of plan years beginning after December 31, 1975.

(c)(1) In the case of a plan maintained on January 1, 1974, pursuant to one or more agreements which the Secretary finds to be collective bargaining agreements between employee organizations and one or more employers, no plan shall be treated as not meeting the requirements of sections 204 and 205 solely by reason of a supplementary or special plan provision (within the meaning of paragraph (2)) for any plan year before the year which begins after the earlier of—

(A) the date on which the last of such agreements relating to the plan terminates (determined without regard to any extension thereof agreed to after the date of the enactment of this Act), or

(B) December 31, 1980.

For purposes of subparagraph (A) and section 306(c), any plan amendment made pursuant to a collective bargaining agreement relating to the plan which amends the plan solely to conform to any requirement contained in this Act or the Internal Revenue Code of 1954 shall not be treated as a termination of such collective bargaining agreement. This paragraph shall not apply unless the Secretary determines that the participation and vesting rules in effect on the date of enactment of this Act are not less favorable to participants, in the aggregate, than the rules provided under sections 202, 203, and 204.

(2) For purposes of paragraph (1), the term "supplementary or special plan provision" means any plan provision which—

(A) provides supplementary benefits, not in excess of one-third of the basic benefit, in the form of an annuity for the life of the participant or

(B) provides that, under a contractual agreement based on medical evidence as to the effects of working in an adverse environment for an extended period of time, a participant having 25 years of service is to be treated as having 30 years of service.

(3) This subsection shall apply with respect to a plan if (and only if) the application of this subsection results in a later effective date for this part than the effective date required by subsection (b).

(d) If the administrator of a plan elects under section 1017(d) of this Act to make applicable to a plan year and to all subsequent plan years the

Sec. 210 (d)

provisions of the Internal Revenue Code of 1954 relating to participation, vesting, funding, and form of benefit, this part shall apply to the first plan year to which such election applies and to all subsequent plan years.

(e)(1) No pension plan to which section 202 applies may make effective any plan amendment with respect to breaks in service (which amendment is made or becomes effective after January 1, 1974, and before the date on which section 202 first becomes effective with respect to such plan) which provides that any employee's participation in the plan would commence at any date later than the later of—

(A) the date on which his participation would commence under the break in service rules of section 202 (b), or

(B) the date on which his participation would commence under the plan as in effect on January 1, 1974.

(2) No pension plan to which section 203 applies may make effective any plan amendment with respect to breaks in service (which amendment is made or becomes effective after January 1, 1974, and before the date on which section 203 first becomes effective with respect to such plan) if such amendment provides that the nonforfeitable benefit derived from employer contributions to which any employee would be entitled is less than the lesser of the nonforfeitable benefit derived from employer contributions to which he would be entitled under—

(A) the break in service rules of section 202(b)(3), or

(B) the plan as in effect on January 1, 1974.

Subparagraph (B) shall not apply if the break in service rules under the plan would have been in violation of any law or rule of law in effect on January 1, 1974.

PART 3—FUNDING

COVERAGE

Sec. 301. (a) This part shall apply to any employee pension benefit plan described in section 4(a), (and not exempted under section 4(b)), other than—

(1) an employee welfare benefit plan;

(2) an insurance contract plan described in subsection (b);

(3) a plan which is unfunded and is maintained by an employer primarily for the purpose of providing deferred compensation for a select group of management or highly compensated employees;

(4)(A) a plan which is established and maintained by a society, order, or association described in section 501(c)(8) or (9) of the Internal Revenue Code of 1954, if no part of the contributions to or under such plan are made by employers of participants in such plan; or

(B) a trust described in section 501(c)(18) of such Code;

(5) a plan which has not at any time after the date of enactment of this Act provided for employer contributions;

(6) an agreement providing payments to a retired partner or deceased partner or a deceased partner's successor in interest as described in section 736 of the Internal Revenue Code of 1954;

(7) an individual retirement account or annuity as described in section 408(a) of the Internal Revenue Code of 1954, or a retirement bond described in section 409 of such Code;

(8) an individual account plan (other than a money purchase plan) and a defined benefit plan to the extent it is treated as an individual account plan (other than a money purchase plan) under section 3(35)(B) of this title; or

(9) an excess benefit plan.

(10) Any plan, fund or program under which an employer, all of whose stock is directly or indirectly owned by

Sec. 301(a)(10)

employees, former employees or their beneficiaries, proposes through an unfunded arrangement to compensate retired employees for benefits which were forfeited by such employees under a pension plan maintained by a former employer prior to the date such pension plan became subject to this Act.

(b) For the purposes of paragraph (2) of subsection (a) a plan is an "insurance contract plan" if—

(1) the plan is funded exclusively by the purchase of individual insurance contracts,

(2) such contracts provide for level annual premium payments to be paid extending not later than the retirement age for each individual participating in the plan, and commencing with the date the individual became a participant in the plan (or, in the case of an increase in benefits, commencing at the time such increase becomes effective),

(3) benefits provided by the plan are equal to the benefits provided under each contract at normal retirement age under the plan and are guaranteed by an insurance carrier (licensed under the laws of a State to do business with the plan) to the extent premiums have been paid,

(4) premiums payable for the plan year, and all prior plan years under such contracts have been paid before lapse or there is reinstatement of the policy,

(5) no rights under such contracts have been subject to a security interest at any time during the plan year, and

(6) no policy loans are outstanding at any time during the plan year.

A plan funded exclusively by the purchase of group insurance contracts which is determined under regulations prescribed by the Secretary of the Treasury to have the same characteristics as contracts described in the preceding sentence shall be treated as a plan described in this subsection.

Sec. 301 (b)

(c) This part applies, with respect to a terminated multiemployer plan to which section 4021 applies, until the last day of the plan year in which the plan terminates, within the meaning of section 4041A(a)(2).

(d) Any amount of any financial assistance from the Pension Benefit Guaranty Corporation to any plan, and any repayment of such amount, shall be taken into account under this section in such manner as determined by the Secretary of the Treasury.

MINIMUM FUNDING STANDARDS

Sec. 302. (a)(1) Every employee pension benefit plan subject to this part shall satisfy the minimum funding standard (or the alternative minimum funding standard under section 305) for any plan year to which this part applies. A plan to which this part applies shall have satisfied the minimum funding standard for such plan for a plan year if as of the end of such plan year the plan does not have an accumulated funding deficiency.

(2) For the purposes of this part, the term "accumulated funding deficiency" means for any plan the excess of the total charges to the funding standard account for all plan years (beginning with the first plan year to which this part applies) over the total credits to such account for such years or, if less, the excess of the total charges to the alternative minimum funding standard account for such plan years over the total credits to such account for such years.

(3) In any plan year in which a multiemployer plan is in reorganization, the accumulated funding deficiency of the plan shall be determined under Section 4243.

(b)(1) Each plan to which this part applies shall establish and maintain a funding standard account. Such account shall be credited and charged solely as provided in this section.

(2) For a plan year, the funding standard account shall be charged with the sum of—

(A) the normal cost of the plan for the plan year,

(B) the amounts necessary to amortize in equal annual installments (until fully amortized)—

(1) in the case of a plan in existence on January 1, 1974, the unfunded past service liability under the plan on the first day of the first plan year to which this part applies, over a period of 40 plan years,

(ii) in the case of a plan which comes into existence after January 1, 1974, the unfunded past service liability under the plan on the first day of the first plan year to which this part applies, over a period of 30 plan years,

(iii) separately, with respect to each plan year, the net increase (if any) in unfunded past service liability under the plan arising from plan amendments adopted in such year, over a period of 30 plan years,

(iv) separately, with respect to each plan year, the net experience loss (if any) under the plan, over a period of 15 plan years, and

(v) separately, with respect to each plan year, the net loss (if any) resulting from changes in actuarial assumptions used under the plan, over a period of 30 plan years,

(C) the amount necessary to amortize each waived funding deficiency (within the meaning of section 303 (c)) for each prior plan year in equal annual installments (until fully amortized) over a period of 15 plan years, and

(D) the amount necessary to amortize in equal annual installments (until fully amortized) over a period of 5 plan years any amount credited to the funding standard account under paragraph (3)(D).

(3) For a plan year, the funding standard account shall be credited with the sum of—

(A) the amount considered contributed by the employer to or under the plan for the plan year,

(B) the amount necessary to amortize in equal annual installments (until fully amortized)—

(i) separately, with respect to each plan year, the net decrease (if any) in unfunded past service liability under the plan arising from plan amendments adopted in such year, over a period of 30 plan years (40 plan years in the case of a multiemployer plan),

(ii) separately, with respect to each plan year, the net experience gain (if any) under the plan, over a period of 15 plan years (20 plan years in the case of a multiemployer plan), and

(iii) separately, with respect to each plan year, the net gain (if any) resulting from changes in actuarial assumptions used under the plan, over a period of 30 plan years,

(C) the amount of the waived funding deficiency (within the meaning of section 303(c)) for the plan year, and

(D) in the case of a plan year for which the accumulated funding deficiency is determined under the funding standard account if such plan year follows a plan year for which such deficiency was determined under the alternative minimum funding standard, the excess (if any) of any debit balance in the funding standard account (determined without regard to this subparagraph) over any debit balance in the alternative minimum funding standard account.

(4) Under regulations prescribed by the Secretary of the Treasury, amounts required to be amortized under paragraph (2) or paragraph (3), as the case may be—

(A) may be combined into one amount under such paragraph to be amortized over a period determined on the basis of the remaining amortization period for all items entering into such combined amount, and

(B) may be offset against amounts required to be amortized under the other such paragraph, with the re-

Sec. 302 (b) (4)

sulting amount to be amortized over a period determined on the basis of the remaining amortization periods for all items entering into whichever of the two amounts being offset is the greater.

(5) The funding standard account (and items therein) shall be charged or credited (as determined under regulations prescribed by the Secretary of the Treasury) with interest at the appropriate rate consistent with the rate or rates of interest used under the plan to determine costs.

(6) In the case of a plan which, immediately before the date of the enactment of the Multiemployer Pension Plan Amendments Act of 1980, was a multiemployer plan (within the meaning of section 3(37) as in effect immediately before such date)—

(A) any amount described in paragraph (2)(B)(ii), (2)(B)(iii), or (3)(B)(i) of this subsection which arose in a plan year beginning before such date shall be amortized in equal annual installments (until fully amortized) over 40 plan years, beginning with the plan year in which the amount arose;

(B) any amount described in paragraph (2)(B)(iv) or (3)(B)(ii) of this subsection which arose in a plan year beginning before such date shall be amortized in equal annual installments (until fully amortized) over 20 plan years, beginning with the plan year in which the amount arose;

(C) any change in past service liability which arises during the period of 3 plan years beginning on or after such date, and results from a plan amendment adopted before such date, shall be amortized in equal annual installments (until fully amortized) over 40 plan years, beginning with the plan year in which the change arises; and

(D) any change in past service liability which arises during the period of 2 plan years beginning on or after such date, and results from the changing of a group of participants from one benefit level to another benefit level under a schedule of plan benefits which—

(i) was adopted before such date, and

(ii) was effective for any plan participant before the beginning of the first plan year beginning on or after such date,

shall be amortized in equal annual installments (until fully amortized) over 40 plan years, beginning with the plan year in which the increase arises.

(7) For purposes of this part—

(A) Any amount received by a multiemployer plan in payment of all or part of an employer's withdrawal liability under part 1 of subtitle E of title IV shall be considered an amount contributed by the employer to or under the plan. The Secretary of the Treasury may prescribe by regulation additional charges and credits to a multiemployer plan's funding standard account to the extent necessary to prevent withdrawal liability payments from being unduly reflected as advance funding for plan liabilities.

(B) If a plan is not in reorganization in the plan year but was in reorganization in the immediately preceding plan year, any balance in the funding standard account at the close of such immediately preceding plan year—

(i) shall be eliminated by an offsetting credit or charge (as the case may be), but

(ii) shall be taken into account in subsequent plan years by being amortized in equal annual installments (until fully amortized) over 30 plan years.

The preceding sentence shall not apply to the extent of any accumulated funding deficiency under section 418B(a) of the Internal Revenue Code of 1954 as of the end of the last plan year that the plan was in reorganization.

(C) Any amount paid by a plan during a plan year to the Pension Benefit Guaranty Corporation pursuant to section 4222 or to a fund exempt under section 501(c)(22) of such Code pursuant to section 4223 shall reduce

Sec. 302 (b) (5)

TEXT OF ERISA

the amount of contributions considered received by the plan for the plan year.

(D) Any amount paid by an employer pending a final determination of the employer's withdrawal liability under part 1 of subtitle E of title IV and subsequently refunded to the employer by the plan shall be charged to the funding standard account in accordance with regulations prescribed by the Secretary.

(E) For purposes of the full funding limitation under subsection (c)(7), unless otherwise provided by the plan, the accrued liability under a multiemployer plan shall not include benefits which are not nonforfeitable under the plan after the termination of the plan (taking into consideration section 411(d)(3) of the Internal Revenue Code of 1954).

(c)(1) For purposes of this part, normal costs, accrued liability, past service liabilities, and experience gains and losses shall be determined under the funding method used to determine costs under the plan.

(2)(A) For purposes of this part, the value of the plan's assets shall be determined on the basis of any reasonable actuarial method of valuation which takes into account fair market value and which is permitted under regulations prescribed by the Secretary of the Treasury.

(B) For purposes of this part, the value of a bond or other evidence of indebtedness which is not in default as to principal or interest may, at the election of the plan administrator, be determined on an amortized basis running from initial cost at purchase to par value at maturity or earliest call date. Any election under this subparagraph shall be made at such time and in such manner as the Secretary of the Treasury shall by regulations provide, shall apply to all such evidences of indebtedness, and may be revoked only with the consent of the Secretary of the Treasury.

(3) For purposes of this part, all costs, liabilities, rates of interest, and other factors under the plan shall be determined on the basis of actuarial assumptions and methods which, in the aggregate, are reasonable (taking into account the experience of the plan and reasonable expectations) and which, in combination, offer the actuary's best estimate of anticipated experience under the plan.

(4) For purposes of this section, if—

(A) a change in benefits under the Social Security Act or in other retirement benefits created under Federal or State law, or

(B) a change in the definition of the term "wages" under section 3121 of the Internal Revenue Code of 1954, or a change in the amount of such wages taken into account under regulations prescribed for purposes of section 401(a)(5) of the Internal Revenue Code of 1954,

results in an increase or decrease in accrued liability under a plan, such increase or decrease shall be treated as an experience loss or gain.

(5) If the funding method for a plan is changed, the new funding method shall become the funding method used to determine costs and liabilities under the plan only if the change is approved by the Secretary of the Treasury. If the plan year for a plan is changed, the new plan year shall become the plan year for the plan only if the change is approved by the Secretary of the Treasury.

(6) If, as of the close of a plan year, a plan would (without regard to this paragraph) have an accumulated funding deficiency (determined without regard to the alternative minimum funding standard account permitted under subsection (g)) in excess of the full funding limitation—

(A) the funding standard account shall be credited with the amount of such excess, and

(B) all amounts described in paragraphs (2), (B), (C), and (D) and (3)(B) of subsection (b) which are required to be amortized shall be

Sec. 302 (c) (6)

considered fully amortized for purposes of such paragraphs.

(7) For purposes of paragraph (6), the term "full funding limitation" means the excess (if any) of—

(A) the accrued liability (including normal cost) under the plan (determined under the entry age normal funding method if such accrued liability cannot be directly calculated under the funding method used for the plan), over

(B) the lesser of the fair market value of the plan's assets or the value of such assets determined under paragraph (2).

(8) For purposes of this part, any amendment applying to a plan year which—

(A) is adopted after the close of such plan year but no later than 2½ months after the close of the plan year (or, in the case of a multiemployer plan, no later than 2 years after the close of such plan year),

(B) does not reduce the accrued benefit of any participant determined as of the beginning of the first plan year to which the amendment applies, and

(C) does not reduce the accrued benefit of any participant determined as of the time of adoption except to the extent required by the circumstances,

shall, at the election of the plan administrator, be deemed to have been made on the first day of such plan year. No amendment described in this paragraph which reduces the accrued benefits of any participant shall take effect unless the plan administrator files a notice with the Secretary notifying him of such amendment and the Secretary has approved such amendment or, within 90 days after the date on which such notice was filed, failed to disapprove such amendment. No amendment described in this subsection shall be approved by the Secretary unless he determines that such amendment is necessary because of a substantial business hardship (as determined under section 303(b)) and that waiver under section 303(a) is unavailable or inadequate.

(9) For purposes of this part, a determination of experience gains and losses and a valuation of the plan's liability shall be made not less frequently than once every 3 years, except that such determination shall be made more frequently to the extent required in particular cases under regulations prescribed by the Secretary of the Treasury.

(10) For purposes of this part, any contributions for a plan year made by an employer after the last day of such plan year, but not later than 2½ months after such day, shall be deemed to have been made on such last day. For purposes of this paragraph, such 2½ month period may be extended for not more than 6 months under regulations prescribed by the Secretary of the Treasury.

(d) Cross Reference—**For alternative amortization method for certain multiemployer plans see section 1013 (d) of this Act.**

VARIANCE FROM MINIMUM FUNDING STANDARD

Sec. 303. (a) If an employer, or in the case of a multiemployer plan, 10 percent or more of the number of employers contributing to or under the plan are unable to satisfy the minimum funding standard for a plan year without substantial business hardship and if application of the standard would be adverse to the interests of plan participants in the aggregate, the Secretary of the Treasury may waive the requirements of section 302(a) for such year with respect to all or any portion of the minimum funding standard other than the portion thereof determined under section 302(b)(2)(C). The Secretary of the Treasury shall not waive the minimum funding standard with respect to a plan for more than 5 of any 15 consecutive plan years.

Sec. 302 (c) (7)

(b) For purposes of this part, the factors taken into account in determining substantial business hardship shall include (but shall not be limited to) whether—

(1) the employer is operating at an economic loss,

(2) there is substantial unemployment or underemployment in the trade or business and in the industry concerned,

(3) the sales and profits of the industry concerned are depressed or declining, and

(4) it is reasonable to expect that the plan will be continued only if the waiver is granted.

(c) For purposes of this part, the term "waived funding deficiency" means the portion of the minimum funding standard determined without regard to subsection (b)(3)(C) of section 302) for a plan year waived by the Secretary of the Treasury and not satisfied by employer contributions.

(d) Cross Reference.—

For corresponding duties of the Secretary of the Treasury with regard to implementation of the Internal Revenue Code of 1954, see section 412(d) of such Code.

EXTENSION OF AMORTIZATION PERIODS

Sec. 304. (a) The period of years required to amortize any unfunded liability (described in any clause of subsection (b)(2)(B) of section 302) of any plan may be extended by the Secretary for a period of time (not in excess of 10 years) if he determines that such extension would carry out the purposes of this Act and would provide adequate protection for participants under the plan and their beneficiaries and if he determines that the failure to permit such extension would—

(1) result in—

(A) a substantial risk to the voluntary continuation of the plan, or

(B) a substantial curtailment of pension benefit levels or employee compensation, and

(2) be adverse to the interests of plan participants in the aggregate.

(b)(1) No amendment of the plan which increases the liabilities of the plan by reason of any increase in benefits, any change in the accrual of benefits, or any change in the rate at which benefits become nonforfeitable under the plan shall be adopted if a waiver under section 303(a) or an extension of time under subsection (a) of this section is in effect with respect to the plan, or if a plan amendment described in section 302(c)(8) has been made at any time in the preceding 12 months (24 months in the case of a multiemployer plan). If a plan is amended in violation of the preceding sentence, any such waiver, or extension of time, shall not apply to any plan year ending on or after the date on which such amendment is adopted.

(2) Paragraph (1) shall not apply to any plan amendment which—

(A) the Secretary determines to be reasonable and which provides for only de minimis increases in the liabilities of the plan,

(B) only repeals an amendment described in section 302(c)(8), or

(C) is required as a condition of qualification under part I of subchapter D, of chapter 1, of the Internal Revenue Code of 1954.

ALTERNATIVE MINIMUM FUNDING STANDARD

Sec. 305. (a) A plan which uses a funding method that requires contributions in all years not less than those required under the entry age normal funding method may maintain an alternative minimum funding standard account for any plan year. Such account shall be credited and charged solely as provided in this section.

(b) For a plan year the alternative minimum funding standard accounts shall be—

(1) charged with the sum of—

(A) the lesser of normal cost under the funding method used under the plan or normal cost determined under the unit credit method,

(B) the excess, if any, of the present value of accrued benefits under the plan over the fair market value of the assets, and

(C) an amount equal to the excess, if any, of credits to the alternative minimum funding standard account for all prior plan years over charges to such account for all such years, and

(2) credited with the amount considered contributed by the employer to or under the plan (within the meaning of section 302(c)(10)) for the plan year.

(c) The alternative minimum funding standard account (and items therein) shall be charged or credited with interest in the manner provided under section 302(b)(5) with respect to the funding standard account.

EFFECTIVE DATES

Sec. 306. (a) Except as otherwise provided in this section, this part shall apply in the case of plan years beginning after the date of the enactment of this Act.

(b) Except as otherwise provided in subsections (c) and (d), in the case of a plan in existence on January 1, 1974, this part shall apply in the case of plan years beginning after December 31, 1975.

(c)(1) In the case of a plan maintained on January 1, 1974, pursuant to one or more agreements which the Secretary finds to be collective bargaining agreements between employee representatives and one or more employers, this part shall apply only with respect to plan years beginning after the earlier of the date specified in subparagraph (A) or (B) of section 211(c)(1).

(2) This subsection shall apply with respect to a plan if (and only if) the application of this subsection results in a later effective date for this part than the effective date required by subsection (b).

(d) In the case of a plan the administrator of which elects under Section 1017(d) of this Act to have the provisions of the Internal Revenue Code of 1954 relating to participation, vesting, funding, and form of benefit to apply to a plan year and to all subsequent plan years, this part shall apply to plan years beginning on the earlier of the first plan year to which such election applies or the first plan year determined under subsections (a), (b), and (c) of this section.

(e) In the case of a plan maintained by a labor organization which is exempt from tax under section 501(c)(5) of the Internal Revenue Code of 1954 exclusively for the benefit of its employees and their beneficiaries, this part shall be applied by substituting for the term "December 31, 1975" in subsection (b), the earlier of—

(1) the date on which the second convention of such labor organization held after the date of the enactment of this Act ends, or

(2) December 31, 1980,

but in no event shall a date earlier than the later of December 31, 1975, or the date determined under subsection (c) be substituted.

PART 4—FIDUCIARY RESPONSIBILITY

COVERAGE

Sec. 401. (a) This part shall apply to any employee benefit plan described in section 4(a) (and not exempted under section 4(b)), other than—

(1) a plan which is unfunded and is maintained by an employer primarily for the purpose of providing deferred compensation for a select group of management or highly compensated employees; or

(2) any agreement described in section 736 of the Internal Revenue Code of 1954, which provides payments to a retired partner or deceased partner or a deceased partner's successor in interest.

Sec. 305 (b) (1)

(b) For purposes of this part:

(1) In the case of a plan which invests in any security issued by an investment company registered under the Investment Company Act of 1940, the assets of such plan shall be deemed to include such security but shall not, solely by reason of such investment, be deemed to include any assets of such investment company.

(2) In the case of a plan to which a guaranteed benefit policy is issued by an insurer, the assets of such plan shall be deemed to include such policy, but shall not, solely by reason of the issuance of such policy, be deemed to include any assets of such insurer. For purposes of this paragraph:

(A) The term "insurer" means an insurance company, insurance service, or insurance organization, qualified to do business in a State.

(B) The term "guaranteed benefit policy" means an insurance policy or contract to the extent that such policy or contract provides for benefits the amount of which is guaranteed by the insurer. Such term includes any surplus in a separate account, but excludes any other portion of a separate account.

ESTABLISHMENT OF PLAN

Sec. 402. (a)(1) Every employee benefit plan shall be established and maintained pursuant to a written instrument. Such instrument shall provide for one or more named fiduciaries who jointly or severally shall have authority to control and manage the operation and administration of the plan.

(2) For purposes of this title, the term "named fiduciary" means a fiduciary who is named in the plan instrument, or who, pursuant to a procedure specified in the plan, is identified as a fiduciary (A) by a person who is an employer or employee organization with respect to the plan or (B) by such an employer and such an employee organization acting jointly.

(b) Every employee benefit plan shall—

(1) provide a procedure for establishing and carrying out a funding policy and method consistent with the objectives of the plan and the requirements of this title,

(2) describe any procedure under the plan for the allocation of responsibilities for the operation and administration of the plan (including any procedure described in section 405(c)(1)),

(3) provide a procedure for amending such plan, and for identifying the persons who have authority to amend the plan, and

(4) specify the basis on which payments are made to and from the plan.

(c) Any employee benefit plan may provide—

(1) that any person or group of persons may serve in more than one fiduciary capacity with respect to the plan (including service both as trustee and administrator);

(2) that a named fiduciary, or a fiduciary designated by a named fiduciary pursuant to a plan procedure described in section 405(c)(1), may employ one or more persons to render advice with regard to any responsibility such fiduciary has under the plan; or

(3) that a person who is a named fiduciary with respect to control or management of the assets of the plan may appoint an investment manager or managers to manage (including the power to acquire and dispose of) any assets of a plan.

ESTABLISHMENT OF TRUST

Sec. 403. (a) Except as provided in subsection (b), all assets of an employee benefit plan shall be held in trust by one or more trustees. Such trustee or trustees shall be either named in the trust instrument or in the plan instrument described in section 402(a) or appointed by a person who is a named fiduciary, and upon acceptance of being named or appointed, the trustee or trustees shall have exclusive authority and discretion to manage and control the assets of the plan, except to the extent that—

(1) the plan expressly provides that the trustee or trustees are subject to the direction of a named fiduciary who is not a trustee, in which case the trustees shall be subject to proper directions of such fiduciary which are made in accordance with the terms of the plan and which are not contrary to this [title,] *Act,* or

(2) authority to manage, acquire, or dispose of assets of the plan is delegated to one or more investment managers pursuant to section 402(c)(3).

(b) The requirements of subsection (a) of this section shall not apply—

(1) to any assets of a plan which consist of insurance contracts or policies issued by an insurance company qualified to do business in a State;

(2) to any assets of such an insurance company or any assets of a plan which are held by such an insurance company;

(3) to a plan—

(i) some or all of the participants of which are employees of described in section 401(c)(1) of the Internal Revenue Code of 1954; or

(ii) which consists of one or more individual retirement accounts described in section 408 of the Internal Revenue Code of 1954, to the extent that such plan's assets are held in one or more custodial accounts which qualify under section 401(f) or 408(h) of such Code, whichever is applicable;

(4) to a plan which the Secretary exempts from the requirement of subsection (a) and which is not subject to any of the following provisions of this Act:

(A) part 2 of this subtitle,
(B) part 3 of this subtitle, or
(C) title IV of this Act; or

(5) to a contract established and maintained under section 403(b) of the Internal Revenue Code of 1954 to the extent that the assets of the contract are held in one or more custodial accounts pursuant to section 403(b)(7) of such Code.

(6) Any plan, fund or program under which an employer, all of whose stock is directly or indirectly owned by employees, former employees or their beneficiaries, proposes through an unfunded arrangement to compensate retired employees for benefits which were forfeited by such employees under a pension plan maintained by a former employer prior to the date such pension plan became subject to this Act.

(c)(1) Except as provided in paragraph (2), (3) or (4) of subsection (d), or under section 4042 and 4044 (relating to termination of insured plans), the assets of a plan shall never inure to the benefit of any employer and shall be held for the exclusive purposes of providing benefits to participants in the plan and their beneficiaries and defraying reasonable expenses of administering the plan.

* (2)(A) In the case of a contribution, or a payment of withdrawal liability under part 1 of subtitle E of part iv—

(i) made by an employer to a plan (other than a multiemployer plan) by a mistake of fact, paragraph (1) shall not prohibit the return of such contribution to the employer within one year after the payment of the contribution, and

---

* [*Editor's Note:* Subsection 403(c)(2)(A) took effect on January 1, 1975, except that in the case of contributions received by a collectively bargained plan maintained by more than one employer before the date of enactment of this Act, any determination by the plan administrator that any such contribution was made by mistake of fact or law before such date shall be deemed to have been made on such date of enactment.]

Sec. 403 (a) (1)

(ii) made by an employer to a multiemployer plan by a mistake of fact or law (other than a mistake relating to whether the plan is described in section 401(a) of the Internal Revenue Code of 1954 or the trust which is part of such plan is exempt from taxation under section 501(a) of such Code), paragraph (1) shall not prohibit the return of such contribution or payment to the employer within 6 months after the plan administrator determines that the contribution was made by such a mistake.

(B) If a contribution is conditioned on qualification of the plan under section 401, 403(a), or 405(a) of the Internal Revenue Code of 1954, and if the plan does not qualify, then paragraph (1) shall not prohibit the return of such contribution to the employer within one year after the date of denial of qualification of the plan.

(C) If a contribution is conditioned upon the deductibility of the contribution under section 404 of the Internal Revenue Code of 1954, then, to the extent the deduction is disallowed, paragraph (1) shall not prohibit the return to the employer of such contribution (to the extent disallowed) within one year after the disallowance of the deduction.

(3) In the case of a contribution which would otherwise be an excess contribution (as defined in section 4972(b) of the Internal Revenue Code of 1954) paragraph (1) shall not prohibit a correcting distribution with respect to such contribution from the plan to the employer to the extent permitted in such section to avoid payment of an excise tax on excess contributions under such section.

(4) In the case of a withdrawal liability payment which has been determined to be an overpayment, paragraph (1) shall not prohibit the return of such payment to the employer within 6 months after the date of such determination.

(d)(1) Upon termination of a pension plan to which section 4021 does not apply at the time of termination and to which this part applies (other than a plan to which no employer contributions have been made) the assets of the plan shall be allocated in accordance with the provisions of section 4044 of this Act, except as otherwise provided in regulations of the Secretary.

(2) The assets of a welfare plan which terminates shall be distributed in accordance with the terms of the plan, except as otherwise provided in regulations of the Secretary.

FIDUCIARY DUTIES

Sec. 404. (a)(1) Subject to sections 403(c) and (d), 4042, and 4044, a fiduciary shall discharge his duties with respect to a plan solely in the interest of the participants and beneficiaries and—

(A) for the exclusive purpose of:

(i) providing benefits to participants and their beneficiaries; and

(ii) defraying reasonable expenses of administering the plan;

(B) with the care, skill, prudence, and diligence under the circumstances then prevailing that a prudent man acting in a like capacity and familiar with such matters would use in the conduct of an enterprise of a like character and with like aims;

(C) by diversifying the investments of the plan so as to minimize the risk of large losses, unless under the circumstances it is clearly prudent not to do so; and

(D) in accordance with the documents and instruments governing the plan insofar as such documents and instruments are consistent with the provisions of this title or title IV.

(2) In the case of an eligible individual account plan (as defined in section 407(d)(3)), the diversification requirement of paragraph (1)(C) and the prudence requirement (only to the extent that it requires diversification) of paragraph (1)(B) is not violated by acquisition or holding of qualifying employer real property or qualifying employer securities (as defined in section 407(d)(4) and (5)).

(b) Except as authorized by the Secretary by regulation, no fiduciary may maintain the indicia of ownership of any assets of a plan outside the jurisdiction of the district courts of the United States.

(c) In the case of a pension plan which provides for individual accounts and permits a participant or beneficiary to exercise control over assets in his account, if a participant or beneficiary exercises control over the assets in his account (as determined under regulations of the Secretary)—

(1) such participant or beneficiary shall not be deemed to be a fiduciary by reason of such exercise, and

(2) no person who is otherwise a fiduciary shall be liable under this part for any loss, or by reason of any breach, which results from such participant's, or beneficiary's exercise of control.

LIABILITY FOR BREACH BY CO-FIDUCIARY

Sec. 405. (a) In addition to any liability which he may have under any other provision of this part, a fiduciary with respect to a plan shall be liable for a breach of fiduciary responsibility of another fiduciary with respect to the same plan in the following circumstances:

(1) if he participates knowingly in, or knowingly undertakes to conceal, an act or omission of such other fiduciary, knowing such act or omission is a breach;

(2) if, by his failure to comply with section 404(a)(1) in the administration of his specific responsibilities which give rise to his status as a fiduciary, he has enabled such other fiduciary to commit a breach; or

(3) if he has knowledge of a breach by such other fiduciary, unless he makes reasonable efforts under the circumstances to remedy the breach.

(b)(1) Except as otherwise provided in subsection (d) and in section 403 (a)(1) and (2), if the assets of a plan are held by two or more trustees—

(A) each shall use reasonable care to prevent a co-trustee from committing a breach; and

(B) they shall jointly manage and control the assets of the plan, except that nothing in this subparagraph (B) shall preclude any agreement, authorized by the trust instrument, allocating specific responsibilities, obligations. or duties among trustees, in which event a trustee to whom certain responsibilities, obligations, or duties have not been allocated shall not be liable by reason of this subparagraph (B) either individually or as a trustee for any loss resulting to the plan arising from the acts or omissions on the part of another trustee to whom such responsibilities, obligations, or duties have been allocated.

(2) Nothing in this subsection shall limit any liability that a fiduciary may have under subsection (a) or any other provision of this part.

(3)(A) In the case of a plan the assets of which are held in more than one trust, a trustee shall not be liable under paragraph (1) except with respect to an act or omission of a trustee of a trust of which he is a trustee.

(B) No trustee shall be liable under this subsection for following instructions referred to in section 403(a)(1).

(c)(1) The instrument under which a plan is maintained may expressly provide for procedures (A) for allocating fiduciary responsibilities (other than trustee responsibilities) among named fiduciaries, and (B) for named fiduciaries to designate persons other than named fiduciaries to carry out fiduciary responsibilities (other than trustee responsibilities) under the plan.

(2) If a plan expressly provides for a procedure described in paragraph (1), and pursuant to such procedure any fiduciary responsibility of a named fiduciary is allocated to any person, or a person is designated to carry out any such responsibility, then such named fiduciary shall not be liable for an act or omission of such person in carrying out such responsibility except to the extent that—

(A) the named fiduciary violated section 404(a)(1)—

Sec. 404 (c)

TEXT OF ERISA

(i) with respect to such allocation or designation,

(ii) with respect to the establishment or implementation of the procedure under paragraph (1), or

(iii) in continuing the allocation or designation; or

(B) the named fiduciary would otherwise be liable in accordance with subsection (a).

(3) For purposes of this subsection, the term "trustee responsibility" means any responsibility provided in the plan's trust instrument (if any) to manage or control the assets of the plan, other than a power under the trust instrument of a named fiduciary to appoint an investment manager in accordance with section 402(c)(3).

(d)(1) If an investment manager or managers have been appointed under section 402(c)(3), then, notwithstanding subsections (a)(2) and (3) and subsection (b), no trustee shall be liable for the acts or omissions of such investment manager or managers, or be under an obligation to invest or otherwise manage any asset of the plan which is subject to the management of such investment manager.

(2) Nothing in this subsection shall relieve any trustee of any liability under this part for any act of such trustee.

PROHIBITED TRANSACTIONS

Sec. 406. (a) Except as provided in section 408:

(1) A fiduciary with respect to a plan shall not cause the plan to engage in a transaction, if he knows or should know that such transaction constitutes a direct or indirect—

(A) sale or exchange, or leasing, of any property between the plan and a party in interest;

(B) lending of money or other extension of credit between the plan and a party in interest;

(C) furnishing of goods, services, or facilities between the plan and a party in interest;

(D) transfer to, or use by or for the benefit of, a party in interest, of any assets of the plan; or

(E) acquisition, on behalf of the plan, of any employer security or employer real property in violation of section 407(a).

(2) No fiduciary who has authority or discretion to control or manage the assets of a plan shall permit the plan to hold any employer security or employer real property if he knows or should know that holding such security or real property violates section 407(a).

(b) A fiduciary with respect to a plan shall not—

(1) deal with the assets of the plan in his own interest or for his own account,

(2) in his individual or any other capacity act in any transaction involving the plan on behalf of a party (or represent a party) whose interests are adverse to the interests of the plan or the interests of its participants or beneficiaries, or

(3) receive any consideration for his own personal account from any party dealing with such plan in connection with a transaction involving the assets of the plan.

(c) A transfer of real or personal property by a party in interest to a plan shall be treated as a sale or exchange if the property is subject to a mortgage or similar lien which the plan assumes or if it is subject to a mortgage or similar lien which a party-in-interest placed on the property within the 10-year period ending on the date of the transfer.

10 PERCENT LIMITATION WITH RESPECT TO ACQUISITION AND HOLDING OF EMPLOYER SECURITIES AND EMPLOYER REAL PROPERTY BY CERTAIN PLANS

Sec. 407. (a) Except as otherwise provided in this section and section 414:

(1) A plan may not acquire or hold—

(A) any employer security which is not a qualifying employer security, or

Sec. 407 (a) (1)

(B) any employer real property which is not qualifying employer real property.

(2) A plan may not acquire any qualifying employer security or qualifying employer real property, if immediately after such acquisition the aggregate fair market value of employer securities and employer real property held by the plan exceeds 10 percent of the fair market value of the assets of the plan.

(3)(A) After December 31, 1984, a plan may not hold any qualifying employer securities or qualifying employer real property (or both) to the extent that the aggregate fair market value of such securities and property determined on December 31, 1984, exceeds 10 percent of the greater of—

(i) the fair market value of the assets of the plan, determined on December 31, 1984, or

(ii) the fair market value of the assets of the plan determined on January 1, 1975.

(B) Subparagraph (A) of this paragraph shall not apply to any plan which on any date after December 31, 1974, and before January 1, 1985, did not hold employer securities or employer real property (or both) the aggregate fair market value of which determined on such date exceeded 10 percent of the greater of

(i) the fair market value of the assets of the plan, determined on such date, or

(ii) the fair market value of the assets of the plan determined on January 1, 1975.

(4)(A) After December 31, 1979, a plan may not hold any employer securities or employer real property in excess of the amount specified in regulations under subparagraph (B). This subparagraph shall not apply to a plan after the earliest date after December 31, 1974, on which it complies with such regulations.

(B) Not later than December 31, 1976, the Secretary shall prescribe regulations which shall have the effect of requiring that a plan divest itself of 50 percent of the holdings of employer securities and employer real property which the plan would be required to divest before January 1, 1985, under paragraph (2) or subsection (c) (whichever is applicable).

(b)(1) Subsection (a) of this section shall not apply to any acquisition or holding of qualifying employer securities or qualifying employer real property by an eligible individual account plan.

(2) Cross References.—

(A) **For exemption from diversification requirements for holding of qualifying employer securities and qualifying employer real property by eligible individual account plans, see** section 404(a)(2).

(B) **For exemption from prohibited transactions for certain acquisitions of qualifying employer securities and qualifying employer real property which are not in violation of the 10 percent limitation, see section 408(e).**

(C) **For transitional rules respecting securities or real property subject to binding contracts in effect on June 30, 1974, see section 414(c).**

(c)(1) A plan which makes the election, under paragraph (3) shall be treated as satisfying the requirement of subsection (a)(3) if and only if employer securities held on any date after December 31, 1974, and before January 1, 1985, have a fair market value, determined as of December 31, 1974, not in excess of 10 percent of the lesser of—

(A) the fair market value of the assets of the plan determined on such date (disregarding any portion of the fair market value of employer securities which is attributable to appreciation of such securities after December 31, 1974) but not less than the fair market value of plan assets on January 1, 1975, or

(B) an amount equal to the sum of (i) the total amount of the contributions to the plan received after December 31, 1974, and prior to such date, plus (ii) the fair market value of the assets of the plan, determined on January 1, 1975.

(2) For purposes of this subsection, in the case of an employer security

Sec. 407 (a) (1) (B)

held by a plan after January 1, 1975, the ownership of which is derived from ownership of employer securities held by the plan on January 1, 1975, or from the exercise of rights derived from such ownership, the value of such security held after January 1, 1975, shall be based on the value as of January 1, 1975, of the security from which ownership was derived. The Secretary shall prescribe regulations to carry out this paragraph.

(3) An election under this paragraph may not be made after December 31, 1975. Such an election shall be made in accordance with regulations prescribed by the Secretary, and shall be irrevocable. A plan may make an election under this paragraph only if on January 1, 1975, the plan holds no employer real property. After such election and before January 1, 1985, the plan may not acquire any employer real property.

(d) For purposes of this section—

(1) The term "employer security" means a security issued by an employer of employees covered by the plan, or by an affiliate of such employer. A contract to which section 408(b)(5) applies shall not be treated as a security for purposes of this section.

(2) The term "employer real property" means real property (and related personal property) which is leased to an employer of employees covered by the plan, or to an affiliate of such employer. For purposes of determining the time at which a plan acquires employer real property for purposes of this section, such property shall be deemed to be acquired by the plan on the date on which the plan acquires the property or on the date on which the lease to the employer (or affiliate) is entered into, whichever is later.

(3)(A) The term "eligible individual account plan" means an individual account plan which is (i) a profit-sharing, stock bonus, thrift, or savings plan; (ii) an employee stock ownership plan; or (iii) a money purchase plan which was in existence on the date of enactment of this Act and which on such date invested primarily in qualifying employer securities. Such term excludes an individual retirement account or annuity described in section 408 of the Internal Revenue Code of 1954.

(B) Notwithstanding subparagraph (A), a plan shall be treated as an eligible individual account plan with respect to the acquisition or holding of qualifying employer real property or qualifying employer securities only if such plan explicitly provides for acquisition and holding of qualifying employer securities or qualifying employer real property (as the case may be). In the case of a plan in existence on the date of enactment of this Act, this subparagraph shall not take effect until January 1, 1976.

(4) The term "qualifying employer real property" means parcels of employer real property—

(A) if a substantial number of the parcels are dispersed geographically;

(B) if each parcel of real property and the improvements thereon are suitable (or adaptable without excessive cost) for more than one use;

(C) even if all of such real property is leased to one lessee (which may be an employer, or an affiliate of an employer); and

(D) if the acquisition and retention of such property comply with the provisions of this part (other than section 404(a)(1)(B) to the extent it requires diversification, and sections 404(a)(1)(C), 406, and subsection (a) of this section).

(5) The term "qualifying employer security" means an employer security which is stock or a marketable obligation (as defined in subsection (e)).

(6) The term "employee stock ownership plan" means an individual account plan—

(A) which is a stock bonus plan which is qualified, or a stock bonus plan and money purchase both of which are qualified, under section 401 of the Internal Revenue Code of 1954, and which is designed to invest primarily in qualifying employee securities, and

Sec. 407 (d) (6)

(B) which meets such other requirements as the Secretary of the Treasury may prescribe by regulation.

(7) A corporation is an affiliate of an employer if it is a member of any controlled group of corporations (as defined in section 1563(a) of the Internal Revenue Code of 1954, except that "applicable percentage" shall be substituted for "80 percent" wherever the latter percentage appears in such section) of which the employer who maintains the plan is a member. For purposes of the preceding sentence, the term "applicable percentage" means 50 percent, or such lower percentage as the Secretary may prescribe by regulation. A person other than a corporation shall be treated as an affiliate of an employer to the extent provided in regulations of the Secretary. An employer which is a person other than a corporation shall be treated as affiliated with another person to the extent provided by regulations of the Secretary. Regulations under this paragraph shall be prescribed only after consultation and coordination with the Secretary of the Treasury.

(8) The Secretary may prescribe regulations specifying the extent to which conversions, splits, the exercise of rights, and similar transactions are not treated as acquisitions.

(e) For purposes of subsection (d) (5), the term "marketable obligation" means a bond, debenture, note, or certificate, or other evidence of indebtedness (hereinafter in this subsection referred to as "obligation") if—

(1) such obligation is acquired—

(A) on the market, either (i) at the price of the obligation prevailing on a national securities exchange which is registered with the Securities and Exchange Commission, or (ii) if the obligation is not traded on such a national securities exchange, at a price not less favorable to the plan than the offering price for the obligation as established by current bid and asked prices quoted by persons independent of the issuer;

(B) from an underwriter, at a price (i) not in excess of the public offering price for the obligation as set forth in a prospectus or offering circular filed with the Securities and Exchange Commission, and (ii) at which a substantial portion of the same issue is acquired by persons independent of the issuer; or

(C) directly from the issuer, at a price not less favorable to the plan than the price paid currently for a substantial portion of the same issue by persons independent of the issuer;

(2) immediately following acquisition of such obligation—

(A) not more than 25 percent of the aggregate amount of obligations issued in such issue and outstanding at the time of acquisition is held by the plan, and

(B) at least 50 percent of the aggregate amount referred to in subparagraph (A) is held by persons independent of the issuer; and

(3) immediately following acquisition of the obligation, not more than 25 percent of the assets of the plan is invested in obligations of the employer or an affiliate of the employer.

EXEMPTIONS FROM PROHIBITED TRANSACTIONS

Sec. 408. (a) The Secretary shall establish an exemption procedure for purposes of this subsection. Pursuant to such procedure, he may grant a conditional or unconditional exemption of any fiduciary or transaction, or class of fiduciaries or transactions, from all or part of the restrictions imposed by sections 406 and 407(a). Action under this subsection may be taken only after consultation and coordination with the Secretary of the Treasury. An exemption granted under this section shall not relieve a fiduciary from any other applicable provision of this Act. The Secretary may not grant an exemption under this subsection unless he finds that such exemption is—

(1) administratively feasible,

(2) in the interests of the plan and of its participants and benefi-

Sec. 407 (d) (7)

TEXT OF ERISA

ciaries, and

(3) protective of the rights of participants and beneficiaries of such plan.

Before granting an exemption under this subsection from section 406(a) or 407(a), the Secretary shall publish notice in the Federal Register of the pendency of the exemption, shall require that adequate notice be given to interested persons, and shall afford interested persons opportunity to present views. The Secretary may not grant an exemption under this subsection from section 406(b) unless he affords an opportunity for a hearing and makes a determination on the record with respect to the findings required by paragraphs (1), (2), and (3) of this subsection.

(b) The prohibitions provided in section 406 shall not apply to any of the following transactions:

(1) Any loans made by the plan to parties in interest who are participants or beneficiaries of the plan if such loans (A) are available to all such participants and beneficiaries on a reasonably equivalent basis, (B) are not made available to highly compensated employees, officers, or shareholders in an amount greater than the amount made available to other employees, (C) are made in accordance with specific provisions regarding such loans set forth in the plan, (D) bear a reasonable rate of interest, and (E) are adequately secured.

(2) Contracting or making reasonable arrangements with a party in interest for office space, or legal, accounting, or other services necessary for the establishment or operation of the plan, if no more than reasonable compensation is paid therefor.

(3) A loan to an employee stock ownership plan (as defined in section 407(d)(6)), if—

(A) such loan is primarily for the benefit of participants and beneficiaries of the plan, and

(B) such loan is at an interest rate which is not in excess of a reasonable rate.

If the plan gives collateral to a party in interest for such loan, such collateral may consist only of qualifying employer securities (as defined in section 407(d)(5)).

(4) The investment of all or part of a plan's assets in deposits which bear a reasonable interest rate in a bank or similar financial institution supervised by the United States or a State, if such bank or other institution is a fiduciary of such plan and if—

(A) the plan covers only employees of such bank or other institution and employees of affiliates of such bank or other institution, or

(B) such investment is expressly authorized by a provision of the plan or by a fiduciary (other than such bank or institution or affiliate thereof) who is expressly empowered by the plan to so instruct the trustee with respect to such investment.

(5) Any contract for life insurance, health insurance, or annuities with one or more insurers which are qualified to do business in a State, if the plan pays no more than adequate consideration, and if each such insurer or insurers is—

(A) the employer maintaining the plan, or

(B) a party in interest which is wholly owned (directly or indirectly) by the employer maintaining the plan, or by any person which is a party in interest with respect to the plan, but only if the total premiums and annuity considerations written by such insurers for life insurance, health insurance, or annuities for all plans (and their employers) with respect to which such insurers are parties in interest (not including premiums or annuity considerations written by the employer maintaining the plan) do not exceed 5 percent of the total premiums and annuity considerations written for all lines of insurance in that year by such insurers (not including premiums or annuity considerations written by the employer maintaining the plan).

(6) The providing of any ancillary service by a bank or similar financial institution supervised by the United States or a State, if such bank or

Sec. 408 (b) (6)

other institution is a fiduciary of such plan, and if—

(A) such bank or similar financial institution has adopted adequate internal safeguards which assure that the providing of such ancillary service is consistent with sound banking and financial practice, as determined by Federal or State supervisory authority, and

(B) the extent to which such ancillary service is provided is subject to specific guidelines issued by such bank or similar financial institution (as determined by the Secretary after consultation with Federal and State supervisory authority), and adherence to such guidelines would reasonably preclude such bank or similar financial institution from providing such ancillary service (i) in an excessive or unreasonable manner, and (ii) in a manner that would be inconsistent with the best interests of participants and beneficiaries of employee benefit plans.

Such ancillary services shall not be provided at more than reasonable compensation.

(7) The exercise of a privilege to convert securities, to the extent provided in regulations of the Secretary, but only if the plan receives no less than adequate consideration pursuant to such conversion.

(8) Any transaction between a plan and (i) a common or collective trust fund or pooled investment fund maintained by a party in interest which is a bank or trust company supervised by a State or Federal agency or (ii) a pooled investment fund of an insurance company qualified to do business in a State, if—

(A) the transaction is a sale or purchase of an interest in the fund,

(B) the bank, trust company, or insurance company receives not more than reasonable compensation, and

(C) such transaction is expressly permitted by the instrument under which the plan is maintained, or by a fiduciary (other than the bank, trust company, or insurance company, or an affiliate thereof) who has authority to manage and control the assets of the plan.

(9) The making by a fiduciary of a distribution of the assets of the plan in accordance with the terms of the plan if such assets are distributed in the same manner as provided under section 4044 of this Act (relating to allocation of assets).

(10) Any transaction required or permitted under part 1 of subtitle E of title IV.

(11) A merger of multiemployer plans, or the transfer of assets or liabilities between multiemployer plans, determined by the Pension Benefit Guaranty Corporation to meet the requirements of section 4231.

(c) Nothing in section 406 shall be construed to prohibit any fiduciary from—

(1) receiving any benefit to which he may be entitled as a participant or beneficiary in the plan, so long as the benefit is computed and paid on a basis which is consistent with the terms of the plan as applied to all other participants and beneficiaries;

(2) receiving any reasonable compensation for services rendered, or for the reimbursement of expenses properly and actually incurred, in the performance of his duties with the plan; except that no person so serving who already receives full-time pay from an employer or an association of employers, whose employees are participants in the plan, or from an employee organization whose members are participants in such plan shall receive compensation from such plan, except for reimbursement of expenses properly and actually incurred; or

(3) serving as a fiduciary in addition to being an officer, employee, agent, or other representative of a party in interest.

(d) Section 407(b) and subsections (a), (b), (c), and (e) of this section shall not apply to any transaction in which a plan, directly or indirectly—

(1) lends any part of the corpus or income of the plan to;

(2) pays any compensation for personal services rendered to the plan to; or

Sec. 408 (b) (7)

(3) acquires for the plan any property from or sells any property to; any person who is with respect to the plan an owner-employee (as defined in section 401(c)(3) of the Internal Revenue Code of 1954), a member of the family (as defined in section 267(c)(4) of such Code) of any such owner-employee, or a corporation controlled by any such owner-employee through the ownership, directly or indirectly, of 50 percent or more of the total combined voting power of all classes of stock entitled to vote or 50 percent or more of the total value of shares of all classes of stock of the corporation. For purposes of this subsection a shareholder employee (as defined in section 1379 of the Internal Revenue Code of 1954 as in effect on the day before the date of the enactment of the Subchapter S Revision Act of 1982) and a participant or beneficiary of an individual retirement annuity, or an individual retirement bond (as defined in section 408 or 409 of the Internal Revenue Code of 1954) and an employer or association of employers which establishes such an account or annuity under section 408(c) of such code shall be deemed to be an owner-employee.

(e) Sections 406 and 407 shall not apply to the acquisition or sale by a plan of qualifying employer securities (as defined in section 407(d)(5)) or acquisition, sale, or lease by a plan of qualifying employer real property (as defined in section 407(d)(4))—

(1) if such acquisition, sale, or lease is for adequate consideration (or in the case of a marketable obligation, at a price not less favorable to the plan than the price determined under section 407(e)(1)),

(2) if no commission is charged with respect thereto, and

(3) if—

(A) the plan is an eligible individual account plan (as defined in section 407(d)(3)), or

(B) in the case of an acquisition or lease of qualifying employer real property by a plan which is not an eligible individual account plan, or of an acquisition of qualifying employer securities by such a plan, the lease or acquisition is not prohibited by section 407(a).

(f) Section 406(b)(2) shall not apply to any merger or transfer described in subsection (b)(11).

LIABILITY FOR BREACH OF FIDUCIARY DUTY

Sec. 409. (a) Any person who is a fiduciary with respect to a plan who breaches any of the responsibilities, obligations, or duties imposed upon fiduciaries by this title shall be personally liable to make good to such plan any losses to the plan resulting from each such breach, and to restore to such plan any profits of such fiduciary which have been made through use of assets of the plan by the fiduciary, and shall be subject to such other equitable or remedial relief as the court may deem appropriate, including removal of such fiduciary. A fiduciary may also be removed for a violation of section 411 of this Act.

(b) No fiduciary shall be liable with respect to a breach of fiduciary duty under this title if such breach was committed before he became a fiduciary or after he ceased to be a fiduciary.

EXCULPATORY PROVISIONS; INSURANCE

Sec. 410. (a) Except as provided in sections 405(b)(1) and 405(d), any provision in an agreement or instrument which purports to relieve a fiduciary from responsibility or liability for any responsibility, obligation, or duty under this part shall be void as against public policy.

(b) Nothing in this subpart shall preclude—

(1) a plan from purchasing insurance for its fiduciaries or for itself to cover liability or losses occurring by reason of the act or omission of a fiduciary, if such insurance permits recourse by the insurer against the fiduciary in the case of a breach of a fiduciary obligation by such fiduciary;

(2) a fiduciary from purchasing

insurance to cover liability under this part from and for his own account; or

(3) an employer or an employee organization from purchasing insurance to cover potential liability of one or more persons who serve in a fiduciary capacity with regard to an employee benefit plan.

PROHIBITION AGAINST CERTAIN PERSONS HOLDING CERTAIN POSITIONS

Sec. 411. (a) No person who has been convicted of, or has been imprisoned as a result of his conviction of, robbery, bribery, extortion, embezzlement, fraud, grand larceny, burglary, arson, a felony violation of Federal or State law involving substances defined in section 102(6) of the Comprehensive Drug Abuse Prevention and Control Act of 1970, murder, rape, kidnaping, perjury, assault with intent to kill, any crime described in section 9(a)(1) of the Investment Company Act of 1940 (15 U.S.C. 80a-9(a)(1)), a violation of any provision of this Act, a violation of section 302 of the Labor-Management Relations Act, 1947 (29 U.S.C. 186), a violation of chapter 63 of title 18, United States Code, a violation of section 874, 1027, 1503, 1505, 1506, 1510, 1951, or 1954 of title 18, United States Code, a violation of the Labor-Management Reporting and Disclosure Act of 1959 (29 U.S.C. 401), or conspiracy to commit any such crimes or attempt to commit any such crimes, or a crime in which any of the foregoing crimes is an element, shall serve or be permitted to serve—

(1) as an administrator, fiduciary, officer, trustee, custodian, counsel, agent, or employee of any employee benefit plan, or

(2) as a consultant to any employee benefit plan,

during or for five years after such conviction or after the end of such imprisonment, whichever is the later, unless prior to the end of such five-year period, in the case of a person so convicted or imprisoned, (A) his citizenship rights, having been revoked as a result of such conviction, have been fully restored, or (B) the Board of Parole of the United States Department of Justice determines that such person's service in any capacity referred to in paragraph (1) or (2) would not be contrary to the purposes of this title. Prior to making any such determination the Board shall hold an administrative hearing and shall give notice of such proceeding by certified mail to the State, county, and Federal prosecuting officials in the jurisdiction or jurisdictions in which such person was convicted. The Board's determnation in any such proceeding shall be final. No person shall knowingly permit any other person to serve in any capacity referred to in paragraph (1) or (2) in violation of this subsection. Notwithstanding the preceding provisions of this subsection, no corporation or partnership will be precluded from acting as an administrator, fiduciary, officer, trustee, custodian, counsel, agent, or employee, of any employee benefit plan or as a consultant to any employee benefit plan without a notice, hearing, and determination by such Board of Parole that such service would be inconsistent with the intention of this section.

(b) Any person who intentionally violates this section shall be fined not more than $10,000 or imprisoned for not more than one year, or both.

(c) For the purposes of this section:

(1) A person shall be deemed to have been "convicted" and under the disability of "conviction" from the date of the judgment of the trial court or the date of the final sustaining of such judgment on appeal, whichever is the later event.

(2) The term "consultant" means any person who, for compensation, advises or represents an employee benefit plan or who provides other assistance to such plan, concerning the establishment or operation of such plan.

(3) A period of parole shall not be considered as part of a period of imprisonment.

Sec. 411

BONDING

Sec. 412. (a) Every fiduciary of an employee benefit plan and every person who handles funds or other property of such a plan (hereafter in this section referred to as "plan official") shall be bonded as provided in this section; except that—

(1) where such plan is one under which the only assets from which benefits are paid are the general assets of a union or of an employer, the administrator, officers, and employees of such plan shall be exempt from the bonding requirements of this section, and

(2) no bond shall be required of a fiduciary (or of any director, officer, or employee of such fiduciary) if such fiduciary—

(A) is a corporation organized and doing business under the laws of the United States or of any State;

(B) is authorized under such laws to exercise trust powers or to conduct an insurance business;

(C) is subject to supervision or examination by Federal or State authority; and

(D) has at all times a combined capital and surplus in excess of such a minimum amount as may be established by regulations issued by the Secretary, which amount shall be at least $1,000,000. Paragraph (2) shall apply to a bank or other financial institution which is authorized to exercise trust powers and the deposits of which are not insured by the Federal Deposit Insurance Corporation, only if such bank or institution meets bonding or similar requirements under State law which the Secretary determines are at least equivalent to those imposed on banks by Federal law.

The amount of such bond shall be fixed at the beginning of each fiscal year of the plan. Such amount shall be not less than 10 per centum of the amount of funds handled. In no case shall such bond be less than $1,000 nor more than $500,000, except that the Secretary, after due notice and opportunity for hearing to all interested parties, and after consideration of the record, may prescribe an amount in excess of $500,000, subject to the 10 per centum limitation of the preceding sentence. For purposes of fixing the amount of such bond, the amount of funds handled shall be determined by the funds handled by the person, group, or class to be covered by such bond and by their predecessor or predecessors, if any, during the preceding reporting year, or if the plan has no preceding reporting year, the amount of funds to be handled during the current reporting year by such person, group, or class, estimated as provided in regulations of the Secretary. Such bond shall provide protection to the plan against loss by reason of acts of fraud or dishonesty on the part of the plan official, directly or through connivance with others. Any bond shall have as surety thereon a corporate surety company which is an acceptable surety on Federal bonds under authority granted by the Secretary of the Treasury pursuant to sections 6 through 13 of title 6, United States Code. Any bond shall be in a form or of a type approved by the Secretary, including individual bonds or schedule or blanket forms of bonds which cover a group or class.

(b) It shall be unlawful for any plan official to whom subsection (a) applies, to receive, handle, disburse, or otherwise exercise custody or control of any of the funds or other property of any employee benefit plan, without being bonded as required by subsection (a) and it shall be unlawful for any plan official of such plan, or any other person having authority to direct the performance of such functions, to permit such functions, or any of them, to be performed by any plan official, with respect to whom the requirements of subsection (a) have not been met.

(c) It shall be unlawful for any person to procure any bond required by subsection (a) from any surety or other company or through any agent or broker in whose business operations such plan or any party in interest in such plan has any control or significant financial interest, direct or indirect.

(d) Nothing in any other provision of law shall require any person, required to be bonded as provided in subsection (a) because he handles funds or other property of an employee benefit plan, to be bonded insofar as the handling by such person of the funds or other property of such plan is concerned.

(e) The Secretary shall prescribe such regulations as may be necessary to carry out the provisions of this section including exempting a plan from the requirements of this section where he finds that (1) other bonding arrangements or (2) the overall financial condition of the plan would be adequate to protect the interests of the beneficiaries and participants. When, in the opinion of the Secretary, the administrator of a plan offers adequate evidence of the financial responsibility of the plan, or that other bonding arrangements would provide adequate protection of the beneficiaries and participants, he may exempt such plan from the requirements of this section.

LIMITATION ON ACTIONS

Sec. 413. (a) No action may be commenced under this title with respect to a fiduciary's breach of any responsibility, duty, or obligation under this part, or with respect to a violation of this part, after the earlier of—

(1) six years after (A) the date of the last action which constituted a part of the breach or violation, or (B) in the case of an omission, the latest date on which the fiduciary could have cured the breach or violation, or

(2) three years after the earliest date (A) on which the plaintiff had actual knowledge of the breach or violation, or (B) on which a report from which he could reasonably be expected to have obtained knowledge of such breach or violation was filed with the Secretary under this title; except that in the case of fraud or concealment, such action may be commenced not later than six years after the date of discovery of such breach or violation.

EFFECTIVE DATE

Sec. 414. (a) Except as provided in subsections (b), (c), and (d), this part shall take effect on January 1, 1975.

(b)(1) The provisions of this part authorizing the Secretary to promulgate regulations shall take effect on the date of enactment of this Act.

(2) Upon application of a plan, the Secretary may postpone until not later than January 1, 1976, the applicability of any provision of sections 402, 403 (other than 403(c)), 405 (other than 405(a) and (d)), and 410(a), as it applies to any plan in existence on the date of enactment of this Act if he determines such postponement is (A) necessary to amend the instrument establishing the plan under which the plan is maintained and (B) not adverse to the interest of participants and beneficiaries.

(3) This part shall take effect on the date of enactment of this Act with respect to a plan which terminates after June 30, 1974, and before January 1, 1975, and to which at the time of termination section 4021 applies.

(c) Section 406 and 407(a) (relating to prohibited transactions) shall not apply—

(1) until June 30, 1984, to a loan of money or other extension of credit between a plan and a party in interest under a binding contract in effect on July 1, 1974 (or pursuant to renewals of such a contract), if such loan or other extension of credit remains at least as favorable to the plan as an arm's-length transaction with an unrelated party would be, and if the execution of the contract, the making of the loan, or the extension of credit was not, at the time of such execution, making, or extension, a prohibited transaction (within the meaning of section 503(b) of the Internal Revenue Code of 1954 or the corresponding provisions of prior law):

(2) until June 30, 1984, to a lease or joint use of property involving the plan and a party in interest pursuant to a binding contract in effect on July 1, 1974 (or pursuant to renewals of such a contract), if such lease or joint use remains at least as favorable to the plan as an arm's-length transaction with an unrelated party would be and if the execution of the contract was not, at the time of such execution, a prohibited transaction (within the meaning of section 503(b) of the Internal Revenue Code of 1954) or the corresponding provisions of prior law;

(3) until June 30, 1984, to the sale, exchange, or other disposition of property described in paragraph (2) between a plan and a party in interest if—

(A) in the case of a sale, exchange, or other disposition of the property by the plan to the party in interest, the plan receives an amount which is not less than the fair market value of the property at the time of such disposition; and

(B) in the case of the acquisition of the property by the plan, the plan pays an amount which is not in excess of the fair market value of the property at the time of such acquisition;

(4) until June 30, 1977, to the provision of services, to which paragraphs (1), (2), and (3) do not apply, between a plan and a party in interest—

(A) under a binding contract in effect on July 1, 1974 (or pursuant to renewals of such contract), or

(B) if the party in interest ordinarily and customarily furnished such services on June 30, 1974, if such provision of services remains at least as favorable to the plan as an arm's-length transaction with an unrelated party would be and if such provision of services was not, at the time of such provision, a prohibited transaction (within the meaning of section 503(b) of the Internal Revenue Code of 1954) or the corresponding provisions of prior law; or

(5) the sale, exchange, or other disposition of property which is owned by a plan on June 30, 1974, and all times thereafter, to a party in interest, if such plan is required to dispose of such property in order to comply with the provisions of section 407(a) (relating to the prohibition against holding excess employer securities and employer real property), and if the plan receives not less than adequate consideration.

(d) Any election, or failure to elect, by a disqualified person under section 2003(c)(1)(B) of this Act shall be treated for purposes of this part (but not for purposes of section 514) as an act or omission occurring before the effective date of this part.

PART 5—ADMINISTRATION AND ENFORCEMENT

CRIMINAL PENALTIES

Sec. 501. Any person who willfully violates any provision of part 1 of this subtitle, or any regulation or order issued under any such provision, shall upon conviction be fined not more than $5,000 or imprisoned not more than one year, or both; except that in the case of such violation by a person not an individual, the fine imposed upon such person shall be a fine not exceeding $100,000.

CIVIL ENFORCEMENT

Sec. 502. (a) A civil action may be brought—

(1) by a participant or beneficiary—

(A) for the relief provided for in subsection (c) of this section, or

(B) to recover benefits due to him under the terms of his plan, to enforce his rights under the terms of the plan, or to clarify his rights to future benefits under the terms of the plan;

(2) by the Secretary, or by a participant, beneficiary or fiduciary for appropriate relief under section 409;

(3) by a participant, beneficiary, or fiduciary, (A) to enjoin any act or practice which violates any provision of this title or the terms of the plan, or (B) to obtain other appropriate

equitable relief (i) to redress such violations or (ii) to enforce any provisions of this title or the terms of the plan;

(4) by the Secretary, or by a participant, or beneficiary for appropriate relief in the case of a violation of 105(c);

(5) except as otherwise provided in subsection (b), by the Secretary (A) to enjoin any act or practice which violates any provision of this title, or (B) to obtain other appropriate equitable relief (i) to redress such violation or (ii) to enforce any provision of this title; or

(6) by the Secretary to collect any civil penalty under subsection (1).

(b) In the case of a plan which is qualified under section 401(a), 403(a), or 405(a) of the Internal Revenue Code of 1954 (or with respect to which an application to so qualify has been filed and has not been finally determined) the Secretary may exercise his authority under subsection (a)(5) with respect to a violation of, or the enforcement of, parts 2 and 3 of this subtitle (relating to participation, vesting, and funding), only if—

(1)(A) requested by the Secretary of the Treasury, or

(B) one or more participants, beneficiaries, or fiduciaries, of such plan request in writing (in such manner as the Secretary shall prescribe by regulation) that he exercise such authority on their behalf. In the case of such a request under this paragraph he may exercise such authority only if he determines that such violation affects, or such enforcement is necessary to protect, claims of participants or beneficiaries to benefits under the plan.

(2) The Secretary shall not initiate an action to enforce section 515.

(c) Any administrator who fails or refuses to comply with a request for any information which such administrator is required by this title to furnish to a participant or beneficiary (unless such failure or refusal results from matters reasonably beyond the control of the administrator) by mailing the material requested to the last known address of the requesting participant or beneficiary within 30 days after such request may in the courts' discretion be personally liable to such participant or beneficiary in the amount of up to $100 a day from the date of such failure or refusal, and the court may in its discretion order such other relief as it deems proper.

(d)(1) An employee benefit plan may sue or be sued under this title as an entity. Service of summons, subpena, or other legal process of a court upon a trustee or an administrator of an employee benefit plan in his capacity as such shall constitute service upon the employee benefit plan. In a case where a plan has not designated in the summary plan description of the plan an individual as agent for the service of legal process, service upon the Secretary shall constitute such service. The Secretary, not later than 15 days after receipt of service under the preceding sentence, shall notify the administrator or any trustee of the plan of receipt of such service.

(2) Any money judgment under this title against an employee benefit plan shall be enforceable only against the plan as an entity and shall not be enforceable against any other person unless liability against such person is established in his individual capacity under this title.

(e)(1) Except for actions under subsection (a)(1)(B) of this section, the district courts of the United States shall have exclusive jurisdiction of civil actions under this title brought by the Secretary or by a participant, beneficiary, or fiduciary. State courts of competent jurisdiction and district courts of the United States shall have concurrent jurisdiction of actions under subsection (a)(1)(B) of this section.

(2) Where an action under this title is brought in a district court of the United States, it may be brought in the district where the plan is administered, where the breach took place, or where a defendant resides or may

Sec. 502 (a) (4)

be found, and process may be served in any other district where a defendant resides or may be found.

(f) The district courts of the United States shall have jurisdiction, without respect to the amount in controversy or the citizenship of the parties, to grant the relief provided for in subsection (a) of this section in any action.

(g)(1) In any action under this title (other than an action described in paragraph (2)) by a participant, beneficiary, or fiduciary, the court in its discretion may allow a reasonable attorney's fee and costs of action to either party.

(2) In any action under this title by a fiduciary for or on behalf of a plan to enforce section 515 in which a judgment in favor of the plan is awarded, the court shall award the plan—

(A) the unpaid contributions,

(B) interest on the unpaid contributions,

(C) an amount equal to the greater of—

(i) interest on the unpaid contributions, or

(ii) liquidated damages provided for under the plan in an amount not in excess of 20 percent (or such higher percentage as may be permitted under Federal or State law) of the amount determined by the court under subparagraph (A),

(D) reasonable attorney's fees and costs of the action, to be paid by the defendant, and

(E) such other legal or equitable relief as the court deems appropriate. For purposes of this paragraph, interest on unpaid contributions shall be determined by using the rate provided under the plan, or, if none, the rate prescribed under section 6621 of the Internal Revenue Code of 1954.

(h) A copy of the complaint in any action under this title by a participant, beneficiary, or fiduciary (other than an action brought by one or more participants or beneficiaries under subsection (a)(1)(B) which is solely for the purpose of recovering benefits due such participants under the terms of the plan) shall be served upon the Secretary and the Secretary of the Treasury by certified mail. Either Secretary shall have the right in his discretion to intervene in any action, except that the Secretary of the Treasury may not intervene in any action under part 4 of this subtitle. If the Secretary brings an action under subsection (a) on behalf of a participant or beneficiary, he shall notify the Secretary of the Treasury.

(i) In the case of a transaction prohibited by section 406 by a party in interest with respect to a plan to which this part applies, the Secretary may assess a civil penalty against such party in interest. The amount of such penalty may not exceed 5 percent of the amount involved (as defined in section 4975(f)(4) of the Internal Revenue Code of 1954); except that if the transaction is not corrected (in such manner as the Secretary shall prescribe by regulation, which regulations shall be consistent with section 4975(f)(5) of such Code) within 90 days after notice from the Secretary (or such long period as the Secretary may permit), such penalty may be in an amount not more than 100 percent of the amount involved. This subsection shall not apply to a transaction with respect to a plan described in section 4975(e)(1) of such Code.

(j) In all civil actions under this title, attorneys appointed by the Secretary may represent the Secretary (except as provided in section 518(a) of title 28, United States Code), but all such litigation shall be subject to the direction and control of the Attorney General.

(k) Suits by an administrator, fiduciary, participant, or beneficiary of an employee benefit plan to review a final order of the Secretary, to restrain the Secretary from taking any action contrary to the provisions of this Act, or to compel him to take action required under this title, may be brought in the district court of the United States for the district where the plan has its principal office, or in the United States District Court for the District of Columbia.

Sec. 502 (k)

CLAIMS PROCEDURE

Sec. 503. In accordance with regulations of the Secretary, every employee benefit plan shall—

(1) provide adequate notice in writing to any participant or beneficiary whose claim for benefits under the plan has been denied, setting forth the specific reasons for such denial, written in a manner calculated to be understood by the participant, and

(2) afford a reasonable opportunity to any participant whose claim for benefits has been denied for a full and fair review by the appropriate named fiduciary of the decision denying the claim.

INVESTIGATIVE AUTHORITY

Sec. 504. (a) The Secretary shall have the power, in order to determine whether any person has violated or is about to violate any provision of this title or any regulation or order thereunder—

(1) to make an investigation, and in connection therewith to require the submission of reports, books, and records, and the filing of data in support of any information required to be filed with the Secretary under this title, and

(2) to enter such places, inspect such books and records and question such persons as he may deem necessary to enable him to determine the facts relative to such investigation, if he has reasonable cause to believe there may exist a violation of this title or any rule or regulation issued thereunder or if the entry is pursuant to an agreement with the plan.

The Secretary may make available to any person actually affected by any matter which is the subject of an investigation under this section, and to any department or agency of the United States, information concerning any matter which may be the subject of such investigation; except that any information obtained by the Secretary pursuant to section 6103(g) of the Internal Revenue Code of 1954 shall be made available only in accordance with regulations prescribed by the Secretary of the Treasury.

(b) The Secretary may not under the authority of this section require any plan to submit to the Secretary any books or records of the plan more than once in any 12 month period, unless the Secretary has reasonable cause to believe there may exist a violation of this title or any regulation or order thereunder.

(c) For the purposes of any investigation provided for in this title, the provisions of sections 9 and 10 (relating to the attendance of witnesses and the production of books, records, and documents) of the Federal Trade Commission Act (15 U.S.C. 49, 50) are hereby made applicable (without regard to any limitation in such sections respecting persons, partnerships, banks, or common carriers) to the jurisdiction, powers, and duties of the Secretary or any officers designated by him. To the extent he considers appropriate, the Secretary may delegate his investigative functions under this section with respect to insured banks acting as fiduciaries of employee benefit plans to the appropriate Federal banking agency (as defined in section 3(q) of the Federal Deposit Insurance Act (12 U.S.C. 1813 (q)).

REGULATIONS

Sec. 505. Subject to title III and section 109, the Secretary may prescribe such regulations as he finds necessary or appropriate to carry out the provisions of this title. Among other things, such regulations may define accounting technical, and trade terms used in such provisions; may prescribe forms; and may provide for the keeping of books and records, and for the inspection of such books and records (subject to section 504(a) and (b)).

OTHER AGENCIES AND DEPARTMENTS

Sec. 506. In order to avoid unnecessary expense and duplication of functions among Government agencies, the Secretary may make such arrangements or agreements for cooperation or mutual assistance in the performance of his functions under

Sec. 503

this title and the functions of any such agency as he may find to be practicable and consistent with law. The Secretary may utilize, on a reimbursable or other basis, the facilities or services of any department, agency, or establishment of the United States or of any State or political subdivision of a State, including the services of any of its employees, with the lawful consent of such department, agency, or establishment; and each department, agency, or establishment of the United States is authorized and directed to cooperate with the Secretary and, to the extent permitted by law, to provide such information and facilities as he may request for his assistance in the performance of his functions under this title. The Attorney General or his representative shall receive from the Secretary for appropriate action such evidence developed in the performance of his functions under this title as may be found to warrant consideration for criminal prosecution under the provisions of this title or other Federal law.

ADMINISTRATION

Sec. 507. (a) Subchapter II of chapter 5, and chapter 7, of title 5, United States Code (relating to administrative procedure), shall be applicable to this title.

(b) Section 5108 of title 5, United States Code, is amended by adding at the end thereof the following new subsection:

"(f) In addition to the number of positions authorized by subsection (a), the Secretary of Labor is authorized, without regard to any other provision of this section, to place 1 position in the Department of Labor in grade GS-18, and a total of 20 positions in the Department of Labor in grades GS-16 and 17."

(c) No employee of the Department of Labor or the Department of the Treasury shall administer or enforce this title or the Internal Revenue Code of 1954 with respect to any employee benefit plan under which he is a participant or beneficiary, any employee organization of which he is a member, or any employer organization in which he has an interest. This subsection does not apply to an employee benefit plan which covers only employees of the United States.

APPROPRIATIONS

Sec. 508. There are hereby authorized to be appropriated such sums as may be necessary to enable the Secretary to carry out his functions and duties under this Act.

SEPARABILITY PROVISIONS

Sec. 509. If any provision of this Act, or the application of such provision to any person or circumstances, shall be held invalid, the remainder of this Act, or the application of such provision to persons or circumstances other than those as to which it is held invalid, shall not be affected thereby.

INTERFERENCE WITH RIGHTS PROTECTED UNDER ACT

Sec. 510. It shall be unlawful for any person to discharge, fine, suspend, expel, discipline, or discriminate against a participant or beneficiary for exercising any right to which he is entitled under the provisions of an employee benefit plan, this title, section 3001, or the Welfare and Pension Plans Disclosure Act, or for the purpose of interfering with the attainment of any right to which such participant may become entitled under the plan, this title, or the Welfare and Pension Plans Disclosure Act. It shall be unlawful for any person to discharge, fine, suspend, expel, or discriminate against any person because he has given information or has testified or is about to testify in any inquiry or proceeding relating to this Act or the Welfare and Pension Plans Disclosure Act. The provisions of section 502 shall be applicable in the enforcement of this section.

COERCIVE INTERFERENCE

Sec. 511. It shall be unlawful for any person through the use of fraud, force, violence, or threat of the use of force or violence, to restrain, coerce, intimidate, or attempt to restrain, coerce, or intimidate any participant or beneficiary for the purpose of interfering with or preventing the exercise of any right to which he is or may become entitled under the plan, this title, section 3001, or the Welfare and Pension Plans Disclosure Act. Any person who willfully violates this section shall be fined $10,000 or imprisoned for not more than one year, or both.

ADVISORY COUNCIL

Sec. 512. (a)(1) There is hereby established an Advisory Council on Employee Welfare and Pension Benefit Plans (hereinafter in this section referred to as the "Council") consisting of fifteen members appointed by the Secretary. Not more than eight members of the Council shall be members of the same political party.

(2) Members shall be persons qualified to appraise the programs instituted under this Act.

(3) Of the members appointed, three shall be representatives of employee organizations (at least one of whom shall be representative of any organization members of which are participants in a multiemployer plan); three shall be representatives of employers (at least one of whom shall be representative of employers maintaining or contributing to multiemployer plans); three representatives shall be appointed from the general public, one of whom shall be a person representing those receiving benefits from a pension plan; and there shall be one representative each from the fields of insurance, corporate trust, actuarial counseling, investment counseling, investment management, and the accounting field.

(4) Members shall serve for terms of three years except that of those first appointed, five shall be appointed for terms of one year, five shall be appointed for terms of two years, and five shall be appointed for terms of three years. A member may be reappointed. A member appointed to fill a vacancy shall be appointed only for the remainder of such term. A majority of members shall constitute a quorum and action shall be taken only by a majority vote of those present and voting.

(b) It shall be the duty of the Council to advise the Secretary with respect to the carrying out of his functions under this Act and to submit to the Secretary recommendations with respect thereto. The Council shall meet at least four times each year and at such other times as the Secretary requests. In his annual report submitted pursuant to section 513(b), the Secretary shall include each recommendation which he has received from the Council during the preceding calendar year.

(c) The Secretary shall furnish to the Council an executive secretary and such secretarial, clerical, and other services as are deemed necessary to conduct its business. The Secretary may call upon other agencies of the Government for statistical data, reports, and other information which will assist the Council in the performance of its duties.

(d)(1) Members of the Council shall each be entitled to receive the daily equivalent of the annual rate of basic pay in effect for grade GS-18 of the General Schedule for each day (including travel time) during which they are engaged in the actual performance of duties vested in the Council.

(2) While away from their homes or regular places of business in the performance of services for Council, members of the Council shall be allowed travel expenses, including per diem in lieu of subsistence, in the same manner as persons employed intermittently in the Government service are allowed expenses under section 5703(b) of title 5 of the United States Code.

(e) Section 14(a) of the Federal Advisory Committee Act (relating to termination) shall not apply to the Council.

Sec. 512

RESEARCH, STUDIES, AND ANNUAL REPORT

Sec. 513. (a)(1) The Secretary is authorized to undertake research and surveys and in connection therewith to collect, compile, analyze and publish data, information, and statistics relating to employee benefit plans, including retirement, deferred compensation, and welfare plans, and types of plans not subject to this Act.

(2) The Secretary is authorized and directed to undertake research studies relating to pension plans, including but not limited to (A) the effects of this title upon the provisions and costs of pension plans, (B) the role of private pensions in meeting the economic security needs of the Nation, and (C) the operation of private pension plans including types and levels of benefits, degree of reciprocity or portability, and financial and actuarial characteristics and practices, and methods of encouraging the growth of the private pension system.

(3) The Secretary may, as he deems appropriate or necessary, undertake other studies relating to employee benefit plans, the matters regulated by this title, and the enforcement procedures provided for under this title.

(4) The research, surveys, studies, and publications referred to in this subsection may be conducted directly, or indirectly through grant or contract arrangements.

(b) The Secretary shall submit annually a report to the Congress covering his administration of this title for the preceding year, and including (1) an explanation of any variances or extensions granted under section 110, 207, 303, or 304 and the projected date for terminating the variance; (2) the status of cases in enforcement status; (3) recommendations received from the Advisory Council during the preceding year; and (4) such information, data, research findings, studies, and recommendations for further legislation in connection with the matters covered by this title as he may find advisable.

(c) The Secretary is authorized and directed to cooperate with the Congress and its appropriate committees, subcommittees, and staff in supplying data and any other information, and personnel and services, required by the Congress in any study, examination, or report by the Congress relating to pension benefit plans established or maintained by States or their political subdivisions.

EFFECT ON OTHER LAWS

SEC. 514. (a) Except as provided in subsection (b) of this section, the provisions of this title and title IV shall supersede any and all State laws insofar as they may now or hereafter relate to any employee benefit plan described in section 4(a) and not exempt under section 4(b). This section shall take effect on January 1, 1975.

(b)(1) This section shall not apply with respect to any cause of action which arose, or any act or omission which occurred, before January 1, 1975.

(2)(A) Except as provided in subparagraph (B), nothing in this title shall be construed to exempt or relieve any person from any law of any State which regulates insurance, banking, or securities.

(B) Neither an employee benefit plan described in section 4(a), which is not exempt under section 4(b) (other than a plan established primarily for the purpose of providing death benefits), nor any trust established under such a plan, shall be deemed to be an insurance company or other insurer, bank, trust company, or investment company or to be engaged in the business of insurance or banking for purposes of any law of any State purporting to regulate insurance companies, insurance contracts, banks, trust companies, or investment companies.

(3) Nothing in this section shall be construed to prohibit use by the Secretary of services or facilities of a State agency as permitted under section 506 of this Act.

(4) Subsection (a) shall not apply to any generally applicable criminal law of a State.

(5) (A) Except as provided in subparagraph (B), subsection (a) shall

not apply to the Hawaii Prepaid Health Care Act (Haw. Rev. Stat. §§ 393-1 through 393-51).

(B) Nothing in subparagraph (A) shall be construed to exempt from subsection (a)—

(i) any State tax law relating to employee benefit plans, or

(ii) any amendment of the Hawaii Prepaid Health Care Act enacted after September 2, 1974, to the extent it provides for more than the effective administration of such Act as in effect on such date.

(C) Notwithstanding subparagraph (A), parts 1 and 4 of this subtitle, and the preceding sections of this part to the extent they govern matters which are governed by the provisions of such parts 1 and 4, shall supersede the Hawaii Prepaid Health Care Act (as in effect on or after the date of the enactment of this paragraph), but the Secretary may enter into cooperative arrangements under this paragraph and section 506 with officials of the State of Hawaii to assist them in effectuating the policies of provisions of such Act which are superseded by such parts.

(6) (A) Notwithstanding any other provision of this section—

(i) in the case of an employee welfare benefit plan which is a multiple employer welfare arrangement and is fully insured (or which is a multiple employer welfare arrangement subject to an exemption under subparagraph (B)), any law of any State which regulates insurance may apply to such arrangement to the extent that such law provides—

(I) standards, requiring the maintenance of specified levels of reserves and specified levels of contributions, which any such plan, or any trust established under such a plan, must meet in order to be considered under such law able to pay benefits in full when due, and

(II) provisions to enforce such standards, and

(ii) in the case of any other employee welfare arrangement, in addition to this title, any law of any State which regulates insurance may apply to the extent not inconsistent with the preceding sections of this title.

(B) The Secretary may, under regulations which may be prescribed by the Secretary, exempt from subparagraph (A)(ii), individually or by class, multiple employer welfare arrangements which are not full insured. Any such exemption may be granted with respect to any arrangement or class of arrangements only if such arrangement or each arrangement which is a member of such class meets the requirements of section 3(1) and section 4 necessary to be considered an employee welfare benefit plan to which this title applies.

(C) Nothing in subparagraph (A) shall affect the manner or extent to which the provisions of this title apply to an employee welfare benefit plan which is not a multiple employer welfare arrangement and which is a plan, fund, or program participating in, subscribing to, or otherwise using a multiple employer welfare arrangement to fund or administer benefits to such plan's participants and beneficiaries.

(D) For purposes of this paragraph, a multiple employer welfare arrangement shall be considered fully insured only if the terms of the arrangement provide for benefits the amount of all of which the Secretary determines are guaranteed under a contract, or policy of insurance, issued by an insurance company, insurance service, or insurance organization, qualified to conduct business in a State.

(c) For purposes of this section:

(1) The term "State law" includes all laws, decisions, rules, regulations, or other State action having the effect of law, of any State. A law of the United State applicable to the District of Columbia shall be treated as a State law rather than a law of the United States.

(2) The term "State" includes a State, any political subdivisions thereof, or any agency or instrumentality of either, which purports to regulate, directly or indirectly, the terms and conditions of employee benefit plans covered by this title.

Sec. 514 (b) (6)

(d) Nothing in this title shall be construed to alter, amend, modify, invalidate, impair, or supersede any law of the United States (except as provided in sections 111 and 507(b)) or any rule or regulation issued under any such law.

DELINQUENT CONTRIBUTIONS
Sec. 515. Every employer who is obligated to make contributions to a multiemployer plan under the terms of the plan or under the terms of a collectively bargained agreement shall, to the extent not inconsistent with law, make such contributions in accordance with the terms and conditions of such plan or such agreement.

*Title II—Amendments to the Internal Revenue Code Relating to Retirement Plans

*[*Editor's Note:* Title II of ERISA amends the Internal Revenue Code. Text of code provisions relevant to pension and benefit plans appears following the text of ERISA as amended. Therefore, most of Title II of ERISA is not reprinted here. What follows are certain transitional rules, effective dates, and conforming code amendments as they were enacted in 1974.]

SEC. 1001. AMENDMENT OF INTERNAL REVENUE CODE OF 1954

Except as otherwise expressly provided, whenever in this title an amendment or repeal is expressed in terms of an amendment to, or repeal of, a section or other provision, the reference shall be considered to be made to a section or other provision of the Internal Revenue Code of 1954.

Subtitle A—Participation, Vesting, Funding, Administration, Etc.

PART 1—PARTICIPATION, VESTING, AND FUNDING

* * *

SEC. 1012. MINIMUM VESTING STANDARDS.

* * *

(c) Variations From Certain Vesting and Accrued Benefits Requirements.—In the case of any plan maintained on January 1, 1974, if, not later than 2 years after the date of the enactment of this Act, the plan administrator petitions the Secretary of Labor, the Secretary of Labor may prescribe an alternate method which shall be treated as satisfying the requirements of subsection (a)(2) of section 411 of the Internal Revenue Code of 1954, or of subsection (b)(1) (other than subparagraph (D) thereof) of such sections 411, or of both such provisions for a period of not more than 4 years. The Secretary may prescribe such alternate method only when he finds that—

(1) the application of such requirements would increase the costs of the plan to such an extent that there would result a substantial risk to the voluntary continuation of the plan or a substantial curtailment of benefit levels or the levels of employees' compensation,

(2) the application of such requirements or discontinuance of the plan would be adverse to the interests of plan participants in the aggregate, and

(3) a waiver or extension of time granted under section 412 (d) or (e) would be inadequate.

In the case of any plan with respect to which an alternate method has been prescribed under the preceding provisions of this subsection for a period of not more than 4 years, if, not later than 1 year before the expiration of such period, the plan administrator petitions the Secretary of Labor for an extension of such alternate method, and the Secretary makes the findings required by the preceding sentence, such alternate method may be extended for not more than 3 years.

SEC. 1013. MINIMUM FUNDING STANDARDS.

* * *

(d) Alternative Amortization Method for Certain Multiemployer Plans.—

(1) General rule.—In the case of any multiemployer plan (as defined in section 414(f) of the Internal Revenue Code of 1954) to which section 412 of such Code applies, if—

(A) on January 1, 1974, the contributions under the plan were based on a percentage of pay,

(B) the actuarial assumptions with respect to pay are reasonably related to past and projected experience, and

(C) the rates of interest under the plan are determined on the basis of reasonable actuarial assumptions,

the plan may elect (in such manner and at such time as may be provided under regulations prescribed by the Secretary of the Treasury or his delegate) to fund the unfunded past service liability under the plan existing as of the date 12 months following the first date on which such section 412 first applies to the plan by charging the funding standard account with an equal annual percentage of the aggregate pay of all participants in the plan in lieu of the level dollar charges to such account required under clauses (i), (ii), and (iii) of section 412(b)(2)(B) of such Code and section 302(b)(2)(B)(i), (ii) and (iii) of this Act.

(2) Limitation.—In the case of a plan which makes an election under paragraph (1), the aggregate of the charges required under such paragraph for a plan year shall not be less than the interest on the unfunded past service liabilities described in clauses (i), (ii), and (iii) of section 412(b)(2)(B) of the Internal Revenue Code of 1954.

* * *

SEC. 1016. CONFORMING AND CLERICAL AMENDMENTS.

(a) Conforming Amendments.—

(1) Section 275(a) (relating to denial of deduction for certain taxes) is amended by adding at the end thereof the following new paragraph:

"(6) Taxes imposed by chapter 42 and chapter 43."

* * *

(6) Section 805(d)(1)(C) (relating to definition of pension plan reserves) is amended by striking out "and (8)" and inserting in lieu thereof "(8), (11), (12), (13), (14), and (15)".

(7) Section 6161(b)(1) (relating to extensions of time for paying tax) is amended by striking out "or 42" and inserting in lieu thereof "42 or 43". The second sentence of section 6161 (b) is amended by striking out "or 42" and inserting in lieu thereof", 42, or chapter 43".

(8) Section 6201(d) (relating to assessment authority) is amended by striking out "and chapter 42" and inserting in lieu thereof ", chapter 42, and chapter 43".

(9) Section 6211 (defining deficiency) is amended—

(A) by striking out so much of subsection (a) as precedes paragraph (1) thereof and inserting in lieu thereof the following:

"*(a) In general.* — For purposes of this title in the case of income, estate, and gift taxes imposed by subtitles A and B and excise taxes imposed by chapters 42 and 43, the term 'deficiency' means the amount by which the tax imposed by subtitle A or B, or chapter 42 or 43, exceeds the excess of—"; and

(B) by striking out "chapter 42" in subsection (b)(2) and inserting in lieu thereof "chapter 42 or 43".

(10) Section 6212 (relating to notice of deficiency) is amended—

(A) by striking out "chapter 42" in subsection (a) and inserting in lieu thereof "chapter 42 or 43",

(B) by striking out "or chapter 42" in subsection (b)(1) and inserting in lieu thereof "chapter 42, or chapter 43",

(C) by striking out "chapter 42, and this chapter" in subsection (b)(1) and inserting in lieu thereof "chapter 42, chapter 43, and this chapter", and

(D) by striking out "of the same decedent," in subsection (c) and inserting in lieu thereof "of the same decedent, of chapter 43 tax for the same taxable years,".

(11) Section 6213 (relating to restrictions applicable to deficiencies and petition to Tax Court) is amended—

(A) by striking out "or chapter 42" in subsection (a) and inserting in lieu thereof ", chapter 42 or 43",

(B) by striking out the heading of subsection (e) and inserting in lieu thereof:

"(e) Suspension of Filing Period for Certain Excise Taxes.—",

(C) by striking out "or 4945 (relating to taxes on taxable expenditures)" in subsection (e) and inserting in lieu thereof "4945 (relating to taxes on taxable expenditures), 4971 (relating to excise taxes on failure to meet minimum funding standard), 4975 (relating to excise taxes on prohibited transactions)"; and

(D) by striking out "or 4945(h)(2)" in subsection (e) and inserting in lieu thereof ", 4945 (i)(2), 4971(c)(3), or 4975(f)(4).",

(12) Section 6214 (relating to determinations by Tax Court) is amended—

(A) by amending the heading of subsection (c) to read as follows:

"(c) Taxes Imposed by Section 507 or Chapter 42 or 43.—",

(B) by inserting after "chapter 42" each place it appears in subsection (c) "or 43"; and

(C) by striking out "chapter 42" in subsection (d) and inserting in lieu thereof "chapter 42 or 43".

(13) Section 6344(a)(1) (relating to cross references) is amended by striking out "chapter 42" and inserting in lieu thereof "chapter 42 or 43".

(14) Section 6501(e)(3) (realting to limitations on assessment and collection) is amended by striking out "chapter 42" and inserting in lieu thereof "chapter 42 or 43".

(15) Section 6503 (relating to suspension of running of period of limitations) is amended—

(A) by striking out "chapter 42 taxes)" in subsection (a)(1) and inserting in lieu thereof "certain excise taxes)", and

(B) by inserting after "section 507" in subsection (h) "or section 4971 or section 4975", and by striking out "or 4945(h)(2)" in subsection (h) and inserting in lieu thereof "4945(i)(2), 4971(c)(3), or 4975(f)(4)".

(16) Section 6512 (relating to limitations in case of petition to Tax Court) is amended by striking out "chapter 42" each place it appears therein and inserting in lieu thereof "chapter 42 or 43".

(17) Section 6601(d) (relating to interest on underpayment, nonpayment, or extensions of time for payment of tax) is amended by—

(A) striking out in the heading thereof "chapter 42" and inserting in lieu thereof "chapter 42 or 43", and

(B) striking out "chapter 42" and inserting in lieu thereof "certain excise".

(18) Section 6653(c)(1) (relating to income, estate, gift, and chapter 42 Taxes) is amended by striking out "chapter 42" each place it appears therein (including the heading) and inserting in lieu thereof "certain excise".

(19) Section 6659(b) (relating to applicable rules) as amended by striking out "chapter 42" and inserting in lieu thereof "certain excise".

(20) Section 6676(b) (relating to failure to supply identifying numbers) is amended by striking out "chapter 42" and inserting in lieu thereof "and certain excise".

(21) Section 6677(b) (relating to failure to file information returns with respect to certain foreign trusts) is amended by striking out "chapter

42" and inserting in lieu thereof "and certain excise".

(22) Section 6679(b) (relating to failure to file returns as to organization or reorganization of foreign corporations and as to acquisitions of their stock) is amended by striking out "chapter 42" and inserting in lieu thereof "and certain excise".

(23) Section 6682(b) (relating to false information with respect to withholding allowances based on itemized deductions) is amended by striking out "chapter 42" and inserting in lieu thereof "and certain excise".

(24) The heading of section 6861 (relating to jeopardy assessments of income, estate, and gift taxes) is amended by striking out "and gift taxes", and inserting in lieu thereof "gift, and certain excise taxes".

(25) Section 6862 (relating to jeopardy assessment of taxes other than income, estate, and gift taxes) is amended—

(A) by striking out "and Gift Taxes.", in the heading and inserting in lieu thereof ", Gift, and Certain Excise Taxes.",

(B) by striking out "and gift tax)" in subsection (a) and inserting in lieu thereof "gift tax, and certain excise taxes)".

(26) Section 7422 (relating to civil actions for refund) is amended—

(A) by striking out "chapter 42" and inserting in lieu thereof "chapter 42 or 43" in subsection (e),

(B) by striking out "Chapter 42" in the heading of subsection (g) and inserting in lieu thereof "Chapter 42 or 43",

(C) by striking out "or 4945" in subsection (g)(1) and inserting in lieu thereof "4945, 4971, or 4975",

(D) by striking out "section 4945 (a) (relating to initial taxes on taxable expenditures)" in subsection (g)(1) and inserting in lieu thereof "section 4945(a) (relating to initial taxes on taxable expenditures), 4971 (a) (relating to initial tax on failure to meet minimum funding standard), 4975(a) (relating to initial tax on prohibited transactions)",

(E) by striking out "or section 4945(b) (relating to additional taxes on taxable expenditures)" in subsection (g)(1) and inserting in lieu thereof "section 4945(b) (relating to additional taxes on taxable expenditures), section 4971(b) (relating to additional tax on failure to meet minimum funding standard), or section 4975(b) (relating to additional tax on prohibited transactions)", and

(F) by striking out "or 4945" in paragraphs (2) and (3) of subsection (g) and inserting in lieu thereof "4945, 4971, or 4975".

(27) Section 6204(b) (relating to supplemental assessments) is amended by striking out "and gift taxes" and inserting in lieu thereof "gift, and certain excise taxes".

(b) Clerical Amendments.—

(1) Part I of subchapter D of chapter 1 is amended by inserting after the heading and before the table of sections the following:

"Subpart A. General rule.
"Subpart B. Special rules.

"Subpart A—General Rule".

(2) The table of chapters for subtitle D is amended by adding at the end thereof the following new item:

"Chapter 43. Qualified pension, etc., plans."

(3) The table of sections for subchapter B of chapter 68 is amended by striking out the item relating to the section captioned "Assessable penalties with respect to information required to be furnished under section 7654" and inserting in lieu thereof:

"Sec. 6688 Assessable Penalties With Respect to Information Required to be Furnished Under Section 7654."

(4) Subchapter B of chapter 68 is amended by striking out the heading of the section immediately preceding section 6689 and inserting in lieu thereof:

Sec. 1016 (a) (22)

"SEC. 6688. ASSESSABLE PENALTIES WITH RESPECT TO INFORMATION REQUIRED TO BE FURNISHED UNDER SECTION 7654."

(5) The table of sections for part II of subchapter A of chapter 70 is amended by striking out "and gift taxes" in the items relating to sections 6861 and 6862 and inserting in lieu thereof "gift, and certain excise taxes".

SEC. 1017. EFFECTIVE DATES AND TRANSITIONAL RULES.

(a) General Rule.—Except as otherwise provided in this section, the amendments made by this part shall apply for plan years beginning after the date of the enactment of this Act.

(b) Existing Plans.—Except as otherwise provided in subsections (c) through (h), in the case of a plan in existence on January 1, 1974, the amendments made by this part shall apply for plan years beginning after December 31, 1975.

(c) Existing Plans Under Collective Bargaining Agreements.—

(1) *Application of vesting rules to certain plan provisions.—*

(A) Waiver of Application.—In the case of a plan maintained on January 1, 1974, pursuant to one or more agreements which the Secretary of Labor finds to be collective bargaining agreements between employee representatives and one or more employers, during the special temporary waiver period the plan shall not be treated as not meeting the requirements of section 411(b)(1) or (2) of the Internal Revenue Code of 1954 solely by reason of a supplementary or special plan provision (within the meaning of subparagraph (D)).

(B) Special temporary waiver period.—For purposes of this paragraph, the term "special temporary waiver period" means plan years beginning after December 31, 1975, and before the earlier of—

(i) the date on which the last of the collective bargaining agreements relating to the plan terminates (determined without regard to any extension thereof agreed to after the date of the enactment of this Act), or

(ii) January 1, 1981.

For purposes of clause (i), any plan amendment made pursuant to a collective bargaining agreement relating to the plan which amends the plan solely to conform to any requirement contained in this Act shall not be treated as a termination of such collective bargaining agreement.

(C) Determination by Secretary of Labor required.—Subparagraph (A) shall not apply unless the Secretary of Labor determines that the participation and vesting rules in effect on the date of the enactment of this Act are not less favorable to the employees, in the aggregate, than the rules provided under sections 410 and 411 of the Internal Revenue Code of 1954.

(D) Supplementary or special plan provisions.—For purposes of this paragraph, the term "supplementary or special plan provision" means any plan provision which—

(i) provides supplementary benefits, not in excess of one-third of the basic benefit, in the form of an annuity for the life of the participant, or

(ii) provides that, under a contractual agreement based on medical evidence as to the effects of working in an adverse environment for an extended period of time, a participant having 25 years of service is to be treated as having 30 years of service.

(2) *Application of funding rules.—*

(A) In general.—In the case of a plan maintained on January 1, 1974, pursuant to one or more agreements which the Secretary of Labor finds to be collective bargaining agreements between employee representatives and one or more employers, section 412 of the Internal Revenue Code of 1954, and other amendments made by this part to the extent such amendments relate to such section 412, shall not apply during the special tem-

porary waiver period (as defined in paragraph (1)(B)).

(B) Waiver of underfunding.—In the case of a plan maintained on January 1, 1974, pursuant to one or more agreements which the Secretary of Labor finds to be collective bargaining agreements between employee representatives and one or more employers, if by reason of subparagraph (A) the requirements of section 401(a)(7) of the Internal Revenue Code of 1954 apply without regard to the amendment of such section 401(a)(7) by section 1016(a)(2)(C) of this Act, the plan shall not be treated as not meeting such requirements solely by reason of the application of the amendments made by sections 1011 and 1012 of this Act or related amendments made by this part.

(C) Labor organization conventions—In the case of a plan maintained by a labor organization, which is exempt from tax under section 501(c)(5) of the Internal Revenue Code of 1954, exclusively for the benefit of its employees and their beneficiaries, section 412 of such Code and other amendments made by this part to the extent such amendments relate to such section 412, shall be applied by substituting for the term "December 31, 1975" in subsection (b), the earlier of—

(i) the date on which the second convention of such labor organization held after the date of the enactment of this Act ends, or

(ii) December 31, 1980, but in no event shall a date earlier than the later of December 31, 1975, or the date determined under subparagraph (A) or (B) be substituted.

(d) Existing Plans May Elect New Provisions.—In the case of a plan in existence on January 1, 1974, the provisions of the Internal Revenue Code of 1954 relating to participation, vesting, funding, and form of benefit (as in effect from time to time) shall apply in the case of the plan year (which begins after the date of the enactment of this Act but before the applicable effective date determined under subsection (b) or (c)) selected by the plan administrator and to all subsequent plan years, if the plan administrator elects (in such manner and at such time as the Secretary of the Treasury or his delegate shall by regulations prescribe) to have such provisions so apply. Any election made under this subsection, once made, shall be irrevocable.

(e) Certain Definitions and Special Rules.—Section 414 of the Internal Revenue Code of 1954 (other than subsections (b) and (c) of such section 414), as added by section 1015(a) of this Act, shall take effect on the date of the enactment of this Act.

(f) Transitional Rules With Respect to Breaks in Service—

(1) Participation.—In the case of a plan to which section 410 of the Internal Revenue Code of 1954 applies, if any plan amendment with respect to breaks in service (which amendment is made or becomes effective after January 1, 1974, and before the date on which such section 410 first becomes effective with respect to such plan) provides that any employee's participation in the plan would commence at any date later than the later of—

(A) the date on which his participation would commence under the break in service rules of section 410(a)(5) of such Code, or

(B) the date on which his participation would commence under the plan as in effect on January 1, 1974,

such plan shall not constitute a plan described in section 403(a) or 405(a) of such Code and a trust forming a part of such plan shall not constitute a qualified trust under section 401(a) of such Code.

(2) Vesting.—In the case of a plan to which section 411 of the Internal Revenue Code of 1954 applies, if any plan amendment with respect to breaks in service (which amendment is made or becomes effective after January 1, 1974, and before the date on which such section 411 first becomes effective with respect to such

Sec. 1017 (d)

TEXT OF ERISA

plan) provides that the nonforfeitable benefit derived from employer contributions to which any employee would be entitled is less than the lesser of the nonforfeitable benefit derived from employer contributions to which he would be entitled under—

(A) the break in service rules of section 411(a)(6) of such Code, or

(B) the plan as in effect on January 1, 1974,

such plan shall not constitute a plan described in section 403(a) or 405(a) of such Code and a trust forming a part of such plan shall not constitute a qualified trust under section 401(a) of such Code. Subparagraph (B) shall not apply if the break in service rules under the plan would have been in violation of any law or rule of law in effect on January 1, 1974.

(g) 3-Year Delay for Certain Provisions.—Subparagraphs (B) and (C) of section 404(a)(1) shall apply only in the case of plan years beginning on or after 3 years after the date of the enactment of this Act.

(h)(1) Except as provided in paragraph (2), section 413 of the Internal Revenue Code of 1954 shall apply to plan years beginning after December 31, 1953.

(2)(A) For plan years beginning before the applicable effective date of section 410 of such Code, the provisions of paragraphs (1) and (8) of subsection (b) of such section 413 shall be applied by substituting "401(a)(3)" for "410".

(B) For plan years beginning before the applicable effective date of section 411 of such Code, the provisions of subsection (b)(2) of such section 413 shall be applied by substituting "401(a)(7)" for "411(d)(3)".

(C)(i) The provisions of subsection (b)(4) of such section 413 shall not apply to plan years beginning before the applicable effective date of section 411 of such Code.

(ii) The provisions of subsection (b)(5) (other than the second sentence thereof) of such section 413 shall not apply to plan years beginning before the applicable effective date of section 412 of such Code.

PART 2—CERTAIN OTHER PROVISIONS RELATING TO QUALIFIED RETIREMENT PLANS

* * *

SEC. 1022. MISCELLANEOUS PROVISIONS.

* * *

(g) Public Inspection of Certain Information With Respect to Pension, Profit-Sharing, and Stock Bonus Plans.—

(1) *Amendment of section 6104(a).*— Paragraph (1) of section 6104(a) (relating to public inspection of applications for tax exemption) is amended—

(A) by redesignating subparagraph (B) as subparagraph (D) and by inserting after subparagraph (A) the following new subparagraphs:

"*(B) Pension, etc., plans.*—The following shall be open to public inspection at such times and in such places as the Secretary or his delegate may prescribe:

"(i) any application filed with respect to the qualification of a pension, profit-sharing, or stock bonus plan under section 401(a), 403(a), or 405(a), an individual retirement account described in section 408(a), or an individual retirement annuity described in section 408(b),

"(ii) any application filed with respect to the exemption from tax under section 501(a) of an organization forming part of a plan or account referred to in clause (i),

"(iii) any papers submitted in support of an application referred to in clause (i) or (ii), and

"(iv) any letter or other document issued by the Internal Revenue Service and dealing with the qualification referred to in clause (i) or the exemption from tax referred to in clause (ii).

Except in the case of a plan participant, this subparagraph shall not apply to any plan referred to in clause

Sec. 1022 (g) (1)

(1) having not more than 25 participants.

"(C) *Certain names and compensation not to be opened to public inspection.*—In the case of any application, document, or other papers, referred to in subparagraph (B), information from which the compensation (including deferred compensation) of any individual may be ascertained shall not be opened to public inspection under subparagraph (B)."

(B) The heading of subparagraph (A) of section 6104(a)(1) is amended to read as follows:

"*(A) Organizations described in section 501.*—".

(C) The heading of subparagraph (D) of section 6104(a)(1) as redesignated by subparagraph (A) of this paragraph is amended to read as follows:

"*(D) Withholding of certain other information.*—".

(D) Subparagraph (D) of section 6104(a)(1) (as so redesignated) is amended by striking out "subparagraph (A)" each place it appears and inserting in lieu thereof "subparagraph (A) or (B)".

(2) Amendment of section 6104(a) (2).—Subparagraph (A) of section 6104 (a)(2) is amended by adding at the end thereof "any application referred to in subparagraph (B) of subsection (a)(1) of this section, and".

(3) Amendment of section 6104(b). —Section 6104(b) (relating to inspection of annual information returns) is amended by striking out "and 6056" and inserting in lieu thereof "6956, and 6058".

(4) Effective Date.—The amendments made by this subsection shall apply to applications filed (or documents issued) after the date of enactment of this Act.

(h) *Publicity of Returns.*—Effective on the date of the enactment of this Act, section 6103 (relating to publicity of returns and disclosure of information as to persons filing income tax returns) is amended by adding at the end thereof a new subsection (g) to read as follows:

"(g) *Disclosure of Information With Respect to Deferred Compensation Plans.*—The Secretary or his delegate is authorized to furnish—

"(1) returns with respect to any tax imposed by this title or information with respect to such returns to the proper officers and employees of the Department of Labor and the Pension Benefit Guaranty Corporation for purposes of administration of Titles I and IV of the Employee Retirement Income Security Act of 1974, and

"(2) registration statements (as described in section 6057) and information with respect to such statements to the proper officers and employees of the Department of Health, Education, and Welfare for purposes of administration of section 1131 of the Social Security Act."

(i) Certain Puerto Rican Pension, Etc., Plans To Be Exempt From Tax Under Section 501(a).—

(1) General rule.—Effective for taxable years beginning after December 31, 1973, for purposes of section 501(a) of the Internal Revenue Code of 1954 (relating to exemption from tax), any trust forming part of a pension, profit-sharing, or stock bonus plan all of the participants of which are residents of the Commonwealth of Puerto Rico shall be treated as an organization described in section 401(a) of such Code if such trust—

(A) forms part of a pension, profit-sharing, or stock bonus plan, and

(B) is exempt from income tax under the laws of the Commonwealth of Puerto Rico.

(2) Election to have provisions of, and amendments made by, title II of this act apply.—

(A) If the administrator of a pension, profit-sharing, or stock bonus plan which is created or organized in Puerto Rico elects, at such time and in such manner as the Secretary of the Treasury may require, to have

Sec. 1022 (g) (2)

TEXT OF ERISA 259

the provisions of this paragraph apply, for plan years beginning after the date of election any trust forming a part of such plan shall be treated as a trust created or organized in the United States for purposes of section 401(a) of the Internal Revenue Code of 1954.

(B) An election under subparagraph (A), once made, is irrevocable.

(C) This paragraph applies to plan years beginning after the date of enactment of this Act.

(D) The source of any distributions made under a plan which makes an election under this paragraph to participants and beneficiaries residing outside of the United States shall be determined, for purposes of subchapter N of chapter 1 of the Internal Revenue Code of 1954, by the Secretary of the Treasury in accordance with regulations prescribed by him. For purposes of this subparagraph the United States means the United States as defined in section 7701(a)(9) of the Internal Revenue Code of 1954.

(j) Year of Deduction for Certain Employer Contributions for Severance Payments Required by Foreign Law.—Effective for taxable years beginning after December 31, 1973, if—

(1) an employer is engaged in a trade or business in a foreign country,

(2) such employer is required by the laws of that country to make payments, based on periods of service, to its employees or their beneficiaries after the employees' retirement, death, or other separation from the service, and

(3) such employer establishes a trust (whether organized within or outside the United States) for the purpose of funding the payments required by such law,

then, in determining for purposes of paragraph (5) of section 404(a) of the Internal Revenue Code of 1954 the taxable year in which any contribution to or under the plan is includible in the gross income of the nonresident alien employees of such employer, such paragraph (5) shall be treated as not requiring that separate accounts be maintained for such nonresident alien employees.

(k) Receipts for Employees.—Section 6051 (relating to receipts for employees) is amended by inserting after "exemption," in subsection (a) the following: "or every employer engaged in a trade or business who pays remuneration for services performed by an employee, including the cash value of such remuneration paid in any medium other than cash,".

* * *

SEC. 1024. EFFECTIVE DATES.

Except as otherwise provided in section 1021, the amendments made by section 1021 shall apply to plan years to which part I applies. Except as otherwise provided in section 1022, the amendments made by section 1022 shall apply to plan years to which part I applies. Section 1023 shall take effect on the date of the enactment of this Act.

PART 3—REGISTRATION AND INFORMATION

SEC. 1031. REGISTRATION AND INFORMATION.

* * *

(b) Sanctions.—

(1) Failure to file registration statements or notification of change in status.—

(A) Section 6652 (relating to failure to file certain information returns) is amended by redesignating subsection (e) as subsection (g) and by inserting after subsection (d) the following new subsections:

"*(e) Annual Registration and Other Notification by Pension Plan.*—

"*(1) Registration.*—In the case of any failure to file a registration statement required under section 6057(a) (relating to annual registration of

Sec. 1031 (b)

certain plans) which includes all participants required to be included in such statement, on the date prescribed therefor (determined without regard to any extension of time for filing), unless it is shown that such failure is due to reasonable cause, there shall be paid (on notice and demand by the Secretary or his delegate and in the same manner as tax) by the person failing so to file, an amount equal to $1 for each participant with respect to whom there is a failure to file, multiplied by the number of days during which such failure continues, but the total amount imposed under this paragraph on any person for any failure to file with respect to any plan year shall not exceed $5,000.

"(2) *Notification of change of status.*—In the case of failure to file a notification required under section 6057(b) (relating to notification of change of status) on the date prescribed therefor (determined without regard to any extension of time for filing), unless it is shown that such failure is due to reasonable cause, there shall be paid (on notice and demand by the Secretary or his delegate and in the same manner as tax) by the person failing so to file, $1 for each day during which such failure continues, but the total amounts imposed under this paragraph on any person for failure to file any notification shall not exceed $1,000.

"*(f) Information Required in Connection With Certain Plans of Deferred Compensation.*—In the case of failure to file a return or statement required under section 6058 (relating to information required in connection with certain plans of deferred compensation) or 6047 (relating to information relating to certain trusts and annuity and bond purchase plans) on the date and in the manner prescribed therefor (determined with regard to any extension of time for filing), unless it is shown that such failure is due to reasonable cause, there shall be paid (on notice and demand by the Secretary or his delegate and in the same manner as tax) by the person failing so to file, $10 for each day during which such failure continues, but the total amount imposed under this subsection on any person for failure to file any return shall not exceed $5,000."

(B)(i) The section heading for section 6652 is amended by adding ", Registration Statements, etc." before the period at the end thereof.

(ii) The item relating to section 6652 in the table of contents for subchapter A of chapter 68 is amended by adding ", registration statements, etc." before the period of the end thereof.

(2) Failure to furnish statement to participant.—

(A) Subchapter B of chapter 68 (relating to assessable penalties) is amended by adding at the end thereof the following new section:

"SEC. 6690. FRAUDULENT STATEMENT OR FAILURE TO FURNISH STATEMENT TO PLAN PARTICIPANT.

"Any person required under section 6057(e) to furnish a statement to a participant who willfully furnishes a false or fraudulent statement, or who willfully fails to furnish a statement in the manner, at the time, and showing the information required under section 6057(e), or regulations prescribed thereunder, shall for each such act, or for each such failure, be subject to a penalty under this subchapter of $50, which shall be assessed and collected in the same manner as the tax on employers imposed by section 3111."

(B) The table of sections for such subchapter B is amended by adding at the end thereof the following new item:

"Sec. 6690. Fraudulent statement or failure to furnish statement to plan participant."

(c) Clerical Amendments.—

(1) The table of subparts for such

Sec. 1031 (b) (1) (A)

part III is amended by adding at the end thereof the following:

"Subpart E. Registration of and information concerning pension, etc., plans."

(2) Section 6033(c) (relating to cross references) is amended by adding at the end thereof the following:

"For provisions relating to information required in connection with certain plans of deferred compensation, see section 6058."

(3) Subsection (d) of section 6047 (relating to information with respect to certain trusts and annuity and bond purchase plans) is amended to read as follows:

"*(d) Cross References.—*

"(1) For provisions relating to penalties for failure to file a return required by this section, see section 6652(f).

"(2) For criminal penalty for furnishing fraudulent information, see section 7207."

SEC. 1032. DUTIES OF SECRETARY OF HEALTH, EDUCATION, AND WELFARE.

Title XI of the Social Security Act (relating to general provisions) is amended by adding at the end of part A thereof the following new section:

"Notification of Social Security Claimant With Respect to Deferred Vested Benefits

"Sec. 1131. (a) Whenever—

"(1) the secretary makes a finding of fact and a decision as to—

"(A) the entitlement of any individual to monthly benefits under section 202, 223, or 228,

"(B) the entitlement of any individual to a lump-sum death payment payable under section 202(i) on account of the death of any person to whom such individual is related by blood, marriage, or adoption, or

"(C) the entitlement under section 226 of any individual to hospital insurance benefits under part A of title XVIII, or

"(2) the Secretary is requested to do so—

"(A) by any individual with respect to whom the Secretary holds information obtained under section 6057 of the Internal Revenue Code of 1954, or

"(B) in the case of the death of the individual referred to in subparagraph (A), by the individual who would be entitled to payment under section 204(d) of this Act,

he shall transmit to the individual referred to in paragraph (1) or the individual making the request under paragraph (2) any information, as reported by the employer, regarding any deferred vested benefit transmitted to the Secretary pursuant to such section 6057 with respect to the individual referred to in paragraph (1) or (2)(A) or the person on whose wages and self-employment income entitlement (or claim of entitlement) is based.

"(b)(1) For purposes of section 201 (g)(1), expenses incurred in the administration of subsection (a) shall be deemed to be expenses incurred for the administration of title II.

"(2) There are hereby authorized to be appropriated to the Federal Old-Age and Survivors Insurance Trust Fund for each fiscal year (commencing with the fiscal year ending June 30, 1974) such sums as the Secretary deems necessary on account of additional administrative expenses resulting from the enactment of the provisions of subsection (a)."

SEC. 1033. REPORTS BY ACTUARIES.

(a) Reports by Actuaries.—Subpart E of part III of subchapter A of chapter 61 (relating to registration of and information concerning pension, etc., plans) as added by section 1031(a) of this Act, is amended by adding at the end thereof the following new section:

"SEC. 6059. PERIODIC REPORT OF ACTUARY.

"*(a) General Rule.*—The actuarial report described in subsection (b) shall be filed by the plan administrator (as defined in section 414(g)) of each defined benefit plan to which section 412 applies, for the first plan year for which section 412 applies to the plan and for each third plan year thereafter (or more frequently if the Secretary or his delegate determines that more frequent reports are necessary).

"*(b) Actuarial Report.*—The actuarial report of a plan required by subsection (a) shall be prepared and signed by an enrolled actuary (within the meaning of section 7701(a)(35)) and shall contain—

"(1) a description of the funding method and actuarial assumptions used to determine costs under the plan,

"(2) a certification of the contribution necessary to reduce the accumulated funding deficiency (as defined in section 412(a)) to zero,

"(3) a statement—

"(A) that to the best of his knowledge the report is complete and accurate, and

"(B) the requirements of section 412(c) (relating to reasonable actuarial assumptions) have been complied with,

"(4) such other information as may be necessary to fully and fairly disclose the actuarial position of the plan, and

"(5) such other information regarding the plan as the Secretary or his delegate may by regulations require.

"*(c) Time and Manner of Filing.*—The actuarial report and statement required by this section shall be filed at the time and in the manner provided by regulations prescribed by the Secretary or his delegate.

"*(d) Cross Reference.*—

"For coordination between the Department of the Treasury and the Department of Labor with respect to the report required to be filed under this section, see section 3004 of title III of the Employee Retirement Income Security Act of 1974.".

(b) Assessable Penalties.—Subchapter B of chapter 68 (relating to assessable penalties) is amended by adding at the end thereof the following new section:

"SEC. 6692. FAILURE TO FILE ACTUARIAL REPORT.

"The plan administrator (as defined in section 414(g)) of each defined benefit plan to which section 412 applies who fails to file the report required by section 6059 at the time and in the manner required by section 6059, shall pay a penalty of $1,000 for each such failure unless it is shown that such failure is due to reasonable cause."

(c) Consolidation of Actuarial Reports.—The Secretary of the Treasury and the Secretary of Labor shall take such steps as may be necessary to assure coordination to the maximum extent feasible between the actuarial reports required by section 6059 of the Internal Revenue Code of 1954 and by section 103(d) of title I of the Employee Retirement Income Security Act of 1974.

(d) Clerical Amendment.—The table of sections for subchapter B of chapter 68 is amended by adding at the end thereof the following new item:

"Sec. 6692. Failure to file actuarial report.".

SEC. 1034. EFFECTIVE DATES.

This part shall take effect upon the date of the enactment of this Act; except that—

(1) the requirements of section 6059 of the Internal Revenue Code of 1954 shall apply only with respect to plan years to which part I of this title applies,

(2) the requirements of section 6057 of such Code shall apply only with respect to plan years beginning after December 31, 1975,

(3) the requirements of section 6058(a) of such Code shall apply only with respect to plan years beginning after the date of the enactment of this Act, and

(4) the amendments made by section 1032 shall take effect on January 1, 1978.

Sec. 1033 (b)

PART 4—Declaratory Judgments Relating to Qualification of Certain Retirement Plans

SEC. 1041. TAX COURT PROCEDURE.

(a) In General.—Subchapter C of chapter 76 (relating to the Tax Court) is amended by adding at the end thereof the following new part:

"Part IV—Declaratory Judgments Relating to Qualification of Certain Retirement Plans

"Sec. 7476. Declaratory judgments.

"SEC. 7476. DECLARATORY JUDGMENTS.

"(a) Creation of Remedy.—In a case of actual controversy involving—

"(1) a determination by the Secretary or his delegate with respect to the initial qualification or continuing qualification of a retirement plan under subchapter D of chapter 1, or

"(2) a failure by the Secretary or his delegate to make a determination with respect to—

"(A) such initial qualification, or

"(B) such continuing qualification if the controversy arises from a plan amendment or plan termination, upon the filing of an appropriate pleading, the United States Tax Court may make a declaration with respect to such initial qualification or continuing qualification. Any such declaration shall have the force and effect of a decision of the Tax Court and shall be reviewable as such.

"(b) Limitations.—

"(1) Petitioner.—A pleading may be filed under this section only by a petitioner who is the employer, the plan administrator, an employee who has qualified under regulations prescribed by the Secretary or his delegate as an interested party for purposes of pursuing administrative remedies within the Internal Revenue Service, or the Pension Benefit Guaranty Corporation.

"(2) Notice.—For purposes of this section, the filing of a pleading by any petitioner may be held by the Tax Court to be premature, unless the petitioner establishes to the satisfaction of the court that he has complied with the requirements prescribed by regulations of the Secretary or his delegate with respect to notice to other interested parties of the filing of the request for a determination referred to in subsection (a).

"(3) Exhaustion of administrative remedies.—The Tax Court shall not issue a declaratory judgment or decree under this section in any proceeding unless it determines that the petitioner has exhausted administrative remedies available to him within the Internal Revenue Service. A petitioner shall not be deemed to have exhausted his administrative remedies with respect to a failure by the Secretary or his delegate to make a determination with respect to initial qualification or continuing qualification of a retirement plan before the expiration of 270 days after the request for such determination was made.

"(4) Plan put into effect.—No proceeding may be maintained under this section unless the plan (and, in the case of a controversy involving the continuing qualification of the plan because of an amendment to the plan, the amendment) with respect to which a decision of the Tax Court is sought has been put into effect before the filing of the pleading. A plan or amendment shall not be treated as not being in effect merely because under the plan the funds contributed to the plan may be refunded if the plan (or the plan as so amended) is found to be not qualified

"(5) Time for bringing action.—If the Secretary or his delegate sends by certified or registered mail notice of his determination with respect to the qualification of the plan to the persons referred to in paragraph (1) (or, in the case of employees referred to in paragraph (1), to any individual

designated under regulations prescribed by the Secretary or his delegate as a representative of such employee), no proceeding may be initiated under this section by any person unless the pleading is filed before the ninety-first day after the day after such notice is mailed to such person (or to his designated representative, in the case of an employee).

"*(c) Commissioners.*—The chief judge of the Tax Court may assign proceedings under this section to be heard by the commissioners of the court, and the court may authorize a commissioner to make the decision of the court with respect to such proceeding, subject to such conditions and review as the court may by rule provide.

"*(d) Retirement Plan.*—For purposes of this section, the term 'retirement plan' means—

"(1) a pension, profit-sharing, or stock bonus plan described in section 401(a) or a trust which is part of such a plan,

"(2) an annuity plan described in section 403(a), or

"(3) a bond purchase plan described in section 405(a).

"*(e) Cross Reference.—*

"For provisions concerning intervention by Pension Benefit Guaranty Corporation and Secretary of Labor in actions brought under this section and right of Pension Benefit Guaranty Corporation to bring action, see section 3001(c) of subtitle A of title III of the Employee Retirement Income Security Act of 1974."

(b) Technical and Conforming Amendments.—

(1) Fee for filing petition.—Section 7451 (relating to fee for filing petition) is amended by striking out "deficiency" and inserting in lieu thereof "deficiency or for a declaratory judgment under part IV of this subchapter".

(2) Date of decision.—Section 7459 (c) (relating to date of decision) is amended by inserting before the period at the end of the first sentence the following: "or, in the case of a declaratory judgment proceeding under part IV of this subchapter, the date of the court's order entering the decision".

(3) Venue for appeal of decision.—

(A) Section 7482(b)(1) (relating to venue) is amended by striking out the period at the end of subparagraph (B) and inserting in lieu thereof ", or" and by inserting after subparagraph (B) the following new subparagraph:

"(C) in the case of a person seeking a declaratory decision under section 7476, the principal place of business, or principal office or agency of the employer."

(B) Section 7482(b)(1) is further amended—

(i) by striking out "neither subparagraph (A) nor (B) applies" and inserting in lieu thereof "subparagraph (A), (B), and (C) do not apply"; and

(ii) by inserting before the period at the end of the last sentence thereof the following: "or as of the time the petition seeking a declaratory decision under section 7476 was filed with the Tax Court".

(c) Clerical Amendment.—The table of parts for subchapter C of chapter 76 (relating to the Tax Court) is amended by adding at the end thereof the following new item:

"**Part IV. Declaratory Judgments Relating to Qualification of Certain Retirement Plans.**"

(d) Effective Date.—The amendments made by this section shall apply to pleadings filed more than 1 year after the date of the enactment of this Act.

PART 5—INTERNAL REVENUE SERVICE

SEC. 1051. ESTABLISHMENT OF OFFICE.

(a) In General.—Section 7802 (relating to Commissioner of Internal Revenue) is amended to read as follows:

"SEC. 7802. COMMISSIONER OF INTERNAL REVENUE; ASSISTANT COMMISSIONER (EMPLOYEE PLANS AND EXEMPT ORGANIZATIONS).

"(a) Commissioner of Internal Revenue.—There shall be in the Department of the Treasury a Commissioner of Internal Revenue, who shall be appointed by the President, by and with the advice and consent of the Senate. The Commissioner of Internal Revenue shall have such duties and powers as may be prescribed by the Secretary.

"(b) Assistant Commissioner for Employee Plans and Exempt Organizations.—There is established within the Internal Revenue Service an office to be known as the 'Office of Employee Plans and Exempt Organizations' to be under the supervision and direction of an Assistant Commissioner of Internal Revenue. As head of the Office, the Assistant Commissioner shall be responsible for carrying out such functions as the Secretary or his delegate may prescribe with respect to organizations exempt from tax under section 501(a) and with respect to plans to which part I of subchapter D of chapter 1 applies (and with respect to organizations designed to be exempt under such section and plans designed to be plans to which such part applies)."

(b) Salaries.—

(1) Assistant commissioner.—Section 5109 of title 5, United States Code, is amended by adding at the end thereof the following new subsection:

"(c) The position held by the employee appointed under section 7802(b) of the Internal Revenue Code of 1954 is classified at GS-18, and is in addition to the number of positions authorized by section 5108(a) of this title."

(2) Classification of positions at GS-16 and 17.—Section 5108 of title 5, United States Code, is amended by adding at the end thereof the following new subsection:

"(e) In addition to the number of positions authorized by subsection (a), the Commissioner of Internal Revenue is authorized, without regard to any other provision of this section, to place a total of 20 positions in the Internal Revenue Service in GS-16 and 17.".

(c) Clerical Amendments. — The item relating to section 7802 in the table of sections for subchapter A of chapter 80 is amended to read as follows:

"Sec. 7802. Commissioner of Internal Revenue; Assistant Commissioner (Employee Plans and Exempt Organizations)."

(d) Effective Date.—The amendments made by this section shall take effect on the 90th day after the date of the enactment of this Act.

SEC. 1052. AUTHORIZATION OF APPROPRIATIONS.

There is authorized to be appropriated to the Department of the Treasury for the purpose of carrying out all functions of the Office of Employee Plans and Exempt Organizations for each fiscal year beginning after June 30, 1974, an amount equal to the sum of—

(1) so much of the collections from the taxes imposed under section 4940 of such Code (relating to excise tax based on investment income) as would have been collected if the rate of tax under such section was 2 percent during the second preceding fiscal year, and

(2) the greater of—

(A) an amount equal to the amount described in paragraph (1), or

(B) $30,000,000.

Subtitle B—Other Amendments To the Internal Revenue Code Relating to Retirement Plans

SEC. 2001. CONTRIBUTIONS ON BEHALF OF SELF-EMPLOYED INDIVIDUALS AND SHAREHOLDER-EMPLOYEES.

* * *

(b) Increase in Maximum Amount Deductible for Shareholder-Employees.—Paragraph (1) of section 1379 (b) (relating to taxability of shareholder-employees) is amended—

(1) by striking out "10 percent" in subparagraph (a) and inserting in lieu thereof "15 percent", and

(2) by striking out "$2,500" in subparagraph (B) and inserting in lieu thereof "$7,500".

* * *

(g) Premature Distributions to Owner-Employees.—

* * *

(2) Conforming Amendments.—

* * *

(B) The second sentence of section 46(a)(3) and the second sentence of section 50A(a)(3), as each is amended by section 2005(c)(4) of this Act, are each amended by inserting after "tax preferences)," the following: "section 72(m)(5)(B) (relating to 10 percent tax on premature distributions to owner-employees),".

(C) The third sentence of section 901(a), as amended by section 2005 (c)(5) of this Act, is amended by striking out "tax preferences)," and inserting in lieu thereof "tax preferences), against the tax imposed for the taxable year under section 72(m) (5)(B) (relating to 10 percent tax on premature distributions to owner-employees),".

(D) Subparagraph (A) of section 56(a)(2) and paragraph (1) of section 56(c), as each is amended by section 2005(c)(7) of this Act, are each amended by striking out "402 (e)" and inserting in lieu of thereof "72(m)(5)(B), 402 (e)".

* * *

(i) Effective Dates.—

(1) The amendments made by subsections (a) and (b) apply to taxable years beginning after December 31, 1973.

(2) The amendments made by subsection (c) apply to—

(A) taxable years beginning after December 31. 1975, and

(B) any other taxable years beginning after December 31, 1973, for which contributions were made under the plan in excess of the amounts permitted to be made under sections 404(e) and 1379(b) as in effect on the day before the date of the enactment of this Act.

(3) The amendments made by subsection (d) apply to taxable years beginning after December 31, 1975.

(4) The amendments made by subsections (e) and (f) apply to contributions made in taxable years beginning after December 31, 1975.

(5) The amendments made by subsection (g) apply to distributions made in taxable years beginning after December 31, 1975.

(6) The amendments made by subsection (h) apply to taxable years ending after the date of enactment of this Act.

SEC. 2002. DEDUCTION FOR RETIREMENT SAVINGS.

* * *

(f) Penalty for Failure To Provide Reports on Individual Retirement Accounts.—Subchapter B of chapter 68 (relating to assessable penalties) is amended by adding at the end thereof the following new section:

"SEC. 6693. FAILURE TO PROVIDE REPORTS ON INDIVIDUAL RETIREMENT ACCOUNTS OR ANNUITIES.

"(a) The person required by section 408(i) to file a report regarding an individual retirement account or individual retirement annuity at the time and in the manner required by section 408(i) shall pay a penalty of $10 for each failure unless it is shown that such failure is due to reasonable cause.

"(b) Deficiency Procedures Not To Apply.—Subchapter B of chapter 63 (relating to deficiency procedures for income, estate, gift, and certain excise taxes) does not apply to the assessment or collection of any penalty imposed by subsection (a)."

(g) Conforming Amendments.—

Sec. 2001 (b)

(1) Section 37(c)(1) (defining retirement income) is amended—

(A) by striking out "and" at the end of subparagraph (D),

(B) by adding at the end of subparagraph (E) the following: "retirement bonds described in section 409, and", and

(C) by adding at the end thereof the following new paragraph:

"(F) an individual retirement account described in section 408(a) or an individual retirement annuity described in section 408(b), or".

(2) The second sentence of section 46(a)(3) and the second sentence of section 50A(a)(3), as each is amended by sections 2001(g)(2)(B) and 2005(c)(4) of this Act, are each amended by inserting after "owner-employees)," the following: "section 408(e) (relating to additional tax on income from certain retirement accounts),".

(3) The third sentence of section 901(a), as amended by section 2005(c)(5) of this Act, is amended by inserting "against the tax imposed for the taxable year by section 408(f) (relating to additional tax on income from certain retirement accounts)," before "against the tax imposed by section 531".

(4) Subparagraph (A) of section 56(a)(2) and paragraph (1) of section 56(c) are each amended by striking out "531" and inserting in lieu thereof "408(f), 531,".

* * *

(7) Section 3401(a)(12) (relating to exemption from collection of income tax at source on certain wages) is amended by adding at the end thereof the following new subparagraph:

"(D) for a payment described in section 219(a) if, at the time of such payment, it is reasonable to believe that the employee will be entitled to a deduction under such section for payment; or".

(8) Section 6047 (relating to information relating to certain trusts and annuity and bond purchase plans) is amended by redesignating subsection (d) as subsection (e) and by inserting after subsection (c) the following new subsection:

"(d) Other Programs. — To the extent provided by regulations prescribed by the Secretary or his delegate, the provisions of this section apply with respect to any payment described in section 219(a) and to transactions of any trust described in section 408(a) or under an individual retirement annuity described in section 408(b).".

(9) Section 805(d)(1) (relating to definition of pension plan reserves) is amended by striking out "or" at the end of subparagraph (C), by striking out "foregoing," at the end of subparagraph (D) and inserting in lieu thereof "foregoing; or", and by adding at the end thereof the following new subparagraph:

"(E) purchased under contracts entered into with trusts which (at the time the contracts were entered into) were individual retirement accounts described in section 408(a) or under contracts entered into with individual retirement annuities described in section 408(b)."

* * *

(11) Section 801(g)(7) (relating to basis of assets held for qualified pension plan contracts) is amended by striking out "or (D)" and inserting in lieu thereof "(D), or (E)".

* * *

SEC. 2003. PROHIBITED TRANSACTIONS.

* * *

(b) Amendment of Section 503.— Section 503 (relating to requirements for exemption) is amended—

(1) by striking out "or (18)" in subsection (a)(1)(A),

(2) by amending subsection (a)(1)(B) by inserting "which is referred to in section 4975(g)(2) or (3)" after "described in section 401(a)",

(3) by striking out "or section 401" in subsection (a)(2) and inserting in lieu thereof "or paragraph (1)(B)",

(4) by striking out "or section 401"

in subection (c) and inserting in lieu thereof "or subsection (a)(1)(B)", and

(5) by striking out subsection (g).

(c) Effective Date and Savings Provisions.—

(1)(A) The amendments made by this section shall take effect on January 1, 1975.

(B) If, before the amendments made by this section take effect, an organization described in section 401 (a) of the Internal Revenue Code of 1954 is denied exemption under section 501(a) of such Code by reason of section 503 of such Code, the denial of such exemption shall not apply if the disqualified person elects (in such manner and at such time as the Secretary or his delegate shall by regulations prescribe) to pay, with respect to the prohibited transaction (within the meaning of section 503 (b) or (g)) which resulted in such denial of exemption, a tax in the amount and in the manner provided with respect to the tax imposed under section 4975 of such Code. An election made under this subparagraph, once made, shall be irrevocable. The Secretary of the Treasury or his delegate shall prescribe such regulations as may be necessary to carry out the purposes of this subparagraph.

(2) Section 4975 of the Internal Revenue Code of 1954 (relating to tax on prohibited transactions) shall not apply to—

(A) a loan of money or other extension of credit between a plan and a disqualified person under a binding contract in effect on July 1, 1974 (or pursuant to renewals of such a contract), until June 30, 1984, if such loan or other extension of credit remains at least as favorable to the plan as an arm's-length transaction with an unrelated party would be, and if the execution of the contract, the making of the loan, or the extension of credit was not, at the time of such execution, making, or extension, a prohibited transaction (within the meaning of section 503(b) of such Code or the corresponding provisions of prior law);

(B) a lease or joint use of property involving the plan and a disqualified person pursuant to a binding contract in effect on July 1, 1974 (or pursuant to renewals of such a contract), until June 30, 1984, if such lease or joint use remains at least as favorable to the plan as an arm's-length transaction with an unrelated party would be and if the execution of the contract was not, at the time of such execution, a prohibited transaction (within the meaning of section 503 (b) of such Code) or the corresponding provisions of prior law;

(C) the sale, exchange, or other disposition of property described in subparagraph (B) between a plan and a disqualified person before June 30, 1984, if—

(i) in the case of a sale, exchange, or other disposition of the property by the plan to the disqualified person, the plan receives an amount which is not less than the fair market value of the property at the time of such disposition; and

(ii) in the case of the acquisition of the property by the plan, the plan pays an amount which is not in excess of the fair market value of the property at the time of such acquisition;

(D) Until June 30, 1977, the provision of services to which subparagraphs (A), (B), and (C) do not apply between a plan and a disqualified person (i) under a binding contract in effect on July 1, 1974 (or pursuant to renewals of such contract), or (ii) if the disqualified person ordinarily and customarily furnished such services on June 30, 1974, if such provision of services remains at least as favorable to the plan as an arm's-length transaction with an unrelated party would be and if the provision of services was not, at the time of such provision, a prohibited transaction (within the meaning of section 503(b) of such Code) or the corresponding provisions of prior law; or

Sec. 2003 (c)

(E) the sale, exchange, or other disposition of property which is owned by a plan on June 30, 1974, and all times thereafter, to a disqualified person, if such plan is required to dispose of such property in order to comply with the provisions of section 407(a)(2)(A) (relating to the prohibition against holding excess employer securities and employer real property) of the Employee Retirement Income Security Act of 1974, and if the plan receives not less than adequate consideration.

For the purposes of this paragraph, the term "disqualified person" has the meaning provided by Section 4975(e)(2) of the Internal Revenue Code of 1954.

SEC. 2004. LIMITATIONS ON BENEFITS AND CONTRIBUTIONS.

(a) Plan Requirements.—

* * *

*(3) Special rule for certain plans in effect on date of enactment.—*In any case in which, on the date of enactment of this Act, an individual is a participant in both a defined benefit plan and a defined contribution plan maintained by the same employer, and the sum of the defined benefit plan fraction and the defined contribution plan fraction for the year during which such date occurs exceeds 1.4, the sum of such fractions may continue to exceed 1.4 if—

(A) the defined benefit plan fraction is not increased, by amendment of the plan or otherwise, after the date of enactment of this Act, and

(B) no contributions are made under the defined contribution plan after such date.

A trust which is part of a pension, profit-sharing, or stock bonus plan described in the preceding sentence shall not be treated as not constituting a qualified trust under section 401(a) of the Internal Revenue Code of 1954 on account of the provisions of section 415(e) of such Code, as long as it is described in the preceding sentence of this subsection.

* * *

(c) Certain Annuity and Bond Purchase Plans.—

* * *

(3) Section 805(d)(1)(C) (relating to pension plan reserves) is amended by striking out "and (15)" and inserting in lieu thereof "(15), (16), and (19)".

* * *

(d) Effective Date.—

*(1) General rule.—*The amendments made by this section shall apply to years beginning after December 31, 1975. The Secretary of the Treasury shall prescribe such regulations as may be necessary to carry out the provisions of this paragraph.

*(2) Transition rule for defined benefit plans.—*In the case of an individual who was an active participant in a defined benefit plan before October 3, 1973, if—

(A) the annual benefit (within the meaning of section 415(b)(2) of the Internal Revenue Code of 1954) payable to such participant on retirement does not exceed 100 percent of his annual rate of compensation on the earlier of (i) October 2, 1973, or (ii) the date on which he separated from the service of the employer,

(B) such annual benefit is no greater than the annual benefit which would have been payable to such participant on retirement if (i) all the terms and conditions of such plan in existence on such date had remained in existence until such retirement, and (ii) his compensation taken into account for any period after October 2, 1973, had not exceeded his annual rate of compensation on such date, and

(C) in the case of a participant who separated from the service of the employer prior to October 2, 1973, such annual benefit is no greater than his vested accrued benefit as of the date he separated from the service,

then such annual benefit shall be treated as not exceeding the limitation of subsection (b) of section 415 of the Internal Revenue Code of 1954.

SEC. 2005. TAXATION OF CERTAIN LUMP SUM DISTRIBUTIONS.

* * *

(c) Conforming Amendments.—

* * *

(4) The second sentence of section 46(a)(3) and the second sentence of section 50A(a)(3) are each amended by inserting after "tax preferences)," the following: "section 402(e) (relating to tax on lump sum distributions),".

(5) The third sentence of section 901(a) is amended by inserting "against the tax imposed by section 402(e) (relating to tax on lump sum distributions)," before "against the tax imposed by section 531".

(6) Subsection 1304(b)(2) (relating to special rules) is amended by striking out paragraph (2) and by redesignating paragraphs (3), (4), (5), and (6) as paragraphs (2), (3), (4), and (5), respectively.

(7) Subparagraph (A) of section 56 (a)(2) and paragraph (1) of section 56(c) are each amended by inserting before "531" the following: "402(e),".

(8) Sections 871(b)(1) and 877(b) are each amended by inserting, "402 (e)(1)," after "section 1".

(9) Section 62 (defining adjusted gross income), is amended by inserting after paragraph (10) the following new paragraph:

"(11) *Certain portion of lump-sum distributions from pension plans taxed under section 402(e).*—The deduction allowed by section 402(e)(3)."

(10) Section 122(b)(2) (relating to consideration for the contract) is amended by striking out "72(o)" and inserting "72(n)".

* * *

(14) Section 1348(b)(1) (relating to earned income) is amended by striking out "72(n), 402(a)(2)" and inserting "402(a)(2), 402(e)".

(15) Section 101(b)(2)(B) is amended by striking out "total distributions payable (as defined in section 402(a)(3)) which are paid to a distributee within one taxable year of the distributee by reason of the employee's death" and inserting in lieu thereof "a lump sum distribution (as defined in section 402(e)(4))".

(d) Effective Date. — The amendments made by this section shall apply only with respect to distributions or payments made after December 31, 1973, in taxable years beginning after such date.

SEC. 2006. SALARY REDUCTION REGULATIONS.

(a) Inclusion of Certain Contributions in Income.—Except in the case of plans or arrangements in existence on June 27, 1974, a contribution made before January 1, 1977, to an employees' trust described in section 401(a), 403(a), or 405(a) of the Internal Revenue Code of 1954 which is exempt from tax under section 501(a) of such Code, or under an arrangement which, but for the fact that it was not in existence on June 27, 1974, would be an arrangement described in subsection (b)(2) of this section, shall be treated as a contribution made by an employee if the contribution is made under an arrangement under which the contribution will be made only if the employee elects to receive a reduction in his compensation or to forego an increase in his compensation.

(b) Administration in the Case of Certain Qualified Pension or Profit-Sharing Plans, Etc., in Existence on June 27, 1974.—No salary reduction regulations may be issued by the Secretary of the Treasury in final form before January 1, 1977, with respect to an arrangement which was in existence on June 27, 1974, and which, on that date—

(1) provided for contributions to an employees' trust described in section 401(a), 403(a), or 405(a) of the Internal Revenue Code of 1954 which is exempt from tax under section 501 (a) of such Code, or

(2) was maintained as part of an arrangement under which an employee was permitted to elect to receive part of his compensation in one or more alternative forms if one of such forms results in the inclusion of amounts in income under the Internal Revenue Code of 1954.

(c) Administration of Law with Respect to Certain Plans.—

(1) Administration in the case of plans described in subsection (b).— Until salary reduction regulations have been issued in final form, the law with respect to plans or arrangements described in subsection (b) shall be administered—

(A) without regard to the proposed salary reduction regulations (37 F.R. 25938) and without regard to any other proposed salary reduction regulations, and

(B) in the manner in which such law was administered before January 1, 1972.

*(2) Administration in the case of qualified profit-sharing plans.—*In the case of plans or arrangements described in subsection (b), in applying this section to the tax treatment of contributions to qualified profit-sharing plans where the contributed amounts are distributable only after a period of deferral, the law shall be administered in a manner consistent with—

(A) Revenue Ruling 56-497 (1956—2 C.B. 284),

(B) Revenue Ruling 63-180 (1963—2 C.B. 189), and

(C) Revenue Ruling 68-89 (1968—1 C.B. 402).

*(d) Limitation on Retroactivity of Final Regulations.—*In the case of any salary reduction regulations which become final after December 31, 1976—

(1) for purposes of chapter 1 of the Internal Revenue Code of 1954 (relating to normal taxes and surtaxes), such regulations shall not apply before January 1, 1977; and

(2) for purposes of chapter 21 of such Code (relating to Federal Insurance Contributions Act) and for purposes of chapter 24 of such Code (relating to collection of income tax at source on wages), such regulations shall not apply before the day on which such regulations are issued in final form.

*(e) Salary Reduction Regulations Defined.—*For purposes of this section, the term "salary reduction regulations" means regulations dealing with the includibility in gross income (at the time of contribution) of amounts contributed to a plan which includes a trust that qualifies under section 401(a), or a plan described in section 403(a) or 405(a), including plans or arrangements described in subsection (b)(2), if the contribution is made under an arrangement under which the contribution will be made only if the employee elects to receive a reduction in his compensation or to forego an increase in his compensation, or under an arrangement under which the employee is permitted to elect to receive part of his compensation in one or more alternative forms (if one of such forms results in the inclusion of amounts in income under the Internal Revenue Code of 1954).

SEC. 2007. RULES FOR CERTAIN NEGOTIATED PLANS.

*(a) Treatment of Certain Participants in the Plan.—*Section 404(c) (relating to certain negotiated plans) is amended by inserting after the first sentence the following new sentences: "For purposes of this chapter and subtitle B, in the case of any individual who before July 1, 1974, was a participant in a plan described in the preceding sentence—

"(A) such individual, if he is or was an employee within the meaning of section 401(c)(1), shall be treated (with respect to service covered by the plan as being an employee other than an employee within the meaning of section 401(c)(1) and as being an employee of a participating employer under the plan,

"(B) earnings derived from service covered by the plan shall be treated as not being earned income within the meaning of section 401(c)(2), and

"(C) such individual shall be treated as an employee of a participating employer under the plan with respect to service before July 1, 1975, covered by the plan.

Section 277 (relating to deductions incurred by certain membership organizations in transactions with members) does not apply to any trust described in this subsection."

(b) Other Amendments to Section 404(c)(1).—

(1) Paragraph (1) of the first sentence of section 404(c) is amended by striking out "and pensions" and inserting in lieu thereof "or pensions".

(2) The last sentence of section 404(c) is amended by striking out "This subsection" and inserting in lieu thereof "The first and third sentences of this subsection".

(c) Effective Date. — The amendments made by this section shall apply to taxable years ending on or after June 30, 1972.

SEC. 2008. CERTAIN ARMED FORCES SURVIVOR ANNUITIES.

(a) In General.—Section 122(a) (relating to certain reduced uniformed services retired pay) is amended to read as follows:

"*(a) General rule.*—In the case of a member or former member of the uniformed services of the United States, gross income does not include the amount of any reduction in his retired or retainer pay pursuant to the provisions of chapter 73 of title 10, United States Code.".

(b) Technical Amendments.—

(1) Section 122(b)(2) is amended by striking out "section 1438" in subparagraph (B) and inserting in lieu thereof "section 1438 or 1452(d)".

(2) Section 72(o) is amended by inserting after "Plan" in the heading of such section "or Survivor Benefit Plan".

(3) Section 101(b)(2)(D) is amended by striking out "if the individual who made the election under such chapter" and inserting in lieu thereof "if the member or former member of the uniformed services by reason of whose death such annuity is payable".

(4) Section 2039(c) is amended by striking out "section 1438" in the last sentence and inserting in lieu thereof "section 1438, or 1452(d)".

(c) Effective Dates. — The amendments made by this section apply to taxable years ending on or after September 21, 1972. The amendments made by paragraphs (3) and (4) of subsection (b) apply with respect to individuals dying on or after such date.

Title III—Jurisdiction, Administration, Enforcement; Joint Pension Task Force, Etc.

Subtitle A—Jurisdiction, Administration, and Enforcement

Procedures in Connection with the Issuance of Certain Determination Letters by The Secretary of the Treasury

Sec. 3001. (a) Before issuing an advance determination of whether a pension, profit-sharing, or stock bonus plan, a trust which is a part of such a plan, or an annuity or bond purchase plan meets the requirements of part I of subchapter D of chapter 1 of the Internal Revenue Code of 1954, the Secretary of the Treasury shall require the person applying for the determination to provide, in addition to any material and information necessary for such determination, such other material and information as may reasonably be made available at the time such application is made as the Secretary of Labor may require under title I of this Act for the administration of that title. The Secretary of the Treasury shall also require that the applicant provide evidence satisfactory to the Secretary that the applicant has notified each employee who qualifies as an interested party (within the meaning of regulations prescribed under section 7476(b)(1) of such Code (relating to declaratory judgments in connection with the qualification of certain retirement plans)) of the application for a determination.

(b) (1) Whenever an application is made to the Secretary of the Treasury for a determination of whether a pension, profit-sharing, or stock bonus plan, a trust which is a part of such a plan, or an annuity or bond purchase plan meets the requirements of part I of subchapter D of chapter 1 of the Internal Revenue Code of 1954, the Secretary shall upon request afford an opportunity to comment on the application at any time within 45 days after receipt thereof to—

(A) any employee or class of employee qualifying as an interested party within the meaning of the regulations referred to in subsection (a).

(B) the Secretary of Labor, and

(C) the Pension Benefit Guaranty Corporation.

(2) The Secretary of Labor may not request an opportunity to comment upon such an application unless he has been requested in writing to do so by the Pension Benefit Guaranty Corporation or by the lesser of—

(A) 10 employees, or

(B) 10 percent of the employees who qualify as interested parties within the meaning of the regulations referred to in subsection (a). Upon receiving such a request, the Secretary of Labor shall furnish a copy of the request to the Secretary of the Treasury within 5 days (excluding Saturdays, Sundays, and legal public holidays (as set forth in section 6103 of title 5, United States Code)).

(3) Upon receiving such a request from the Secretary of Labor, the Secretary of the Treasury shall furnish to the Secretary of Labor such infor-

mation held by the Secretary of the Treasury relating to the application as the Secretary of Labor may request.

(4) The Secretary of Labor shall, within 30 days after receiving a request from the Pension Benefit Guaranty Corporation of from the necessary number of employees who qualify as interested parties, notify the Secretary of the Treasury, the Pension Benefit Guaranty Corporation, and such employees with respect to whether he is going to comment on the application to which the request relates and with respect to any matters raised in such request on which he is not going to comment. If the Sceretary of Labor indicates in the notice required under the preceding sentence that he is not going to comment on all or part of the matters raised in such request, the Secretary of the Treasury shall afford the corporations, and such employees, an opportunity to comment on the application with respect to any matter on which the Secretary of Labor has declined to comment.

(c) The Pension Benefit Guaranty Corporation and, upon petition of a group of employees referred to in subsection (b)(2), the Secretary of Labor, may intervene in any action brought for declaratory judgment under section 7476 of the Internal Revenue Code of 1954 in accordance with the provisions of such section. The Pension Benefit Guaranty Corporation is permitted to bring an action under such section 7476 under such rules as may be prescribed by the United States Tax Court.

(d) If the Secretary of the Treasury determines that a plan or trust to which this section applies meets the applicable requirements of part I of subchapter D of chapter 1 of the Internal Revenue Code of 1954 and issues a determination letter to the applicant, the Secretary shall notify the Secretary of Labor of his determination and furnish such information and material relating to the application and determination held by the Secretary of the Treasury as the Secretary of Labor may request for the proper administration of title I of this Act. The Secretary of Labor shall accept the determination of the Secretary of the Treasury as prima facie evidence of initial compliance by the plan with the standards of parts 2, 3, and 4 of subtitle B of title I of this Act. If an application for such a determination is withdrawn, or if the Secretary of the Treasury issues a determination that the plan or trust does not meet the requirements of such part I, the Secretary shall notify the Secretary of Labor of the withdrawal or determination.

(e) This section does not apply with respect to an application for any plan received by the Secretary of the Treasury before the date on which section 410 of the Internal Revenue Code of 1954 applies to the plan, or on which such section will apply if the plan is determined by the Secretary to be a qualified plan.

Procedures with Respect to Continued Compliance with Requirements Relating to Participation, Vesting, and Funding Standards

Sec. 3002. (a) In carrying out the provisions of part I of subchapter D of chapter 1 of the Internal Revenue Code of 1954 with respect to whether a plan or a trust meets the requirements of section 410(a) or 411 of such Code (relating to minimum participation standards and minimum vesting standards, respectively), the Secretary of the Treasury shall notify the Secretary of Labor when the Secretary of the Treasury issues a preliminary notice of intent to disqualify related to the plan or trust or, if earlier, at the time of commencing any proceeding to determine whether the plan or trust satisfies such requirements. Unless the Secretary of the Treasury finds that the collection of a tax imposed under the Internal Revenue Code of 1954 is in jeopardy, the Secretary of the Treasury shall

Sec. 3001 (b) (4)

not issue a determination that the plan or trust does not satisfy the requirements of such section until the expiration of a period of 60 days after the date on which he notifies the Secretary of Labor of such review. The Secretary of the Treasury, in his discretion, may extend the 60-day period referred to in the preceding sentence if he determines that such an extension would enable the Secretary of Labor to obtain compliance with such requirements by the plan within the extension period. Except as otherwise provided in this Act, the Secretary of Labor shall not generally apply part 2 of title I of this Act to any plan or trust subject to sections 410(a) and 411 of such Code, but shall refer alleged general violations of the vesting or participation standards to the Secretary of the Treasury. (The preceding sentence shall not apply to matters relating to individuals benefits.)

(b) Unless the Secretary of the Treasury finds that the collection of a tax is in jeopardy, in carrying out the provisions of section 4971 of the Internal Revenue Code of 1954 (relating to taxes on the failure to meet minimum funding standards), the Secretary of the Treasury shall notify the Secretary of Labor before sending a notice of deficiency with respect to any tax imposed under that section on an employer and, in accordance with the provisions of subsection (d) of that section, afford the Secretary of Labor an opportunity to comment on the imposition of the tax in the case. The Secretary of the Treasury may waive the imposition of the tax imposed under section 4971 (b) of such Code in appropriate cases. Upon receiving a written request from the Secretary of Labor or from the Pension Benefit Guaranty Corporation, the Secretary of the Treasury shall cause an investigation to be commenced expeditiously with respect to whether the tax imposed under section 4971 of such Code should be applied with respect to any employer to which the request relates. The Secretary of the Treasury and the Secretary of Labor shall consult with each other from time to time with respect to the provisions of section 412 of the Internal Revenue Code of 1954 (relating to minimum funding standards) and with respect to the funding standards applicable under title I of this Act in order to coordinate the rules applicable under such standards.

(c) Regulations prescribed by the Secretary of the Treasury under sections 410(a), 411, and 412 of the Internal Revenue Code of 1954 (relating to minimum participation standards, minimum vesting standards, and minimum funding standards, respectively) shall also apply to the minimum participation, vesting, and funding standards set forth in parts 2 and 3 of subtitle B of title I of this Act. Except as otherwise expressly provided in this Act, the Secretary of Labor shall not prescribe other regulations under such parts, or apply the regulations prescribed by the Secretary of the Treasury under sections 410(a), 411, 412 of the Internal Revenue Code of 1954 and applicable to the minimum participation, vesting, and funding standards under such parts in a manner inconsistent with the way such regulations apply under sections 410(a), 411, and 412 of such Code.

(d) The Secretary of Labor and the Pension Benefit Guaranty Corporation, before filing briefs in any case involving the construction or application of minimum participation standards, minimum vesting standards, or minimum funding standards under title I of this Act, shall afford the Secretary of the Treasury a reasonable opportunity to review any such brief. The Secretary of the Treasury shall have the right to intervene in any such case.

(e) The Secretary of the Treasury shall consult with the Pension Benefit Guaranty Corporation with respect to any proposed or final regulation au-

Sec. 3002 (e)

thorized by subpart C of part I of subchapter D of chapter 1 of the Internal Revenue Code of 1954, or by sections 4241 through 4245 of this Act, before publishing any such proposed or final regulation.

Procedures in Connection with Prohibited Transactions

Sec. 3003. (a) Unless the Secretary of the Treasury finds that the collection of a tax is in jeopardy, in carrying out the provisions of section 4975 of the Internal Revenue Code of 1954 (relating to tax on prohibited transactions) the Secretary of the Treasury shall, in accordance with the provisions of subsection (h) of such section, notify the Secretary of Labor before sending a notice of deficiency with respect to the tax imposed by subsection (a) or (b) of such section, and, in accordance with the provisions of subsection (h) of such section, afford the Secretary an opportunity to comment on the imposition of the tax in any case. The Secretary of the Treasury shall have authority to waive the imposition of the tax imposed under section 4975(b) in appropriate cases. Upon receiving a written request from the Secretary of Labor or from the Pension Benefit Guaranty Corporation, the Secretary of the Treasury shall cause an investigation to be carried out with respect to whether the tax imposed by section 4975 of such Code should be applied to any person referred to in the request.

(b) The Secretary of the Treasury and the Secretary of Labor shall consult with each other from time to time with respect to the provisions of section 4975 of the Internal Revenue Code of 1954 (relating to tax on prohibited transactions) and with respect to the provisions of title I of this Act relating to prohibited transactions and exemptions therefrom in order to coordinate the rules applicable under such standards.

(c) Whenever the Secretary of Labor obtains information indicating that a party-in-interest or disqualified person is violating section 406 of this Act, he shall transmit such information to the Secretary of the Treasury.

Coordination Between the Department of the Treasury and the Department of Labor

Sec. 3004. (a) Whenever in this Act or in any provision of law amended by this Act the Secretary of the Treasury and the Secretary of Labor are required to carry out provisions relating to the same subject matter (as determined by them) they shall consult with each other and shall develop rules, regulations, practices, and forms which, to the extent appropriate for the efficient administration of such provisions, are designed to reduce duplication of effort, duplication of reporting, conflicting or overlapping requirements, and the burden of compliance with such provisions by plan administrators, employers, and participants and beneficiaries.

(b) In order to avoid unnecessary expense and duplication of functions among Government agencies, the Secretary of the Treasury and the Secretary of Labor may make such arrangements or agreements for cooperation or mutual assistance in the performance of their functions under this Act, and the functions of any such agency as they find to be practicable and consistent with law. The Secretary of the Treasury and the Secretary of Labor may utilize, on a reimbursable or other basis, the facilities or services, of any department, agency, or establishment of the United States or of any State or political subdivision of a State, including the services, of any of its employees, with the lawful consent of such department, agency, or establishment; and each department, agency, or establishment of the United States is authorized and directed to cooperate with the Secretary of the Treasury and the Secretary of Labor and, to the extent permitted by law, to provide such information and facilities as they may request for their assistance in the performance of their functions under this Act. The Attorney General or his representative shall receive from the Secretary of the Treasury and the Secretary of Labor for appropriate action such evidence developed in the performance of their functions under this Act as may be found to warrant consideration for criminal prosecution under the provisions of this title or other Federal law.

Subtitle B—Joint Pension Task Force; Studies

PART 1—JOINT PENSION TASK FORCE

Establishment

Sec. 3021. The staffs of the Committee on Ways and Means and the Committee on Education and Labor of the House of Representatives, the Joint Committee on Internal Revenue Taxation, and the Committee on Finance and the Committee on Labor and Public Welfare of the Senate shall carry out the duties assigned under this title to the Joint Pension Task Force. By agreement among the chairmen of such Committees, the Joint Pension Task Force shall be furnished with office space, clerical personnel, and such supplies and equipment as may be necessary for the Joint Pension Task Force to carry out its duties under this title.

Duties

Sec. 3022. (a) The Joint Pension Task Force shall, within 24 months after the date of enactment of this Act, make a full study and review of—
(1) the effect of the requirements of section 411 of the Internal Revenue Code of 1954 and of section 203 of this Act to determine the extent of discrimination, if any, among employees in various age groups resulting from the application of such requirements;

(2) means of providing for the portability of pension rights among different pension plans;
(3) the appropriate treatment under title IV of this Act (relating to termination insurance) of plans established and maintained by small employers;
(4) the effects and desirability of the Federal preemption of State and local law with respect to matters relating to pension and similar plans; and
(5) such other matter as any of the committees referred to in section 3021 may refer to it.

(b) The Joint Pension Task Force shall report the results of its study and review to each of the committees referred to in section 3021.

PART 2—OTHER STUDIES

Congressional Study

Sec. 3031. (a) The Committee on Education and Labor and the Committee on Ways and Means of the House of Representatives and the Committee on Finance and the Committee on Labor and Public Welfare of the Senate shall study retirement plans established and maintained or financed (directly or indirectly) by the Government of the United States, by any State (including the District of Columbia) or political subdivision thereof, or by any agency or instrumentality of any of the foregoing. Such study shall include an analysis of—

(1) the adequacy of existing levels of participation, vesting, and financing arrangements,
(2) existing fiduciary standards, and
(3) the necessity for Federal legislation and standards with respect to such plans.

In determining whether any such plan is adequately financed, each committee shall consider the necessity for minimum funding standards, as well as the taxing power of the government maintaining the plan.

Sec. 3031 (a) (3)

(b) Not later than December 31, 1976, the Committee on Education and Labor and the Committee on Ways and Means shall each submit to the House of Representatives the results of the studies conducted under this section, together with such recommendations as they deem appropriate. The Committee on Finance and the Committee on Labor and Public Welfare shall each submit to the Senate the results of the studies conducted under this section together with such recommendations as they deem appropriate not later than such date.

Protection for Employees under Federal Procurement, Construction, and Research Contracts and Grants

Sec. 3032. (a) The Secretary of Labor shall, during the 2-year period beginning on the date of the enactment of this Act, conduct a full and complete study and investigation of the steps necessary to be taken to insure that professional, scientific, and technical personnel and others working in associated occupations employed under Federal procurement, construction, or research contracts or grants will, to the extent feasible, be protected against forfeitures of pension or retirement rights or benefits, otherwise provided, as a consequence of job transfers or loss of employment resulting from terminations or modifications of Federal contracts, grants, or procurement policies. The Secretary of Labor shall report the results of his study and investigation to the Congress within 2 years after the date of the enactment of this Act. The Secretary of Labor is authorized, to the extent provided by law, to obtain the services of private research institutions and such other persons by contract or other arrangement as he determines necessary in carrying out the provisions of this section.

(b) In the course of conducting the study and investigation described in subsection (a), and in developing the regulations referred to in subsection (c), the Secretary of Labor shall consult—

(1) with appropriate professional societies, business organizations, and labor organizations, and

(2) with the heads of interested Federal departments and agencies.

(c) Within 1 year after the date on which he submits his report to the Congress under subsection (a), the Secretary of Labor shall, if he determines it to be feasible, develop regulations which will provide the protection of pension and retirement rights and benefits referred to in subsection (a).

(d)(1) Any regulations developed pursuant to subsection (c) shall take effect if, and only if—

(A) the Secretary of Labor, not later than the day which is 3 years after the date of the enactment of this Act, delivers a copy of such regulations to the House of Representatives and a copy to the Senate, and

(B) before the close of the 120-day period which begins on the day on which the copies of such regulations are delivered to the House of Representatives and to the Senate, neither the House of Representatives nor the Senate adopts, by an affirmative vote of a majority of those present and voting in that House, a resolution of disapproval.

(2) For purposes of this subsection, the term "resolution of disapproval" means only a resolution of either House of Congress, the matter after the resolving clause of which is as follows: "That the —— does not favor the taking effect of the regulations transmitted to the Congress by the Secretary of Labor on ——", the first blank space therein being filled with the name of the resolving House and the second blank space therein being filled with the day and year.

(3) A resolution of disapproval in the House of Representatives shall be referred to the Committee on Education and Labor. A resolution of disapproval in the Senate shall be re-

Sec. 3031 (b)

ferred to the Committee on Labor and Public Welfare.

(4) (A) If the committee to which a resolution of disapproval has been referred has not reported it at the end of 7 calendar days after its introduction, it is in order to move either to discharge the committee from further consideration of the resolution or to discharge the committee from further consideration of any other resolution of disapproval which has been referred to the committee.

(B) A motion to discharge may be made only by an individual favoring the resolution, is highly privileged (except that it may not be made after the committee has reported a resolution of disapproval), and debate thereon shall be limited to not more than 1 hour, to be divided equally between those favoring and those opposing the resolution. An amendment to the motion is not in order, and it is not in order to move to reconsider the vote by which the motion is agreed to or disagreed to.

(C) If the motion to discharge is agreed to or disagreed to, the motion may not be renewed, nor may another motion to discharge the committee be made with respect to any other resolution of disapproval.

(5) (A) When the committee has reported, or has been discharged from further consideration of, a resolution of disapproval, it is at any time thereafter in order (even though a previous motion to the same effect has been disagreed to) to move to proceed to the consideration of the resolution. The motion is highly privileged and is not debatable. An amendment to the motion is not in order, and it is not in order to move to reconsider the vote by which the motion is agreed to or disagreed to.

(B) Debate on the resolution of disapproval shall be limited to not more than 10 hours, which shall be divided equally between those favoring and those opposing the resolution. A motion further to limit debate is not debatable. An amendment to, or motion to recommit, the resolution is not in order, and it is not in order to move to reconsider the vote by which the resolution is agreed to or disagreed to.

(6) (A) Motions to postpone, made with respect to the discharge from committee or the consideration of a resolution of disapproval, and motions to proceed to the consideration of other business, shall be decided without debate.

(B) Appeals from the decisions of the Chair relating to the application of the rules of the House of Representatives or the Senate, as the case may be, to the procedure relating to any resolution of disapproval shall be decided without debate.

(7) Whenever the Secretary of Labor transmits copies of the regulations to the Congress, a copy of such regulations shall be delivered to each House of Congress on the same day and shall be delivered to the Clerk of the House of Representatives if the House is not in session and to the Secretary of the Senate if the Senate is not in session.

(8) The 120 day period referred to in paragraph (1) shall be computed by excluding—

(A) the days on which either House is not in session because of an adjournment of more than 3 days to a day certain or an adjournment of the Congress sine die, and

(B) any Saturday and Sunday, not excluded under subparagraph (A), when either House is not in session.

(9) This subsection is enacted by the Congress—

(A) as an exercise of the rulemaking power of the House of Representatives and the Senate, respectively, and as such they are deemed a part of the rules of each House, respectively, but applicable only with respect to the procedure to be followed in that House in the case of resolutions of disapproval described in paragraph (2); and they supersede other rules only to the extent that they are inconsistent therewith; and

Sec. 3032 (d) (9)

(B) with full recognition of the constitutional right of either House to change the rules (so far as relating to the procedure of that House) at any time, in the same manner and to the same extent as in the case of any other rule of that House.

Subtitle C—Enrollment of Actuaries

Establishment of Joint Board for the Enrollment of Actuaries

Sec. 3041. The Secretary of Labor and the Secretary of the Treasury shall, not later than the last day of the first calendar month beginning after the date of the enactment of this Act, establish a Joint Board for the Enrollment of Actuaries (hereinafter in this part referred to as the "Joint Board").

Enrollment by Joint Board

Sec. 3042. (a) The Joint Board shall, by regulations, establish reasonable standards and qualifications for persons performing actuarial services with respect to plans in which this Act applies and, upon application by any individual, shall enroll such individual if the Joint Board finds that such individual satisfies such standards and qualifications. With respect to individuals applying for enrollment before January 1, 1976, such standards and qualifications shall include a requirement for an appropriate period of responsible actuarial experience relating to pension plans. With respect to individuals applying for enrollment on or after January 1, 1976, such standards and qualifications shall include—

(1) education and training in actuarial mathematics and methodology, as evidenced by—

(A) a degree in actuarial mathematics or its equivalent from an accredited college or university,

(B) successful completion of an examination in actuarial mathematics and methodology to be given by the Joint Board, or

(C) successful completion of other actuarial examinations deemed adequate by the Joint Board, and

(2) an appropriate period of responsible actuarial experience. Notwithstanding the preceding provisions of this subsection, the Joint Board may provide for the temporary enrollment for the period ending on January 1, 1976, of actuaries under such interim standards as it deems adequate.

(b) The Joint Board may, after notice and an opportunity for a hearing, suspend or terminate the enrollment of an individual under this section if the Joint Board finds that such individual—

(1) has failed to discharge his duties under this Act, or

(2) does not satisfy the requirements for enrollment as in effect at the time of his enrollment.

The Joint Board may also, after notice and opportunity for hearing, suspend or terminate the temporary enrollment of an individual who fails to discharge his duties under this Act or who does not satisfy the interim enrollment standards.

Amendment of Internal Revenue Code

Sec. 3043. Section 7701(a) of the Internal Revenue Code of 1954 (relating to definitions) is amended by adding at the end thereof the following new paragraph:

"(35) **Enrolled actuary.**—The term 'enrolled actuary' means a person who is enrolled by the Joint Board for the Enrollment of Actuaries established under subtitle C of the title III of the Employee Retirement Income Security Act of 1974."

Sec. 3032 (d) (9) (B)

Title IV—Plan Termination Insurance

Subtitle A—Pension Benefit Guaranty Corporation

Definitions

Sec. 4001. (a) For purposes of this title, the term—

(1) "administrator" means the person or persons described in paragraph (16) of section 3 of this Act;

(2) "substantial employer" means for any plan year an employer (treating employers who are members of the same affiliated group, within the meaning of section 1563(a) of the Internal Revenue Code of 1954, determined without regard to section 1563(a)(4) and (e)(3)(C) of such Code, as one employer) who has made contributions to or under a plan under which more than one employer (other than a multiemployer plan) makes contributions for each of—

(A) the two immediately preceding plan years, or

(B) the second and third preceding plan years, equaling or exceeding 10 percent of all employer contributions said to or under that plan for each such year;

(3) "multiemployer plan" means a plan—

(A) to which more than one employer is required to contribute,

(B) which is maintained pursuant to one or more collective bargaining agreements between one or more employee organizations and more than one employer, and

(C) which satisfies such other requirements as the Secretary of Labor may prescribe by regulation,
except that, in applying this paragraph—

(i) a plan shall be considered a multiemployer plan on and after its termination date if the plan was a multiemployer plan under this paragraph for the plan year preceding such termination, and

(ii) for any plan year which began before the date of the enactment of the Multiemployer Pension Plan Amendments Act of 1980, the term "multiemployer plan" means a plan described in section 414(f) of the Internal Revenue Code of 1954 as in effect immediately before such date;

(4) "corporation", except where the context clearly requires otherwise, means the Pension Benefit Guaranty Corporation established under section 4002;

(5) "fund" means the appropriate fund established under section 4005;

(6) "basic benefits" means benefits guaranteed under section 4022 (other than under section 4022(c)), or under section 4022A (other than under section 4022A(g));

(7) "non-basic benefits" means benefits guaranteed under section 4022(c) or 4022A(g);

(8) "nonforfeitable benefit" means, with respect to a plan, a benefit for which a participant has satisfied the conditions for entitlement under the plan or the requirements of this Act (other than submission of a formal application, retirement, completion of a required waiting period, or death in the case of a benefit which returns all or a portion of a participant's accumulated mandatory employee contributions upon the participant's death), whether or not the benefit may subsequently be reduced or suspended by a plan amendment, an occurrence of any condition, or operation of this Act or the Internal Revenue Code of 1954;

(9) "reorganization index" means

the amount determined under section 4241(b);

(10) "plan sponsor" means, with respect to a multiemployer plan—

(A) the plan's joint board of trustees, or

(B) if the plan has no joint board of trustees, the plan administrator;

(11) "contribution base unit" means a unit with respect to which an employer has an obligation to contribute under a multiemployer plan, as defined in regulations prescribed by the Secretary of the Treasury; and

(12) "outstanding claim for withdrawal liability" means a plan's claim for the unpaid balance of the liability determined under part 1 of subtitle E for which demand has been made, valued in accordance with regulations prescribed by the corporation.

[Editor's Note: In early stages of deliberations over MPPAA, Congress redesignated Sec. 4001(b) as 4001(c) and inserted a new Sec. 4001(b). That section was later deleted.]

(c)(1) An individual who owns the entire interest in an unincorporated trade or business is treated as his own employer, and a partnership is treated as the employer of each partner who is an employee within the meaning of section 401(c)(1) of the Internal Revenue Code of 1954. For purposes of this title, under regulations prescribed by the corporation, all employees of trades or businesses (whether or not incorporated) which are under common control shall be treated as employed by a single employer and all such trades and businesses as a single employer. The regulations prescribed under the preceding sentence shall be consistent and coextensive with regulations prescribed for similar purposes by the Secretary of the Treasury under section 414(c) of the Internal Revenue Code of 1954.

(2) For purposes of this title, "single-employer plan" means, except as otherwise specifically provided in this title, any plan which is not a multiemployer plan.

(3) For purposes of this title, except as otherwise provided in this title, contributions or other payments shall be considered made under a plan for a plan year if they are made within the period prescribed under section 412(c)(10) of the Internal Revenue Code of 1954.

(4) For purposes of subtitle E, "Secretary of the Treasury" means the Secretary of the Treasury or such Secretary's delegate.

Pension Benefit Guaranty Corporation

Sec. 4002. (a) There is established within the Department of Labor a body corporate to be known as the Pension Benefit Guaranty Corporation. In carrying out its functions under this title, the corporation shall be administered by the chairman of the board of directors in accordance with policies established by the board. The purposes of this title, which are to be carried out by the corporation, are—

(1) to encourage the continuation and maintenance of voluntary private pension plans for the benefit of their participants,

(2) to provide for the timely and uninterrupted payment of pension benefits to participants and beneficiaries under plans to which this title applies, and

(3) to maintain premiums established by the corporation under section 4006 at the lowest level consistent with carrying out its obligations under this title.

(b) To carry out the purposes of this title, the corporation has the powers conferred on a nonprofit corporation under the District of Columbia Nonprofit Corporation Act and, in addition to any specific power granted to the corporation elsewhere in this title or under that Act, the corporation has the power—

(1) to sue and be sued, complain and defend, in its corporate name and through its own counsel, in any court, State or Federal;

Sec. 4001 (a) (10)

(2) to adopt, alter, and use a corporate seal, which shall be judicially noticed;

(3) to adopt, amend, and repeal, by the board of directors, bylaws, rules, and regulations relating to the conduct of its business and the exercise of all other rights and powers granted to it by this Act and such other bylaws, rules and regulations as may be necessary to carry out the purposes of this title;

(4) to conduct its business (including the carrying on of operations and the maintenance of offices) and to exercise all other rights and powers granted to it by this Act in any State or other jurisdiction without regard to qualification, licensing, or other requirements imposed by law in such State or other jurisdiction;

(5) to lease, purchase, accept gifts or donations of, or otherwise to acquire, to own, hold, improve, use, or otherwise deal in or with, and to sell, convey, mortgage, pledge, lease, exchange, or otherwise dispose of, any property, real, personal, or mixed, or any interest therein wherever situated;

(6) to appoint and fix the compensation of such officers, attorneys, employees, and agents as may be required, to determine their qualifications, to define their duties, and, to the extent desired by the corporation, require bonds for them and fix the penalty thereof, and to appoint and fix the compensation of experts and consultants in accordance with the provisions of section 3109 of title 5, United States Code;

(7) to utilize the personnel and facilities of any other agency or department of the United States Government, with or without reimbursement, and the consent of the head of such agency or department; and

(8) to enter into contracts, to execute instruments, to incur liabilities, and to do any and all other acts and things as may be necessary or incidental to the conduct of its business and the exercise of all other rights and powers granted to the corporation by this Act.

(c) The board of directors of the corporation consists of the Secretary of the Treasury, the Secretary of Labor, and the Secretary of Commerce. Members of the board shall serve without compensation, but shall be reimbursed for travel, subsistence, and other necessary expenses incurred in the performance of their duties as members of the board. The Secretary of Labor is the chairman of the board of directors.

(d) The board of directors shall meet at the call of its chairman, or as otherwise provided by the bylaws of the corporation.

(e) As soon as practicable, but not later than 180 days after the date of enactment of this Act, the board of directors shall adopt initial bylaws and rules relating to the conduct of the business of the corporation. Thereafter, the board of directors may alter, supplement, or repeal any existing bylaw or rule, and may adopt additional bylaws and rules from time to time as may be necessary. The chairman of the board shall cause a copy of the bylaws of the corporation to be published in the Federal Register not less often than once each year.

(f)(1) The corporation, its property, its franchise, capital, reserves, surplus, and its income (including, but not limited to, any income of any fund established under section 4005), shall be exempt from all taxation now or hereafter imposed by the United States (other than taxes imposed under chapter 21 of Title 26, relating to Federal Insurance Contributions Act and chapter 23 of Title 26, relating to Federal Unemployment Tax Act) or by any State or local taxing authority, except that any real property and any tangible personal property (other than cash and securities) of the corporation shall be subject to State and local taxation to the same extent according to its value as other real and tangible personal property is taxed.

(2) The receipts and disbursements of the corporation in the discharge of its functions shall be included in the totals of the budget of the United States Government. The United States is not liable for any obligation or liability incurred by the corporation.

(g)(1) There is established an advisory committee to the corporation, for the purpose of advising the corporation as to its policies and procedures relating to (A) the appointment of trustees in termination proceedings, (B) investment of moneys, (C) whether plans being terminated should be liquidated immediately or continued in operation under a trustee, and (D) such other issues as the corporation may request from time to time. The advisory committee may also recommend persons for appointment as trustees in termination proceedings, make recommendations with respect to the investment of moneys in the funds, and advise the corporation as to whether a plan subject to being terminated should be liquidated immediately or continued in operation under a trustee.

(2) The advisory committee consists of seven members appointed, from among individuals recommended by the board of directors, by the President. Of the seven members, two shall represent the interests of employee organizations, two shall represent the interests of employers who maintain pension plans, and three shall represent the interests of the general public. The president shall designate one member as chairman at the time of the appointment of that member.

(3) Members shall serve for terms of 3 years each, except that, of the members first appointed, one of the members representing the interests of employee organizations, one of the members representing the interests of employers, and one of the members representing the interests of the general public shall be appointed for terms of 2 years each, one of the members representing the interests of the general public shall be appointed for a term of 1 year, and the other members shall be appointed to full-3-year terms. The advisory committee shall meet at least six times each year and at such other times as may be determined by the chairman or requested by any three members of the advisory committee.

(4) Members shall be chosen on the basis of their experience with employee organizations, with employers who maintain pension plans, with the administration of pension plans, or otherwise on account of outstanding demonstrated ability in related fields. Of the members serving on the advisory committee at any time, no more than four shall be affiliated with the same political party.

(5) An individual appointed to fill a vacancy occurring other than by the expiration of a term of office shall be appointed only for the unexpired term of the member he succeeds. Any vacancy occurring in the office of a member of the advisory committee shall be filled in the manner in which that office was originally filled.

(6) The advisory committee shall appoint and fix the compensation of such employees as it determines necessary to discharge its duties, including experts and consultants in accordance with the provisions of section 3109 of title 5, United States Code. The corporation shall furnish to the advisory committee such professional, secretarial, and other services as the committee may request.

(7) Members of the advisory committee shall, for each day (including traveltime) during which they are attending meetings or conferences of the committee or otherwise

Sec. 4002 (f) (2)

engaged in the business of the committee, be compensated at a rate fixed by the corporation which is not in excess of the daily equivalent of the annual rate of basic pay in effect for grade GS-18 of the General Schedule, and while away from their homes or regular places of business they may be allowed travel expenses, including per diem in lieu of subsistence, as authorized by section 5703 of title 5, United States Code.

(8) The Federal Advisory Committee Act does not apply to the advisory committee established by this subsection.

Investigatory Authority; Cooperation With Other Agencies; Civil Actions

Sec. 4003. (a) The corporation may make such investigations as it deems necessary to enforce any provision of this title or any rule or regulation thereunder, and may require or permit any person to file with it a statement in writing under oath or otherwise as the corporation shall determine, as to all the facts and circumstances concerning the matter to be investigated.

(b) For the purpose of any such investigation, or any other proceeding under this title, any member of the board of directors of the corporation, or any officer designated by the chairman, may administer oaths and affirmations, subpena witnesses, compel their attendance, take evidence, and require the production of any books, papers, correspondence, memoranda, or other records which the corporation deems relevant or material to the inquiry.

(c) In case of contumacy by, or refusal to obey a subpena issued to, any person, the corporation may invoke the aid of any court of the United States within the jurisdiction of which such investigation or proceeding is carried on, or where such person resides or carries on business, in requiring the attendance and testimony of witnesses and the production of books, papers, correspondence, memoranda, and other records. The court may issue an order requiring such person to appear before the corporation, or member or officer designated by the corporation, and to produce records or to give testimony related to the matter under investigation or in question. Any failure to obey such order of the court may be punished by the court as a contempt thereof. All process in any such case may be served in the judicial district in which such person is an inhabitant or may be found.

(d) In order to avoid unnecessary expense and duplication of functions among government agencies, the corporation may make such arrangements or agreements for cooperation or mutual assistance in the performance of its functions under this title as is practicable and consistent with law. The corporation may utilize the facilities or services any department, agency, or establishment of the United States or of any State or political subdivision of a State, including the services of any of its employees, with the lawful consent of such department, agency, or establishment. The head of each department, agency, or establishment of the United States shall cooperate with the corporation and, to the extent permitted by law, provide such information and facilities as it may request for its assistance in the performance of its functions under this title. The Attorney General or his representative shall receive from the corporation for appropriate action such evidence developed in the performance of its functions under this title as may be found to warrant consideration for criminal prosecution under the provisions of this or any other Federal law.

(e)(1) Civil actions may be brought by the corporation for appropriate relief, legal or equitable or both, to enforce the provisions of this title.

(2) Except as otherwise provided in this title, where such an action is brought in a district court of the United States, it may be brought in the district where the plan is ad-

Sec. 4003 (e)

ministered, where the violation took place, or where a defendant resides or may be found, and process may be served in any other district where a defendant resides or may be found.

(3) The district courts of the United States shall have jurisdiction of actions brought by the corporation under this title without regard to the amount in controversy in any such action.

(4) Upon application by the corporation to a court of the United States for expedited handling of any case in which the corporation is a party, it is the duty of that court to assign such case for hearing at the earliest practical date and to cause such case to be in every way expedited.

(5) In any action brought under this title, whether to collect premiums, penalties, and interest under section 4007 or for any other purpose, the court may award to the corporation all or a portion of the costs of litigation incurred by the corporation in connection with such action.

(f) Except as provided in section 4301(a)(2), any participant, beneficiary, plan administrator, or employee adversely affected by any action of the corporation, or by a receiver or trustee appointed by the corporation, with respect to a plan in which such participant, beneficiary, plan administrator or employee has an interest, may bring an action against the corporation, receiver, or trustee in the appropriate court. For purposes of this subsection the term "appropriate court" means the United States district court before which proceedings under section 4041 or 4042 of this title are being conducted, or if no such proceedings are being conducted the United States district court for the district in which the plan has its principal office, or the United States district court for the District of Columbia. The district courts of the United States have jurisdiction of actions brought under this subsection without regard to the amount in controversy.

Sec. 4003 (f)

In any suit, action, or proceeding in which the corporation is a party, or intervenes under section 4301, in any State court, the corporation may, without bond or security, remove such suit, action, or proceeding from the State court to the United States District Court for the district or division embracing the place where the same is pending by following any procedure for removal now or hereafter in effect.

Temporary Authority for Initial Period

Sec. 4004. (a) Notwithstanding anything to the contrary in this title, the corporation may, upon receipt of notice that a plan is to be terminated or upon making a determination described in section 4042, appoint a receiver whose powers shall take effect immediately. The receiver shall assume control of such plan and its assets, protecting the interests of all interested persons during subsequent proceedings.

(b)(1) Within a reasonable time, not exceeding 20 days, after the appointment of a receiver under subsection (a), the corporation shall apply to an appropriate United States district court for a decree approving such appointment. The court to which application is made shall issue a decree approving such appointment unless it determines that such approval would not be in the best interests of the participants and beneficiaries of the plan.

(2) If the court to which application is made under paragraph (1) dismisses the application with prejudice, or if the corporation fails to apply for a decree under paragraph (1) within 20 days after the appointment of the receiver, the receiver shall transfer all assets and records of the plan held by him to the plan administrator within 3 business days after such dismissal or the expiration of the 20 day period. The receiver shall not be liable to the plan or to any other person for his acts as receiver other than for willful misconduct, or

for conduct in violation of the provisions of part 4 of subpart B of title I of this Act (except to the extent that the provisions of section 4042(d)(1)(A) provide otherwise).

(c) The corporation is authorized, as an alternative to appointing a receiver under subsection (a), to direct a plan administrator to apply to a district court of the United States for the appointment of a receiver to assume control of the plan and its assets for the purpose of protecting the interests of all interested persons until the plan can be terminated under the provisions of this title.

(d) A receiver appointed under this section has the powers of a trustee under section 4042(d)(1)(A) and (B), and shall report to the corporation and the court on the plan from time to time as required by the corporation or the court. As soon as practicable after his appointment, a receiver appointed under this section shall determine whether the assets of the plan are sufficient to discharge when due all obligations of the plan with respect to benefits guaranteed under this title in accordance with the requirements of section 4044. If the determination of the receiver is approved by the corporation and the court, the receiver shall proceed as if he were a trustee appointed under section 4042.

(e) A receiver may not be appointed under this section more than 270 days after the date of enactment of this Act.

(f) In addition to its other powers under this title, for only the first 270 days after the date of enactment of this Act the corporation may—

(1) contract for printing without regard to the provisions of chapter 5 of title 44, United States Code,

(2) waive any notice required under this title if the corporation finds that a waiver is necessary or appropriate,

(3) extend the 90-day period referred to in section 4041(a) for an additional 90 days without the agreement of the plan administrator and without application to a court as required under section 4041(d), and

(4) waive the application of the provisions of sections 4062, 4063, and 4064 to, or reduce the liability imposed under such sections on, any employer with respect to a plan terminating during that 270 day period if the corporation determines that such waiver or reduction is necessary to avoid unreasonable hardship in any case in which the employer was not able, as a practical matter, to continue the plan.

Establishment of Pension Benefit Guaranty Funds

Sec. 4005. (a) There are established on the books of the Treasury of the United States four revolving funds to be used by the corporation in carrying out its duties under this title. One of the funds shall be used with respect to basic benefits guaranteed under section 4022, one of the funds shall be used with respect to basic benefits guaranteed under section 4022A, one of the funds shall be used with respect to nonbasic benefits guaranteed under section 4022 (if any), and the remaining fund shall be used with respect to nonbasic benefits guaranteed under section 4022A (if any), other than subsection (g)(2) thereof (if any). Whenever in this title reference is made to the term "fund" the reference shall be considered to refer to the appropriate fund established under this subsection.

(b)(1) Each fund established under this section shall be credited with the appropriate portion of—

(A) funds borrowed under subsection (c),

(B) premiums, penalties, interest, and charges collected under this title,

(C) the value of the assets of a plan administered under section 4042 by a trustee to the extent that they exceed the liabilities of such plan,

Sec. 4005 (b)

(D) the amount of any employer liability payments collected under subtitle D, to the extent that such payments exceed liabilities of the plan (taking into account all other plan assets),

(E) earnings on investments of the fund or on assets credited to the fund under this subsection, and

(F) receipts from any other operations under this title.

(2) Subject to the provisions of subsection (a), each fund shall be available—

(A) for making such payments as the corporation determines are necessary to pay benefits guaranteed under section 4022, or 4022A,

(B) to purchase assets from a plan being terminated by the corporation when the corporation determines such purchase will best protect the interests of the corporation, participants in the plan being terminated, and other insured plans,

(C) to repay to the Secretary of the Treasury such sums as may be borrowed (together with interest thereon) under subsection (c), and

(D) to pay the operational and administrative expenses of the corporation, including reimbursement of the expenses incurred by the Department of the Treasury in maintaining the funds, and the Comptroller General in auditing the corporation.

(3) Whenever the corporation determines that the moneys of any fund are in excess of current needs, it may request the investment of such amounts as it determines advisable by the Secretary of the Treasury in obligations issued or guaranteed by the United States but, until all borrowings under subsection (c) have been repaid, the obligations in which such excess moneys are invested may not yield a rate of return in excess of the rate of interest payable on such borrowings.

(c) The corporation is authorized to issue to the Secretary of the Treasury notes or other obligations in an aggregate amount of not to exceed $100,000,000, in such forms and denominations, bearing such maturities, and subject to such terms and conditions as may be prescribed by the Secretary of the Treasury. Such notes or other obligations shall bear interest at a rate determined by the Secretary of the Treasury, taking into consideration the current average market yield on outstanding marketable obligations of the United States of comparable maturities during the month preceding the issuance of such notes or other obligations of the corporation. The Secretary of the Treasury is authorized and directed to purchase any notes or other obligations issued by the corporation under this subsection, and for that purpose he is authorized to use as a public debt transaction the proceeds from the sale of any securities issued under the Second Liberty Bond Act, as amended, and the purposes for which securities may be issued under that Act, as amended, are extended to include any purchase of such notes and obligations. The Secretary of the Treasury may at any time sell any of the notes or other obligations acquired by him under this subsection. All redemptions, purchases, and sales by the Secretary of the Treasury of such notes or other obligations shall be treated as public debt transactions of the United States.

(d)(1) A fifth fund shall be established for the reimbursement of uncollectible withdrawal liability under section 4222, and shall be credited with the appropriate—

(A) premiums, penalties, and interest charges collected under this title, and

(B) earnings on investments of the fund or on assets credited to the fund. The fund shall be available to make payments pursuant to the supplemental program established under section 4222, including those expenses and other charges determined to be appropriate by the corporation.

(2) The corporation may invest amounts of the fund in such obligations as the corporation considers appropriate.

Sec. 4005 (b) (1) (D)

(e)(1) A sixth fund shall be established for the supplemental benefit guarantee program provided under section 4022A(g)(2).

(2) Such fund shall be credited with the appropriate—

(A) premiums, penalties, and interest charges collected under section 4022A(g)(2), and

(B) earnings on investments of the fund or on assets credited to the fund. The fund shall be available for making payments pursuant to the supplemental benefit guarantee program established under section 4022(g)(2), including those expenses and other charges determined to be appropriate by the corporation.

(3) The corporation may invest amounts of the fund in such obligations as the corporation considers appropriate.

(f)(1) Amounts in any fund established under this section may be used only for the purposes for which such fund was established and may not be used to make loans to (or on behalf of) any other fund or to finance any other activity of the corporation.

(2) None of the funds borrowed under subsection (c) may be used to make loans to (or on behalf of) any fund other than a fund described in the second sentence of subsection (a).

(3) Any repayment to the corporation of any amount paid out of any fund in connection with a multiemployer plan shall be deposited in such fund.

Premium Rates
Sec. 4006.
(a)(1) The corporation shall prescribe such schedules of premium rates and bases for the application of those rates as may be necessary to provide sufficient revenue to the fund for the corporation to carry out its functions under this title. The premium rates charged by the corporation for any period shall be uniform for all plans, other than multiemployer plans, insured by the corporation with respect to basic benefits guaranteed by it under section 4022, and shall be uniform for all multiemployer plans with respect to basic benefits guaranteed by it under section 4022A. In establishing annual premiums with respect to plans, other than multiemployer plans, paragraphs (5) and (6) of this subsection (as in effect before the enactment of the Multiemployer Pension Plan Amendments Act of 1980) shall continue to apply.

(2) The corporation shall maintain separate schedules of premium rates, and bases for the application of those rates, for—

(A) basic benefits guaranteed by it under section 4022 for single-employer plans,

(B) basic benefits guaranteed by it under section 4022A for multiemployer plans,

(C) nonbasic benefits guaranteed by it under section 4022 for single-employer plans,

(D) nonbasic benefits guaranteed by it under section 4022A for multiemployer plans, and

(E) reimbursements of uncollectible withdrawal liability under section 4222. The corporation may revise such schedules whenever it determines that revised schedules are necessary. Except as provided in section 4022A(f), in order to place a revised schedule described in subparagraph (A) or (B) in effect, the corporation shall proceed in accordance with subsection (b)(1), and such schedule shall apply only to plan years beginning more than 30 days after the date on which the Congress approves such revised schedule by a concurrent resolution.

(3)(A) Except as provided in subparagraph (C), the annual premium rate payable to the corporation by all plans for basic benefits guaranteed under this title is—

(i) in the case of a single-employer plan, for plan years beginning after December 31, 1977, an amount equal to $2.60 for each individual who is a participant in such plan during the plan year;

(ii) in the case of a multiemployer plan, for the plan year within which the date of enactment of the Multiemployer Pension Plan Amendments Act of 1980 falls, an amount for each individual who is a participant in such plan, for such plan year equal to the sum of—

(I) 50 cents, multiplied by a fraction the numerator of which is the number of months in such year ending on or before such date and the denominator of which is 12—and

(II) $1.00, multiplied by a fraction equal to 1 minus the fraction determined under clause (i),

(iii) in the case of a multiemployer plan for plan years after the date of enactment of the Multiemployer Pension Plan Amendments Act of 1980, an amount equal to—

(I) $1.40 for each participant, for the first, second, third, and fourth plan years,

(II) $1.80 for each participant, for the fifth and sixth plan years,

(III) $2.20 for each participant, for the seventh and eighth plan years, and

(IV) $2.60 for each participant, for the ninth plan year, and for each succeeding plan year.

(B) The corporation may prescribe by regulation the extent to which the rate described in subparagraph (A)(i) applies more than once for any plan year to an individual participating in more than one plan maintained by the same employer, and the corporation may prescribe regulations under which the rate described in subparagraph (A)(iii) will not apply to the same participant in any multiemployer plan more than once for any plan year.

(C)(i) If the sum of—
(I) the amounts in any fund for basic benefits guaranteed for multiemployer plans, and
(II) the value of any assets held by the corporation for payment of basic benefits guaranteed for multiemployer plans, is for any calendar year less than 2 times the amount of basic benefits guaranteed by the corporation under this title for multiemployer plans which were paid out of any such fund or assets during the preceding calendar year, the annual premium rates under subparagraph (A) shall be increased to the next highest premium level necessary to insure that such sum will be at least 2 times greater than such amount during the following calendar year.

(ii) If the board of directors of the corporation determines that an increase in the premium rates under subparagraph (A) is necessary to provide assistance to plans which are receiving assistance under section 4261 and to plans the board finds are reasonably likely to require such assistance, the board may order such increase in the premium rates.

(iii) The maximum annual premium rate which may be established under this subparagraph is $2.60 for each participant.

(iv) The provisions of this subparagraph shall not apply if the annual premium rate is increased to a level in excess of $2.60 per participant under any other provisions of this title.

(D)(i) Not later than 120 days before the date on which an increase under subparagraph (C)(ii) is to become effective, the corporation shall publish in the Federal Register a notice of the determination described in subparagraph (C)(ii), the basis for the determination, the amount of the increase in the premium, and the anticipated increase in premium income that would result from the increase in the premium rate. The notice shall invite public comment, and shall provide for a public hearing if one is requested. Any such hearing shall be commenced not later than 60 days be-

Sec. 4006 (a) (3) (A) (i)

fore the date on which the increase is to become effective.

(ii) The board of directors shall review the hearing record established under clause (i) and shall, not later than 30 days before the date on which the increase is to become effective, determine (after consideration of the comments received) whether the amount of the increase should be changed and shall publish its determination in the Federal Register.

(4) The corporation may prescribe, subject to approval by the Congress in accordance with this section or section 4022A(f), alternative schedules of premium rates, and bases for the application of those rates, for basic benefits guaranteed by it under sections 4022 and 4022A based, in whole or in part, on the risks insured by the corporation in each plan.

(5)(A) In carrying out its authority under paragraph (1) to establish schedules of premium rates, and bases for the application of those rates, for nonbasic benefits guaranteed under sections 4022 and 4022A, the premium rates charged by the corporation for any period for nonbasic benefits guaranteed shall—

(i) be uniform by category of nonbasic benefits guaranteed,

(ii) be based on the risks insured in each category, and

(iii) reflect the experience of the corporation (including experience which may be reasonably anticipated) in guaranteeing such benefits.

(B) Notwithstanding subparagraph (A), premium rates charged to any multiemployer plan by the corporation for any period for supplemental guarantees under section 4022A(g)(2) may reflect any reasonable considerations which the corporation determines to be appropriate.

(b)(1) In order to place a revised schedule (other than a schedule described in subsection (a)(2)(C), (D), or (E) in effect, the corporation shall transmit the proposed schedule, its proposed effective date, and the reasons for its proposal to the Committee on Ways and Means and the Committee on Education and Labor of the House of Representatives, and to the Committee on Finance and the Committee on Labor and Human Resources of the Senate.

(2) The succeeding paragraphs of this subsection are enacted by Congress as an exercise of the rulemaking power of the Senate and the House of Representatives, respectively, and as such they shall be deemed a part of the rules of each House, respectively, but applicable only with respect to the procedure to be followed in that House in the case of resolutions described in paragraph (3). They shall supersede other rules only to the extent that they are inconsistent therewith. They are enacted with full recogniton of the constitutional right of either House to change the rules (so far as relating to the procedure of that House) at any time, in the same manner and to the same extent as in the case of any rule of that House.

(3) For the purpose of the succeeding paragraphs of this subsection, "resolution" means only a concurrent resolution, the matter after the resolving clause of which is as follows: "That the Congress favors the proposed revised [coverage] schedule transmitted to Congress by the Pension Benefit Guaranty Corporation on ———.", the blank space therein being filled with the date on which the corporation's message proposing the rate was delivered.

(4) A resolution shall be referred to the Committee on Ways and Means and the Committee on Education and Labor of the House of Representatives and to the Committee on Finance and the Committee on Labor and Human Resources of the Senate.

(5) If a committee to which has been referred a resolution has not reported it before the expiration of 10 calendar days after its introduction, it shall then (but not before) be in order to move to discharge the commitee from further consideration

Sec. 4006 (b) (5)

of that resolution, or to discharge the committee from further consideration of any other resolution with respect to the proposed adjustment which has been referred to the committee. The motion to discharge may be made only by a person favoring the resolution, shall be highly privileged (except that it may not be made after the committee has reported a resolution with respect to the same proposed rate), and debate thereon shall be limited to not more than 1 hour, to be divided equally between those favoring and those opposing the resolution. An amendment to the motion is not in order, and it is not in order to move to reconsider the vote by which the motion is agreed to or disagreed to. If the motion to discharge is agreed to or disagreed to, the motion may not be renewed, nor may another motion to discharge the committee be made with respect to any other resolution with respect to the same proposed rate.

(6) When a committee has reported, or has been discharged from further consideration of a resolution, it is at any time thereafter in order (even though a previous motion to the same effect has been disagreed to) to move to proceed to the consideration of the resolution. The motion is highly privileged and is not debatable. An amendment to the motion is not in order, and it is not in order to move to reconsider the vote by which the motion is agreed to or disagreed to. Debate on the resolution shall be limited to not more than 10 hours, which shall be divided equally between those favoring and those opposing the resolution. A motion further to limit debate is not debatable. An amendment to, or motion to recommit, the resolution is not in order, and it is not in order to move to reconsider the vote by which the resolution is agreed to or disagreed to.

(7) Motions to postpone, made with respect to the discharge from committee, or the consideration of, a resolution and motions to proceed to the consideration of other business shall be decided without debate. Appeals from the decisions of the Chair relating to the application of the rules of the Senate or the House of Representatives, as the case may be, to the procedure relating to a resolution shall be decided without debate.

(c)(1) Except as provided in subsection (a)(3), and subject to paragraph (2), the rate for all plans for basic benefits guaranteed under this title with respect to plan years ending after September 2, 1974, is—

(A) in the case of each plan which was not a multiemployer plan in a plan year, an amount equal to $1 for each individual who was a participant in such plan during the plan year, and

(B) in the case of each plan which was a multiemployer plan in a plan year, an amount equal to 50 cents for each individual who was a participant in such plan during the plan year.

(2) The rate applicable under this subsection for the plan year preceding September 1, 1975, is the product of—

(A) the rate described in the preceding sentence; and

(B) a fraction—

(i) the numerator of which is the number of calendar months in the plan year which ends after September 2, 1974, and before the date on which the new plan year commences, and

(ii) the denominator of which is 12.

Payment of Premiums

Sec. 4007. (a) The plan administrator of each plan shall pay the premiums imposed by the corporation under this title with respect to that plan when they are due. Premiums under this title are payable at the time, and on an estimated, advance, or other basis, as determined by the corporation. Premiums imposed by this title on the date of enactment (appli-

Sec. 4006 (b) (6)

cable to that portion of any plan year during which such date occurs) are due within 30 days after such date. Premiums imposed by this title on the first plan year commencing after the date of enactment of this Act are due within 30 days after such plan year commences. Premiums shall continue to accrue until a plan's assets are distributed pursuant to a termination procedure, or until a trustee is appointed pursuant to section 4042, whichever is earlier. The corporation may waive or reduce premiums for a multiemployer plan for any plan year during which such plan receives financial assistance from the corporation under section 4261, except that any amount so waived or reduced shall be treated as financial assistance under such section.

(b) If any basic benefit premium is not paid when it is due the corporation is authorized to assess a late payment charge of not more than 100 percent of the premium payment which was not timely paid. The preceding sentence shall not apply to any payment of premium made within 60 days after the date on which payment is due, if before such date, the plan administrator obtains a waiver from the corporation based upon a showing of substantial hardship arising from the timely payment of the premium. The corporation is authorized to grant a waiver under this subsection upon application made by the plan administrator, but the corporation may not grant a waiver if it appears that the plan administrator will be unable to pay the premium within 60 days after the date on which it is due. If any premium is not paid by the last date prescribed for a payment, interest on the amount of such premium at the rate imposed under section 6601(a) of the Internal Revenue Code of 1954 (relating to interest on underpayment, nonpayment, or extensions of time for payment of tax) shall be paid for the period from such last date to the date paid.

(c) If any plan administrator fails to pay a premium when due, the corporation is authorized to bring a civil action in any district court of the United States within the jurisdiction of which the plan assets are located, the plan is administered, or in which a defendant resides or is found for the recovery of the amount of the premium, penalty, and interest, and process may be served in any other district. The district courts of the United States shall have jurisdiction over actions brought under this subsection by the corporation without regard to the amount in controversy.

(d) The corporation shall not cease to guarantee basic benefits on account of the failure of a plan administrator to pay any premium when due.

Report by the Corporation

Sec. 4008. As soon as practicable after the close of each fiscal year the corporation shall transmit to the President and the Congress a report relative to the conduct of its business under this title for that fiscal year. The report shall include financial statements setting forth the finances of the corporation at the end of such fiscal year and the result of its operations (including the source and application of its funds) for the fiscal year and shall include an actuarial evaluation of the expected operations and status of the funds established under section 4005 for the next five years (including a detailed statement of the actuarial assumptions and methods used in making such evaluation).

Portability Assistance

Sec. 4009. The corporation shall provide advice and assistance to individuals with respect to evaluating the economic desirability of establishing individual retirement accounts or other forms of individual retirement savings for which a deduction is allowable under section 219 of the Internal Revenue Code of 1954 and with respect to evaluating the desirability, in particular cases, of transferring amounts representing an employee's interest in a qualified plan to such an account upon the employee's separation from service with an employer.

SUBTITLE B—COVERAGE

Plans Covered

Sec. 4021. (a) Except as provided in subsection (b), this section applies to any plan (including a successor plan) which, for a plan year—

(1) is an employee pension benefit plan (as defined in paragraph (2) of section 3 of this Act) established or maintained—

(A) by an employer engaged in commerce or in any industry or activity affecting commerce, or

(B) by any employee organization, or organization representing employees, engaged in commerce or in any industry or activity affecting commerce, or

(C) by both,

which has, in practice, met the requirements of part I of subchapter D of chapter 1 of the Internal Revenue Code of 1954 (as in effect for the preceding 5 plan years of the plan) applicable to plans described in paragraph (2) for the preceding 5 plan years; or

(2) is, or has been determined by the Secretary of the Treasury to be, a plan described in section 401(a) of the Internal Revenue Code of 1954, or which meets, or has been determined by the Secretary of the Treasury to meet, the requirements of section 404(a)(2) of such Code.

For purposes of this title, a successor plan is considered to be a continuation of a predecessor plan. For this purpose, unless otherwise specifically indicated in this title, a successor plan is a plan which covers a group of employees which includes substantially the same employees as a previously established plan, and provides substantially the same benefits as that plan provided.

(b) This section does not apply to any plan—

(1) which is an individual account plan, as defined in paragraph (34) of section 3 of this Act,

(2) established and maintained for its employees by the Government of the United States, by the government of any State or political subdivision thereof, or by any agency or instrumentality of any of the foregoing, or to which the Railroad Retirement Act of 1935 or 1937 applies and which is financed by contributions required under that Act,

(3) which is a church plan as defined in section 414(e) of the Internal Revenue Code of 1954, unless that plan has made an election under section 410(d) of such Code, and has notified the corporation in accordance with procedures prescribed by the corporation, that it wishes to have the provisions of this part apply to it,

(4)(A) established and maintained by a society, order, or association described in section 501(c)(8) or (9) of the Internal Revenue Code of 1954, if no part of the contributions to or under the plan is made by employers of participants in the plan, or

(B) of which a trust described in section 501(c)(18) of such Code is a part;

(5) which has not at any time after the date of enactment of this Act provided for employer contributions;

(6) which is unfunded and which is maintained by an employer primarily for the purpose of providing deferred compensation for a select group of management or highly compensated employees;

(7) which is established and maintained outside of the United States primarily for the benefit of individuals substantially all of whom are nonresident aliens;

(8) which is maintained by an employer solely for the purpose of providing benefits for certain employees in excess of the limitations on contributions and benefits imposed by section 415 of the Internal Revenue Code of 1954 on plans to which that section applies, without regard to whether the plan is funded, and, to

Sec. 4021 (a)

the extent that a separable part of a plan (as determined by the corporation) maintained by an employer is maintained for such purpose, that part shall be treated for purposes of this title, as a separate plan which is an excess benefit plan;

(9) which is established and maintained exclusively for substantial owners as defined in section 4022(b)(6);

(10) of an international organization which is exempt from taxation under the International Organizations Immunities Act;

(11) maintained solely for the purpose of complying with applicable workmen's compensation laws or unemployment compensation or disability insurance laws;

(12) which is a defined benefit plan, to the extent that it is treated as an individual account plan under paragraph (35)(B) of section 3 of this Act; or

(13) established and maintained by a professional service employer which does not at any time after the date of enactment of this Act have more than 25 active participants in the plan.

(c)(1) For purposes of subsection (b)(1), the term "individual account plan" does not include a plan under which a fixed benefit is promised if the employer or his representative participated in the determination of that benefit.

(2) For purposes of this paragraph and for purposes of subsection (b)(13)—

(A) the term "professional service employer" means any proprietorship, partnership, corporation, or other association or organization (i) owned or controlled by professional individuals or by executors or administrators of professional individuals, (ii) the principal business of which is the performance of professional services, and

(B) the term "professional individuals" includes but is not limited to, physicians, dentists, chiropractors, osteopaths, optometrists, other licensed practitioners of the healing arts, attorneys at law, public accountants, public engineers, architects, draftsmen, actuaries, psychologists, social or physical scientists, and performing artists.

(3) In the case of a plan established and maintained by more than one professional service employer, the plan shall not be treated as a plan described in subsection (b)(13) if, at any time after the date of enactment of this Act the plan has more than 25 active participants.

Single Employer Plan Benefits Guaranteed

Sec. 4022. (a) Subject to the limitations contained in subsection (b), the corporation shall guarantee in accordance with this section the payment of all nonforfeitable benefits (other than benefits becoming nonforfeitable solely on account of the termination of a plan) under a single employer plan which terminates at a time when section 4021 applies to it.

(b)(1) Except to the extent provided in paragraph (7)—

(A) no benefits provided by a plan which has been in effect for less than 60 months at the time the plan terminates shall be guaranteed under this section, and

(B) any increase in the amount of benefits under a plan resulting from a plan amendment which was made, or became effective, whichever is later, within 60 months before the date on which the plan terminates shall be disregarded.

(2) For purposes of this subsection, the time a successor plan (within the meaning of section 4021(a)) has been in effect includes the time a previously established plan (within the meaning of section 4021(a)) was in effect. For purposes of determining what benefits are guaranteed under this section in the case of a plan to which section 4021 does not apply on the day after the date of enactment of this Act, the 60 month period referred to in paragraph (1) shall be computed

beginning on the first date on which such section does apply to the plan.

(3) The amount of monthly benefits described in subsection (a) provided by a plan, which are guaranteed under this section with respect to a participant, shall not have an actuarial value which exceeds the actuarial value of a monthly benefit in the form of a life annuity commencing at age 65 equal to the lesser of—

(A) his average monthly gross income from his employer during the 5 consecutive calendar year period (or, if less, during the number of calendar years in such period in which he actively participates in the plan) during which his gross income from that employer was greater than during any other such period with that employer determined by dividing 1/12 of the sum of all such gross income by the number of such calendar years in which he had such gross income, or

(B) $750 multiplied by a fraction, the numerator of which is the contribution and benefit base (determined under section 230 of the Social Security Act) in effect at the time the plan terminates and the denominator of which is such contribution and benefit base in effect in calendar year 1974.

The provisions of this paragraph do not apply to non-basic benefits.

(4)(A) The actuarial value of a benefit, for purposes of this subsection, shall be determined in accordance with regulations prescribed by the corporation.

(B) For purposes of paragraph (3)—

(i) the term "gross income" means "earned income" within the meaning of section 911(b) of the Internal Revenue Code of 1954 (determined without regard to any community property laws),

(ii) in the case of a participant in a plan under which contributions are made by more than one employer, amounts received as gross income from any employer under that plan shall be aggregated with amounts received from any other employer under that plan during the same period, and

(iii) any non-basic benefit shall be disregarded.

(5)(A) For purposes of this title, the term "substantial owner" means an individual who—

(i) owns the entire interest in an unincorporated trade or business,

(ii) in the case of a partnership, is a partner who owns, directly or indirectly, more than 10 percent of either the capital interest or the profits interests in such partnership, or

(iii) in the case of a corporation, owns, directly or indirectly, more than 10 percent in value of either the voting stock of that corporation or all the stock of that corporation.

For purposes of clause (iii) the constructive ownership rules of section 1563(e) of the Internal Revenue Code of 1954 shall apply (determined without regard to section 1563(e)(3)(C)). For purposes of this title an individual is also treated as a substantial owner with respect to a plan if, at any time within the 60 months preceding the date on which the determination is made, he was a substantial owner under the plan.

(B) In the case of a participant in a plan under which benefits have not been increased by reason of any plan amendments and who is covered by the plan as a substantial owner, the amount of benefits guaranteed under this section shall not exceed the product of—

(i) a fraction (not to exceed 1) the numerator of which is the number of years the substantial owner was an active participant in the plan, and the denominator of which is 30, and

(ii) the amount of the substantial owner's monthly benefits guaranteed under subsection (a) (as limited under paragraph (3) of this subsection).

(C) In the case of a participant in a plan, other than a plan described in subparagraph (B), who is covered by the plan as a substantial owner, the amount of the benefit guaranteed under this section shall, under regulations prescribed by the corpora-

Sec. 4022 (b) (3)

tion, treat each benefit increase attributable to a plan amendment as if it were provided under a new plan. The benefits guaranteed under this section with respect to all such amendments shall not exceed the amount which would be determined under subparagraph (B) if subparagraph (B) applied.

(6)(A) No benefits accrued under a plan after the date on which the Secretary of the Treasury issues notice that he has determined that any trust which is a part of a plan does not meet the requirements of section 401(a) of the Internal Revenue Code of 1954, or that the plan does not meet the requirements of section 404(a)(2) of such Code, are guaranteed under this section unless such determination is erroneous. This subparagraph does not apply if the Secretary subsequently issues a notice that such trust meets the requirements of section 401(a) of such Code or that the plan meets the requirements of section 404(a)(2) of such Code and if the Secretary determines that the trust or plan has taken action necessary to meet such requirements during the period between the issuance of the notice referred to in the preceding sentence and the issuance of the notice referred to in this sentence.

(B) No benefits accrued under a plan after the date on which an amendment of the plan is adopted which causes the Secretary of the Treasury to determine that any trust under the plan has ceased to meet the requirements of section 401(a) of the Internal Revenue Code of 1954 or that the plan has ceased to meet the requirements of section 404(a)(2) of such Code, are guaranteed under this section unless such determination is erroneous. This subparagraph shall not apply if the amendment is revoked as of the date it was first effective or amended to comply with such requirements.

(7) Benefits described in paragraph (1) are guaranteed only to the extent of the greater of—

(A) 20 percent of the amount which, but for the fact that the plan or amendment has not been in effect for 60 months or more, would be guaranteed under this section, or

(B) $20 per month,

multiplied by the number of years (but not more than 5) the plan or amendment, as the case may be, has been in effect. In determining how many years a plan or amendment has been in effect for purposes of this paragraph, the first 12 months following the date on which the plan or amendment is made or first becomes effective (whichever is later) constitutes one year, and each consecutive period of 12 months thereafter constitutes an additional year. This paragraph does not apply to benefits payable under a plan unless the corporation finds substantial evidence that the plan was terminated for a reasonable business purpose and not for the purpose of obtaining the payment of benefits by the corporation under this title.

(c) The corporation is authorized to guarantee the payment of such other classes of benefits and to establish the terms and conditions under which such other classes of benefits are guaranteed as it determines to be appropriate.

Multiemployer Plan Benefits Guaranteed

Sec. 4022A. (a) The corporation shall guarantee, in accordance with this section, the payment of all nonforfeitable benefits (other than benefits becoming nonforfeitable solely on account of the termination of a plan) under a multiemployer plan—

(1) to which section 4021 applies, and

(2) which is insolvent under section 4245(b) or 4281(d)(2).

(b)(1)(A) For purposes of this section, a benefit or benefit increase which has been in effect under a plan for less than 60 months is not eligible for the corporation's guarantee. For purposes of this paragraph, any month of any plan year during which the plan was insolvent or terminated (within the meaning of section 4041 (a)(2)) shall not be taken into account.

(B) For purposes of this section, a benefit or benefit increase which has been in effect under a plan for less than 60 months before the first day of the plan year for which an amendment reducing the benefit or the benefit increase is taken into account under section 4244A(a)(2) in determining the minimum contribution requirement for the plan year under section 4243(b) is not eligible for the corporation's guarantee.

(2) For purposes of this section—

(A) the date on which a benefit or a benefit increase under a plan is first in effect is the later of—

(i) the date on which the documents establishing or increasing the benefit were executed, or

(ii) the effective date of the benefit or benefit increase;

(B) the period of time for which a benefit or a benefit increase has been in effect under a successor plan includes the period of time for which the benefit or benefit increase was in effect under a previously established plan; and

(C) in the case of a plan to which section 4021 did not apply on September 3, 1974, the time periods referred to in this section are computed beginning on the date on which section 4021 first applies to the plan.

(c)(1) Except as provided in subsection (g), the monthly benefit of a participant or a beneficiary which is guaranteed under this section by the corporation with respect to a plan is the product of—

(A) 100 percent of the accrual rate up to $5, plus 75 percent of the lesser of—

(i) $15, or

(ii) the accrual rate, if any, in excess of $5, and

(B) the number of the participant's years of credited service.

(2) Except as provided in paragraph (6) of this subsection and in subsection (g), in applying paragraph (1) with respect to a plan described in paragraph (5)(A), the term "65 percent" shall be substituted in paragraph (1)(A) for the term "75 percent."

(3) For purposes of this section, the accrual rate is—

(A) the monthly benefit of the participant or beneficiary which is described in subsection (a) and which is eligible for the corporation's guarantee under subsection (b), except that such benefit shall be—

(i) no greater than the monthly benefit which would be payable under the plan at normal retirement age in the form of a single life annuity, and

(ii) determined without regard to any reduction under section 411(a) (3)(E) of the Internal Revenue Code of 1954; divided by

(B) the participant's years of credited service.

(4) For purposes of this subsection—

(A) a year of credited service is a year in which the participant completed—

(i) a full year of participation in the plan, or

(ii) any period of service before participation which is credited for purposes of benefit accrual as the equivalent of a full year of participation;

(B) any year for which the participant is credited for purposes of benefit accrual with a fraction of the equivalent of a full year of participation shall be counted as such a fraction of a year of credited service; and

(C) years of credited service shall be determined by including service which may otherwise be disregarded by the plan under section 411(a) (3)(E) of the Internal Revenue Code of 1954.

(5)(A) A plan is described in this subparagraph if—

(i) the first plan year—

(I) in which the plan is insolvent under section 4245(b) or 4281(d)(2), and

(II) for which benefits are required to be suspended under section 4245, or reduced or suspended under section 4281, until they do not exceed the lev-

Sec. 4022A (b) (1) (B)

els provided in this subsection, begins before the year 2000; and

(ii) the plan sponsor has not established to the satisfaction of the corporation that, during the period of 10 consecutive plan years (or of such lesser number of plan years for which the plan was maintained) immediately preceding the first plan year to which the minimum funding standards of section 412 of the Internal Revenue Code of 1954 apply, the total amount of the contributions required under the plan for each plan year was at least equal to the sum of—

(I) the normal cost for that plan year, and

(II) the interest for the plan year (determined under the plan) on the unfunded past service liability for that plan year, determined as of the beginning of that plan year.

(B) A plan shall not be considered to be described in subparagraph (A) if—

(i) it is established to the satisfaction of the corporation that—

(I) the total amount of the contributions received under the plan for the plan years for which the actuarial valuations (performed during the period described in subparagraph (A)(ii) were performed was at least equal to the sum described in subparagraph (A)(ii); or

(II) the rates of contribution to the plan under the collective bargaining agreements negotiated when the findings of such valuations were available were reasonably expected to provide such contributions;

(ii) the number of actuarial valuations performed during the period described in subparagraph (A)(ii) is—

(I) at least 2, in any case in which such period consists of more than 6 plan years, and

(II) at least 1, in any case in which such period consists of 6 or fewer plan years; and

(iii) if the proposition described in clause (i)(I) is to be established, the plan sponsor certifies that to the best of the plan sponsor's knowledge there is no information available which establishes that the total amount of the contributions received under the plan for any plan year during the period described in subparagraph (A)(ii) for which no valuation was performed is less than the sum described in subparagraph (A)(ii).

(6) Notwithstanding paragraph (2), in the case of a plan described in paragraph (5)(A), if for any period of 3 consecutive plan years beginning with the first plan year to which the minimum funding standards of section 412 of the Internal Revenue Code of 1954 apply, the value of the assets of the plan for each such plan year is an amount equal to at least 8 times the benefit payments for such plan year—

(A) paragraph (2) shall not apply to such plan; and

(B) the benefit of a participant or beneficiary guaranteed by the corporation with respect to the plan shall be an amount determined under paragraph (1).

(d) In the case of a benefit which has been reduced under section 411 (a)(3)(E) of the Internal Revenue Code of 1954, the corporation shall guarantee the lesser of—

(1) the reduced benefit, or

(2) the amount determined under subsection (c).

(e) The corporation shall not guarantee benefits under a multiemployer plan which, under section 4022(b)(6), would not be guaranteed under a single-employer plan.

(f)(1) No later than 5 years after the date of the enactment of the Multiemployer Pension Plan Amendments Act of 1980, and at least every fifth year thereafter, the corporation shall—

(A) conduct a study to determine—

(i) the premiums needed to maintain the basic-benefit guarantee levels for multiemployer plans described in subsection (c), and

(ii) whether the basic-benefit guarantee levels for multiemployer plans may be increased without increasing the basic-benefit premiums for multiemployer plans under this title; and

(B) report such determinations to the Committee on Ways and Means

Sec. 4022A (f) (1)

and the Committee on Education and Labor of the House of Representatives and to the Committee on Finance and the Committee on Labor and Human Resources of the Senate.

(2)(A) If the last report described in paragraph (1) indicates that a premium increase is necessary to support the existing basic-benefit guarantee levels for multiemployer plans, the corporation shall transmit to the Committee on Ways and Means and the Committee on Education and Labor of the House of Representatives and to the Committee on Finance and the Committee on Labor and Human Resources of the Senate by March 31 of any calendar year in which congressional action under this subsection is requested—

(i) a revised schedule of basic-benefit guarantees for multiemployer plans which would be necessary in the absence of an increase in premiums approved in accordance with section 4006(b),

(ii) a revised schedule of basic-benefit premiums for multiemployer plans which is necessary to support the existing basic-benefit guarantees for such plans, and

(iii) a revised schedule of basic-benefit guarantees for multiemployer plans for which the schedule of premiums necessary is higher than the existing premium schedule for such plans but lower than the revised schedule of premiums for such plans specified in clause (ii), together with such schedule of premiums.

(B) The revised schedule of increased premiums referred to in subparagraph (A)(ii) or (A)(iii) shall go into effect as approved by the Congress by concurrent resolution.

(C) If an increase in premiums is not approved, the revised guarantee schedule described in subparagraph (A)(i) shall go into effect on the first day of the second calendar year following the year in which such revised guarantee schedule was submitted to the Congress.

(3)(A) If the last report described in paragraph (1) indicates that basic-benefit guarantees for multiemployer plans can be increased without increasing the basic-benefit premiums for multiemployer plans under this title, the corporation shall submit to the Committee on Ways and Means and the Committee on Education and Labor of the House of Representatives and to the Committee on Finance and the Committee on Labor and Human Resources of the Senate by March 31 of the calendar year in which congressional action under this paragraph is requested—

(i) a revised schedule of increases in the basic-benefit guarantees which can be supported by the existing schedule of basic-benefit premiums for multiemployer plans, and

(ii) a revised schedule of basic-benefit premiums sufficient to support the existing basic-benefit guarantees.

(B) The revised schedules referred to in subparagraph (A)(i) or subparagraph (A)(ii) shall go into effect as approved by the Congress by a concurrent resolution.

(4)(A) The succeeding subparagraphs of this paragraph, are enacted by the Congress as an exercise of the rulemaking power of the Senate and the House of Representatives, respectively, and as such they shall be deemed a part of the rules of each House, respectively, but applicable only with respect to the procedure to be followed in that House in the case of concurrent resolutions (as defined in subparagraph (B)). Such subparagraphs shall supersede other rules only to the extent that they are inconsistent therewith. They are enacted with full recognition of the constitutional right of either House to change the rules (so far as relating to the procedure of that House) at any time, in the same manner, and to the same extent as in the case of any rule of that House.

(B) For purposes of this subsection, "concurrent resolution" means only a concurrent resolution, the matter after the resolving clause of which is as follows: "That the Congress favors the proposed schedule described in

Sec. 4022A (f) (2) (A)

transmitted to the Congress by the Pension Benefit Guaranty Corporation on   .", the first blank space therein being filled with section 4022 A(f)(2)(A)(ii) of the Employee Retirement Income Security Act of 1974", "section 4022A(f)(2)(A)(iii) of the Employee Retirement Income Security Act of 1974", "section 4022A(f)(3)(A)(i) of the Employee Retirement Income Security Act of 1974", or "section 4022A(f)(3)(A)(ii) of the Employee Retirement Income Security Act of 1974" (whichever is applicable), and the second blank space therein being filled with the date on which the corporation's message proposing the revision was submitted.

(C) The procedure for disposition of a concurrent resolution shall be the procedure described in section 4006(b)(4) through (7).

(g)(1) The corporation may guarantee the payment of such other classes of benefits under multiemployer plans, and establish the terms and conditions under which those other classes of benefits are guaranteed, as it determines to be appropriate.

(2)(A) The corporation shall prescribe regulations to establish a supplemental program to guarantee benefits under multiemployer plans which would be guaranteed under this section but for the limitations in subsection (c). Such regulations shall be proposed by the corporation no later than the end of the 18th calendar month following the date of the enactment of the Multiemployer Pension Plan Amendments Act of 1980. The regulations shall make coverage under the supplemental program available no later than January 1, 1983. Any election to participate in the supplemental program shall be on a voluntary basis, and a plan electing such coverage shall continue to pay the premiums required under section 4006(a)(2)(B) to the revolving fund used pursuant to section 4005 in connection with benefits otherwise guaranteed under this section. Any such election shall be irrevocable, except to the extent otherwise provided by regulations prescribed by the corporation.

(B) The regulations prescribed under this paragraph shall provide—

(i) that a plan must elect coverage under the supplemental program within the time permitted by the regulations;

(ii) unless the corporation determines otherwise, that a plan may not elect supplemental coverage unless the value of the assets of the plan as of the end of the plan year preceding the plan year in which the election must be made is an amount equal to 15 times the total amount of the benefit payments made under the plan for that year; and

(iii) such other reasonable terms and conditions for supplemental coverage, including funding standards and any other reasonable limitations with respect to plans or benefits covered or to means of program financing, as the corporation determines are necessary and appropriate for a feasible supplemental program consistent with the purposes of this title.

(3) Any benefits guaranteed under this subsection shall be considered nonbasic benefits for purposes of this title.

(4)(A) No revised schedule of premiums under this subsection, after the initial schedule, shall go into effect unless—

(i) the revised schedule is submitted to the Congress, and

(ii) a concurrent resolution described in subparagraph (B) is not adopted before the close of the 60th legislative day after such schedule is submitted to the Congress.

(B) For purposes of subparagraph (A), a concurrent resolution described in this subparagraph is a concurrent resolution the matter after the resolving clause of which is as follows: "That the Congress disapproves the revised premium schedule transmitted to the Congress by the Pension Benefit Guaranty Corporation under section 4022A(g)(4) of the Employee Retirement Income Security Act of 1974 on

.", the blank space therein being filled with the date on which the revised schedule was submitted.

(C) For purposes of subparagraph (A), the term "legislative day" means any calendar day other than a day on which either House is not in session because of a sine die adjournment or an adjournment of more than 3 days to a day certain.

(D) The procedure for disposition of a concurrent resolution described in subparagraph (B) shall be the procedure described in paragraphs (4) through (7) of section 4006(b).

(5) Regulations prescribed by the corporation to carry out the provisions of this subsection, may, to the extent provided therein, supersede the requirements of sections 4245, 4261, and 4281, and the requirements of section 418E of the Internal Revenue Code of 1954, but only with respect to benefits guaranteed under this subsection.

(h)(1) Except as provided in paragraph (3), subsections (b) and (c) shall not apply with respect to the nonforfeitable benefits accrued as of July 29, 1980, with respect to a participant or beneficiary under a multiemployer plan—

(1) who is in pay status on July 29, 1980, or

(2) who is within 36 months of the normal retirement age and has a nonforfeitable right to a pension as of that date.

(2) The benefits described in paragraph (1) shall be guaranteed by the corporation in the same manner and to the same extent as benefits are guaranteed by the corporation under section 4022 (without regard to this section).

(3) This subsection does not apply with respect to a plan for plan years following a plan year—

(A) in which the plan has terminated within the meaning of section 4041A(a)(2), or

(B) in which it is determined by the corporation that substantially all the employers have withdrawn from the plan pursuant to an agreement or arrangement to withdraw.

Sec. 4022A (g) (4) (C)

Aggregate Limit on Benefits Guaranteed

Sec. 4022B. (a) Notwithstanding sections 4022 and 4022A, no person shall receive from the corporation pursuant to a guarantee by the corporation of basic benefits with respect to a participant under all multiemployer and single employer plans an amount, or amounts, with an actuarial value which exceeds the actuarial value of a monthly benefit in the form of a life annuity commencing at age 65 equal to the amount determined under section 4022(b)(3)(B) as of the date of the last plan termination.

(b) For purposes of this section—

(1) the receipt of benefits under a multiemployer plan receiving financial assistance from the corporation shall be considered the receipt of amounts from the corporation pursuant to a guarantee by the corporation of basic benefits except to the extent provided in regulations prescribed by the corporation, and

(2) the date on which a multiemployer plan, whether or not terminated, begins receiving financial assistance from the corporation shall be considered a date of plan termination.

Plan Fiduciaries

Sec. 4023. Notwithstanding any other provision of this Act, a fiduciary of a plan to which section 4021 applies is not in violation of the fiduciary's duties as a result of any act or of any withholding of action required by this title.

Contingent Liability Coverage
[Repealed]

SUBTITLE C—TERMINATIONS

Termination of Single Employer Plans

Sec. 4041. (a) Before the effective date of the termination of a single employer plan, the plan administrator shall file a notice with the corporation that the plan is to be terminated on a proposed date (which may not be earlier than 10 days after the filing of the notice), and for a period of 90 days after the proposed termination date the plan administrator shall pay no amount pursuant to the termination procedure of the plan unless, before the expiration of such period, he receives a notice of sufficiency under subsection (b). Upon receiving such a notice, the plan administrator may proceed with the termination of the plan in a manner consistent with this subtitle.

(b) If the corporation determines that, after application of section 4044, the assets held under the plan are sufficient to discharge when due all obligations of the plan with respect to basic benefits, it shall notify the plan administrator of such determination as soon as practicable.

(c) If, within such 90-day period, the corporation finds that it is unable to determine that, if the assets of the plan are allocated in accordance with the provisions of section 4044, the assets held under the plan are sufficient to discharge when due all oblgiations of the plan with respect to basic benefits, it shall notify the plan administrator within such 90-day period of that finding. When the corporation issues a notice under this subsection, it shall commence proceeding in accordance with the provisions of section 4042. Upon receiving a notice under this subsection, the plan administrator shall refrain from taking any action under the proposed termination.

(d) The corporation and the plan administrator may agree to extend the 90-day period provided by this section by a written agreement signed by the corporation and the plan administrator before the expiration of the 90-day period, or the corporation may apply to an appropriate court (as defined in section 4042(g)) for an order extending the 90-day period provided by this section. The 90-day period shall be extended as provided in the agreement or in any court order obtained by the corporation. The 90-day period may be further extended by subsequent written agreements signed by the corporation and the plan administrator made before the expiration of a previously agreed upon extension of the 90-day period, or by subsequent order of the court. Any extension may be made upon such terms and conditions (including the payment of benefits) as are agreed upon by the corporation and the plan administrator or as specified in the court order.

(e) If, after the plan administrator has begun to terminate the plan as authorized by this section, the corporation or the plan administrator finds that the plan is unable, or will be unable, to pay basic benefits when due, the plan administrator shall notify the corporation of such finding as soon as practicable thereafter. If the corporation makes such a finding or concurs with the finding of the plan administrator, it shall institute appropriate proceedings under section 4042. The plan administrator terminating a plan shall furnish such reports to the corporation as it may require for purposes of its duties under this section.

(f) For purposes of subsection (a), a plan with respect to which basic benefits are guaranteed shall be treated as terminated upon the adoption of an amendment to such plan, if, after giving effect to such amendment, the plan is a plan described in section 4021(b)(1).

Termination of Multiemployer Plans

Sec. 4041A. (a) Termination of a multiemployer plan under this section occurs as a result of—

(1) the adoption after the date of enactment of the Multiemployer Pension Plan Amendments Act of 1980 of a plan amendment which provides that participants will receive no credit for any purpose under the plan for service with any employer after the date specified by such amendment;

(2) the withdrawal of every employer from the plan, within the meaning of section 4203, or the cessation of the obligation of all employers to contribute under the plan; or

(3) the adoption of an amendment to the plan which causes the plan to become a plan described in section 4021(b)(1).

(b)(1) The date on which a plan terminates under paragraph (1) or (3) of subsection (a) is the later of—

(A) the date on which the amendment is adopted, or

(B) the date on which the amendment takes effect.

(2) The date on which a plan terminates under paragraph (2) of subsection (a) is the earlier of—

(A) the date on which the last employer withdraws, or

(B) the first day of the first plan year for which no employer contributions were required under the plan.

(c) Except as provided in subsection (f)(1), the plan sponsor of a plan which terminates under paragraph (2) of subsection (a) shall—

(1) limit the payment of benefits to benefits which are nonforfeitable under the plan as of the date of the termination, and

(2) pay benefits attributable to employer contributions, other than death benefits, only in the form of an annuity, unless the plan assets are distributed in full satisfaction of all nonforfeitable benefits under the plan.

(d) The plan sponsor of a plan which terminates under paragraph (2) of subsection (a) shall reduce benefits and suspend benefit payments in accordance with section 4281.

(e) In the case of a plan which terminates under paragraph (1) or (3) of subsection (a), the rate of an employer's contributions under the plan for each plan year beginning on or after the plan termination date shall equal or exceed the highest rate of employer contributions at which the employer had an obligation to contribute under the plan in the 5 preceding plan years ending on or before the plan termination date, unless the corporation approves a reduction in the rate based on a finding that the plan is or soon will be fully funded.

(f)(1) The plan sponsor of a terminated plan may authorize the payment other than in the form of an annuity of a participant's entire nonforfeitable benefit attributable to employer contributions, other than a death benefit, if the value of the entire nonforfeitable benefit does not exceed $1,750. The corporation may authorize the payment of benefits under the terms of a terminated plan other than nonforfeitable benefits, or the payment other than in the form of an annuity of benefits having a value greater than $1,750, if the corporation determines that such payment is not adverse to the interest of the plan's participants and beneficiaries generally and does not unreasonably increase the corporation's risk of loss with respect to the plan.

(2) The corporation may prescribe reporting requirements for terminated plans, and rules and standards for the administration of such plans, which the corporation considers appropriate to protect the interests of plan participants and beneficiaries or to prevent unreasonable loss to the corporation.

Termination By Corporation

Sec. 4042. (a) The corporation may institute proceedings under this section to terminate a plan whenever it determines that—

(1) the plan has not met the minimum funding standard required under section 412 of the Internal Revenue Code of 1954, or has been notified by the Secretary of the Treasury that a notice of deficiency under section 6212 of such Code has been mailed with respect to the tax imposed under section 4971(a) of such Code,

(2) the plan is unable to pay benefits when due,

(3) the reportable event described in section 4043(b)(7) has occurred, or

Sec. 4041A (b)

(4) the possible long-run loss of the corporation with respect to the plan may reasonably be expected to increase unreasonably if the plan is not terminated.

The corporation may prescribe a simplified procedure to follow in terminating small plans as long as that procedure includes substantial safeguards for the rights of the participants and beneficiaries under the plans, and for the employers who maintain such plans (including the requirement for a court decree under subsection (c)). The corporation is authorized to pool the assets of terminated plans for purposes of administration and such other purposes, not inconsistent with its duties to the plan participants and the employer maintaining the plan under this title, as it determines to be required for the efficient administration of this title.

(b)(1) Whenever the corporation makes a determination under subsection (a) with respect to a plan it may, upon notice to the plan, apply to the appropriate United States district court for the appointment of a trustee to administer the plan with respect to which the determination is made pending the issuance of a decree under subsection (c) ordering the termination of the plan. If within 3 business days after the filing of an application under this subsection, or such other period as the court may order, the administrator of the plan consents to the appointment of a trustee, or fails to show why a trustee should not be appointed, the court may grant the application and appoint a trustee to administer the plan in accordance with its terms until the corporation determines that the plan should be terminated or that termination is unnecessary. The corporation may request that it be appointed as trustee of a plan in any case.

(2) Notwithstanding any other provision of this title—

(A) upon the petition of a plan administrator or the corporation, the appropriate United States district court may appoint a trustee in accordance with the provisions of this section if the interests of the plan participants would be better served by the appointment of the trustee, and

(B) upon the petition of the corporation, the appropriate United States district court shall appoint a trustee proposed by the corporation for a multiemployer plan which is in reorganization or to which section 4041A (d) applies, unless such appointment would be adverse to the interests of the plan participants and beneficiaries in the aggregate.

(3) The corporation and plan administrator may agree to the appointment of a trustee without proceeding in accordance with the requirements of paragraphs (1) and (2).

(c) If the corporation has issued a notice under this section to a plan administrator and (whether or not a trustee has been appointed under subsection (b)) has determined that the plan should be terminated, it may, upon notice to the plan administrator, apply to the appropriate United States district court for a decree adjudicating that the plan must be terminated in order to protect the interests of the participants or to avoid any unreasonable deterioration of the financial condition of the plan or any unreasonable increase in the liability of the fund. If the trustee appointed under subsection (b) disagrees with the determination of the corporation under the preceding sentence he may intervene in the proceeding relating to the application for the decree, or make application for such decree himself. Upon granting a decree for which the corporation or trustee has applied under this subsection the court shall authorize the trustee appointed under subsection (b) (or appoint a trustee if one has not been appointed under such subsection and authorize him) to terminate the plan in accordance with the provisions of this subtitle. If the

Sec. 4042 (c)

corporation and the plan administrator agree that a plan should be terminated and agree to the appointment of a trustee without proceeding in accordance with the requirements of this subsection (other than this sentence) the trustee shall have the power described in subsection (d)(1) and, in addition to any other duties imposed on the trustee under law or by agreement between the corporation and the plan administrator, the trustee is subject to the duties described in subsection (d)(3). Whenever a trustee appointed under this title is operating a plan with discretion as to the date upon which final distribution of the assets is to be commenced, the trustee shall notify the corporation at least 10 days before the date on which he proposes to commence such distribution.

(d)(1)(A) A trustee appointed under subsection (b) shall have the power—

(i) to do any act authorized by the plan or this title to be done by the plan administrator or any trustee of the plan;

(ii) to require the transfer of all (or any part) of the assets and records of the plan to himself as trustee;

(iii) to invest any assets of the plan which he holds in accordance with the provisions of the plan, regulations of the corporation, and applicable rules of law;

(iv) to limit payment of benefits under the plan to basic benefits or to continue payment of some or all of the benefits which were being paid prior to his appointment;

(v) in the case of a multiemployer plan, to reduce benefits or suspend benefit payments under the plan, give appropriate notices, amend the plan, and perform other acts required or authorized by subtitle (E) to be performed by the plan sponsor or administrator;

(vi) to do such other acts as he deems necessary to continue operation of the plan without increasing the potential liability of the corporation, if such acts may be done under the provisions of the plan.

If the court to which application is made under subsection (c) dismisses the application with prejudice, or if the corporation fails to apply for a decree under subsection (c) within 30 days after the date on which the trustee is appointed under subsection (b), the trustee shall transfer all assets and records of the plan held by him to the plan administrator within 3 business days after such dismissal or the expiration of such 30-day period, and shall not be liable to the plan or any other person for his acts as trustee except for willful misconduct, or for conduct in violation of the provisions of part 4 of subtitle B of title I of this Act (except as provided in subsection (d)(1)(A)(v)). The 30-day period referred to in this subparagraph may be extended as provided by agreement between the plan administrator and the corporation or by court order obtained by the corporation and

(vii) to require the plan sponsor, the plan administrator, any contributing or withdrawn employer, and any employee organization representing plan participants to furnish any information with respect to the plan which the trustee may reasonably need in order to administer the plan.

(B) If the court to which an application is made under subsection (c) issues the decree requested in such application, in addition to the powers described in subparagraph (A), the trustee shall have the power—

(i) to pay benefits under the plan in accordance with the requirements of this title;

(ii) to collect for the plan any amounts due the plan;

(iii) to receive any payment made by the corporation to the plan under this title;

(iv) to commence, prosecute, or defend on behalf of the plan any suit or proceeding involving the plan;

Sec. 4042 (d)

(v) to issue, publish, or file such notices, statements, and reports as may be required by the corporation or any order of the court;

(vi) to liquidate the plan assets;

(vii) to recover payments under section 4045(a); and

(viii) to do such other acts as may be necessary to comply with this title or any order of the court and to protect the interests of plan participants and beneficiaries.

(2) As soon as practicable after his appointment, the trustee shall give notice to interested parties of the institution of proceedings under this title to determine whether the plan should be terminated or to terminate the plan, whichever is applicable. For purposes of this paragraph, the term "interested party" means—

(A) the plan administrator,

(B) each participant in the plan and each beneficiary of a deceased participant,

(C) each employer who may be subject to liability under section 4062, 4063, or 4064,

(D) each employer who is or may be liable to the plan under section part 1 of subtitle E,

(E) each employer who has an obligation to contribute, within the meaning of section 4212(a), under a multiemployer plan, and

(F) each employee organization which, for purposes of collective bargaining, represents plan participants employed by an employer described in subparagraph (C), (D), or (E).

(3) Except to the extent inconsistent with the provisions of this Act, or as may be otherwise ordered by the court, a trustee appointed under this section shall be subject to the same duties as a trustee appointed under section 47 of the Bankruptcy Act, and shall be, with respect to the plan, a fiduciary within the meaning of paragraph (21) of section 3 of this Act and under section 4975(e) of the Internal Revenue Code of 1954 (except to the extent that the provisions of this title are inconsistent with the requirements applicable under part 4 of subtitle B of title I of this Act and of such section 4975).

(e) An application by the corporation under this section may be filed notwithstanding the pendency in the same or any other court of any bankruptcy, mortgage foreclosure, or equity receivership proceeding, or any proceeding to reorganize, conserve, or liquidate such plan or its property, or any proceeding to enforce a lien against property of the plan.

(f) Upon the filing of an application for the appointment of a trustee or the issuance of a decree under this section, the court to which an application is made shall have exclusive jurisdiction of the plan involved and its property wherever located with the powers, to the extent consistent with the purposes of this section, of a court of the United States having jurisdiction over cases under chapter 11 of title 11. Pending an adjudication under subsection (c) of this section such court shall stay, and upon appointment by it of a trustee, as provided in this section such court shall continue the stay of, any pending mortgage foreclosure, equity receivership, or other proceeding to reorganize, conserve, or liquidate the plan or its property and any other suit against any receiver, conservator, or trustee of the plan or its property. Pending such adjudication and upon the appointment by it of such trustee, the court may stay any proceeding to enforce a lien against property of the plan or any other suit against the plan.

(g) An action under this subsection may be brought in the judicial district where the plan administrator resides or does business or where any asset of the plan is situated. A district court in which such action is brought may issue process with respect to such action in any other judicial district.

(h)(1) The amount of compensation paid to each trustee appointed under the provisions of this title shall require the prior approval of the corporation, and, in the case of a trustee appointed by a court, the consent of that court.

(2) Trustees shall appoint, retain, and compensate accountants, actuaries, and other professional service personnel in accordance with regulations prescribed by the corporation.

Reportable Events

Sec. 4043. (a) Within 30 days after the plan administrator knows or has reason to know that a reportable event described in subsection (b) has occurred, he shall notify the corporation that such event has occurred. The corporation is authorized to waive the requirement of the preceding sentence with respect to any or all reportable events with respect to any plan, and to require the notification to be made by including the event in the annual report made by the plan. Whenever an employer making contributions under a plan to which section 4021 applies knows or has reason to know that a reportable event has occurred he shall notify the plan administrator immediately.

(b) For purposes of this section a reportable event occurs—

(1) when the Secretary of the Treasury issues notice that a plan has ceased to be a plan described in section 4021(a)(2), or when the Secretary of Labor determines the plan is not in compliance with title I of this Act;

(2) when an amendment of the plan is adopted if, under the amendment, the benefit payable with respect to any participant may be decreased;

(3) when the number of active participants is less than 80 percent of the number of such participants at the beginning of the plan year, or is less than 75 percent of the number of such participants at the beginning of the previous plan year;

(4) when the Secretary of the Treasury determines that there has been a termination or partial termination of the plan within the meaning of section 411(d)(3) of the Internal Revenue Code of 1954, but the occurrence of such a termination or partial termination does not, by itself, constitute or require a termination of a plan under this title;

(5) when the plan fails to meet the minimum funding standards under section 412 of such Code (without regard to whether the plan is a plan described in section 4021(a)(2) of this Act) or under section 302 of this Act;

(6) when the plan is unable to pay benefits thereunder when due;

(7) when there is a distribution under the plan to a participant who is a substantial owner as defined in section 4022(b)(6) if—

(A) such distribution has a value of $10,000 or more;

(B) such distribution is not made by reason of the death of the participant; and

(C) immediately after the distribution, the plan has nonforfeitable benefits which are not funded;

(8) when a plan merges, consolidates, or transfers its assets under section 208 of this Act, or when an alternative method of compliance is prescribed by the Secretary of Labor under section 110 of this Act; or

(9) when any other event occurs which the corporation determines may be indicative of a need to terminate the plan.

For purposes of paragraph (7), all distributions to a participant within any 24-month period are treated as a single distribution.

(c) The Secretary of the Treasury shall notify the corporation—

(1) whenever a reportable event described in paragraph (1), (4), or (5) of subsection (b) occurs, or

(2) whenever any other event occurs which the Secretary of the Treasury believes indicates that the plan may not be sound.

(d) The Secretary of Labor shall notify the corporation—

(1) whenever a reportable event de-

Sec. 4043

scribed in paragraph (1), (5), or (8) of subsection (b) occurs, or

(2) whenever any other event occurs which the Secretary of Labor believes indicates that the plan may not be sound.

Allocation of Assets

Sec. 4044. (a) In the case of the termination of a single employer defined benefit plan, the plan administrator shall allocate the assets of the plan (available to provide benefits) among the participants and beneficiaries of the plan in the following order:

(1) First, to that portion of each individual's accrued benefit which is derived from the participant's contributions to the plan which were not mandatory contributions.

(2) Second, to that portion of each individual's accrued benefit which is derived from the participant's mandatory contributions.

(3) Third, in the case of benefits payable as an annuity—

(A) in the case of the benefit of a participant or beneficiary which was in pay status as of the beginning of the 3-year period ending on the termination date of the plan, to each such benefit, based on the provisions of the plan (as in effect during the 5-year period ending on such date) under which such benefit would be the least,

(B) in the case of a participant's or beneficiary's benefit (other than a benefit described in subparagraph (A)) which would have been in pay status as of the beginning of such 3-year period if the participant had retired prior to the beginning of the 3-year period and if his benefits had commenced (in the normal form of annuity under the plan) as of the beginning of such period, to each such benefit based on the provisions of the plan (as in effect during the 5-year period ending on such date) under which such benefit would be the least.

For purposes of subparagraph (A), the lowest benefit in pay status during a 3-year period shall be considered the benefit in pay status for such period.

(4) Fourth—

(A) to all other benefits (if any) of individuals under the plan guaranteed under this title (determined without regard to section 4022(b)(5)), and

(B) to the additional benefits (if any) which would be determined under subparagraph (A) if section 4022(b)(6) did not apply.

For purposes of this paragraph, section 4021 shall be applied without regard to subsection (c) thereof.

(5) Fifth, to all other nonforfeitable benefits under the plan.

(6) Sixth, to all other benefits under the plan.

(b) For purposes of subsection (a)—

(1) The amount allocated under any paragraph of subsection (a) with respect to any benefit shall be properly adjusted for any allocation of assets with respect to that benefit under a prior paragraph of subsection (a).

(2) If the assets available for allocation under any paragraph of subsection (a) (other than paragraphs (5) and (6)) are insufficient to satisfy in full the benefits of all individuals which are described in that paragraph, the assets shall be allocated pro rata among such individuals on the basis of the present value (as of the termination date) of their respective benefits described in that paragraph.

(3) This paragraph applies if the assets available for allocation under paragraph (5) of subsection (a) are not sufficient to satisfy in full the benefits of individuals described in that paragraph.

(A) If this paragraph applies, except as provided in subparagraph (B), the assets shall be allocated to the benefits of individuals described in such paragraph (5) on the basis of the benefits of individuals which would have been described in such paragraph (5) under the plan as in effect at the beginning of the 5-year period ending on the date of plan termination.

(B) If the assets available for allocation under subparagraph (A) are sufficient to satisfy in full the benefits described in such subparagraph (without regard to this subparagraph), then for purposes of subparagraph (A), benefits of individuals described in such subparagraph shall be determined on the basis of the plan as amended by the most recent plan amendment effective during such 5-year period under which the assets available for allocation are sufficient to satisfy in full the benefits of individuals described in subparagraph (A) and any assets remaining to be allocated under such subparagraph shall be allocated under subparagraph (A) on the basis of the plan as amended by the next succeeding plan amendment effective during such period.

(4) If the Secretary of the Treasury determines that the allocation made pursuant to this section (without regard to this paragraph) results in discrimination prohibited by section 401(a)(4) of the Internal Revenue Code of 1954 then, if required to prevent the disqualification of the plan (or any trust under the plan) under section 401(a), 403(a), or 405(a) of such Code, the assets allocated under subsection (a)(4)(B), (a)(5), and (a)(6) shall be reallocated to the extent necessary to avoid such discrimination.

(5) The term "mandatory contributions" means amounts contributed to the plan by a participant which are required as a condition of employment, as a condition of participation in such plan, or as a condition of obtaining benefits under the plan attributable to employer contributions. For this purpose, the total amount of mandatory contributions of a participant is the amount of such contributions reduced (but not below zero) by the sum of the amounts paid or distributed to him under the plan before its termination.

(6) A plan may establish subclasses and categories within the classes described in paragraphs (1) through (6)

of subsection (a) in accordance with regulations prescribed by the corporation.

(c) Any increase or decrease in the value of the assets of a single employer plan occurring during the period beginning on the later of (1) the date a trustee is appointed under section 4042(b) or (2) the date on which the plan is terminated is to be allocated between the plan and the corporation in the manner determined by the court (in the case of a court-appointed trustee) or as agreed upon by the corporation and the plan administrator in any other case. Any increase or decrease in the value of the assets of a single employer plan occurring after the date on which the plan is terminated shall be credited to, or suffered by, the corporation.

(d)(1) Any residual assets of a single employer plan may be distributed to the employer if—

(A) all liabilities of the plan to participants and their beneficiaries have been satisfied,

(B) the distribution does not contravene any provision of law, and

(C) the plan provides for such a distribution in these circumstances.

(2) Notwithstanding the provisions of paragraph (1), if any assets of the plan attributable to employee contributions remain after all liabilities of the plan to participants and their beneficiaries have been satisfied, such assets shall be equitably distributed to the employees who made such contributions (or their beneficiaries) in accordance with their rate of contributions.

Recapture of Certain Payments

Sec. 4045. (a) Except as provided in subsection (c), the trustee is authorized to recover for the benefit of a plan from a participant the recoverable amount (as defined in subsection (b)) of all payments from the plan to him which commenced within the 3-year period immediately preceding the time the plan is terminated.

(b) For purposes of subsection (a) the recoverable amount is the excess

Sec. 4044 (b) (4)

TEXT OF ERISA

of the amount determined under paragraph (1) over the amount determined under paragraph (2).

(1) The amount determined under this paragraph is the sum of the amount of the actual payments received by the participant within the 3-year period.

(2) The amount determined under this paragraph is the sum of—

(A) the sum of the amount such participant would have received during each consecutive 12-month period within the 3 years if the participant received the benefit in the form described in paragraph (3),

(B) the sum for each of the consecutive 12-month periods of the lesser of—

(i) the excess, if any, of $10,000 over the benefit in the form described in paragraph (3), or

(ii) the excess of the actual payment, if any, over the benefit in the form described in paragraph (3), and

(C) the present value at the time of termination of the participant's future benefits guaranteed under this title as if the benefits commenced in the form described in paragraph (3).

(3) The form of benefit for purposes of this subsection shall be the monthly benefit the participant would have received during the consecutive 12-month period, if he had elected at the time of the first payment made during the 3-year period, to receive his interest in the plan as a monthly benefit in the form of a life annuity commencing at the time of such first payment.

(c)(1) In the event of a distribution described in section 4043(b)(7) the 3-year period referred to in subsection (b) shall not end sooner than the date on which the corporation is notified of the distribution.

(2) The trustee shall not recover any payment made from a plan after or on account of the death of a participant, or to a participant who is disabled (within the meaning of section 72(m)(7) of the Internal Revenue Code of 1954).

(3) The corporation is authorized to waive, in whole or in part, the recovery of any amount which the trustee is authorized to recover for the benefit of a plan under this section in any case in which it determines that substantial economic hardship would result to the participant or his beneficiaries from whom such amount is recoverable.

Reports to Trustee

Sec. 4046. The corporation and the plan administrator of any plan to be terminated under this subtitle shall furnish to the trustee such information as the corporation or the plan administrator has and, to the extent practicable, can obtain regarding—

(1) the amount of benefits payable with respect to each participant under a plan to be terminated,

(2) the amount of basic benefits guaranteed under section 4022 or 4022A which are payable with respect to each participant in the plan,

(3) the present value, as of the time of termination, of the aggregate amount of basic berrefits payable under section 4022 or 4022A (determined without regard to section 4022B),

(4) the fair market value of the assets of the plan at the time of termination,

(5) the computations under section 4044, and all actuarial assumptions under which the items described in paragraphs (1) through (4) were computed, and

(6) any other information with respect to the plan the trustee may require in order to terminate the plan.

Restoration of Plans

Sec. 4047. Whenever the corporation determines that a plan which is to be terminated, or which is in the process of being terminated, under this subtitle should not be terminated as a result of such circumstances as the corporation determines to be relevant, the corporation is authorized to cease any activities undertaken to terminate the plan, and to take whatever action is necessary and

Sec. 4047

within its power to restore the plan to its status prior to the determination that the plan was to be terminated. In the case of a plan which has been terminated under section 4042 the corporation is authorized in any such case in which the corporation determines such action to be appropriate and consistent with its duties under this title, to take such action as may be necessary to restore the plan to its pretermination status, including, but not limited to, the transfer to the employer or a plan administrator of control of part or all of the remaining assets and liabilities of the plan.

Date of Termination

Sec. 4048. (a) For purposes of this title the date of termination of a single employer plan is—

(1) in the case of a plan terminated in accordance with the provisions of section 4041, the date established by the plan administrator and agreed to by the corporation,

(2) in the case of a plan terminated in accordance with the provisions of section 4042, the date established by the corporation and agreed to by the plan administrator, **or**

(3) in the case of a plan terminated in accordance with the provisions of either section in any case in which no agreement is reached between the plan administrator and the corporation (or the trustee), the date established by the court.

(b) For purposes of this title, the date of termination of a multiemployer plan is—

(1) in the case of a plan terminated in accordance with the provisions of section 4041A, the date determined under subsection (b) of that section; or

Sec. 4048

(2) in the case of a plan terminated in accordance with the provisions of section 4042, the date agreed to between the plan administrator and the corporation (or the trustee appointed under section 4042(b)(2), if any), or, if no agreement is reached, the date established by the court.

SUBTITLE D—LIABILITY

Amounts Payable by the Corporation

Sec. 4061. The corporation shall pay benefits under a single-employer plan terminated under this title subject to the limitations and requirements of subtitle B of this title. The corporation shall provide financial assistance to pay benefits under a multiemployer plan which is insolvent under section 4245 or 4281(d)(2)(A), subject to the limitations and requirements of subtitles, B, C, and E of this title. Amounts guaranteed by the corporation under sections 4022 and 4022A shall be paid by the corporation only out of the appropriate fund. The corporation shall make payments under the supplemental program to reimburse multiemployer plans for uncollectible withdrawal liability only out of the fund established under section 4005(e).

Liability of Employer

Sec. 4062. (a) This section applies to any employer who maintained a single employer plan at the time it was terminated, but does not apply—

(1) to an employer who maintained a plan with respect to which he paid the annual premium described in section 4006(a)(2)(B) for each of the 5 plan years immediately preceding the plan year during which the plan terminated unless the conditions imposed by the corporation on the payment of coverage under section 4023 do not permit such coverage to apply under the circumstances, or

(2) to the extent of any liability arising out of the insolvency of an insurance company with respect to an insurance contract.

(b) Any employer to which this section applies shall be liable to the corporation, in an amount equal to the lesser of—

(1) the excess of—

(A) the current value of the plan's benefits guaranteed under this title on the date of termination over

(B) the current value of the plan's assets allocable to such benefits on the date of termination, or

(2) 30 percent of the net worth of the employer determined as of a day, chosen by the corporation but not more than 120 days prior to the date of termination, computed without regard to any liability under this section.

(c) For purposes of subsection (b) (2) the net worth of an employer is—

(1) determined on whatever basis best reflects, in the determination of the corporation, the current status of the employer's operations and prospects at the time chosen for determining the net worth of the employer, and

(2) increased by the amount of any transfers of assets made by the employer determined by the corporation to be improper under the circumstances, including any such transfers which would be inappropriate under title 11 if the employer were a debtor in a case under chapter 7 of such title.

(d) For purposes of this section the following rules apply in the case of certain corporate reorganizations.

(1) If an employer ceases to exist by reason of a reorganization which involves a mere change in identity, form, or place of organization, however effected, a successor corporation resulting from such reorganization shall be treated as the employer to whom this section applies.

(2) If an employer ceases to exist by reason of a liquidation into a parent corporation, the parent corporation shall be treated as the employer to whom this section applies.

(3) If an employer ceases to exist by reason of a merger, consolidation, or division, the successor corporation or corporations shall be treated as the employer to whom this section applies.

(e) If an employer ceases operations at a facility in any location and, as a result of such cessation of operations, more than 20 percent of the total number of his employees who are participants under a plan established and maintained by him are separated from employment, the employer shall be treated with respect to that plan as if he were a substantial employer under a plan under which more than one employer makes contributions and the provisions of sections 4063, 4064, and 4065 shall apply.

Liability of Substantial Employer for Withdrawal

Sec. 4063. (a) Except as provided in subsection (d), the plan administrator of a plan under which more than one employer makes contributions (other than a multiemployer plan)—

(1) shall notify the corporation of the withdrawal of a substantial employer from the plan, within 60 days after such withdrawal, and

(2) request that the corporation determine the liability of such employer under this subtitle with respect to such withdrawal.

The corporation shall, as soon as practicable thereafter, determine whether such employer is liable for any amount under this subtitle with respect to the withdrawal and notify such employer of such liability.

(b) Except as provided in subsection (c), an employer who withdraws from a plan to which section 4021 applies, during a plan year for which he was a substantial employer, and who is notified by the corporation as provided by subsection (a), shall be liable to the corporation in accordance with the provisions of section 4062 and this section. The amount of such employer's liability shall be

Sec. 4063 (b)

computed on the basis of an amount determined by the corporation to be the amount described in section 4062 for the entire plan, as if the plan had been terminated by the corporation on the date of the employer's withdrawal, multiplied by a fraction—

(1) the numerator of which is the total amount required to be contributed to the plan by such employer for the last 5 years ending prior to the withdrawal, and

(2) the denominator of which is the total amount required to be contributed to the plan by all employers for such last 5 years.

In addition to and in lieu of the manner prescribed in the preceding sentence, the corporation may also determine the liability of each such employer on any other equitable basis prescribed by the corporation in regulations. Any amount collected by the corporation under this subsection shall be held in escrow subject to disposition in accordance with the provisons of paragraphs (2) and (3) of subsection (c).

(c)(1) In lieu of payment of his liability under this section the employer may be required to furnish a bond to the corporation in an amount not exceeding 150 percent of his liability to insure payment of his liability under this section. The bond shall have as surety thereon a corporate surety company which is an acceptable surety on Federal bonds under authority granted by the Secretary of the Treasury under sections 6 through 13 of title 6, United States Code. Any such bond shall be in a form or of a type approved by the Secretary including individual bonds or schedule or blanket forms of bonds which cover a group or class.

(2) If the plan is not terminated within the 5-year period commencing on the day of withdrawal, the liability of such employer is abated and any payment held in escrow shall be refunded without interest to the employer (or his bond cancelled) in accordance with bylaws or rules prescribed by the corporation.

(3) If the plan terminates within the 5-year period commencing on the day of withdrawal, the corporation shall—

(A) demand payment or realize on the bond and hold such amount in escrow for the benefit of the plan;

(B) treat any escrowed payments under this section as if they were plan assets and apply them in a manner consistent with this subtitle; and

(C) refund any amount to the employer which is not required to meet any obligation of the corporation with respect to the plan.

(d) The provisions of this subsection apply in the case of a withdrawal described in subsection (a), and the provisions of subsections (b) and (c) shall not apply, if the corporation determines that the procedure provided for under this subsection is consistent with the purposes of this section and section 4064 and is more appropriate in the particular case. Upon a showing by the plan administrator of a plan (other than a multiemployer plan) that the withdrawal from the plan by any employer or employers has resulted, or will result, in a significant reduction in the amount of aggregate contributions to or under the plan by employers, the corporation may—

(1) require the plan fund to be equitably allocated between those participants no longer working in covered service under the plan as a result of their employer's withdrawal, and those participants who remain in covered service under the plan;

(2) treat that portion of the plan funds allocable under paragraph (1) to participants no longer in covered service as a termination; and

(3) treat that portion of the plan fund allocable to participants remaining in covered service as a separate plan.

(e) The corporation is authorized to waive the application of the provisions of subsections (b), (c), and (d) of this section to any employer or plan administrator whenever it determines that there is an indemnity

Sec. 4063 (c)

agreement in effect among all other employers under the plan which is adequate to satisfy the purposes of this section and of section 4064.

Liability of Employers on Termination of Plan Maintained by More than One Employer

Sec. 4064. (a) This section applies to all employers who maintain a plan under which more than one employer makes contributions (other than a multiemployer plan) at the time such plan is terminated, or who, at any time within the 5 plan years preceding the date of termination, made contributions under the plan.

(b) The corporation shall determine the liability of each such employer in a manner consistent with section 4062 except that the amount of the liability determined under section 4062(b)(1) with respect to the entire plan shall be allocated to each employer by multiplying such amounts by a fraction—

(1) the numerator of which is the amount required to be contributed to the plan by each employer for the last 5 plan years ending prior to the termination, and

(2) the denominator of which is the total amount required to be contributed to the plan by all such employers for such last 5 years,

and the limitation described in section 4062(b)(2) shall be applied separately to each employer. The corporation may also determine the liability of each such employer on any other equitable basis prescribed by the corporation in regulations.

Annual Report of Plan Administrator

Sec. 4065. For each plan year for which section 4021 applies to a plan, the plan administrator shall file with the corporation, on a form prescribed by the corporation, an annual report which identifies the plan and plan administrator and which includes—

(1) a copy of each notification required under section 4063 with respect to such year,

(2) a statement disclosing whether any reportable event (described in section 4043(b) occurred during the plan year except to the extent the corporation waives such requirement, and

(3) in the case of a multiemployer plan, information with respect to such plan which the corporation determines is necessary for the enforcement of subtitle E and requires by regulation, which may include—

(A) a statement certified by the plan's enrolled actuary of—

(i) the value of all vested benefits under the plan as of the end of the plan year, and

(ii) the value of the plan's assets as of the end of the plan year;

(B) a statement certified by the plan sponsor of each claim for outstanding withdrawal liability (within the meaning of section 4001(a)(12)) and its value as of the end of that plan year and as of the end of the preceding plan year; and

(C) the number of employers having an obligation to contribute to the plan and the number of employers required to make withdrawal liability payments.

The report shall be filed within 6 months after the close of the plan year to which it relates. The corporation shall cooperate with the Secretary of the Treasury and the Secretary of Labor in an endeavor to coordinate the timing and content, and possibly obtain the combination, of reports under this section with reports required to be made by plan administrators to such Secretaries.

Annual Notification to Substantial Employers

Sec. 4066. The plan administrator of each plan under which contributions are made by more than one employer (other than a multiemployer plan) shall notify, within 6 months after the close of each plan year, any employer making contributions under that plan who is described in section 4001(a)(2) that he is a substantial employer for that year.

Recovery of Employer Liability for Plan Termination

Sec. 4067. The corporation is authorized to make arrangements with employers who are liable under section 4062, 4063, or 4064 for payment of their liability, including arrangements for deferred payment on such terms and for such periods as the corporation deems equitable and appropriate.

Lien for Liability of Employer

Sec. 4068. (a) If any employer or employers liable to the corporation under section 4062, 4063, or 4064 neglect or refuse to pay, after demand, the amount of such liability (including interest), there shall be a lien in favor of the corporation upon all property and rights to property, whether real or personal, belonging to such employer or employers.

(b) The lien imposed by subsection (a) arises on the date of termination of a plan, and continues until the liability imposed under section 4062, 4063, or 4064 is satisfied or becomes unenforceable by reason of lapse of time.

(c)(1) Except as otherwise provided under this section, the priority of the lien imposed under subsection (a) shall be determined in the same manner as under section 6323 of the Internal Revenue Code of 1954. Such section 6323 shall be applied by substituting "lien imposed by section 4068 of the Employee Retirement Income Security Act of 1974" for "lien imposed by section 6321"; "corporation" for "Secretary or his delegate"; "employer liability lien" for "tax lien"; "employer" for "taxpayer"; "lien arising under section 4068(a) of the Employee Retirement Income Security Act of 1974" for "assessment of the tax"; and "payment of the loan value is made to the corporation" for "satisfaction of a levy pursuant to section 6332(b)"; each place such terms appear.

(2) In a case under title II of the United States Code or in insolvency proceedings, the lien imposed under subsection (a) of this section shall be treated in the same manner as a tax due and owing to the United States for purposes of title 11 or section 191 of title 131.

(3) For purposes of applying section 6323(a) of the Internal Revenue Code of 1954 to determine the priority between the lien imposed under subsection (a) and a Federal tax lien, each lien shall be treated as a judgment lien arising as of the time notice of such lien is filed.

(4) For purposes of this subsection, notice of the lien imposed by subsection (a) shall be filed in the same manner as under section 6323(f) and (g) of the Internal Revenue Code of 1954.

(d)(1) In any case where there has been a refusal or neglect to pay the liability imposed under section 4062, 4063, or 4064, the corporation may bring civil action in a district court of the United States to enforce the lien of the corporation under this section with respect to such liability or to subject any property, of whatever nature, of the employer, or in which he has any right, title, or interest to the payment of such liability.

(2) The liability imposed by section 4062, 4063, or 4064 may be collected by a proceeding in court if the proceeding is commenced within 6 years after the date upon which the plan was terminated or prior to the expiration of any period for collection agreed upon in writing by the corporation and the employer before the expiration of such 6-year period. The period of limitations provided under this paragraph shall be suspended for the period the assets of the employer are in the control or custody of any court of the United States, or of any State, or of the District of Columbia, and for 6 months thereafter, and for any period during which the employer is outside the United States if such period of absence is for a continuous period of at least 6 months.

(e) If the corporation determines, with the consent of the board of directors, that release of the lien or subordination of the lien to any other creditor of the employer or employers would not adversely affect the collection of the liability imposed under section 4062, 4063, or 4064, or that the amount realizable by the corporation from the property to which the lien attaches will ultimately be increased by such release or subordination, and that the ultimate collection of the liability will be facilitated by such release or subordination, the corporation may issue a certificate of release or subordination of the lien with respect to such property, or any part thereof.

SUBTITLE E—SPECIAL PROVISIONS FOR MULTIEMPLOYER PLANS

PART 1—EMPLOYER WITHDRAWALS

Withdrawal Liability Established

Sec. 4201. (a) If an employer withdraws from a multiemployer plan in a complete withdrawal or a partial withdrawal, then the employer is liable to the plan in the amount determined under this part to be the withdrawal liability.

(b) For purposes of subsection (a)—

(1) The withdrawal liability of an employer to a plan is the amount determined under section 4211 to be the allocable amount of unfunded vested benefits, adjusted—

(A) first, by any de minimis reduction applicable under section 4209,

(B) next, in the case of a partial withdrawal, in accordance with section 4206,

(C) then, to the extent necessary to reflect the limitation on annual payments under section 4219(c)(1)(B), and

(D) finally, in accordance with section 4225.

(2) The term "complete withdrawal" means a partial withdrawal described in section 4203.

(3) The term "partial withdrawal" means a partial withdrawal described in section 4205.

Determination and Collection of Liability; Notification of Employer

Sec. 4202. When an employer withdraws from a multiemployer plan, the plan sponsor, in accordance with this part, shall—

(1) determine the amount of the employer's withdrawal liability,

(2) notify the employer of the amount of the withdrawal liability, and

(3) collect the amount of the withdrawal liability from the employer.

Complete Withdrawal

Sec. 4203. (a) For purposes of this part, a complete withdrawal from a multiemployer plan occurs when an employer—

(1) permanently ceases to have an obligation to contribute under the plan, or

(2) permanently ceases all covered operations under the plan.

(b)(1) Notwithstanding subsection (a), in the case of an employer that has an obligation to contribute under a plan for work performed in the building and construction industry, a complete withdrawal occurs only as described in paragraph (2), if—

(A) substantially all the employees with respect to whom the employer has an obligation to contribute under the plan perform work in the building and construction industry, and

(B) the plan—

(i) primarily covers employees in the building and construction industry, or

(ii) is amended to provide that this subsection applies to employers described in this paragraph.

(2) A withdrawal occurs under this paragraph if—

(A) an employer ceases to have an obligation to contribute under the plan, and

(B) the employer—

(i) continues to perform work in the jurisdiction of the collective bargaining agreement of the type for which contributions were previously required, or

(ii) resumes such work within 5 years after the date on which the obligation to contribute under the plan ceases, and does not renew the obligation at the time of the resumption.

(3) In the case of a plan terminated

by mass withdrawal (within the meaning of section 4041A(a)(2)), paragraph (2) shall be applied by substituting "3 years" for "5 years" in subparagraph (B)(ii).

(c)(1) Notwithstanding subsection (a), in the case of an employer that has an obligation to contribute under a plan for work performed in the entertainment industry, primarily on a temporary or project-by-project basis, if the plan primarily covers employees in the entertainment industry, a complete withdrawal occurs only as described in subsection (b)(2) applied by substituting "plan" for "collective bargaining agreement" in subparagraph (B)(i) thereof.

(2) For purposes of this subsection, the term "entertainment industry" means—

(A) theater, motion picture (except to the extent provided in regulations prescribed by the corporation), radio, television, sound or visual recording, music, and dance, and

(B) such other entertainment activities as the corporation may determine to be appropriate.

(3) The corporation may by regulation exclude a group or class of employers described in the preceding sentence from the application of this subsection if the corporation determines that such exclusion is necessary—

(A) to protect the interest of the plan's participants and beneficiaries, or

(B) to prevent a significant risk of loss to the corporation with respect to the plan.

(4) A plan may be amended to provide that this subsection shall not apply to a group or class of employers under the plan.

(d)(1) Notwithstanding subsection (a), in the case of an employer who—

(A) has an obligation to contribute under a plan described in paragraph (2) primarily for work described in such paragraph, and

(B) does not continue to perform work within the jurisdiction of the plan,

a complete withdrawal occurs only as described in paragraph (3).

(2) A plan is described in this paragraph if substantially all of the contributions required under the plan are made by employers primarily engaged in the long and short haul trucking industry, the household goods moving industry, or the public warehousing industry.

(3) A withdrawal occurs under this paragraph if—

(A) an employer permanently ceases to have an obligation to contribute under the plan or permanently ceases all covered operations under the plan, and

(B) either—

(i) the corporation determines that the plan has suffered substantial damage to its contribution base as a result of such cessation, or

(ii) the employer fails to furnish a bond issued by a corporate surety company that is an acceptable surety for purposes of section 412, or an amount held in escrow by a bank or similar financial institution satisfactory to the plan, in an amount equal to 50 percent of the withdrawal liability of the employer.

(4) If, after an employer furnishes a bond or escrow to a plan under paragraph (3)(B)(ii), the corporation determines that the cessation of the employer's obligation to contribute under the plan (considered together with any cessations by other employers), or cessation of covered operations under the plan, has resulted in substantial damage to the contribution base of the plan, the employer shall be treated as having withdrawn from the plan on the date on which the obligation to contribute or covered operations ceased, and such bond or escrow shall be paid to the plan. The corporation shall not make a determination under this paragraph more than 60 months after the date on which such obligation to contribute or covered operations ceased.

(5) If the corporation determines that the employer has no further liability under the plan either—

(A) because it determines that the contribution base of the plan has not suffered substantial damage as a result of the cessation of the employer's obligation to contribute or cessation of covered operations (considered together with any cessation of contribution obligation, or of covered operations, with respect to other employers), or

(B) because it may not make a determination under paragraph (4) because of the last sentence thereof,

then the bond shall be cancelled or the escrow refunded.

(6) Nothing in this subsection shall be construed as a limitation on the amount of the withdrawal liability of any employer.

(e) For purposes of this part, the date of a complete withdrawal is the date of the cessation of the obligation to contribute or the cessation of covered operations.

(f)(1) The corporation may prescribe regulations under which plans in industries other than the construction or entertainment industries may be amended to provide for special withdrawal liability rules similar to the rules described in subsections (b) and (c).

(2) Regulations under paragraph (1) shall permit use of special withdrawal liability rules—

(A) only in industries (or portions thereof) in which, as determined by the corporation, the characteristics that would make use of such rules appropriate are clearly shown, and

(B) only if the corporation determines, in each instance in which special withdrawal liability rules are permitted, that use of such rules will not pose a significant risk to the corporation under this title.

Sale of Assets

Sec. 4204. (a)(1) A complete or partial withdrawal of an employer (hereinafter in this section referred to as the 'seller') under this section does not occur solely because, as a result of a bona fide, arm's-length sale of assets to an unrelated party (hereinafter in this section referred to as the 'purchaser'), the seller ceases covered operations or ceases to have an obligation to contribute for such operations, if—

(A) the purchaser has an obligation to contribute to the plan with respect to the operations for substantially the same number of contribution base units for which the seller had an obligation to contribute to the plan;

(B) the purchaser provides to the plan for a period of 5 plan years commencing with the first plan year beginning after the sale of assets, a bond issued by a corporate surety company that is an acceptable surety for purposes of section 412 of this Act, or an amount held in escrow by a bank or similar financial institution, satisfactory to the plan, in an amount equal to the greater of—

(i) the average annual contribution required to be made by the seller with respect to the operations under the plan for the 3 plan years preceding the plan year in which the sale of the employer's assets occurs, or

(ii) the annual contribution that the seller was required to make with respect to the operations under the plan for the last plan year before the plan year in which the sale of the assets occurs,

which bond or escrow shall be paid to the plan if the purchaser withdraws from the plan, or fails to make a contribution to the plan when due, at any time during the first 5 plan years beginning after the sale; and

(C) the contract for sale provides that, if the purchaser withdraws in a complete withdrawal, or a partial withdrawal with respect to operations, during such first 5 plan years, the seller is secondarily liable for any withdrawal liability it would have had to the plan with respect to the operations (but for this section) if the liability of the purchaser with respect to the plan is not paid.

(2) If the purchaser—

(A) withdraws before the last day of the fifth plan year beginning after the sale, and

(B) fails to make any withdrawal liability payment when due, then the seller shall pay to the plan an amount equal to the payment that would have been due from the seller but for this section.

(3)(A) If all, or substantially all, of the seller's assets are distributed, or if the seller is liquidated before the end of the 5 plan year period described in paragraph (1)(C), then the seller shall provide a bond or amount in escrow equal to the present value of the withdrawal liability the seller would have had but for this subsection.

(B) If only a portion of the seller's assets are distributed during such period, then a bond or escrow shall be required, in accordance with regulations prescribed by the corporation, in a manner consistent with subparagraph (A).

(4) The liability of the party furnishing a bond or escrow under this subsection shall be reduced, upon payment of the bond or escrow to the plan, by the amount thereof.

(b)(1) For the purposes of this part, the liability of the purchaser shall be determined as if the purchaser had been required to contribute to the plan in the year of the sale and the 4 plan years preceding the sale the amount the seller was required to contribute for such operations for such 5 plan years.

(2) If the plan is in reorganization in the plan year in which the sale of assets occurs, the purchaser shall furnish a bond or escrow in an amount equal to 200 percent of the amount described in subsection (a)(1)(B).

(c) The corporation may by regulation vary the standards in subparagraphs (B) and (C) of subsection (a)(1) if the variance would more effectively or equitably carry out the purposes of this title. Before it promulgates such regulations, the corporation may grant individual or class variances or exemptions from the requirements of such subparagraphs if the particular case warrants it. Before granting such an individual or class variance or exemption, the corporation—

(1) shall publish notice in the Federal Register of the pendency of the variance or exemption,

(2) shall require that adequate notice be given to interested persons, and

(3) shall afford interested persons an opportunity to present their views.

(d) For purposes of this section, the term "unrelated party" means a purchaser or seller who does not bear a relationship to the seller or purchaser, as the case may be, that is described in section 267(b) of the Internal Revenue Code of 1954, or that is described in regulations prescribed by the corporation applying principles similar to to the principles of such section.

Partial Withdrawals

* Sec. 4205. (a) Except as otherwise provided in this section, there is a partial withdrawal by an employer from a plan on the last day of a plan year if for such plan year—

(1) there is a 70-percent contribution decline, or

(2) there is a partial cessation of the employer's contribution obligation.

(b) For purposes of subsection (a)—

(1)(A) There is a 70-percent contribution decline for any plan year if during each plan year in the 3-year testing period the employer's contribution base units do not exceed 30 percent of the employer's contribution base units for the high base year.

(B) For purposes of subparagraph (A)—

(i) The term "3-year testing period" means the period consisting of the plan year and the immediately preceding 2 plan years.

(ii) The number of contribution base units for the high base year is the average number of such units for the 2 plan years for which the employer's contribution base units were the highest within the 5 plan years immediately preceding the beginning of the 3-year testing period.

(2)(A) There is a partial cessation of the employer's contribution obligation for the plan year if, during such year—

Sec. 4204 (b)

(i) the employer permanently ceases to have an obligation to contribute under one or more but fewer than all collective bargaining agreements under which the employer has been obligated to contribute under the plan but continues to perform work in the jurisdiction of the collective bargaining agreement of the type for which contributions were previously required or transfers such work to another location, or

(ii) an employer permanently ceases to have an obligation to contribute under the plan with respect to work performed at one or more but fewer than all of its facilities, but continues to perform work at the facility of the type for which the obligation to contribute ceased.

(B) For purposes of subparagraph (A), a cessation of obligations under a collective bargaining agreement shall not be considered to have occurred solely because, with respect to the same plan, one agreement that requires contributions to the plan has been substituted for another agreement.

(c)(1) In the case of a plan in which a majority of the covered employees are employed in the retail food industry, the plan may be amended to provide that this section shall be applied with respect to such plan—

(A) by substituting "35 percent" for "70 percent" in subsections (a) and (b), and

(B) by substituting "65 percent" for "30 percent" in subsection (b).

(2) Any amendment adopted under paragraph (1) shall provide rules for the equitable reduction of withdrawal liability in any case in which the number of the plan's contribution base units, in the 2 plan years following the plan year of withdrawal of the employer, is higher than such number immediately after the withdrawal.

(3) Section 4208 shall not apply to a plan which has been amended under paragraph (1).

(d) In the case of a plan described in section 404(c) of the Internal Revenue Code of 1954, or a continuation thereof, the plan may be amended to provide rules setting forth other conditions consistent with the purposes of this Act under which an employer has liability for partial withdrawal.

* [*Editor's Note:* The following special provisions of PL 96-364 are exceptions to Section 4205:

(2)(A) For the purpose of applying section 4205 of the Employee Retirement Income Security Act of 1974 in the case of an employer described in subparagraph (B)—

(i) "more than 75 percent" shall be substituted for "70 percent" in subsections (a) and (b) of such section,

(ii) "25 percent or less" shall be substituted for "30 percent" in subsection (b) of such section, and

(iii) the number of contribution units for the high base year shall be the average annual number of such units for calendar years 1970 and 1971.

(B) An employer is described in this subparagraph if—

(i) the employer is engaged in the trade or business of shipping bulk cargoes in the Great Lakes Maritime Industry, and whose fleet consists of vessels the gross registered tonnage of which was at least 7,800, as stated in the American Bureau of Shipping Record, and

(ii) whose fleet during any 5 years from the period 1970 through and including 1979 has experienced a 33 percent or more increase in the contribution units as measured from the average annual contribution units for the calendar years 1970 and 1971.

(3)(A) For the purpose of determining the withdrawal liability of an employer under title IV of the Employee Retirement Income Security Act of 1974 from a plan that terminates while the plan is insolvent (within the meaning of section 4245 of such Act), the plan's unfunded vested benefits shall be reduced by an amount equal to the sum of all overburden credits that were applied in determining the plan's accumulated funding deficiency for all plan years preceding the first plan year in which the plan is insolvent, plus interest thereon.

(B) The provisions of subparagraph (A) apply only if—

(i) the plan would have been eligible for the overburden credit in the last plan year beginning before the date of the enactment of this Act, if section 4243 of the Employee Retirement Income Security Act of 1974 had been in effect for that plan year, and

(ii) the Pension Benefit Guaranty Corporation determines that the reduction of unfunded vested benefits under subparagraph (A) would not significantly increase the risk of loss to the corporation.

(4) In the case of an employer who withdrew before the date of enactment of this Act from a multiemployer plan covering employees in the seagoing industry (as determined by the corporation), sections 4201 through 4219 of the Employee Retirement Income Security Act of 1974, as added by this Act, are effective as of May 3, 1979. For the purpose of applying section 4217 for purposes of the preceding sentence, the date "May 2, 1979," shall be substituted for "April 28, 1980," and the date "May 3, 1979" shall be substituted for April 29, 1980". For purposes of this paragraph, terms which are used in title IV of the Employee Retirement Income Security Act of 1974, or in regulations prescribed under that title, and which are used in the preceding sentence have the same meaning as when used in that Act or those regulations. For purposes of this paragraph, the term "employer" includes only a substantial employer covering employees in the seagoing industry (as so determined) in connection with ports on the West Coast of the United States, but does not include an employer who withdrew from a plan because of a change in the collective bargaining representative.

(d) For purposes of section 4205 of the Employee Retirement Income Security Act of 1974—

(1) subsection (a) (1) of such section shall not apply to any plan year beginning before April 29, 1982,

(2) subsection (a) (2) of such section shall not apply with respect to any cessation of contribution obligations occurring before April 29, 1980, and

(3) in applying subsection (b) of such section, the employer's contribution base units for any plan year ending before April 29, 1980, shall be deemed to be equal to the employer's contribution base units for the last plan year ending before such date.

(e)(1) In the case of a partial withdrawal under section 4205 of the Employee Retirement Income Security Act of 1974, an employer who—

Adjustment for Partial Withdrawal

Sec. 4206. (a) The amount of an employer's liability for a partial withdrawal, before the application of sections 4219(c)(1) and 4225, is equal to the product of—

(1) the amount determined under section 4211, and adjusted under section 4209 if appropriate, determined as if the employer had withdrawn from the plan in a complete withdrawal—

(A) on the date of the partial withdrawal, or

(B) in the case of a partial withdrawal described in section 4205(a)(1) (relating to 70-percent contribution decline), on the last day of the first plan year in the 3-year testing period, multiplied by

(2) a fraction which is 1 minus a fraction—

(A) the numerator of which is the employer's contribution base units for the plan year following the plan year in which the partial withdrawal occurs, and

(B) the denominator of which is the average of the employer's contribution base units for—

(i) except as provided in clause (ii),

Sec. 4206

the 5 plan years immediately preceding the plan year in which the partial withdrawal occurs, or

(ii) in the case of a partial withdrawal described in section 4205(a)(1) (relating to 70-percent contribution decline), the 5 plan years immediately preceding the beginning of the 3-year testing period.

(b)(1) In the case of an employer that has withdrawal liability for a partial withdrawal from a plan, any withdrawal liability of that employer for a partial or complete withdrawal from that plan in a subsequent plan year shall be reduced by the amount of any partial withdrawal liability (reduced by any abatement or reduction of such liability) of the employer with respect to the plan for a previous plan year.

(2) The corporation shall prescribe such regulations as may be necessary to provide for proper adjustments in the reduction provided by paragraph (1) for—

(A) changes in unfunded vested benefits arising after the close of the prior year for which partial withdrawal liability was determined,

(B) changes in contribution base units occurring after the close of the

---

(A) before December 13, 1979, had publicly announced the total cessation of covered operations at a facility in a State (and such cessation occurred within 12 months after the announcement),

(B) had not been obligated to make contributions to the plan on behalf of the employees at such facility for more than 8 years before the discontinuance of contributions, and

(C) after the discontinuance of contributions does not within 1 year after the date of the partial withdrawal perform work in the same State of the type for which contributions were previously required,

shall be liable under such section with respect to such partial withdrawal in an amount not greater than the amount determined under paragraph (2).

(2) The amount determined under this paragraph is the excess (if any) of—

(A) the present value (on the withdrawal date) of the benefits under the plan which—

(i) were vested on the withdrawal date (or, if earlier, at the time of separation from service with the employer at the facility),

(ii) were accrued by employees who on December 13, 1979 (or, if earlier, at the time of separation from service with the employer at the facility), were employed at the facility, and

(iii) are attributable to service with the withdrawing employer, over

(B)(i) the sum of—

(I) all employer contributions to the plan on behalf of employees at the facility before the withdrawal date,

(II) interest (to the withdrawal date) on amounts described in subclause (I), and

(III) $100,000, reduced by

(ii) the sum of—

(I) the benefits paid under the plan on or before the withdrawal date with respect to former employees who separated from employment at the facility, and

(II) interest (to the withdrawal date) on amounts described in subclause (I).

(3) For purposes of paragraph (2)—

(A) actuarial assumptions shall be those used in the last actuarial report completed before December 13, 1979,

(B) the term "withdrawal date" means the date on which the employer ceased work at the facility of the type for which contributions were previously required, and

(C) the term "facility" means the facility referred to in paragraph (1).]

Sec. 4206 (b) (2)

prior year for which partial withdrawal liability was determined, and

(C) any other factors for which it determines adjustment to be appropriate,
so that the liability for any complete or partial withdrawal in any subsequent year (after the application of the reduction) properly reflects the employer's share of liability with respect to the plan.

Reduction or Waiver of Complete Withdrawal Liability

Sec. 4207. (a) The corporation shall provide by regulation for the reduction or waiver of liability for a complete withdrawal in the event that an employer who has withdrawn from a plan subsequently resumes covered operations under the plan or renews an obligation to contribute under the plan, to the extent that the corporation determines that reduction or waiver of withdrawal liability is consistent with the purposes of this Act.

(b) The corporation shall prescribe by regulation a procedure and standards for the amendment of plans to provide alternative rules for the reduction or waiver of liability for a complete withdrawal in the event that an employer who has withdrawn from the plan subsequently resumes covered operations or renews an obligation to contribute under the plan. The rules may apply only to the extent that the rules are consistent with the purposes of this Act.

Reduction of Partial Withdrawal Liability

Sec. 4208. (a)(1) If, for any 2 consecutive plan years following the plan year in which an employer has partially withdrawn from a plan under section 4205(a)(1) (referred to elsewhere in this section as the "partial withdrawal year"), the number of contribution base units with respect to which the employer has an obligation to contribute under the plan for each such year is not less than 90 percent of the total number of contribution base units with respect to which the employer had an obligation to contribute under the plan for the high base year (within the meaning of section 4205(b)(1)(B)(ii)), then the employer shall have no obligation to make payments with respect to such partial withdrawal (other than delinquent payments) for plan years beginning after the second consecutive plan year following the partial withdrawal year.

(2)(A) For any plan year for which the number of contribution base units with respect to which an employer who has partially withdrawn under section 4205(a)(1) has an obligation to contribute under the plan equals or exceeds the number of units for the highest year determined under paragraph (1) without regard to "90 percent of", the employer may furnish (in lieu of payment of the partial withdrawal liability determined under section 4206) a bond to the plan in the amount determined by the plan sponsor (not exceeding 50 percent of the annual payment otherwise required).

(B) If the plan sponsor determines under paragraph (1) that the employer has no further liability to the plan for the partial withdrawal, then the bond shall be cancelled.

(C) If the plan sponsor determines under paragraph (1) that the employer continues to have liability to the plan for the partial withdrawal, then—

(i) the bond shall be paid to the plan,

(ii) the employer shall immediately be liable for the outstanding amount of liability due with respect to the plan

Sec. 4207

year for which the bond was posted, and

(iii) the employer shall continue to make the partial withdrawal liability payments as they are due.

(b) If—

(1) for any 2 consecutive plan years following a partial withdrawal under section 4205(a)(1), the number of contribution base units with respect to which the employer has an obligation to contribute for each such year exceeds 30 percent of the total number of contribution base units with respect to which the employer had an obligation to contribute for the high base year (within the meaning of section 4205(b)(1)(B)(ii)), and

(2) the total number of contribution base units with respect to which all employers under the plan have obligations to contribute in each of such 2 consecutive years is not less than 90 percent of the total number of contribution base units for which all employers had obligations to contribute in the partial withdrawal plan year;

then, the employer shall have no obligation to make payments with respect to such partial withdrawal (other than delinquent payments) for plan years beginning after the second such consecutive plan year.

(c) In any case in which, in any plan year following a partial withdrawal under section 4205(a)(1), the number of contribution base units with respect to which the employer has an obligation to contribute for such year equals or exceeds 110 percent (or such other percentage as the plan may provide by amendment and which is not prohibited under regulations prescribed by the corporation) of the number of contribution base units with respect to which the employer had an obligation to contribute in the partial withdrawal year, then the amount of the employer's partial withdrawal liability payment for such year shall be reduced pro rata, in accordance with regulations prescribed by the corporation.

(d)(1) An employer to whom section 4202(b) (relating to the building and construction industry) applies is liable for a partial withdrawal only if the employer's obligation to contribute under the plan is continued for no more than an insubstantial portion of its work in the craft and area jurisdiction of the collective bargaining agreement of the type for which contributions are required.

(2) An employer to whom section 4202(c) (relating to the entertainment industry) applies shall have no liability for a partial withdrawal except under the conditions and to the extent prescribed by the corporation by regulation.

(e)(1) The corporation may prescribe regulations providing for the reduction or elimination of partial withdrawal liability under any conditions with respect to which the corporation determines that reduction or elimination of partial withdrawals liability is consistent with the purposes of this Act.

(2) Under such regulations, reduction of withdrawal liability shall be provided only with respect to subsequent changes in the employer's contributions for the same operations, or under the same collective bargaining agreement, that gave rise to the partial withdrawal, and changes in the employer's contribution base units with respect to other facilities or other collective bargaining agreements shall not be taken into account.

(3) The corporation shall prescribe by regulation a procedure by which a plan may by amendment adopt rules for the reduction or elimination of partial withdrawal liability under any other conditions, subject to the approval of the corporation based on its determination that adoption of such rules by the plan is consistent with the purposes of this Act.

De Minimis Rule

Sec. 4209. (a) Except in the case of a plan amended under subsection (b), the amount of the unfunded vested benefits allocable under section 4211 to an employer who withdraws from a plan shall be reduced by the smaller of—

(1) ¾ of 1 percent of the plan's unfunded vested obligations (determined as of the end of the plan year ending before the date of withdrawal), or

(2) $50,000,

reduced by the amount, if any, by which the unfunded vested benefits allowable to the employer, determined without regard to this subsection, exceeds $100,000.

(b) A plan may be amended to provide for the reduction of the amount determined under section 4211 by not more than the greater of—

(1) the amount determined under subsection (a), or

(2) the lesser of—

(A) the amount determined under subsection (a)(1), or

(B) $100,000,

reduced by the amount, if any, by which the amount determined under section 4211 for the employer, determined without regard to this subsection, exceeds $150,000.

(c) This section does not apply—

(1) to an employer who withdraws in a plan year in which substantially all employers withdraw from the plan, or

(2) in any case in which substantially all employers withdraw from the plan during a period of one or more plan years pursuant to an agreement or arrangement to withdraw, to an employer who withdraws pursuant to such agreement or arrangement.

(d) In any action or proceeding to determine or collect withdrawal liability, if substantially all employers have withdrawn from a plan within a period of 3 plan years, an employer who has withdrawn from such plan during such period shall be presumed to have withdrawn from the plan pursuant to an agreement or arrangement, unless the employer proves otherwise by a preponderance of the evidence.

No Withdrawal Liability for Certain Temporary Contribution Obligation Periods

Sec. 4210. (a) An employer who withdraws from a plan in complete or partial withdrawal is not liable to the plan if the employer—

(1) first had an obligation to contribute to the plan after the date of the enactment of the Multiemployer Pension Plan Amendments Act of 1980,

(2) had an obligation to contribute to the plan for no more than the lesser of—

(A) 6 consecutive plan years preceding the date on which the employer withdraws, or

(B) the number of years required for vesting under the plan,

(3) was required to make contributions to the plan for each such plan year in an amount equal to less than 2 percent of the sum of all employer contributions made to the plan for each such year, and

(4) has never avoided withdrawal liability because of the application of this section with respect to the plan.

(b) Subsection (a) shall apply to an employer with respect to a plan only if—

(1) the plan is not a plan which primarily covers employees in the building and construction industry;

(2) the plan is amended to provide that subsection (a) applies;

(3) the plan provides, or is amended to provide, that the reduction under section 411(a)(3)(E) of the Internal Revenue Code of 1954 applies with respect to the employees of the employer; and

(4) the ratio of the assets of the plan for the plan year preceding the first plan year for which the employer was required to contribute to the plan to the benefit payments made during that plan year was at least 8 to 1.

Methods for Computing Withdrawal Liability

Sec. 4211. (a) The amount of the unfunded vested benefits allocable to an employer that withdraws from a plan shall be determined in accordance with subsection (b), (c), or (d) of this section.

(b)(1) Except as provided in subsections (c) and (d), the amount of unfunded vested benefits allocable to an employer that withdraws is the sum of—

(A) the employer's proportional share of the unamortized amount of the change in the plan's unfunded vested benefits for plan years ending after April 28, 1980, as determined under paragraph (2),

(B) the employer's proportional share, if any, of the unamortized amount of the plan's unfunded vested benefits at the end of the plan year ending before April 29, 1980, as determined under paragraph (3); and

(C) the employer's proportional share of the unamortized amounts of the reallocated unfunded vested benefits (if any) as determined under paragraph (4).

If the sum of the amounts determined with respect to an employer under paragraphs (2), (3), and (4) is negative, the unfunded vested benefits allocable to the employer shall be zero.

(2)(A) An employer's proportional share of the unamortized amount of the change in the plan's unfunded vested benefits for plan years ending after April 28, 1980, is the sum of the employer's proportional shares of the unamortized amount of the change in unfunded vested benefits for each plan year in which the employer has an obligation to contribute under the plan ending—

(i) after such date, and
(ii) before the plan year in which the withdrawal of the employer occurs.

(B) The change in a plan's unfunded vested benefits for a plan year is the amount by which—

(i) the unfunded vested benefits at the end of the plan year; exceeds
(ii) the sum of—
(I) the unamortized amount of the unfunded vested benefits for the last plan year ending before April 29, 1980, and
(II) the sum of the unamortized amounts of the change in unfunded vested benefits for each plan year ending after April 28, 1980, and preceding the plan year for which the change is determined.

(C) The unamortized amount of the change in a plan's unfunded vested benefits with respect to a plan year is the change in unfunded vested benefits for the plan year, reduced by 5 percent of such change for each succeeding plan year.

(D) The unamortized amount of the unfunded vested benefits for the last plan year ending before April 29, 1980, is the amount of the unfunded vested benefits as of the end of that plan year reduced by 5 percent of such amount for each succeeding plan year.

(E) An employer's proportional share of the unamortized amount of a change in unfunded vested benefits is the product of—

(i) the unamortized amount of such change (as of the end of the plan year preceding the plan year in which the employer withdraws); multiplied by
(ii) a fraction—
(I) the numerator of which is the sum of the contributions required to be made under the plan by the employer for the year in which such change arose and for the 4 preceding plan years, and
(II) the denominator of which is the sum for the plan year in which such change arose and the 4 preceding plan years of all contributions made by employers who had an obligation to contribute under the plan for the plan year in which such change arose reduced by the contributions made in such years by employers who had withdrawn from the plan in the year in which the change arose.

(3) An employer's proportional share of the unamortized amount of the plan's unfunded vested benefits for the last plan year ending before April 29, 1980, is the product of—

(A) such unamortized amount; multiplied by—
(B) a fraction—
(i) the numerator of which is the sum of all contributions required to be made by the employer under the plan for the most recent 5 plan years ending before April 29, 1980, and

Sec. 4211 (b) (3)

(ii) the denominator of which is the sum of all contributions made for the most recent 5 plan years ending before April 29, 1980, by all employers—

(I) who had an obligation to contribute under the plan for the first plan year ending on or after such date, and

(II) who had not withdrawn from the plan before such date.

(4)(A) An employer's proportional share of the unamortized amount of the reallocated unfunded vested benefits is the sum of the employer's proportional shares of the unamortized amount of the reallocated unfunded vested benefits for each plan year ending before the plan year in which the employer withdrew from the plan.

(B) Except as otherwise provided in regulations prescribed by the corporation, the reallocated unfunded vested benefits for a plan year is the sum of—

(i) any amount which the plan sponsor determines in that plan year to be uncollectible for reasons arising out of cases or proceedings under title 11, United States Code, or similar proceedings.

(ii) any amount which the plan sponsor determines in that plan year will not be assessed as a result of the operation of section 4209, 4219(c)(1)(B), or section 4225 against an employer to whom a notice described in section 4219 has been sent, and

(iii) any amount which the plan sponsor determines to be uncollectible or unassessable in that plan year for other reasons under standards not inconsistent with regulations prescribed by the corporation.

(C) The unamortized amount of the reallocated unfunded vested benefits with respect to a plan year is the reallocated unfunded vested benefits for the plan year, reduced by 5 percent of such reallocated unfunded vested benefits for each succeeding plan year.

(D) An employer's proportional share of the unamortized amount of the reallocated unfunded vested benefits with respect to a plan year is the product of—

(i) the unamortized amount of the reallocated unfunded vested benefits (as of the end of the plan year preceding the plan year in which the employer withdraws); multiplied by

(ii) the fraction defined in paragraph (2)(E)(ii).

(c)(1) A multiemployer plan, other than a plan which primarily covers employees in the building and construction industry, may be amended to provide that the amount of unfunded vested benefits allocable to an employer that withdraws from the plan is an amount determined under paragraph (2), (3), (4), or (5) of this subsection, rather than under subsection (b) or (d). A plan prescribed in section 4203(b)(1)(B)(i) (relating to the building and construction industry) may be amended, to the extent provided in regulations prescribed by the corporation, to provide that the amount of the unfunded vested benefits allocable to an employer not described in section 4203(b)(1)(A) shall be determined in a manner different from that provided in subsection (b).

(2)(A) The amount of the unfunded vested benefits allocable to any employer under this paragraph is the sum of the amounts determined under subparagraphs (B) and (C).

(B) The amount determined under this subparagraph is the product of—

(i) the plan's unfunded vested benefits as of the end of the last plan year ending before April 29, 1980, reduced as if those obligations were being fully amortized in level annual installments over 15 years beginning with the first plan year ending on or after such date; multiplied by

(ii) a fraction—

(I) the numerator of which is the sum of all contributions required to be made by the employer under the plan for the last 5 plan years ending before April 29, 1980, and

(II) the denominator of which is the sum of all contributions made for the last 5 plan years ending before April 29, 1980, by all employers who had an obligation to contribute under the plan for the first plan year end-

Sec. 4211 (b) (4)

ing after April 28, 1980, and who had not withdrawn from the plan before such date.

(C) The amount determined under this subparagraph is the product of—

(i) an amount equal to—

(I) the plan's unfunded vested benefits as of the end of the plan year preceding the plan year in which the employer withdraws, less

(II) the sum of the value as of such date of all outstanding claims for withdrawal liability which can reasonably be expected to be collected, with respect to employers withdrawing before such plan year, and that portion of the amount determined under subparagraph (B)(i) which is allocable to employers who have an obligation to contribute under the plan in the plan year preceding the plan year in which the employer withdraws and who also had an obligation to contribute under the plan for the first plan year ending after April 28, 1980; multiplied by

(ii) a fraction—

(I) the numerator of which is the total amount required to be contributed under the plan by the employer for the last 5 plan years ending before the date on which the employer withdraws, and

(II) the denominator of which is the total amount contributed under the plan by all employers for the last 5 plan years ending before the date on which the employer withdraws, increased by the amount of any employer contributions owed with respect to earlier periods which were collected in those plan years, and decreased by any amount contributed by an employer who withdrew from the plan under this part during those plan years.

(D) The corporation may by regulation permit adjustments in any denominator under this section, consistent with the purposes of this title, where such adjustment would be appropriate to ease administrative burdens of plan sponsors in calculating such denominators.

(3) The amount of the unfunded vested benefits allocable to an employer under this paragraph is the product of—

(A) the plan's unfunded vested benefits as of the end of the plan year preceding the plan year in which the employer withdraws, less the value as of the end of such year of all outstanding claims for withdrawal liability which can reasonably be expected to be collected from employers withdrawing before such year; multiplied by

(B) a fraction—

(i) the numerator of which is the total amount required to be contributed by the employer under the plan for the last 5 plan years ending before the withdrawal, and

(ii) the denominator of which is the total amount contributed under the plan by all employers for the last 5 plan years ending before the withdrawal, increased by any employer contributions owed with respect to earlier periods which were collected in those plan years, and decreased by any amount contributed to the plan during those plan years by employers who withdrew from the plan under this section during those plan years.

(4)(A) The amount of the unfunded vested benefits allocable to an employer under this paragraph is equal to the sum of—

(i) the plan's unfunded vested benefits which are attributable to participants' service with the employer (determined as of the end of the plan year preceding the plan year in which the employer withdraws), and

(ii) the employer's proportional share of any unfunded vested benefits which are not attributable to service with the employer or other employers who are obligated to contribute under the plan in the plan year preceding the plan year in which the employer withdraws (determined as of the end of the plan year preceding the plan year in which the employer withdraws).

(B) The plan's unfunded vested benefits which are attributable to participants' service with the employer is the amount equal to the value of nonforfeitable benefits under the plan which are attributable to participants' service with such employer (determined under plan rules not inconsistent with regulations of the corporation) decreased by the share of plan assets determined under subparagraph (C) which is allocated to the employer as provided under subparagraph (D).

(C) The value of plan assets determined under this subparagraph is the value of plan assets allocated to nonforfeitable benefits which are attributable to service with the employers who have an obligation to contribute under the plan in the plan year preceding the plan year in which the employer withdraws, which is determined by multiplying—

(i) the value of the plan assets as of the end of the plan year preceding the plan year in which the employer withdraws, by

(ii) a fraction—

(I) the numerator of which is the value of nonforfeitable benefits which are attributable to service with such employers, and

(II) the denominator of which is the value of all nonforfeitable benefits under the plan

as of the end of the plan year.

(D) The share of plan assets, determined under subparagraph (C), which is allocated to the employer shall be determined in accordance with one of the following methods which shall be adopted by the plan by amendment:

(i) by multiplying the value of plan assets determined under subparagraph (C) by a fraction

(I) the numerator of which is the value of the nonforfeitable benefits which are attributable to service with the employer, and

(II) the denominator of which is the value of the nonforfeitable benefits which are attributable to service with all employers who have an obligation to contribute under the plan in the plan year preceding the plan year in which the employer withdraws;

(ii) by multiplying the value of plan assets determined under subparagraph (C) by a fraction—

(I) the numerator of which is the sum of all contributions (accumulated with interest) which have been made to the plan by the employer for the plan year preceding the plan year in which the employer withdraws and all preceding plan years; and

(II) the denominator of which is the sum of all contributions (accumulated with interest) which have been made to the plan (for the plan year preceding the plan year in which the employer withdraws and all preceding plan years) by all employers who have an obligation to contribute to the plan for the plan year preceding the plan year in which the employer withdraws; or

(iii) by multiplying the value of plan assets under subparagraph (C) by a fraction—

(I) the numerator of which is the amount determined under clause (ii) (I) of this subparagraph, less the sum of benefit payments (accumulated with interest) made to participants (and their beneficiaries) for the plan years described in such clause (ii)(I) which are attributable to service with the employer; and

(II) the denominator of which is the amount determined under clause (ii) (II) of this subparagraph, reduced by the sum of benefit payments (accumulated with interest) made to participants (and their beneficiaries) for the plan years described in such clause (ii)(II) which are attributable to service with respect to the employers described in such clause (ii)(II).

(E) The amount of the plan's unfunded vested benefits for a plan year preceding the plan year in which an employer withdraws, which is not attributable to service with employers who have an obligation to contribute under the plan in the plan year preceding the plan year in which such employer withdraws, is equal to—

(i) an amount equal to—

Sec. 4211 (c) (4) (C)

(I) the value of all nonforfeitable benefits under the plan at the end of such plan year, reduced by

(II) the value of nonforfeitable benefits under the plan at the end of such plan year which are attributable to participants' service with employers who have an obligation to contribute under the plan for such plan year; reduced by

(ii) an amount equal to—

(I) the value of the plan assets as of the end of such plan year, reduced by

(II) the value of plan assets as of the end of such plan year as determined under subparagraph (C); reduced by

(iii) the value of all outstanding claims for withdrawal liability which can reasonably be expected to be collected with respect to employers withdrawing before the year preceding the plan year in which the employer withdraws.

(F) The employer's proportional share described in subparagraph (A)(ii) for a plan year is the amount determined under subparagraph (E) for the employer, but not in excess of an amount which bears the same ratio to the sum of the amounts determined under subparagraph (E) for all employers under the plan as the amount determined under subparagraph (C) for the employer bears to the sum of the amounts determined under subparagraph (C) for all employers under the plan.

(G) The corporation may prescribe by regulation other methods which a plan may adopt for allocating assets to determine the amount of the unfunded vested benefits attributable to service with the employer and to determine the employer's share of unfunded vested benefits not attributable to service with employers who have an obligation to contribute under the plan in the plan year in which the employer withdraws.

(5)(A) The corporation shall prescribe by regulation a procedure by which a plan may, by amendment, adopt any other alternative method for determining an employer's allocable share of unfunded vested benefits under this section, subject to the approval of the corporation based on its determination that adoption of the method by the plan would not significantly increase the risk of loss to plan participants and beneficiaries or to the corporation.

(B) The corporation may prescribe by regulation standard approaches for alternative methods, other than those set forth in the preceding paragraphs of this subsection, which a plan may adopt under subparagraph (A), for which the corporation may waive or modify the approval requirements of subparagraph (A). Any alternative method shall provide for the allocation of substantially all of a plan's unfunded vested benefits among employers who have an obligation to contribute under the plan.

(C) Unless the corporation by regulation provides otherwise, a plan may be amended to provide that a period of more than 5 but not more than 10 plan years may be used for determining the numerator and denominator of any fraction which is used under any method authorized under this section for determining an employer's allocable share of unfunded vested benefits under this section.

(D) The corporation may by regulation permit adjustments in any denominator under this section, consistent with the purposes of this title, where such adjustment would be appropriate to ease administrative burdens of plan sponsors in calculating such denominators.

(d)(1) The method of calculating an employer's allocable share of unfunded vested benefits set forth in subsection (c)(3) shall be the method for calculating an employer's allocable share of unfunded vested benefits under a plan to which section 404(c) of the Internal Revenue Code of 1954, or a continuation of such a plan, applies, unless the plan is amended to adopt

Sec. 4211 (d)

another method authorized under subsection (b) or (c).

(2) Sections 4204, 4209, 4219(c)(1)(B), and 4225 shall not apply with respect to the withdrawal of an employer from a plan described in paragraph (1) unless the plan is amended to provide that any of such sections apply.

(e) In the case of a transfer of liabilities to another plan incident to an employer's withdrawal or partial withdrawal, the withdrawn employer's liability under this part shall be reduced in an amount equal to the value, as of the end of the last plan year ending on or before the date of the withdrawal, of the transferred unfunded vested benefits.

(f) In the case of a withdrawal following a merger of multiemployer plans, subsection (b), (c) or (d) shall be applied in accordance with regulations prescribed by the corporation; except that, if a withdrawal occurs in the first plan year beginning after a merger of multiemployer plans, the determination under this section shall be made as if each of the multiemployer plans had remained separate plans.

Obligation to Contribute; Special Rules

Sec. 4212. (a) For purposes of this part, the term "obligation to contribute" means an obligation to contribute arising—

(1) under one or more collective bargaining (or related) agreements, or

(2) as a result of a duty under applicable labor-management relations law, but

does not include an obligation to pay withdrawal liability under this section or to pay delinquent contributions.

(b) Payments of withdrawal liability under this part shall not be considered contributions for purposes of this part.

(c) If a principal purpose of any transaction is to evade or avoid liability under this part, this part shall be applied (and liability shall be determined and collected) without regard to such transaction.

Actuarial Assumptions, Etc.

Sec. 4213. (a) The corporation may prescribe by regulation actuarial assumptions which may be used by a plan actuary in determining the unfunded vested benefits of a plan for purposes of determining an employer's withdrawal liability under this part. Withdrawal liability under this part shall be determined by each plan on the basis of—

(1) actuarial assumptions and methods which, in the aggregate, are reasonable (taking into account the experience of the plan and reasonable expectations) and which, in combination, offer the actuary's best estimate of anticipated experience under the plan, or

(2) actuarial assumptions and methods set forth in the corporation's regulations for purposes of determining an employer's withdrawal liability.

(b) In determining the unfunded vested benefits of a plan for purposes of determining an employer's withdrawal liability under this part, the plan actuary may—

(1) rely on the most recent complete actuarial valuation used for purposes of section 412 of the Internal Revenue Code of 1954 and reasonable estimates for the interim years of the unfunded vested benefits, and

(2) in the absence of complete data, rely on the data available or on data secured by a sampling which can reasonably be expected to be representative of the status of the entire plan.

(c) For purposes of this part, the term "unfunded vested benefits" means with respect to a plan, an amount equal to—

(A) the value of nonforfeitable benefits under the plan, less

(B) the value of the assets of the plan.

Application of Plan Amendments

Sec. 4214. (a) No plan rule or amendment adopted after January 31, 1981, under section 4209 or 4211(c) may be applied without the employer's consent with respect to liability for a withdrawal or partial withdrawal which occurred before the date on which the rule or amendment was adopted.

(b) All plan rules and amendments authorized under this part shall operate and be applied uniformly with respect to each employer, except that special provisions may be made to take into account the creditworthiness of an employer. The plan sponsor shall give notice to all employers who have an obligation to contribute under the plan and to all employee organizations representing employees covered under the plan of any plan rules or amendments adopted pursuant to this section.

Plan Notification to Corporation of Potentially Significant Withdrawals

Sec. 4215. The corporation may, by regulation, require the plan sponsor of a multiemployer plan to provide notice to the corporation when the withdrawal from the plan by any employer has resulted, or will result, in a significant reduction in the amount of aggregate contributions under the plan made by employers.

Special Rules for Section 404(c) Plans

Sec. 4216. (a) In the case of a plan described in subsection (b)—

(1) if an employer withdraws prior to a termination described in section 4041A(a)(2), the amount of withdrawal liability to be paid in any year by such employer shall be an amount equal to the greater of—

(A) the amount determined under section 4219(c)(1)(C)(i), or

(B) the product of—

(i) the number of contribution base units for which the employer would have required to make contributions for the prior plan year if the employer had not withdrawn, multiplied by

(ii) the contribution rate for the plan year which would be required to meet the amortization schedules contained in section 4243(d)(3)(B)(ii) (determined without regard to any limitation on such rate otherwise provided by this title)

except that an employer shall not be required to pay an amount in excess of the withdrawal liability computed with interest; and

(2) the withdrawal liability of an employer who withdraws after December 31, 1983, as a result of a termination described in section 4041A(a)(2) which is agreed to by the labor organization that appoints the employee representative on the joint board of trustees which sponsors the plan, shall be determined under subsection (c) if—

(A) as a result of prior employer withdrawals in any plan year commencing after January 1, 1980, the number of contribution base units is reduced to less than 67 percent of the average number of such units for the calendar years 1974 through 1979; and

(B) at least 50 percent of the withdrawal liability attributable to the first 33 percent decline described in subparagraph (A) has been determined by the plan sponsor to be uncollectible within the meaning of regulations of the corporation of general applicability; and

(C) the rate of employer contributions under the plan for each plan year following the first plan year beginning after the date of enactment of the Multiemployer Pension Plan Amendments Act of 1980 and preceding the termination date equals or exceeds the rate described in section 4243(d)(3).

(b) A plan is described in this subsection if—

(1) it is a plan described in section 404(c) of the Internal Revenue Code of 1954 or a continuation thereof; and

(2) participation in the plan is substantially limited to individuals who retired prior to January 1, 1976.

(c)(1) The amount of an employer's liability under this paragraph is the product of—

(A) the amount of the employer's withdrawal liability determined without regard to this section, and

(B) the greater of 90 percent, or a fraction—

Sec. 4216 (b)

(i) the numerator of which is an amount equal to the portion of the plan's unfunded vested benefits that is attributable to plan participants who have a total of 10 or more years of signatory service, and

(ii) the denominator of which is an amount equal to the total unfunded vested benefits of the plan.

(2) For purposes of paragraph (1), the term "a year of signatory service" means a year during any portion of which a participant was employed for an employer who was obligated to contribute in that year, or who was subsequently obligated to contribute.

Application of Part in Case of Certain Pre-1980 Withdrawals

Sec. 4217. (a) For the purpose of determining the amount of unfunded vested benefits allocable to an employer for a partial or complete withdrawal from a plan which occurs after April 28, 1980, and for the purpose of determining whether there has been a partial withdrawal after such date, the amount of contributions, and the number of contribution base units, of such employer properly allocable—

(1) to work performed under a collective bargaining agreement for which there was a permanent cessation of the obligation to contribute before April 29, 1980, or

(2) to work performed at a facility at which all covered operations permanently ceased before April 29, 1980, or for which there was a permanent cessation of the obligation to contribute before that date,

shall not be taken into account.

(b) A plan may, in a manner not inconsistent with regulations, which shall be prescribed by the corporation, adjust the amount of unfunded vested benefits allocable to other employers under a plan maintained by an employer described in subsection (a).

Withdrawal Not to Occur Merely Because of Change in Business Form or Suspension of Contributions During Labor Dispute

Sec. 4218. Notwithstanding any other provision of this part, an employer shall not be considered to have withdrawn from a plan solely because—

(1) an employer ceases to exist by reason of—

(A) a change in corporate structure described in section 4062(d), or

(B) a change to an unincorporated form of business enterprise,

if the change causes no interruption in employer contributions or obligations to contribute under the plan, or

(2) an employer suspends contributions under the plan during a labor dispute involving its employees.

For purposes of this part, a successor or parent corporation or other entity resulting from any such change shall be considered the original employer.

Notice, Collection, Etc., of Withdrawal Liability

Sec. 4219. (a) An employer shall, within 30 days after a written request from the plan sponsor, furnish such information as the plan sponsor reasonably determines to be necessary to enable the plan sponsor to comply with the requirements of this part.

(b)(1) As soon as practicable after an employer's complete or partial withdrawal, the plan sponsor shall—

(A) notify the employer of—

(i) the amount of the liability, and

(ii) the schedule for liability payments, and

(B) demand payment in accordance with the schedule.

(2)(A) No later than 90 days after the employer receives the notice described in paragraph (1), the employer—

(i) may ask the plan sponsor to review any specific matter relating to the determination of the employer's liability and the schedule of payments,

(ii) may identify any inaccuracy in the determination of the amount of the unfunded vested benefits allocable to the employer, and

(iii) may furnish any additional relevant information to the plan sponsor.

Sec. 4217

(B) After a reasonable review of any matter raised, the plan sponsor shall notify the employer of—
(i) the plan sponsor's decision,
(ii) the basis for the decision, and
(iii) the reason for any change in the determination of the employer's liability or schedule of liability payments.

(c)(1)(A)(i) Except as provided in subparagraphs (B) and (D) of this paragraph and in paragraphs (4) and (5), an employer shall pay the amount determined under section 4211, adjusted if appropriate first under section 4209 and then under section 4206 over the period of years necessary to amortize the amount in level annual payments determined under subparagraph (C), calculated as if the first payment were made on the first day of the plan year following the plan year in which the withdrawal occurs and as if each subsequent payment were made on the first day of each subsequent plan year. Actual payment shall commence in accordance with paragraph (2).
(ii) The determination of the amortization period described in clause (i) shall be based on the assumptions used for the most recent actuarial valuation for the plan.
(B) In any case in which the amortization period described in subparagraph (A) exceeds 20 years, the employer's liability shall be limited to the first 20 annual payments determined under subparagraph (C).
(C)(i) Except as provided in subparagraph (E), the amount of each annual payment shall be the product of—
(I) the average annual number of contribution base units for the period of 3 consecutive plan years, during the period of 10 consecutive plan years ending before the plan year in which the withdrawal occurs, in which the number of contribution base units for which the employer had an obligation to contribute under the plan is the highest, and
(II) the highest contribution rate at which the employer had an obligation to contribute under the plan during the 10 plan years ending with the plan year in which the withdrawal occurs. For purposes of the preceding sentence, a partial withdrawal described in section 4205(a)(1) shall be deemed to occur on the last day of the first year of the 3-year testing period described in section 4205(b)(1)(B)(i).
(ii)(I) A plan may be amended to provide that for any plan year ending before 1986 the amount of each annual payment shall be (in lieu of the amount determined under clause (i)) the average of the required employer contributions under the plan for the period of 3 consecutive plan years (during the period of 10 consecutive plan years ending with the plan year preceding the plan year in which the withdrawal occurs) for which such required contributions were the highest.
(II) Subparagraph (B) shall not apply to any plan year to which this clause applies.
(III) This clause shall not apply in the case of any withdrawal described in subparagraph (D).
(IV) If under a plan this clause applies to any plan year but does not apply to the next plan year, this clause shall not apply to any plan year after such next plan year.
(V) For purposes of this clause, the term "required contributions" means, for any period, the amounts which the employer was obligated to contribute for such period (not taking into account any delinquent contribution for any other period).
(iii) A plan may be amended to provide that for the first plan year ending on or after April 29, 1980, the number "5" shall be substituted for the number "10" each place it appears in clause (i) or clause (ii) (whichever is appropriate). If the plan is so amended, the number "5" shall be increased by one for each succeeding plan year until the number "10" is reached.

(D) In any case in which a multiemployer plan terminates by the withdrawal of every employer from the plan, or in which substantially all the employers withdraw from a plan pursuant to an agreement or arrangement to withdraw from the plan—

(i) the liability of each such employer who has withdrawn shall be determined (or redetermined) under this paragraph without regard to subparagraph (B), and

(ii) notwithstanding any other provision of this part, the total unfunded vested benefits of the plan shall be fully allocated among all such employers in a manner not inconsistent with regulations which shall be prescribed by the corporation.

Withdrawal by an employer from a plan, during a period of 3 consecutive plan years within which substantially all the employers who have an obligation to contribute under the plan withdraw, shall be presumed to be a withdrawal pursuant to an agreement or arrangement, unless the employer proves otherwise by a preponderance of the evidence.

(E) In the case of a partial withdrawal described in section 4205(a), the amount of each annual payment shall be the product of—

(i) the amount determined under subparagraph (C) (determined without regard to this subparagraph), multiplied by

(ii) the fraction determined under section 4206(a)(2).

(2) Withdrawal liability shall be payable in accordance with the schedule set forth by the plan sponsor under subsection (b)(1) beginning no later than 60 days after the date of the demand notwithstanding any request for review or appeal of determinations of the amount of such liability or of the schedule.

(3) Each annual payment determined under paragraph (1)(C) shall be payable in 4 equal installments due quarterly, or at other intervals specified by plan rules. If a payment is not made when due, interest on the payment shall accrue from the due date until the date on which the payment is made.

(4) The employer shall be entitled to prepay the outstanding amount of the unpaid annual withdrawal liability payments determined under paragraph (1)(C), plus accrued interest, if any, in whole or in part, without penalty. If the prepayment is made pursuant to a withdrawal which is later determined to be part of a withdrawal described in paragraph (1)(D), the withdrawal liability of the employer shall not be limited to the amount of the prepayment.

(5) In the event of a default, a plan sponsor may require immediate payment of the outstanding amount of an employer's withdrawal liability, plus accrued interest on the total outstanding liability from the due date of the first payment which was not timely made. For purposes of this section, the term "default" means—

(A) the failure of an employer to make, when due, any payment under this section, if the failure is not cured within 60 days after the employer receives written notification from the plan sponsor of such failure, and

(B) any other event defined in rules adopted by the plan which indicates a substantial likelihood that an employer will be unable to pay its withdrawal liability.

(6) Except as provided in paragraph (1)(A)(ii), interest under this subsection shall be charged at rates based on prevailing market rates for comparable obligations, in accordance with regulations prescribed by the corporation.

(7) A multiemployer plan may adopt rules for other terms and conditions for the satisfaction of an employer's withdrawal liability if such rules—

(A) are consistent with this Act, and

(B) are not inconsistent with regulations of the corporation.

(8) In the case of a terminated multiemployer plan, an employer's obligation to make payments under this section ceases at the end of the plan year in which the assets of the plan (exclusive of withdrawal liability claims) are sufficient to meet all obligations of the plan, as determined by the corporation.

Sec. 4219 (c) (1) (D) (i)

(d) The prohibitions provided in section 406(a) do not apply to any action required or permitted under this part.

Approval of Amendments

Sec. 4220. (a) Except as provided in subsection (b), if an amendment to a multiemployer plan authorized by any preceding section of this part is adopted more than 36 months after the effective date of this section, the amendment shall be effective only if the corporation approves the amendment, or, within 90 days after the corporation receives notice and a copy of the amendment from the plan sponsor, fails to disapprove the amendment.

(b) An amendment permitted by section 4211(c)(5) may be adopted only in accordance with that section.

(c) The corporation shall disapprove an amendment referred to in subsection (a) or (b) only if the corporation determines that the amendment creates an unreasonable risk of loss to plan participants and beneficiaries or to the corporation.

Resolution of Disputes

Sec. 4221. (a)(1) Any dispute between an employer and the plan sponsor of a multiemployer plan concerning a determination made under sections 4201 through 4219 shall be resolved through arbitration. Either party may initiate the arbitration proceeding within a 60-day period after the earlier of—

(A) the date of notification to the employer under section 4219(b)(2)(B), or

(B) 120 days after the date of the employer's request under section 4219(b)(2)(A).

The parties may jointly initiate arbitration within the 180-day period after the date of the plan sponsor's demand under section 4219(b)(1).

(2) An arbitration proceeding under this section shall be conducted in accordance with fair and equitable procedures to be promulgated by the corporation. The plan sponsor may purchase insurance to cover potential liability of the arbitrator. If the parties have not provided for the costs of the arbitration, including arbitrator's fees, by agreement, the arbitrator shall assess such fees. The arbitrator may also award reasonable attorney's fees.

(3)(A) For purposes of any proceeding under this section, any determination made by a plan sponsor under sections 4201 through 4219 and section 4225 is presumed correct unless the party contesting the determination shows by a preponderance of the evidence that the determination was unreasonable or clearly erroneous.

(B) In the case of the determination of a plan's unfunded vested benefits for a plan year, the determination is presumed correct unless a party contesting the determination shows by a preponderance of evidence that—

(i) the actuarial assumptions and methods used in the determination were, in the aggregate, unreasonable (taking into account the experience of the plan and reasonable expectations), or

(ii) the plan's actuary made a significant error in applying the actuarial assumptions or methods.

(b)(1) If no arbitration proceeding has been initiated pursuant to subsection (a), the amounts demanded by the plan sponsor under section 4219(b)(1) shall be due and owing on the schedule set forth by the plan sponsor. The plan sponsor may bring an action in a State or Federal court of competent jurisdiction for collection.

(2) Upon completion of the arbitration proceedings in favor of one of the parties, any party thereto may bring an action, no later than 30 days after the issuance of an arbitrator's award, in an appropriate United States district court in accordance with section 4301 to enforce, vacate, or modify the arbitrator's award.

(3) Any arbitration proceedings under this section shall, to the extent consistent with this title, be conducted in the same manner, subject to the same limitations, carried out with the same powers (including subpoena power), and enforced in United States

courts as an arbitration proceeding carried out under title 9, United States Code.

(c) In any proceeding under subsection (b), there shall be a presumption, rebuttable only by a clear preponderance of the evidence, that the findings of fact made by the arbitrator were correct.

(d) Payments shall be made by an employer in accordance with the determinations made under this part until the arbitrator issues a final decision with respect to the determination submitted for arbitration, with any necessary adjustments in subsequent payments for overpayments or underpayments arising out of the decision of the arbitrator with respect to the determination. If the employer fails to make timely payment in accordance with such final decision, the employer shall be treated as being delinquent in the making of a contribution required under the plan (within the meaning of section 515).

(e) If any employer requests in writing that the plan sponsor make available to the employer general information necessary for the employer to compute its withdrawal liability with respect to the plan (other than information which is unique to that employer), the plan sponsor shall furnish the information to the employer without charge. If any employer requests in writing that the plan sponsor make an estimate of such employer's potential withdrawal liability with respect to the plan or to provide information unique to that employer, the plan sponsor may require the employer to pay the reasonable cost of making such estimate or providing such information.

Reimbursements for Uncollectible Withdrawal Liability

Sec. 4222. (a) By May 1, 1982, the corporation shall establish by regulation a supplemental program to reimburse multiemployer plans for withdrawal liability payments which are due from employers and which are determined to be uncollectible for reasons arising out of cases or proceedings involving the employers under title 11, United States Code, or similar cases or proceedings. Participation in the supplemental program shall be on a voluntary basis, and a plan which elects coverage under the program shall pay premiums to the corporation in accordance with a premium schedule which shall be prescribed from time to time by the corporation. The premium schedule shall contain such rates and bases for the application of such rates as the corporation considers to be appropriate.

(b) The corporation may provide under the program for reimbursement of amounts of withdrawal liability determined to be uncollectible for any other reasons the corporation considers appropriate.

(c) The cost of the program (including such administrative and legal costs as the corporation considers appropriate) may be paid only out of premiums collected under such program.

(d) The supplemental program may be offered to eligible plans on such terms and conditions, and with such limitations with respect to the payment of reimbursements (including the exclusion of de minimis amounts of uncollectible employer liability, and the reduction or elimination of reimbursements which cannot be paid from collected premiums) and such restrictions on withdrawal from the program, as the corporation considers necessary and appropriate.

(e) The corporation may enter into arrangements with private insurers to carry out in whole or in part the program authorized by this section and may require plans which elect coverage under the program to elect coverage by those private insurers.

Withdrawal Liability Payment Fund

Sec. 4223. (a) The plan sponsors of multiemployer plans may establish or participate in a withdrawal liability payment fund.

(b) For purposes of this section, the term "withdrawal liability payment fund", and the term "fund", mean a trust which—

(1) is established and maintained under section 501(c)(22) of the Internal Revenue Code of 1954,

(2) maintains agreements which cover a substantial portion of the participants who are in multiemployer plans which (under the rules of the trust instrument) are eligible to participate in the fund,

(3) is funded by amounts paid by the plans which participate in the fund, and

(4) is administered by a Board of Trustees, and in the administration of the fund there is equal representation of—

(A) trustees representing employers who are obligated to contribute to the plans participating in the fund, and

(B) trustees representing employees who are participants in plans which participate in the fund.

(c)(1) If an employer withdraws from a plan which participates in a withdrawal liability payment fund, then, to the extent provided in the trust, the fund shall pay to that plan—

(A) the employer's unattributable liability,

(B) the employer's withdrawal liability payments which would have been due but for section 4208, 4209, 4219, or 4225,

(C) the employer's withdrawal liability payments to the extent they are uncollectible.

(2) The fund may provide for the payment of the employer's attributable liability if the fund—

(A) provides for the payment of both the attributable and the unattributable liability of the employer in a single payment, and

(B) is subrogated to all rights of the plan against the employer.

(3) For purposes of this section, the term—

(A) "attributable liability" means the excess, if any, determined under the provisions of a plan not inconsistent with regulations of the corporation, of—

(i) the value of vested benefits accrued as a result of service with the employer, over

(ii) the value of plan assets attributed to the employer, and

(B) "unattributable liability" means the excess of withdrawal liability over attributable liability.

Such terms may be further defined, and the manner in which they shall be applied may be prescribed, by the corporation by regulation.

(4)(A) The trust of a fund shall be maintained for the exclusive purpose of paying—

(i) any amount described in paragraph (1) and paragraph (2), and

(ii) reasonable and necessary administrative expenses in connection with the establishment and operation of the trust and the processing of claims against the fund.

(B) The amounts paid by a plan to a fund shall be deemed a reasonable expense of administering the plan under sections 403(c)(1) and 404(a)(1)(A)(ii), and the payments made by a fund to a participating plan shall be deemed services necessary for the operation of the plan within the meaning of section 408(b)(2) or within the meaning of section 4975(d)(2) of the Internal Revenue Code of 1954.

(d)(1) For purposes of this part—

(A) only amounts paid by the fund to a plan under subsection (c)(1)(A) shall be credited to withdrawal liability otherwise payable by the employer, unless the plan otherwise provides, and

(B) any amounts paid by the fund under subsection (c) to a plan shall be treated by the plan as a payment of withdrawal liability to such plan.

(2) For purposes of applying provisions relating to the funding standard accounts (and minimum contribution requirements), amounts paid from the plan to the fund shall be applied to reduce the amount treated as contributed to the plan.

(e) The fund shall be subrogated to the rights of the plan against the employer that has withdrawn from the plan for amounts paid by a fund to a plan under—

Sec. 4223 (e)

(1) subsection (c)(1)(A), to the extent not credited under subsection (d)(1)(A), and

(2) subsection (c)(1)(C).

(f) Notwithstanding any other provision of this Act, a fiduciary of the fund shall discharge the fiduciary's duties with respect to the fund in accordance with the standards for fiduciaries prescribed by this Act (to the extent not inconsistent with the purposes of this section), and in accordance with the documents and instruments governing the fund insofar as such documents and instruments are consistent with the provisions of this Act (to the extent not inconsistent with the purposes of this section). The provisions of the preceding sentence shall supersede any and all State laws relating to fiduciaries insofar as they may now or hereafter relate to a fund to which this section applies.

(g) No payments shall be made from a fund to a plan on the occasion of a withdrawal or partial withdrawal of an employer from such plan if the employees representing the withdrawn contribution base units continue, after such withdrawal, to be represented under section 9 of the National Labor Relations Act (or other applicable labor laws) in negotiations with such employer by the labor organization which represented such employees immediately preceding such withdrawal.

(h) Nothing in this section shall be construed to prohibit the purchase of insurance by an employer from any other person, to limit the circumstances under which such insurance would be payable, or to limit in any way the terms and conditions of such insurance.

(i) The corporation may provide by regulation rules not inconsistent with this section governing the establishment and maintenance of funds, but only to the extent necessary to carry out the purposes of this part (other than section 4222).

Alternative Method of Withdrawal Liability Payments

Sec. 4224. A multiemployer plan may adopt rules providing for other terms and conditions for the satisfaction of an employer's withdrawal liability if such rules are consistent with this Act and with such regulations as may be prescribed by the corporation.

Limitation on Withdrawal Liability

Sec. 4225. (a)(1) In the case of bona fide sale of all or substantially all of the employer's assets in an arm's-length transaction to an unrelated party (within the meaning of section 4204(d)), the unfunded vested benefits allocable to an employer (after the application of all sections of this part having a lower number designation than this section), other than an employer undergoing reorganization under title 11, United States Code, or similar provisions of State law, shall not exceed the greater of—

(A) a portion (determined under paragraph (2)) of the liquidation or dissolution value of the employer (determined after the sale or exchange of such assets), or

(B) the unfunded vested benefits attributable to employees of the employer.

(2) For purposes of paragraph (1), the portion shall be determined in accordance with the following table:

If the liquidation or dissolution value of the employer after the sale or exchange is—

Not more than $2,000,000 ....
More than $2,000,000, but not more than $4,000,000.
More than $4,000,000, but not more than $6,000,000.
More than $6,000,000, but not more than $7,000,000.
More than $7,000,000, but not more than $8,000,000.
More than $8,000,000, but not more than $9,000,000.
More than $9,000,000, but not more than $10,000,000.
More than $10,000,000 ....

The portion is—
30 percent of the amount.

Sec. 4223 (f)

$600,000, plus 35 percent of the amount in excess of $2,000,000.
$1,300,000, plus 40 percent of the amount in excess of $4,000,000.
$2,100,000, plus 45 percent of the amount in excess of $6,000,000.
$2,550,000, plus 50 percent of the amount in excess of $7,000,000.
$3,050,000, plus 60 percent of the amount in excess of $8,000,000.
$3,650,000, plus 70 percent of the amount in excess of $9,000,000.
$4,350,000, plus 80 percent of the amount in excess of $10,000,000.

(b) In the case of an insolvent employer undergoing liquidation or dissolution, the unfunded vested benefits allocable to that employer shall not exceed an amount equal to the sum of—

(1) 50 percent of the unfunded vested benefits allocable to the employer (determined without regard to this section), and

(2) that portion of 50 percent of the unfunded vested benefits allocable to the employer (as determined under paragraph (1)) which does not exceed the liquidation or dissolution value of the employer determined—

(A) as of the commencement of liquidation or dissolution, and

(B) after reducing the liquidation or dissolution value of the employer by the amount determined under paragraph (1).

(c) To the extent that the withdrawal liability of an employer is attributable to his obligation to contribute to or under a plan as an individual (whether as a sole proprietor or as a member of a partnership), property which may be exempt from the estate under section 522 of title 11, United States Code, or under similar provisions of law, shall not be subject to enforcement of such liability.

(d) For purposes of this section—

(1) an employer is insolvent if the liabilities of the employer, including withdrawal liability under the plan (determined without regard to subsection (b)), exceed the assets of the employer (determined as of the commencement of the liquidation or dissolution), and

(2) the liquidation or dissolution value of the employer shall be determined without regard to such withdrawal liability.

(e) In the case of one or more withdrawals of an employer attributable to the same sale, liquidation, or dissolution, under regulations prescribed by the corporation—

(1) all such withdrawals shall be treated as a single withdrawal for the purpose of applying this section, and

(2) the withdrawal liability of the employer to each plan shall be an amount which bears the same ratio to the present value of the withdrawal liability payments to all plans (after the application of the preceding provisions of this section) as the withdrawal liability of the employer to such plan (determined without regard to this section) bears to the withdrawal liability of the employer to all such plans (determined without regard to this section).

PART 2—MERGER OR TRANSFER OF PLAN ASSETS OR LIABILITIES

Mergers and Transfers Between Multiemployer Plans

Sec. 4231. (a) Unless otherwise provided in regulations prescribed by the corporation, a plan sponsor may not cause a multiemployer plan to merge with one or more multiemployer plans, or engage in a transfer of assets and liabilities to or from another multiemployer plan, unless such merger or transfer satisfies the requirements of subsection (b).

(b) A merger or transfer satisfies the requirements of this section if—

(1) in accordance with regulations of the corporation, the plan sponsor of a multiemployer plan notifies the corporation of a merger with or transfer of plan assets or liabilities to another multiemployer plan at least 120 days before the effective date of the merger or transfer;

(2) no participant's or beneficiary's accrued benefit will be lower immedi-

ately after the effective date of the merger or transfer than the benefit imediately before that date;

(3) the benefits of participants and beneficiaries are not reasonably expected to be subject to suspension under section 4245; and

(4) an actuarial valuation of the assets and liabilities of each of the affected plans has been performed during the plan year preceding the effective date of the merger or transfer, based upon the most recent data available as of the day before the start of that plan year, or other valuation of such assets and liabilities performed under such standards and procedures as the corporation may prescribe by regulation.

(c) The merger of multiemployer plans or the transfer of assets or liabilities between multiemployer plans, shall be deemed not to constitute a violation of the provisions of section 406(a) or section 406(b)(2) if the corporation determines that the merger or transfer otherwise satisfies the requirements of this section.

(d) A plan to which liabilities are transferred under this section is a successor plan for purposes of section 4022A(b)(2)(B).

Transfers Between a Multiemployer Plan and a Single-Employer Plan

Sec. 4232. (a) A transfer of assets or liabilities between, or a merger of, a multiemployer plan and a single-employer plan shall satisfy the requirements of this section.

(b) No accrued benefit of a participant or beneficiary may be lower immediately after the effective date of a transfer or merger described in subsection (a) than the benefit immediately before that date.

(c)(1) Except as provided in paragraphs (2) and (3), a multiemployer plan which transfers liabilities to a single-employer plan shall be liable to the corporation if the single-employer plan terminates within 60 months after the effective date of the transfer. The amount of liability shall be the lesser of—

(A) the amount of the plan asset insufficiency of the terminated single-employer plan, less 30 percent of the net worth of the employer who maintained the single-employer plan, determined in accordance with section 4062 or 4064, or

(B) the value, on the effective date of the transfer, of the unfunded benefits transferred to the single-employer plan which are guaranteed under section 4022.

(2) A multiemployer plan shall be liable to the corporation as provided in paragraph (1) unless, within 180 days after the corporation receives an application (together with such information as the corporation may reasonably require for purposes of such application) from the multiemployer plan sponsor for a determination under this paragraph—

(A) the corporation determines that the interests of the plan participants and beneficiaries and of the corporation are adequately protected, or

(B) fails to make any determination regarding the adequacy with which such interests are protected with respect to such transfer of liabilities.

If, after the receipt of such application, the corporation requests from the plan sponsor additional information necessary for the determination, the running of the 180-day period shall be suspended from the date of such request until the receipt by the corporation of the additional information requested. The corporation may by regulation prescribe procedures and standards for the issuance of determinations under this paragraph. This paragraph shall not apply to any application submitted less than 180 days after the date of enactment of the Multiemployer Pension Plan Amendments Act of 1980.

(3) A multiemployer plan shall not be liable to the corporation as provided in paragraph (1) in the case of a transfer from the multiemployer plan to a single-employer plan of liabilities which accrued under a single-employer plan which merged with the

Sec. 4231 (c)

multiemployer plan, if, the value of liabilities transferred to the single-employer plan does not exceed the value of the liabilities for benefits which accrued before the merger, and the value of the assets transferred to the single-employer plan is substantially equal to the value of the assets which would have been in the single-employer plan if the employer had maintained and funded it as a separate plan under which no benefits accrued after the date of the merger.

(4) The corporation may make equitable arrangements with multiemployer plans which are liable under this subsection for satisfaction of their liability.

(d) Benefits under a single-employer plan to which liabilities are transferred in accordance with this section are guaranteed under section 4022 to the extent provided in that section as of the effective date of the transfer and the plan is a successor plan.

(e)(1) Except as provided in paragraph (2), a multiemployer plan may not transfer liabilities to a single-employer plan unless the plan sponsor of the plan to which the liabilities would be transferred agrees to the transfer.

(2) In the case of a transfer described in subsection (c)(3), paragraph (1) of this subsection is satisfied by the advance agreement to the transfer by the employer who will be obligated to contribute to the single-employer plan.

(f)(1) The corporation may prescribe by regulation such additional requirements with respect to the transfer of assets or liabilities as may be necessary to protect the interests of plan participants and beneficiaries and the corporation.

(2) Except as otherwise determined by the corporation, a transfer of assets or liabilities to a single-employer plan from a plan in reorganization under section 4241 is not effective unless the corporation approves such transfer.

(3) No transfer to which this section applies, in connection with a termination described in section 4041A (a)(2) shall be effective unless the transfer meets such requirements as may be established by the corporation to prevent an increase in the risk of loss to the corporation.

Partition

Sec. 4233. (a) The corporation may order the partition of a multiemployer plan in accordance with this section.

(b) A plan sponsor may apply to the corporation for an order partitioning a plan. The corporation may not order the partition of a plan except upon notice to the plan sponsor and the participants and beneficiaries whose vested benefits will be affected by the partition of the plan, and upon finding that—

(1) a substantial reduction in the amount of aggregate contributions under the plan has resulted or will result from a case or proceeding under title 11, United States Code, with respect to an employer;

(2) the plan is likely to become insolvent;

(3) contributions will have to be increased significantly in reorganization to meet the minimum contribution requirement and prevent insolvency; and

(4) partition would significantly reduce the likelihood that the plan will become insolvent.

(c) The corporation may order the partition of a plan notwithstanding the pendency of a proceeding described in subsection (b)(1).

(d) The corporation's partition order shall provide for a transfer of no more than the nonforfeitable benefits directly attributable to service with the employer referred to in subsection (b)(1) and an equitable share of assets.

(e) The plan created by the partition is—

(1) a successor plan to which section 4022A applies, and

(2) a terminated multiemployer plan to which section 4041A(d) applies,

with respect to which only the employer described in subsection (b)(1) has withdrawal liability, and to which section 4068 applies.

(f) The corporation may proceed under section 4042(c) through (h) for a decree partitioning a plan and appointing a trustee for the terminated portion of a partitioned plan. The court may order the partition of a plan upon making the findings described in subsection (b)(1) through (4), and subject to the conditions set forth in subsections (c) through (e).

Asset Transfer Rules

Sec. 4234. (a) A transfer of assets from a multiemployer plan to another plan shall comply with asset-transfer rules which shall be adopted by the multiemployer plan and which—

(1) do not unreasonably restrict the transfer of plan assets in connection with the transfer of plan liabilities, and

(2) operate and are applied uniformly with respect to each proposed transfer, except that the rules may provide for reasonable variations taking into account the potential financial impact of a proposed transfer on the multiemployer plan.

Plan rules authorizing asset transfers consistent with the requirements of section 4232(c)(3) shall be considered to satisfy the requirements of this subsection.

(b) The corporation shall prescribe regulations which exempt de minimis transfers of assets from the requirements of this part.

(c) This part shall not apply to transfers of assets pursuant to written reciprocity agreements, except to the extent provided in regulations prescribed by the corporation.

Transfers Pursuant to Change in Bargaining Representative

Sec. 4235. (a) In any case in which an employer has completely or partially withdrawn from a multiemployer plan (hereafter in this section referred to as the "old plan") as a result of a certified change of collective bargaining representative occurring after April 28, 1980, if participants of the old plan who are employed by the employer will, as a result of that change, participate in another multiemployer plan (hereafter in this section referred to as the "new plan"), the old plan shall transfer assets and liabilities to the new plan in accordance with this section.

(b)(1) The employer shall notify the plan sponsor of the old plan of a change in multiemployer plan participation described in subsection (a) no later than 30 days after the employer determines that the change will occur.

(2) The plan sponsor of the old plan shall—

(A) notify the employer of—

(i) the amount of the employer's withdrawal liability determined under part 1 with respect to the withdrawal,

(ii) the old plan's intent to transfer to the new plan the nonforfeitable benefits of the employees who are no longer working in covered service under the old plan as a result of the change of bargaining representative, and

(iii) the amount of assets and liabilities which are to be transferred to the new plan, and

(B) notify the plan sponsor of the new plan of the benefits, assets, and liabilities which will be transferred to the new plan.

(3) Within 60 days after receipt of the notice described in paragraph (2)(B), the new plan may file an appeal with the corporation to prevent the transfer. The transfer shall not be made if the corporation determines that the new plan would suffer substantial financial harm as a result of the transfer. Upon notification described in paragraph (2), if—

(A) the employer fails to object to the transfer within 60 days after receipt of the notice described in paragraph (2)(A), or

(B) the new plan either—

(i) fails to file such an appeal, or

(ii) the corporation, pursuant to such an appeal, fails to find that the new plan would suffer substantial fi-

nancial harm as a result of the transfer described in the notice under paragraph (2)(B) within 180 days after the date on which the appeal is filed,
then the plan sponsor of the old plan shall transfer the appropriate amount of assets and liabilities to the new plan.

(c) If the plan sponsor of the old plan transfers the appropriate amount of assets and liabilities under this section to the new plan, then the amount of the employer's withdrawal liability (as determined under section 4201(b) without regard to such transfer and this section) with respect to the old plan shall be reduced by the amount by which—

(1) the value of the unfunded vested benefits allocable to the employer which were transferred by the plan sponsor of the old plan to the new plan, exceeds

(2) the value of the assets transferred.

(d) In any case in which there is a complete or partial withdrawal described in subsection (a), if—

(1) the new plan files an appeal with the corporation under subsection (b)(3), and

(2) the employer is required by section 4219 to begin making payments of withdrawal liability before the earlier of—

(A) the date on which the corporation finds that the new plan would not suffer substantial financial harm as a result of the transfer, or

(B) the last day of the 180-day period beginning on the date on which the new plan files its appeal,

then the employer shall make such payments into an escrow held by a bank or similar financial institution satisfactory to the old plan. If the transfer is made, the amounts paid into the escrow shall be returned to the employer. If the transfer is not made, the amounts paid into the escrow shall be paid to the old plan and credited against the employer's withdrawal liability.

(e)(1) Notwithstanding subsection (b), the plan sponsor shall not transfer any assets to the new plan if—

(A) the old plan is in reorganization (within the meaning of section 4241(a)), or

(B) the transfer of assets would cause the old plan to go into reorganization (within the meaning of section 4241(a)).

(2) In any case in which a transfer of assets from the old plan to the new plan is prohibited by paragraph (1), the plan sponsor of the old plan shall transfer—

(A) all nonforfeitable benefits described in subsection (b)(2), if the value of such benefits does not exceed the withdrawal liability of the employer with respect to such withdrawal, or

(B) such nonforfeitable benefits having a value equal to the withdrawal liability of the employer, if the value of such benefits exceeds the withdrawal liability of the employer.

(f)(1) Notwithstanding subsections (b) and (e), the plan sponsors of the old plan and the new plan may agree to a transfer of assets and liabilities that complies with sections 4231 and 4234, rather than this section, except that the employer's liability with respect to the withdrawal from the old plan shall be reduced under subsection (c) as if assets and liabilities had been transferred in accordance with this section.

(2) If the employer withdraws from the new plan within 240 months after the effective date of a transfer of assets and liabilities described in this section, the amount of the employer's withdrawal liability to the new plan shall be the greater of—

(A) the employer's withdrawal liability determined under part 1 with respect to the new plan, or

(B) the amount by which the employer's withdrawal liability to the old plan was reduced under subsection (c), reduced by 5 percent for each 12-month period following the effective date of the transfer and ending before

Sec. 4235 (f)

the date of the withdrawal from the new plan.

(g) For purposes of this section—

(1) "appropriate amount of assets" means the amount by which the value of the nonforfeitable benefits to be transferred exceeds the amount of the employer's withdrawal liability to the old plan (determined under part 1 without regard to section 4211(e)), and

(2) "certified change of collective bargaining representative" means a change of collective bargaining representative certified under the Labor-Management Relations Act, 1947, or the Railway Labor Act.

PART 3—REORGANIZATION; MINIMUM CONTRIBUTION REQUIREMENT FOR MULTIEMPLOYER PLANS

Reorganization Status

Sec. 4241. (a) A multiemployer plan is in reorganization for a plan year if the plan's reorganization index for that year is greater than zero.

(b)(1) A plan's reorganization index for any plan year is the excess of—

(A) the vested benefits charge for such year, over

(B) the net charge to the funding standard account for such year.

(2) For purposes of this part, the net charge to the funding standard account for any plan year is the excess (if any) of—

(A) the charges to the funding standard account for such year under section 412(b)(2) of the Internal Revenue Code of 1954, over

(B) the credits to the funding standard account under Section 412(b)(3)(B) of such Code.

(3) For purposes of this part, the vested benefits charge for any plan year is the amount which would be necessary to amortize the plan's unfunded vested benefits as of the end of the base plan year in equal annual installments—

(A) over 10 years, to the extent such benefits are attributable to persons in pay status, and

(B) over 25 years, to the extent such benefits are attributable to other participants.

(4)(A) The vested benefits charge for a plan year shall be based on an actuarial valuation of the plan as of the end of the base plan year, adjusted to reflect—

(i) any—

(I) decrease of 5 percent or more in the value of plan assets, or increase of 5 percent or more in the number of persons in pay status, during the period beginning on the first day of the plan year following the base plan year and ending on the adjustment date, or

(II) at the election of the plan sponsor, actuarial valuation of the plan as of the adjustment date or any later date not later than the last day of the plan year for which the determination is being made,

(ii) any change in benefits under the plan which is not otherwise taken into account under this subparagraph and which is pursuant to any amendment—

(I) adopted before the end of the plan year for which the determination is being made, and

(II) effective after the end of the base plan year and on or before the end of the plan year referred to in subclause (I), and

(iii) any other event (including an event described in subparagraph (B)(i)(I)) which, as determined in accordance with regulations prescribed by the Secretary, would substantially increase the plan's vested benefit charge.

(B)(i) In determining the vested benefits charge for a plan year following a plan year in which the plan was not in reorganization, any change in benefits which—

(I) results from the changing of a group of participants from one benefit level to another benefit level under a schedule of plan benefits as a result of changes in a collective bargaining agreement, or

(II) results from any other change in a collective bargaining agreement,

Sec. 4235 (g)

shall not be taken into account except to the extent provided in regulations prescribed by the Secretary of the Treasury.

(ii) Except as otherwise determined by the Secretary of the Treasury, in determining the vested benefits charge for any plan year following any plan year in which the plan was in reorganization, any change in benefits—

(I) described in clause (i)(I), or

(II) described in clause (i)(II) as determined under regulations prescribed by the Secretary of the Treasury,

shall, for purposes of subparagraph (A)(ii), be treated as a change in benefits pursuant to an amendment to a plan.

(5)(A) For purposes of this part, the base plan year for any plan year is—

(i) if there is a relevant collective bargaining agreement, the last plan year ending at least 6 months before the relevant effective date, or

(ii) if there is no relevant collective bargaining agreement, the last plan year ending at least 12 months before the beginning of the plan year.

(B) For purposes of this part, a relevant collective bargaining agreement is a collective bargaining agreement—

(i) which is in effect for at least 6 months during the plan year, and

(ii) which has not been in effect for more than 36 months as of the end of the plan year.

(C) For purposes of this part, the relevant effective date is the earliest of the effective dates for the relevant collective bargaining agreements.

(D) For purposes of this part, the adjustment date is the date which is—

(i) 90 days before the relevant effective date, or

(ii) if there is no relevant effective date, 90 days before the beginning of the plan year.

(6) For purposes of this part, the term "person in pay status" means—

(A) a participant or beneficiary on the last day of the base plan year who, at any time during such year, was paid an early, late, normal, or disability retirement benefit (or a death benefit related to a retirement benefit), and

(B) to the extent provided in regulations prescribed by the Secretary of the Treasury, any other person who is entitled to such a benefit under the plan.

(7) For purposes of paragraph (3)—

(A) in determining the plan's unfunded vested benefits, plan assets shall first be allocated to the vested benefits attributable to persons in pay status, and

(B) the vested benefits charge shall be determined without regard to reductions in accrued benefits under section 4244A which are first effective in the plan year.

(8) For purposes of this part, any outstanding claim for withdrawal liability shall not be considered a plan asset, except as otherwise provided in regulations prescribed by the Secretary of the Treasury.

(9) For purposes of this part, the term "unfunded vested benefits" means with respect to a plan, an amount (determined in accordance with regulations prescribed by the Secretary of the Treasury) equal to—

(A) the value of nonforfeitable benefits under the plan, less

(B) the value of assets of the plan.

(c) Except as provided in regulations prescribed by the corporation, while a plan is in reorganization a benefit with respect to a participant (other than a death benefit) which is attributable to employer contributions and which has a value of more than $1,750 may not be paid in a form other than an annuity which (by itself or in combination with social security, railroad retirement, or workers' compensation benefits) provides substantially level payments over the life of the participant.

(d) Any multiemployer plan which terminates under section 4041A(a)(2) shall not be considered in reorganization after the last day of the plan year in which the plan is treated as having terminated.

Sec. 4241 (d)

Notice of Reorganization and Funding Requirements

Sec. 4242. (a)(1) If—

(A) a multiemployer plan is in reorganization for a plan year, and

(B) section 4243 would require an increase in contributions for such plan year,

the plan sponsor shall notify the persons described in paragraph (2) that the plan is in reorganization and that, if contributions to the plan are not increased, accrued benefits under the plan may be reduced or an excise tax may be imposed (or both such reduction and imposition may occur).

(2) The persons described in this paragraph are—

(A) each employer who has an obligation to contribute under the plan (within the meaning of section 4201(h)(5)), and

(B) each employee organization which, for purposes of collective bargaining, represents plan participants employed by such an employer.

(3) The determination under paragraph (1)(B) shall be made without regard to the overburden credit provided by section 4244.

(b) The corporation may prescribe additional or alternative requirements for assuring, in the case of a plan with respect to which notice is required by subsection (a)(1), that the persons described in subsection (a)(2)—

(1) receive appropriate notice that the plan is in reorganization,

(2) are adequately informed of the implications of reorganization status, and

(3) have reasonable access to information relevant to the plan's reorganization status.

Minimum Contribution Requirement

Sec. 4243. (a)(1) For any plan year for which a plan is in reorganization—

(A) the plan shall continue to maintain its funding standard account while it is in reorganization, and

(B) the plan's accumulated funding deficiency under section 302(a) for such plan year shall be equal to the excess (if any) of—

(i) the sum of the minimum contribution requirement for such plan year (taking into account any overburden credit under section 4244(a)) plus the plan's accumulated funding deficiency for the preceding plan year (determined under this section if the plan was in reorganization during such year or under section 302(a) if the plan was not in reorganization), over

(ii) amounts considered contributed by employers to or under the plan for the plan year (increased by any amount waived under subsection (f) for the plan year).

(2) For purposes of paragraph (1), withdrawal liability payments (whether or not received) which are due with respect to withdrawals before the end of the base plan year shall be considered amounts contributed by the employer to or under the plan if, as of the adjustment date, it was reasonable for the plan sponsor to anticipate that such payments would be made during the plan year.

(b)(1) Except as otherwise provided in this section, for purposes of this part the minimum contribution requirement for a plan year in which a plan is in reorganization is an amount equal to the excess of—

(A) the sum of—

(i) the plan's vested benefits charge for the plan year, and

(ii) the increase in normal cost for the plan year determined under the entry age normal funding method which is attributable to plan amendments adopted while the plan was in reorganization, over

(B) the amount of the overburden credit (if any) determined under section 4244 for the plan year.

(2) If the plan's current contribution base for the plan year is less than the plan's valuation contribution base for the plan year, the minimum contribution requirement for such plan year shall be equal to the product of the amount determined under paragraph (1) (after any adjustment required by this part other than this paragraph) and a fraction—

(A) the numerator of which is the

Sec. 4242

plan's current contribution base for the plan year, and

(B) the denominator of which is the plan's valuation contribution base for the plan year.

(3)(A) If the vested benefits charge for a plan year of a plan in reorganization is less than the plan's cash-flow amount for the plan year, the plan's minimum contribution requirement for the plan year is the amount determined under paragraph (1) (determined before the application of paragraph (2)) after substituting the term "cash-flow amount" for the term "vested benefits charge" in paragraph (1)(A).

(B) For purposes of subparagraph (A), a plan's cash-flow amount for a plan year is an amount equal to—

(i) the amount of the benefits payable under the plan for the base plan year, plus the amount of the plan's administrative expenses for the base plan year, reduced by

(ii) the value of the available plan assets for the base plan year determined under regulations prescribed by the Secretary of the Treasury,

adjusted in a manner consistent with section 4241(b)(4).

(c)(1) For purposes of this part, a plan's current contribution base for a plan year is the number of contribution base units with respect to which contributions are required to be made under the plan for that plan year, determined in accordance with regulations prescribed by the Secretary of the Treasury.

(2)(A) Except as provided in subparagraph (B), for purposes of this part a plan's valuation contribution base is the number of contribution base units for which contributions were received for the base plan year—

(i) adjusted to reflect declines in the contribution base which have occurred (or could reasonably be anticipated) as of the adjustment date for the plan year referred to in paragraph (1),

(ii) adjusted upward (in accordance with regulations prescribed by the Secretary of the Treasury) for any contribution base reduction in the base plan year caused by a strike or lockout or by unusual events, such as fire, earthquake, or severe weather conditions, and

(iii) adjusted (in accordance with regulations prescribed by the Secretary of the Treasury) for reductions in the contribution base resulting from transfers of liabilities.

(B) For any plan year—

(i) in which the plan is insolvent (within the meaning of section 4245(b)(1)), and

(ii) beginning with the first plan year beginning after the expiration of all relevant collective bargaining agreements which were in effect in the plan year in which the plan became insolvent,

the plan's valuation contribution base is the greater of the number of contribution base units for which contributions were received for the first or second plan year preceding the first plan year in which the plan is insolvent, adjusted as provided in clause (ii) or (iii) of subparagraph (A).

(d)(1) Under regulations prescribed by the Secretary of the Treasury, the minimum contribution requirement applicable to any plan for any plan year which is determined under subsection (b) (without regard to subsection (b)(2)) shall not exceed an amount which is equal to the sum of—

(A) the greater of—

(i) the funding standard requirement for such plan year, or

(ii) 107 percent of—

(I) if the plan was not in reorganization in the preceding plan year, the funding standard requirement for such preceding plan year, or

(II) if the plan was in reorganization in the preceding plan year, the sum of the amount determined under this subparagraph for the preceding plan year and the amount (if any) determined under subparagraph (B) for the preceding plan year, plus

(B) if for the plan year a change in benefits is first required to be consid-

Sec. 4243 (d)

ered in computing the charges under section 412(b)(2)(A) or (B) of the Internal Revenue Code of 1954, the sum of—

(i) the increase in normal cost for a plan year determined under the entry age normal funding method due to increases in benefits described in section 4241(b)(4)(A)(ii) (determined without regard to section 4241(b)(4)(B)(i)), and

(ii) the amount necessary to amortize in equal annual installments the increase in the value of vested benefits under the plan due to increases in benefits described in clause (i) over—

(I) 10 years, to the extent such increase in value is attributable to persons in pay status, or

(II) 25 years, to the extent such increase in value is attributable to other participants.

(2) For purposes of paragraph (1), the funding standard requirement for any plan year is an amount equal to the net charge to the funding standard account for such plan year (as defined in section 4241(b)(2)).

(3)(A) In the case of a plan described in section 4216(b), if a plan amendment which increases benefits is adopted after January 1, 1980—

(i) paragraph (1) shall apply only if the plan is a plan described in subparagraph (B), and

(ii) the amount under paragraph (1) shall be determined without regard to paragraph (1)(B).

(B) A plan is described in this subparagraph if—

(i) the rate of employer contributions under the plan for the first plan year beginning on or after the date on which an amendment increasing benefits is adopted, multiplied by the valuation contribution base for that plan year, equals or exceeds the sum of—

(I) the amount that would be necessary to amortize fully, in equal annual installments, by July 1, 1986, the unfunded vested benefits attributable to plan provisions in effect on July 1, 1977 (determined as of the last day of the base plan year); and

(II) the amount that would be necessary to amortize fully, in equal annual installments, over the period described in subparagraph (C), beginning with the first day of the first plan year beginning on or after the date on which the amendment is adopted, the unfunded vested benefits (determined as of the last day of the base plan year) attributable to each plan amendment after July 1, 1977; and

(ii) the rate of employer contributions for each subsequent plan year is not less than the lesser of—

(I) the rate which when multiplied by the valuation contribution base for that subsequent plan year produces the annual amount that would be necessary to complete the amortization schedule described in clause (i), or

(II) the rate for the plan year immediately preceding such subsequent plan year, plus 5 percent of such rate.

(C) The period determined under this subparagraph is the lesser of—

(i) 12 years, or

(ii) a period equal in length to the average of the remaining expected lives of all persons receiving benefits under the plan.

(4) Paragraph (1) shall not apply with respect to a plan, other than a plan described in paragraph (3), for the period of consecutive plan years in each of which the plan is in reorganization, beginning with a plan year in which occurs the earlier of the date of the adoption or the effective date of any amendment of the plan which increases benefits with respect to service performed before the plan year in which the adoption of the amendment occurred.

(e) In determining the minimum contribution requirement with respect to a plan for a plan year under subsection (b), the vested benefits charge may be adjusted to reflect a plan amendment reducing benefits under section 412(c)(8) of the Internal Revenue Code of 1954.

(f)(1) The Secretary of the Treasury may waive any accumulated funding deficiency under this section in accordance with the provisions of section 303(a).

(2) Any waiver under paragraph (1) shall not be treated as a waived funding deficiency (within the meaning of section 303(c)).

(g) For purposes of making any determination under this part, the requirements of section 302(c)(3) shall apply.

Overburden Credit Against Minimum Contribution Requirement

Sec. 4244. (a) For purposes of determining the minimum contribution requirement under section 4243 (before the application of section 4243(b)(2) or (d)) the plan sponsor of a plan which is overburdened for the plan year shall apply an overburden credit against the plan's minimum contribution requirement for the plan year (determined without regard to section 4243(b)(2) or (d) and without regard to this section).

(b) A plan is overburdened for a plan year if—

(1) the average number of pay status participants under the plan in the base plan year exceeds the average of the number of active participants in the base plan year and the 2 plan years preceding the base plan year, and

(2) the rate of employer contributions under the plan equals or exceeds the greater of—

(A) such rate for the preceding plan year, or

(B) such rate for the plan year preceding the first year in which the plan is in reorganization.

(c) The amount of the overburden credit for a plan year is the product of—

(1) one-half of the average guaranteed benefit paid for the base plan year, and

(2) the overburden factor for the plan year.

The amount of the overburden credit for a plan year shall not exceed the amount of the minimum contribution requirement for such year (determined without regard to this section).

(d) For purposes of this section, the overburden factor of a plan for the plan year is an amount equal to—

(1) the average number of pay status participants for the base plan year, reduced by

(2) the average of the number of active participants for the base plan year and for each of the 2 plan years preceding the base plan year.

(e) For purposes of this section—

(1) The term "pay status participant" means, with respect to a plan, a participant receiving retirement benefits under the plan.

(2) The number of active participants for a plan year shall be the sum of—

(A) the number of active employees who are participants in the plan and on whose behalf contributions are required to be made during the plan year;

(B) the number of active employees who are not participants in the plan but who are in an employment unit covered by a collective bargaining agreement which requires the employees' employer to contribute to the plan, unless service in such employment unit was never covered under the plan or a predecessor thereof, and

(C) the total number of active employees attributed to employers who made payments to the plan for the plan year of withdrawal liability pursuant to part 1, determined by dividing—

(i) the total amount of such payments, by

(ii) the amount equal to the total contributions received by the plan during the plan year divided by the average number of active employees who were participants in the plan during the plan year.

The Secretary of the Treasury shall by regulation provide alternative methods of determining active participants where (by reason of irregular employment, contributions on a unit basis, or otherwise) this paragraph does not yield a representative basis for determining the credit.

(3) The term "average number"

means, with respect to pay status participants for a plan year, a number equal to one-half the sum of—

(A) the number with respect to the plan as of the beginning of the plan year, and

(B) the number with respect to the plan as of the end of the plan year.

(4) The average guaranteed benefit paid is 12 times the average monthly pension payment guaranteed under section 4022A(c)(1) determined under the provisions of the plan in effect at the beginning of the first plan year in which the plan is in reorganization and without regard to section 4022A(c)(2).

(5) The first year in which the plan is in reorganization is the first of a period of 1 or more consecutive plan years in which the plan has been in reorganization not taking into account any plan years the plan was in reorganization prior to any period of 3 or more consecutive plan years in which the plan was not in reorganization.

(f)(1) Notwithstanding any other provision of this section, a plan is not eligible for an overburden credit for a plan year if the Secretary of the Treasury finds that the plan's current contribution base for the plan year was reduced, without a corresponding reduction in the plan's unfunded vested benefits attributable to pay status participants, as a result of a change in an agreement providing for employer contributions under the plan.

(2) For purposes of paragraph (1), a complete or partial withdrawal of an employer (within the meaning of part 1) does not impair a plan's eligibility for an overburden credit, unless the Secretary of the Treasury finds that a contribution base reduction described in paragraph (1) resulted from a transfer of liabilities to another plan in connection with the withdrawal.

(g) Notwithstanding any other provision of this section, if 2 or more multiemployer plans merge, the amount of the overburden credit which may be applied under this section with respect to the plan resulting from the merger for any of the 3 plan years ending after the effective date of the merger shall not exceed the sum of the used overburden credit for each of the merging plans for its last plan year ending before the effective date of the merger. For purposes of the preceding sentence, the used overburden credit is that portion of the credit which does not exceed the excess of the minimum contribution requirement (determined without regard to any overburden requirement under this section) over the employer contributions required under the plan.

Adjustments in Accrued Benefits

Sec. 4244A. (a)(1) Notwithstanding sections 203 and 204, a multiemployer plan in reorganization may be amended in accordance with this section, to reduce or eliminate accrued benefits attributable to employer contributions which, under section 4022A(b), are not eligible for the corporation's guarantee. The preceding sentence shall only apply to accrued benefits under plan amendments (or plans) adopted after March 26, 1980, or under collective bargaining agreements entered into after March 26, 1980.

(2) In determining the minimum contribution requirement with respect to a plan for a plan year under section 4243(b), the vested benefits charge may be adjusted to reflect a plan amendment reducing benefits under this section or section 412(c)(8) of the Internal Revenue Code of 1954, but only if the amendment is adopted and effective no later than 2½ months after the end of the plan year, or within such extended period as the Secretary of the Treasury may prescribe by regulation under section 412(c)(10) of such Code.

(b)(1) Accrued benefits may not be reduced under this section unless—

(A) notice has been given, at least 6 months before the first day of the plan year in which the amendment reducing benefits is adopted, to—

(i) plan participants and beneficiaries,

Sec. 4244 (e) (4)

(ii) each employer who has an obligation to contribute (within the meaning of section 4212(a)) under the plan, and

(iii) each employee organization which, for purposes of collective bargaining, represents plan participants employed by such an employer,

that the plan is in reorganization and that, if contributions under the plan are not increased, accrued benefits under the plan will be reduced or an excise tax bill will be imposed on employers;

(B) in accordance with regulations prescribed by the Secretary of the Treasury—

(i) any category of accrued benefits is not reduced with respect to inactive participants to a greater extent proportionally than such category of accrued benefits is reduced with respect to active participants,

(ii) benefits attributable to employer contributions other than accrued benefits and the rate of future benefit accruals are reduced at least to an extent equal to the reduction in accrued benefits of inactive participants, and

(iii) in any case in which the accrued benefit of a participant or beneficiary is reduced by changing the benefit form or the requirements which the participant or beneficiary must satisfy to be entitled to the benefit, such reduction is not applicable to—

(I) any participant or beneficiary in pay status on the effective date of the amendment, or the beneficiary of such a participant, or

(II) any participant who has attained normal retirement age, or who is within 5 years of attaining normal retirement age, on the effective date of the amendment, or the beneficiary of any such participant; and

(C) the rate of employer contributions for the plan year in which the amendment becomes effective and for all succeeding plan years in which the plan is in reorganization equals or exceeds the greater of—

(i) the rate of employer contributions, calculated without regard to the amendment, for the plan year in which the amendment becomes effective, or

(ii) the rate of employer contributions for the plan year preceding the plan year in which the amendment becomes effective.

(2) The plan sponsors shall include in any notice required to be sent to plan participants and beneficiaries under paragraph (1) information as to the rights and remedies of plan participants and beneficiaries as well as how to contact the Department of Labor for further information and assistance where appropriate.

(c) A plan may not recoup a benefit payment which is in excess of the amount payable under the plan because of an amendment retroactively reducing accrued benefits under this section.

(d)(1)(A) A plan which has been amended to reduce accrued benefits under this section may be amended to increase or restore accrued benefits, or the rate of future benefit accruals, only if the plan is amended to restore levels of previously reduced accrued benefits of inactive participants and of participants who are within 5 years of attaining normal retirement age to at least the same extent as any such increase in accrued benefits or in the rate of future benefit accruals.

(B) For purposes of this subsection, in the case of a plan which has been amended under this section to reduce accrued benefits—

(i) an increase in a benefit, or in the rate of future benefit accruals, shall be considered a benefit increase to the extent that the benefit, or the accrual rate, is thereby increased above the highest benefit level, or accrual rate, which was in effect under the terms of the plan before the effective date of the amendment reducing accrued benefits, and

(ii) an increase in a benefit, or in the rate of future benefit accruals, shall be considered a benefit restoration to the extent that the bene-

Sec. 4244A (d)

fit, or the accrual rate, is not thereby increased above the highest benefit level, or accrual rate, which was in effect under the terms of the plan immediately before the effective date of the amendment reducing accrued benefits.

(2) If a plan is amended to partially restore previously reduced accrued benefit levels, or the rate of future benefit accruals, the benefits of inactive participants shall be restored in at least the same proportions as other accrued benefits which are restored.

(3) No benefit increase under a plan may take effect in a plan year in which an amendment reducing accrued benefits under the plan, in accordance with this section, is adopted or first becomes effective.

(4) A plan is not required to make retroactive benefit payments with respect to that portion of an accrued benefit which was reduced and subsequently restored under this section.

(e) For purposes of this section, "inactive participant" means a person not in covered service under the plan who is in pay status under the plan or who has a nonforfeitable benefit under the plan.

(f) The Secretary of the Treasury may prescribe rules under which, notwithstanding any other provision of this section, accrued benefit reductions or benefit increases for different participant groups may be varied equitably to reflect variations in contribution rates and other relevant factors reflecting differences in negotiated levels of financial support for plan benefit obligations.

Insolvent Plans

Sec. 4245. (a) Notwithstanding sections 203 and 204, in any case in which benefit payments under an insolvent multiemployer plan exceed the resource benefit level, any such payments of benefits which are not basic benefits shall be suspended, in accordance with this section, to the extent necessary to reduce the sum of such payments and the payments of such basic benefits to the greater of the resource benefit level or the level of basic benefits, unless an alternative procedure is prescribed by the corporation under section 4022A(g)(5).

(b) For purposes of this section, for a plan year—

(1) a multiemployer plan is insolvent if the plan's available resources are not sufficient to pay benefits under the plan when due for the plan year, or if the plan is determined to be insolvent under subsection (d);

(2) "resource benefit level" means the level of monthly benefits determined under subsections (c)(1) and (3) and (d)(3) to be the highest level which can be paid out of the plan's available resources;

(3) "available resources" means the plan's cash, marketable assets, contributions, withdrawal liability payments, and earnings, less reasonable administrative expenses and amounts owed for such plan year to the corporation under section 4261(b)(2); and

(4) "insolvency year" means a plan year in which a plan is insolvent.

(c)(1) The plan sponsor of a plan in reorganization shall determine in writing the plan's resource benefit level for each insolvency year, based on the plan sponsor's reasonable projection of the plan's available resources and the benefits payable under the plan.

(2) The suspension of benefit payments under this section shall, in accordance with regulations prescribed by the Secretary of the Treasury, apply in substantially uniform proportions to the benefits of all persons in pay status (within the meaning of section 4241(b)(6)) under the plan, except that the Secretary of the Treasury may prescribe rules under which benefit suspensions for different participant groups may be varied equitably to reflect variations in contribution rates and other relevant factors including differences in negotiated levels of financial support for plan benefit obligations.

(3) Notwithstanding paragraph (2), if a plan sponsor determines in writing a resource benefit level for a plan year

which is below the level of basic benefits, the payment of all benefits other than basic benefits must be suspended for that plan year.

(4)(A) If, by the end of an insolvency year, the plan sponsor determines in writing that the plan's available resources in that insolvency year could have supported benefit payments above the resource benefit level for that insolvency year, the plan sponsor shall distribute the excess resources to the participants and beneficiaries who received benefit payments from the plan in that insolvency year, in accordance with regulations prescribed by the Secretary of the Treasury.

(B) For purposes of this paragraph, the term "excess resources" means available resources above the amount necessary to support the resource benefit level, but no greater than the amount necessary to pay benefits for the plan year at the benefit levels under the plan.

(5) If, by the end of an insolvency year, any benefit has not been paid at the resource benefit level, amounts up to the resource benefit level which were unpaid shall be distributed to the participants and beneficiaries, in accordance with regulations prescribed by the Secretary of the Treasury, to the extent possible taking into account the plan's total available resources in that insolvency year.

(6) Except as provided in paragraph (4) or (5), a plan is not required to make retroactive benefit payments with respect to that portion of a benefit which was suspended under this section.

(d)(1) As of the end of the first plan year in which a plan is in reorganization, and at least every 3 plan years thereafter (unless the plan is no longer in reorganization), the plan sponsor shall compare the value of plan assets (determined in accordance with section 4243(b)(3)(B)(ii)) for that plan year with the total amount of benefit payments made under the plan for that plan year. Unless the plan sponsor determines that the value of plan assets exceeds 3 times the total amount of benefit payments, the plan sponsor shall determine whether the plan will be insolvent in any of the next 3 plan years.

(2) If, at any time, the plan sponsor of a plan in reorganization reasonably determines, taking into account the plan's recent and anticipated financial experience, that the plan's available resources are not sufficient to pay benefits under the plan when due for the next plan year, the plan sponsor shall make such determination available to interested parties.

(3) The plan sponsor of a plan in reorganization shall determine in writing for each insolvency year the resource benefit level and the level of basic benefits no later than 3 months before the insolvency year.

(e)(1) If the plan sponsor of a plan in reorganization determines under subsection (d)(1) or (2) that the plan may become insolvent (within the meaning of subsection (b)(1)), the plan sponsor shall—

(A) notify the Secretary of the Treasury, the corporation, the parties described in section 4242(a)(2), and the plan participants and beneficiaries of that determination, and

(B) inform the parties described in section 4242(a)(2) and the plan participants and beneficiaries that if insolvency occurs certain benefit payments will be suspended, but that basic benefits will continue to be paid.

(2) No later than 2 months before the first day of each insolvency year, the plan sponsor of a plan in reorganization shall notify the Secretary of the Treasury, the corporation, and the parties described in paragraph (1)(B) of the resource benefit level determined in writing for that insolvency year.

(3) In any case in which the plan sponsor anticipates that the resource benefit level for an insolvency year may not exceed the level of basic benefits, the plan sponsor shall notify the corporation.

(4) Notice required by this subsec-

tion shall be given in accordance with regulations prescribed by the corporation, except that notice to the Secretary of the Treasury shall be given in accordance with regulations prescribed by the Secretary of the Treasury.

(5) The corporation may prescribe a time other than the time prescribed by this section for the making of a determination or the filing of a notice under this section.

(f)(1) If the plan sponsor of an insolvent plan, for which the resource benefit level is above the level of basic benefits, anticipates that, for any month in an insolvency year, the plan will not have funds sufficient to pay basic benefits, the plan sponsor may apply for financial assistance from the corporation under section 4261.

(2) A plan sponsor who has determined a resource benefit level for an insolvency year which is below the level of basic benefits shall apply for financial assistance from the corporation under section 4261.

PART 4—FINANCIAL ASSISTANCE

Financial Assistance

Sec. 4261. (a) If, upon receipt of an application for financial assistance under section 4245(f) or section 4281(d), the corporation verifies that the plan is or will be insolvent and unable to pay basic benefits when due, the corporation shall provide the plan financial assistance in an amount sufficient to enable the plan to pay basic benefits under the plan.

(b)(1) Financial assistance shall be provided under such conditions as the corporation determines are equitable and are appropriate to prevent unreasonable loss to the corporation with respect to the plan.

(2) A plan which has received financial assistance shall repay the amount of such assistance to the corporation on reasonable terms consistent with regulations prescribed by the corporation.

(c) Pending determination of the amount described in subsection (a), the corporation may provide financial assistance in such amounts as it considers appropriate in order to avoid undue hardship to plan participants and beneficiaries.

PART 5—BENEFITS AFTER TERMINATION

Benefits Under Certain Terminated Plans

Sec. 4281. (a) Notwithstanding sections 203 and 204, the plan sponsor of a terminated multiemployer plan to which section 4041A(d) applies shall amend the plan to reduce benefits, and shall suspend benefit payments, as required by this section.

(b)(1) The value of nonforfeitable benefits under a terminated plan referred to in subsection (a), and the value of the plan's assets, shall be determined in writing, in accordance with regulations prescribed by the corporation, as of the end of the plan year during which section 4041A(d) becomes applicable to the plan, and each plan year thereafter.

(2) For purposes of this section, plan assets include outstanding claims for withdrawal liability (within the meaning of section 4001(a)(12)).

(c)(1) If, according to the determination made under subsection (b), the value of nonforfeitable benefits exceeds the value of the plan's assets, the plan sponsor shall amend the plan to reduce benefits under the plan to the extent necessary to ensure that the plan's assets are sufficient, as determined and certified in accordance with regulations prescribed by the corporation, to discharge when due all of the plan's obligations with respect to nonforfeitable benefits.

(2) Any plan amendment required by this subsection shall, in accordance with regulations prescribed by the Secretary of the Treasury—

(A) reduce benefits only to the extent necessary to comply with paragraph (1);

(B) reduce accrued benefits only to the extent that those benefits are not eligible for the corporation's guarantee under section 4022A(b);

(C) comply with the rules for and

limitations on benefit reductions under a plan in reorganization, as prescribed in section 4244A, except to the extent that the corporation prescribes other rules and limitations in regulations under this section; and

(D) take effect no later than 6 months after the end of the plan year for which it is determined that the value of nonforfeitable benefits exceeds the value of the plan's assets.

(d)(1) In any case in which benefit payments under a plan which is insolvent under paragraph (2)(A) exceed the resource benefit level, any such payments which are not basic benefits shall be suspended, in accordance with this subsection, to the extent necessary to reduce the sum of such payments and such basic benefits to the greater of the resource benefit level or the level of basic benefits, unless an alternative procedure is prescribed by the corporation in connection with a supplemental guarantee program established under section 4022A(g)(2).

(2) For the purposes of this subsection, for a plan year—

(A) a plan is insolvent if—

(i) the plan has been amended to reduce benefits to the extent permitted by subsection (c), and

(ii) the plan's available resources are not sufficient to pay benefits under the plan when due for the plan year; and

(B) "resource benefit level" and "available resources" have the meanings set forth in paragraphs (2) and (3), respectively, of section 4245(b).

(3) The plan sponsor of a plan which is insolvent (within the meaning of paragraph (2)(A)) shall have the powers and duties of the plan sponsor of a plan in reorganization which is insolvent (within the meaning of section 4245(b)(1)), except that regulations governing the plan sponsor's exercise of those powers and duties under this section shall be prescribed by the corporation, and the corporation shall prescribe by regulation notice requirements which assure that plan participants and beneficiaries receive adequate notice of benefit suspensions.

(4) A plan is not required to make retroactive benefit payments with respect to that portion of a benefit which was suspended under this subsection, except that the provisions of section 4245(c)(4) and (5) shall apply in the case of plans which are insolvent under paragraph (2)(A), in connection with the plan year during which such section 4041A(d) first became applicable to the plan and every year thereafter, in the same manner and to the same extent as such provisions apply to insolvent plans in reorganization under section 4245, in connection with insolvency years under such section 4245.

PART 6—ENFORCEMENT

Civil Actions

Sec. 4301. (a)(1) A plan fiduciary, employer, plan participant, or beneficiary, who is adversely affected by the act or omission of any party under this subtitle with respect to a multiemployer plan, or an employee organization which represents such a plan participant or beneficiary for purposes of collective bargaining, may bring an action for appropriate legal or equitable relief, or both.

(2) Notwithstanding paragraph (1), this section does not authorize an action against the Secretary of the Treasury, the Secretary of Labor, or the corporation.

(b) In any action under this section to compel an employer to pay withdrawal liability, any failure of the employer to make any withdrawal liability payment within the time prescribed shall be treated in the same manner as a delinquent contribution (within the meaning of section 515).

(c) The district courts of the United States shall have exclusive jurisdiction of an action under this section without regard to the amount in controversy, except that State courts of competent jurisdiction shall have concurrent jurisdiction over an action brought by

Sec. 4301 (c)

a plan fiduciary to collect withdrawal liability.

(d) An action under this section may be brought in the district where the plan is administered or where a defendant resides or does business, and process may be served in any district where a defendant resides, does business, or may be found.

(e) In any action under this section, the court may award all or a portion of the costs and expenses incurred in connection with such action, including reasonable attorney's fees, to the prevailing party.

(f) An action under this section may not be brought after the later of—

(1) 6 years after the date on which the cause of action arose, or

(2) 3 years after the earliest date on which the plaintiff acquired or should have acquired actual knowledge of the existence of such cause of action; except that in the case of fraud or concealment, such action may be brought not later than 6 years after the date of discovery of the existence of such cause of action.

(g) A copy of the complaint in any action under this section or section 4221 shall be served upon the corporation by certified mail. The corporation may intervene in any such action.

Penalty for Failure to Provide Notice

Sec. 4302. Any person who fails, without reasonable cause, to provide a notice required under this subtitle or any implementing regulations shall be liable to the corporation in an amount up to $100 for each day for which such failure continues. The corporation may bring a civil action against any such person in the United States District Court for the District of Columbia or in any district court of the United States within the jurisdiction of which the plan assets are located, the plan is administered, or a defendant resides or does business, and process may be served in any district where a defendant resides, does business, or may be found.

Election of Plan Status

Sec. 4303. (a) Within one year after the date of the enactment of the Multiemployer Pension Plan Amendments Act of 1980, a multiemployer plan may irrevocably elect, pursuant to procedures established by the corporation, that the plan shall not be treated as a multiemployer plan for any purpose under this Act or the Internal Revenue Code of 1954, if for each of the last 3 plan years ending prior to the effective date of the Multiemployer Pension Plan Amendments Act of 1980—

(1) the plan was not a multiemployer plan because the plan was not a plan described in section 3(37)(A)(iii) of this Act and section 414(f)(1)(C) of the Internal Revenue Code of 1954 (as such provisions were in effect on the day before the date of the enactment of the Multiemployer Pension Plan Amendments Act of 1980); and

(2) the plan had been identified as a plan that was not a multiemployer plan in substantially all its filings with the corporation, the Secretary of Labor and the Secretary of the Treasury.

(b) An election described in subsection (a) shall be effective only if—

(1) the plan is amended to provide that it shall not be treated as a multiemployer plan for all purposes under this Act and the Internal Revenue Code of 1954, and

(2) written notice of the amendment is provided to the corporation within 60 days after the amendment is adopted.

(c) An election described in subsection (a) shall be treated as being effective as of the date of the enactment of the Multiemployer Pension Plan Amendments Act of 1980.

SUBTITLE F—TRANSITION RULES AND EFFECTIVE DATES

Amendments to Internal Revenue Code of 1954

Sec. 4401. (a) Section 404 of the Internal Revenue Code of 1954 (relating to deduction for contributions of an employer to employees' trust or annu-

Sec. 4301 (d)

ity plan in compensation under a deferred-payment plan) is amended by adding at the end thereof the following new subsection:

(g) Certain Employer Liability Payments Considered as Contributions.—For purposes of this section any amount paid by an employer under section 4062, 4063, or 4064 of the Employee Retirement Income Security Act of 1974 shall be treated as a contribution to which this section applies by such employer to or under a stock bonus, pension, profit-sharing, or annuity plan.

(b) Section 6511(d) of the Internal Revenue Code of 1954 (relating to special rules applicable to income taxes) is amended by adding at the end thereof the following new paragraph:

(8) Special period of limitation with respect to amounts included in income subsequently recaptured under qualified plan termination.—If the claim for credit or refund relates to an overpayment of tax imposed by subtitle A on account of the recapture, under section 4045 of the Employee Retirement Income Security Act of 1974, of amounts included in income for a prior taxable year, the 3-year period of limitation prescribed in subsection (a) shall be extended, for purposes of permitting a credit or refund of the amount of the recapture, until the date which occurs one year after the date on which such recaptured amount is paid by the taxpayer.

Effective Date; Special Rules

Sec. 4402. (a) The provisions of this title take effect on the date of enactment of this Act.

(b) Notwithstanding the provisions of subsection (a), the corporation shall pay benefits guaranteed under this title with respect to any plan—

(1) which is not a multiemployer plan,

(2) which terminates after June 30, 1974, and before the date of enactment of this Act,

(3) to which section 4021 would apply if that section were effective beginning on July 1, 1974, and

(4) with respect to which a notice is filed with the Secretary of Labor and received by him not later than 10 days after the date of enactment of this Act, except that, for reasonable cause shown, such notice may be filed with the Secretary of Labor and received by him not later than October 31, 1974, stating that the plan is a plan described in paragraphs (1), (2), and (3).

The corporation shall not pay benefits guaranteed under this title with respect to a plan described in the preceding sentence unless the corporation finds substantial evidence that the plan was terminated for a reasonable business purpose and not for the purpose of obtaining the payment of benefits by the corporation under this title or for the purpose of avoiding the liability which might be imposed under subtitle D if the plan terminated on or after September 2, 1974. The provisions of subtitle D do not apply in the case of such plan which terminates before September 2, 1974. For purposes of determining whether a plan is a plan described in paragraph (2), the provisions of section 4048 shall not apply, but the corporation shall make the determination on the basis of the date on which benefits ceased to accrue or on any other reasonable basis consistent with the purposes of this subsection.

(c)(1) Except as provided in paragraphs (2), (3), and (4), the corporation shall not pay benefits guaranteed under this title with respect to a multiemployer plan which terminates before August 1, 1980. Whenever the corporation exercises the authority granted under paragraph (2) or (3), the corporation shall notify the Committee on Education and Labor and the Committee on Ways and Means of the House of Representatives, and the Committee on Labor and Human Resources and the Committee on Finance of the Senate.

(2) The corporation may, in its discretion, pay benefits guaranteed under

this title with respect to a multiemployer plan which terminates after the date of enactment of this Act and before August 1, 1980, if—

(A) the plan was maintained during the 60 months immediately preceding the date on which the plan terminates, and

(B) the corporation determines that the payment by the corporation of benefits guaranteed under this title with respect to that plan will not jeopardize the payments the corporation anticipates it may be required to make in connection with benefits guaranteed under this title with respect to multiemployer plans which terminate after July 31, 1980.

(3) Notwithstanding any provision of section 4021 or 4022 which would prevent such payments, the corporation, in carrying out its authority under paragraph (2), may pay benefits guaranteed under this title with respect to a multiemployer plan described in paragraph (2) in any case in which those benefits would otherwise not be payable if—

(A) the plan has been in effect for at least 5 years,

(B) the plan has been in substantial compliance with the funding requirements for a qualified plan with respect to the employees and former employees in those employment units on the basis of which the participating employers have contributed to the plan for the preceding 5 years, and

(C) the participating employers and employee organization or organizations had no reasonable recourse other than termination.

(4) If the corporation determines, under paragraph (2) or (3), that it will pay benefits guaranteed under this title with respect to a multiemployer plan which terminates before August 1, 1980, the corporation—

(A) may establish requirements for the continuation of payments which commenced before January 2, 1974, with respect to retired participants under the plan,

(B) may not, notwithstanding any other provision of this title, make payments with respect to any participant under such a plan who, on January 1, 1974, was receiving payment of retirement benefits, in excess of the amounts and rates payable with respect to such participant on that date,

(C) may not make any payments with respect to benefits guaranteed under this title in connection with such a plan which are derived, directly or indirectly, from amounts borrowed under section 4005(c), and

(D) shall review from time to time payments made under the authority granted to it by paragraphs (2) and (3), and reduce or terminate such payments to the extent necessary to avoid jeopardizing the ability of the corporation to make payments of benefits guaranteed under this title in connection with multiemployer plans which terminate after July 31, 1980, without increasing premium rates for such plans.

(d) Notwithstanding any other provision of this title, guaranteed benefits payable by the corporation pursuant to its discretionary authority under this section shall continue to be paid at the level guaranteed under section 4022, without regard to any limitation on payment under subparagraph (C) or (D) of subsection (c)(4).

(e)(1) Except as provided in paragraphs (2), (3), and (4), the amendments to this Act made by the Multiemployer Pension Plan Amendments Act of 1980 shall take effect on the date of the enactment of that Act.

(2)(A) Except as provided in this paragraph, part 1 of subtitle E, relating to withdrawal liability, takes effect on April 29, 1980.

(B) For purposes of determining withdrawal liability under part 1 of subtitle E, an employer who has withdrawn from a plan shall be considered to have withdrawn from a multiemployer plan if, at the time of the withdrawal, the plan was a multiemployer

Sec. 4402 (c) (3)

plan as defined in section 4001(a)(3) as in effect at the time of the withdrawal.

(3) Sections 4241 through 4245, relating to multiemployer plan reorganization, shall take effect, with respect to each plan, on the first day of the first plan year beginning on or after the earlier of—

(A) the date on which the last collective bargaining agreement providing for employer contributions under the plan, which was in effect on the date of the enactment of the Multiemployer Pension Plan Amendments Act of 1980, expires, without regard to extensions agreed to on or after the date of the enactment of that Act, or

(B) 3 years after the date of the enactment of the Multiemployer Pension Plan Amendments Act of 1980.

(4) Section 4235 shall take effect on April 29, 1980.

(f)(1) In the event that before the date of enactment of the Multiemployer Pension Plan Amendments Act of 1980, the corporation has determined that—

(A) an employer has withdrawn from a multiemployer plan under section 4063, and

(B) the employer is liable to the corporation under such section, the corporation shall retain the amount of liability paid to it or furnished in the form of a bond and shall pay such liability to the plan in the event the plan terminates in accordance with section 4041A(a)(2) before the earlier of April 29, 1985, or the day after the 5-year period commencing on the date of such withdrawal.

(2) In any case in which the plan is not so terminated within the period described in paragraph (1), the liability of the employer is abated and any payment held in escrow shall be refunded without interest to the employer or the employer's bond shall be cancelled.

(g)(1) In any case in which an employer or employers withdrew from a multiemployer plan before the effective date of part 1 of subtitle E, the corporation may—

(A) apply section 4063(d), as in effect before the amendments made by the Multiemployer Pension Plan Amendments Act of 1980, to such plan,

(B) assess liability against the withdrawn employer with respect to the resulting terminated plan,

(C) guarantee benefits under the terminated plan under section 4022, as in effect before such amendments, and

(D) if necessary, enforce such action through suit brought under section 4003.

(2) The corporation shall use the revolving fund used by the corporation with respect to basic benefits guaranteed under section 4022A in guaranteeing benefits under a terminated plan described in this subsection.

[*Editor's Note:* Sections 412 and 413 of PL 96-364, The Multiemployer Pension Plan Amendments Act of 1980, do not amend ERISA or the Internal Revenue Code. They establish requirements for studies to be conducted by the Pension Benefit Guaranty Corporation and the General Accounting Office. Section 415 deals with unemployment benefits for former members of the armed forces. Section 416 amends the Federal-State Extended Unemployment Compensation Act of 1970.

Text of the four sections follows:

SEC. 412. STUDIES BY PENSION BENEFIT GUARANTY CORPORATION AND SECRETARY OF LABOR.

(a)(1) The Pension Benefit Guaranty Corporation shall conduct a seperate study with respect to—

(A) the advantages and disadvantages of establishing a graduated premium rate schedule under section 4006 of the Employee Retirement Income and Security Act of 1974 which is based on risk, and

(B) the necessity of adopting special rules in cases of union-mandated withdrawal from multiemployer pension plans.

(2) The Corporation shall report to the Congress the results of the studies conducted under paragraph (1), including its recommendations with respect thereto.

(b)(1) The Secretary of Labor shall study the feasibility of requiring collective bargaining on both the issues of contributions to, and benefits from, multiemployer plans.

(2) The Secretary shall submit a report on the study conducted under paragraph (1) to the Congress within 3 years of the date of the enactment of this Act.

SEC. 413. STUDY BY GENERAL ACCOUNTING OFFICE; HEARINGS REQUIRED.

(a)(1) The Comptroller General of the United States shall conduct a study of the effects of the amendments made by, and the provisions of, this Act on—

(A) participants, beneficiaries, employers, employee organizations, and other parties affected by this Act, and

(B) the self-sufficiency of the fund established under section 4005 of the Employee Retirement Income Security Act of 1974 with respect to benefits guaranteed under section 4022A of such Act, taking into account the financial conditions of multiemployer plans and employers.

(2)(A) The Comptroller General shall report to the Congress no later than June 30, 1985, the results of the study conducted under paragraph (1), including his recommendations with respect thereto.

(B) The report submitted under subparagraph (A) shall be made available to the public.

(b) In conducting the study under subsection (a)(1), the Comptroller General shall consult with the Committees on Finance and Labor and Human Resources of the Senate and the Committees on Education and Labor and Ways and Means of the House of Representatives.

(c) The committees described in subsection (b) shall conduct hearings on the report and recommendations submitted under subsection (a)(2).

(d) For purposes of conducting the study required by this section, the Comptroller General, or any of his duly authorized representatives, shall have access to and the right to examine and copy any books, documents, papers, records, or other recorded information—

(1) within the possession or control of the administrator or the sponsor of any plan, and

(2) which the Comptroller General or his representative finds, in his own judgment, pertinent to such study.

The Comptroller General shall not disclose the identity of any individual in making any information obtained under this subsection available to the public.

SEC. 415. INCREASE IN LENGTH OF SERVICE IN ARMED FORCES REQUIRED FOR EX-SERVICEMEN TO BE ELIGIBLE FOR UNEMPLOYMENT BENEFITS.

(a) General Rule.—Subparagraph (A) of section 8521(a)(1) of title 5 of the United States Code is amended by striking out "90 days or more" and inserting in lieu thereof "365 days or more".

(b) Effective Date.—The amendment made by subsection (a) shall apply with respect to determinations of Federal service in the case of individuals filing claims for unemployment compensation on or after October 1, 1980.

SEC. 416. CESSATION OF EXTENDED BENEFITS WHEN PAID UNDER AN INTERSTATE CLAIM IN A STATE WHERE EXTENDED BENEFIT PERIOD IS NOT IN EFFECT.

(a) General Rule.—Section 202 of the Federal-State Extended Unemployment Compensation Act of 1970 is amended by adding at the end thereof the following new subsection:

Cessation of Extended Benefits When Paid Under an Interstate Claim in a State Where Extended Benefit Period Is Not in Effect

MPPAA Sec. 413

(c)(1) Except as provided in paragraph (2), payment of extended compensation shall not be made to any individual for any week if—

(A) extended compensation would (but for this subsection) have been payable for such week pursuant to an interstate claim filed in any State under the interstate benefit payment plan, and

(B) an extended benefit period is not in effect for such week in such State.

(2) Paragraph (1) shall not apply with respect to the first 2 weeks for which extended compensation is payable (determined without regard to this subsection) pursuant to an interstate claim filed under the interstate benefit payment plan to the individual from the extended compensation account established for the benefit year.

(3) Section 3304(a)(9)(A) of the Internal Revenue Code of 1954 shall not apply to any denial of compensation required under this subsection.

(b) Effective Date.—

(1) In General.—The amendment made by subsection (a) shall apply to weeks of unemployment beginning after October 1, 1980; except that such amendment shall not be a requirement of any State law under section 3304(a)(11) of the Internal Revenue Code of 1954 for any week which begins before June 1, 1981.

(2) Special rule for certain states.—In the case of any State the legislature of which does not meet in a regular session which begins during calendar year 1981 and before April 1, 1981, paragraph (1) shall be applied by substituting "June 1, 1982" for "June 1, 1981."]

Speaker of the
House of Representatives.
Vice President of the
United States and
President of the Senate.

MPPAA Sec. 416 (b)

Part III   IRC Excerpts

IRC Finding List

IRC Sections
Section

Subtitle A—Income Taxes

Chapter I—Normal Taxes and Surtaxes
Subchapter B—Computation of Taxable Income

Part II—Items Specifically Included in Gross Income

72.	Annuities; Certain proceeds of endowment and life insurance contracts	367

* * *

79.	Group-term life insurance contracts	375

Part III—Items Specifically Excluded from Gross Income

125.	Cafeteria plans	376

Part VI—Itemized Deductions for Individuals and Corporations

194.	Contributions to employer liability trusts	377

Part VII—Additional Itemized Deductions for Individuals

219.	Retirement savings	378

Subchapter D—Deferred Compensation, Etc.
Part I—Pension, Profit Sharing, Stock Bonus Plans, Etc.
Subpart A—General Rule

401.	Qualified pension, profit sharing, and stock bonus plans	381
402.	Taxability of beneficiary of employees' trust	395
403.	Taxation of employee annuities	401
404.	Deduction for contributions of an employer to an employees' trust or annuity plan and compensation under a deferred payment plan	405
405.	Qualified bond purchase plans	414
406.	Certain employees of foreign subsidiaries	416
407.	Certain employees of domestic subsidiaries engaged in business outside the U.S.	417
408.	Individual retirement accounts	419
409.	Retirement bonds	426
409A.	Qualification for tax credit employee stock ownership plans	427

IRC FINDING LIST 365

Section

Subpart B—Special Rules
410.	Minimum participation standards	431
411.	Minimum vesting standards	434
412.	Minimum funding standards	442
413.	Collectively bargained plans	448
414.	Definitions and special rules	449
415.	Limitations on benefits and contributions under qualified plans	454
416.	Special rules for top-heavy plans	463

Subpart C—Special Rules for Multiemployer Plans
418.	Reorganization status	468
418A.	Notice of reorganization and funding requirements	469
418B.	Minimum contribution requirement	470
418C.	Overburden credit against minimum contribution requirement	473
418D.	Adjustments in accrued benefits	474
418E.	Insolvent plans	476

Part II—Certain Stock Options
421.	General rules	478
422.	Qualified stock options	479
422A.	Incentive stock options	481
423.	Employee stock purchase plans	483
424.	Restricted stock options	485
425.	Definitions and special rules	486

Subchapter F—Exempt Organizations

Part I—General Rule
501.	Exemption from tax on corporations, certain trusts, etc.	489

Subtitle B—Estate and Gift Taxes

Chapter 11—Estate Tax

Subchapter A—Estate of Citizens or Residents

Part III—Gross Estate
2039.	Annuities	496

Subtitle C—Employment Taxes

Chapter 23—Federal Unemployment Tax Act
3304(a).	Approval of state laws	498
3405.	Special rules for pensions, annuities, and certain other deferred income	501

Section

Subtitle D—Miscellaneous Excise Taxes

Chapter 43—Qualified Pension, Etc., Plans

4971.	Taxes on failure to meet minimum funding standards	503
4972.	Tax on excess contributions for self-employed individuals	504
4973.	Tax on excess contributions to individual retirement accounts, certain 403(b) contracts, certain individual retirement annuities, and certain retirement bonds	505
4974.	Excise tax on certain accumulations in individual retirement accounts	506
4975.	Tax on prohibited transactions	507

* * *

Chapter 61—Information and Returns

Subpart E—Registration of and Information Concerning Pension, Etc., Plans

6057.	Annual registration, etc.	512
6058.	Information required in connection with certain plans of deferred compensation	513
6059.	Periodic report of actuary	514

PERTINENT SECTIONS OF THE INTERNAL REVENUE CODE

SUBTITLE A—INCOME TAXES

CHAPTER I—NORMAL TAXES AND SURTAXES

* * *

Subchapter B—Computation of Taxable Income

* * *

Part II—Items Specifically Included in Gross Income

* * *

SEC. 72. ANNUITIES; CERTAIN PROCEEDS OF ENDOWMENT AND LIFE INSURANCE CONTRACTS.

(a) General Rule for Annuities.—Except as otherwise provided in this chapter, gross income includes any amount received as an annuity (whether for a period certain or during one or more lives) under an annuity, endowment, or life insurance contract.

(b) Exclusion Ratio.—Gross income does not include that part of any amount received as an annuity under an annuity, endowment, or life insurance contract which bears the same ratio to such amount as the investment in the contract (as of the annuity starting date) bears to the expected return under the contract (as of such date). This subsection shall not apply to any amount to which subsection (d)(1) (relating to certain employee annuities) applies.

(c) Definitions.—

(1) Investment in the contract.—For purposes of subsection (b), the investment in the contract as of the annuity starting date is—
(A) the aggregate amount of premiums or other consideration paid for the contract, minus
(B) the aggregate amount received under the contract before such date, to the extent that such amount was excludable from gross income under this subtitle or prior income tax laws.

(2) Adjustment in investment where there is refund feature.—If—
(A) the expected return under the contract depends in whole or in part on the life expectancy of one or more individuals;
(B) the contract provides for payments to be made to a beneficiary (or to the estate of an annuitant) on or after the death of the annuitant or annuitants; and
(C) such payments are in the nature of a refund of the consideration paid,
then the value (computed without discount for interest) of such payments on the annuity starting date shall be subtracted from the amount determined under paragraph (1). Such value shall be computed in accordance with actuarial tables prescribed by the Secretary. For purposes of this paragraph and of subsection (e)(2)(A), the term "refund of the consideration paid" includes amounts payable after the death of an annuitant by reason of a provision in the contract for a life annuity with minimum period of payments certain, but (if part of the consideration was contributed by an employer) does not include that part of any payment to a beneficiary (or to the estate of the annuitant) which is not attributable to the consideration paid by the employee for the contract as determined under paragraph (1)(A).

(3) Expected return.—For purposes of subsection (b), the expected return under the contract shall be determined as follows:
(A) Life expectancy.—If the expected return under the contract, for the period on and after the annuity starting date, depends in whole or in part on the life expectancy of one or more individuals, the expected return shall be computed with reference to actuarial tables prescribed by the Secretary.
(B) Installment payments.—If subparagraph (A) does not apply, the expected return is the aggregate of the amounts receivable under the contract as an annuity.

(4) Annuity starting date.—For purposes of this section, the annuity starting date in the case of any contract is the first day of the first period for which an amount is received as an annuity under the contract; except that if such date was before January 1, 1954, then the annuity starting date is January 1, 1954.

(d) Employees Annuities.—

(1) Employee's contributions recoverable in 3 years.—Where—

(A) part of the consideration for an annuity, endowment, or life insurance contract is contributed by the employer, and

(B) during the 3-year period beginning on the date on which an amount is first received under the contract as an annuity, the aggregate amount receivable by the employee under the terms of the contract is equal to or greater than the consideration for the contract contributed by the employee,

then all amounts received as an annuity under the contract shall be excluded from gross income until there has been so excluded an amount equal to the consideration for the contract contributed by the employee. Thereafter all amounts so received under the contract shall be included in gross income.

(2) Special rules for application of paragraph (1).—For purposes of paragraph (1)—

(A) if the employee died before any amount was received as an annuity under the contract, the words "receivable by the employee" shall be read as "receivable by a beneficiary of the employee"; and

(B) any contribution made with respect to the contract while the employee is an employee within the meaning of section 401(c)(1) which is not allowed as a deduction under section 404 shall be treated as consideration for the contract contributed by the employee.

(3) Cross reference.—

For certain rules for determining whether amounts contributed by employer are includible in the gross income of the employee, see part I of subchapter D (sec. 401 and following, relating to pension, profit-sharing, and stock bonus plans, etc.).

*(e) Amounts Not Received as Annuities.—

(1) Application of subsection.—

(A) In general.—This subsection shall apply to any amount which—

(i) is received under an annuity, endowment, or life insurance contract, and

(ii) is not received as an annuity,

if no provision of this subtitle (other than this subsection) applies with respect to such amount.

(B) Dividends.—For purposes of this section, any amount received which is in the nature of a dividend or similar distribution shall be treated as an amount not received as an annuity.

(2) General rule.—Any amount to which this subsection applies—

(A) if received on or after the annuity starting date, shall be included in gross income, or

(B) if received before the annuity starting date—

(i) shall be included in gross income to the extent allocable to income on the contract, and

(ii) shall not be included in gross income to the extent allocable to the investment in the contract.

(3) Allocation of amounts to income and investment.—For purposes of paragraph (2)(B)—

(A) Allocation to income.—Any amount to which this subsection applies shall be treated as allocable to income on the contract to the extent that such amount does not exceed the excess (if any) of—

(i) the cash value of the contract (determined without regard to any surrender charge) immediately before the amount is received, over

(ii) the investment in the contract at such time.

(B) Allocation to investment.—Any amount to which this subsection applies shall be treated as allocable to investment in the contract to the extent that such amount is not allocated to income under subparagraph (A).

(4) Special rules for application of paragraph (2)(B).—For purposes of paragraph (2)(B)—

(A) Loans treated as distributions.—If, during any taxable year, an individual—

(i) receives (directly or indirectly) any amount as a loan under any contract to

*[*Editor's Note:* Section 72(e) is effective Aug. 18, 1982.]

which this subsection applies, or

(ii) assigns or pledges (or agrees to assign or pledge) any portion of the value of any such contract,

such amount or portion shall be treated as received under the contract as an amount not received as an annuity.

(B) Treatment of policyholder dividends.—Any amount described in paragraph (1)(B) shall not be included in gross income under paragraph (2)(B)(i) to the extent such amount is retained by the insurer as a premium or other consideration paid for the contract.

(5) Retention of existing rules in certain cases.—

(A) In general.—In any case to which this paragraph applies—

(i) paragraphs (2)(B) and (4)(A) shall not apply, and

(ii) if paragraph (2)(A) does not apply,

the amount shall be included in gross income, but only to the extent it exceeds the investment in the contract.

(B) Existing contracts.—This paragraph shall apply to contracts entered into before August 14, 1982. Any amount allocable to investment in the contract after August 13, 1982, shall be treated as from a contract entered into after such date.

(C) Certain life insurance and endowment contracts.—Except to the extent prescribed by the Secretary by regulations, this paragraph shall apply to any amount not received as an annuity which is received under a life insurance or endowment contract.

(D) Contracts under qualified plans.— This paragraph shall apply to any amount received—

(i) from a trust described in section 401(a) which is exempt from tax under section 501(a),

(ii) from a contract—

(I) purchased by a trust described in clause (i),

(II) purchased as part of a plan described in section 403(a),

(III) described in section 403(b), or

(IV) provided for employees of a life insurance company under a plan described in section 805(d)(3), or

(iii) from an individual retirement account or an individual retirement annuity.

(E) Full refunds, surrenders, redemptions, and maturities.—This paragraph shall apply to—

(i) any amount received, whether in a single sum or otherwise, under a contract in full discharge of the obligation under the contract which is in the nature of a refund of the consideration paid for the contract, and

(ii) any amount received under a contract on its complete surrender, redemption, or maturity.

In the case of any amount to which the preceding sentence applies, the rule of paragraph (2)(A) shall not apply.

(6) Investment in the contract.—For purposes of this subsection, the investment in the contract as of any date is—

(A) the aggregate amount of premiums or other consideration paid for the contract before such date, minus

(B) the aggregate amount received under the contract before such date, to the extent that such amount was excludable from gross income under this subtitle or prior income tax laws.

(f) Special Rules for Computing Employees' Contributions.—In computing, for purposes of subsection (c)(1)(A), the aggregate amount of premiums or other consideration paid for the contract, for purposes of subsection (d)(1), the consideration for the contract contributed by the employee, and for purposes of subsection (e)(1)(B), the aggregate premiums or other consideration paid, amounts contributed by the employer shall be included, but only to the extent that—

(1) such amounts were includible in the gross income of the employee under this subtitle or prior income tax laws; or

(2) if such amounts had been paid directly to the employee at the time they were contributed, they would not have been includible in the gross income of the employee under the law applicable at the time of such contribution.

Paragraph (2) shall not apply to amounts which were contributed by the employer after December 31, 1962, and which would not have been includible in the gross income of the employee by reason of the application of section 911 if such amounts had been paid directly to the employee at the time of contribution. The preceding sentence shall not apply to amounts which were con-

Code Sec. 72 (f)

tributed by the employer, as determined under regulations prescribed by the Secretary, to provide pension or annuity credits, to the extent such credits are attributable to services performed before January 1, 1963, and are provided pursuant to pension or annuity plan provisions in existence on March 12, 1962, and on that date applicable to such services.

(g) **Rules for Transferee Where Transfer Was for Value.**—Where any contract (or any interest therein) is transferred (by assignment or otherwise) for a valuable consideration, to the extent that the contract (or interest therein) does not, in the hands of the transferee, have a basis which is determined by reference to the basis in the hands of the transferor, then—

(1) for purposes of this section, only the actual value of such consideration, plus the amount of the premiums and other consideration paid by the transferee after the transfer, shall be taken into account in computing the aggregate amount of the premiums or other consideration paid for the contract;

(2) for purposes of subsection (c)(1)(B), there shall be taken into account only the aggregate amount received under the contract by the transferee before the annuity starting date, to the extent that such amount was excludable from gross income under this subtitle or prior income tax laws; and

(3) the annuity starting date is January 1, 1954, or the first day of the first period for which the transferee received an amount under the contract as an annuity, whichever is the later.

For purposes of this subsection, the term "transferee" includes a beneficiary of, or the estate of, the transferee.

(h) **Option to Receive Annuity in Lieu of Lump Sum.**—If—

(1) a contract provides for payment of a lump sum in full discharge of an obligation under the contract, subject to an option to receive an annuity in lieu of such lump sum;

(2) the option is exercised within 60 days after the day on which such lump sum first became payable; and

(3) part or all of such lump sum would (but for this subsection) be includible in gross income by reason of subsection (e)(1), then, for purposes of this subtitle, no part of such lump sum shall be considered as includible in gross income at the time such lump sum first became payable.

(i) **[Repealed.]**

(j) **Interest.**—Notwithstanding any other provision of this section, if any amount is held under an agreement to pay interest thereon, the interest payments shall be included in gross income.

(k) **Payments in Discharge of Alimony.**—

(1) **In general.**—This section shall not apply to so much of any payment under an annuity, endowment, or life insurance contract (or any interest therein) as is includible in the gross income of the wife under section 71 or section 682 (relating to income of an estate or trust in case of divorce, etc.).

(2) **Cross reference.**—

For definition of "wife", see section 7701(a)(17).

(l) **Face-Amount Certificates.**—For purposes of this section, the term "endowment contract" includes a face-amount certificate, as defined in section 2(a)(15) of the Investment Company Act of 1940 (15 U.S.C., sec. 80a-2), issued after December 31, 1954.

(m) **Special Rules Applicable to Employee Annuities and Distributions Under Employee Plans.**—

(1) **[Repealed.]**

(2) **Computation of consideration paid by the employee.**—In computing—

(A) the aggregate amount of premiums or other consideration paid for the contract for purposes of subsection (c)(1)(A) (relating to the investment in the contract),

(B) the consideration for the contract contributed by the employee for purposes of subsection (d)(1) (relating to employee's contributions recoverable in 3 years), and

(C) the aggregate premiums or other consideration paid for purposes of subsection (e)(1)(B) (relating to certain amounts not received as an annuity),

any amount allowed as a deduction with respect to the contract under section 404 which was paid while the employee was an employee within the meaning of section 401(c)(1) shall be treated as consideration contributed by the employer, and there

Code Sec. 72 (g)

shall not be taken into account any portion of the premiums or other consideration for the contract paid while the employee was an owner-employee which is properly allocable (as determined under regulations prescribed by the Secretary) to the cost of life, accident, health, or other insurance.

(3) Life insurance contracts.—

(A) This paragraph shall apply to any life insurance contract—

(i) purchased as a part of a plan described in section 403(a), or

(ii) purchased by a trust described in section 401(a) which is exempt from tax under section 501(a) if the proceeds of such contract are payable directly or indirectly to a participant in such trust or to a beneficiary of such participant.

(B) Any contribution to a plan described in subparagraph (A)(i) or a trust described in subparagraph (A)(ii) which is allowed as a deduction under section 404, and any income of a trust described in subparagraph (A)(ii), which is determined in accordance with regulations prescribed by the Secretary to have been applied to purchase the life insurance protection under a contract described in subparagraph (A), is includible in the gross income of the participant for the taxable year when so applied.

(C) In the case of the death of an individual insured under a contract described in subparagraph (A), an amount equal to the cash surrender value of the contract immediately before the death of the insured shall be treated as a payment under such plan or a distribution by such trust, and the excess of the amount payable by reason of the death of the insured over such cash surrender value shall not be includible in gross income under this section and shall be treated as provided in section 101.

(4) Amounts constructively received.— [Repealed.]

(5) Penalties applicable to certain amounts received by owner-employees.—

(A) This paragraph shall apply—

(i) to amounts (other than any amount received by an individual in his capacity as a policyholder of an annuity, endowment, or life insurance contract which is in the nature of a dividend or similar distribution) which are received from a qualified trust described in section 401(a) or under a plan described in section 403(a) and which are received by an individual, who is, or has been, a key employee, before such individual attains the age of 59½ years, for any reason other than the individual's becoming disabled (within the meaning of paragraph (7) of this subsection), but only to the extent that such amounts are attributable to contributions paid on behalf of such individual (other than contributions made by him as an owner-employee) while he was a key employee in a top-heavy plan, and

(ii) to amounts which are received from a qualified trust described in section 401(a) or under a plan described in section 403(a) at any time by an individual who is, or has been, a key employee, or by the successor of such individual, but only to the extent that such amounts are determined, under regulations prescribed by the Secretary, to exceed the benefits provided for such individual under the plan formula.

(B) If a person receives an amount to which this paragraph applies, his tax under this chapter for the taxable year in which such amount is received shall be increased by an amount equal to 10 percent of the portion of the amount so received which is includible in his gross income for such taxable year.

(C) For purposes of this paragraph, the terms "key employee" and "top-heavy plan" have the same meanings as when used in section 416.

(6) Owner-employee defined.—For purposes of this subsection, the term "owner-employee" has the meaning assigned to it by section 401(c)(3) and includes an individual for whose benefit an individual retirement account or annuity described in section 408(a) or (b) is maintained. For purposes of the preceding sentence, the term "owner-employee" shall include an employee within the meaning of section 401(c)(1).

(7) Meaning of disabled.—For purposes of this section, an individual shall be considered to be disabled if he is unable to engage in any substantial gainful activity by reason of any medically determinable physical or mental impairment which can be expected to result in death or to be of long-continued and indefinite duration. An individual shall not be considered to be disabled unless he furnishes proof of the existence thereof in such form and manner as the Secretary may require.

(8) Loans to owner-employees.—[Repealed.]

(9) Return of excess contributions before due date of return.—
(A) In general.—If an excess contribution is distributed in a qualified distribution—
(i) such distribution of such excess contribution shall not be included in gross income, and
(ii) this section (other than this paragraph) shall be applied as if such excess contribution and such distribution had not been made.
(B) Excess contribution.—For purposes of this paragraph, the term "excess contribution" means any contribution to a qualified trust described in section 401(a) or under a plan described in section 403(a) or 405(a) made on behalf of an employee (within the meaning of section 401(c)) for any taxable year to the extent such contribution exceeds the amount allowable as a deduction under section 404(a).
(C) Qualified distribution.—The term "qualified distribution" means any distribution of an excess contribution which meets requirements similar to the requirements of subparagraphs (A), (B), and (C) of section 408(d)(4). In the case of such distribution, the rules of the last sentence of section 408(d)(4) shall apply.

(n) Annuities Under Retired Serviceman's Family Protection Plan or Survivor Benefit Plan.—Subsections (b) and (d) shall not apply in the case of amounts received after December 31, 1965, as an annuity under chapter 73 of title 10 of the United States Code, but all such amounts shall be excluded from gross income until there has been so excluded (under section 122(b)(1) or this section, including amounts excluded before January 1, 1966) an amount equal to the consideration for the contract (as defined by section 122(b)(2)), plus any amount treated pursuant to section 101(b)(2)(D) as additional consideration paid by the employee. Thereafter all amounts so received shall be included in gross income.

(o) Special Rules for Distributions From Qualified Plans to Which Employee Made Deductible Contributions.—

(1) Treatment of contributions.—For purposes of this section and sections 402, 403, and 405, notwithstanding section 414(h), any deductible employee contribution made to a qualified employer plan or government plan shall be treated as an amount contributed by the employer which is not includible in the gross income of the employee.

(2) Additional tax if amount received before age 59½.—If—
(A) any accumulated deductible employee contributions are received from a qualified employer plan or government plan,
(B) such amount is received by the employee before the employee attains the age of 59½, and
(C) such amount is not attributable to such employee's becoming disabled (within the meaning of subsection (m)(7)),
then the employee's tax under this chapter for the taxable year in which such amount is received shall be increased by an amount equal to 10 percent of the amount so received to the extent that such amount is includible in gross income. For purposes of this title, any tax imposed by this paragraph shall be treated as a tax imposed by subsection (m)(5)(B).

(3) Amounts constructively received.—
(A) In general.—For purposes of this subsection, rules similar to the rules provided by subsection (p) shall apply.
(B) Purchase of life insurance.—To the extent any amount of accumulated deductible employee contributions of an employee are applied to the purchase of life insurance contracts, such amount shall be treated as distributed to the employee in the year so applied.

(4) Special rule for treatment of rollover amounts.—For purposes of sections 402(a)(5), 402(a)(7), 403(a)(4), 408(d)(3), and 409(b)(3)(C), the Secretary shall prescribe regulations providing for such allocations of amounts attributable to accumulated deductible employee contributions, and for such other rules, as may be necessary to insure that such accumulated deductible employee contributions do not

Code Sec. 72 (m) (8)

become eligible for additional tax benefits (or freed from limitations) through the use of rollovers.

(5) Definitions and special rules.—For purposes of this subsection—

(A) Deductible employee contributions.—The term "deductible employee contributions" means any qualified voluntary employee contribution (as defined in section 219(e)(2)) made after December 31, 1981, in a taxable year beginning after such date and allowable as a deduction under section 219(a) for such taxable year.

(B) Accumulated deductible employee contributions.—The term "accumulated deductible employee contributions" means the deductible employee contributions—

(i) increased by the amount of income and gain allocable to such contributions, and

(ii) reduced by the sum of the amount of loss and expense allocable to such contributions and the amounts distributed with respect to the employee which are attributable to such contributions (or income or gain allocable to such contributions).

(C) Qualified employer plan.—The term "qualified employer plan" has the meaning given to such term by section 219(e)(3).

(D) Government plan.—The term "government plan" has the meaning given such term by section 219(e)(4).

(6) Ordering rules.—Unless the plan specifies otherwise, any distribution from such plan shall not be treated as being made from the accumulated deductible employee contributions until all other amounts to the credit of the employee have been distributed.

*(p) Loans Treated as Distributions.—For purposes of this section—

(1) Treatment as distributions.—

(A) Loans.—If during any taxable year a participant or beneficiary receives (directly or indirectly) any amount as a loan from a qualified employer plan, such amount shall be treated as having been received by such individual as a distribution under such plan.

(B) Assignments or pledges.—If during any taxable year a participant or beneficiary assigns (or agrees to assign) or pledges (or agrees to pledge) any portion of his interest in a qualified employer plan, such portion shall be treated as having been received by such individual as a loan from such plan.

(2) Exception for certain loans.—

(A) General rule.—Paragraph (1) shall not apply to any loan to the extent that such loan (when added to the outstanding balance of all other loans from such plan whether made on, before, or after August 13, 1982), does not exceed the lesser of—

(i) $50,000, or

(ii) ½ of the present value of the nonforfeitable accrued benefit of the employee under the plan (but not less than $10,000).

(B) Requirement that loan be repayable within 5 years.—

(i) In general.—Subparagraph (A) shall not apply to any loan unless such loan, by its terms, is required to be repaid within 5 years.

(ii) Exception for home loans.—Clause (i) shall not apply to any loan used to acquire, construct, reconstruct, or substantially rehabilitate any dwelling unit which within a reasonable time is to be used (determined at the time the loan is made) as a principal residence of the participant or a member of the family (within the meaning of section 267(c)(4)) of the participant.

(C) Related employers and related plans.—For purposes of this paragraph—

(i) the rules of subsections (b), (c), and (m) of section 414 shall apply, and

(ii) all plans of an employer (determined after the application of such subsections) shall be treated as 1 plan.

(3) Qualified employer plan, etc.—For purposes of this subsection, the term "qualified employer plan" means any plan which was (or was determined to be) a qualified employer plan as defined in section 219(e)(3). For purposes of this subsection, such term includes any government plan (as defined in section 219(e)(4)).

(4) Special rules for loans, etc., from certain contracts.—For purposes of this subsection, any amount received as a loan under a contract purchased under a qualified employer plan (and any assign-

---

*[*Editor's Note:* Section 236(c) of TEFRA (PL 97-248), on the effective date of code section 72(p), reads as follows:

ment or pledge with respect to such a contract) shall be treated as a loan under such employer plan.

***(q) 5-Percent Penalty for Premature Distributions From Annuity Contracts.—**

(1) Imposition of penalty.—
(A) In general.—If any taxpayer receives any amount under an annuity contract, the taxpayer's tax under this chapter for the taxable year in which such amount is received shall be increased by an amount equal to 5 percent of the portion of such amount includible in gross income which is properly allocable to any investment in the annuity contract made during the 10-year period ending on the date such amount was received by the taxpayer.

(B) Allocation on first-in, first-out basis. —For purposes of subparagraph (A), the amount includible in gross income shall be allocated to the earliest investment in the contract with respect to which amounts have not been previously fully allocated under this paragraph.

(2) Subsection not to apply to certain distributions.—This subsection shall not apply to any distribution—
(A) made on or after the date on which the taxpayer attains age 59½,
(B) made to a beneficiary (or to the estate of an annuitant) on or after the death of an annuitant,
(C) attributable to the taxpayer's becoming disabled within the meaning of subsection (m)(7),
(D) which is one of a series of substantially equal periodic payments made for the life of a taxpayer or over a period extending for at least 60 months after the annuity starting date,

*[*Editor's Note:* Section 72(q) applies to distributions after December 31, 1982.]

(c) **Effective Date.—**

(1) **In general.**—The amendments made by this section shall apply to loans, assignments, and pledges made after August 13, 1982. For purposes of the preceding sentence, the outstanding balance of any loan which is renegotiated, extended, renewed, or revised after such date shall be treated as an amount received as a loan on the date of such renegotiation, extension, renewal, or revision.

(2) **Exception for certain loans used to repay outstanding obligations.—**
(A) In general.—Any qualified refunding loan shall not be treated as a distribution by reason of the amendments made by this section to the extent such loan is repaid before August 14, 1983.
(B) Qualified refunding loan.—For purposes of subparagraph (A), the term "qualified refunding loan" means any loan made after August 13, 1982, and before August 14, 1983, to the extent such loan is used to make a required principal payment.
(C) Required principal payment.—For purposes of subparagraph (B), the term "required principal payment" means any principal repayment on a loan made under the plan which was outstanding on August 13, 1982, if such repayment is required to be made after August 13, 1982, and before August 14, 1983.

(3) **Treatment of certain renegotiations.**—If—
(A) the taxpayer after August 13, 1982, and before September 4, 1982, borrows money from a government plan (as defined in section 219(e)(4) of the Internal Revenue Code of 1954),
(B) under the applicable State law, such loan requires the renegotiation of all outstanding prior loans made to the taxpayer under such plan, and
(C) the renegotiation described in subparagraph (B) does not change the interest rate on or extend the duration of, any such outstanding prior loan,
then the renegotiation described in subparagraph (B) shall not be treated as a renegotiation, extension, renewal, or revision for purposes of paragraph (1). If the renegotiation described in subparagraph (B) does not meet the requirements of subparagraph (C) solely because it extends the duration of any such outstanding prior loan, the requirements of subparagraph (C) shall be treated as met with respect to such renegotiation if, before April 1, 1983, such extension is eliminated.]

Code Sec. 72 (q)

(E) from a plan, contract, account, trust, or annuity described in subsection (e)(5)(D), or

(F) allocable to investment in the contract before August 14, 1982.

(r) **Cross Reference.**—For limitation on adjustments to basis of annuity contracts sold, see section 1021.

* * *

SEC. 79. GROUP-TERM LIFE INSURANCE PURCHASED FOR EMPLOYEES.

(a) **General Rule.**—There shall be included in the gross income of an employee for the taxable year an amount equal to the cost of group-term life insurance on his life provided for part or all of such year under a policy (or policies) carried directly or indirectly by his employer (or employers); but only to the extent that such cost exceeds the sum of—

(1) the cost of $50,000 of such insurance, and

(2) the amount (if any) paid by the employee toward the purchase of such insurance.

(b) **Exceptions.**—Subsection (a) shall not apply to—

(1) the cost of group-term life insurance on the life of an individual which is provided under a policy carried directly or indirectly by an employer after such individual has terminated his employment with such employer and either has reached the retirement age with respect to such employer or is disabled (within the meaning of section 72(m)(7)),

(2) the cost of any portion of the group-term life insurance on the life of an employee provided during part or all of the taxable year of the employee under which—

(A) the employer is directly or indirectly the beneficiary, or

(B) a person described in section 170(c) is the sole beneficiary,

for the entire period during such taxable year for which the employee receives such insurance, and

(3) the cost of any group-term life insurance which is provided under a contract to which section 72(m)(3) applies.

*[*Editor's Note:* Section 79(d) is effective for taxable years beginning after Dec. 31, 1983.]

(c) **Determination of Cost of Insurance.**—For purposes of this section and section 6052, the cost of group-term insurance on the life of an employee provided during any period shall be determined on the basis of uniform premiums (computed on the basis of 5-year age brackets) prescribed by regulations by the Secretary. In the case of an employee who has attained age 64, the cost prescribed shall not exceed the cost with respect to such individual if he were age 63.

*(d) **Nondiscrimination Requirements.**—

(1) **In general.**—In the case of discriminatory group-term life insurance plan, paragraph (1) of subsection (a) shall not apply with respect to any key employee.

(2) **Discriminatory group-term life insurance plan.**—For purposes of this subsection, the term "discriminatory group-term life insurance plan" means any plan of an employer for providing group-term life insurance unless—

(A) the plan does not discriminate in favor of key employees as to eligibility to participate, and

(B) the type and amount of benefits available under the plan do not discriminate in favor of participants who are key employees.

(3) **Nondiscriminatory eligibility classification.**—

(A) In general.—A plan does not meet requirements of subparagraph (A) of paragraph (2) unless—

(i) such plan benefits 70 percent or more of all employees of the employer,

(ii) at least 85 percent of all employees who are participants under the plan are not key employees,

(iii) such plan benefits such employees as qualify under a classification set up by the employer and found by the Secretary not to be discriminatory in favor of key employees, or

(iv) in the case of a plan which is part of a cafeteria plan, the requirements of section 125 are met.

(B) Exclusion of certain employees.—For purposes of subparagraph (A), there may be excluded from consideration—

(i) employees who have not completed 3 years of service;

Code Sec. 79 (d) (3)

(ii) part-time or seasonal employees;

(iii) employees not included in the plan who are included in a unit of employees covered by an agreement between employee representatives and one or more employers which the Secretary finds to be a collective bargaining agreement, if the benefits provided under the plan were the subject of good faith bargaining between such employee representatives and such employer or employers; and

(iv) employees who are nonresident aliens and who receive no earned income (within the meaning of section 911(d)(2)) from the employer which constitutes income from sources within the United States (within the meaning of section 861(a)(3)).

(4) Nondiscriminatory benefits.—A plan does not meet the requirements of paragraph (2)(B) unless all benefits available to participants who are key employees are available to all other participants.

(5) Special rule.—A plan shall not fail to meet the requirements of paragraph (2)(B) merely because the amount of life insurance on behalf of the employees under the plan bears a uniform relationship to the total compensation or the basic or regular rate of compensation of such employees.

(6) Key employee defined.—For purposes of this subsection, the term "key employee" has the meaning given to such term by paragraph (1) of section 416(i), except that subparagraph (A)(iv) of such paragraph shall be applied by not taking into account employees described in paragraph (3)(B) who are not participants in the plan.

(7) Certain controlled groups, etc.—All employees who are treated as employed by a single employer under subsection (b), (c), or (m) of section 414 shall be treated as employed by a single employer for purposes of this section.

* * *

Part III—Items Specifically Excluded From Gross Income

* * *

SEC. 125. CAFETERIA PLANS.

(a) In General.—Except as provided in subsection (b), no amount shall be included in the gross income of a participant in a cafeteria plan solely because, under the plan, the participant may choose among the benefits of the plan.

(b) Exception for Highly Compensated Participants Where Plan Is Discriminatory.—

(1) In general.—In the case of a highly compensated participant, subsection (a) shall not apply to any benefit attributable to a plan year for which the plan discriminates in favor of—

(A) highly compensated individuals as to eligibility to participate, or

(B) highly compensated participants as to contributions and benefits.

(2) Year of inclusion.—For purposes of determining the taxable year of inclusion, any benefit described in paragraph (1) shall be treated as received or accrued in the participant's taxable year in which the plan year ends.

(c) Discrimination as to Benefits or Contributions.—For purposes of subparagraph (B) of subsection (b)(1), a cafeteria plan does not discriminate where nontaxable benefits and total benefits (or employer contributions allocable to nontaxable benefits and employer contributions for total benefits) do not discriminate in favor of highly compensated participants.

(d) Cafeteria Plan Defined.—For purposes of this section—

(1) In general.—The term "cafeteria plan" means a written plan under which—

(A) all participants are employees, and

(B) the participants may choose among two or more benefits.

The benefits which may be chosen may be nontaxable benefits, or cash, property, or other taxable benefits.

(2) Deferred compensation plans excluded.—The term "cafeteria plan" does not include any plan which provides for deferred compensation. The preceding sentence shall not apply in the case of a profit-sharing or stock bonus plan which includes a qualified cash or deferred arrangement (as defined in section 401(k)(2)) to the extent of amounts which a covered employee may elect to have the employer pay as contributions to a trust under such plan on behalf of the employee.

Code Sec. 79 (d) (4)

(e) Highly Compensated Participant and Individual Defined.—For purposes of this section—

(1) Highly compensated participant.—The term "highly compensated participant" means a participant who is—

(A) an officer,
(B) a shareholder owning more than 5 percent of the voting power or value of all classes of stock of the employer,
(C) highly compensated, or
(D) a spouse or dependent (within the meaning of section 152) of an individual described in subparagraph (A), (B), or (C).

(2) Highly compensated individual.—The term "highly compensated individual" means an individual who is described in subparagraph (A), (B), (C), or (D) of paragraph (1).

(f) Nontaxable Benefit Defined.—For purposes of this section, the term "nontaxable benefit" means any benefit which, with the application of subsection (a), is not includible in the gross income of the employee.

(g) Special Rules.—

(1) Collectively bargained plan not considered discriminatory.—For purposes of this section, a plan shall not be treated as discriminatory if the plan is maintained under an agreement which the Secretary finds to be a collective bargaining agreement between employee representatives and one or more employers.

(2) Health benefits.—For purposes of subparagraph (B) of subsection (b)(1), a cafeteria plan which provides health benefits shall not be treated as discriminatory if—

(A) contributions under the plan on behalf of each participant include an amount which—
  (i) equals 100 percent of the cost of the health benefit coverage under the plan of the majority of the highly compensated participants similarly situated, or
  (ii) equals or exceeds 75 percent of the cost of the health benefit coverage of the participant (similarly situated) having the highest cost health benefit coverage under the plan, and
(B) contributions or benefits under the plan in excess of those described in subparagraph (A) bear a uniform relationship to compensation.

(3) Certain participation eligibility rules not treated as discriminatory.—For purposes of subparagraph (A) of subsection (b)(1), a classification shall not be treated as discriminatory if the plan—
(A) benefits a group of employees described in subparagraph (B) of section 410 (b)(1), and
(B) meets the requirements of clauses (i) and (ii):
  (i) No employee is required to complete more than 3 years of employment with the employer or employers maintaining the plan as a condition of participation in the plan, and the employment requirement for each employee is the same.
  (ii) Any employee who has satisfied the employment requirement of clause (i) and who is otherwise entitled to participate in the plan commences participation no later than the first day of the first plan year beginning after the date the employment requirement was satisfied unless the employee was separated from service before the first day of that plan year.

(4) Certain controlled groups, etc.—All employees who are treated as employed by a single employer under subsection (b), (c), or (m) of section 414 shall be treated as employed by a single employer for purposes of this section.

(h) Regulations.—The Secretary shall prescribe such regulations as may be necessary to carry out the provisions of this section.

* * *

Part VI—Itemized Deductions for Individuals and Corporations

* * *

SEC. 194. CONTRIBUTIONS TO EMPLOYER LIABILITY TRUSTS.

(a) Allowance of Deduction.—There shall be allowed as a deduction for the taxable year an amount equal to the amount—
(1) which is contributed by an employer to a trust described in section 501(c)(22) (relating to withdrawal liability payment

fund) which meets the requirements of section 4223(h) of the Employee Retirement Income Security Act of 1974, and

(2) which is properly allocable to such taxable year.

(b) **Allocation to Taxable Year.**—In the case of a contribution described in subsection (a) which relates to any specified period of time which includes more than one taxable year, the amount properly allocable to any taxable year in such period shall be determined by prorating such amounts to such taxable years under regulations prescribed by the Secretary.

(c) **Disallowance of Deduction.**—No deduction shall be allowed under subsection (a) with respect to any contribution described in subsection (a) which does not relate to any specified period of time.

* * *

Part VII—Additional Itemized Deductions for Individuals

* * *

SEC. 219. RETIREMENT SAVINGS.

(a) **Allowance of Deduction.**—In the case of an individual, there shall be allowed as a deduction an amount equal to the qualified retirement contributions of the individual for the taxable year.

(b) **Maximum Amount of Deduction.**—

(1) **In general.**—The amount allowable as a deduction under subsection (a) to any individual for any taxable year shall not exceed the lesser of—
(A) $2,000, or
(B) an amount equal to the compensation includible in the individual's gross income for such taxable year.

(2) **Special rules for employer contributions under simplified employee pensions.**—

(A) Limitation.—If there is an employer contribution on behalf of the employee to a simplified employee pension, an employee shall be allowed as a deduction under subsection (a) (in addition to the amount allowable under paragraph (1)) an amount equal to the lesser of—
(i) 15 percent of the compensation from such employer includible in the employee's gross income for the taxable year (determined without regard to the employer contribution to the simplified employee pension), or
(ii) the amount contributed by such employer to the simplified employee pension and included in gross income (but not in excess of $15,000).

(B) Certain limitations do not apply to employer contribution.—Paragraph (1) of this subsection and paragraph (1) of subsection (d) shall not apply with respect to the employer contribution to a simplified employee pension.

(C) Special rule for applying subparagraph (A)(ii).—In the case of an employee who is an officer, shareholder, or owner-employee described in section 408(k)(3), the $15,000 amount specified in subparagraph (A)(ii) shall be reduced by the amount of tax taken into account with respect to such individual under subparagraph (D) of section 408(k)(3).

(3) **Special rule for individual retirement plans.**—If the individual has paid any qualified voluntary employee contributions for the taxable year, the amount of the qualified retirement contributions (other than employer contributions to a simplified employee pension) which are paid for the taxable year to an individual retirement plan and which are allowable as a deduction under subsection (a) for such taxable year shall not exceed—
(A) the amount determined under paragraph (1) for such taxable year, reduced by
(B) the amount of the qualified voluntary employee contributions for the taxable year.

(4) **Certain divorced individuals.**—
(A) In general.—In the case of an individual to whom this paragraph applies, the limitation of paragraph (1) shall not be less than the lesser of—
(i) $1,125, or
(ii) the sum of the amount referred to in paragraph (1)(B) and any qualifying alimony received by the individual during the taxable year.
(B) Qualifying alimony.—For purposes of this paragraph, the term "qualifying alimony" means amounts includible in the individual's gross income under paragraph (1) of section 71(a) (relating to decree of divorce or separate maintenance).
(C) Individuals to whom paragraph ap-

plies.—This paragraph shall apply to an individual if—

(i) an individual retirement plan was established for the benefit of the individual at least 5 years before the beginning of the calendar year in which the decree of divorce or separate maintenance was issued, and

(ii) for at least 3 of the former spouse's most recent 5 taxable years ending before the taxable year in which the decree was issued, such former spouse was allowed a deduction under subsection (c) (or the corresponding provisions of prior law) for contributions to such individual retirement plan.

(c) **Special Rules for Certain Married Individuals.**—

(1) **In general.**—In the case of any individual with respect to whom a deduction is otherwise allowable under subsection (a)—

(A) who files a joint return under section 6013 for a taxable year, and

(B) whose spouse has no compensation (determined without regard to section 911) for such taxable year,

there shall be allowed as a deduction any amount paid in cash for the taxable year by or on behalf of the individual to an individual retirement plan established for the benefit of his spouse.

(2) **Limitation.**—The amount allowable as a deduction under paragraph (1) shall not exceed the excess of—

(A) the lesser of—

(i) $2,250, or

(ii) an amount equal to the compensation includible in the individual's gross income for the taxable year, over

(B) the amount allowable as a deduction under subsection (a) for the taxable year (determined without regard to so much of the employer contributions to a simplified employee pension as is allowable by reason of paragraph (2) of subsection (b)).

(d) **Other Limitations and Restrictions.**—

(1) **Beneficiary must be under age 70½.**—No deduction shall be allowed under this section with respect to any qualified retirement contribution for the benefit of an individual if such individual has attained age 70½ before the close of such individual's taxable year for which the contribution was made.

(2) **Recontributed amounts.**—No deduction shall be allowed under this section with respect to a rollover contribution described in section 402(a)(5), 402(a)(7), 403(a)(4), 403(b)(8), 405(d)(3), 408(d)(3), or 409(b)(3)(C).

(3) **Amounts contributed under endowment contract.**—In the case of an endowment contract described in section 408(b), no deduction shall be allowed under this section for that portion of the amounts paid under the contract for the taxable year which is properly allocable, under regulations prescribed by the Secretary, to the cost of life insurance.

*(4) **Denial of deduction for amount contributed to inherited annuities or accounts.**—No deduction shall be allowed under this section with respect to any amount paid to an inherited individual retirement account or individual retirement annuity (within the meaning of section 408(d)(3)(C)(ii)).

(e) **Definition of Retirement Savings Contributions, Etc.**—For purposes of this section—

(1) **Qualified retirement contribution.**—The term "qualified retirement contribution" means—

(A) any qualified voluntary employee contribution paid in cash by the individual for the taxable year, and

(B) any amount paid in cash for the taxable year by or on behalf of such individual for his benefit to an individual retirement plan.

For purposes of the preceding sentence, the term "individual retirement plan" includes a retirement bond described in section 409 only if the bond is not redeemed within 12 months of its issuance.

(2) **Qualified voluntary employee contribution.**—

(A) In general.—The term "qualified voluntary employee contribution" means any voluntary contribution—

*[*Editor's Note:* Section 219(d)(4) is effective for taxable years beginning after Dec. 31, 1983.]

Code Sec. 219 (e) (2)

(i) which is made by an individual as an employee under a qualified employer plan or government plan, which plan allows an employee to make contributions which may be treated as qualified voluntary employee contributions under this section, and

(ii) with respect to which the individual has not designated such contribution as a contribution which should not be taken into account under this section.

(B) Voluntary contribution.—For purposes of subparagraph (A), the term "voluntary contribution" means any contribution which is not a mandatory contribution (within the meaning of section 411(c)(2)(C)).

(C) Designation.—For purposes of determining whether or not an individual has made a designation described in subparagraph (A)(ii) with respect to any contribution during any calendar year under a qualified employer plan or government plan, such individual shall be treated as having made such designation if he notifies the plan administrator of such plan, not later than the earlier of—

(i) April 15 of the succeeding calendar, year, or

(ii) the time prescribed by the plan administrator,

that the individual does not want such contribution taken into account under this section. Any designation or notification referred to in the preceding sentence shall be made in such manner as the Secretary shall by regulations prescribe and, after the last date on which such designation or notification may be made, shall be irrevocable for such taxable year.

(3) **Qualified employer plan.**—The term "qualified employer plan" means—

(A) a plan described in section 401(a) which includes a trust exempt from tax under section 501(a),

(B) an annuity plan described in section 403(a),

(C) a qualified bond purchase plan described in section 405(a), and

(D) a plan under which amounts are contributed by an individual's employer for an annuity contract described in section 403(b).

(4) **Government plan.**—The term "government plan" means any plan, whether or not qualified, established and maintained for its employees by the United States, by a State or political subdivision thereof, or by an agency or instrumentality of any of the foregoing.

(5) **Payments for certain plans.**—The term "amounts paid to an individual retirement plan" includes amounts paid for an individual retirement annuity or a retirement bond.

(f) **Other Definitions and Special Rules.—**

(1) **Compensation.**—For purposes of this section, the term "compensation" includes earned income (as defined in section 401(c)(2)) reduced by any amount allowable as a deduction to the individual in computing adjusted gross income under paragraph (7) of section 62. The "compensation" does not include any amount received as a pension or annuity and does not include any amount received as deferred compensation.

(2) **Married individuals.**—The maximum deduction under subsections (b) and (c) shall be computed separately for each individual, and this section shall be applied without regard to any community property laws.

(3) **Time when contributions deemed made.—**

(A) Individual retirement plans.—For purposes of this section, a taxpayer shall be deemed to have made a contribution to an individual retirement plan on the last day of the preceding taxable year if the contribution is made on account of such taxable year and is made not later than the time prescribed by law for filing the return for such taxable year (including extensions thereof).

(B) Qualified employer or government plans.—For purposes of this section, if a qualified employer or government plan elects to have the provisions of this subparagraph apply, a taxpayer shall be deemed to have made a voluntary contribution to such plan on the last day of the preceding calendar year (if, without regard to this paragraph, such contribution may be made on such date) if the contribution is made on account of the taxable year which includes such last day and by April 15 of the

Code Sec. 219 (e) (3)

calendar year or such earlier time as is provided by the plan administrator.

(4) **Reports.**—The Secretary shall prescribe regulations which prescribe the time and the manner in which reports to the Secretary and plan participants shall be made by the plan administrator of a qualified employer or government plan receiving qualified voluntary employee contributions.

(5) **Employer payments.**—For purposes of this title, any amount paid by an employer to an individual retirement plan shall be treated as payment of compensation to the employee (other than a self-employed individual who is an employee within the meaning of section 401(c)(1)) includible in his gross income in the taxable year for which the amount was contributed, whether or not a deduction for such payment is allowable under this section to the employee.

(6) **Excess contributions treated as contribution made during subsequent year for which there is an unused limitation.**—

(A) In general.—If for the taxable year the maximum amount allowable as a deduction under this section for contributions to an individual retirement plan exceeds the amount contributed, then the taxpayer shall be treated as having made an additional contribution for the taxable year in an amount equal to the lesser of—

(i) the amount of such excess, or

(ii) the amount of the excess contributions for such taxable year (determined under section 4973(b)(2) without regard to subparagraph (C) thereof).

(B) Amount contributed.—For purposes of this paragraph, the amount contributed—

(i) shall be determined without regard to this paragraph, and

(ii) shall not include any rollover contribution.

(C) Special rule where excess deduction was allowed for closed year.—Proper reduction shall be made in the amount allowable as a deduction by reason of this paragraph for any amount allowed as a deduction under this section for a prior taxable year for which the period for assessing deficiency has expired if the amount so allowed exceeds the amount which should have been allowed for such prior taxable year.

(g) **Cross Reference.**—For failure to provide required reports, see section 6652(h).

* * *

Subchapter D—Deferred Compensation, Etc.

Part I. Pension, Profit-sharing, stock bonus plans, etc.
Subpart A. General rule.
Subpart B. Special rules.
Subpart C. Special rules for multiemployer plans.
Part II. Certain stock options.

Part I—Pension, Profit-Sharing, Stock Bonus Plans, Etc.

Section
401. Qualified pension, profit-sharing, and stock bonus plans.
402. Taxability of beneficiary of employees' trust.
403. Taxation of employee annuities.
404. Deduction for contributions of an employer to an employee's trust or annuity plan and compensation under a deferred-payment plan.
404A. Deduction for certain foreign deferred compensation plans.
405. Qualified bond purchase plans.
406. Certain employees of foreign subsidiaries.
407. Certain employees of domestic subsidiaries engaged in business outside the United States.
408. Individual retirement accounts.
409. Retirement bonds.
409A. Qualification for tax credit employee Stock ownership plans.

SEC. 401. QUALIFIED PENSION, PROFIT-SHARING, AND STOCK BONUS PLANS.

(a) **Requirements for Qualification.**—A trust created or organized in the United States and forming part of a stock bonus, pension, or profit-sharing plan of an employer for the exclusive benefit of his employees or their beneficiaries shall constitute a qualified trust under this section—

(1) If contributions are made to the trust by such employer, or employees, or both, or by another employer who is entitled to deduct his contributions under section 404(a)(3)(B) (relating to deduction for contributions to profit-sharing and stock bonus plans), for the purpose of distributing to such employees or their beneficiaries the corpus and income of the fund accumulated by the trust in accordance with such plan;

(2) If under the trust instrument it is impossible, at any time prior to the satisfaction of all liabilities with respect to employees and their beneficiaries under the trust, for any part of the corpus or income to be (within the taxable year or thereafter) used for, or diverted to, purposes other than for the exclusive benefit of his employees or their beneficiaries but this paragraph shall not be construed, in the case of a multiemployer plan, to prohibit the return of a contribution within 6 months after the plan administrator determines that the contribution was made by a mistake of fact or law (other than a mistake relating to whether the plan is described in section 401(a) or the trust which is part of such plan is exempt from taxation under section 501(a), or the return of any withdrawal liability payment determined to be an overpayment within 6 months of such determination);

(3) if the plan of which such trust is a part satisfies the requirements of section 410 (relating to minimum participation standards); and

(4) if the contributions or the benefits provided under the plan do not discriminate in favor of employees who are—

(A) officers,
(B) shareholders, or
(C) highly compensated.

For purposes of this paragraph, there shall be excluded from consideration employees described in section 410(b)(3)(A) and (C).

(5) A classification shall not be considered discriminatory within the meaning of paragraph (4) or section 410(b) (without regard to paragraph (1)(A) thereof) merely because it excludes employees the whole of whose remuneration constitutes "wages" under section 3121(a)(1) (relating to the Federal Insurance Contributions Act) or merely because it is limited to salaried or clerical employees. Neither shall a plan be considered discriminatory within the meaning of such provisions merely because the contributions or benefits of or on behalf of the employees under the plan bear a uniform relationship to the total compensation, or the basic or regular rate of compensation, of such employees, or merely because the contributions or benefits based on that part of an employee's remuneration which is excluded from "wages" by section 3121(a)(1) differ from the contributions or benefits based on employee's remuneration not so excluded, or differ because of any retirement benefits created under State or Federal law. For purposes of this paragraph and paragraph (10), the total compensation of an individual who is an employee within the meaning of subsection (c)(1) means such individual's earned income (as defined in subsection (c)(2)), and the basic or regular rate of compensation of such an individual shall be determined, under regulations prescribed by the Secretary, with respect to that portion of his earned income which bears the same ratio to his earned income as the basic or regular compensation of the employees under the plan bears to the total compensation of such employees. For purposes of determining whether two or more plans of an employer satisfy the requirements of paragraph (4) when considered as a single plan, if the amount of contributions on behalf of the employees allowed as a deduction under section 404 for the taxable year with respect to such plans, taken together, bears a uniform relationship to the total compensation, or the basic or regular rate of compensation, of such employees, the plans shall not be considered discriminatory merely because the rights of employees to, or derived from, the employer contributions under the separate plans do not become nonforfeitable at the same rate. For the purposes of determining whether two or more plans for an employer satisfy the requirements of paragraph (4) when considered as a single plan, if the employees' rights to benefits under the separate plans do not become nonforfeitable at the same rate, but the levels of benefits provided by the separate plans satisfy the requirements of regulations prescribed by the Secretary to take account of the differences in such rates, the plans shall not be considered discriminatory merely because of the difference in such

Code Sec. 401 (a) (1)

IRC EXCERPTS

rates. For purposes of determining whether one or more plans of an employer satisfy the requirements of paragraph (4) and of section 410(b), an employer may take into account all simplified employee pensions to which only the employer contributes.

(6) A plan shall be considered as meeting the requirements of paragraph (3) during the whole of any taxable year of the plan if on one day in each quarter it satisfied such requirements.

(7) A trust shall not constitute a qualified trust under this section unless the plan of which such trust is a part satisfies the requirements of section 411 (relating to minimum vesting standards).

(8) A trust forming part of a pension plan shall not constitute a qualified trust under this section unless the plan provides that forfeitures must not be applied to increase the benefits any employee would otherwise receive under the plan.

*(9) **Required distributions.—**
(A) Before death.—A trust forming part of a plan shall not constitute a qualified trust under this section unless the plan provides that the entire interest of each employee—
(i) either will be distributed to him not later than his taxable year in which he attains age 70½ or, in the case of an employee other than a key employee who is a participant in a top-heavy plan, in which he retires, whichever is the later, or
(ii) will be distributed, commencing not later than such taxable year—
(I) in accordance with regulations prescribed by the Secretary, over the life of such employee or over the lives of such employee and his spouse, or
(II) in accordance with such regulations, over a period not extending beyond the life expectancy of such employee or the life expectancy of such employee and his spouse.

(B) After death.—A trust forming part of a plan shall not constitute a qualified trust under this section unless the plan provides that if—
(i) an employee dies before his entire interest has been distributed to him, or
(ii) distribution has been commenced in accordance with subparagraph (A)(ii) to his surviving spouse and such surviving spouse dies before his entire interest has been distributed to such surviving spouse,
his entire interest (or the remaining part of such interest if distribution thereof has commenced) will be distributed within 5 years after his death (or the death of his surviving spouse). The preceding sentence shall not apply if the distribution of the interest of the employee has commenced and such distribution is for a term certain over a period permitted under subparagraph (A)(ii)(II).

(10) **Other requirements.—**
(A) Plans benefiting owner-employees.—In the case of any plan which provides contributions or benefits for employees some or all of whom are owner-employees (as defined in subsection (c)(3)), a trust forming part of such plan shall constitute a qualified trust under this section only if the requirements of subsection (d) are also met.
(B) Top-heavy plans.—
(i) In general.—In the case of any top-

---

*[*Editor's Note:* Section 242(a) of TEFRA (PL 97-248) amended code section 401(a)(9). Section 242(b) of the act, which provided effective dates and transition rules, reads as follows:

(b) Effective Date.—

(1) In general.—The amendment made by subsection (a) shall apply to plan years beginning after December 31, 1983.

(2) Transition rule.—A trust forming part of a plan shall not be disqualified under paragraph (9) of section 401(a) of the Internal Revenue Code of 1954, as amended by subsection (a), by reason of distributions under a designation (before January 1, 1984) by any employee of a method of distribution—
(A) which does not meet the requirements of such paragraph (9), but
(B) which would not have disqualified such trust under paragraph (9) of section 401(a) of such Code as in effect before the amendment made by subsection (a).]

Code Sec. 401 (a) (10)

heavy plan, a trust forming part of such plan shall constitute a qualified trust under this section only if the requirements of section 416 are met.

(ii) Plans which may become top-heavy.— Except to the extent provided in regulations, a trust forming part of a plan (whether or not a top-heavy plan) shall constitute a qualified trust under this section only if such plan contains provisions—

(I) which will take effect if such plan becomes a top-heavy plan, and

(II) which meet the requirements of section 416.

(11)(A) A trust shall not constitute a qualified trust under this section if the plan of which such trust is a part provides for the payment of benefits in the form of an annuity unless such plan provides for the payment of annuity benefits in a form having the effect of a qualified joint and survivor annuity.

(B) Notwithstanding the provisions of subparagraph (A), in the case of a plan which provides for the payment of benefits before the normal retirement age (as defined in section 411(a)(8)), the plan is not required to provide for the payment of annuity benefits in a form having the effect of a qualified joint and survivor annuity during the period beginning on the date on which the employee enters into the plan as a participant and ending on the later of—

(i) the date the employee reaches the earliest retirement age under the plan, or

(ii) the first day of the 120th month beginning before the date on which the employee reaches normal retirement age.

(C) A plan described in subparagraph (B) does not meet the requirements of subparagraph (A) unless, under the plan, a participant has a reasonable period during which he may elect the qualified joint and survivor annuity form with respect to the period beginning on the date on which the period described in subparagraph (B) ends and ending on the date on which he reaches normal retirement age (as defined in section 411(a)(8)) if he continues his employment during that period. A plan does not meet the requirements of this subparagraph unless, in the case of such an election, the payments under the survivor annuity are not less than the payments which would have been made under the joint annuity to which the participant would have been entitled if he made an election described in this subparagraph immediately prior to his retirement and if his retirement had occurred on the day before his death and within the period within which an election can be made.

(D) A plan shall not be treated as not satisfying the requirements of this paragraph solely because the spouse of the participant is not entitled to receive a survivor annuity (whether or not an election described in subparagraph (C) has been made under subparagraph (C)) unless the participant and his spouse have been married throughout the 1-year period ending on the date of such participant's death.

(E) A plan shall not be treated as satisfying the requirements of this paragraph unless, under the plan, each participant has a reasonable period (as prescribed by the Secretary by regulations) before the annuity starting date during which he may elect in writing (after having received a written explanation of the terms and conditions of the joint and survivor annuity and the effect of an election under this subparagraph) not to take such joint and survivor annuity.

(F) A plan shall not be treated as not satisfying the requirements of this paragraph solely because under the plan there is a provision that any election described in subparagraph (C) or (E), and any revocation of any such election, does not become effective (or ceases to be effective) if the participant dies within a period (not in excess of 2 years) beginning on the date of such election or revocation, as the case may be. The preceding sentence does not apply unless the plan provision described in the preceding sentence also provides that such an election or revocation will be given effect in any case in which—

(i) the participant dies from accidental causes,

(ii) a failure to give effect to the election or revocation would deprive the participant's survivor of a survivor annuity, and

(iii) such election or revocation is made before such accident occurred.

(G) For purposes of this paragraph—

(i) the term "annuity starting date" means the first day of the first period for which an amount is received as an annuity (whether by reason of retirement or by reason of disability),

(ii) the term "earliest retirement age"

Code Sec. 401 (a) (11)

means the earliest date on which, under the plan, the participant could elect to receive retirement benefits, and

(iii) the term "qualified joint and survivor annuity" means an annuity for the life of the participant within a survivor annuity for the life of his spouse which is not less than one-half of, or greater than, the amount of the annuity payable during the joint lives of the participant and his spouse and which is the actuarial equivalent of a single life annuity for the life of the participant.

For purposes of this paragraph, a plan may take into account in any equitable manner (as determined by the Secretary) any increased costs resulting from providing joint and survivor annuity benefits.

(H) This paragraph shall apply only if—

(i) the annuity starting date did not occur before the effective date of this paragraph, and

(ii) the participant was an active participant in the plan on or after such effective date.

(12) A trust shall not constitute a qualified trust under this section unless the plan of which such trust is a part provides that in the case of any merger or consolidation with, or transfer of assets or liabilities to, any other plan after September 2, 1974, each participant in the plan would (if the plan then terminated) receive a benefit immediately after the merger, consolidation, or transfer which is equal to or greater than the benefit he would have been entitled to receive immediately before the merger, consolidation, or transfer (if the plan had then terminated). [This paragraph shall apply in the case of a multiemployer plan only to the extent determined by the Pension Benefit Guaranty Corporation.] The preceding sentence does not apply to any multiemployer plan with respect to any transaction to the extent that participants either before or after the transaction are covered under a multiemployer plan to which title IV of the Employee Retirement Income Security Act of 1974 applies.

(13) A trust shall not constitute a qualified trust under this section unless the plan of which such trust is a part provides that benefits provided under the plan may not be assigned or alienated. For purposes of the preceding sentence, there shall not be taken into account any voluntary and revocable assignment of not to exceed 10 percent of any benefit payment made by any participant who is receiving benefits under the plan unless the assignment or alienation is made for purposes of defraying plan administration costs. For purposes of this paragraph a loan made to a participant or beneficiary shall not be treated as an assignment or alienation if such loan is secured by the participant's accrued nonforfeitable benefit and is exempt from the tax imposed by section 4975 (relating to tax on prohibited transactions) by reason of section 4975(d)(1). This paragraph shall take effect on January 1, 1976 and shall not apply to assignments which were irrevocable on September 2, 1974.

(14) A trust shall not constitute a qualified trust under this section unless the plan of which such trust is a part provides that, unless the participant otherwise elects, the payment of benefits under the plan to the participant will begin not later than the 60th day after the latest of the close of the plan year in which—

(A) the date on which the participant attains the earlier of age 65 or the normal retirement age specified under the plan,

(B) occurs the 10th anniversary of the year in which the participant commenced participation in the plan, or

(C) the participant terminates his service with the employer.

In the case of a plan which provides for the payment of an early retirement benefit, a trust forming a part of such plan shall not constitute a qualified trust under this section unless a participant who satisfied the service requirements for such early retirement benefit, but separated from the service (with any nonforfeitable right to an accured benefit) before satisfying the age requirement for such early retirement benefit, is entitled upon satisfaction of such age requirement to receive a benefit not less than the benefit to which he would be entitled at the normal retirement age, actuarially reduced under regulations prescribed by the Secretary.

(15) A trust shall not constitute a qualified trust under this section unless under the plan of which such trust is a part—

(A) in the case of a participant or beneficiary who is receiving benefits under such plan, or

Code Sec. 401 (a) (15)

(B) in the case of a participant who is separated from the service and who has nonforfeitable rights to benefits, such benefits are not decreased by reason of any increase in the benefit levels payable under title II of the Social Security Act or any increase in the wage base under such title II, if such increase takes place after September 2, 1974, or (if later) the earlier of the date of first receipt of such benefits or the date of such separation, as the case may be.

(16) A trust shall not constitute a qualified trust under this section if the plan of which such trust is a part provides for benefits or contributions which exceed the limitations of section 415.

(17) [Repealed.]

(18) Repealed.]

(19) A trust shall not constitute a qualified trust under this section if under the plan of which such trust is a part any part of a participant's accrued benefit derived from employer contributions (whether or not otherwise nonforfeitable), is forfeitable solely because of withdrawal by such participant of any amount attributable to the benefit derived from contributions made by such participant. The preceding sentence shall not apply to the accrued benefit of any participant unless, at the time of such withdrawal, such participant has a nonforfeitable right to at least 50 percent of such accrued benefit (as determined under section 411). The first sentence of this paragraph shall not apply to the extent that an accrued benefit is permitted to be forfeited in accordance with section 411(a)(3)(D)(iii) (relating to proportional forfeitures of benefits accrued before September 2, 1974, in the event of withdrawal of certain mandatory contributions).

(20) A trust forming part of a pension plan shall not be treated as failing to constitute a qualified trust under this section merely because the pension plan of which such trust is a part makes a qualifying rollover distribution (determined as if section 402(a)(5)(D)(i) did not contain subclause (II) thereof) described in section 402(a)(5)(A)(i) or 403(a)(4)(A)(i). This paragraph shall not apply to a defined benefit plan unless the employer maintaining such plan files a notice with the Pension Benefit Guaranty Corporation (at the time and in the manner prescribed by the Pension Benefit Guaranty Corporation) notifying the Corporation of such payment or distribution and the Corporation has approved such payment or distribution or, within 90 days after the date on which such notice was filed, has failed to disapprove such payment or distribution.

(21) A trust forming part of a tax credit employee stock ownership plan shall not fail to be considered a permanent program merely because employer contributions under the plan are determined solely by reference to the amount of credit—

(A) under section 46(a) if the employer made the transfer described in section 48(n)(1), or

(B) under section 44G if the employer made the transfer described in section 44G(c)(1)(B).

(22) If a defined contribution plan (other than a profit sharing plan)—

(A) is established by an employer whose stock is not publicly traded, and

(B) after acquiring securities of the employer, more than 10 percent of the total assets of the plan are securities of the employer,

any trust forming part of such plan shall not constitute a qualified trust under this section unless the plan meets the requirements of subsection (e) of section 409A.

(23) A stock bonus plan which otherwise meets the requirements of this section shall not be considered to fail to meet the requirements of this section because it provides a cash distribution option to participants if that option meets the requirements of section 409A(h), except that in applying section 409A(h) for purposes of this paragraph, the term "employer securities" shall include any securities of the employer held by the plan.

*(24) Any group trust which otherwise meets the requirements of this section shall not be treated as not meeting such requirements on account of the participation or inclusion in such trust of the moneys of any plan or governmental unit described in section 805(d)(6).

(b) **Certain Retroactive Changes in Plan.**—A stock bonus, pension, profit-

*[*Editor's Note:* Section 401(a)(24) is effective for taxable years beginning after Dec. 31, 1981.]

sharing, or annuity plan shall be considered as satisfying the requirements of subsection (a) for the period beginning with the date on which it was put into effect, or for the period beginning with the earlier of the date on which there was adopted or put into effect any amendment which caused the plan to fail to satisfy such requirements, and ending with the time prescribed by law for filing the return of the employer for his taxable year in which such plan or amendment was adopted (including extensions thereof) or such later time as the Secretary may designate, if all provisions of the plan which are necessary to satisfy such requirements are in effect by the end of such period and have been made effective for all purposes for the whole of such period.

(c) Definitions and Rules Relating to Self-Employed Individuals and Owner-Employees.—For purposes of this section—

(1) Self-employed individual treated as employee.—

(A) In general.—The term 'employee' includes, for any taxable year, an individual who is a self-employed individual for such taxable year.

(B) Self-employed individual.—The term "self-employed individual" means, with respect to any taxable year, an individual who has earned income as defined in paragraph (2)) for such taxable year. To the extent provided in regulations prescribed by the Secretary, such term also includes, for any taxable year—

(i) an individual who would be a self-employed individual within the meaning of the preceding sentence but for the fact that the trade or business carried on by such individual did not have net profits for the taxable year, and

(ii) an individual who has been a self-employed individual within the meaning of the preceding sentence for any prior taxable year.

(2) Earned income.—

(A) In general.—The term "earned income" means the net earnings from self-employment (as defined in section 1402(a)), but such net earnings shall be determined—

(i) only with respect to a trade or business in which personal services of the taxpayer are a material income-producing factor,

(ii) without regard to paragraphs (4) and (5) of section 1402(c),

(iii) in the case of any individual who is treated as an employee under sections 3121(d)(3)(A), (C), or (D), without regard to paragraph (2) of section 1402(c),

(iv) without regard to items which are not included in gross income for purposes of this chapter, and the deductions properly allocable to or chargeable against such items.

For purposes of this subparagraph, section 1402, as in effect for a taxable year ending on December 31, 1962, shall be treated as having been in effect for all taxable years ending before such date —,

(v) with regard to the deductions allowed by sections 404 and 405(c) to the taxpayer.

(B) [Repealed.]

(C) Income from disposition of certain property.—For purposes of this section, the term "earned income" includes gains (other than any gain which is treated under any provision of this chapter as gain from the sale or exchange of a capital asset) and net earnings derived from the sale or other disposition of, the transfer of any interest in, or the licensing of the use of property (other than good will) by an individual whose personal efforts created such property.

(3) Owner-employee.—The term "owner-employee" means an employee who—

(A) owns the entire interest in an unincorporated trade or business, or

(B) in the case of a partnership, is a partner who owns more than 10 percent of either the capital interest or the profits interest in such partnership.

To the extent provided in regulations prescribed by the Secretary, such term also means an individual who has been an owner-employee within the meaning of the preceding sentence.

(4) Employer.—An individual who owns the entire interest in an unincorporated trade or business shall be treated as his own employer. A partnership shall be treated as the employer of each partner who is an employee within the meaning of paragraph (1).

(5) Contributions on behalf of owner-employees.—The term "contribution on behalf of an owner-employee" includes, except as the context otherwise requires, a contribution under a plan—

Code Sec. 401 (c) (5)

(A) by the employer for an owner-employee, and

(B) by an owner-employee as an employee.

*(d) Additional Requirements for Qualification of Trusts and Plans Benefiting Owner-Employees.—A trust forming part of a pension or profit-sharing plan which provides contributions or benefits for employees some or all of whom are owner-employees shall constitute a qualified trust under this section only if, in addition to meeting the requirements of subsection (a), the following requirements of this subsection are met by the trust and by the part of which such trust is a part:

(1) In the case of a trust which is created on or after October 10, 1962, or which was created before such date but is not exempt from tax under section 501(a) as an organization described in subsection (a) on the day before such date, the assets thereof are held by a bank or other person who demonstrates to the satisfaction of the Secretary that the manner in which he will administer the trust will be consistent with the requirements of this section. A trust shall not be disqualified under this paragraph merely because a person (including the employer) other than the trustee or custodian so ad-

---

*[Editor's Note: Section 401(d) was amended by TEFRA (PL 97-248) effective Jan. 1, 1984, to read as follows.

(d) Additional Requirements for Qualification of Trustees and Plans Benefiting Owner-Employees.—A trust forming part of a pension or profit-sharing plan which provides contributions or benefits for employees some or all of whom are owner-employees shall constitute a qualified trust under this section only if, in addition to meeting the requirements of subsection (a), the following requirements of this subsection are met by the trust and by the plan of which such trust is a part:

(1)(A) If the plan provides contributions or benefits for an owner-employee who controls, or for two or more owner-employees who together control, the trade or business with respect to which the plan is established, and who also control as an owner-employee or as owner-employees one or more other trades or businesses, such plan and the plans established with respect to such other trades or businesses, when coalesced, constitute a single plan which meets the requirements of subsection (a) (including paragraph (10) thereof) and of this subsection with respect to the employees of all such trades or businesses (including the trade or business with respect to which the plan intended to qualify under this section is established).

(B) For purposes of subparagraph (A), an owner-employee, or two or more owner-employees, shall be considered to control a trade or business if such owner-employee, or such two or more owner-employees together—
(i) own the entire interest in an unincorporated trade or business, or
(ii) in the case of a partnership, own more than 50 percent of either the capital interest or the profits interest in such partnership.

For purposes of the preceding sentence, an owner-employee, or two or more owner-employees, shall be treated as owning any interest in a partnership which is owned, directly or indirectly, by a partnership which such owner-employee, or such two or more owner-employees, are considered to control within the meaning of the preceding sentence.

(2) The plan does not provide contributions or benefits for any owner-employee who controls (within the meaning of paragraph (1)(B)), or for two or more owner-employees who together control, as an owner-employee or as owner-employees, any other trade or business, unless the employees of each trade or business which such owner-employee or such owner-employees control are included under a plan which meets the requirements of subsection (a) (including paragraph (10) thereof) and of this subsection, and provides contributions and benefits for employees which are not less favorable than contributions and benefits provided for owner-employees under the plan.

(3) Under the plan, contributions on behalf of any owner-employee may be made only with respect to the earned income of such owner-employee which is derived from the trade or business with respect to which such plan is established.]

Code Sec. 401 (d)

ministering the trust may be granted, under the trust instrument, the power to control the investment of the trust funds either by directing investments (including reinvestments, disposals, and exchanges) or by disapproving proposed investments (including reinvestments, disposals, and exchanges). This paragraph shall not apply to a trust created or organized outside the United States before October 10, 1962, if, under section 402(c), it is treated as exempt from tax under section 501(a) on the day before such date; or, to the extent provided under regulations prescribed by the Secretary, to a trust which uses annuity, endowment, or life insurance contracts of a life insurance company exclusively to fund the benefits prescribed by the trust, if the life insurance company supplies annually such information about trust transactions affecting owner-employees as the Secretary shall by forms or regulations prescribe. For purposes of this paragraph, the term "bank" means a bank as defined in section 581, an insured credit union (within the meaning of section 101(6) of the Federal Credit Union Act), a corporation which under the laws of the State of its incorporation is subject to supervision and examination by the commissioner of banking or other officer of such State in charge of the administration of the banking laws of such State, and, in the case of a trust created or organized outside the United States, a bank or trust company, wherever incorporated, exercising fiduciary powers and subject to supervision and examination by governmental authority.

(2) Under the plan—

(A) the employees' rights to or derived from the contributions under the plan are nonforfeitable at the time the contributions are paid to or under the plan; and

(B) in the case of a profit-sharing plan, there is a definite formula for determining the contributions to be made by the employer on behalf of employees (other than owner-employees).

Subparagraph (A) shall not apply to contributions which, under provisions of the plan adopted pursuant to regulations prescribed by the Secretary to preclude the discrimination prohibited by subsection (a)(4), may not be used to provide benefits for designated employees in the event of early termination of the plan.

(3)(A) The plan benefits each employee having 3 or more years of service (within the meaning of section 410(a)(3)).

(B) For purposes of subparagraph (A), the term "employee" does not include—

(i) any employee included in a unit of employees covered by a collective-bargaining agreement described in section 410(b)(2)(A), and

(ii) any employee who is a nonresident alien individual described in section 410(b)(2)(C).

(4) Under the plan—

(A) contributions or benefits are not provided for any owner-employee unless such owner-employee has consented to being included under the plan; and

(B) no benefits in excess of contributions made by an owner-employee as an employee may be paid to any owner-employee, except in the case of his becoming disabled (within the meaning of section 72(m)(7) prior to his attaining the age of 59½ years. Subparagraph (B) shall not apply to any distribution to which section 72(m)(9) applies.

(5) The plan does not permit—

(A) contributions to be made by the employer on behalf of any owner-employee in excess of the amounts which may be deducted under section 404 for the taxable year;

(B) in the case of a plan which provides contributions or benefits only for owner-employees, contributions to be made on behalf of any owner-employee in excess of the amounts which may be deducted under section 404 for the taxable year; and

(C) if a distribution under the plan is made to any employee and if any portion of such distribution is an amount described in section 72(m)(5)(A)(i), contributions to be made on behalf of such employee for the 5 taxable years succeeding the taxable year in which such distribution is made.

Subparagraphs (A) and (B) do not apply to contributions described in subsection (e). Subparagraph (C) shall not apply to a distribution on account of the termination of the plan.

(6) Except as provided in this paragraph, the plan meets the requirements of subsection (a)(4) without taking into account for any purpose contributions or benefits under chapter 2 (relating to tax on self-

Code Sec. 401 (d) (6)

employment income), chapter 21 (relating to Federal Insurance Contributions Act), title II of the Social Security Act, as amended, or any other Federal or State law. If—

(A) of the contributions deductible under section 404, not more than one-third is deductible by reason of contributions by the employer on behalf of owner-employees, and

(B) taxes paid by the owner-employees under chapter 2 (relating to tax on self-employment income), and the taxes which would be payable under such chapter 2 by the owner-employees for paragraphs (4) and (5) of section 1402(c), are taken into account as contributions by the employer on behalf of such owner-employees,

then taxes paid under section 3111 (relating to tax on employers) with respect to an employee may, for purposes of subsection (a)(4), be taken into account as contributions by the employer for such employee under the plan.

(7) Under the plan, if an owner-employee dies before his entire interest has been distributed to him, or if distribution has been commenced in accordance with subsection (a)(9)(B) to his surviving spouse and such surviving spouse dies before his entire interest has been distributed to such surviving spouse, his entire interest (or the remaining part of such interest if distribution thereof has commenced) will, within 5 years after his death (or the death of his surviving spouse), be distributed, or applied to the purchase of an immediate annuity for his beneficiary or beneficiaries (or a beneficiary or beneficiaries of his surviving spouse) which will be payable for the life of such beneficiary or beneficiaries (or for a term certain not extending beyond the life expectancy of such beneficiary or beneficiaries) and which will be immediately distributed to such beneficiary or beneficiaries. The preceding sentence shall not apply if distribution of the interest of an owner-employee has commenced and such distribution is for a term certain over a period permitted under subsection (a)(9)(B)(ii).

(8) [Repealed.]

(9)(A) If the plan provides contributions or benefits for an owner-employee who controls, or for two or more owner-employees who together control, the trade or business with respect to which the plan is established, and who also control as an owner-employee or as owner-employees one or more other trades or businesses, such plan and the plans established with respect to such other trades or businesses, when coalesced, constitute a single plan which meets the requirements of subsection (a) (including paragraph (10) thereof) and of this subsection with respect to the employees of all such trades or businesses (including the trade or business with respect to which the plan intended to qualify under this section is established).

(B) For purposes of subparagraph (A), an owner-employee, or two or more owner-employees, shall be considered to control a trade or business if such owner-employee, or such two or more owner-employees together—

(i) own the entire interest in an unincorporated trade or business, or

(ii) in the case of a partnership, own more than 50 percent of either the capital interest or the profits interest in such partnership.

For purposes of the preceding sentence, an owner-employee, or two or more owner-employees, shall be treated as owning any interest in a partnership which is owned, directly or indirectly, by a partnership which such owner-employee, or such two or more owner-employees, are considered to control within the meaning of the preceding sentence.

(10) The plan does not provide contributions or benefits for any owner-employee who controls (within the meaning of paragraph (q)(B)), or for two or more owner-employees who together control, as an owner-employee or as owner-employees, any other trade or business, unless the employees of each trade or business which such owner-employee or such owner-employees control are included under a plan which meets the requirements of subsection (a) (including paragraph (10) thereof) and of this subsection, and provides contributions and benefits for employees which are not less favorable than contributions and benefits provided for owner-employees under the plan.

(11) Under the plan, contributions on behalf of any owner-employee may be made only with respect to the earned income of such owner-employee which is

Code Sec. 401 (d) (7)

derived from the trade or business with respect to which such plan is established.

(e) Contributions for Premiums on Annuity, Etc., Contracts.—A contribution by the employer on behalf of an owner-employee is described in this subsection if—

(1) under the plan such contribution is required to be applied (directly or through a trustee) to pay premiums or other consideration for one or more annuity, endowment, or life insurance contracts on the life of such owner-employee issued under the plan.

(2) the amount of such contribution exceeds the amount deductible under section 404 with respect to contributions made by the employer on behalf of such owner-employee under the plan, and

(3) the amount of such contribution does not exceed the average of the amounts which were deductible under section 404 with respect to contributions made by the employer on behalf of such owner-employee under the plan (or which would have been deductible if such section had been in effect) for the first three taxable years (A) preceding the year in which the last such annuity, endowment, or life insurance contract was issued under the plan, and (B) in which such owner-employee derived earned income from the trade or business with respect to which the plan is established, or for so many of such taxable years as such owner-employee was engaged in such trade or business and derived earned income therefrom.

In the case of any individual on whose behalf contributions described in paragraph (1) are made under more than one plan as an owner-employee during any taxable year, the preceding sentence does not apply if the amount of such contributions under all such plans for all such years exceeds $15,000. Any contribution which is described in this subsection shall, for purposes of section 4972(b), be taken into account as a contribution made by such owner-employee as an employee to the extent that the amount of such contribution is not deductible under section 404 for the taxable year, but only for the purpose of applying section 4972(b) to other contributions made by such owner-employee as an employee.

(f) Certain Custodial Accounts and Contracts.—For purposes of this title, a custodial account, an annuity contract, or a contract (other than a life, health or accident, property, casualty, or liability insurance contract) issued by an insurance company qualified to do business in a State shall be treated as a qualified trust under this section if—

(1) the custodial account or contract would, except for the fact that it is not a trust, constitute a qualified trust under this section, and

(2) in the case of a custodial account the assets thereof are held by a bank (as defined in subsection (d)(1)) or another person who demonstrates, to the satisfaction of the Secretary, that the manner in which he will hold the assets will be consistent with the requirements of this section.

For purposes of this title, in the case of a custodial account or contract treated as a qualified trust under this section by reason of this subsection, the person holding the assets of such account or holding such contract shall be treated as the trustee thereof.

(g) Annuity Defined.—For purposes of this section and sections 402, 403, and 404, the term "annuity" includes a face-amount certificate, as defined in section 2(a)(15) of the Investment Company Act of 1940 (15 U.S.C., sec. 80a-2); but does not include any contract or certificate issued after December 31, 1962, which is transferable, if any person other than the trustee of a trust described in section 401(a) which is exempt from tax under section 501(a) is the owner of such contract or certificate.

(h) Medical, etc., Benefits for Retired Employees and Their Spouses and Dependents.—Under regulations prescribed by the Secretary, a pension or annuity plan may provide for the payment of benefits for sickness, accident hospitalization, and medical expenses of retired employees, their spouses and their dependents, but only if—

(1) such benefits are subordinate to the retirement benefits provided by the plan,

(2) a separate account is established and maintained for such benefit,

(3) the employer's contributions to such separate account are reasonable and ascertainable,

(4) it is impossible, at any time prior to the satisfaction of all liabilities under the plan to provide such benefits, for any part

Code Sec. 401 (h)

of the corpus or income of such separate account to be (within the taxable year or thereafter) used for, or diverted to, any purposes other than the providing of such benefits, and

(5) not withstanding the provisions of subsection (a)(2), upon the satisfaction of all liabilities under the plan to provide such benefits, any amount remaining in such separate account must, under the terms of the plan, be returned to the employer.

(i) Certain Union-Negotiated Pension Plans.—In the case of a trust forming part of a pension plan which has been determined by the Secretary to constitute a qualified trust under subsection (a) and to be exempt from taxation under section 501(a) for a period beginning after contributions are first made to or for such trust, if it is shown to the satisfaction of the Secretary that—

(1) such trust was created pursuant to a collective bargaining agreement between employee representatives and one or more employers,

(2) any disbursements of contributions, made to or for such trust before the time as of which the Secretary determined that the trust constituted a qualified trust, substantially complied with the terms of the trust, and the plan of which the trust is a part, as subsequently qualified, and

(3) before the time as of which the Secretary determined that the trust constitutes a qualified trust, the contributions to or for such trust were not used in a manner which would jeopardize the interests of its beneficiaries,

then such trust shall be considered as having constituted a qualified trust under subsection (a) and as having been exempt from taxation under section 501(a) for the period beginning on the date on which contributions were first made to or for such trust and ending on the date such trust first constituted (without regard to this subsection) a qualified trust under subsection (a).

*(j) Defined Benefit Plans Providing Benefits for Self-Employed Individuals and Shareholder-Employees.—

(1) In general.—A defined benefit plan satisfies the requirements of this subsection only if the basic benefit accruing under the plan for each plan year of participation by an employee within the meaning of subsection (c)(1) (or a shareholder-employee) is permissible under regulations prescribed by the Secretary under this subsection to insure that there will be reasonable comparability (assuming level funding) between the maximum retirement benefits which may be provided with favorable tax treatment under this title for such employees under—

(A) defined contribution plans,
(B) defined benefit plans, and
(C) a combination of defined contribution plans and defined benefit plans.

(2) Guidelines for regulations.—The regulations prescribed under this subsection shall provide that a plan does not satisfy the requirements of this subsection if, under the plan, the basic benefit of any employee within the meaning of subsection (c)(1) (or a shareholder-employee) may exceed the sum of the products for each plan year of participation of—

(A) his annual compensation (not in excess of $100,000 for such year, and
(B) the applicable percentage determined under paragraph (3).

(3) Applicable percentage.—

(A) Table.—For purposes of paragraph (2), the applicable percentage for any individual for any plan year shall be based on the percentage shown on the following table opposite his age when his current period of participation in the plan began.

Age when participation began:	Applicable percentage
30 or less	6.5
35	5.4
40	4.4
45	3.6
50	3.0
55	2.5
60 or over	2.0

(B) Additional requirements.—The regulations prescribed under this subsection shall include provisions—

(i) for applicable percentages for ages between any two ages shown on the table,
(ii) for adjusting the applicable per-

---

*[Editor's Note: Section 401(j) was repealed by TEFRA (PL 97-248) effective Jan. 1, 1984.]

centages in the case of plans providing benefits other than a basic benefit,

(iii) that any increase in the rate of accrual, and any increase in the compensation base which may be taken into account, shall, with respect only to such increase, begin a new period of participation in the plan, and

(iv) when appropriate, in the case of periods beginning after December 31, 1977, for adjustments in the applicable percentages based on changes in prevailing interest and mortality rates occurring after 1973.

For purposes of this paragraph, a change in the annual compensation taken into account under paragraph (A) of paragraph (j)(2) shall be treated as beginning a new period of plan participation with respect only to such change.

(4) Certain contributions and benefits may not be taken into account.—A defined benefit plan which provides contributions or benefits for owner-employees does not satisfy the requirements of this subsection unless such plan meets the requirements of subsection (a)(4) without taking into account contributions or benefits under chapter 2 (relating to tax on self-employment income), chapter 21 (relating to Federal Insurance Contributions Act), title II of the Social Security Act, or any other Federal or State law.

(5) Definitions.—For purposes of this subsection—

(A) Basic benefit.—The term "basic benefit" means a benefit in the form of a straight life annuity commencing at the later of—

(i) age 65, or

(ii) the day 5 years after the day the participant's current period of participation began

under a plan which provides no ancillary benefits and to which employees do not contribute.

(B) Shareholder-employee.—The term "shareholder-employee" has the same meaning as when used in section 1379(d).

(C) Compensation.—The term "compensation" means—

(i) in the case of an employee within the meaning of subsection (c)(1), the earned income of such individual, or

(ii) in the case of a shareholder-employee, the compensation received or accrued by the individual from the electing small business corporation.

(6) Special rules.—Section 404(e) (relating to special limitations for self-employed individuals) and section 1379(b) (relating to taxability of shareholder-employee beneficiaries) do not apply to a trust to which this subsection applies.

(k) Cash or Deferred Arrangements.—

(1) General rule.—A profit-sharing or stock bonus plan shall not be considered as not satisfying the requirements of subsection (a) merely because the plan includes a qualified cash or deferred arrangement.

(2) Qualified cash or deferred arrangement.—A qualified cash or deferred arrangement is any arrangement which is part of a profit-sharing or stock bonus plan which meets the requirements of subsection (a)—

(A) under which a covered employee may elect to have the employer make payments as contributions to a trust under the plan on behalf of the employee, or to the employee directly in cash;

(B) under which amounts held by the trust which are attributable to employer contributions made pursuant to the employee's election may not be distributable to participants or other beneficiaries earlier than upon retirement, death, disability, or separation from service, hardship or the attainment of age 59½, and will not be distributable merely by reason of the completion of a stated period of participation or the lapse of a fixed number of years; and

(C) which provides that an employee's right to his accrued benefit derived from employer contributions made to the trust pursuant to his election are [is] non-forfeitable.

(3) Application of participation and discrimination standards.—

(A) A qualified cash or deferred arrangement shall be considered to satisfy the requirements of subsection (a)(4), with respect to the amount of contributions, and of subparagraph (B) of section 410(b)(1) for a plan year if those employees eligible to benefit under the plan satisfy the provisions of subparagraph (A) or (B) of section 410(b)(1) and if the actual deferral percentage for highly compensated employees (as defined in paragraph (4)) for such plan year bears a relationship to the actual deferral percentage for all other eligible employees for such plan year which meets either of the following tests:

(i) The actual deferral percentage for the group of highly compensated employees is not more than the actual deferral percentage of all other eligible employees multiplied by 1.5.

(ii) The excess of the actual deferral percentage for the group of highly compensated employees over that of all other eligible employees is not more than 3 percentage points, and the actual deferral percentage for the group of highly compensated employees is not more than the actual deferral percentage of all other eligible employees multiplied by 2.5.

(B) For purposes of subparagraph (A), the actual deferral percentage for a specified group of employees for a plan year shall be the average of the ratios (calculated separately for each employee in such group) of—

(i) the amount of employer contributions actually paid over to the trust on behalf of each such employee for such plan year to

(ii) the employee's compensation for such plan year.

For purposes of the preceding sentence, the compensation of any employee for a plan year shall be the amount of his compensation which is taken into account under the plan in calculating the contribution which may be made on his behalf for such plan year.

(4) **Highly compensated employee.**—For purposes of this subsection, the term "highly compensated employee" means any employee who is more highly compensated than two-thirds of all eligible employees, taking into account only compensation which is considered in applying paragraph (3).

*(l) **Nondiscriminatory Coordination of Defined Contribution Plans With OASDI.**—

(1) **In general.**—Notwithstanding subsection (a)(5), the coordination of a defined contribution plan with OASDI meets the requirements of subsection (a)(4) only if the total contributions with respect to each participant, when increased by the OASDI contributions, bear a uniform relationship—

(A) to the total compensation of such employee, or

(B) to the basic or regular rate of compensation of such employee.

(2) **Definitions.**—For purposes of paragraph (1)—

(A) OASDI contributions.—The term "OASDI contributions" means the product of—

(i) so much of the remuneration paid by the employer to the employee during the plan year as—

(I) constitutes wages (within the meaning of section 3121(a) without regard to paragraph (1) thereof), and

(II) does not exceed the contribution and benefit base applicable under OASDI at the beginning of the plan year, multiplied by

(ii) the rate of tax applicable under section 3111(a) (relating to employer's OASDI tax) at the beginning of the plan year.

In the case of an individual who is an employee within the meaning of subsection (c)(1), the preceding sentence shall be applied by taking into account his earned income (as defined in subsection (c)(2)).

(B) OASDI.—The term "OASDI" means the system of old-age, survivors, and disability insurance established under title II of the Social Security Act and the Federal Insurance Contributions Act.

(C) Remuneration.—The term "remuneration" means—

(i) total compensation, or

(ii) basic or regular rate of compensation,

whichever is used in determining contributions or benefits under the plan.

(3) **Determination of compensation, etc., of self-employed individuals.**—For purposes of this subsection, in the case of an individual who is an employee within the meaning of subsection (c)(1)—

(A) his total compensation shall include his earned income (as defined in subsection (c)(2)), and

(B) his basic or regular rate of compensation shall be determined (under regulations prescribed by the Secretary) with respect to that portion of his earned income which bears the same ratio to his earned income as

---

*[Editor's Note: Section 401(l) is effective for taxable years beginning after Dec. 31, 1983.]

the basic or regular compensation of the employees under the plan (other than employees within the meaning of subsection (c)(1)) bears to the total compensation of such employees.

(o)[m] Cross Reference.—

For exemption from tax of a trust qualified under this section, see Section 501(a).

SEC. 402. TAXABILITY OF BENEFICIARY OF EMPLOYEES' TRUST.

(a) Taxability of Beneficiary of Exempt Trust.—

(1) General rule.—Except as provided in paragraphs (2) and (4), the amount actually distributed to any distributee by any employees' trust described in section 401(a) which is exempt from tax under section 501(a) shall be taxable to him, in the year in which so distributed, under section 72 (relating to annuities). The amount actually distributed to any distributee shall not include net unrealized appreciation in securities of the employer corporation attributable to the amount contributed by the employee (other than deductible employee contributions within the meaning of section 72(o)(5)). Such net unrealized appreciation and the resulting adjustments to basis of such securities shall be determined in accordance with regulations prescribed by the Secretary.

(2) Capital gains treatment for portion of lump sum distributions.—In the case of an employee trust described in section 401(a), which is exempt from tax under section 501(a), so much of the total taxable amount (as defined in subparagraph (D) of subsection (e)(4)) of a lump sum distribution as is equal to the product of such total taxable amount multiplied by a fraction—

(A) the numerator of which is the number of calendar years of active participation by the employee in such plan before January 1, 1974, and

(B) the denominator of which is the number of calendar years of active participation by the employee in such plan,

shall be treated as a gain from the sale or exchange of a capital asset held for more than 1 year. For purposes of computing the fraction described in this paragraph and the fraction under subsection (e)(4)(E), the Secretary may prescribe regulations under which plan years may be used in lieu of calendar years. For purposes of this paragraph, in the case of an individual who is an employee without regard to section 401(c)(1), determination of whether or not any distribution is a lump sum distribution shall be made without regard to the requirement that an election be made under subsection (e)(4)(B), but no distribution to any taxpayer other than an individual estate, or trust may be treated as a lump sum distribution under this paragraph.

(3) Definitions.—For purposes of this subsection—

(A) The term "securities" means only shares of stock and bonds or debentures issued by a corporation with interest coupons or in registered form.

(B) The term "securities of the employer corporation" includes securities of a parent or subsidiary corporation (as defined in subsections (e) and (f) of section 425) of the employer corporation.

(4) Distributions by United States to nonresident aliens.—The amount includible under paragraph (1) or (2) of this subsection in the gross income of a nonresident alien individual with respect to a distribution made by the United States in respect of services performed by an employee of the United States shall not exceed an amount which bears the same ratio to the amount includible in gross income without regard to this paragraph as—

(A) the aggregate basic pay paid by the United States to such employee for such services, reduced by the amount of such basic pay which was not includible in gross income by reason of being from sources without the United States, bears to

(B) the aggregate basic pay paid by the United States to such employee for such services.

In the case of distributions under the civil service retirement laws, the term "basic pay" shall have the meaning provided in section 8331(3) of title 5, United States Code.

(5) Rollover amounts.—

(A) General rule.—If—

(i) the balance to the credit of an employee in a qualified trust is paid to him in a qualifying rollover distribution,

(ii) the employee transfers any portion of

the property he receives in such distribution to an eligible retirement plan, and

(iii) in the case of a distribution of property other than money, the amount so transferred consists of the property distributed,

then such distribution (to the extent so transferred) shall not be includible in gross income for the taxable year in which paid.

(B) Maximum amount which may be rolled over.—In the case of any qualifying rollover distribution, the maximum amount transferred to which subparagraph (A) applies shall not exceed the fair market value of all property the employee receives in the distribution, reduced by the employee contributions (other than accumulated deductible employee contributions within the meaning of section 72(o)(5)).

(C) Transfer must be made within 60 days of receipt.—Subparagraph (A) shall not apply to any transfer of a distribution made after the 60th day following the day on which the employee received the property distributed.

(D) Definitions.—For purposes of this paragraph—

(i) Qualifying rollover distribution.—The term "qualifying rollover distribution" means 1 or more distributions—

(I) within 1 taxable year of the employee on account of a termination of the plan of which the trust is a part or, in the case of a profit-sharing or stock bonus plan, a complete discontinuance of contributions under such plan, or

(II) which constitute a lump sum distribution within the meaning of subsection (e)(4)(A) (determined without reference to subparagraphs (B) and (H) of subsection (e)(4)), or

(III) which constitute a distribution of accumulated deductible employee contributions (within the meaning of section 72(o)(5)).

(ii) Employee contributions.—The term "employee contributions" means—

(I) the excess of the amounts considered contributed by the employee (determined by applying section 72(f)), over

(II) any amounts theretofore distributed to the employee which were not includible in gross income.

(iii) Qualified trust.—The term "qualified trust" means an employees' trust described in section 401(a) which is exempt from tax under section 501(a).

(iv) Eligible retirement plan.—The term "eligible retirement plan" means—

(I) an individual retirement account described in section 408(a),

(II) an individual retirement annuity described in section 408(b) (other than an endowment contract),

(III) a retirement bond described in section 409,

(IV) a qualified trust, and

(V) an annuity plan described in section 403(a).

(v) Rollover of partial distributions of deductible employee contributions permitted.—In the case of any qualifying rollover distribution described in subclause (III) of clause (i), clause (i) of subparagraph (A) shall be applied by substituting "any portion of the balance" for "the balance."

(E) Special rules.—

(i) Transfer treated as rollover contribution under section 408.—For purposes of this title, a transfer described in subparagraph (A) to an eligible retirement plan described in subclause (I), (II), or (III) of subparagraph (D)(iv) shall be treated as a rollover contribution described in section 408(d)(3).

(ii) Self-employed individuals and owner-employees.—An eligible retirement plan described in subclause (IV) or (V) of subparagraph (D)(iv) shall not be treated as an eligible retirement plan for the transfer of a distribution if any part of the distribution is attributable to a trust forming part of a plan under which the employee was an employee within the meaning of section 401(c)(1) at the time contributions were made on his behalf under the plan.

(6) Special rollover rules.—

(A) Time of termination.—For purposes of paragraph (5)(D)(i), a complete discontinuance of contributions under a profit-sharing or stock bonus plan shall be deemed to occur on the day the plan administrator notifies the Secretary (in accordance with regulations prescribed by the Secretary) that all contributions to the plan have been completely discontinued. For purposes of section 411(d)(3), the plan shall be considered to be terminated no later than the day such notice is filed with the Secretary.

(B) Sale of subsidiary or assets.—For purposes of paragraph (5)(D)(i)—

Code Sec. 402 (a) (5) (B)

(i) A payment of the balance to the credit of an employee of a corporation (hereinafter referred to as the employer corporation) which is a subsidiary corporation (within the meaning of section 425(f)) or which is a member of a controlled group of corporations (within the meaning of section 1563(a), determined by substituting "50 percent" for "80 percent" each place it appears therein) in connection with the liquidation, sale, or other means of terminating the parent-subsidiary or controlled group relationship of the employer corporation with the parent corporation or controlled group, or

(ii) a payment of the balance to the credit of an employee of a corporation (hereinafter referred to as the acquiring corporation) in connection with the sale or other transfer to the acquiring corporation of all or substantially all of the assets used by the previous employer of the employee (hereinafter referred to as the selling corporation) in a trade or business conducted by the selling corporation;

shall be treated as a payment or distribution on account of the termination of the plan with respect to such employee if the employees of the employer corporation or the acquiring corporation (whichever applies) are not active participants in such plan at the time of such payment or distribution. For purposes of this subparagraph, in no event shall a payment or distribution be deemed to be in connection with a sale or other transfer of assets, or a liquidation, sale, or other means of terminating such parent-subsidiary or controlled group relationship, if such payment or distribution is made later than the end of the second calendar year after the calendar year in which occurs such sale or other transfer of assets, or such liquidation, sale, or other means of terminating such parent-subsidiary or controlled group relationship.

(C) Treatment of portion not rolled over.—If any portion of a lump sum distribution is transferred in a transfer to which paragraph (5)(A) applies, paragraph (2) of subsection (a), and paragraphs (1) and (3) of subsection (e) shall not apply with respect to such lump sum distribution.

(D) Sales of distributed property.—For purposes of subparagraphs (5) and (7)—

(i) Transfer of proceeds from sale of distributed property treated as transfer of distributed property.—The transfer of an amount equal to any portion of the proceeds from the sale of property received in the distribution shall be treated as the transfer of property received in the distribution.

(ii) Proceeds attributable to increase in value.—The excess of fair market value of property on sale over its fair market value on distribution shall be treated as property received in the distribution.

(iii) Designation where amount of distribution exceeds rollover contribution.—In any case where part or all of the distribution consists of property other than money, the taxpayer may designate—

(I) the portion of the money or other property which is to be treated as attributable to employee contributions, and

(II) the portion of the money or other property which is to be treated as included in the rollover contribution.

Any designation under this clause for a taxable year shall be made not later than the time prescribed by law for filing the return for such taxable year (including extensions thereof). Any such designation, once made, shall be irrevocable.

(iv) Treatment where no designation.—In any case where part or all of the distribution consists of property other than money and the taxpayer fails to make a designation under clause (iii) within the time provided therein, then—

(I) the portion of the money or other property which is to be treated as attributable to employee contributions, and

(II) the portion of the money or other property which is to be treated as included in the rollover contribution

shall be determined on a ratable basis.

(v) Nonrecognition of gain or loss.—In the case of any sale described in clause (i), to the extent that an amount equal to the proceeds is transferred pursuant to paragraph (5)(B) or (7)(B) (as the case may be), neither gain nor loss on such sale shall be recognized.

(E) Special rule where employer maintains money purchase pension plan and other pension plan.—

(i) In general.—In the case of any distribution from a money purchase pension plan which is maintained by an employer, for purposes of paragraph (5)(D)(i)(II), subsection (e)(4)(C) shall be applied by not

Code Sec. 402 (a) (6) (E)

taking into account any pension plan maintained by such employer which is not a money purchase pension plan. The preceding sentence shall not apply to any distribution which is a qualifying rollover distribution without regard to this subparagraph.

(ii) Treatment of subsequent distributions.—If—

(I) any distribution of the balance to the credit of an employee from a money purchase pension plan maintained by an employer is treated as a qualifying rollover distribution by reason of clause (i), and

(II) any portion of such distribution is transferred in a transfer to which paragraph (5)(A) applies,

then paragraph (2) of subsection (a), and paragraphs (1) and (3) of subsection (e), shall not apply to any distribution (after the taxable year in which the distribution described in subparagraph (A) of paragraph (5) is made) of the balance to the credit of such employee from any other pension plan maintained by such employer.

(7) Rollover where spouse receives lump-sum distribution at death of employee.—

(A) General rule.—If—

(i) any portion of a qualifying rollover distribution attributable to an employee is paid to the spouse of the employee after the employee's death,

(ii) the spouse transfers any portion of the property which the spouse receives in such distribution to an individual retirement plan, and

(iii) in the case of a distribution of property other than money, the amount so transferred consists of the property distributed,

then such distribution (to the extent so transferred) shall not be includible in gross income for the taxable year in which paid.

(B) Certain rules made applicable.—Rules similar to the rules of subparagraphs (B) through (E) of paragraph (5) and of paragraph (6) shall apply for purposes of this paragraph.

(8) Cash or deferred arrangements.—For purposes of this title, contributions made by an employer on behalf of an employee to a trust which is a part of a qualified cash or deferred arrangement (as defined in section 401(k)(2)) shall not be treated as distributed or made available to the employee nor as contributions made to the trust by the employee merely because the arrangement includes provisions under which the employee has an election whether the contribution will be made to the trust or received by the employee in cash.

(b) Taxability of Beneficiary of Nonexempt Trust.—Contributions to an employee's trust made by an employer during a taxable year of the employer which ends within or with a taxable year of the trust for which the trust is not exempt from tax under section 501(a) shall be included in the gross income of the employee in accordance with section 83 (relating to property transferred in connection with performance of services), except that the value of the employee's interest in the trust shall be substituted for the fair market value of the property for purposes of applying such section. The amount actually distributed or made available to any distributee by any such trust shall be taxable to him in the year in which so distributed or made available, under section 72 (relating to annuities), except that distributions of income of such trust before the annuity starting date (as defined in section 72(c)(4)) shall be included in the gross income of the employee without regard to section 72(e)(1) (relating to amount not received as annuities). A beneficiary of any such trust shall not be considered the owner of any portion of such trust under subpart E of part I of subchapter J (relating to grantors and others treated as substantial owners).

(c) Taxability of Beneficiary of Certain Foreign Situs Trusts.—For purposes of subsections (a) and (b), a stock bonus, pension, or profit-sharing trust which would qualify for exemption from tax under section 501(a) except for the fact that it is a trust created or organized outside the United States shall be treated as if it were a trust exempt from tax under section 501(a).

(d) [Repealed.]

(e) Tax on Lump Sum Distributions.—

(1) Imposition of separate tax on lump sum distributions.—

(A) Separate tax.—There is hereby imposed a tax (in the amount determined under subparagraph (B)) on the ordinary income portion of a lump sum distribution.

Code Sec. 402 (a) (7)

(B) Amount of tax.—The amount of tax imposed by subparagraph (A) for any taxable year shall be an amount equal to the amount of the initial separate tax for such taxable year multiplied by a fraction, the numerator of which is the ordinary income portion of the lump sum distribution for the taxable year and the denominator of which is the total taxable amount of such distribution for such year.

(C) Initial separate tax.—The initial separate tax for any taxable year is an amount equal to 10 times the tax which would be imposed by subsection (c) of section 1 if the recipient were an individual referred to in such subsection and the taxable income were an amount equal to the zero bracket amount applicable to such an individual for the taxable year plus one-tenth of the excess of—

(i) the total taxable amount of the lump sum distribution for the taxable year, over

(ii) the minimum distribution allowance.

(D) Minimum distribution allowance.—For purposes of this paragraph, the minimum distribution allowance for the taxable year is an amount equal to—

(i) the lesser of $10,000 or one-half of the total taxable amount of the lump sum distribution for the taxable year, reduced (but not below zero) by

(ii) 20 percent of the amount (if any) by which such total taxable amount exceeds $20,000.

(E) Liability for tax.—The recipient shall be liable for the tax imposed by this paragraph.

(2) **Multiple distributions and distributions of annuity contracts.**—In the case of any recipient of a lump sum distribution for the taxable year with respect to whom during the 6-taxable-year period ending on the last day of the taxable year there has been one or more other lump sum distributions after December 31, 1973, or if the distribution (or any part thereof) is an annuity contract, in computing the tax imposed by paragraph (1)(A), the total taxable amounts of all such distributions during such 6-taxable-year period shall be aggregated, but the amount of tax so computed shall be reduced (but not below zero) by the sum of—

(A) the amount of the tax imposed by paragraph (1)(A) paid with respect to such other distributions, plus

(B) that portion of the tax on the aggregated total taxable amounts which is attributable to annuity contracts.

For purposes of this paragraph, a beneficiary of a trust to which a lump sum distribution is made shall be treated as the recipient of such distribution if the beneficiary is an employee (including an employee within the meaning of section 401(c)(1)) with respect to the plan under which the distribution is made or if the beneficiary is treated as the owner of such trust for purposes of subpart E of part I of subchapter J. In the case of the distribution of an annuity contract, the taxable amount of such distribution shall be deemed to be the current actuarial value of the contract, determined on the date of such distribution. In the case of a lump sum distribution with respect to any individual which is made only to two or more trusts, the tax imposed by paragraph (1)(A) shall be computed as if such distribution was made to a single trust, but the liability for such tax shall be apportioned among such trusts according to the relative amounts received by each. The Secretary shall prescribe such regulations as may be necessary to carry out the purposes of this paragraph.

(3) **Allowance of deduction.**—The ordinary income portion of a lump sum distribution for the taxable year shall be allowed as a deduction from gross income for such taxable year, but only to the extent included in the taxpayer's gross income for such taxable year.

(4) **Definitions and special rules.**—

(A) Lump sum distribution.—For purposes of this section and section 403, the term "lump sum distribution" means the distribution or payment within one taxable year of the recipient of the balance to the credit of an employee which becomes payable to the recipient—

(i) on account of the employee's death,

(ii) after the employee attains age 59½,

(iii) on account of the employee's separation from the service, or

(iv) after the employee has become disabled (within the meaning of section 72(m)(7))

from a trust which forms a part of a plan described in section 401(a) and which is exempt from tax under section 501 or from a plan described in section 403(a). Clause (iii)

Code Sec. 402 (e) (4)

of this subparagraph shall be applied only with respect to an individual who is an employee without regard to section 401(c)(1), and clause (iv) shall be applied only with respect to an employee within the meaning of section 401(c)(1). Except for purposes of subsection (a)(2) and section 403(a)(2), a distribution of an annuity contract from a trust or annuity plan referred to in the first sentence of this subparagraph shall be treated as a lump sum distribution. For purposes of this subparagraph, a distribution to two or more trusts shall be treated as a distribution to one recipient. For purposes of this subsection, subsection (a)(2) of this section, and subsection (a)(2) of section 403, the balance to the credit of the employee does not include the accumulated deductible employee contribution under the plan (within the meaning of section 72(o)(5)).

(B) Election of lump sum treatment.—For purposes of this section and section 403, no amount which is not an annuity contract may be treated as a lump sum distribution under subparagraph (A) unless the taxpayer elects for the taxable year to have all such amounts received during such year so treated at the time and in the manner provided under regulations prescribed by the Secretary. Not more than one election may be made under this subparagraph with respect to any individual after such individual has attained age 59½. No election may be made under this subparagraph by any taxpayer other than an individual, an estate, or a trust. In the case of a lump sum distribution made with respect to an employee to two or more trusts, the election under this subparagraph shall be made by the personal representative of the employee.

(C) Aggregation of certain trusts and plans.—For purposes of determining the balance to the credit of an employee under subparagraph (A)—

(i) all trusts which are part of a plan shall be treated as a single trust, all pension plans maintained by the employer shall be treated as a single plan, all profit-sharing plans maintained by the employer shall be treated as a single plan, and all stock bonus plans maintained by the employer shall be treated as a single plan, and

(ii) trusts which are not qualified trusts under section 401(a) and annuity contracts which do not satisfy the requirements of section 404(a)(2) shall not be taken into account.

(D) Total taxable amount.—For purposes of this section and section 403, the term "total taxable amount" means, with respect to a lump sum distribution, the amount of such distribution which exceeds the sum of—

(i) the amounts considered contributed by the employee (determined by applying section 72(f)), which employee contributions shall be reduced by any amounts theretofore distributed to him which were not includible in gross income, and

(ii) the net unrealized appreciation attributable to that part of the distribution which consists of the securities of the employer corporation so distributed.

(E) Ordinary income portion.—For purposes of this section, the term "ordinary income portion" means, with respect to a lump sum distribution, so much of the total taxable amount of such distribution as is equal to the product of such total taxable amount multiplied by a fraction—

(i) the numerator of which is the number of calendar years of active participation by the employee in such plan after December 31, 1973, and

(ii) the denominator of which is the number of calendar years of active participation by the employee in such plan.

(F) Employee.—For purposes of this subsection and subsection (a)(2), except as otherwise provided in subparagraph (A), the term "employee" includes an individual who is an employee within the meaning of section 401(c)(1) and the employer of such individual is the person treated as his employer under section 401(c)(4).

(G) Community property laws.—The provisions of this subsection, other than paragraph (3), shall be applied without regard to community property laws.

(H) Minimum period of service.—For purposes of this subsection (but not for purposes of subsection (a)(2) or section 403(a)(2)(A)), no amount distributed to an employee from or under a plan may be treated as a lump sum distributed under subparagraph (A) unless he has been a participant in the plan for 5 or more taxable years before the taxable year in which such amounts are distributed.

(I) Amounts subject to penalty.—This

subsection shall not apply to amounts described in clause (ii) of subparagraph (A) of section 72(m)(5) to the extent that section 72(m)(5) applies to such amounts.

(J) Unrealized appreciation of employer securities.—In the case of any distribution including securities of the employer corporation which, without regard to the requirement of subparagraph (H), would be treated as a lump sum distribution under subparagraph (A), there shall be excluded from gross income the net unrealized appreciation attributable to that part of the distribution which consists of securities of the employer corporation so distributed. In the case of any such distribution or any lump sum distribution including securities of the employer corporation, the amount of net unrealized appreciation of such securities and the resulting adjustments to the basis of such securities shall be determined under regulations prescribed by the Secretary. This subparagraph shall not apply to distributions of accumulated deductible employee contributions (within the meaning of section 72(o)(5)).

(K) Securities.—For purposes of this subsection, the terms "securities" and "securities of the employer corporation" have the respective meanings provided by subsection (a)(3).

(L) Election to treat pre-1974 participation as post-1973 participation.—For purposes of subparagraph (E), subsection (a)(2), and section 403(a)(2), if a taxpayer elects (at the time and in the manner provided under regulations prescribed by the Secretary), all calendar years of an employee's active participation in all plans in which the employee has been an active participant shall be considered years of active participation by such employee after December 31, 1973. An election made under this subparagraph, once made, shall be irrevocable and shall apply to all lump-sum distributions received by the taxpayer with respect to the employee. This subparagraph shall not apply if the taxpayer received a lump-sum distribution in a previous taxable year of the employee beginning after December 31, 1975, unless no portion of such lump-sum distribution was treated under section 402(a)(2) or section 403(a)(2) as gain from the sale or exchange of a capital asset held for more than 1 year.

SEC. 403. TAXATION OF EMPLOYEE ANNUITIES.

(a) Taxability of Beneficiary Under a Qualified Annuity Plan.—

(1) General rule.—Except as provided in paragraph (2), if an annuity contract is purchased by an employer for an employee under a plan which meets the requirements of section 404(a)(2) (whether or not the employer deducts the amounts paid for the contract under such section), the employee shall include in his gross income the amounts received under such contract for the year received as provided in section 72 (relating to annuities).

(2) Capital gains treatment for certain distributions.—

(A) General rule.—If—

(i) an annuity contract is purchased by an employer for an employee under a plan described in paragraph (1);

(ii) such plan requires that refunds of contributions with respect to annuity contracts purchased under such plan be used to reduce subsequent premiums on the contracts under the plan; and

(iii) a lump sum distribution (as defined in section 402(e)(4)(A)) is paid to the recipient,

so much of the total taxable amount (as defined in section 402(e)(4)(D)) of such distribution as is equal to the product of such total taxable amount multiplied by the fraction described in section 402(a)(2) shall be treated as a gain from the sale or exchange of a capital asset held for more than 1 year. For purposes of this paragraph, in the case of an individual who is an employee without regard to section 401(c)(1), determination of whether or not any distribution is a lump sum distribution shall be made without regard to the requirement that an election be made under subsection (e)(4)(B) of section 402, but no distribution to any taxpayer other than an individual, estate, or trust may be treated as a lump sum distribution under this paragraph.

(B) Cross reference.—

For imposition of separate tax on ordinary income portion of lump sum distribution, see section 402(e).

(3) Self-employed individuals.—For purposes of this subsection, the term, "employee" includes an individual who is an employee within the meaning of section 401(c)(1), and the employer of such individual is the person treated as his employer under section 401(c)(4).

(4) Rollover amounts.—

(A) General rule.—If—

(i) the balance to the credit of an employee in an employee annuity described in paragraph (1) is paid to him in a qualifying rollover distribution,

(ii) the employee transfers any portion of the property he receives in such distribution to an eligible retirement plan, and

(iii) in the case of a distribution of property other than money, the amount so transferred consists of the property distributed,

then such distribution (to the extent so transferred) shall not be includible in gross income for the taxable year in which paid.

(B) Certain rules made applicable.— Rules similar to the rules of subparagraphs (B) through (E) of section 402(a)(5) and of paragraphs (6) and (7) of section 402(a) shall apply for purposes of subparagraph (A).

(b) Taxability of Beneficiary Under Annuity Purchased by Section 501(c)(3) Organization or Public School.—

(1) General rule.—If—

(A) an annuity contract is purchased—

(i) for an employee by an employer described in section 501(c)(3) which is exempt from tax under section 501(a), or

(ii) for an employee (other than an employee described in clause (i)), who performs services for an educational organization described in section 170(b)(1)(A)(ii), by an employer which is a State, a political subdivision of a State, or an agency or instrumentality of any one or more of the foregoing,

(B) such annuity contract is not subject to subsection (a), and

(C) the employee's rights under the contract are nonforfeitable, except for failure to pay future premiums,

then amounts contributed by such employer for such annuity contract on or after such rights become nonforfeitable shall be excluded from the gross income of the employee for the taxable year to the extent that the aggregate of such amounts does not exceed the exclusion allowance for such taxable year. The employee shall include in his gross income the amounts received under such contract for the year received as provided in section 72 (relating to annuities). For purposes of applying the rules of this subsection to amounts contributed by an employer for a taxable year, amounts transferred to a contract described in this paragraph by reason of a rollover contribution described in paragraph (8) of this subsection or section 408(d)(3)(A)(iii) or 409(b)(3)(C) shall not be considered contributed by such employer.

(2) Exclusion allowance.—

(A) In general.—For purposes of this subsection, the exclusion allowance for any employee for the taxable year is an amount equal to the excess, if any, of—

(i) the amount determined by multiplying 20 percent of his includible compensation by the number of years of service over

(ii) the aggregate of amounts contributed by the employer for annuity contracts and excludable from the gross income of the employee for any prior taxable year.

(B) Election to have allowance determined under section 415 rule.—In the case of an employee who makes an election under section 415(c)(4)(D) to have the provisions of section 415(c)(4)(C) (relating to special rule for section 403(b) contracts purchased by educational institutions, hospitals, home health service agencies and certain churches, etc.) apply, the exclusion allowance for any such employee for the taxable year is the amount which could be contributed (under section 415 without regard to section 415(c)(8)) by his employer under a plan described in section 403(a) if the annuity contract for the benefit of such employee were treated as a defined contribution plan maintained by the employer.

*(C) Number of years of service for duly ordained, commissioned, or licensed

---

*[Editor's Note: Section 403(b)(2)(C), added by TEFRA (PL 98-248), is effective for taxable years beginning after Dec. 31, 1981. Section 251(d) of TEFRA provided a correction rule for church plans that reads as follows:

ministers or lay employees.—For purposes of this subsection and section 415(c)(4)(A)—
(i) all years of service by—
(I) a duly ordained, commissioned, or licensed minister of a church, or
(II) a lay person,
as an employee of a church, a convention or association of churches, including an organization described in section 414(e)(3)(B)(ii), shall be considered as years of service for 1 employer, and
(ii) all amounts contributed for annuity contracts by each such church (or convention or association of churches) or such organization during such years for such minister or lay person shall be considered to have been contributed by 1 employer.
For purposes of the preceding sentence, the terms 'church' and 'convention or association of churches' have the same meaning as when used in section 414(e).
(D) Alternative exclusion allowance.—
(i) In general.—In the case of any individual described in subparagraph (C), the amount determined under subparagraph (A) shall not be less than the lesser of—
(I) $3,000, or
(II) the includible compensation of such individual.
(ii) Subparagraph not to apply to individuals with adjusted gross income over $17,000.—This subparagraph shall not apply with respect to any taxable year to any individual whose adjusted gross income for such taxable year (determined separately and without regard to any community property laws) exceeds $17,000.

(iii) Special rule for foreign missionaries.—In the case of an individual described in subparagraph (C)(i) performing services outside the United States, there shall be included as includible compensation for any year under clause (i)(II) any amount contributed during such year by a church (or convention or association of churches) for an annuity contract with respect to such individual.

(3) **Includible compensation.**—For purposes of this subsection, the term "includible compensation" means, in the case of any employee, the amount of compensation which is received from the employer described in paragraph (1)(A), and which is includible in gross income (computed without regard to section 105(d) and 911) for the most recent period (ending not later than the close of the taxable year) which under paragraph (4) may be counted as one year of service. Such term does not include any amount contributed by the employer for any annuity contract to which this subsection applies.

(4) **Years of service.**—In determining the number of years of service for purposes of this subsection, there shall be included—
(A) one year for each full year during which the individual was a full-time employee of the organization purchasing the annuity for him, and
(B) a fraction of a year (determined in accordance with regulations prescribed by the Secretary) for each full year during which such individual was a part-time employee of such organization and for each

---

(d) **Correction Period for Church Plans.**—A church plan (within the meaning of section 414(e) of the Internal Revenue Code of 1954) shall not be treated as not meeting the requirements of section 401 or 403 of such Code if—
(1) by reason of any change in any law, regulation, ruling, or otherwise such plan is required to be amended to meet such requirements, and
(2) such plan is so amended at the next earliest church convention or such other time as the Secretary of the Treasury or his delegate may prescribe.

Section 241(e)(5) provided a special rule for defined benefit plans that reads as follows:

(5) **Special rule for existing defined benefit arrangements.**—Any defined benefit arrangement which is established by a church or a convention or association of churches (including an organization described in section 414(e)(3)(B)(ii) of the Internal Revenue Code of 1954) and which is in effect on the date of the enactment of this Act shall not be treated as failing to meet the requirements of section 403(b)(2) of such Code merely because it is a defined benefit arrangement.]

part of a year during which such individual was a full-time or part-time employee of such organization.

In no case shall the number of years of service be less than one.

(5) Application to more than one annuity contract.—If for any taxable year of the employee this subsection applies to 2 or more annuity contracts purchased by the employer, such contracts shall be treated as one contract.

(6) Forfeitable rights which become nonforfeitable.—For purposes of this subsection and section 72(f) (relating to special rules for computing employees' contributions to annuity contracts), if rights of the employee under an annuity contract described in subparagraphs (A) and (B) of paragraph (1) change from forfeitable to nonforfeitable rights, then the amount (determined without regard to this subsection) includible in gross income by reason of such change shall be treated as an amount contributed by the employer for such annuity contract as of the time such rights become nonforfeitable.

(7) Custodial accounts for regulated investment company stock.—

(A) Amounts paid treated as contributions.—For purposes of this title, amounts paid by an employer described in paragraph (1)(A) to a custodial account which satisfies the requirements of section 401(f)(2) shall be treated as amounts contributed by him for an annuity contract for his employee if—

(i) the amounts are to be invested in regulated investment company stock to be held in that custodial account, and

(ii) under the custodial account no such amounts may be paid or made available to any distributee before the employee dies, attains age 59½, separates from service, becomes disabled (within the meaning of section 72(m)(7)), or encounters financial hardship.

(B) Account treated as plan.—For purposes of this title, a custodial account which satisfies the requirements of section 401(f)(2) shall be treated as an organization described in section 401(a) solely for purposes of subchapter F and subtitle F with respect to amounts received by it (and income from investment thereof).

(C) Regulated investment company.—For purposes of this paragraph, the term "regulated investment company" means a domestic corporation which is a regulated investment company within the meaning of section 851(a).

(8) Rollover Amounts.—

(A) General Rule.—If—

(i) the balance to the credit of an employee is paid to him in a qualifying distribution,

(ii) the employee transfers any portion of the property he receives in such distribution to an individual retirement plan or to an annuity contract described in paragraph (1), and

(iii) in the case of a distribution of property other than money, the property so transferred consists of the property distributed,

then such distribution (to the extent so transferred) shall not be includible in gross income for the taxable year in which paid.

(B) Qualifying distribution defined.—

(i) In general.—For purposes of subparagraph (A), the term "qualifying distribution" means 1 or more distributions from an annuity contract described in paragraph (1) which would constitute a lump sum distribution within the meaning of section 402(e)(4)(A) (determined without regard to subparagraphs (B) and (H) of section 402(e)(4)) if such annuity contract were described in subsection (a), or 1 or more distributions of accumulated deductible employee contributions (within the meaning of section 72(o)(5)).

(ii) Aggregation of annuity contracts.—For purposes of this paragraph, all annuity contracts described in paragraph (1) purchased by an employer shall be treated as a single contract, and section 402(e)(4)(C) shall not apply.

(C) Certain rules made applicable.—Rules similar to the rules of subparagraphs (B), (C), and (D)(v), and (E)(i) of section 402(a)(5) and of paragraphs (6) and (7) of section 402(a) shall apply for purposes of subparagraph (A).

***(9) Retirement income accounts provided by churches, etc.**—

---

*[Editor's Note: Section 403(b)(9), added by TEFRA (PL 97-248), is effective for taxable years beginning after Dec. 31, 1974.]

(A) Amounts paid treated as contributions.—For purposes of this title—
(i) a retirement income account shall be treated as an annuity contract described in this subsection, and
(ii) amounts paid by an employer described in paragraph (1)(A) to a retirement income account shall be treated as amounts contributed by the employer for an annuity contract for the employee on whose behalf such account is maintained.
(B) Retirement income account.—For purposes of this paragraph, the term 'retirement income account' means a defined contribution program established or maintained by a church, a convention or association of churches, including an organization described in section 414(e)(3)(A), to provide benefits under section 403(b) for an employee described in paragraph (1) or his beneficiaries.

(c) **Taxability of Beneficiary Under Nonqualified Annuities or Under Annuities Purchased by Exempt Organizations.**— Premiums paid by an employer for an annuity contract which is not subject to subsection (a) shall be included in the gross income of the employee in accordance with section 83 (relating to property transferred in connection with performance of services), except that the value of such contract shall be substituted for the fair market value of the property for purposes of applying such section. The preceding sentence shall not apply to that portion of the premiums paid which is excluded from gross income under subsection (b). The amount actually paid or made available to any beneficiary under such contract shall be taxable to him in the year in which so paid or made available under section 72 (relating to annuities).

SEC. 404. DEDUCTION FOR CONTRIBUTIONS OF AN EMPLOYER TO AN EMPLOYEES' TRUST OR ANNUITY PLAN AND COMPENSATION UNDER A DEFERRED-PAYMENT PLAN.

(a) **General Rule.**—If contributions are paid by an employer to or under a stock bonus, pension, profit-sharing or annuity plan, or if compensation is paid or accrued on account of any employee under a plan deferring the receipt of such compensation, such contributions or compensation shall not be deductible under section 162 (relating to trade or business expenses) or section 212 (relating to expenses for the production of income); but if they satisfy the conditions of either of such sections, they shall be deductible under this section, subject, however, to the following limitations as to the amounts deductible in any year:

(1) **Pension trusts.**—
(A) In general.—In the taxable year when paid, if the contributions are paid into a pension trust, and if such taxable year ends within or with a taxable year of the trust for which the trust is exempt under section 501(a), in an amount determined as follows:
(i) the amount necessary to satisfy the minimum funding standard provided by section 412(a) for plan years ending within or with such taxable year (or for any prior plan year), if such amount is greater than the amount determined under clause (ii) or (iii) (whichever is applicable with respect to the plan),
(ii) the amount necessary to provide with respect to all of the employees under the trust the remaining unfunded cost of their past and current service credits distributed as a level amount, or a level percentage of compensation, over the remaining future service of each such employee, as determined under regulations prescribed by the Secretary, but if such remaining unfunded cost with respect to any 3 individuals is more than 50 percent of such remaining unfunded cost, the amount of such unfunded cost attributable to such individuals shall be distributed over a period of at least 5 taxable years,
(iii) an amount equal to the normal cost of the plan, as determined under regulations prescribed by the Secretary, plus, if past service or other supplementary pension or annuity credits are provided by the plan, an amount necessary to amortize such credits in equal annual payments (until fully amortized) over 10 years, as determined under regulations prescribed by the Secretary.

In determining the amount deductible in such year under the foregoing limitations the funding method and the actuarial assumptions used shall be those used for

Code Sec. 404 (a) (1)

such year under section 412, and the maximum amount deductible for such year shall be an amount equal to the full funding limitation for such year determined under section 412.

(B) Special rule in case of certain amendments.—In the case of a plan which the Secretary of Labor finds to be collectively bargained which makes an election under this subparagraph (in such manner and at such time as may be provided under regulations prescribed by the Secretary), if the full funding limitation determined under section 412(c)(7) for such year is zero, if as a result of any plan amendment applying to such plan year, the amount determined under section 412(c)(7)(B) exceeds the amount determined under section 412(c)(7)(A), and if the funding method and the actuarial assumptions used are those used for such year under section 412, the maximum amount deductible in such year under the limitations of this paragraph shall be an amount equal to the lesser of—

(i) the full funding limitation for such year determined by applying section 412(c)(7) but increasing the amount referred to in subparagraph (A) thereof by the decrease in the present value of all unamortized liabilities resulting from such amendment, or

(ii) the normal cost under the plan reduced by the amount necessary to amortize in equal annual installments over 10 years (until fully amortized) the decrease described in clause (i).

In the case of any election under this subparagraph, the amount deductible under the limitations of this paragraph with respect to any of the plan years following the plan year for which such election was made shall be determined as provided under such regulations as may be prescribed by the Secretary to carry out the purposes of this subparagraph.

(C) Certain collectively-bargained plans.—In the case of a plan which the Secretary of Labor finds to be collectively bargained, established or maintained by an employer doing business in not less than 40 States and engaged in the trade or business of furnishing or selling services described in section 167(l)(3)(A)(iii), with respect to which the rates have been established or approved by a State or political subdivision thereof, by any agency or instrumentality of the United States, or by a public service or public utility commission or other similar body of any State or political subdivision thereof, and in the case of any employer which is a member of a controlled group with such employer, subparagraph (B) shall be applied by substituting for the words "plan amendment" the words "plan amendment or increase in benefits payable under title II of the Social Security Act." For purposes of this subparagraph, the term "controlled group" has the meaning provided by section 1563(a), determined without regard to section 1563(a)(4) and (e)(3)(C).

(D) Carryover.—Any amount paid in a taxable year in excess of the amount deductible in such year under the foregoing limitations shall be deductible in the succeeding taxable years in order of time to the extent of the difference between the amount paid and deductible in each such succeeding year and the maximum amount deductible for such year under the foregoing limitations.

(2) **Employees' annuities.**—In the taxable year when paid, in an amount determined in accordance with paragraph (l), if the contributions are paid toward the purchase of retirement annuities, or retirement annuities and medical benefits as described in Sec. 401(h), and such purchase is a part of a plan which meets the requirements of section 401(a)(3), (4), (5), (6), (7), (8), (9), (11), (12), (13), (14), (15), (16), (19), (20) and (22) and, if applicable, the requirements of section 401(a)(10) and of section 401(d), and if refunds of premiums, if any, are applied within the current taxable or next succeeding taxable year towards the purchase of such retirement annuities, or such retirement annuities and medical benefits.

(3) **Stock bonus and profit-sharing trusts.—**

(A) Limits on deductible contributions.—In the taxable year when paid, if the contributions are paid into a stock bonus or profit-sharing trust, and if such taxable year ends within or with a taxable year of the trust with respect to which the trust is exempt under section 501(a), in an amount not in excess of 15 percent of the compensation otherwise paid or accrued during the taxable year to all employees under the

Code Sec. 404 (a) (1) (B)

stock bonus or profit-sharing plan. If in any taxable year there is paid into the trust, or a similar trust then in effect, amounts less than the amounts deductible under the preceding sentence, the excess, or if no amount is paid, the amounts deductible, shall be carried forward and be deductible when paid in the succeeding taxable years in order of time, but the amount so deductible under this sentence in any such succeeding taxable year shall not exceed 15 percent of the compensation otherwise paid or accrued during such succeeding taxable year to the beneficiaries under the plan, but the amount so deductible under this sentence in any one succeeding taxable year together with the amount so deductible under the first sentence of this subparagraph shall not exceed 25 percent of the compensation otherwise paid or accrued during such taxable year to the beneficiaries under the plan. In addition, any amount paid into the trust in any taxable year in excess of the amount allowable with respect to such year under the preceding provisions of this subparagraph shall be deductible in the succeeding taxable years in order of time, but the amount so deductible under this sentence in any one such succeeding taxable year together with the amount allowable under the first sentence of this subparagraph shall not exceed 15 percent of the compensation otherwise paid or accrued during such taxable year to the beneficiaries under the plan. The term "stock bonus or profit-sharing trust", as used in this subparagraph, shall not include any trust designed to provide benefits upon retirement and covering a period of years, if under the plan the amounts to be contributed by the employer can be determined actuarially as provided in paragraph (l). If the contributions are made to 2 or more stock bonus or profit-sharing trusts, such trusts shall be considered a single trust for purposes of applying the limitations in this subparagraph.

(B) Profit-sharing Plan of Affiliated Group.—In the case of a profit-sharing plan, or a stock bonus plan in which contributions are determined with reference to profits, of a group of corporations which is an affiliated group within the meaning of section 1504, if any member of such affiliated group is prevented from making a contribution which it would otherwise have made under the plan, by reason of having no current or accumulated earnings or profits or because such earnings or profits are less than the contributions which it would otherwise have made, then so much of the contribution which such member was so prevented from making may be made, for the benefit of the employees of such member, by the other members of the group, to the extent of current or accumulated earnings or profits, except that such contribution by each such other member shall be limited, where the group does not file a consolidated return, to that proportion of its total current and accumulated earnings or profits remaining after adjustment for its contribution deductible without regard to this subparagraph which the total prevented contribution bears to the total current and accumulated earnings or profits of all the members of the group remaining after adjustment for all contributions deductible without regard to this subparagraph. Contributions made under the preceding sentence shall be deductible under subparagraph (A) of this paragraph by the employer making such contribution, and, for the purpose of determining amounts which may be carried forward and deducted under the second sentence of subparagraph (A) of this paragraph in succeeding taxable years, shall be deemed to have been made by the employer on behalf of whose employees such contributions were made.

The term 'compensation otherwise paid or accrued during the taxable year to all employees' shall include any amount with respect to which an election under section 415(c)(3)(C) is in effect, but only to the extent that any contribution with respect to such amount is nonforfeitable.

(4) **Trusts created or organized outside the United States.**—If a stock bonus, pension, or profit-sharing trust would qualify for exemption under section 501(a) except for the fact that it is a trust created or organized outside the United States, contributions to such a trust by an employer which is a resident, or corporation, or other entity of the United States, shall be deductible under the preceding paragraphs.

(5) **Other plans.**—If the plan is not one included in paragraph (1), (2), or (3), in the taxable year in which an amount attribu-

table to the contribution is includible in the gross income of employees participating in the plan, but, in the case of a plan in which more than one employee participates only if separate accounts are maintained for each employee.

(6) Time when contributions deemed made.—For purposes of paragraphs (1), (2), and (3), a taxpayer shall be deemed to have made a payment on the last day of the preceding taxable year if the payment is on account of such taxable year and is made not later than the time prescribed by law for filing the return for such taxable year (including extensions thereof).

(7) Limit on deductions.—If amounts are deductible under paragraphs (1) and (3), or (2) and (3), or (1), (2), and (3), in connection with 2 or more trusts, or one or more trusts and an annuity plan, the total amount deductible in a taxable year under such trusts and plans shall not exceed the greater of 25 percent of the compensation otherwise paid or accrued during the taxable year to the beneficiaries of the trusts or plans, or the amount of contributions made to or under the trusts or plans to the extent such contributions do not exceed the amount of employer contributions necessary to satisfy the minimum funding standard provided by section 412 for the plan year which ends with or within such taxable year (or for any prior plan year). In addition, any amount paid into such trust or under such annuity plans in any taxable year in excess of the amount allowable with respect to such year under the preceding provisions of this paragraph shall be deductible in the succeeding taxable years in order of time, but the amount so deductible under this sentence in any one such succeeding taxable year together with the amount allowable under the first sentence of this paragraph shall not exceed 25 percent of the compensation otherwise paid or accrued during such taxable years to the beneficiaries under the trusts or plans. This paragraph shall not have the effect of reducing the amount otherwise deductible under paragraphs (1), (2), and (3), if no employee is a beneficiary under more than one trust, or a trust and an annuity plan.

(8) Self-employed individuals.—In the case of a plan included in paragraph (1), (2), or (3) which provides contributions or benefits for employees some or all of whom are employees within the meaning of section 401(c)(1), for purposes of this section—

(A) the term "employee" includes an individual who is an employee within the meaning of section 401(c)(1), and the employer of such individual is the person treated as his employer under section 401(c)(4);

(B) the term "earned income" has the meaning assigned to it by section 401(c)(2);

(C) the contributions to such plan on behalf of an individual who is an employee within the meaning of section 401(c)(1) shall be considered to satisfy the conditions of section 162 or 212 to the extent that such contributions do not exceed the earned income of such individual derived from the trade or business with respect to which such plan is established, and to the extent that such contributions are not allocable (determined in accordance with regulations prescribed by the Secretary) to the purchase of life, accident, health or other insurance; and

(D) any reference to compensation shall, in the case of an individual who is an employee within the meaning of section 401(c)(1), be considered to be a reference to the earned income of such individual derived from the trade or business with respect to which the plan is established.

(9) Plans benefiting self-employed individuals.—In the case of a plan included in paragraph (1), (2), or (3) which provides contributions or benefits for employees some or all of whom are employees within the meaning of section 401(c)(1)—

(A) the limitations provided by paragraphs (1), (2), and (7) on the amounts deductible for any taxable year shall be computed, with respect to contributions on behalf of employees (other than employees within the meaning of section 401(c)(1)), as if such employees were the only employees for whom contributions and benefits are provided under the plan;

(B) the limitations provided by paragraphs (1), (2), (3), and (7) on the amounts deductible for any taxable year shall be computed, with respect to contributions on behalf of employees within the meaning of section 401(c)(1)—

Code Sec. 404 (a) (6)

(i) as if such employees were the only employees for whom contributions and benefits are provided under the plan, and

(ii) without regard to the second sentence of paragraph (3); and

(C) the amounts deductible under paragraphs (1), (2), (3), and (7), with respect to contributions on behalf of any employee within the meaning of section 401(c)(1), shall not exceed the applicable limitation provided in subsection (e).

(10) Certain contributions to employee stock ownership plans.—

(A) Principal payments.—Notwithstanding the provisions of paragraphs (3) and (7), if contributions are paid into a trust which forms a part of an employee stock ownership plan (as described in section 4975(e)(7)), and such contributions are, on or before the time prescribed in paragraph (6), applied by the plan to the repayment of the principal of a loan incurred for the purpose of acquiring qualifying employer securities (as described in section 4975(e)(8)), such contributions shall be deductible under this paragraph for the taxable year determined under paragraph (6). The amount deductible under this paragraph shall not, however, exceed 25 percent of the compensation otherwise paid or accrued during the taxable year to the employees under such employee stock ownership plan. Any amount paid into such trust in any taxable year in excess of the amount deductible under this paragraph shall be deductible in the succeeding taxable years in order of time to the extent of the difference between the amount paid and deductible in each such succeeding year and the maximum amount deductible for such year under the preceding sentence.

(B) Interest payment.—Notwithstanding the provisions of paragraphs (3) and (7), if contributions are made to an employee stock ownership plan (described in subparagraph (A)) and such contributions are applied by the plan to the repayment of interest on a loan incurred for the purpose of acquiring qualifying employer securities (as described in subparagraph (A)), such contributions shall be deductible for the taxable year with respect to which such contributions are made as determined under paragraph (6).

(b) Method of Contribution, Etc., Having the Effect of a Plan.—If there is no plan but a method of employer contributions or compensation has the effect of a stock bonus, pension, profit-sharing, or annuity plan, or other plan deferring the receipt of compensation, subsection (a) shall apply as if there were such a plan.

(c) Certain Negotiated Plans.—If contributions are paid by an employer—

(1) under a plan under which such contributions are held in trust for the purpose of paying (either from principal or income or both) for the benefit of employees and their families and dependents at least medical or hospital care, or pensions on retirement or death of employees; and

(2) such plan was established prior to January 1, 1954, as a result of an agreement between employee representatives and the Government of the United States during a period of Government operation, under seizure powers, of a major part of the productive facilities of the industry in which such employer is engaged,

such contributions shall not be deductible under this section nor be made nondeductible by this section, but the deductibility thereof shall be governed solely by section 162 (relating to trade or business expenses). For purposes of this chapter and subtitle B, in the case of any individual who before July 1, 1974, was a participant in a plan described in the preceding sentence—

(A) such individual, if he is or was an employee within the meaning of section 401(c)(1), shall be treated (with respect to service covered by the plan) as being an employee other than an employee within the meaning of section 401(c)(1) and as being an employee of a participating employer under the plan,

(B) earnings derived from service covered by the plan shall be treated as not being earned income within the meaning of section 401(c)(2), and

(C) such individual shall be treated as an employee of a participating employer under the plan with respect to service before July 1, 1975, covered by the plan.

Section 277 (relating to deductions incurred by certain membership organizations in transactions with members) does not apply to any trust described in this subsection. The first and third sentences of this subsec-

Code Sec. 404 (c)

tion shall have no application with respect to amounts contributed to a trust on or after any date on which such trust is qualified for exemption from tax under section 501(a).

(d) Deductibility of Payments of Deferred Compensation, Etc., to Independent Contractors.—If a plan would be described in so much of subsection (a) as precedes paragraph (1) thereof (as modified by subsection (b)) but for the fact that there is no employer-employee relationship, the contributions or compensation—

(1) shall not be deductible by the payor thereof under section 162 or 212, but

(2) shall (if they would be deductible under section 162 or 212 but for paragraph (1)) be deductible under this subsection for the taxable year in which an amount attributable to the contribution or compensation is includible in the gross income of the persons participating in the plan.

(e) Contributions Allocable to Life Insurance Protection for Self-Employed Individuals.—In the case of a self-employed individual described in section 401(c)(1), contributions which are allocable (determined under regulations prescribed by the Secretary) to the purchase of life, accident, health, or other insurance shall not be taken into account under this section.

(f) Certain Loan Repayments Considered as Contributions.—For purposes of this section, any amount paid, directly or indirectly, by an owner-employee (within the meaning of section 401(c)(3)) in repayment of any loan which under section 72(m)(4)(B) was treated as an amount received under a contract purchased by a trust described in section 401(a) which is exempt from tax under section 501(a) or purchased as a part of a plan described in section 403(a) shall be treated as a contribution to which this section applies on behalf of such owner-employee to such trust or to or under such plan.

***(g) Certain Employer Liability Payments Considered as Contributions.**—

(1) **In General.**—For purposes of this section, any amount paid by an employer under section 4062, 4063, or 4064, or part 1 of subtitle E of title IV of the Employee Retirement Income Security Act of 1974 shall be treated as a contribution to which this section applies by such employer to or under a stock bonus, pension, profit-sharing, or annuity plan.

(2) **Controlled Group Deductions.**—In the case of a payment described in paragraph (1) made by an entity which is liable because it is a member of a commonly controlled group of corporations, trades, or businesses, within the meaning of subsection (b) or (c) of section 414, the fact that the entity did not directly employ participants of the plan with respect to which the liability payment was made shall not affect the deductibility of a payment which otherwise satisfies the conditions of section 162 (relating to trade or business expenses) or section 212 (relating to expenses for the production of income).

*[*Editor's Note:* Section 408 of the Multiemployer Pension Plan Amendments Act of 1980 (PL 96-364) reads as follows:

SEC. 408. DEDUCTIBILITY OF PAYMENTS TO PLAN BY A CORPORATION OPERATING PUBLIC TRANSPORTATION SYSTEM ACQUIRED BY A STATE.

(a) For purposes of subsection (g) of section 404 of the Internal Revenue Code of 1954 (relating to certain employer liability payments considered as contributions), as amended by section 205 of this Act, any payment made to a plan covering employees of a corporation operating a public transportation system shall be treated as a payment described in paragraph (1) of such subsection if—

(1) such payment is made to fund accrued benefits under the plan in conjunction with an acquisition by a State (or agency or instrumentality thereof) of the stock or assets of such corporation, and

(2) such acquisition is pursuant to a State public transportation law enacted after June 30, 1979, and before January 1, 1980.

(b) The provisions of this section shall apply to payments made after June 29, 1980.]

IRC EXCERPTS

(3) Coordination With Subsection (a).— Any payment described in paragraph (1) shall (subject to the last sentence of subsection (a)(1)(A)) be deductible under this section when paid.

(h) Special Rules for Simplified Employee Pensions.—

(1) In General.—Employer contributions to a simplified employee pension shall be treated as if they are made to a plan subject to the requirements of this section. Employer contributions to a simplified employee pension are subject to the following limitations:

(A) Contributions made for a calendar year are deductible for the taxable year with which or within which the calendar year ends.

(B) Contributions made within 3½ months after the close of a calendar year are treated as if they were made on the last day of such calendar year if they are made on account of such calendar year.

(C) The amount deductible in a taxable year for a simplified employee pension shall not exceed 15 percent of the compensation paid to the employees during the calendar year ending with or within the taxable year. The excess of the amount contributed over the amount deductible for a taxable year shall be deductible in the succeeding taxable years in order of time, subject to the 15 percent limit of the preceding sentence.

(2) Effect on stock bonus and profit-sharing trust.—For any taxable year for which the employer has a deduction under paragraph (1), the otherwise applicable limitations in subsection (a)(3)(A) shall be reduced by the amount of the allowable deductions under paragraph (1) with respect to participants in the stock bonus or profit-sharing trust.

(3) Effect on limit on deductions.—For any taxable year for which the employer has a deduction under paragraph (1), the otherwise applicable 25 percent limitations in subsection (a)(7) shall be reduced by the amount of the allowable deductions under paragraph (1) with respect to participants in the stock bonus or profit-sharing trust.

(4) Effect on self-employed individuals or shareholder-employees.—The limitations described in paragraphs (1), (2)(A) and (4) of subsection (e) or described in section 1379(b)(1) for any taxable year shall be reduced by the amount of the allowable deductions under paragraph (1) with respect to an employee within the meaning of section 401(c)(1) or a shareholder-employee (as defined in section 1379(d)).

*(i) Deductibility of Unused Portions of Employee Stock Ownership Credit.—

(1) Unused credit carryovers.—There shall be allowed as a deduction (without regard to any limitations provided under this section) for the last taxable year to which an unused employee stock ownership credit carryover (within the meaning of section 44G(b)(2)(A)) may be carried, an amount equal to the portion of such unused credit carryover which expires at the close of such taxable year.

(2) Reductions in credit.—There shall be allowed as a deduction (subject to the limitations provided under this section) an amount equal to any reduction of the credit allowed under section 44G resulting from a final determination of such credit to the extent such reduction is not taken into account in section 44G(c)(2).

(j) Special Rules Relating to Application With Section 415.—

(1) No deduction in excess of section 415 limitation.—In computing the amount of any deduction allowable under paragraph (1), (2), (3), (4), (7), or (10) of subsection (a) for any year—

(A) in the case of a defined benefit plan, there shall not be taken into account any benefits for any year in excess of any limitation on such benefits under section 415 for such year, or

(B) in the case of a defined contribution plan, the amount of any contributions otherwise taken into account shall be reduced by any annual additions in excess of the limitation under section 415 for such year.

(2) No advance funding of cost-of-living adjustments.—For purposes of clause (i), (ii) or (iii) of subsection (a)(1)(A), and in computing the full funding limitation, there

*[*Editor's Note:* Section 404(i), added by ERTA (PL 94-37) is effective for taxable years after Dec. 31, 1982.]

Code Sec. 404 (j) (2)

shall not be taken into account any adjustments under section 415(d)(1) for any year before the year for which such adjustment first takes effect.

SEC. 404A. DEDUCTION FOR CERTAIN FOREIGN DEFERRED COMPENSATION PLANS.

(a) General Rule.—Amounts paid or accrued by an employer under a qualified foreign plan—

(1) shall not be allowable as a deduction under section 162, 212, or 404, but

(2) if they satisfy the conditions of section 162, shall be allowed as a deduction under this section for the taxable year for which such amounts are properly taken into account under this section.

(b) Rules for Qualified Funded Plans.—For purposes of this section—

(1) **In general.**—Except as otherwise provided in this section, in the case of a qualified funded plan contributions are properly taken into account for the taxable year in which paid.

(2) **Payment after close of taxable year.**—For purposes of paragraph (1), a payment made after the close of a taxable year shall be treated as made on the last day of such year if the payment is made—

(A) on account of such year, and

(B) not later than the time prescribed by law for filing the return for such year (including extensions thereof).

(3) **Limitations.**—In the case of a qualified funded plan, the amount allowable as a deduction for the taxable year shall be subject to—

(A) in the case of—

(i) a plan under which the benefits are fixed or determinable, limitations similar to those contained in clauses (ii) and (iii) of subparagraph (A) of section 404(a)(1) (determined without regard to the last sentence of such subparagraph (A)), or

(ii) any other plan, limitations similar to the limitations contained in paragraph (3) of section 404(a), and

(B) limitations similar to those contained in paragraph (7) of section 404(a).

(4) **Carryover.**—If—

(A) the aggregate of the contributions paid during the taxable year reduced by any contributions not allowable as a deduction under paragraphs (1) and (2) of subsection (g), exceeds

(B) the amount allowable as a deduction under subsection (a) (determined without regard to subsection (d)),

such excess shall be treated as an amount paid in the succeeding taxable year.

(5) **Amounts must be paid to qualified trust, etc.**—In the case of a qualified funded plan, a contribution shall be taken into account only if it is paid—

(A) to a trust (or the equivalent of a trust) which meets the requirements of section 401(a)(2),

(B) for a retirement annuity, or

(C) to a participant or beneficiary.

(c) Rules Relating to Qualified Reserve Plans.—For purposes of this section—

(1) **In general.**—In the case of a qualified reserve plan, the amount properly taken into account for the taxable year is the reasonable addition for such year to a reserve for the taxpayer's liability under the plan. Unless otherwise required or permitted in regulations prescribed by the Secretary, the reserve for the taxpayer's liability shall be determined under the unit credit method modified to reflect the requirements of paragraphs (3) and (4). All benefits paid under the plan shall be charged to the reserve.

(2) **Income item.**—In the case of a plan which is or has been a qualified reserve plan, an amount equal to that portion of any decrease for the taxable year in the reserve which is not attributable to the payment of benefits shall be included in gross income.

(3) **Rights must be nonforfeitable, etc.**—In the case of a qualified reserve plan, an item shall be taken into account for a taxable year only if—

(A) there is no substantial risk that the rights of the employee will be forfeited, and

(B) such item meets such additional requirements as the Secretary may by regulations prescribe as necessary or appropriate to ensure that the liability will be satisfied.

Code Sec. 404 A

(4) Spreading of certain increases and decreases in reserves.—There shall be amortized over a 10-year period any increase or decrease to the reserve on account of—

(A) the adoption of the plan or a plan amendment,

(B) experience gains and losses, and

(C) any change in actuarial assumptions,

(D) changes in the interest rate under subsection (g)(3)(B), and

(E) such other factors as may be prescribed by regulations.

(d) Amounts Taken Into Account Must Be Consistent With Amounts Allowed Under Foreign Law.—

(1) General Rule.—In the case of any plan, the amount allowed as a deduction under subsection (a) for any taxable year shall equal—

(A) the lesser of—

(i) the cumulative United States amount, or

(ii) the cumulative foreign amount, reduced by

(B) the aggregate amount determined under this section for all prior taxable years.

(2) Cumulative amounts defined.—For purposes of paragraph (1)—

(A) Cumulative United States amount.—The term "cumulative United States amount" means the aggregate amount determined with respect to the plan under this section for the taxable year and for all prior taxable years to which this section applies. Such determination shall be made for each taxable year without regard to the application of paragraph (1).

(B) Cumulative foreign amount.—The term "cumulative foreign amount" means the aggregate amount allowed as a deduction under the appropriate foreign tax laws for the taxable year and all prior taxable years to which this section applies.

(3) Effect on earnings and profits, etc.—In determining the earnings and profits and accumulated profits of any foreign corporation with respect to a qualified foreign plan, the amount determined under paragraph (1) with respect to any plan for any taxable year shall in no event exceed the amount allowed as a deduction under the appropriate foreign tax laws for such taxable year.

(e) Qualified Foreign Plan.—For purposes of this section, the term "qualified foreign plan" means any written plan of an employer for deferring the receipt of compensation but only if—

(1) such plan is for the exclusive benefit of the employer's employees or their beneficiaries,

(2) 90 percent or more of the amounts taken into account for the taxable year under the plan are attributable to services—

(A) performed by nonresident aliens, and

(B) the compensation for which is not subject to tax under this chapter, and

(3) the employer elects (at such time and in such manner as the Secretary shall by regulations prescribe) to have this section apply to such plan.

(f) Funded and Reserve Plans.—For purposes of this section—

(1) Qualified funded plan.—The term "qualified funded plan" means a qualified foreign plan which is not a qualified reserve plan.

(2) Qualified reserve plan.—The term "qualified reserve plan" means a qualified foreign plan with respect to which an election made by the taxpayer is in effect for the taxable year. An election under the preceding sentence shall be made in such manner and form as the Secretary may by regulations prescribe and, once made, may be revoked only with the consent of the Secretary.

(g) Other Special Rules.—

(1) No deduction for certain amounts.—Except as provided in section 404(a)(5), no deduction shall be allowed under this section for any item to the extent such item is attributable to services—

(A) performed by a citizen or resident of the United States who is an officer, shareholder, or highly compensated, or

(B) performed in the United States the compensation for which is subject to tax under this chapter.

(2) Taxpayer must furnish information.—

(A) In general.—No deduction shall be allowed under this section with respect to any plan for any taxable year unless the taxpayer furnishes to the Secretary with

Code Sec. 404 A (g)

respect to such plan (at such time as the Secretary may by regulations prescribe)—

(i) a statement from the foreign tax authorities specifying the amount of the deduction allowed in computing taxable income under foreign law for such year with respect to such plan,

(ii) if the return under foreign tax law shows the deduction for plan contributions or reserves as a separate, identifiable item, a copy of the foreign tax return for the taxable year, or

(iii) such other statement, return, or other evidence as the Secretary prescribes by regulation as being sufficient to establish the amount of the deduction under foreign law.

(B) Redetermination where foreign tax deduction is adjusted.—If the deduction under foreign tax law is adjusted, the taxpayer shall notify the Secretary of such adjustment on or before the date prescribed by regulations, and the Secretary shall redetermine the amount of the tax year or years affected. In any case described in the preceding sentence, rules similar to the rules of subsection (c) of section 905 shall apply.

(3) Actuarial assumptions must be reasonable; full funding.—

(A) In general.—Except as provided in subparagraph (B), principles similar to those set forth in paragraphs (3) and (7) of section 412(c) shall apply for purposes of this section.

(B) Interest rate for reserve plan.—

(i) In general.—In the case of a qualified reserve plan, in lieu of taking rates of interest into account under subparagraph (A), the rate of interest for the plan shall be the rate selected by the taxpayer which is within the permissible range.

(ii) Rate remains in effect so long as it falls within permissible range.—Any rate selected by the taxpayer for the plan under this subparagraph shall remain in effect for such plan until the first taxable year for which such rate is no longer within the permissible range. At such time, the taxpayer shall select a new rate of interest which is within the permissible range applicable at such time.

(iii) Permissible range.—For purposes of this subparagraph, the term "permissible range" means a rate of interest which is not more than 20 percent above, and not more than 20 percent below, the average rate of interest for long-term corporate bonds in the appropriate country for the 15-year period ending on the last day before the beginning of the taxable year.

(4) Accounting method.—Any change in the method (but not the actuarial assumptions) used to determine the amount allowed as a deduction under subsection (a) shall be treated as a change in accounting method under section 446(e).

(5) Section 481 applies to election.—For purposes of section 481, any election under this section shall be treated as a change in the taxpayer's method of accounting. In applying section 481 with respect to any such election, the period for taking into account any increase or decrease in accumulated profits, earnings and profits or taxable income resulting from the application of section 481(a)(2) shall be the year for which the election is made and the fourteen succeeding years.

(h) Regulations.—The Secretary shall prescribe such regulations as may be necessary to carry out the purposes of this section (including regulations providing for the coordination of the provisions of this section with section 404 in the case of a plan which has been subject to both of such sections).

SEC. 405. QUALIFIED BOND PURCHASE PLANS.

(a) Requirements for Qualification.—A plan of an employer for the purchase for and distribution to his employees or their beneficiaries of United States bonds described in subsection (b) shall constitute a qualified bond purchase plan under this section if—

(1) the plan meets the requirements of section 401(a)(3), (4), (5), (6), (7), (8), (16), and (19) and, if applicable, the requirements of section 401(a)(9) and (10) and of section 401(d) (other than paragraphs (1), (5)(B), and (8)); and

(2) contributions under the plan are used solely to purchase for employees or their beneficiaries United States bonds described in subsection (b).

(b) Bonds to Which Applicable.—

(1) Characteristics of bonds.—This section shall apply only to a bond issued under the Second Liberty Bond Act, as amended, which by its terms, or by regulations prescribed by the Secretary under such Act—

(A) provides for payment of interest, or investment yield, only upon redemption;

(B) may be purchased only in the name of an individual;

(C) ceases to bear interest, or provide investment yield, not later than 5 years after the death of the individual in whose name it is purchased;

(D) may be redeemed before the death of the individual in whose name it is purchased only if such individual—

(i) has attained the age of 59½ years, or

(ii) has become disabled (within the meaning of section 72(m)(7)); and

(E) is nontransferable.

(2) Must be purchased in name of employee.—This section shall apply to a bond described in paragraph (1) only if it is purchased in the name of the employee.

(c) Deduction for Contributions to Bond Purchase Plans.

—Contributions paid by an employer to or under a qualified bond purchase plan shall be allowed as a deduction in an amount determined under section 404 in the same manner and to the same extent as if such contributions were made to a trust described in section 401(a) which is exempt from tax under section 501(a).

(d) Taxability of Beneficiary of Qualified Bond Purchase Plan.—

(1) Gross income not to include bonds at time of distribution.—For purposes of this chapter, in the case of a distributee of a bond described in subsection (b) under a qualified bond purchase plan, or from a trust described in section 401(a) which is exempt from tax under section 501(a), gross income does not include any amount attributable to the receipt of such bond. Upon redemption of such bond, except as provided in paragraph (3), the proceeds shall be subject to taxation under this chapter, but the provisions of section 72 (relating to annuities, etc.) and section 1232 (relating to bonds and other evidences of indebtedness) shall not apply.

(2) Basis.—The basis of any bond received by a distributee under a qualified bond purchase plan—

(A) if such bond is distributed to an employee, or with respect to an employee, who at the time of purchase of the bond, was an employee other than an employee within the meaning of section 401(c)(1), shall be the amount of the contributions by the employee which were used to purchase the bond, and

(B) if such bond is distributed to an employee, or with respect to an employee, who, at the time of purchase of the bond, was an employee within the meaning of section 401(c)(1), shall be the amount of the contributions used to purchase the bond which were made on behalf of such employee and were not allowed as a deduction under subsection (c).

The basis of any bond described in subsection (b) received by a distributee from a trust described in section 401(a) which is exempt from tax under section 501(a) shall be determined under regulations prescribed by the Secretary.

(3) Rollover into an individual retirement account or annuity.—

(A) In General.—If—

(i) any qualified bond is redeemed,

(ii) any portion of the excess of the proceeds from such redemption over the basis of such bond is transferred to an individual retirement plan which is maintained for the benefit of the individual redeeming such bond, and

(iii) such transfer is made on or before the 60th day after the day on which the individual received the proceeds of such redemption,

then, gross income shall not include the proceeds to the extent so transferred and the transfer shall be treated as a rollover contribution described in section 408(d)(3).

(B) Qualified bond.—For purposes of this paragraph, the term "qualified bond" means any bond described in subsection (b) which is distributed under a qualified bond purchase plan or from a trust described in subsection (b) which is distributed under a qualified bond purchase plan or from a trust described in section 401(a) which is exempt from tax under section 501(a).

Code Sec. 405 (d) (3)

(e) **Capital Gains Treatment and Limitation of Tax Not to Apply to Bonds Distributed by Trusts.**—Subsections (a)(2) and (e) of section 402 shall not apply to any bond described in subsection (b) distributed to any distributee and, for purposes of applying such sections, any such bond distributed to any distributee and any such bond to the credit of any employee shall not be taken into account.

(f) **Employee Defined.**—For purposes of this section, the term "employee" includes an individual who is an employee within the meaning of section 401(c)(1), and the employer of such individual shall be the person treated as his employer under section 401(c)(4).

(g) **Proof of Purchase.**—At the time of purchase of any bond to which this section applies, proof of such purchase shall be furnished in such form as will enable the purchaser, and the employee in whose name such bond is purchased, to comply with the provisions of this section.

(h) **Regulations.**—The Secretary shall prescribe such regulations as may be necessary to carry out the provisions of this section.

SEC. 406. CERTAIN EMPLOYEES OF FOREIGN SUBSIDIARIES.

(a) **Treatment as Employees of Domestic Corporation.**—For purposes of applying this part with respect to a pension, profit-sharing, or stock bonus plan described in section 401(a), an annuity plan described in section 403(a), or a bond purchase plan described in section 405(a), of a domestic corporation, an individual who is a citizen of the United States and who is an employee of a foreign subsidiary (as defined in section 3121(l)(8)) of such domestic corporation shall be treated as an employee of such domestic corporation, if—

(1) such domestic corporation has entered into an agreement under section 3121(l) which applies to the foreign subsidiary of which such individual is an employee;

(2) the plan of such domestic corporation expressly provides for contributions or benefits for individuals who are citizens of the United States and who are employees of its foreign subsidiaries to which an agreement entered into by such domestic corporation under section 3121(l) applies; and

(3) contributions under a funded plan of deferred compensation (whether or not a plan described in section 401(a), 403(a) or 405(a)) are not provided by any other person with respect to the remuneration paid to such individual by the foreign subsidiary.

(b) **Special Rules for Application of Section 401(a).**—

(1) **Nondiscrimination requirements.**—For purposes of applying section 401(a)(4) and section 410(b) (without regard to paragraph (1)(A) thereof) with respect to an individual who is treated as an employee of a domestic corporation under subsection (a)—

(A) if such individual is an officer, shareholder, or person whose principal duties consist in supervising the work of other employees of a foreign subsidiary of such domestic corporation, he shall be treated as having such capacity with respect to such domestic corporation; and

(B) the determination of whether such individual is a highly compensated employee shall be made by treating such individual's total compensation (determined with the application of paragraph (2) of this subsection) as compensation paid by such domestic corporation and by determining such individual's status with regard to such domestic corporation.

(2) **Determination of compensation.**—For purposes of applying paragraph (5) of section 401(a) with respect to an individual who is treated as an employee of a domestic corporation under subsection (a)—

(A) the total compensation of such individual shall be the remuneration paid to such individual by the foreign subsidiary which would constitute his total compensation if his services had been performed for such domestic corporation, and the basic or regular rate of compensation of such individual shall be determined under regulations prescribed by the Secretary; and

(B) such individual shall be treated as having paid the amount paid by such domestic corporation which is equivalent to the tax imposed by section 3101.

Code Sec. 405 (e)

(c) **Termination of Status as Deemed Employee Not to be Treated as Separation from Service for Purposes of Capital Gain Provisions and Limitation of Tax.**—For purposes of applying subsections (a)(2) and (e) of section 402, and section 403(a)(2) with respect to an individual who is treated as an employee of a domestic corporation under subsection (a), such individual shall not be considered as separated from the service of such domestic corporation solely by reason of the fact that—

(1) the agreement entered into by such domestic corporation under section 3121(l) which covers the employment of such individual is terminated under the provisions of such section,

(2) such individual becomes an employee of a foreign subsidiary with respect to which such agreement does not apply,

(3) such individual ceases to be an employee of the foreign subsidiary by reason of which he is treated as an employee of such domestic corporation, if he becomes an employee of another corporation controlled by such domestic corporation, or

(4) the provision of the plan described in subsection (a)(2) is terminated.

(d) **Deductibility of Contributions.**—For purposes of applying sections 404 and 405(c) with respect to contributions made to or under a pension, profit-sharing, stock bonus, annuity, or bond purchase plan by a domestic corporation, or by another corporation which is entitled to deduct its contributions under section 404(a)(3)(B), on behalf of an individual who is treated as an employee of such domestic corporation under subsection (a)—

(1) except as provided in paragraph (2), no deduction shall be allowed to such domestic corporation or to any other corporation which is entitled to deduct its contributions under such sections,

(2) there shall be allowed as a deduction to the foreign subsidiary of which such individual is an employee an amount equal to the amount which (but for paragraph (1)) would be deductible under section 404 (or section 405(c)) by the domestic corporation if he were an employee of the domestic corporation, and

(3) any reference to compensation shall be considered to be a reference to the total compensation of such individual (determined with the application of subsection (b)(2)).

Any amount deductible by a foreign subsidiary under this subsection shall be deductible for its taxable year with or within which the taxable year of such domestic corporation ends.

(e) **Treatment as Employee Under Related Provisions.**—An individual who is treated as an employee of a domestic corporation under subsection (a) shall also be treated as an employee of such domestic corporation, with respect to the plan described in subsection (a)(2), for purposes of applying the following provisions of this title:

(1) Section 72(d) (relating to employees' annuities).

(2) Section 72(f) (relating to special rules for computing employees' contributions).

(3) Section 101(b) (relating to employees' death benefits).

(4) Section 2039 (relating to annuities).

(5) Section 2517 (relating to certain annuities under qualified plans).

SEC. 407. CERTAIN EMPLOYEES OF DOMESTIC SUBSIDIARIES ENGAGED IN BUSINESS OUTSIDE THE UNITED STATES.

(a) **Treatment as Employees of Domestic Parent Corporation.—**

(1) **In general.**—For purpose of applying this part with respect to a pension, profit-sharing, or stock bonus plan described in section 401(a), an annuity plan described in section 403(a), or a bond purchase plan described in section 405(a), of a domestic parent corporation, an individual who is a citizen of the United States and who is an employee of a domestic subsidiary (within the meaning of paragraph (2)) of such domestic parent corporation shall be treated as an employee of such domestic parent corporation, if—

(A) the plan of such domestic parent corporation expressly provides for contributions or benefits for individuals who are citizens of the United States and who are employees of its domestic subsidiaries; and

(B) contributions under a funded plan of deferred compensation (whether or not a plan described in section 401(a), 403(a), or

405(a)) are not provided by any other person with respect to the remuneration paid to such individual by the domestic subsidiary.

(2) **Definitions.**—For purposes of this section—

(A) Domestic subsidiary.—A corporation shall be treated as a domestic subsidiary for any taxable year only if—

(i) such corporation is a domestic corporation 80 percent or more of the outstanding voting stock of which is owned by another domestic corporation;

(ii) 95 percent or more of its gross income for the three-year period immediately preceding the close of its taxable year which ends on or before the close of the taxable year of such other domestic corporation (or for such part of such period during which the corporation was in existence) was derived from sources without the United States; and

(iii) 90 percent or more of its gross income for such period (or such part) was derived from the active conduct of a trade or business.

If for the period (or part thereof) referred to in clauses (ii) and (iii) such corporation has no gross income, the provisions of clauses (ii) and (iii) shall be treated as satisfied if it is reasonable to anticipate that, with respect to the first taxable year thereafter for which such corporation has gross income, the provisions of such clauses will be satisfied.

(B) Domestic parent corporation.—The domestic parent corporation of any domestic subsidiary is the domestic corporation which owns 80 percent or more of the outstanding voting stock of such domestic subsidiary.

(b) **Special Rules for Application of Section 401(a).**—

(1) **Nondiscrimination requirements.**—For purposes of applying section 401(a)(4) and section 410(b) (without regard to paragraph (1)(A) thereof) with respect to an individual who is treated as an employee of a domestic parent corporation under subsection (a)—

(A) if such individual is an officer, shareholder, or person whose principal duties consist in supervising the work of other employees of a domestic subsidiary, he shall be treated as having such capacity with respect to such domestic parent corporation; and

(B) the determination of whether such individual is a highly compensated employee shall be made by treating such individual's total compensation (determined with the application of paragraph (2) of this subsection) as compensation paid by such domestic parent corporation and by determining such individual's status with regard to such domestic parent corporation.

(2) **Determination of compensation.**—For purposes of applying paragraph (5) of section 401(a) with respect to an individual who is treated as an employee of a domestic parent corporation under subsection (a), the total compensation of such individual shall be the remuneration paid to such individual by the domestic subsidiary which would constitute his total compensation if his services had been performed for such domestic parent corporation, and the basic or regular rate of compensation of such individual shall be determined under regulations prescribed by the Secretary.

(c) **Termination of Status as Deemed Employee Not To Be Treated as Separation From Service for Purposes of Capital Gain Provisions and Limitation of Tax.**—For purposes of applying subsections (a)(2) and (e) of section 402, and section 403(a)(2) with respect to an individual who is treated as an employee of a domestic parent corporation under subsection (a), such individual shall not be considered as separated from the service of such domestic parent corporation solely by reason of the fact that—

(1) the corporation for which such individual is an employee ceases, for any taxable year, to be a domestic subsidiary within the meaning of subsection (a)(2)(A),

(2) such individual ceases to be an employee of a domestic subsidiary of such domestic parent corporation, if he becomes an employee of another corporation controlled by such domestic parent corporation, or

(3) the provision of the plan described in subsection (a)(1)(A) is terminated.

(d) **Deductibility of Contributions.**—For purposes of applying sections 404 and 405(c) with respect to contributions made to or under a pension, profit-sharing, stock

IRC EXCERPTS

bonus, annuity, or bond purchase plan by a domestic parent corporation, or by another corporation which is entitled to deduct its contributions under section 404(a)(3)(B), on behalf of an individual who is treated as an employee of such domestic corporation under subsection (a)—

(1) except as provided in paragraph (2), no deduction shall be allowed to such domestic parent corporation or to any other corporation which is entitled to deduct its contributions under such sections,

(2) there shall be allowed as a deduction to the domestic subsidiary of which such individual is an employee an amount equal to the amount which (but for paragraph (1)) would be deductible under section 404 (or section 405(c)) by the domestic parent corporation if he were an employee of the domestic parent corporation, and

(3) any reference to compensation shall be considered to be a reference to the total compensation of such individual (determined with the application of subsection (b)(2)).

Any amount deductible by a domestic subsidiary under this subsection shall be deductible for its taxable year with or within which the taxable year of such domestic parent corporation ends.

(e) Treatment as Employee Under Related Provisions.—An individual who is treated as an employee of a domestic parent corporation under subsection (a) shall also be treated as an employee of such domestic parent corporation, with respect to the plan described in subsection (a)(1)(A), for purposes of applying the following provisions of this title:

(1) Section 72(d) (relating to employees' annuities).

(2) Section 72(f) (relating to special rules for computing employees' contributions).

(3) Section 101(b) (relating to employees' death benefits).

(4) Section 2039 (relating to annuities).

(5) Section 2517 (relating to certain annuities under qualified plans).

SEC. 408. INDIVIDUAL RETIREMENT ACCOUNTS.

(a) Individual Retirement Account.—For purposes of this section, the term "individual retirement account" means a trust created or organized in the United States for the exclusive benefit of an individual or his beneficiaries, but only if the written governing instrument creating the trust meets the following requirements:

(1) Except in the case of a rollover contribution described in subsection (d)(3), in section 402(a)(5), 402(a)(7), 403(a)(4), 403(b)(8), 405(d)(3), or 409(b)(3)(C), no contribution will be accepted unless it is in cash, and contributions will not be accepted for the taxable year in excess of $2,000 on behalf of any individual.

(2) The trustee is a bank (as defined in subsection (n)) or such other person who demonstrates to the satisfaction of the Secretary that the manner in which such other person will administer the trust will be consistent with the requirements of this section.

(3) No part of the trust funds will be invested in life insurance contracts.

(4) The interest of an individual in the balance in his account is nonforfeitable.

(5) The assets of the trust will not be commingled with other property except in a common trust fund or common investment fund.

(6) The entire interest of an individual for whose benefit the trust is maintained will be distributed to him not later than the close of his taxable year in which he attains age 70½, or will be distributed, commencing before the close of such taxable year, in accordance with regulations prescribed by the Secretary, over—

(A) the life of such individual or the lives of such individual and his spouse, or

(B) a period not extending beyond the life expectancy of such individual or the life expectancy of such individual and his spouse.

*(7) If—

(A) an individual for whose benefit the trust is maintained dies before his entire interest has been distributed to him, or

(B) distribution has been commenced as provided in paragraph (6) to his surviving spouse and such surviving spouse dies before the entire interest has been distributed to such spouse,

the entire interest (or the remaining part of such interest if distribution thereof has commenced) will be distributed within 5

*[*Editor's Note:* Section 408(a)(7) applies in the case of individuals dying after Dec. 31, 1983.]

Code Sec. 408 (a) (7)

years after his death (or the death of the surviving spouse). The preceding sentence shall not apply if distributions over a term certain commenced before the death of the individual for whose benefit the trust was maintained and the term certain is for a period permitted under paragraph (6).

(b) Individual Retirement Annuity.—For purposes of this section, the term "individual retirement annuity" means an annuity contract, or an endowment contract (as determined under regulations prescribed by the Secretary), issued by an insurance company which meets the following requirements:

(1) The contract is not transferable by the owner.

(2) Under the Contract—

(A) the premiums are not fixed,

(B) the annual premium on behalf of any individual will not exceed $2,000, and

(C) any refund of premiums will be applied before the close of the calendar year following the year of the refund toward the payment of future premiums or the purchase of additional benefits.

(3) The entire interest of the owner will be distributed to him not later than the close of his taxable year in which he attains age 70½, or will be distributed, in accordance with regulations prescribed by the Secretary, over—

(A) the life of such owner or the lives of such owner and his spouse, or

(B) a period not extending beyond the life expectancy of such owner or the life expectancy of such owner and his spouse.

*(4) If—

(A) the owner dies before his entire interest has been distributed to him, or

(B) distribution has been commenced as provided in paragraph (3) to his surviving spouse and such surviving spouse dies before the entire interest has been distributed to such spouse,

the entire interest (or the remaining part of such interest if distribution thereof has commenced) will be distributed within 5 years after his death (or the death of his surviving spouse). The preceding sentence shall not apply if distributions over a term certain commenced before the death of the owner and the term certain is for a period permitted under paragraph (3).

(5) The entire interest of the owner is nonforfeitable.

Such term does not include such an annuity contract for any taxable year of the owner in which it is disqualified on the application of subsection (e) or for any subsequent taxable year. For purposes of this subsection, no contract shall be treated as an endowment contract if it matures later than the taxable year in which the individual in whose name such contract is purchased attains age 70½; if it is not for the exclusive benefit of the individual in whose name it is purchased or his beneficiaries; or if the aggregate annual premiums under all such contracts purchased in the name of such individual for any taxable year exceed $2,000.

(c) Accounts Established by Employers and Certain Associations of Employees.—A trust created or organized in the United States by an employer for the exclusive benefit of his employees or their beneficiaries, or by an association of employees (which may include employees within the meaning of section 401(c)(1)) for the exclusive benefit of its members or their beneficiaries, shall be treated as an individual retirement account (described in subsection (a)), but only if the written governing instrument creating the trust meets the following requirements:

(1) The trust satisfies the requirements of paragraphs (1) through (7) of subsection (a).

(2) There is a separate accounting for the interest of each employee or member (or spouse of an employee or member).

The assets of the trust may be held in a common fund for the account of all individuals who have an interest in the trust.

(d) Tax Treatment of Distributions.—

(1) In general.—Except as otherwise provided in this subsection, any amount paid or distributed out of an individual retirement account or under an individual retirement annuity shall be included in gross income by the payee or distributee, as the case may be, for the taxable year in which the payment or distribution is received. Notwithstanding any other provision of this title (including chapters 11 and 12), the basis any person in such an account of annuity is zero.

*[*Editor's Note:* Section 408(b)(4) applies in the case of individuals dying after Dec. 31, 1983.]

Code Sec. 408 (b)

(2) Distributions of annuity contracts.—Paragraph (1) does not apply to any annuity contract which meets the requirements of paragraphs (1), (3), (4), and (5) of subsection (b) and which is distributed from an individual retirement account. Section 72 applies to any such annuity contract, and for purposes of section 72 the investment in such contract is zero.

(3) Rollover contribution.—An amount is described in this paragraph as a rollover contribution if it meets the requirements of subparagraphs (A) and (B).

(A) In general.—Paragraph (1) does not apply to any amount paid or distributed out of an individual retirement account or individual retirement annuity to the individual for whose benefit the account or annuity is maintained if—

(i) the entire amount received (including money and any other property) is paid into an individual retirement account or individual retirement annuity (other than an endowment contract) or retirement bond for the benefit of such individual not later than the 60th day after the day on which he receives the payment or distribution;

(ii) the entire amount received (including money and any other property) represents the entire amount in the account or the entire value of the annuity and no amount in the account and no part of the value of the annuity is attributable to any source other than a rollover contribution from an employee's trust described in section 401(a) which is exempt from tax under section 501(a) (other than a trust forming part of a plan under which the individual was an employee within the meaning of section 401(c)(1) at the time contributions were made on his behalf under the plan), or an annuity plan described in section 403(a), (other than a plan under which the individual was an employee within the meaning of section 401(c)(1) at the time contributions were made on his behalf under the plan) and any earnings on such sums and the entire amount thereof is paid into another such trust (for the benefit of such individual) or annuity plan not later than the 60th day on which he receives the payment or distribution; or

(iii)(I) the entire amount received (including money and other property) represents the entire interest in the account or the entire value of the annuity,

(II) no amount in the account and no part of the value of the annuity is attributable to any source other than a rollover contribution from an annuity contract described in section 403(b) and any earnings on such rollover, and

(III) the entire amount thereof is paid into another annuity contract described in section 403(b) (for the benefit of such individual) not later than the 60th day after he receives the payment or distribution.

(B) Limitation.—This paragraph does not apply to any amount described in subparagraph (A)(i) received by an individual from an individual retirement account or individual retirement annuity if at any time during the 1-year period ending on the day of such receipt such individual received any other amount described in that subparagraph from an individual retirement account, individual retirement annuity, or a retirement bond which was not includible in his gross income because of the application of this paragraph. Clause (ii) of subparagraph (A) shall not apply to any amount paid or distributed out of an individual retirement account or an individual retirement annuity to which an amount was contributed which was treated as a rollover contribution by section 402(a)(7) (or in the case of an individual retirement annuity, such section as made applicable by section 403(a)(4)(B)).

*(C) Denial of rollover treatment for inherited accounts, etc.—

(i) In general.—In the case of an inherited individual retirement account or individual retirement annuity—

(I) this paragraph shall not apply to any amount received by an individual from such an account or annuity (and no amount transferred from such account or annuity to another individual retirement account or annuity shall be excluded from gross income by reason of such transfer), and

(II) such inherited account or annuity shall not be treated as an individual retirement account or annuity for purposes of determining whether any other amount is a rollover contribution.

(ii) Inherited individual retirement account or annuity.—An individual retirement account or individual retirement annuity shall be treated as inherited if—

Code Sec. 408 (d) (3) (C)

(I) the individual for whose benefit the account or annuity is maintained acquired such account by reason of the death of another individual, and

(II) such individual was not the surviving spouse of such other individual.

*(C) Partial rollovers permitted.—

(i) In general.—If any amount paid or distributed out of an individual retirement account or individual retirement annuity would meet the requirements of subparagraph (A) but for the fact that the entire amount was not paid into an eligible plan as required by clause (i), (ii), or (iii) of subparagraph (A), such amount shall be treated as meeting the requirements of subparagraph (A) to the extent it is paid into an eligible plan referred to in such clause not later than the 60th day referred to in such clause.

(ii) Eligible plan.—For purposes of clause (i), the term 'eligible plan' means any account, annuity, bond, contract, or plan referred to in subparagraph (A).

(4) Excess contributions returned before due date of return.—Paragraph (1) does not apply to the distribution of any contribution paid during a taxable year to an individual retirement account or for an individual retirement annuity to the extent that such contribution exceeds the amount allowable as a deduction under section 219 if—

(A) such distribution is received on or before the day prescribed by law (including extensions of time) for filing such individual's return for such taxable year,

(B) no deduction is allowed under section 219 with respect to such excess contribution, and

(C) such distribution is accompanied by the amount of net income attributable to such excess contribution.

In the case of such a distribution, for purposes of section 61, any net income described in subparagraph (C) shall be deemed to have been earned and receivable in the taxable year in which such excess contribution is made.

(5) Certain distributions of excess contributions after due date for taxable year.—

(A) In general.—In the case of any individual, if the aggregate contributions (other than rollover contributions) paid for any taxable year to an individual retirement account or for an individual retirement annuity do not exceed $2,250, paragraph (1) shall not apply to the distribution of any such contribution to the extent that such contribution exceeds the amount allowable as a deduction under section 219 for the taxable year for which the contribution was paid—

(i) if such distribution is received after the date described in paragraph (4),

(ii) but only to the extent that no deduction has been allowed under section 219 with respect to such excess contribution.

If employer contributions on behalf of the individual are paid for the taxable year to a simplified employee pension, the dollar limitation of the preceding sentence shall be increased by the lesser of the amount of such contributions or $15,000.

(B) Excess rollover contributions attributable to erroneous information.—If—

(i) the taxpayer reasonably relies on information supplied pursuant to subtitle F for determining the amount of a rollover contribution, but

(ii) the information was erroneous, subparagraph (A) shall be applied by increasing the dollar limit set forth therein by that portion of the excess contribution which was attributable to such information.

(6) Transfer of account incident to divorce.—The transfer of an individual's interest in an individual retirement account, individual retirement annuity, or retirement bond to his former spouse under a divorce decree or under a written instrument incident to such divorce is not to be considered a taxable transfer made by such individual notwithstanding any other provision of this subtitle, and such interest at the time of the transfer is to be treated as an individual

---

*[Editor's Note: Paragraph 408(d)(3)(C), on denial of rollover treatment, was added by section 243(b) of TEFRA (PL 97-248). It is effective for taxable years beginning after Dec. 31, 1983. Paragraph 408(d)(3)(C), on partial rollovers, was added by section 335 of TEFRA. It is effective for distributions made after Dec. 31, 1982, in taxable years ending after that date.

Code Sec. 408 (d) (4)

retirement account of such spouse, and not of such individual. Thereafter such account, annuity, or bond for purposes of this subtitle is to be treated as maintained for the benefit of such spouse.

(e) Tax Treatment of Accounts and Annuities.—

(1) Exemption from tax.—Any individual retirement account is exempt from taxation under this subtitle unless such account has ceased to be an individual retirement account by reason of paragraph (2) or (3). Notwithstanding the preceding sentence, any such account is subject to the taxes imposed by section 511 (relating to imposition of tax on unrelated business income of charitable, etc. organizations).

(2) Loss of exemption of account where employee engages in prohibited transaction.—

(A) In general.—If, during any taxable year of the individual for whose benefit any individual retirement account is established, that individual or his beneficiary engages in any transaction prohibited by section 4975 with respect to such account, such account ceases to be an individual retirement account as of the first day of such taxable year. For purposes of this paragraph—

(i) the individual for whose benefit any account was established is treated as the creator of such account, and

(ii) the separate account for any individual within an individual retirement account maintained by an employer or association of employees is treated as a separate individual retirement account.

(B) Account treated as distributing all its assets.—In any case in which any account ceases to be an individual retirement account by reason of subparagraph (A) as of the first day of any taxable year, paragraph (1) of subsection (d) applies as if there were a distribution on such first day in an amount equal to the fair market value (on such first day) of all assets in the account (on such first day).

(3) Effect of borrowing on annuity contract.—If during any taxable year the owner of an individual retirement annuity borrows any money under or by use of such contract, the contract ceases to be an individual retirement annuity as of the first day of such taxable year. Such owner shall include in gross income for such year an amount equal to the fair market value of such contract as of such first day.

(4) Effect of pledging account as security.—If, during any taxable year of the individual for whose benefit an individual retirement account is established, that individual uses the account or any portion thereof as security for a loan, the portion so used is treated as distributed to that individual.

(5) Purchase of endowment contract by individual retirement account.—If the assets of an individual retirement account or any part of such assets are used to purchase an endowment contract for the benefit of the individual for whose benefit the account is established—

(A) to the extent that the amount of the assets involved in the purchase are not attributable to the purchase of life insurance, the purchase is treated as a rollover contribution described in subsection (d)(3), and

(B) to the extent that the amount of the assets involved in the purchase are attributable to the purchase of life, health, accident, or other insurance, such amounts are treated as distributed to that individual (but the provisions of subsection (f) do not apply).

(6) Commingling individual retirement account amounts in certain common trust funds and common investment funds.—Any common trust fund or common investment fund of individual retirement account assets which is exempt from taxation under this subtitle does not cease to be exempt on account of the participation or inclusion of assets of a trust exempt from taxation under section 501(a) which is described in section 401(a).

(f) Additional Tax on Certain Amounts Included in Gross Income Before Age 59½.—

(1) Early distributions from an individual retirement account, etc.—If a distribution from an individual retirement account or under an individual retirement annuity to the individual for whose benefit such account or annuity was established is made before such individual attains age 59½, his tax under this chapter for the taxable year in which such distribution is

Code Sec. 408 (f)

received shall be increased by an amount equal to 10 percent of the amount of the distribution which is includible in his gross income for such taxable year.

(2) Disqualification cases.—If an amount is includible in gross income for a taxable year under subsection (e) and the taxpayer has not attained age 59½ before the beginning of such taxable year, his tax under this chapter for such taxable year shall be increased by an amount equal to 10 percent of such amount so required to be included in his gross income.

(3) Disability cases.—Paragraphs (1) and (2) do not apply if the amount paid or distributed, or the disqualification of the account or annuity under subsection (e), is attributable to the taxpayer becoming disabled within the meaning of section 72(m)(7).

(g) Community Property Laws.—This section shall be applied without regard to any community property laws.

(h) Custodial Accounts.—For purposes of this section, a custodial account shall be treated as a trust if the assets of such account are held by a bank (as defined in section 401(d)(1)) or another person who demonstrates, to the satisfaction of the Secretary, that the manner in which he will administer the account will be consistent with the requirements of this section, and if the custodial account would, except for the fact that it is not a trust, constitute an individual retirement account described in subsection (a). For purposes of this title, in the case of a custodial account treated as a trust by reason of the preceding sentence, the custodian of such account shall be treated as the trustee thereof.

(i) Reports.—The trustee of an individual retirement account and the issuer of an endowment contract described in subsection (b) or an individual retirement annuity shall make such reports regarding such account, contract, or annuity to the Secretary and to the individual for whom the account, contract, or annuity is, or is to be, maintained with respect to the contributions, distributions, and such other matters as the Secretary may require under regulations. The reports required by this subsection shall be filed at such time and in such manner and furnished to such individuals at such time and in such manner as may be required by those regulations.

(j) Increase in Maximum Limitations for Simplified Employee Pensions.—In the case of any simplified employee pension, subsections (a)(1) and (b)(2) of this section shall be applied by increasing the $2,000 amounts contained therein by the amount of the limitation in effect under section 415(c)(1)(A).

(k) Simplified Employee Pension Defined.—

(1) In general.—For purposes of this title, the term "simplified employee pension" means an individual retirement account or individual retirement annuity with respect to which the requirements of paragraphs (2), (3), (4), and (5) of this subsection are met.

(2) Participation requirements.—This paragraph is satisfied with respect to a simplified employee pension for a calendar year only if for such year the employer contributes to the simplified employee pension of each employee who—

(A) has attained age 25, and

(B) has performed service for the employer during at least 3 of the immediately preceding 5 calendar years. For purposes of this paragraph, there shall be excluded from consideration employees described in subparagraph (A) or (C) of section 410(b)(3).

(3) Contributions may not discriminate in favor of the highly compensated, etc.—

(A) In general.—The requirements of this paragraph are met with respect to a simplified employee pension for a calendar year if for such year the contributions made by the employer to simplified employee pensions for his employees do not discriminate in favor of any employee who is—

(i) an officer,
(ii) a shareholder,
(iii) a self-employed individual, or
(iv) highly compensated.

(B) Special rules.—For purposes of subparagraph (A)—

(i) there shall be excluded from consideration employees described in subparagraph (A) or (C) of section 410(b)(3), and

Code Sec. 408 (f) (2)

(ii) an individual shall be considered a shareholder if he owns (with the application of section 318) more than 10 percent of the value of the stock of the employer.

(C) Contributions must bear uniform relationship to total compensation.—For purposes of subparagraph (A), employer contributions to simplified employee pensions shall be considered discriminatory unless contributions thereto bear a uniform relationship to the total compensation (not in excess of the first $200,000) of each employee (other than an employee within the meaning of section 401(c)(1)) maintaining a simplified employee pension.

(D) Treatment of certain contributions and taxes.—Except as provided in this subparagraph, employer contributions do not meet the requirements of this paragraph unless such contributions meet the requirements of this paragraph without taking into account contributions or benefits under chapter 2 (relating to tax on self-employment income), chapter 21 (relating to Federal Insurance Contribution Act), title II of the Social Security Act, or any other Federal or State law. If the employer does not maintain an integrated plan at any time during the taxable year, taxes paid under section 3111 (relating to tax on employers) with respect to an employee may, for purposes of this paragraph, be taken into account as a contribution by the employer to an employee's simplified employee pension. If contributions are made to the simplified employee pension of an owner-employee, the preceding sentence shall not apply unless taxes paid by all such owner-employees under chapter 2, and the taxes which would be payable under chapter 2 by such owner-employees but for paragraphs (4) and (5) of section 1402(c), are taken into account as contributions by the employer on behalf of such owner-employees.

(E) Integrated plan defined.—For purposes of subparagraph (D), the term "integrated plan" means a plan which meets the requirements of section 401(a), 403(a), or 405(a) but would not meet such requirements if contributions or benefits under chapter 2 (relating to tax on self-employment income), chapter 21 (relating to Federal Insurance Contributions Act), title II of the Social Security Act, or any other Federal or State law were not taken into account.

(4) Withdrawals must be permitted.—A simplified employee pension meets the requirements of this paragraph only if—

(A) employer contributions thereto are not conditioned on the retention in such pension of any portion of the amount contributed, and

(B) there is no prohibition imposed by the employer on withdrawals from the simplified employee pension.

(5) Contributions must be made under written allocation formula.—The requirements of this paragraph are met with respect to a simplified employee pension only if employer contributions to such pension are determined under a definite written allocation formula which specifies—

(A) the requirements which an employee must satisfy to share in an allocation, and

(B) the manner in which the amount allocated is computed.

(6) Employer may not maintain plan to which section 401(j) applies.—[Repealed]

(7) Definitions.—For purposes of this subsection and subsection (1)—

(A) Employee, employer, or owner-employee.—The terms "employee," "employer," and "owner-employee" shall have the respective meanings given such terms by section 401(c).

(B) Compensation.—The term "compensation" means, in the case of an employee within the meaning of section 401(c)(1), earned income within the meaning of section 401(c)(2).

(l) Simplified Employer Reports.—An employer who makes a contribution on behalf of an employee to a simplified employee pension shall provide such simplified reports with respect to such contributions as the Secretary may require by regulations. The reports required by this subsection shall be filed at such time and in such manner, and information with respect to such contributions shall be furnished to the employee at such time and in such manner, as may be required by regulations.

(m) Investment in Collectibles Treated as Distributions.—

Code Sec. 408 (m)

(1) In general.—The acquisition by an individual retirement account or by an individually-directed account under a plan described in section 401(a) of any collectible shall be treated (for purposes of this section and section 402) as a distribution from such account in an amount equal to the cost to such account of such collectible.

(2) Collectible defined.—For purposes of this subsection, the term "collectible" means—

(A) any work of art,
(B) any rug or antique,
(C) any metal or gem,
(D) any stamp or coin,
(E) any alcoholic beverage, or
(F) any other tangible personal property specified by the Secretary for purposes of this subsection.

(n) Bank.—For purposes of subsection (a)(2), the term 'bank' means—

(1) any bank (as defined in section 581),
(2) an insured credit union (within the meaning of section 101(6) of the Federal Credit Union Act), and
(3) a corporation which, under the laws of the State of its incorporation, is subject to supervision and examination by the Commissioner of Banking or other officer of such State in charge of the administration of the banking laws of such State.

(o) Cross References.—

(1) For tax on excess contributions in individual retirement accounts or annuities, see section 4973.

(2) For tax on certain accumulations in individual retirement accounts or annuities, see section 4974.

SEC. 409. RETIREMENT BONDS.

(a) Retirement Bond.—For purposes of this section and section 219(a), the term "retirement bond" means a bond issued under the Second Liberty Bond Act, as amended, which by its terms, or by regulations prescribed by the Secretary under such Act—

(1) provides for payment of interest, or investment yield, only on redemption;
(2) provides that no interest, or investment yield, is payable if the bond is redeemed within 12 months after the date of its issuance;
(3) provides that it ceases to bear interest, or provide investment yield on the earlier of—
   (A) the date on which the individual in whose name it is purchased (hereinafter in this section referred to as the "registered owner") attains age 70½; or
   (B) 5 years after the date on which the registered owner dies, but not later than the date on which he would have attained the age 70½ had he lived;
(4) provides that, except in the case of a rollover contribution described in subsection (b)(3)(C) or in section 402(a)(5), 402(a)(7), 403(a)(4), 403(b)(8), or 408(d)(3) the registered owner may not contribute on behalf of any individual for the purchase of such bonds in excess of $2,000 for any taxable year; and
(5) is not transferable.

(b) Income Tax Treatment of Bonds.—

(1) In general.—Except as otherwise provided in this subsection, on the redemption of a retirement bond the entire proceeds shall be included in the gross income of the taxpayer entitled to the proceeds on redemption. If the registered owner has not tendered it for redemption before the close of the taxable year in which he attains age 70½, such individual shall include in his gross income for such taxable year the amount of proceeds he would have received if the bond had been redeemed at age 70½. The provisions of section 72 (relating to annuities) and section 1232 (relating to bonds and other evidences of indebtedness) shall not apply to a retirement bond.

(2) Basis.—The basis of a retirement bond is zero.

(3) Exceptions.—

(A) Redemption within 12 months.—If a retirement bond is redeemed within 12 months after the date of its issuance, the proceeds are excluded from gross income if no deduction is allowed under section 219 on account of the purchase of such bond. The preceding sentence shall not apply to the extent that the bond was purchased with a rollover contribution described in subparagraph (C) of this paragraph or in section 402(a)(5), 402(a)(7), 403(a)(4), 403(b)(8), 405(b)(3), or 408(d)(3).

(B) Redemption after age 70½.—If a retirement bond is redeemed after the close of the taxable year in which the registered owner attains age 70½, the proceeds from the redemption of the bond are excluded from the gross income of the registered owner to the extent that such proceeds were includible in his gross income for such taxable year.

(C) Rollover into an individual retirement account or annuity or a qualified plan.—If a retirement bond is redeemed at any time before the close of the taxable year in which the registered owner attains age 70½, and the registered owner transfers the entire amount of the proceeds from the redemption of the bond to an individual retirement account described in section 408(a) or to an individual retirement annuity described in section 408(b) (other than an endowment contract) which is maintained for the benefit of the registered owner of the bond, or to an employees' trust described in section 401(a) which is exempt from tax under section 501(a), an annuity plan described in section 403(a), or an annuity contract described in section 403(b) for the benefit of the registered owner, on or before the 60th day after the day on which he received the proceeds of such redemption, then the proceeds shall be excluded from gross income and the transfer shall be treated as a rollover contribution described in section 408(d)(3). This subparagraph does not apply in the case of a transfer to such an employees' trust or such an annuity plan unless no part of the value of such proceeds is attributable to any source other than a rollover contribution from such an employees' trust or annuity plan (other than an annuity plan or a trust forming part of a plan under which the individual was an employee within the meaning of section 401(c)(1) at the time contributions were made on his behalf under the plan). This subparagraph does not apply in the case of a transfer to an annuity contract described in section 403(b) unless no part of the value of such proceeds is attributable to any source other than a rollover contribution from such an annuity contract. This subparagraph shall not apply to any retirement bond if such bond is acquired by the owner by reason of the death of another individual and the owner was not the surviving spouse of such other individual.

*(D) partial rollovers permitted.—Rules similar to the rules of section 408(d)(3)(C) shall apply for purposes of subparagraph (C).

(c) Additional Tax on Certain Redemptions Before Age 59½.—

(1) **Early redemption of bond.**—If a retirement bond is redeemed by the registered owner before he attains age 59½, his tax under this chapter for the taxable year in which the bond is redeemed shall be increased by an amount equal to 10 percent of the amount of the proceeds of the redemption includible in his gross income for the taxable year.

(2) **Disability cases.**—Paragraph (1) does not apply for any taxable year during which the retirement bond is redeemed if, for that taxable year, the registered owner is disabled within the meaning of section 72(m)(7).

(3) **Redemption within one year.**—Paragraph (1) does not apply if the registered owner tenders the bond for redemption within 12 months after the date of its issuance.

SEC. 409A. QUALIFICATIONS FOR TAX CREDIT EMPLOYEE STOCK OWNERSHIP PLANS.

(a) **Tax Credit Employee Stock Ownership Plan Defined.**—Except as otherwise provided in this title, for purposes of this title, the term "tax credit employee stock ownership plan" means a defined contribution plan which—

(1) meets the requirements of section 401(a),

(2) is designed to invest primarily in employer securities, and

(3) meets the requirements of subsections (b), (c), (d), (e), (f), (g), and (h) of this section.

**(b) Required Allocation of Employer Securities.—

---

*[Editor's Note: The last sentence of section 409(b)(3)(C) is effective for taxable years beginning after Dec. 31, 1982. Section 409(b)(3)(D) applies to distributions made after Dec. 31, 1982, in taxable years ending after that date.]

**[Editor's Note: Sections 409A(b), (g), (i)(1)(A), (m), and (n) are effective for taxable years ending after Dec. 31, 1982.]

Code Sec. 409A (b)

(1) **In general.**—A plan meets the requirements of this subsection if—

(A) the plan provides for the allocation for the plan year of all employer securities transferred to it or purchased by it (because of the requirements of section 48(n)(1)(A) or 44(G)(c)(1)(B)) to the accounts of all participants who are entitled to share in such allocation, and

(B) for the plan year the allocation to each participant so entitled is an amount which bears substantially the same proportion to the amount of all such securities allocated to all such participants in the plan for that year as the amount of compensation paid to such participant during that year bears to the compensation paid to all such participants during that year.

(2) **Compensation in excess of $100,000 disregarded.**—For purposes of paragraph (1), compensation of any participant in excess of the first $100,000 per year shall be disregarded.

(3) **Determination of compensation.**—For purposes of this subsection, the amount of compensation paid to a participant for any period is the amount of such participant's compensation (within the meaning of section 415(c)(3)) for such period.

(4) **Suspension of allocation in certain cases.**—Notwithstanding paragraph (1), the allocation to the account of any participant which is attributable to the basic employee plan credit or the credit allowed under section 44G (relating to the employee stock ownership credit) may be extended over whatever period may be necessary to comply with the requirements of section 415.

(c) **Participants Must Have Nonforfeitable Rights.**—A plan meets the requirements of this subsection only if it provides that each participant has a nonforfeitable right to any employer security allocated to his account.

(d) **Employer Securities Must Stay in the Plan.**—A plan meets the requirements of this subsection only if it provides that no employer security allocated to a participant's account under subsection (b) (or allocated to a participant's account in connection with matched employer and employee contributions) may be distributed from that account before the end of the 84th month beginning after the month in which the security is allocated to the account. To the extent provided in the plan, the preceding sentence shall not apply in the case of—

(1) death, disability, or separation from service;

(2) a transfer of a participant to the employment of an acquiring employer from the employment of the selling corporation in the case of a sale to the acquiring corporation of substantially all of the assets used by the selling corporation in a trade or business conducted by the selling corporation, or

(3) with respect to the stock of a selling corporation, a disposition of such selling corporation's interest in a subsidiary when the participant continues employment with such subsidiary.

(e) **Voting Rights.**—

(1) **In general.**—A plan meets the requirements of this subsection if it meets the requirements of paragraph (2) or (3), whichever is applicable.

(2) **Requirements where employer has a registration-type class of securities.**—If the employer has a registration-type class of securities, the plan meets the requirements of this paragraph only if each participant in the plan is entitled to direct the plan as to the manner in which employer securities which are entitled to vote and are allocated to the account of such participant are to be voted.

(3) **Requirement for other employers.**—If the employer does not have a registration-type class of securities, the plan meets the requirements of this paragraph only if each participant in the plan is entitled to direct the plan as to the manner in which voting rights under employer securities which are allocated to the account of such participant are to be exercised with respect to a corporate matter which (by law or charter) must be decided by more than a majority vote of outstanding common shares voted.

(4) **Registration-type class of securities defined.**—For purposes of this subsection,

Code Sec. 409A (b) (1)

the term "registration-type class of securities" means—

(A) a class of securities required to be registered under section 12 of the Securities Exchange Act of 1934, and

(B) a class of securities which would be required to be so registered except for the exemption from registration provided in subsection (g)(2)(H) of such section 12.

(f) Plan Must Be Established Before Employer's Due Date.—

(1) In general.—A plan meets the requirements of this subsection only if it is established on or before the due date (including any extension of such date) for the filing of the employer's tax return for the first taxable year of the employer for which an employee plan credit is claimed by the employer with respect to the plan.

(2) Special rule for first year.—A plan which otherwise meets the requirements of this section shall not be considered to have failed to meet the requirements of section 401(a) merely because it was not established by the close of the first taxable year of the employer for which an employee plan credit is claimed by the employer with respect to the plan.

(g) Transferred Amounts Must Stay in Plan Even Though Investment Credit is Redetermined or Recaptured.—A plan meets the requirement of this subsection only if it provides that amounts which are transferred to the plan (because of the requirements of section 48(n)(1) or 44G(c)(1)(B)) shall remain in the plan (and, if allocated under the plan, shall remain so allocated) even though part or all of the employee plan credit or the credit allowed under section 44G (relating to employee stock ownership credit) is recaptured or redetermined.

(h) Right to Demand Employer Securities; Put Option.—

(1) In general.—A plan meets the requirements of this subsection if a participant who is entitled to a distribution from the plan—

(A) has a right to demand that his benefits be distributed in the form of employer securities, and

(B) if the employer securities are not readily tradable on an established market, has a right to require that the employer repurchase employer securities under a fair valuation formula.

(2) Plan may distribute cash in certain cases.—A plan which otherwise meets the requirements of this subsection or of section 4975(e)(7) shall not be considered to have failed to meet the requirements of section 401(a) merely because under the plan the benefits may be distributed in cash or in the form of employer securities. In the case of an employer whose charter or bylaws restrict the ownership of substantially all outstanding employer securities to employees or to a trust described in section 401(a), a plan which otherwise meets the requirements of this subsection or section 4975(e)(7) shall not be considered to have failed to meet the requirements of this subsection or of section 401(a) merely because it does not permit a participant to exercise the right described in paragraph (1)(A) if such plan provides that participants entitled to a distribution from the plan shall have a right to receive such distribution in cash.

(3) Special rule for banks.—In the case of a plan established and maintained by a bank (as defined in section 581) which is prohibited by law from redeeming or purchasing its own securities, the requirements of paragraph (1)(B) shall not apply if the plan provides that participants entitled to a distribution from the plan shall have a right to receive a distribution in cash.

(4) Put option period.—An employer shall be deemed to satisfy the requirements of paragraph (1)(B) if it provides a put option for a period of at least 60 days following the date of distribution of stock of the employer and, if the put option is not exercised within such 60-day period, for an additional period of at least 60 days in the following plan year (as provided in regulations promulgated by the Secretary).

(i) Reimbursement for Expenses of Establishing and Administering Plan.—A plan which otherwise meets the requirements of this section shall not be treated as failing to meet such requirements merely because it provides that—

(1) Expenses of establishing plan.—As reimbursement for the expenses of establishing the plan, the employer may withhold from amounts due the plan for the taxable year for which the plan is established (or the plan may pay) so much of the amounts paid or incurred in connection with the establishment of the plan as does not exceed the sum of—

(A) 10 percent of the first $100,000 which the employer is required to transfer to the plan for that taxable year under section 48(n)(1) or 44(G)(c)(1)(B), and

(B) 5 percent of any amount so required to be transferred in excess of the first $100,000; and

(2) Administrative expenses.—As reimbursement for the expenses of administering the plan, the employer may withhold from amounts due the plan (or the plan may pay) so much of the amounts paid or incurred during the taxable year as expenses of administering the plan as does not exceed the lesser of—

(A) the sum of—

(i) 10 percent of the first $100,000 of the dividends paid to the plan with respect to stock of the employer during the plan year ending with or within the employer's taxable year, and

(ii) 5 percent of the amount of such dividends in excess of $100,000 or

(B) $100,000.

(j) Conditional Contributions to the Plan.—A plan which otherwise meets the requirements of this section shall not be treated as failing to satisfy such requirements (or as failing to satisfy the requirements of section 401(a) of this title or of section 403(c)(1) of the Employee Retirement Income Security Act of 1974) merely because of the return of a contribution (or a provision permitting such a return) if—

(1) the contribution to the plan is conditioned on a determination by the Secretary that such plan meets the requirements of this section,

(2) the application for a determination described in paragraph (1) is filed with the Secretary not later than 90 days after the date on which an employee plan credit is claimed, and

(3) the contribution is returned within 1 year after the date on which the Secretary issues notice to the employer that such plan does not satisfy the requirements of this section.

(k) Requirements Relating to Certain Withdrawals.—Notwithstanding any other law or rule of law—

(1) the withdrawal from a plan which otherwise meets the requirements of this section by the employer of an amount contributed for purposes of the matching employee plan credit shall not be considered to make the benefits forfeitable, and

(2) the plan shall not, by reason of such withdrawal, fail to be for the exclusive benefit of participants or their beneficiaries,

if the withdrawn amounts were not matched by employee contributions or were in excess of the limitations of section 415. Any withdrawal described in the preceding sentence shall not be considered to violate the provisions of section 403(c)(1) of the Employee Retirement Income Security Act of 1974.

(l) Employer Securities Defined.—For purposes of this section—

(1) In general.—The term "employer securities" means common stock issued by the employer (or by a corporation which is a member of the same controlled group) which is readily tradable on an established securities market.

(2) Special rule where there is no readily tradable common stock.—If there is no common stock which meets the requirements of paragraph (1), the term "employer securities" means common stock issued by the employer (or by a corporation which is a member of the same controlled group) having a combination of voting power and dividend rights equal to or in excess of—

(A) that class of common stock of the employer (or of any other such corporation) having the greatest voting power, and

(B) that class of common stock of the employer (or of any other such corporation) having the greatest dividend rights.

(3) Preferred stock may be issued in certain cases.—Noncallable preferred stock shall be treated as employer securities if such stock is convertible at any time into stock which meets the requirements of paragraph (1) or (2) (whichever is applicable) and if such conversion is at a conversion price which (as of the date of the acquisition by the tax credit employee stock ownership plan) is reasonable. For purposes of the preceding sentence, under regulations prescribed by the Secretary, preferred stock shall be treated as noncallable if after the call there will be a reasonable opportunity for a conversion which meets the requirements of the preceding sentence.

(4) **Application to controlled group of corporations.**—

(A) In general.—For purposes of this subsection, the term "controlled group of corporations" has the meaning given to such term by section 1563(a) (determined without regard to subsections (a)(4) and (e)(3)(C) of section 1563).

(B) Where common parent owns at least 50 percent of first tier subsidiary.—For purposes of subparagraph (A), if the common parent owns directly stock possessing at least 50 percent of the voting power of all classes of stock and at least 50 percent of each class of nonvoting stock in a first tier subsidiary, such subsidiary (and all other corporations below it in the chain which would meet the 80 percent test of section 1563(a) if the first tier subsidiary were the common parent) shall be treated as includible corporations.

(C) Where common parent owns 100 percent of first tier subsidiary.—For purposes of subparagraph (A), if the common parent owns directly stock possessing all of the voting power of all classes of stock and all of the nonvoting stock, in a first tier subsidiary, and if the first tier subsidiary owns directly stock possessing at least 50 percent of the voting power of all classes of stock, and at least 50 percent of each class of nonvoting stock, in a second tier subsidiary of the common parent, such second tier subsidiary (and all other corporations below it in the chain which would meet the 80 percent test of section 1563(a) if the second tier subsidiary were the common parent) shall be treated as includible corporations.

(m) **Nonrecognition of Gain or Loss on Contribution of Employer Securities to Tax Credit Employee Stock Ownership Plan.**—No gain or loss shall be recognized to the taxpayer with respect to the transfer of employer securities to a tax credit employee stock ownership plan maintained by the taxpayer to the extent that such transfer is required under section 44G(c)(1)(B), or subparagraph (A) or (B) of section 48(n)(1).

(n) **Cross References.**—

(1) **For requirements for allowance of employee plan credit, see section 48(n).**

(2) **For assessable penalties for failure to meet requirements of this section, or for failure to make contributions required with respect to the allowance of an employee plan credit or employee stock ownership credit, see section 6699.**

(3) **For requirements for allowance of an employee stock ownership credit, see section 44G.**

Subpart B—Special Rules

Section
410. Minimum participation standards.
411. Minimum vesting standards.
412. Minimum funding standards.
413. Collectively bargained plans.
414. Definitions and special rules.
415. Limitations on benefits and contributions under qualified plans.
416. Special rules for top-heavy plans.

SEC. 410. MINIMUM PARTICIPATION STANDARDS.

(a) **Participation.**—

(1) **Minimum age and service conditions.**—

(A) General rule.—A trust shall not constitute a qualified trust under section 401(a) if the plan of which it is a part requires, as a condition of participation in the plan, that an employee complete a period of service with employer or employers maintaining the plan extending beyond the later of the following dates—

(i) the date on which the employee attains the age of 25; or

(ii) the date on which he completes 1 year of service.

(B) Special rules for certain plans.—

(i) In the case of any plan which provides that after not more than 3 years of service each participant has a right to 100 percent of his accrued benefit under the plan which is nonforfeitable (within the meaning of section 411) at the time such benefit accrues, clause (ii) of subparagraph (A) shall be applied by substituting "3 years of service" for "1 year of service."

(ii) In the case of any plan maintained exclusively for employees of an educational institution (as defined in section 170(b)(1)(A)(ii)) by an employer which is exempt from tax under section 501(a) which provides that each participant having at least 1 year of service has a right to 100 percent of his accrued benefit under the plan which is nonforfeitable (within the meaning of section 411) at the time such benefit accrues, clause (i) of subparagraph (A) shall be applied by substituting "30" for "25". This clause shall not apply to any plan to which clause (i) applies.

(2) Maximum age conditions.—A trust shall not constitute a qualified trust under section 401(a) if the plan of which it is a part excludes from participation (on the basis of age) employees who have attained a specified age, unless—

(A) the plan is a—

(i) defined benefit plan, or

(ii) target benefit plan (as defined under regulations prescribed by the Secretary), and

(B) such employees begin employment with the employer after they have attained a specified age which is not more than 5 years before the normal retirement age under the plan.

(3) Definition of year of service.—

(A) General rule.—For purposes of this subsection, the term "year of service" means a 12-month period during which the employee has not less than 1,000 hours of service. For purposes of this paragraph, computation of any 12-month period shall be made with reference to the date on which the employee's employment commenced, except that, under regulations prescribed by the Secretary of Labor, such computation may be made by reference to the first day of a plan year in the case of an employee who does not complete 1,000 hours of service during the 12-month period beginning on the date his employment commenced.

(B) Seasonal industries.—In the case of any seasonal industry where the customary period of employment is less than 1,000 hours during a calendar year, the term "year of service" shall be such period as may be determined under regulations prescribed by the Secretary of Labor.

(C) Hours of service.—For purposes of this subsection the term "hours of service" means a time of service determined under regulations prescribed by the Secretary of Labor.

(D) Maritime industries.—For purposes of this subsection, in the case of any maritime industry, 125 days of service shall be treated as 1,000 hours of service. The Secretary of Labor may prescribe regulations to carry out this subparagraph.

(4) Time of participation.—A plan shall be treated as not meeting the requirements of paragraph (1) unless it provides that any employee who has satisfied the minimum age and service requirements specified in such paragraph, and who is otherwise entitled to participate in the plan, commences participation in the plan no later than the earlier of—

(A) the first day of the first plan year beginning after the date on which such employee satisfied such requirements, or

(B) the date 6 months after the date on which he satisfied such requirements, unless such employee was separated from the service before the date referred to in subparagraph (A) or (B), whichever is applicable.

(5) Breaks in service.—

(A) General rule.—Except as otherwise provided in subparagraphs (B), (C), and (D), all years of service with the employer or employers maintaining the plan shall be taken into account in computing the period of service for purposes of paragraph (1).

(B) Employees under 3-year 100 percent vesting.—In the case of any employee who has any 1-year break in service (as defined in section 411(a)(6)(A)) under a plan to which the service requirements of clause (i) of paragraph (1)(B) apply, if such employee has not satisfied such requirements, service before such break shall not be required to be taken into account.

(C) 1-year break in service.—In computing an employee's period of service for purposes of paragraph (1) in the case of any participant who has any 1-year break in service (as defined in section 411(a)(6)(A)), service before such break shall not be required to be taken into account under the plan until he has completed a year of service (as defined in paragraph (3)) after his return.

Code Sec. 410 (a) (2)

(D) Nonvested participants.—In the case of a participant who does not have any nonforfeitable right to an accrued benefit derived from employer contributions, years of service with the employer or employers maintaining the plan before a break in service shall not be required to be taken into account in computing the period of service for purposes of paragraph (1) if the number of consecutive 1-year breaks in service equals or exceeds the aggregate number of such years of service before such break. Such aggregate number of years of service before such break shall be deemed not to include any years of service not required to be taken into account under this subparagraph by reason of any prior break in service.

(b) Eligibility.—

(1) In general.—A trust shall not constitute a qualified trust under section 401(a) unless the trust, or two or more trusts, or the trust or trusts and annuity plan or plans are designated by the employer as constituting parts of a plan intended to qualify under section 401(a) which benefits either—

(A) 70 percent or more of all employees, or 80 percent or more of all the employees who are eligible to benefit under the plan if 70 percent or more of all the employees are eligible to benefit under the plan, excluding in each case employees who have not satisfied the minimum age and service requirements, if any, prescribed by the plan as a condition of participation, or

(B) such employees as qualify under a classification set up by the employer and found by the Secretary not to be discriminatory in favor of employees who are officers, shareholders, or highly compensated.

(2) Special rule for certain plans.—A trust which is part of a tax credit employee stock ownership plan which is the only plan of an employer intended to qualify under section 401(a) shall not be treated as not a qualified trust under section 401(a) solely because it fails to meet the requirements of paragraph (1) if—

(A) it benefits 50 percent or more of all the employees who are eligible under the plan (excluding employees who have not satisfied the minimum age and service requirements, if any, prescribed by the plan as a condition of participation), and

(B) the sum of the amounts allocated to each participant's account for the year does not exceed 2 percent of the compensation of that participant for the year.

(3) Exclusion of certain employees.—For purposes of paragraphs (1) and (2), there shall be excluded from consideration—

(A) employees not included in the plan who are included in a unit of employees covered by an agreement which the Secretary of Labor finds to be a collective bargaining agreement between employee representatives and one or more employers, if there is evidence that retirement benefits were the subject of good faith bargaining between such employee representatives and such employer or employers,

(B) in the case of a trust established or maintained pursuant to an agreement which the Secretary of Labor finds to be a collective bargaining agreement between air pilots represented in accordance with title II of the Railway Labor Act and one or more employers, all employees not covered by such agreement, and

(C) employees who are nonresident aliens and who receive no earned income (within the meaning of section 911(d)(2)) from the employer which constitutes income from sources within the United States (within the meaning of section 861(a)(3)).

Subparagraph (B) shall not apply in the case of a plan which provides contributions or benefits for employees whose principal duties are not customarily performed aboard aircraft in flight.

(c) Application of Participation Standards to Certain Plans.—

(1) The provisions of this section (other than paragraph (2) of this subsection) shall not apply to—

(A) a governmental plan (within the meaning of section 414(d)),

(B) a church plan (within the meaning of section 414(e)) with respect to which the election provided by subsection (d) of this section has not been made,

(C) a plan which has not at any time after September 2, 1974 provided for employer contributions, and

(D) a plan established and maintained by a society, order, or association described in section 501(c)(8) or (9) if no part of the contributions to or under such plan are made by employers of participants in such plan.

Code Sec. 410 (c)

(2) A plan described in paragraph (1) shall be treated as meeting the requirements of this section, for purposes of section 401(a), if such plan meets the requirements of section 401(a)(3) as in effect on September 1, 1974.

(d) **Election by Church to Have Participation, Vesting, Funding, etc., Provisions Apply.—**

(1) **In general.**—If the church or convention or association of churches which maintains any church plan makes an election under this subsection (in such form and manner as the Secretary may by regulations prescribe), then the provisions of this title relating to participation, vesting, funding, etc. (as in effect from time to time) shall apply to such church plan as if such provisions did not contain an exclusion for church plans.

(2) **Election irrevocable.**—An election under this subsection with respect to any church plan shall be binding with respect to such plan, and, once made, shall be irrevocable.

SEC. 411. MINIMUM VESTING STANDARDS.

(a) **General Rule.**—A trust shall not constitute a qualified trust under section 401(a) unless the plan of which such trust is a part provides that an employee's right to his normal retirement benefit is nonforfeitable upon the attainment of normal retirement age (as defined in paragraph (8)) and in addition satisfies the requirements of paragraphs (1) and (2) of this subsection and the requirements of paragraph (2) of subsection (b), and in the case of a defined benefit plan, also satisfies the requirements of paragraph (1) of subsection (b).

(1) **Employee contributions.**—A plan satisfies the requirements of this paragraph if an employee's rights in his accrued benefit derived from his own contributions are nonforfeitable.

(2) **Employer contributions.**—A plan satisfies the requirements of this paragraph if it satisfies the requirements of subparagraph (A), (B), or (C).

(A) 10-year vesting.—A plan satisfies the requirements of this subparagraph if an employee who has at least 10 years of service has a nonforfeitable right to 100 percent of his accrued benefit derived from employer contributions.

(B) 5- to 15-year vesting.—A plan satisfies the requirements of this subparagraph if an employee who has completed at least 5 years of service has a nonforfeitable right to a percentage of his accrued benefit derived from employer contributions which percentage is not less than the percentage determined under the following table:

Years of service:	Nonforfeitable percentage
5	25
6	30
7	35
8	40
9	45
10	50
11	60
12	70
13	80
14	90
15 or more	100

(C) Rule of 45.—

(i) A plan satisfies the requirements of this subparagraph if an employee who is not separated from the service, who has completed at least 5 years of service, and with respect to whom the sum of his age and years of service equals or exceeds 45, has a nonforfeitable right to a percentage of his accrued benefit derived from employer contributions determined under the following table:

If years of service equal or exceed—	and sum of age and service equals or exceeds—	then the nonforfeitable percentage is—
5	45	50
6	47	60
7	49	70
8	51	80
9	53	90
10	55	100

(ii) Notwithstanding clause (i), a plan shall not be treated as satisfying the requirements of this subparagraph unless any employee who has completed at least 10 years of service has a nonforfeitable right to not less than 50 percent of his accrued benefit derived from employer contributions and to not less than an additional 10

IRC EXCERPTS

percent for each additional year of service thereafter.

(3) Certain permitted forfeitures, suspensions, etc.—For purposes of this subsection—

(A) Forfeiture on account of death.—A right to an accrued benefit derived from employer contributions shall not be treated as forfeitable solely because the plan provides that it is not payable if the participant dies (except in the case of a survivor annuity which is payable as provided in section 401(a)(11)).

(B) Suspension of benefits from reemployment of retiree.—A right to an accrued benefit derived from employer contributions shall not be treated as forfeitable solely because the plan provides that the payment of benefits is suspended for such period as the employee is employed, subsequent to the commencement of payment of such benefits—

(i) in the case of a plan other than a multiemployer plan, by the employer who maintains the plan under which such benefits were being paid; and

(ii) in the case of a multiemployer plan, in the same industry, the same trade or craft, and the same geographic area covered by the plan as when such benefits commenced.

The Secretary of Labor shall prescribe such regulations as may be necessary to carry out the purposes of this subparagraph, including regulations with respect to the meaning of the term "employed."

(C) Effect of retroactive plan amendments.—A right to an accrued benefit derived from employer contributions shall not be treated as forfeitable solely because plan amendments may be given retroactive application as provided in section 412(c)(8).

(D) Withdrawal of mandatory contribution.—

(i) A right to an accrued benefit derived from employer contributions shall not be treated as forfeitable solely because the plan provides that, in the case of a participant who does not have a nonforfeitable right to at least 50 percent of his accrued benefit derived from employer contributions, such accrued benefit may be forfeited on account of the withdrawal by the participant of any amount attributable to the benefit derived from mandatory contributions (as defined in subsection (c)(2)(C)) made by such participant.

(ii) Clause (i) shall not apply to a plan unless the plan provides that any accrued benefit forfeited under a plan provision described in such clause shall be restored upon repayment by the participant of the full amount of the withdrawal described in such clause plus, in the case of a defined benefit plan, interest. Such interest shall be computed on such amount at the rate determined for purposes of subsection (c)(2)(C) on the date of such repayment (computed annually from the date of such withdrawal). In the case of a defined contribution plan, the plan provision required under this clause may provide that such repayment must be made before the participant has any one-year break in service commencing after the withdrawal.

(iii) In the case of accrued benefits derived from employer contributions which accrued before September 2, 1974, a right to such accrued benefit derived from employer contributions shall not be treated as forfeitable solely because the plan provides that an amount of such accrued benefit may be forfeited on account of the withdrawal by the participant of an amount attributable to the benefit derived from mandatory contributions (as defined in subsection (c)(2)(C)) made by such participant before September 2, 1974 if such amount forfeited is proportional to such amount withdrawn. This clause shall not apply to any plan to which any mandatory contribution is made after September 2, 1974. The Secretary shall prescribe such regulations as may be necessary to carry out the purposes of this clause.

(iv) For purposes of this subparagraph, in the case of any class-year plan, a withdrawal of employee contributions shall be treated as a withdrawal of such contributions on a plan year by plan year basis in succeeding order of time.

(v) For nonforfeitability where the employee has a nonforfeitable right to at least 50 percent of his accrued benefit, see section 401(a)(19).

(E) Cessation of contributions under a multiemployer plan.—A right to an accrued benefit derived from employer contributions under a multiemployer plan shall not be treated as forfeitable solely because the plan provides that benefits acccrued as a

Code Sec. 411 (a) (3) (E)

result of service with the participant's employer before the employer had an obligation to contribute under the plan may not be payable if the employer ceases contributions to the multiemployer plan.

(F) Reduction and suspension of benefits by a multiemployer plan.—A participant's right to an accrued benefit derived from employer contributions under a multiemployer plan shall not be treated as forfeitable solely because—

(i) the plan is amended to reduce benefits under section 418D or under section 4281 of the Employee Retirement Income Security Act of 1974, or

(ii) benefit payments under the plan may be suspended under section 418E or under section 4281 of the Employee Retirement Income Security Act of 1974.

(4) Service included in determination of nonforfeitable percentage.—In computing the period of service under the plan for purposes of determining the nonforfeitable percentage under paragraph (2), all of an employee's years of service with the employer or employers maintaining the plan shall be taken into account, except that the following may be disregarded:

(A) years of service before age 22, except that in the case of a plan which does not satisfy subparagraph (A) or (B) of paragraph (2), the plan may not disregard any such year of service during which the employee was a participant;

(B) years of service during a period for which the employee declined to contribute to a plan requiring employee contributions;

(C) years of service with an employer during any period for which the employer did not maintain the plan or a predecessor plan (as defined under regulations prescribed by the Secretary);

(D) service not required to be taken into account under paragraph (6);

(E) years of service before January 1, 1971, unless the employee has had at least 3 years of service after December 31, 1970;

(F) years of service before the first plan year to which this section applies, if such service would have been disregarded under the rules of the plan with regard to breaks in service as in effect on the applicable date; and

(G) in the case of a multiemployer plan, years of service—

(i) with an employer after—

(I) a complete withdrawal of that employer from the plan (within the meaning of section 4203 of the Employee Retirement Income Security Act of 1974), or

(II) to the extent permitted in regulations prescribed by the Secretary, a partial withdrawal described in section 4205(b)(2)(A)(i) of such Act in conjunction with the decertification of the collective bargaining representative, and

(ii) with any employer under the plan after the termination date of the plan under section 4048 of such Act.

(5) Year of service.—

(A) General rule.—For purposes of this subsection, except as provided in subparagraph (C), the term "year of service" means a calendar year, plan year, or other 12-consecutive month period designated by the plan (and not prohibited under regulations prescribed by the Secretary of Labor) during which the participant has completed 1,000 hours of service.

(B) Hours of service.—For purposes of this subsection, the term "hour of service" has the meaning provided by section 410(a)(3)(C).

(C) Seasonal industries.—In the case of any seasonal industry where the customary period of employment is less than 1,000 hours during a calendar year, the term "year of service" shall be such period as may be determined under regulations prescribed by the Secretary of Labor.

(D) Maritime industries.—For purposes of this subsection, in the case of any maritime industry, 125 days of service shall be treated as 1,000 hours of service. The Secretary of Labor may prescribe regulations to carry out the purposes of this subparagraph.

(6) Breaks in service.—

(A) Definition of 1-year break in service. —For purposes of this paragraph, the term "1-year break in service" means a calendar year, plan year, or other 12-consecutive-month period designated by the plan (and not prohibited under regulations prescribed by the Secretary of Labor) during which the participant has not completed more than 500 hours of service.

(B) 1 year of service after 1-year break in service.—For purposes of paragraph (4), in

Code Sec. 411 (a) (4)

the case of any employee who has any 1-year break in service, years of service before such break shall not be required to be taken into account until he has completed a year of service after his return.

(C) 1-year break in service under defined contribution plan.—For purposes of paragraph (4), in the case of any participant in a defined contribution plan, or an insured defined benefit plan which satisfies the requirements of subsection (b)(1)(F), who has any 1-year break in service, years of service after such break shall not be required to be taken into account for purposes of determining the nonforfeitable percentage of his accrued benefit derived from employer contributions which accrued before such break.

(D) Nonvested participants.—For purposes of paragraph (4), in the case of a participant who, under the plan, does not have any nonforfeitable right to an accrued benefit derived from employer contributions, years of service before any 1-year break in service shall not be required to be taken into account if the number of consecutive 1-year breaks in service equals or exceeds the aggregate number of such years of service prior to such break. Such aggregate number of years of service before such break shall be deemed not to include any years of service not required to be taken into account under this subparagraph by reason of any prior break in service.

(7) Accrued benefit.—

(A) In general.—For purposes of this section, the term "accrued benefit" means—

(i) in the case of a defined benefit plan, the employee's accrued benefit determined under the plan and, except as provided in subsection (c)(3), expressed in the form of an annual benefit commencing at normal retirement age, or

(ii) in the case of a plan which is not a defined benefit plan, the balance of the employee's account.

(B) Effect of certain distributions.—Notwithstanding paragraph (4), for purposes of determining the employee's accrued benefit under the plan, the plan may disregard service performed by the employee with respect to which he has received—

(i) a distribution of the present value of his entire nonforfeitable benefit if such distribution was in an amount (not more than $1,750) permitted under regulations prescribed by the Secretary, or

(ii) a distribution of the present value of his nonforfeitable benefit attributable to such service which he elected to receive.

Clause (i) of this subparagraph shall apply only if such distribution was made on termination of the employee's participation in the plan. Clause (ii) of this subparagraph shall apply only if such distribution was made on termination of the employee's participation in the plan or under such other circumstances as may be provided under regulations prescribed by the Secretary.

(C) Repayment of subparagraph (B) distributions.—For purposes of determining the employee's accrued benefit under a plan, the plan may not disregard service as provided in subparagraph (B) unless the plan provides an opportunity for the participant to repay the full amount of the distribution described in such subparagraph (B) with, in the case of a defined benefit plan, interest at the rate determined for purposes of subsection (c)(2)(C) and provides that upon such repayment the employee's accrued benefit shall be recomputed by taking into account service so disregarded. This subparagraph shall apply only in the case of a participant who—

(i) received such a distribution in any plan year to which this section applies, which distribution was less than the present value of his accrued benefit,

(ii) resumes employment covered under the plan, and

(iii) repays the full amount of such distribution with, in the case of a defined benefit plan, interest at the rate determined for purposes of subsection (c)(2)(C).

In the case of a defined contribution plan, the plan provision required under this subparagraph may provide that such repayment must be made before the participant has any one-year break in service commencing after such withdrawal.

(8) Normal retirement age.—For purposes of this section, the term "normal retirement age" means the earlier of—

(A) the time a plan participant attains normal retirement age under the plan, or

(B) the later of—

(i) the time a plan participant attains age 65, or

Code Sec. 411 (a) (8)

(ii) the 10th anniversary of the time a plan participant commenced participation in the plan.

(9) Normal retirement benefit.—For purposes of this section, the term "normal retirement benefit" means the greater of the early retirement benefit under the plan, or the benefit under the plan commencing at normal retirement age. The normal retirement benefit shall be determined without regard to—
(A) medical benefits, and
(B) disability benefits not in excess of the qualified disability benefit.
For purposes of this paragraph, a qualified disability benefit is a disability benefit provided by a plan which does not exceed the benefit which would be provided for the participant if he separated from the service at normal retirement age. For purposes of this paragraph, the early retirement benefit under a plan shall be determined without regard to any benefits commencing before benefits payable under title II of the Social Security Act become payable which—
(i) do not exceed such social security benefits, and
(ii) terminate when such social security benefits commence.

(10) Changes in vesting schedule.—
(A) General rule.—A plan amendment changing any vesting schedule under the plan shall be treated as not satisfying the requirements of paragraph (2) if the nonforfeitable percentage of the accrued benefit derived from employer contributions (determined as of the later of the date such amendment is adopted, or the date such amendment becomes effective) of any employee who is a participant in the plan is less than such nonforfeitable percentage computed under the plan without regard to such amendment.
(B) Election of former schedule.—A plan amendment changing any vesting schedule under the plan shall be treated as not satisfying the requirements of paragraph (2) unless each participant having not less than 5 years of service is permitted to elect, within a reasonable period after the adoption of such amendment, to have his nonforfeitable percentage computed under the plan without regard to such amendment.

(b) Accrued Benefit Requirements.—

(1) General rules.—
(A) 3-percent method.—A defined benefit plan satisfies the requirements of this paragraph if the accrued benefit to which each participant is entitled upon his separation from the service is not less than—

(i) 3 percent of the normal retirement benefit to which he would be entitled if he commenced participation at the earliest possible entry age under the plan and served continuously until the earlier of age 65 or the normal retirement age specified under the plan, multiplied by

(ii) the number of years (not in excess of $33\frac{1}{3}$) of his participation in the plan.
In the case of a plan providing retirement benefits based on compensation during any period, the normal retirement benefit to which a participant would be entitled shall be determined as if he continued to earn annually the average rate of compensation which he earned during consecutive years of service, not in excess of 10, for which his compensation was the highest. For purposes of this subparagraph, social security benefits and all other relevant factors used to compute benefits shall be treated as remaining constant as of the current year for all years after such current year.

(B) $133\frac{1}{3}$ percent rule.—A defined benefit plan satisfies the requirements of this paragraph for a particular plan year if under the plan the accrued benefit payable at the normal retirement age is equal to the normal retirement benefit and the annual rate at which any individual who is or could be a participant can accrue the retirement benefits payable at normal retirement age under the plan for any later plan year is not more than $133\frac{1}{3}$ percent of the annual rate at which he can accrue benefits for any plan year beginning on or after such particular plan year and before such later plan year. For purposes of this subparagraph—

(i) any amendment to the plan which is in effect for the current year shall be treated as in effect for all other plan years;

(ii) any change in an accrual rate which does not apply to any individual who is or could be a participant in the current year shall be disregarded;

(iii) the fact that benefits under the plan may be payable to certain employees before normal retirement age shall be disregarded; and

(iv) social security benefits and all other relevant factors used to compute benefits shall be treated as remaining constant as of the current year for all years after the current year.

(C) Fractional rule.—A defined benefit plan satisfies the requirements of this paragraph if the accrued benefit to which any participant is entitled upon his separation from the service is not less than a fraction of the annual benefit commencing at normal retirement age to which he would be entitled under the plan as in effect on the date of his separation if he continued to earn annually until normal retirement age the same rate of compensation upon which his normal retirement benefit would be computed under the plan, determined as if he had attained normal retirement age on the date on which any such determination is made (but taking into account no more than the 10 years of service immediately preceding his separation from service). Such fraction shall be a fraction, not exceeding 1, the numerator of which is the total number of his years of participation in the plan (as of the date of his separation from the service) and the denominator of which is the total number of years he would have participated in the plan if he separated from the service at the normal retirement age. For purposes of this subparagraph, social security benefits and all other relevant factors used to compute benefits shall be treated as remaining constant as of the current year for all years after such current year.

(D) Accrual for service before effective date.—Subparagraphs (A), (B), and (C) shall not apply with respect to years of participation before the first plan year to which this section applies, but a defined benefit plan satisfies the requirements of this subparagraph with respect to such years of participation only if the accrued benefit of any participant with respect to such years of participation is not less than the greater of—

(i) his accrued benefit determined under the plan, as in effect from time to time prior to September 2, 1974, or

(ii) an accrued benefit which is not less than one-half of the accrued benefit to which such participant would have been entitled if subparagraph (A), (B), or (C) applied with respect to such years of participation.

(E) First two years of service.—Notwithstanding subparagraphs (A), (B), and (C) of this paragraph, a plan shall not be treated as not satisfying the requirements of this paragraph solely because the accrual of benefits under the plan does not become effective until the employee has two continuous years of service. For purposes of this subparagraph, the term "years of service" has the meaning provided by section 410(a)(3)(A).

(F) Certain insured defined benefit plans.—Notwithstanding subparagraphs (A), (B), and (C), a defined benefit plan satisfies the requirements of this paragraph if such plan—

(i) is funded exclusively by the purchase of insurance contracts, and

(ii) satisfies the requirements of paragraphs (2) and (3) of section 412(i) (relating to certain insurance contract plans),

but only if an employee's accrued benefit as of any applicable date is not less than the cash surrender value his insurance contracts would have on such applicable date if the requirements of paragraphs (4), (5), and (6) of section 412(i) were satisfied.

(G) Accrued benefit may not decrease on account of increasing age or service.—Notwithstanding the preceding subparagraphs, a defined benefit plan shall be treated as not satisfying the requirements of this paragraph if the participant's accrued benefit is reduced on account of any increase in his age or service. The preceding sentence shall not apply to benefits under the plan commencing before entitlement to benefits payable under title II of the Social Security Act which benefits under the plan—

(i) do not exceed such social security benefits, and

(ii) terminate when such social security benefits commence.

(2) Separate accounting required in certain cases.—A plan satisfies the requirements of this paragraph if—

(A) in the case of a defined benefit plan, the plan requires separate accounting for the portion of each employee's accrued benefit derived from any voluntary employee contributions permitted under the plan; and

(B) in the case of any plan which is not a defined benefit plan, the plan requires separate accounting for each employee's accrued benefit.

(3) **Year of participation.**—
(A) Definition.—For purposes of determining an employee's accrued benefit, the term "year of participation" means a period of service (beginning at the earliest date on which the employee is a participant in the plan and which is included in a period of service required to be taken into account under section 410(a)(5)) as determined under regulations prescribed by the Secretary of Labor which provide for the calculation of such period on any reasonable and consistent basis.
(B) Less than full time service.—For purposes of this paragraph, except as provided in subparagraph (C), in the case of any employee whose customary employment is less than full time, the calculation of such employee's service on any basis which provides less than a ratable portion of the accrued benefit to which he would be entitled under the plan if his customary employment were full time shall not be treated as made on a reasonable and consistent basis.
(C) Less than 1,000 hours of service during year.—For purposes of this paragraph, in the case of any employee whose service is less than 1,000 hours during any calendar year, plan year or other 12-consecutive month period designated by the plan (and not prohibited under regulations prescribed by the Secretary of Labor) the calculation of his period of service shall not be treated as not made on a reasonable and consistent basis solely because such service is not taken into account.
(D) Seasonal industries.—In the case of any seasonal industry where the customary period of employment is less than 1,000 hours during a calendar year, the term "year of participation" shall be such period as determined under regulations prescribed by the Secretary of Labor.
(E) Maritime industries.—For purposes of this subsection, in the case of any maritime industry, 125 days of service shall be treated as a year of participation. The Secretary of Labor may prescribe regulations to carry out the purposes of this subparagraph.

(c) **Allocation of Accrued Benefits Between Employer and Employee Contributions.**—

(1) **Accrued benefit derived from employer contributions.**—For purposes of this section, an employee's accrued benefit derived from employer contributions as of any applicable date is the excess, if any, of the accrued benefit for such employee as of such applicable date over the accrued benefit derived from contributions made by such employee as of such date.

(2) **Accrued benefit derived from employee contributions.**—
(A) Plans other than defined benefit plans.—In the case of a plan other than a defined benefit plan, the accrued benefit derived from contributions made by an employee as of any applicable date is—
(i) except as provided in clause (ii), the balance of the employee's separate account consisting only of his contributions and the income, expenses, gains, and losses attributable thereto, or
(ii) if a separate account is not maintained with respect to an employee's contributions under such a plan, the amount which bears the same ratio to his total accrued benefit as the total amount of the employee's contributions (less withdrawals) bears to the sum of such contributions and the contributions made on his behalf by the employer (less withdrawals).
(B) Defined benefit plans.—
(i) In general.—In the case of a defined benefit plan providing an annual benefit in the form of a single life annuity (without ancillary benefits) commencing at normal retirement age, the accrued benefit derived from contributions made by an employee as of any applicable date is the annual benefit equal to the employee's accumulated contributions multiplied by the appropriate conversion factor.
(ii) Appropriate conversion factor.—For purposes of clause (i), the term "appropriate conversion factor" means the factor necessary to convert an amount equal to the accumulated contributions to a single life annuity (without ancillary benefits) commencing at normal retirement age and shall be 10 percent for a normal retirement age of 65 years. For other normal retirement ages the conversion factor

shall be determined in accordance with regulations prescribed by the Secretary.

(C) Definition of accumulated contributions.—For purposes of this subsection, the term "accumulated contributions" means the total of—

(i) all mandatory contributions made by the employee,

(ii) interest (if any) under the plan to the end of the last plan year to which subsection (a)(2) does not apply (by reason of the applicable effective date), and

(iii) interest on the sum of the amounts determined under clauses (i) and (ii) compounded annually at the rate of 5 percent per annum from the beginning of the first plan year to which subsection (a)(2) applies (by reason of the applicable effective date) to the date upon which the employee would attain normal retirement age.

For purposes of this subparagraph, the term "mandatory contributions" means amounts contributed to the plan by the employee which are required as a condition of employment, as a condition of participation in such plan, or as a condition of obtaining benefits under the plan attributable to employer contributions.

(D) Adjustments.—The Secretary is authorized to adjust by regulation the conversion factor described in subparagraph (B), the rate of interest described in clause (iii) of subparagraph (C), or both, from time to time as he may deem necessary. The rate of interest shall bear the relationship to 5 percent which the Secretary determines to be comparable to the relationship which the long-term money rates and investment yields for the last period of 10 calendar years ending at least 12 months before the beginning of the plan year bear to the long-term money rates and investment yields for the 10-calendar year period 1964 through 1973. No such adjustment shall be effective for a plan year beginning before the expiration of 1 year after such adjustment is determined and published.

(E) Limitation.—The accrued benefit derived from employee contributions shall not exceed the greater of—

(i) the employee's accrued benefit under the plan, or

(ii) the accrued benefit derived from employee contributions determined as though the amounts calculated under clauses (ii) and (iii) of subparagraph (C) were zero.

(3) Actuarial adjustment.—For purposes of this section, in the case of any defined benefit plan, if an employee's accrued benefit is to be determined as an amount other than an annual benefit commencing at normal retirement age, or if the accrued benefit derived from contributions made by an employee is to be determined with respect to a benefit other than an annual benefit in the form of a single life annuity (without ancillary benefits) commencing at normal retirement age, the employee's accrued benefit, or the accrued benefits derived from contributions made by an employee, as the case may be, shall be the actuarial equivalent of such benefit or amount determined under paragraph (1) or (2).

(d) Special Rules.—

(1) Coordination with section 401(a)(4). —A plan which satisfies the requirements of this section shall be treated as satisfying any vesting requirements resulting from the application of section 401(a)(4) unless—

(A) there has been a pattern of abuse under the plan (such as dismissal of employees before their accrued benefits become nonforfeitable) tending to discriminate in favor of employees who are officers, shareholders, or highly compensated, or

(B) there have been, or there is reason to believe there will be, an accrual of benefits or forfeitures tending to discriminate in favor of employees who are officers, shareholders, or highly compensated.

(2) Prohibited discrimination.—Subsection (a) shall not apply to benefits which may not be provided for designated employees in the event of early termination of the plan under provisions of the plan adopted pursuant to regulations prescribed by the Secretary to preclude the discrimination prohibited by section 401(a)(4).

(3) Termination or partial termination; discontinuance of contributions.—Notwithstanding the provisions of subsection (a), a trust shall not constitute a qualified trust under section 401(a) unless the plan of which such trust is a part provides that—

Code Sec. 411 (d) (3)

(A) upon its termination or partial termination, or

(B) in the case of a plan to which section 412 does not apply, upon complete discontinuance of contributions under the plan, the rights of all affected employees to benefits accrued to the date of such termination, partial termination, or discontinuance, to the extent funded as of such date, or the amounts credited to the employees' accounts, are nonforfeitable. This paragraph shall not apply to benefits or contributions which, under provisions of the plan adopted pursuant to regulations prescribed by the Secretary to preclude the discrimination prohibited by section 401(a)(4), may not be used for designated employees in the event of early termination of the plan.

(4) **Class year plans.**—The requirements of subsection (a)(2) shall be deemed to be satisfied in the case of a class year plan if such plan provides that 100 percent of each employee's right to or derived from the contributions of the employer on his behalf with respect to any plan year are nonforfeitable not later than the end of the 5th plan year following the plan year for which such contributions were made. For purposes of this section, the term "class year plan" means a profit-sharing, stock bonus, or money purchase plan which provides for the separate nonforfeitability of employees' rights to or derived from the contributions for each plan year.

(5) **Treatment of voluntary employee contributions.**—In the case of a defined benefit plan which permits voluntary employee contributions, the portion of an employee's accrued benefit derived from such contributions shall be treated as an accrued benefit derived from employee contributions under a plan other than a defined benefit plan.

(6) **Accrued benefit not to be decreased by amendment.**—A plan shall be treated as not satisfying the requirements of this section if the accrued benefit of a participant is decreased by an amendment of the plan, other than an amendment described in section 412(c)(8), or section 4281 of the Employee Retirement Income Security Act of 1974.

(e) Application of Vesting Standards to Certain Plans.—

(1) The provisions of this section (other than paragraph (2)) shall not apply to—

(A) a governmental plan (within the meaning of section 414(d)),

(B) a church plan (within the meaning of section 414(e)) with respect to which the election provided by section 410(d) has not been made,

(C) a plan which has not, at any time after September 2, 1974, provided for employer contributions, and

(D) a plan established and maintained by a society, order, or association described in section 501(c)(8) or (9), if no part of the contributions to or under such plan are made by employers of participants in such plan.

(2) A plan described in paragraph (1) shall be treated as meeting the requirements of this section, for purposes of section 401(a), if such plan meets the vesting requirements resulting from the application of section 401(a)(4) and 401(a)(7) as in effect on September 1, 1974.

SEC. 412. MINIMUM FUNDING STANDARDS.

(a) General Rule.—Except as provided in subsection (h), this section applies to a plan if, for any plan year beginning on or after the effective date of this section for such plan—

(1) Such plan included a trust which qualified (or was determined by the Secretary to have qualified) under section 401(a), or

(2) such plan satisfied (or was determined by the Secretary to have satisfied) the requirements of section 403(a) or 405(a).

A plan to which this section applies shall have satisfied the minimum funding standard for such plan for a plan year if as of the end of such plan year, the plan does not have an accumulated funding deficiency. For purposes of this section and section 4971, the term "accumulated funding deficiency" means for any plan the excess of the total charges to the funding standard account for all plan years (beginning with the first plan year to which this section applies) over the total credits to such account for such years or, if less, the excess of the total charges to the alternative minimum funding standard account for such plan

Code Sec. 411 (d) (4)

years over the total credits to such account for such years. In any plan year in which a multiemployer plan is in reorganization, the accumulated funding deficiency of the plan shall be determined under section 418B.

(b) Funding Standard Account.—

(1) Account required.—Each plan to which this section applies shall establish and maintain a funding standard account. Such account shall be credited and charged solely as provided in this section.

(2) Charges to account.—For a plan year, the funding standard account shall be charged with the sum of—
(A) the normal cost of the plan for the plan year,
(B) the amounts necessary to amortize in equal annual installments (until fully amortized)—
(i) in the case of a plan in existence on January 1, 1974, the unfunded past service liability under the plan on the first day of the first plan year to which this section applies, over a period of 40 plan years,
(ii) in the case of a plan which comes into existence after January 1, 1974, the unfunded past service liability under the plan on the first day of the first plan year to which this section applies, over a period of 30 plan years,
(iii) separately, with respect to each plan year, the net increase (if any) in unfunded past service liability under the plan arising from plan amendments adopted in such year, over a period of 30 plan years,
(iv) separately with respect to each plan year, the net experience loss (if any) under the plan, over a period of 15 years, and
(v) separately, with respect to each plan year, the net loss (if any) resulting from changes in actuarial assumptions used under the plan, over a period of 30 plan years,
(C) the amount necessary to amortize each waived funding deficiency (within the meaning of subsection (d)(3)) for each prior plan year in equal annual installments (until fully amortized) over a period of 15 plan years, and
(D) the amount necessary to amortize in equal annual installments (until fully amortized) over a period of 5 plan years any amount credited to the funding standard account under paragraph (3)(D).

(3) Credits to account.—For a plan year, the funding standard account shall be credited with the sum of—
(A) the amount considered contributed by the employer to or under the plan for the plan year,
(B) the amount necessary to amortize in equal annual installments (until fully amortized)—
(i) separately, with respect to each plan year, the net decrease (if any) in unfunded past service liability under the plan arising from plan amendments adopted in such year, over a period of 30 plan years,
(ii) separately, with respect to each plan year, the net experience gain (if any) under the plan, over a period of 15 plan years,
(iii) separately, with respect to each plan year, the net gain (if any) resulting from changes in actuarial assumptions used under the plan, over a period of 30 plan years,
(C) the amount of the waived funding deficiency (within the meaning of subsection (d)(3)) for the plan year, and
(D) in the case of a plan year for which the accumulated funding deficiency is determined under the funding standard account if such plan year follows a plan year for which such deficiency was determined under the alternative minimum funding standard, the excess (if any) of any debit balance in the funding standard account (determined without regard to this subparagraph) over any debit balance in the alternative minimum funding standard account.

(4) Combining and offsetting amounts to be amortized.—Under regulations prescribed by the Secretary, amounts required to be amortized under paragraph (2) or paragraph (3), as the case may be—
(A) may be combined into one amount under such paragraph to be amortized over a period determined on the basis of the remaining amortization period for all items entering into such combined amount, and
(B) may be offset against amounts required to be amortized under the other such paragraph, with the resulting amount to be amortized over a period determined on the basis of the remaining amortization periods for all items entering into whichever of the two amounts being offset is the greater.

Code Sec. 412 (b) (4)

(5) Interest.—The funding standard account (and items therein) shall be charged or credited (as determined under regulations prescribed by the Secretary) with interest at the appropriate rate consistent with the rate or rates of interest used under the plan to determine costs.

(6) Certain amortization charges and credits.—In the case of a plan which, immediately before the date of the enactment of the Multiemployer Pension Plan Amendments Act of 1980, was a multiemployer plan (within the meaning of section 414(f) as in effect immediately before such date)—

(A) any amount described in paragraph (2)(B)(ii), (2)(B)(iii), or (3)(B)(i) of this subsection which arose in a plan year beginning before such date shall be amortized in equal annual installments (until fully amortized) over 40 plan years, beginning with the plan year in which the amount arose;

(B) any amount described in paragraph (2)(B)(iv) or (3)(B)(ii) of this subsection which arose in a plan year beginning before such date shall be amortized in equal annual installments (until fully amortized) over 20 plan years, beginning with the plan year in which the amount arose;

(C) any change in past service liability which arises during the period of 3 plan years beginning on or after such date, and results from a plan amendment adopted before such date, shall be amortized in equal annual installments (until fully amortized) over 40 plan years, beginning with the plan year in which the change arises; and

(D) any change in past service liability which arises during the period of 2 plan years beginning on or after such date, and results from the changing of a group of participants from one benefit level to another benefit level under a schedule of plan benefits which—

(i) was adopted before such date, and

(ii) was effective for any plan participant before the beginning of the first plan year beginning on or after such date,

shall be amortized in equal annual installments (until fully amortized) over 40 plan years, beginning with the plan year in which the change arises.

(7) Special rules for multiemployer plans.—For purposes of this section—

(A) Withdrawal liability.—Any amount received by a multiemployer plan in payment of all or part of an employer's withdrawal liability under part 1 of subtitle E of title IV of the Employee Retirement Income Security Act of 1974 shall be considered an amount contributed by the employer to or under the plan. The Secretary may prescribe by regulation additional charges and credits to a multiemployer plan's funding standard account to the extent necessary to prevent withdrawal liability payments from being unduly reflected as advance funding for plan liabilities.

(B) Adjustments when a multiemployer plan leaves reorganization.—If a multiemployer plan is not in reorganization in the plan year but was in reorganization in the immediately preceding plan year, any balance in the funding standard account at the close of such immediately preceding plan year—

(i) shall be eliminated by an offsetting credit or charge (as the case may be), but

(ii) shall be taken into account in subsequent plan years by being amortized in equal annual installments (until fully amortized) over 30 plan years.

The preceding sentence shall not apply to the extent of any accumulated funding deficiency under section 418B(a) as of the end of the last plan year that the plan was in reorganization.

(C) Plan payments to supplemental program or withdrawal liability payment fund.—Any amount paid by a plan during a plan year to the Pension Benefit Guaranty Corporation pursuant to section 4222 of such Act or to a fund exempt under section 501(c)(22) pursuant to section 4223 of such Act shall reduce the amount of contributions considered received by the plan for the plan year.

(D) Interim withdrawal liability payments.—Any amount paid by an employer pending a final determination of the employer's withdrawal liability under part 1 of subtitle E of title IV of such Act and subsequently refunded to the employer by the plan shall be charged to the funding standard account in accordance with regulations prescribed by the Secretary.

(E) For purposes of the full funding limitation under subsection (c)(7), unless otherwise provided by the plan, the accrued liability under a multiemployer plan shall not include benefits which are not nonforfeitable under the plan after the termination of the plan (taking into consideration 411(d)(3)).

(c) Special Rules.—

(1) Determinations to be made under funding method.—For purposes of this section, normal costs, accrued liability, past service liabilities, and experience gains and losses shall be determined under the funding method used to determine costs under the plan.

(2) Valuation of assets.—

(A) In general.—For purposes of this section, the value of the plan's assets shall be determined on the basis of any reasonable actuarial method of valuation which takes into account fair market value and which is permitted under regulations prescribed by the Secretary.

(B) Election with respect to bonds.—The value of a bond or other evidence of indebtedness which is not in default as to principal or interest may, at the election of the plan administrator, be determined on an amortized basis running from initial cost at purchase to par value at maturity or earliest call date. Any election under this subparagraph shall be made at such time and in such manner as the Secretary shall by regulations provide, shall apply to all such evidences of indebtedness, and may be revoked only with the consent of the Secretary.

(3) Actuarial assumptions must be reasonable.—For purposes of this section, all costs, liabilities, rates of interest, and other factors under the plan shall be determined on the basis of actuarial assumptions and methods which, in the aggregate, are reasonable (taking into account the experience of the plan and reasonable expectations) and which, in combination, offer the actuary's best estimate of anticipated experience under the plan.

(4) Treatment of certain changes as experience gain or loss.—For purposes of this section, if—
(A) a change in benefits under the Social Security Act or in other retirement benefits created under Federal or State law, or
(B) a change in the definition of the term "wages" under section 3121, or a change in the amount of such wages taken into account under regulations prescribed for purposes of section 401(a)(5),
results in an increase or decrease in accrued liability under a plan, such increase or decrease shall be treated as an experience loss or gain.

(5) Change in funding method or in plan year requires approval.—If the funding method for a plan is changed, the new funding method shall become the funding method used to determine costs and liabilities under the plan only if the change is approved by the Secretary. If the plan year for a plan is changed, the new plan year shall become the plan year for the plan only if the change is approved by the Secretary.

(6) Full funding.—If, as of the close of a plan year, a plan would (without regard to this paragraph) have an accumulated funding deficiency (determined without regard to the alternative minimum funding standard account permitted under subsection (g)) in excess of the full funding limitation—
(A) the funding standard account shall be credited with the amount of such excess, and
(B) all amounts described in paragraphs (2)(B), (C), and (D) and (3)(B) of subsection (b) which are required to be amortized shall be considered fully amortized for purposes of such paragraphs.

(7) Full funding limitation.—For purposes of paragraph (6), the term "full funding limitation" means the excess (if any) of—
(A) the accrued liability (including normal cost) under the plan (determined under the entry age normal funding method if such accrued liability cannot be directly calculated under the funding method used for the plan), over
(B) the lesser of the fair market value of the plan's assets or the value of such assets determined under paragraph (2).

(8) Certain retroactive plan amendments.—For purposes of this section, any amendment applying to a plan year which—
(A) is adopted after the close of such plan year but no later than 2 and one-half months after the close of the plan year (or, in the case of a multiemployer plan, no

later than 2 years after the close of such plan year),

(B) does not reduce the accrued benefit of any participant determined as of the beginning of the first plan year to which the amendment applies, and

(C) does not reduce the accrued benefit of any participant determined as of the time of adoption except to the extent required by the circumstances,

shall, at the election of the plan administrator, be deemed to have been made on the first day of such plan year. No amendment described in this paragraph which reduces the accrued benefit of any participant shall take effect unless the plan administrator files a notice with the Secretary of Labor notifying him of such amendment and the Secretary of Labor has approved such amendment, or within 90 days after the date on which such notice was filed, failed to disapprove such amendment. No amendment described in this subsection shall be approved by the Secretary of Labor unless he determines that such amendment is necessary because of a substantial business hardship (as determined under subsection (d)(2)) and that a waiver under subsection (d)(1) is unavailable or inadequate.

(9) 3-year valuation.—For purposes of this section, a determination of experience gains and losses and a valuation of the plan's liability shall be made not less frequently than once every 3 years, except that such determination shall be made more frequently to the extent required in particular cases under regulations prescribed by the Secretary.

(10) Time when certain contributions deemed made.—For purposes of this section, any contributions for a plan year made by an employer after the last day of such plan year, but not later than two and one-half months after such day, shall be deemed to have been made on such last day. For purposes of this paragraph, such two and one-half month period may be extended for not more than six months under regulations prescribed by the Secretary.

(d) Variance from Minimum Funding Standard.—

(1) Waiver in case of substantial business hardship.—If an employer, or in the case of a multiemployer plan, 10 percent or more of the number of employers contributing to or under the plan, are unable to satisfy the minimum funding standard for a plan year without substantial business hardship and if application of the standard would be adverse to the interests of plan participants in the aggregate, the Secretary may waive the requirements of subsection (a) for such year with respect to all or any portion of the minimum funding standard other than the portion thereof determined under subsection (b)(2)(C). The Secretary shall not waive the minimum funding standards with respect to a plan for more than 5 of any 15 consecutive plan years.

(2) Determination of substantial business hardship.—For purposes of this section, the factors taken into account in determining substantial business hardship shall include (but shall not be limited to) whether or not—

(A) the employer is operating at an economic loss,

(B) there is substantial unemployment or underemployment in the trade or business and in the industry concerned,

(C) the sales and profits of the industry concerned are depressed or declining, and

(D) it is reasonable to expect that the plan will be continued only if the waiver is granted.

(3) Waived funding deficiency.—For purposes of this section, the term "waived funding deficiency" means the portion of the minimum funding standard (determined without regard to subsection (b)(3)(C)) for a plan year waived by the Secretary and not satisfied by employer contributions.

(e) Extension of Amortization Periods. —The period of years required to amortize any unfunded liability (described in any clause of subsection (b)(2)(B)) of any plan may be extended by the Secretary of Labor for a period of time (not in excess of 10 years) if he determines that such extension would carry out the purposes of the Employee Retirement Income Security Act of 1974 and would provide adequate protection for participants under the plan and their beneficiaries and if he determines that the failure to permit such extension would—

Code Sec. 412 (c) (9)

(1) result in—
(A) a substantial risk to the voluntary continuation of the plan, or
(B) a substantial curtailment of pension benefit levels or employee compensation, and
(2) be adverse to the interests of plan participants in the aggregate.

(f) Benefits May Not be Increased During Waiver or Extension Period.—

(1) In general.—No amendment of the plan which increases the liabilities of the plan by reason of any increase in benefits, any change in the accrual of benefits, or any change in the rate at which benefits become nonforfeitable under the plan shall be adopted if a waiver under subsection (d)(1) or an extension of time under subsection (e) is in effect with respect to the plan, or if a plan amendment described in subsection (c)(8) has been made at any time in the preceding 12 months (24 months for multiemployer plans). If a plan is amended in violation of the preceding sentence, any such waiver or extension of time shall not apply to any plan year ending on or after the date on which such amendment is adopted.

(2) Exception.—Paragraph (1) shall not apply to any plan amendment which—
(A) the Secretary of Labor determines to be reasonable and which provides for only de minimis increases in the liabilities of the plan,
(B) only repeals an amendment described in subsection (c)(8), or
(C) is required as a condition of qualification under this part.

(g) Alternative Minimum Funding Standard.—

(1) In general.—A plan which uses a funding method that requires contributions in all years not less than those required under the entry age normal funding method may maintain an alternative minimum funding standard account for any plan year. Such account shall be credited and charged solely as provided in this subsection.

(2) Charges and credits to account.—For a plan year the alternative minimum funding standard account shall be—

(A) charged with the sum of—
(i) the lesser of normal cost under the funding method used under the plan or normal cost determined under the unit credit method,
(ii) the excess, if any, of the present value of accrued benefits under the plan over the fair market value of the assets, and
(iii) an amount equal to the excess (if any) of credits to the alternative minimum standard account for all prior plan years over charges to such account for all such years, and
(B) credited with the amount considered contributed by the employer to or under the plan for the plan year.

(3) Special rules.—The alternative minimum funding standard account (and items therein) shall be charged or credited with interest in the manner provided under subsection (b)(5) with respect to the funding standard account.

(h) Exceptions.—This section shall not apply to—
(1) any profit-sharing or stock bonus plan,
(2) any insurance contract plan described in subsection (i),
(3) any governmental plan (within the meaning of section 414(d)),
(4) any church plan (within the meaning of section 414(e)) with respect to which the election provided by section 410(d) has not been made,
(5) any plan which has not, at any time after September 2, 1974, provided for employer contributions, or
(6) any plan established and maintained by a society, order, or association described in section 501(c)(8) or (9), if no part of the contributions to or under such plan are made by employers of participants in such plan.
No plan described in paragraph (3), (4), or (6) shall be treated as a qualified plan for purposes of section 401(a) unless such plan meets the requirements of section 401(a)(7) as in effect on September 1, 1974.

(i) Certain Insurance Contract Plans.—A plan is described in this subsection if—
(1) the plan is funded exclusively by the purchase of individual insurance contracts,
(2) such contracts provided for level annual premium payments to be paid extend-

ing not later than the retirement age for each individual participating in the plan, and commencing with the date the individual became a participant in the plan (or, in the case of an increase in benefits, commencing at the time such increase becomes effective),

(3) benefits provided by the plan are equal to the benefits provided under each contract at normal retirement age under the plan and are guaranteed by an insurance carrier (licensed under the laws of a State to do business with the plan) to the extent premiums have been paid,

(4) premiums payable for the plan year, and all prior plan years, under such contracts have been paid before lapse or there is reinstatement of the policy,

(5) no rights under such contracts have been subject to a security interest at any time during the plan year, and

(6) no policy loans are outstanding at any time during the plan year.

A plan funded exclusively by the purchase of group insurance contracts which is determined under regulations prescribed by the Secretary to have the same characteristics as contracts described in the preceding sentence shall be treated as a plan described in this subsection.

(j) Certain Terminated Multiemployer Plans.—This section applies with respect to a terminated multiemployer plan to which section 4021 of the Employee Retirement Income Security Act of 1974 applies, until the last day of the plan year in which the plan terminates, within the meaning of secton 4041A(a)(2) of that Act.

(k) Financial Assistance.—Any amount of any financial assistance from the Pension Benefit Guaranty Corporation to any plan, and any repayment of such amount, shall be taken into account under this section in such manner as determined by the Secretary.

SEC. 413. COLLECTIVELY BARGAINED PLANS, ETC.

(a) Application of Subsection (b).—Subsection (b) applies to—

(1) a plan maintained pursuant to an agreement which the Secretary of Labor finds to be a collective-bargaining agreement between employee representatives and one or more employers, and

(2) each trust which is a part of such plan.

(b) General Rule.—If this subsection applies to a plan, notwithstanding any other provision of this title—

(1) Participation.—Section 410 shall be applied as if all employees of each of the employers who are parties to the collective-bargaining agreement and who are subject to the same benefit computation formula under the plan were employed by a single employer.

(2) Discrimination, etc.—Sections 401(a)(4) and 411(d)(3) shall be applied as if all participants who are subject to the same benefit computation formula and who are employed by employers who are parties to the collective-bargaining agreement were employed by a single-employer.

(3) Exclusive benefit.—For purposes of section 401(a), in determining whether the plan of an employer is for the exclusive benefit of his employees and their beneficiaries, all plan participants shall be considered to be his employees.

(4) Vesting.—Section 411 (other than subsection (d)(3)) shall be applied as if all employers who have been parties to the collective-bargaining agreement constituted a single employer, except that the application of any rules with respect to breaks in service shall be made under regulations prescribed by the Secretary of Labor.

(5) Funding.—The minimum funding standard provided by section 412 shall be determined as if all participants in the plan were employed by a single employer.

(6) Liability for funding tax.—For a plan year the liability under section 4971 of each employer who is a party to the collective-bargaining agreement shall be determined in a reasonable manner not inconsistent with regulations prescribed by the Secretary—

(A) first on the basis of their respective delinquencies in meeting required employer contributions under the plan, and

(B) then on the basis of their respective liabilities for contributions under the plan. For purposes of this subsection and the last

IRC EXCERPTS

sentence of section 4971(a), an employer's withdrawal liability under part 1 of subtitle E of title IV of the Employee Retirement Income Security Act of 1974 shall not be treated as a liability for contributions under the plan.

(7) **Deduction limitations.**—Each applicable limitation provided by section 404(a) shall be determined as if all participants in the plan were employed by a single employer. The amounts contributed to or under the plan by each employer who is a party to the agreement, for the portion of his taxable year which is included within such a plan year, shall be considered not to exceed such a limitation if the anticipated employer contributions for such plan year (determined in a manner consistent with the manner in which actual employer contributions for such plan year are determined) do not exceed such limitation. If such anticipated contributions exceed such a limitation, the portion of each such employer's contributions which is not deductible under section 404 shall be determined in accordance with regulations prescribed by the Secretary.

(8) **Employees of labor unions.**—For purposes of this subsection, employees of employee representatives shall be treated as employees of an employer described in subsection (a)(1) if such representatives meet the requirements of sections 401(a)(4) and 410 with respect to such employees.

(c) **Plans Maintained by More Than One Employer.**—In the case of a plan maintained by more than one employer—

(1) **Participation.**—Section 410(a) shall be applied as if all employees of each of the employers who maintain the plan were employed by a single employer.

(2) **Exclusive benefit.**—For purposes of section 401(a), in determining whether the plan of an employer is for the exclusive benefit of his employees and their beneficiaries all plan participants shall be considered to be his employees.

(3) **Vesting.**—Section 411 shall be applied as if all employers who maintain the plan constituted a single employer, except that the application of any rules with respect to breaks in service shall be made

under regulations prescribed by the Secretary of Labor.

(4) **Funding.**—The minimum funding standard provided by section 412 shall be determined as if all participants in the plan were employed by a single employer.

(5) **Liability for funding tax.**—For a plan year the liability under section 4971 of each employer who maintains the plan shall be determined in a reasonable manner not inconsistent with regulations prescribed by the Secretary—

(A) first on the basis of their respective delinquencies in meeting required employer contributions under the plan, and

(B) then on the basis of their respective liabilities for contributions under the plan.

(6) **Deduction limitations.**—Each applicable limitation provided by section 404(a) shall be determined as if all participants in the plan were employed by a single employer. The amounts contributed to or under the plan by each employer who maintains the plan, for the portion of this taxable year which is included within such a plan year, shall be considered not to exceed such a limitation if the anticipated employer contributions for such plan year (determined in a reasonable manner not inconsistent with regulations prescribed by the Secretary) do not exceed such limitation. If such anticipated contributions exceed such a limitation, the portion of each such employer's contributions which is not deductible under section 404 shall be determined in accordance with regulations prescribed by the Secretary.

Allocations of amounts under paragraphs (4), (5), and (6), among the employers maintaining the plan, shall not be inconsistent with regulations prescribed for this purpose by the Secretary.

SEC. 414. DEFINITIONS AND SPECIAL RULES.

(a) **Service for Predecessor Employer.**—For purposes of this part—

(1) in any case in which the employer maintains a plan of a predecessor employer, service for such predecessor shall be treated as service for the employer, and

(2) in any case in which the employer maintains a plan which is not the plan main-

tained by a predecessor employer, service for such predecessor shall, to the extent provided in regulations prescribed by the Secretary, be treated as service for the employer.

(b) Employees of Controlled Group of Corporations.—For purposes of sections 401, 408(k), 410, 411, 415, and 416, all employees of all corporations which are members of a controlled group of corporations (within the meaning of section 1563(a), determined without regard to section 1563(a)(4) and (e)(3)(C)) shall be treated as employed by a single employer. With respect to a plan adopted by more than one such corporation, the minimum funding standard of section 412, the tax imposed by section 4971, and the applicable limitations provided by section 404(a) shall be determined as if all such employers were a single employer, and allocated to each employer in accordance with regulations prescribed by the Secretary.

(c) Employees of Partnerships, Proprietorships, etc., which are Under Common Control.—For purposes of sections 401, 408(k), 410, 411, 415, and 416, under regulations prescribed by the Secretary, all employees of trades or businesses (whether or not incorporated) which are under common control shall be treated as employed by a single employer. The regulations prescribed under this subsection shall be based on principles similar to the principles which apply in the case of subsection (b).

(d) Governmental Plan.—For purposes of this part, the term "governmental plan" means a plan established and maintained for its employees by the Government of the United States, by the government of any State or political subdivision thereof, or by any agency or instrumentality of any of the foregoing. The term "governmental plan" also includes any plan to which the Railroad Retirement Act of 1935 or 1937 applies and which is financed by contributions required under that Act and any plan of an international organization which is exempt from taxation by reason of the International Organizations Immunities Act (59 Stat. 669).

(e) Church Plan.—

(1) In General.—For purposes of this part, the term 'church plan' means a plan established and maintained (to the extent required in paragraph (2)(B)) for its employees (or their beneficiaries) by a church or by a convention or association of churches which is exempt from tax under section 501.

(2) Certain plans excluded.—The term "church plan" does not include a plan—

(A) which is established and maintained primarily for the benefit of employees (or their beneficiaries) of such church or convention or association of churches who are employed in connection with one or more unrelated trades or businesses (within the meaning of section 513); or

(B) if less than substantially all of the individuals included in the plan are individuals described in paragraph (1) or (3)(B) (or their beneficiaries).

(3) Definitions and other provisions.—For purposes of this subsection—

(A) Treatment as church plan.—A plan established and maintained for its employees (or their beneficiaries) by a church or by a convention or association of churches includes a plan maintained by an organization, whether a civil law corporation or otherwise, the principal purpose or function of which is the administration or funding of a plan or program for the provision of retirement benefits or welfare benefits, or both, for the employees of a church or a convention or association of churches, if such organization is controlled by or associated with a church or a convention or association of churches.

(B) Employee defined.—The term employee of a church or a convention or association of churches shall include—

(i) a duly ordained, commissioned, or licensed minister of a church in the exercise of his ministry, regardless of the source of his compensation;

(ii) an employee of an organization, whether a civil law corporation or otherwise, which is exempt from tax under section 501 and which is controlled by or associated with a church or a convention or association of churches; and

(iii) an individual described in subparagraph (E).

(C) Church treated as employer.—A church or a convention or association of churches which is exempt from tax under section 501 shall be deemed the employer of

Code Sec. 414 (b)

any individual included as an employee under subparagraph (B).

(D) Association with church.—An organization, whether a civil law corporation or otherwise, is associated with a church or a convention or association of churches if it shares common religious bonds and convictions with that church or convention or association of churches.

(E) Special rule in case of separation from plan.—If an employee who is included in a church plan separates from the service of a church or a convention or association of churches or an organization described in clause (ii) of paragraph (3)(B), the church plan shall not fail to meet the requirements of this subsection merely because the plan—

(i) retains the employee's accrued benefit or account for the payment of benefits to the employee or his beneficiaries pursuant to the terms of the plan; or

(ii) receives contributions on the employee's behalf after the employee's separation from such service, but only for a period of 5 years after such separation, unless the employee is disabled (within the meaning of the disability provisions of the church plan or, if there are no such provisions in the church plan, within the meaning of section 72(m)(7)) at the time of such separation from service.

(4) Correction of failure to meet church plan requirements.—

(A) In general.—If a plan established and maintained for its employees (or their beneficiaries) by a church or by a convention or association of churches which is exempt from tax under section 501 fails to meet one or more of the requirements of this subsection and corrects its failure to meet such requirements within the correction period, the plan shall be deemed to meet the requirements of this subsection for the year in which the correction was made and for all prior years.

(B) Failure to correct.—If a correction is not made within the correction period, the plan shall be deemed not to meet the requirements of this subsection beginning with the date on which the earliest failure to meet one or more of such requirements occurred.

(C) Correction period defined.—The term "correction period" means—

(i) the period ending 270 days after the date of mailing by the Secretary of a notice of default with respect to the plan's failure to meet one or more of the requirements of this subsection;

(ii) any period set by a court of competent jurisdiction after a final determination that the plan fails to meet such requirements, or, if the court does not specify such period, any reasonable period determined by the Secretary on the basis of all the facts and circumstances, but in any event not less than 270 days after the determination has become final; or

(iii) any additional period which the Secretary determines is reasonable or necessary for the correction of the default,

whichever has the latest ending date.

(f) Multiemployer Plan.—

(1) Definition.—For purposes of this part, the term "multiemployer plan" means a plan—

(A) to which more than one employer is required to contribute,

(B) which is maintained pursuant to one or more collective bargaining agreements between one or more employee organizations and more than one employer, and

(C) which satisfies such other requirements as the Secretary of Labor may prescribe by regulation.

(2) Cases of common control.—For purposes of this subsection, all trades or businesses (whether or not incorporated) which are under common control within the meaning of subsection (c) are considered a single employer.

(3) Continuation of status after termination.—Notwithstanding paragraph (1), a plan is a multiemployer plan on and after its termination date under title IV of the Employee Retirement Income Security Act of 1974 if the plan was a multiemployer plan under this subsection for the plan year preceding its termination date.

(4) Transitional rule.—For any plan year which began before the date of the enactment of the Multiemployer Pension Plan Amendments Act of 1980, the term "multiemployer plan" means a plan described in this subsection as in effect immediately before that date.

Code Sec. 414 (f) (4)

(5) Special election.—Within one year after the date of the enactment of the Multiemployer Pension Plan Amendments Act of 1980, a multiemployer plan may irrevocably elect, pursuant to procedures established by the Pension Benefit Guaranty Corporation and subject to the provisions of section 4403(b) and (c) of the Employee Retirement Income Security Act of 1974, that the plan shall not be treated as a multiemployer plan for any purpose under such Act or this title, if for each of the last 3 plan years ending prior to the effective date of the Multiemployer Pension Plan Amendments Act of 1980—

(A) the plan was not a multiemployer plan because the plan was not a plan described in section 3(37)(A)(iii) of the Employee Retirement Income Security Act of 1974 and section 414(f)(1)(C) (as such provisions were in effect on the day before the date of the enactment of the Multiemployer Pension Plan Amendments Act of 1980); and

(B) the plan had been identified as a plan that was not a multiemployer plan in substantially all its filings with the Pension Benefit Guaranty Corporation, the Secretary of Labor and the Secretary.

(g) Plan Administrator.—For purposes of this part, the term "plan administrator" means—

(1) the person specifically so designated by the terms of the instrument under which the plan is operated;

(2) in the absence of a designation referred to in paragraph (1)—

(A) in the case of a plan maintained by a single employer, such employer,

(B) in the case of a plan maintained by two or more employers or jointly by one or more employers and one or more employee organizations, the association, committee, joint board of trustees, or other similar group of representatives of the parties who maintained the plan, or

(C) in any case to which subparagraph (A) or (B) does not apply, such other person as the Secretary may by regulation, prescribe.

(h) Tax Treatment of Certain Contributions.—

(1) **In general.**—Effective with respect to taxable years beginning after December 31, 1973, for purposes of this title, any amount contributed—

(A) to an employees' trust described in section 401(a), or

(B) under a plan described in section 403(a) or 405(a), shall not be treated as having been made by the employer if it is designated as an employee contribution.

(2) **Designation by units of government.** —For purposes of paragraph (1), in the case of any plan established by the government of any State or political subdivision thereof, or by any agency or instrumentality of any of the foregoing, where the contributions of employing units are designated as employee contributions but where any employing unit picks up the contributions, the contributions so picked up shall be treated as employer contributions.

(i) Defined Contribution Plan.—For purposes of this part, the term "defined contribution plan" means a plan which provides for an individual account for each participant and for benefits based solely on the amount contributed to the participant's account, and any income, expenses, gains and losses, and any forfeitures of accounts of other participants which may be allocated to such participant's account.

(j) Defined Benefit Plan.—For purposes of this part, the term "defined benefit plan" means any plan which is not a defined contribution plan.

(k) Certain Plans.—A defined benefit plan which provides a benefit derived from employer contributions which is based partly on the balance of the separate account of a participant shall—

(1) for purposes of section 410 (relating to minimum participation standards), be treated as a defined contribution plan,

(2) for purposes of sections 411(a)(7)(A) (relating to minimum vesting standards) and 415 (relating to limitations on benefits and contributions under qualified plans), be treated as consisting of a defined contribution plan to the extent benefits are based on the separate account of a participant and as a defined benefit plan with respect to the remaining portion of benefits under the plan, and

(3) for purposes of section 4975 (relating to tax on prohibited transactions), be treated as a defined benefit plan.

Code Sec. 414 (g)

(l) Mergers and Consolidations of Plans or Transfers of Plan Assets.—A trust which forms a part of a plan shall not constitute a qualified trust under section 401 and a plan shall be treated as not described in section 403(a) or 405 unless in the case of any merger or consolidation of the plan with, or in the case of any transfer of assets or liabilities of such plan to, any other trust plan after September 2, 1974, each participant in the plan would (if the plan then terminated) receive a benefit immediately after the merger, consolidation, or transfer which is equal to or greater than the benefit he would have been entitled to receive immediately before the merger, consolidation, or transfer (if the plan had then terminated). The preceding sentence does not apply to any multiemployer plan with respect to any transaction to the extent that participants either before or after the transaction are covered under a multiemployer plan to which title IV of the Employee Retirement Income Security Act of 1974 applies.

(m) Employees of an Affiliated Service Group.—

(1) In general.—For purposes of the employee benefit requirements listed in paragraph (4), except to the extent otherwise provided in regulations, all employees of the members of an affiliated service group shall be treated as employed by a single employer.

(2) Affiliated service group.—For purposes of this subsection, the term "affiliated service group" means a group consisting of a service organization (hereinafter in this paragraph referred to as the "first organization") and one or more of the following:

(A) any service organization which—

(i) is a shareholder or partner in the first organization, and

(ii) regularly performs services for the first organization or is regularly associated with the first organization in performing services for third persons, and

(B) any other organization if—

(i) a significant portion of the business of such organization is the performance of services (for the first organization, for organizations described in subparagraph (A), or for both) of a type historically performed in such service field by employees, and

(ii) 10 percent or more of the interests in such organization is held by persons who are officers, highly compensated employees, or owners of the first organization or an organization described in subparagraph (A).

(3) Service organizations.—For purposes of this subsection, the term "service organization" means an organization the principal business of which is the performance of services.

(4) Employee benefit requirements.—For purposes of this subsection, the employee benefit requirements listed in this paragraph are—

(A) paragraphs (3), (4), (7), and (16) of section 401(a),

(B) sections 408(k), 410, 411, 415, and 416,

(C) section 105(h), and

(D) section 125.

*(5) Certain organizations performing management functions.—For purposes of this subsection, the term 'affiliated service group' also includes a group consisting of—

(A) an organization the principal business of which is performing, on a regular and continuing basis, management functions for 1 organization (or for 1 organization and other organizations related to such 1 organization), and

(B) the organization (and related organizations) for which such functions are so performed by the organization described in subparagraph (A).

For purposes of this paragraph, the term 'related organizations' has the same meaning as the term 'related persons' when used in section 103(b)(6)(C).

(6) Other definitions.—For purposes of this subsection—

(A) Organization defined.—The term "organization" means a corporation, partnership, or other organization.

(B) Ownership.—In determining ownership, the principles of section 267(c) shall apply.

*[*Editor's Note:* Section 414(m)(5) is effective for taxable years beginning after Dec. 31, 1983.]

(7) Prevention of avoidance.—The Secretary shall prescribe such regulations as may be necessary to prevent the avoidance with respect to service organizations, through the use of separate organizations, of any employee benefit requirement listed in paragraph (4).

*(n) Employee Leasing.—

(1) In general.—For purposes of the pension requirements listed in paragraph (3), except to the extent otherwise provided in regulations, with respect to any person (hereinafter in this subsection referred to as the 'recipient') for whom a leased employee performs services—

(A) the leased employee shall be treated as an employee of the recipient, but

(B) contributions or benefits provided by the leasing organization which are attributable to services performed for the recipient shall be treated as provided by the recipient.

(2) Leased employee.—For purposes of paragraph (1), the term 'leased employee' means any person who provides services to the recipient if—

(A) such services are provided pursuant to an agreement between the recipient and any other person (in this subsection referred to as the 'leasing organization'),

(B) such person has performed such services for the recipient (or for the recipient and related persons) on a substantially full-time basis for a period of at least 1 year, and

(C) such services are of a type historically performed, in the business field of the recipient, by employees.

(3) Pension requirements.—For purposes of this subsection, the pension requirements listed in this paragraph are—

(A) paragraphs (3), (4), (7), and (16) of section 401(a), and

(B) sections 408(k), 410, 411, 415, and 416.

(4) Time when leased employee is first considered as employee.—In the case of any leased employee, paragraph (1) shall apply only for purposes of determining whether the pension requirements listed in paragraph (3) are met for periods after the close of the 1-year period referred to in paragraph (2); except that years of service for the recipient shall be determined by taking into account the entire period for which the leased employee performed services for the recipient (or related persons).

(5) Safe harbor.—This subsection shall not apply to any leased employee if such employee is covered by a plan which is maintained by the leasing organization if, with respect to such employee, such plan—

(A) is a money purchase pension plan with a nonintegrated employer contribution rate of at least 7½ percent, and

(B) provides for immediate participation and for full and immediate vesting.

(6) Related persons.—For purposes of this subsection, the term 'related persons' has the same meaning as when used in section 103(b)(6)(C).

**SEC. 415. LIMITATIONS ON BENEFITS AND CONTRIBUTIONS UNDER QUALIFIED PLANS.

(a) General Rule.—

(1) Trusts.—A trust which is a part of a pension, profit-sharing, or stock bonus

---

*[*Editor's Note:* Section 414(n) is effective for taxable years beginning after Dec. 31, 1983.]

**[*Editor's Note:* Section 235 of TEFRA (PL 97-248), amended Internal Revenue Code Section 415 to reduce the limitations on benefits and contributions under qualified plans. Section 235(g) of the act, which provided certain effective dates and transition rules, reads as follows:

(g) Effective Dates.—

(1) In general.—

(A) New plans.—In the case of any plan which is not in existence on July 1, 1982, the amendments made by this section shall apply to years ending after July 1, 1982.

(B) Existing plans.—

(i) In the case of any plan which is in existence on July 1, 1982, the amendments made by this section shall apply to years beginning after December 31, 1982.

Code Sec. 414 (m) (7)

(ii) Plan requirements.—A plan shall not be treated as failing to meet the requirements of section 401(a)(16) of the Internal Revenue Code of 1954 for any year beginning before January 1, 1984, merely because such plan provides for benefit or contribution limits which are in excess of the limitations under section 415 of such Code, as amended by this section. The preceding sentence shall not apply to any plan which provides such limits in excess of the limitation under section 415 of such Code before such amendments.

(2) Amendments related to cost-of-living adjustments.—
(A) In general.—Except as provided in subparagraph (b), the amendments made by subsection (b) shall apply to adjustments for years beginning after December 31, 1982.

(B) Adjustment procedures.—The amendments made by subsections (b)(1) and (b)(2)(B) shall apply to adjustments for years beginning after December 31, 1985.

(3) Transition rule where the sum of defined contribution and defined benefit plan fractions exceeds 1.0.—In the case of a plan which satisfied the requirements of section 415 of the Internal Revenue Code of 1954 for the last year beginning before January 1, 1983, the Secretary of the Treasury or his delegate shall prescribe regulations under which an amount is subtracted from the numerator of the defined contribution plan fraction (not exceeding such numerator) so that the sum of the defined benefit plan fraction and the defined contribution plan fraction computed under section 415(e)(1) of the Internal Revenue Code of 1954 (as amended by the Tax Equity and Fiscal Responsibility Act of 1982) does not exceed 1.0 for such year.

(4) Right to higher accrued defined benefit preserved.—
(A) In general.—In the case of an individual who is a participant before January 1, 1983, in a defined benefit plan which is in existence on July 1, 1982, and with respect to which the requirements of section 415 of such Code have been met for all years, if such individual's current accrued benefit under such plan exceeds the limitation of subsection (b) of section 415 of the Internal Revenue Code of 1954 (as amended by this section), then (in the case of such plan) for purposes of subsections (b) and (e) of such section, the limitation of such subsection (b) with respect to such individual shall be equal to such current accrued benefit.

(B) Current accrued benefit defined.—
(i) In general.—For purposes of this paragraph, the term "current accrued benefit" means the individual's accrued benefit (at the close of the last year beginning before January 1, 1983) when expressed as an annual benefit (within the meaning of section 415(b)(2) of such Code as in effect before the amendments made by this Act).

(ii) Special Rule.—For purposes of determining the amount of any individual's current accrued benefit—

(I) no change in the terms and conditions of the plan after July 1, 1982, and

(II) no cost-of-living adjustment occurring after July 1, 1982,

shall be taken into account.

(5) Special rule for collective bargaining agreements.—In the case of a plan maintained on the date of the enactment of this Act pursuant to 1 or more collective bargaining agreements between employee representatives and 1 or more employers, the amendments made by this section and section 242 (relating to age 70½) shall not apply to years beginning before the earlier of—

(A) the date on which the last of the collective bargaining agreements relating to the plan terminates (determined without regard to any extension thereof agreed to after the date of the enactment of this Act), or

(B) January 1, 1986.

For purposes of subparagraph (A), any plan amendment made pursuant to a collective bargaining agreement relating to the plan which amends the plan solely to conform to any requirement added by this section and section 253 shall not be treated as a termination of such collective bargaining agreement.]

Code Sec. 415 (a) (1)

plan shall not constitute a qualified trust under section 401(a) if—

(A) in the case of a defined benefit plan, the plan provides for the payment of benefits with respect to a participant which exceed the limitation of subsection (b),

(B) in the case of a defined contribution plan, contributions and other additions under the plan with respect to any participant for any taxable year exceed the limitation of subsection (c), or

(C) in any case in which an individual is a participant in both a defined benefit plan and a defined contribution plan maintained by the employer, the trust has been disqualified under subsection (g).

(2) Section applies to certain annuities and accounts.—In the case of—

(A) an employee annuity plan described in section 403(a),

(B) an annuity contract described in section 403(b),

(C) a simplified employee pension described in section 408(k), or

(D) a plan described in section 405(a), such a contract, plan, or pension shall not be considered to be described in section 403(a), 403(b), 405(a), or 408(k), as the case may be, unless it satisfies the requirements of subparagraph (A) or subparagraph (B) of paragraph (1), whichever is appropriate, and has not been disqualified under subsection (g). In the case of an annuity contract described in section 403(b), the preceding sentence shall apply only to the portion of the annuity contract which exceeds the limitation of subsection (b) or the limitation of subsection (c), whichever is appropriate, and the amount of the contribution for such portion shall reduce the exclusion allowance as provided in section 403(b)(2).

(b) Limitation for Defined Benefit Plans.—

(1) In general.—Benefits with respect to a participant exceed the limitation of this subsection if, when expressed as an annual benefit (within the meaning of paragraph (2)), such annual benefit is greater than the lesser of—

(A) $90,000, or

(B) 100 percent of the participant's average compensation for his high 3 years.

(2) Annual benefit.—

(A) In general.—For purposes of paragraph (1), the term "annual benefit" means a benefit payable annually in the form of a straight life annuity (with no ancillary benefits) under a plan to which employees do not contribute and under which no rollover contributions (as defined in sections 402(a)(5), 403(a)(4), 408(d)(3), and 409(b)(3)(C) are made.

(B) Adjustment for certain other forms of benefit.—If the benefit under the plan is payable in any form other than the form described in subparagraph (A), or if the employees contribute to the plan or make rollover contributions (as defined in sections 402(a)(5), 403(a)(4), 408(d)(3) and 409(b)(3)(C)), the determinations as to whether the limitation described in paragraph (1) has been satisfied shall be made, in accordance with regulations prescribed by the Secretary, by adjusting such benefit so that it is equivalent to the benefit described in subparagraph (A). For purposes of this subparagraph, any ancillary benefit which is not directly related to retirement income benefits shall not be taken into account; and that portion of any joint and survivor annuity which constitutes a qualified joint and survivor annuity (as defined in section 401(a)(11)(G)(iii) shall not be taken into account.

(C) Adjustment to $90,000 limit where benefit begins before age 62.—If the retirement income benefit under the plan begins before age 62, the determination as to whether the $90,000 limitation set forth in paragraph (1)(A) has been satisfied shall be made, in accordance with regulations prescribed by the Secretary, by adjusting such benefit so that it is equivalent to such a benefit beginning at age 62. The reduction under this subparagraph shall not reduce the limitation of paragraph (1)(A) below—

(i) if the benefit begins at or after age 55, $75,000, or

(ii) if the benefit begins before age 55, the amount which is the equivalent of the $75,000 limitation for age 55.

(D) **Adjustment to $90,000 limitation where benefit begins after age 65.**—If the retirement income benefit under the plan begins after age 65, the determination as to whether the $90,000 limitation set forth in paragraph (1)(A) has been satisfied shall be made, in accordance with regulations prescribed by the Secretary, by adjusting such benefit so that it is equivalent to such a benefit beginning at age 65.

(E) **Limitation on certain assumptions.**—

(i) For purposes of adjusting any benefit under subparagraph (B) or (C), the interest rate assumption shall not be less than the greater of 5 percent or the rate specified in the plan.

(ii) For purposes of adjusting any benefit under subparagraph (D), the interest rate assumption shall not be greater than the lesser of 5 percent or the rate specified in the plan.

(iii) For purposes of adjusting any benefit under subparagraph (B), (C), or (D), no adjustments under subsection (d)(1) shall be taken into account before the year for which such adjustment first takes effect.

(3) **Average compensation for high 3 years.**—For purposes of paragraph (1), a participant's high 3 years shall be the period of consecutive calendar years (not more than 3) during which the participant both was an active participant in the plan and had the greatest aggregate compensation from the employer. In the case of an employee within the meaning of section 401(c)(1), the preceding sentence shall be applied by substituting for "compensation from the employer" the following: "the participant's earned income (within the meaning of section 401(c)(2) but determined without regard to any exclusion under section 911)".

(4) **Total annual benefit not in excess of $10,000.**—Notwithstanding the preceding provisions of this subsection, the benefits payable with respect to a participant under any defined benefit plan shall be deemed not to exceed the limitation of this subsection if—

(A) the retirement benefits payable with respect to such participant under such plan and under all other defined benefit plans of the employer do not exceed $10,000 for the plan year, or for any prior plan year, and

(B) the employer has not at any time maintained a defined contribution plan in which the participant participated.

(5) **Reduction for service less than 10 years.**—In the case of an employee who has less than 10 years of service with the employer, the limitation referred to in paragraph (1), and the limitation referred to in paragraph (4), shall be the limitation determined under such paragraph (without regard to this paragraph), multiplied by a fraction, the numerator of which is the number of years (or part thereof) of service with the employer and the denominator of which is 10.

(6) **Computation of benefits and contributions.**—The computation of—

(A) benefits under a defined contribution plan, for purposes of section 401(a)(4),

(B) contributions made on behalf of a participant in a defined benefit plan, for purposes of section 401(a)(4), and

(C) contributions and benefits provided for a participant in a plan described in section 414(k), for purposes of this section

shall not be made on a basis inconsistent with regulations prescribed by the Secretary.

(7) **Benefits under certain collectively bargained plans.**—For a year, the limitation referred to in paragraph (1)(B) shall not apply to benefits with respect to a participant under a defined benefit plan—

(A) which is maintained for such year pursuant to a collective bargaining agreement between employee representatives and one or more employers,

(B) which, at all times during such year, has at least 100 participants,

(C) under which benefits are determined solely by reference to length of service, the particular years during which service was rendered, age at retirement, and date of retirement,

(D) which provides that an employee who has at least 4 years of service has a nonforfeitable right to 100 percent of his accrued benefit derived from employer contributions, and

(E) which requires, as a condition of participation in the plan, that an employee complete a period of not more than 60 consecutive days of service with the employer or employers maintaining the plan.

Code Sec. 415 (b) (7)

This paragraph shall not apply to a participant whose compensation for any 3 years during the 10-year period immediately preceding the year in which he separates from service exceeded the average compensation for such 3 years of all participants in such plan. This paragraph shall not apply to a participant for any period for which he is a participant under another plan to which this section applies which is maintained by an employer maintaining this plan. For any year for which the paragraph applies to benefits with respect to a participant, paragraph (1)(A) and subsection (d)(1)(A) shall be applied with respect to such participant by substituting the greater of $68,212 or one-half the amount otherwise applicable for such year under paragraph (1)(A) for $90,000.

(c) **Limitation for Defined Contribution Plans.**—

(1) **In general.**—Contributions and other additions with respect to a participant exceed the limitation of this subsection if, when expressed as an annual addition (within the meaning of paragraph (2)) to the participant's account, such annual addition is greater than the lesser of—
(A) $30,000 or
(B) 25 percent of the participant's compensation.

(2) **Annual addition.**—For purposes of paragraph (1), the term "annual addition" means the sum for any year of—
(A) employer contributions,
(B) the lesser of—
(i) the amount of the employee contributions in excess of 6 percent of his compensation, or
(ii) one-half of the employee contributions, and
(C) forfeitures.
For the purposes of this paragraph, employee contributions under subparagraph (B) are determined without regard to any rollover contributions (as defined in sections 402(a)(5), 403(a)(4), 403(b)(8), 405(d)(3), 408(d)(3), and 409(b)(3)(C) without regard to employee contributions to a simplified employee pension allowable as a deduction under section 219(a), and without regard to deductible

*[*Editor's Note:* Section 415(c)(3) is effective for taxable years beginning after Dec. 31, 1982.]

employee contributions within the meaning of section 72(o)(5).

*(3) **Participant's compensation.**—For purposes of paragraph (1)—
(A) **In general.**—The term 'participant's compensation' means the compensation of the participant from the employer for the year.
(B) **Special rule for self-employed individuals.**—In the case of an employee within the meaning of section 401(c)(1), subparagraph (A) shall be applied by substituting 'the participant's earned income (within the meaning of section 401(c)(2) but determined without regard to any exclusion under section 911)' for 'compensation of the participant from the employer'.
(C) **Special rules for permanent and total disability.**—In the case of a participant—
(i) who is permanently and totally disabled (as defined in section 105(d)(4)),
(ii) who is not an officer, owner, or highly compensated, and
(iii) with respect to whom the employer elects, at such time and in such manner as the Secretary may prescribe, to have this subparagraph apply,
the term 'participant's compensation' means the compensation the participant would have received for the year if the participant was paid at the rate of compensation paid immediately before becoming permanently and totally disabled. This subparagraph shall only apply if contributions made with respect to such participant are nonforfeitable when made.

(4) **Special election for section 403(b) contracts purchased by educational organizations, hospitals, home health service agencies and certain churches, etc.**—
(A) In the case of amounts contributed for an annuity contract described in section 403(b) for the year in which occurs a participant's separation from the service with an educational organization, a hospital, a home health service agency, or a church, convention or association of churches, or an organization described in section 414(e)(3)(B)(ii), at the election of the participant there is substituted for the amount specified in paragraph (1)(B) the amount of the exclusion allowance which would be determined under section 403(b)(2)

Code Sec. 415 (c)

(without regard to this section) for the participant's taxable year in which such separation occurs if the participant's years of service were computed only by taking into account his service for the employer (as determined for purposes of section 403(b)(2)) during the period of years (not exceeding ten) ending on the date of such separation.

(B) In the case of amounts contributed for an annuity contract described in section 403(b) for any year in the case of a participant who is an employee of an educational organization, a hospital, a home health service agency, or a church, convention or association of churches, or an organization described in section 414(e)(3)(B)(ii), at the election of the participant there is substituted for the amount specified in paragraph (1)(B) the least of—

(i) 25 percent of the participant's includible compensation (as defined in section 403(b)(3)) plus $4,000,

(ii) the amount of the exclusion allowance determined for the year under section 403(b)(2), or

(iii) $15,000.

(C) In the case of amounts contributed for an annuity contract described in section 403(b) for any year for a participant who is an employee of an educational organization, a hospital, a home health service agency, or a church, convention or association of churches, or an organization described in section 414(e)(3)(B)(ii), at the election of the participant the provisions of section 403(b)(2)(A) shall not apply.

(D)(i) The provisions of this paragraph apply only if the participant elects its application at the time and in the manner provided under regulations prescribed by the Secretary. Not more than one election may be made under subparagraph (A) by any participant. A participant who elects to have the provisions of subparagraph (A), (B), or (C) of this paragraph apply to him may not elect to have any other subparagraph of this paragraph apply to him. Any election made under this paragraph is irrevocable.

(ii) For purposes of this paragraph the term "educational organization" means an educational organization as described in section 170(b)(1)(A)(ii).

(iii) For purposes of this paragraph the term "home health service agency" means an organization described in subsection 501(c)(3) which is exempt from tax under section 501(a) and which has been determined by the Secretary of Health, Education, and Welfare to be a home health agency (as defined in section 1861(o) of the Social Security Act).

(iv) For purposes of this paragraph, the terms 'church' and 'convention or association of churches' have the same meaning as when used in section 414(e).

(5) [Repealed].

(6) **Special limitation for employee stock ownership plan.**—

(A) In the case of an employee stock ownership plan (as defined in subparagraph (B)), under which no more than one-third of the employer contributions for a year are allocated to the group of employees consisting of officers, shareholders owning more than 10 percent of the employer's stock (determined under subparagraph (B)(iv)), or employees described in subparagraph (B)(iii), the amount described in paragraph (c)(1)(A) (as adjusted for such year pursuant to subsection (d)(1)) for a year with respect to any participant shall be equal to the sum of (i) the amount described in paragraph (c)(1)(A) (as so adjusted) determined without regard to this paragraph and (ii) the lesser of the amount determined under clause (i) or the amount of employer securities contributed or purchased with cash contributed to the employee stock ownership plan.

(B) For purposes of this paragraph—

(i) the term "employee stock ownership plan" means a [an] employee stock ownership plan (within the meaning of section 4975(e)(7)) or a tax credit employee stock ownership plan,

(ii) the term "employer securities" has the meaning given to such term by section 409A,

(iii) an employee described in this clause is any participant whose compensation for a year exceeds an amount equal to twice the amount described in paragraph (c)(1)(A) for such year (as adjusted for such year pursuant to subsection (d)(1)), determined without regard to subparagraph (A) of this paragraph, and

(iv) an individual shall be considered to own more than 10 percent of the employer's stock if, without regard to stock held under the employee stock ownership plan, he

Code Sec. 415 (c) (6)

owns (after application of section 1563(e)) more than 10 percent of the total combined voting power of all classes of stock entitled to vote or more than 10 percent of the total value of shares of all classes of stock.

(C) In the case of an employee stock ownership plan (as described in section 4975(e)(7)), under which no more than one-third of the employer contributions for a year which are deductible under paragraph (10) of section 404(a) are allocated to the group of employees consisting of officers, shareholders owning more than 10 percent of the employer's stock (determined under subparagraph (B)(iv)), or employees described in subparagraph (B)(iii), the limitations imposed by this section shall not apply to—

(i) forfeitures of employer securities under an employee stock ownership plan (as described in section 4975(e)(7)) if such securities were acquired with the proceeds of a loan (as described in section 404(a)(10)(A)), or

(ii) employer contributions to such an employee stock ownership plan which are deductible under section 404(a)(10)(B) and charged against the participant's account.

(7) Certain level premium annuity contracts under plans benefiting owner-employees.—Paragraph (1)(B) shall not apply to a contribution described in section 401(e) which is made on behalf of a participant for a year to a plan which benefits an owner-employee (within the meaning of section 401(c)(3)), if—

(A) the annual addition determined under this section with respect to the participant for such year consists solely of such contribution, and

(B) the participant is not an active participant at any time during such year in a defined benefit plan maintained by the employer.

For purposes of this section and section 401(e), in the case of a plan which provides contributions or benefits for employees who are not owner-employees, such plan will not be treated as failing to satisfy section 401(a)(4) merely because contributions made on behalf of employees who are not owner-employees are not permitted to exceed the limitations of paragraph (1)(B).

*[*Editor's Note:* Section 415(c)(8) is effective for taxable years beginning after Dec. 31, 1981.]

*(8) Certain contributions by church plans not treated as exceeding limits.—

(A) Alternative exclusion allowance.—Any contribution or addition with respect to any participant, when expressed as an annual addition, which is allocable to the application of section 403(b)(2)(D) to such participant for such year, shall be treated as not exceeding the limitations of paragraph (1).

(B) Contributions not in excess of $40,000 ($10,000 per year).—

(i) In general.—Notwithstanding any other provision of this subsection, at the election of a participant who is an employee of a church, a convention or association of churches, including an organization described in section 414(e)(3)(B)(ii), contributions and other additions for an annuity contract or retirement income account described in section 403(b) with respect to such participant, when expressed as an annual addition to such participant's account, shall be treated as not exceeding the limitation of paragraph (1) if such annual addition is not in excess of $10,000.

(ii) $40,000 aggregate limitation.—The total amount of additions with respect to any participant which may be taken into account for purposes of this subparagraph for all years may not exceed $40,000.

(iii) No election if paragraph (4)(A) election made.—No election may be made under this subparagraph for any year if an election is made under paragraph (4)(A) for such year.

(C) Annual addition.—For purposes of this paragraph, the term 'annual addition' has the meaning given such term by paragraph (2).

(d) Cost-of-Living Adjustments.—
Code Sec. 415(c)(6)(B)(ii)

(1) In general.—The Secretary shall adjust annually—

(A) the $90,000 amount in subsection (b)(1)(A),

(B) the $30,000 amount in subsection (c)(1)(A), and

(C) in the case of a participant who is separated from service, the amount taken into account under subsection (b)(1)(B).

for increases in the cost of living in accordance with regulations prescribed by the

Secretary. Such regulations shall provide for adjustment procedures which are similar to the procedures used to adjust benefit amounts under section 215(i)(2)(A) of the Social Security Act.

(2) Base periods.—The base period taken into account—

(A) for purposes of subparagraphs (A) and (B) of paragraph (1) is the calendar quarter beginning October 1, 1984, and

(B) for purposes of subparagraph (C) of paragraph (1) is the last calendar quarter of the calendar year before the calendar year in which the participant is separated from service.

(3) Freeze on adjustment to defined contribution and benefit limits.—The Secretary shall not make any adjustment under subparagraph (A) or (B) of paragraph (1) with respect to any year beginning after December 31, 1982, and before January 1, 1986.

(e) Limitation in Case of Defined Benefit Plan and Defined Contribution Plan for Same Employee.—

(1) In general.—In any case in which an individual is a participant in both a defined benefit plan and a defined contribution plan maintained by the same employer, the sum of the defined benefit plan fraction and the defined contribution plan fraction for any year may not exceed 1.0.

(2) Defined benefit plan fraction.—For purposes of this subsection, the defined benefit plan fraction for any year is a fraction—

(A) the numerator of which is the projected annual benefit of the participant under the plan (determined as of the close of the year), and

(B) the denominator of which is the lesser of—

(i) the product of 1.25, multiplied by the dollar limitation in effect under subsection (b)(1)(A) for such year, or

(ii) the product of—

(I) 1.4, multiplied by

(II) the amount which may be taken into account under subsection (b)(1)(B) with respect to such individual under the plan for such year.

(3) Defined contribution plan fraction. —For purposes of this subsection, the defined contribution plan fraction for any year is a fraction—

(A) the numerator of which is the sum of the annual additions to the participant's account as of the close of the year, and

(b) the denominator of which is the sum of the lesser of the following amounts determined for such year and for each prior year of service with the employer:

(i) the product of 1.25, multiplied by the dollar limitation in effect under subsection (c)(1)(A) for such year (determined without regard to subsection (c)(6)), or

(ii) the product of—

(I) 1.4, multiplied by—

(II) the amount which may be taken into account under subsection (c)(1)(B) (or subsection (c)(7) or (8), if applicable) with respect to such individual under such plan for such year.

(4) Special transition rules for defined contribution fraction.—In applying paragraph (3) with respect to years beginning before January 1, 1976—

(A) the aggregate amount taken into account under paragraph (3)(A) may not exceed the aggregate amount taken into account under paragraph (3)(B), and

(B) the amount taken into account under subsection (c)(2)(B)(i) for any year concerned is an amount equal to—

(i) the excess of the aggregate amount of employee contributions for all years beginning before January 1, 1976, during which the employee was an active participant of the plan, over 10 percent of the employee's aggregate compensation for all such years, multiplied by

(ii) a fraction the numerator of which is 1 and the denominator of which is the number of years beginning before January 1, 1976, during which the employee was an active participant in the plan.

Employee contributions made on or after October 2, 1973, shall be taken into account under subparagraph (B) of the preceding sentence only to the extent that the amount of such contributions does not exceed the maximum amount of contributions permissible under the plan as in effect on October 2, 1973.

(5) Special rules for sections 403(b) and 408.—For purposes of this section, any annuity contract described in section 403(b) (except in the case of a participant who has

Code Sec. 415 (e) (5)

elected under subsection (c)(4)(D) to have the provisions of subsection (c)(4)(C) apply) for the benefit of a participant shall be treated as a defined contribution plan maintained by each employer with respect to which the participant has the control required under subsection (b) or (c) of section 414 (as modified by subsection (h)). For purposes of this section, any contribution by an employer to a simplified employee pension for an individual for a taxable year shall be treated as an employer contribution to a defined contribution plan for such individual for such year. In the case of any annuity contract described in section 403(b), the amount of the contribution disqualified by reason of subsection (g) shall reduce the exclusion allowance as provided in section 403(b)(2).

(6) Special transition rule for defined contribution fraction for years ending after December 31, 1982.—
(A) In general.—At the election of the plan administrator, in applying paragraph (3) with respect to any year ending after December 31, 1982, the amount taken into account under paragraph (3)(B) with respect to each participant for all years ending before January 1, 1983, shall be an amount equal to the product of—
(i) the amount determined under paragraph (3)(B) (as in effect for the year ending in 1982) for the year ending in 1982, multiplied by
(ii) the transition fraction.
(B) Transition fraction.—The term 'transition fraction' means a fraction—
(i) the numerator of which is the lesser of—
(I) $51,875, or
(II) 1.4, multiplied by 25 percent of the compensation of the participant for the year ending in 1981, and
(ii) the denominator of which is the lesser of—
(I) $41,500, or
(II) 25 percent of the compensation of the participant for the year ending in 1981.

(f) Combining of Plans.—

(1) In general.—For purposes of applying the limitations of subsections (b), (c), and (e)—
(A) all defined benefit plans (whether or not terminated) of an employer are to be treated as one defined benefit plan, and
(B) all defined contribution plans (whether or not terminated) of an employer are to be treated as one defined benefit plan, and

(2) Annual compensation taken into account for defined benefit plans.—If the employer has more than one defined benefit plan—
(A) subsection (b)(1)(B) shall be applied separately with respect to each such plan, but
(B) in applying subsection (b)(1)(B) to the aggregate of such defined benefit plans for purposes of this subsection, the high 3 years of compensation taken into account shall be the period of consecutive calendar years (not more than 3) during which the individual had the greatest aggregate compensation from the employer.

(g) Aggregation of Plans.—The Secretary, in applying the provisions of this section to benefits or contributions under more than one plan maintained by the same employer, and to any trusts, contracts, accounts, or bonds referred to in subsection (a)(2), with respect to which the participant has the control required under section 414(b) or (c), as modified by subsection (h), shall, under regulations prescribed by the Secretary, disqualify one or more trusts, plans, contracts, accounts, or bonds, or any combination thereof until such benefits or contributions do not exceed the limitations contained in this section. In addition to taking into account such other factors as may be necessary to carry out the purposes of subsections (e) and (f), the regulations prescribed under this paragraph shall provide that no plan which has been terminated shall be disqualified until all other trusts, plans, contracts, accounts, or bonds have been disqualified.

(h) 50 Percent Control.—For purposes of applying subsections (b) and (c) of section 414 to this section, the phrase "more than 50 percent" shall be substituted for the phrase "at least 80 percent" each place it appears in section 1563(a)(1).

(i) Records Not Available For Past Periods.—Where for the period before Janu-

Code Sec. 415 (e) (6)

IRC EXCERPTS

ary 1, 1976, or (if later) the first day of the first plan year of the plan, the records necessary for the application of this section are not available, the Secretary may by regulations prescribe alternative methods for determining the amounts to be taken into account for such period.

(j) **Regulations; Definition of Year.**—The Secretary shall prescribe such regulations as may be necessary to carry out the purposes of this section, including, but not limited to, regulations defining the term "year" for purposes of any provision of this section.

(k) **Special Rules.**—

(1) **Defined benefit plan and defined contribution plan.**—For purposes of this title, the term "defined contribution plan" or "defined benefit plan" means a defined contribution plan (within the meaning of section 414(i)) or a defined benefit plan (within the meaning of section 414(j)), whichever applies, which is—
(A) a plan described in section 401(a) which includes a trust which is exempt from tax under section 501(a),
(B) an annuity plan described in section 403(a),
(C) a qualified bond purchase plan described in section 405(a),
(D) an annuity contract described in section 403(b),
(E) an individual retirement account described in section 408(a),
(F) an individual retirement annuity described in section 408(b),
(G) a simplified employee pension, or
(H) an individual retirement bond described in section 409.

*SEC. 416. SPECIAL RULES FOR TOP-HEAVY PLANS.

(a) **General Rule.**—A trust shall not constitute a qualified trust under section 401(a) for any plan year if the plan of which it is a part is a top-heavy plan for such plan year unless such plan meets—
(1) the vesting requirements of subsection (b),
(2) the minimum benefit requirements of subsection (c), and
(3) the limitation on compensation requirement of subsection (d).

(b) **Vesting Requirements.**—

(1) **In general.**—A plan satisfies the requirements of this subsection if it satisfies the requirements of either of the following subparagraphs:
(A) 3-year vesting.—A plan satisfies the requirements of this subparagraph if an employee who has completed at least 3 years of service with the employer or employers maintaining the plan has a nonforfeitable right to 100 percent of his accrued benefit derived from employer contributions.
(B) 6-year graded vesting.—A plan satisfies the requirements of this subparagraph if an employee has a nonforfeitable right to a percentage of his accrued benefit derived from employer contributions determined under the following table:

Years of Service	The nonforfeitable percentage is:
2	20
3	40
4	60
5	80
6 or more	100

*[*Editor's Note:* Section 240 of TEFRA (PL 97-248) added Internal Revenue Code Section 416 to provide special rules for top heavy plans. Section 241 of the act, on effective dates for the top heavy plan rules, reads as follows:

SEC. 241. EFFECTIVE DATES.

(a) **General Rule.**—Except as provided in subsection (b), the amendments made by this part shall apply to years beginning after December 31, 1983.

(b) **Allowance of Exclusion of Death Benefit for Self-Employed Individuals.**—The amendment made by section 239 shall apply with respect to decedents dying after December 31, 1983. *Note:* Section 239 amended code section 101(b)(3) to provide that the term "employee" does not include a self-employed individual described in section 401(c)(1).]

Code Sec. 416 (b) (1)

(2) Certain rules made applicable.—Except to the extent inconsistent with the provisions of this subsection, the rules of section 411 shall apply for purposes of this subsection.

(c) Plan Must Provide Minimum Benefits.—

(1) Defined benefit plans.—
(A) In general.—A defined benefit plan meets the requirements of this subsection if the accrued benefit derived from employer contributions of each participant who is a non-key employee, when expressed as an annual retirement benefit, is not less than the applicable percentage of the participant's average compensation for years in the testing period.

(B) Applicable percentage.—For purposes of subparagraph (A), the term 'applicable percentage' means the lesser of—

(i) 2 percent multiplied by the number of years of service with the employer, or

(ii) 20 percent.

(C) Years of service.—For purposes of this paragraph—

(i) In general.—Except as provided in clause (ii), years of service shall be determined under the rules of paragraphs (4), (5), and (6) of section 411(a).

(ii) Exception for years during which plan was not top-heavy.—A year of service with the employer shall not be taken into account under this paragraph if—

(I) the plan was not a top-heavy plan for any plan year ending during such year of service, or

(II) such year of service was completed in a plan year beginning before January 1, 1984.

(D) Average compensation for high 5 years.—For purposes of this paragraph—

(i) In general.—A participant's testing period shall be the period of consecutive years (not exceeding 5) during which the participant had the greatest aggregate compensation from the employer.

(ii) Year must be included in year of service.—The years taken into account under clause (i) shall be properly adjusted for years not included in a year of service.

(iii) Certain years not taken into account.—Except to the extent provided in the plan, a year shall not be taken into account under clause (i) if—

(I) such year ends in a plan year beginning before January 1, 1984, or

(II) such year begins after the close of the last year in which the plan was a top-heavy plan.

(E) Annual retirement benefit.—For purposes of this paragraph, the term 'annual retirement benefit' means a benefit payable annually in the form of a single life annuity (with no ancillary benefits) beginning at the normal retirement age under the plan.

(2) Defined contribution plans.—
(A) In general.—A defined contribution plan meets the requirements of the subsection if the employer contribution for the year for each participant who is a non-key employee is not less than 3 percent of such participant's compensation (within the meaning of section 415).

(B) Special rule where maximum contribution less than 3 percent.—

(i) In general.—The percentage referred to in subparagraph (A) for any year shall not exceed the percentage at which contributions are made (or required to be made) under the plan for the year for the key employee for whom such percentage is the highest for the year.

(ii) Determination of percentage.—The determination referred to in clause (i) shall be determined for each key employee by dividing the contributions for such employee by so much of his total compensation for the year as does not exceed $200,000.

(iii) Treatment of aggregation groups.—

(I) For purposes of this subparagraph, all defined contribution plans required to be included in an aggregation group under subsection (g)(2)(A)(i) shall be treated as one plan.

(II) This subparagraph shall not apply to any plan required to be included in an aggregation group if such plan enables a defined benefit plan required to be included in such group to meet the requirements of section 401(a)(4) or 410.

(C) Certain amounts not taken into account.—For purposes of this paragraph, any employer contribution attributable to a salary reduction or similar arrangement shall not be taken into account.

Code Sec. 416 (c)

(d) Not More Than $200,000 in Annual Compensation Taken Into Account.—

(1) In general.—A plan meets the requirements of this subsection if the annual compensation of each employee taken into account under the plan does not exceed the first $200,000.

(2) Cost-of-living adjustments.—The Secretary shall annually adjust the $200,000 amount contained in paragraph (1) of this subsection and in clause (ii) of subsection (c)(2)(B) in the same manner as he adjusts the dollar amount contained in section 415(c)(1)(A).

(e) Plan Must Meet Requirements Without Taking Into Account Social Security and Similar Contributions and Benefits.—A top-heavy plan shall not be treated as meeting the requirement of subsection (b) or (c) unless such plan meets such requirement without taking into account contributions or benefits under chapter 2 (relating to tax on self-employment income), chapter 21 (relating to Federal Insurance Contributions Act), title II of the Social Security Act, or any other Federal or State law.

(f) Coordination Where Employer Has 2 or More Plans.—The Secretary shall prescribe such regulations as may be necessary or appropriate to carry out the purposes of this section where the employer has 2 or more plans including (but not limited to) regulations to prevent inappropriate omissions or require duplication of minimum benefits or contributions.

(g) Top-Heavy Plan Defined.—For purposes of this section—

(1) In general.—
(A) Plans not required to be aggregated.—Except as provided in subparagraph (B), the term 'top-heavy plan' means, with respect to any plan year—
(i) any defined benefit plan if, as of the determination date, the present value of the cumulative accrued benefits under the plan for key employees exceeds 60 percent of the present value of the cumulative accrued benefits under the plan for all employees, and
(ii) any defined contribution plan if, as of the determination date, the aggregate of the accounts of key employees under the plan exceeds 60 percent of the aggregate of the accounts of all employees under such plan.
(B) Aggregated plans.—Each plan of an employer required to be included in an aggregation group shall be treated as a top-heavy plan if such group is a top-heavy group.

(2) Aggregation.—For purposes of this subsection—
(A) Aggregation group.—
(i) Required aggregation—The term 'aggregation group' means—
(I) each plan of the employer in which a key employee is a participant, and
(II) each other plan of the employer which enables any plan described in subclause (I) to meet the requirements of section 401(a)(4) or 410.
(ii) Permissive aggregation.—The employer may treat any plan not required to be included in an aggregation group under clause (i) as being part of such group if such group would continue to meet the requirements of sections 401(a)(4) and 410 with such plan being taken into account.
(B) Top-heavy group.—The term 'top-heavy group' means any aggregation group if—
(i) the sum (as of the determination date) of—
(I) the present value of the cumulative accrued benefits for key employees under all defined benefit plans included in such group, and
(II) the aggregate of the accounts of key employees under all defined contribution plans included in such group,
(ii) exceeds 60 percent of a similar sum determined for all employees.

(3) Distributions during last 5 years taken into account.—For purposes of determining—
(A) the present value of the cumulative accrued benefit for any employee, or
(B) the amount of the account of any employee,
such present value or amount shall be increased by the aggregate distributions made with respect to such employee under the plan during the 5-year period ending on the determination date.

(4) Other special rules.—For purposes of this subsection—

Code Sec. 416 (g) (4)

(A) Rollover contributions to plan not taken into account.—Except to the extent provided in regulations, any rollover contribution (or similar transfer) initiated by the employee and made after December 31, 1983, to a plan shall not be taken into account with respect to the transferee plan for purposes of determining whether such plan is a top-heavy plan (or whether any aggregation group which includes such plan is a top-heavy group).

(B) Benefits not taken into account if employee ceases to be key employee.—If any individual is a non-key employee with respect to any plan for any plan year, but such individual was a key employee with respect to such plan for any prior plan year, any accrued benefit for such employee (and the account of such employee) shall not be taken into account.

(C) Determination date.—The term 'determination date' means, with respect to any plan year—

(i) the last day of the preceding plan year, or

(ii) in the case of the first plan year of any plan, the last day of such plan year.

(D) Years.—To the extent provided in regulations, this section shall be applied on the basis of any year specified in such regulations in lieu of plan years.

(h) Adjustments in Section 415 Limits for Top-Heavy Plans.—

(1) In general.—In the case of any top-heavy plan, paragraphs (2)(B) and (3)(B) of section 415(e) shall be applied by substituting '1.0' for '1.25'.

(2) Exception where benefits for key employees do not exceed 90 percent of total benefits and additional contributions are made for non-key employees.—Paragraph (1) shall not apply with respect to any top-heavy plan if the requirements of subparagraphs (A) and (B) of this paragraph are met with respect to such plan.

(A) Minimum benefit requirements.—

(i) In general.—The requirements of this subparagraph are met with respect to any top-heavy plan if such plan (and any plan required to be included in an aggregation group with such plan) meets the requirements of subsection (c) as modified by clause (ii).

(ii) Modifications.—For purposes of clause (i)—

(I) paragraph (1)(B) of subsection (c) shall be applied by substituting '3 percent' for '2 percent', and by increasing (but not by more than 10 percentage points) 20 percent by 1 percentage point for each year for which such plan was taken into account under this subsection, and

(II) paragraph (2)(A) shall be applied by substituting '4 percent' for '3 percent'.

(B) Benefits for key employees cannot exceed 90 percent of total benefits.—A plan meets the requirements of this subparagraph if such plan would not be a top-heavy plan if '90 percent' were substituted for '60 percent' each place it appears in paragraphs (1)(A) and (2)(B) of subsection (g).

(3) Transition rule.—If, but for this paragraph, paragraph (1) would begin to apply with respect to any top-heavy plan, the application of paragraph (1) shall be suspended with respect to any individual so long as there are no—

(A) employer contributions, forfeitures, or voluntary nondeductible contributions allocated to such individual, or

(B) accruals for such individual under the defined benefit plan.

(4) Coordination with transitional rule under section 415.—In the case of any top-heavy plan to which paragraph (1) applies, section 415(e)(6)(B)(i) shall be applied by substituting '$41,500' for '$51,875'.

(i) Definitions.—For purposes of this section—

(1) Key employee.—

(A) In general.—The term 'key employee' means any participant in an employer plan who, at any time during the plan year or any of the 4 preceding plan years, is—

(i) an officer of the employer,

(ii) 1 of the 10 employees owning (or considered as owning within the meaning of section 318) the largest interests in the employer,

(iii) a 5-percent owner of the employer, or

(iv) a 1-percent owner of the employer having an annual compensation from the employer of more than $150,000.

Code Sec. 416 (h)

For purposes of clause (i), no more than 50 employees (or, if lesser, the greater of 3 or 10 percent of the employees) shall be treated as officers.

(B) Percentage owners.—

(i) 5-percent owner.—For purposes of this paragraph, the term '5-percent owner' means—

(I) if the employer is a corporation, any person who owns (or is considered as owning within the meaning of section 318) more than 5 percent of the outstanding stock of the corporation or stock possessing more than 5 percent of the total combined voting power of all stock of the corporation, or

(II) if the employer is not a corporation, any person who owns more than 5 percent of the capital or profits interest in the employer.

(ii) 1-percent owner.—For purposes of this paragraph, the term '1-percent owner' means any person who would be described in clause (i) if '1 percent' were substituted for '5 percent' each place it appears in clause (i).

(iii) Constructive ownership rules.—For purposes of this subparagraph and subparagraph (A)(ii)(II)—

(I) subparagraph (C) of section 318(a)(2) shall be applied by substituting '5 percent' for '50 percent', and

(II) in the case of any employer which is not a corporation, ownership in such employer shall be determined in accordance with regulations prescribed by the Secretary which shall be based on principles similar to the principles of section 318 (as modified by subclause (I)).

(C) Aggregation rules do not apply for purposes of determining 5-percent or 1-percent owners.—The rules of subsections (b), (c), and (m) of section 414 shall not apply for purposes of determining ownership in the employer.

(2) **Non-key employee.**—The term 'non-key employee' means any employee who is not a key employee.

(3) **Self-employed individuals.**—In the case of a self-employed individual described in section 401(c)(1)—

(A) such individual shall be treated as an employee, and

(B) such individual's earned income (within the meaning of section 401(c)(2)) shall be treated as compensation.

(4) **Treatment of employees covered by collective bargaining agreements.**—The requirements of subsections (b), (c), and (d) shall not apply with respect to any employee included in a unit of employees covered by an agreement which the Secretary of Labor finds to be a collective bargaining agreement between employee representatives and 1 or more employers if there is evidence that retirement benefits were the subject of good faith bargaining between such employee representatives and such employer or employers.

(5) **Treatment of beneficiaries.**—The terms 'employee' and 'key employee' include their beneficiaries.

(6) **Treatment of simplified employee pensions.**—

(A) Treatment as defined contribution plans.—A simplified employee pension shall be treated as a defined contribution plan.

(B) Election to have determinations based on employer contributions.—In the case of a simplified employee pension, at the election of the employer, paragraphs (1)(A)(ii) and (2)(B) of subsection (g) shall be applied by taking into account aggregate employer contributions in lieu of the aggregate of the accounts of employees.

*Subpart C—Special Rules for Multiemployer Plans

Section
418. Reorganization status.
418A. Notice of reorganization and funding requirements.
418B. Minimum contribution requirement.
418C. Overburden credit against minimum contribution requirement.
418D. Adjustments in accrued benefits.
418E. Insolvent plans.

---

*[*Editor's Note:* The effective date of this subpart, as provided in section 210(b) of the Multiemployer Pension Plan Amendments Act of 1980, is as follows:

Code Sec. 416 (i) (6)

SEC. 418. REORGANIZATION STATUS.

(a) **General Rule.**—A multiemployer plan is in reorganization for a plan year if the plan's reorganization index for that year is greater than zero.

(b) **Reorganization Index.**—For purposes of this subpart—

(1) **In general.**—A plan's reorganization index for any plan year is the excess of—
(A) the vested benefits charge for such year, over
(B) the net charge to the funding standard account for such year.

(2) **Net charge to funding standard account.**—The net charge to the funding standard account for any plan year is the excess (if any) of—
(A) the charges to the funding standard account for such year under section 412(b)(2), over
(B) the credits to the funding standard account under section 412(b)(3)(B).

(3) **Vested benefits charge.**—The vested benefits charge for any plan year is the amount which would be necessary to amortize the plan's unfunded vested benefits as of the end of the base plan year in equal annual installments—
(A) over 10 years, to the extent such benefits are attributable to persons in pay status, and
(B) over 25 years, to the extent such benefits are attributable to other participants.

(4) **Determination of vested benefits charge.**—
(A) In general.—The vested benefits charge for a plan year shall be based on an actuarial valuation of the plan as of the end of the base plan year, adjusted to reflect—
(i) any—
(I) decrease of 5 percent or more in the value of plan assets, or increase of 5 percent or more in the number of persons in pay status, during the period beginning on the first day of the plan year following the base plan year and ending on the adjustment date, or
(II) at the election of the plan sponsor, actuarial valuation of the plan as of the adjustment date or any later date not later than the last day of the plan year for which the determination is being made.
(ii) any change in benefits under the plan which is not otherwise taken into account under this subparagraph and which is pursuant to any amendment—
(I) adopted before the end of the plan year for which the determination is being made, and
(II) effective after the end of the base plan year and on or before the end of the plan year referred to in subclause (I), and
(iii) any other event (including an event described in subparagraph (B)(i)(I)) which, as determined in accordance with regulations prescribed by the Secretary, would substantially increase the plan's vested benefit charge.

(B) Certain changes in benefit levels.—
(i) In general.—In determining the vested benefits charge for a plan year following a plan year in which the plan was not in reorganization, any change in benefits which—
(I) results from the changing of a group of participants from one benefit level to another benefit level under a schedule of plan benefits as a result of changes in a collective bargaining agreement, or
(II) results from any change in a collective bargaining agreement,
shall not be taken into account except to the extent provided in regulations prescribed by the Secretary.
(ii) Plan in reorganization.—Except as otherwise determined by the Secretary, in determining the vested benefits charge for any plan year following any plan year in which the plan was in reorganization, any change in benefits—

(b) Subpart C of part I of subchapter D of chapter 1 of such Code (as added by this Act) shall take effect, with respect to each plan, on the first day of the first plan year beginnng on or after the earlier of—
(1) the date on which the last collective-bargaining agreement providing for employer contributions under the plan, which was in effect on the date of the enactment of this Act, expires, without regard to extensions agreed to after such date of enactment, or
(2) 3 years after the date of the enactment of this Act.]

Code Sec. 418 (a)

(I) described in clause (i)(I), or
(II) described in clause (i)(II) as determined under regulations prescribed by the Secretary,

shall, for purposes of subparagraph (A)(ii), be treated as a change in benefits pursuant to an amendment to a plan.

(5) Base plan year.—
(A) In general.—The base plan year for any plan year is—
(i) if there is a relevant collective bargaining agreement, the last plan year ending at least 6 months before the relevant effective date, or
(ii) if there is no relevant collective bargaining agreement, the last plan year ending at least 12 months before the beginning of the plan year.
(B) Relevant collective bargaining agreement.—A relevant collective bargaining agreement is a collective bargaining agreement—
(i) which is in effect for at least 6 months during the plan year, and
(ii) which has not been in effect for more than 36 months as of the end of the plan year.
(C) Relevant effective date.—The relevant effective date is the earliest of the effective dates for the relevant collective bargaining agreements.
(D) Adjustment date.—The adjustment date is the date which is—
(i) 90 days before the relevant effective date, or
(ii) if there is no relevant effective date, 90 days before the beginning of the plan year.

(6) Person in pay status.—The term "person in pay status" means—
(A) a participant or beneficiary on the last day of the base plan year who, at any time during such year, was paid an early, late, normal, or disability retirement benefit (or a death benefit related to a retirement benefit), and
(B) to the extent provided in regulations prescribed by the Secretary, any other person who is entitled to such a benefit under the plan.

(7) Other definitions and special rules.—
(A) Unfunded vested benefits.—The term "unfunded vested benefits" means, in connection with a plan, an amount (determined in accordance with regulations prescribed by the Secretary) equal to—
(i) the value of vested benefits under the plan, less
(ii) the value of the assets of the plan.
(B) Vested benefits.—The term "vested benefits" means any nonforfeitable benefit within the meaning of section 4001(a)(8) of the Employee Retirement Income Security Act of 1974).
(C) Allocation of assets.—In determining the plan's unfunded vested benefits, plan assets shall first be allocated to the vested benefits to persons in pay status.
(D) Treatment of certain benefit reductions.—The vested benefits charge shall be determined without regard to reductions in accrued benefits under section 418D which are first effective in the plan year.
(E) Withdrawal liability.—For purposes of this part, any outstanding claim for withdrawal liability shall not be considered a plan asset, except as otherwise provided in regulations prescribed by the Secretary.

(c) Prohibition of Nonannuity Payments.—Except as provided in regulations prescribed by the Pension Benefit Guaranty Corporation, while a plan is in reorganization a benefit with respect to a participant (other than a death benefit) which is attributable to employer contributions and which has a value of more than $1,750 may not be paid in a form other than an annuity which (by itself or in combination with social security, railroad retirement, or workers' compensation benefits) provides substantially level payments over the life of the participant.

(d) Terminated Plans.—Any multiemployer plan which terminates under section 4041A(a)(2) of the Employee Retirement Income Security Act of 1974 shall not be considered in reorganization after the last day of the plan year in which the plan is treated as having terminated.

SEC. 418A. NOTICE OF REORGANIZATION AND FUNDING REQUIREMENTS.

(a) Notice Requirement.—

(1) In general.—If—
(A) a multiemployer plan is in reorganization for a plan year, and

(B) section 418B would require an increase in contributions for such plan year, the plan sponsor shall notify the persons described in paragraph (2) that the plan is in reorganization and that, if contributions to the plan are not increased, accrued benefits under the plan may be reduced or an excise tax may be imposed (or both such reduction and imposition may occur).

(2) **Persons to whom notice is to be given.**—The persons described in this paragraph are—

(A) each employer who has an obligation to contribute under the plan (within the meaning of section 4212(a) of the Employee Retirement Income Security Act of 1974), and

(B) each employee organization which, for purposes of collective bargaining, represents plan participants employed by such an employer.

(3) **Overburden credit not taken into account.**—The determination under paragraph (1)(B) shall be made without regard to the overburden credit provided by section 418C.

(b) **Additional Requirements.**—The Pension Benefit Guaranty Corporation may prescribe additional or alternative requirements for assuring, in the case of a plan with respect to which notice is required by subsection (a)(1), that the persons described in subsection (a)(2)—

(1) receive appropriate notice that the plan is in reorganization,

(2) are adequately informed of the implications of reorganization status, and

(3) have reasonable access to information relevant to the plan's reorganization status.

SEC. 418B. MINIMUM CONTRIBUTION REQUIREMENT.

(a) **Accumulated Funding Deficiency in Reorganization.**—

(1) **In general.**—For any plan year in which a multiemployer plan is in reorganization—

(A) the plan shall continue to maintain its funding standard account, and

(B) the plan's accumulated funding deficiency under section 412(a) for such plan year shall be equal to the excess (if any) of—

(i) the sum of the minimum contribution requirement for such plan year (taking into account any overburden credit under section 418C(a)) plus the plan's accumulated funding deficiency for the preceding plan year (determined under this section if the plan was in reorganization during such plan year or under section 412(a), if the plan was not in reorganization), over

(ii) amounts considered contributed by employers to or under the plan for the plan year (increased by any amount waived under subsection (f) for the plan year).

(2) **Treatment of withdrawal liability payments.**—For purposes of paragraph (1), withdrawal liability payments (whether or not received) which are due with respect to withdrawals before the end of the base plan year shall be considered amounts contributed by the employer to or under the plan if, as of the adjustment date, it was reasonable for the plan sponsor to anticipate that such payments would be made during the plan year.

(b) **Minimum Contribution Requirement.**—

(1) **In general.**—Except as otherwise provided in this section for purposes of this subpart the minimum contribution requirement for a plan year in which a plan is in reorganization is an amount equal to the excess of—

(A) the sum of—

(i) the plan's vested benefits charge for the plan year; and

(ii) the increase in normal cost for the plan year determined under the entry age normal funding method which is attributable to plan amendments adopted while the plan was in reorganization, over

(B) the amount of the overburden credit (if any) determined under section 418C for the plan year.

(2) **Adjustment for reductions in contribution base units.**—If the plan's current contribution base for the plan year is less than the plan's valuation contribution base for the plan year, the minimum contribution requirement for such plan year shall be equal to the product of the amount determined under paragraph (1) (after any ad-

IRC EXCERPTS

justment required by this subpart other than this paragraph) multiplied by a fraction—
(A) the numerator of which is the plan's current contribution base for the plan year, and
(B) the denominator of which is the plan's valuation contribution base for the plan year.

(3) Special rule where cash-flow amount exceeds vested benefits charge.—
(A) In general.—If the vested benefits charge for a plan year of a plan in reorganization is less than the plan's cash-flow amount for the plan year, the plan's minimum contribution requirement for the plan year is the amount determined under paragraph (1) (determined before the application of paragraph (2)) after substituting the term "cash-flow amount" for the term "vested benefits charge" in paragraph (1)(A).
(B) Cash-flow amount.—For purposes of subparagraph (A), a plan's cash-flow amount for a plan year is an amount equal to—
(i) the amount of the benefits payable under the plan for the base plan year, plus the amount of the plan's administrative expenses for the base plan year, reduced by
(ii) the value of the available plan assets for the base plan year determined under regulations prescribed by the Secretary, adjusted in a manner consistent with section 418(b)(4).

(c) Current Contribution Base; Valuation Contribution Base.—

(1) Current contribution base.—For purposes of this subpart, a plan's current contribution base for a plan year is the number of contribution base units with respect to which contributions are required to be made under the plan for that plan year determined in accordance with regulations prescribed by the Secretary.

(2) Valuation contribution base.—
(A) In general.—Except as provided in subparagraph (B), for purposes of this subpart a plan's valuation contribution base is the number of contribution base units for which contributions were received for the base plan year—

(i) adjusted to reflect declines in the contribution base which have occurred (or could reasonably be anticipated) as of the adjustment date for the plan year referred to in paragraph (1),
(ii) adjusted upward (in accordance with regulations prescribed by the Secretary) for any contribution base reduction in the base plan year caused by a strike or lockout or by unusual events, such as fire, earthquake, or severe weather conditions, and
(iii) adjusted (in accordance with regulations prescribed by the Secretary) for reductions in the contribution base resulting from transfers of liabilities.
(B) Insolvent plans.—For any plan year—
(i) in which the plan is insolvent (within the meaning of section 418E(b)(1)), and
(ii) beginning with the first plan year beginning after the expiration of all relevant collective bargaining agreements which were in effect in the plan year in which the plan became insolvent,
the plan's valuation contribution base is the greater of the number of contribution base units for which contributions were received for the first or second plan year preceding the first plan year in which the plan is insolvent, adjusted as provided in clause (ii) or (iii) of subparagraph (A).

(3) Contribution base unit.—For purposes of this subpart, the term "contribution base unit" means a unit with respect to which an employer has an obligation to contribute under a multiemployer plan (as defined in regulations prescribed by the Secretary).

(d) Limitation on Required Increases in Rate of Employer Contributions.—

(1) In general.—Under regulations prescribed by the Secretary, the minimum contribution requirement applicable to any plan for any plan year which is determined under subsection (b) (without regard to subsection (b)(2)) shall not exceed an amount which is equal to the sum of—
(A) the greater of—
(i) the funding standard requirement for such plan year, or
(ii) 107 percent of—
(I) if the plan was not in reorganization in the preceding plan year, the funding

Code Sec. 418B (d)

standard requirement for such preceding plan year, or

(II) if the plan was in reorganization in the preceding plan year, the sum of the amount determined under this subparagraph for the preceding plan year and the amount (if any) determined under subparagraph (B) for the preceding plan year, plus

(B) if for the plan year a change in benefits is first required to be considered in computing the charges under section 412(b)(2)(A) or (B), the sum of—

(i) the increase in normal cost for a plan year determined under the entry age normal funding method due to increases in benefits described in section 418(b)(4)(A)(ii) (determined without regard to section 418(b)(4)(B)(ii)), and

(ii) the amount necessary to amortize in equal annual installments the increase in the value of vested benefits under the plan due to increases in benefits described in clause (i) over—

(I) 10 years, to the extent such increase in value is attributable to persons in pay status, or

(II) 25 years, to the extent such increase in value is attributable to other participants.

(2) Funding standard requirement.—For purposes of paragraph (1), the funding standard requirement for any plan year is an amount equal to the net charge to the funding standard account for such plan year (as defined in section 418(b)(2)).

(3) Special rule for certain plans.—

(A) In general.—In the case of a plan described in section 4216(b) of the Employee Retirement Income Security Act of 1974, if a plan amendment which increases benefits is adopted after January 1, 1980—

(i) paragraph (1) shall apply only if the plan is a plan described in subparagraph (B), and

(ii) the amount under paragraph (1) shall be determined without regard to subparagraph (1)(B).

(B) Eligible plans.—A plan is described in this subparagraph if—

(i) the rate of employer contributions under the plan for the first plan year beginning on or after the date on which an amendment increasing benefits is adopted,

multiplied by the valuation contribution base for that plan year, equals or exceeds the sum of—

(I) the amount that would be necessary to amortize fully, in equal annual installments, by July 1, 1986, the unfunded vested benefits attributable to plan provisions in effect on July 1, 1977 (determined as of the last day of the base plan year); and

(II) the amount that would be necessary to amortize fully, in equal annual installments, over the period described in subparagraph (C), beginning with the first day of the first plan year beginning on or after the date on which the amendment is adopted, the unfunded vested benefits (determined as of the last day of the base plan year) attributable to each plan amendment after July 1, 1977; and

(ii) the rate of employer contributions for each subsequent plan year is not less than the lesser of—

(I) the rate which when multiplied by the valuation contribution base for that subsequent plan year produces the annual amount that would be necessary to complete the amortization schedule described in clause (i), or

(II) the rate for the plan year immediately preceding such subsequent plan year, plus 5 percent of such rate.

(C) Period.—The period determined under this subparagraph is the lesser of—

(i) 12 years, or

(ii) a period equal in length to the average of the remaining expected lives of all persons receiving benefits under the plan.

(4) Exception in case of certain benefit increases.—Paragraph (1) shall not apply with respect to a plan, other than a plan described in paragraph (3), for the period of consecutive plan years in each of which the plan is in reorganization, beginning with a plan year in which occurs the earlier of the date of the adoption or the effective date of any amendment of the plan which increases benefits with respect to service performed before the plan year in which the adoption of the amendment occurred.

(e) Certain Retroactive Plan Amendments.—In determining the minimum contribution requirement with respect to a plan for a plan year under subsection (b), the vested benefits charge may be adjusted to

Code Sec. 418B (d) (2)

reflect a plan amendment reducing benefits under section 412(c)(8).

(f) Waiver of Accumulated Funding Deficiency.—

(1) In general.—The Secretary may waive any accumulated funding deficiency under this section in accordance with the provisions of section 412(d)(1).

(2) Treatment of waiver.—Any waiver under paragraph (1) shall not be treated as a waived funding deficiency (within the meaning of section 412(d)(3)).

(g) Actuarial Assumptions Must Be Reasonable.—For purposes of making any determination under this subpart, the requirements of section 412(c)(3) shall apply.

SEC. 418C. OVERBURDEN CREDIT AGAINST MINIMUM CONTRIBUTION REQUIREMENT.

(a) General Rule.—For purposes of determining the contribution under section 418B (before the application of section 418B(b)(2) or (d)), the plan sponsor of a plan which is overburdened for the plan year shall apply an overburden credit against the plan's minimum contribution requirement for the plan year (determined without regard to section 418B(b)(2) or (d) and without regard to this section).

(b) Definition of Overburdened Plan.—A plan is overburdened for a plan year if—

(1) the average number of pay status participants under the plan in the base plan year exceeds the average of the number of active participants in the base plan year and the 2 plan years preceding the base plan year, and

(2) the rate of employer contributions under the plan equals or exceeds the greater of—

(A) such rate for the preceding plan year, or

(B) such rate for the plan year preceding the first year in which the plan is in reorganization.

(c) Amount of Overburden Credit.—The amount of the overburden credit for a plan year is the product of—

(1) one-half of the average guaranteed benefit paid for the base plan year, and

(2) the overburden factor for the plan year.

The amount of the overburden credit for a plan year shall not exceed the amount of the minimum contribution requirement for such year (determined without regard to this section).

(d) Overburden Factor.—For purposes of this section, the overburden factor of a plan for the plan year is an amount equal to—

(1) the average number of pay status participants for the base plan year, reduced by

(2) the average of the number of active participants for the base plan year and for each of the 2 plan years preceding the base plan year.

(e) Definitions.—For purposes of this section—

(1) Pay status participant.—The term "pay status participant" means, with respect to a plan, a participant receiving retirement benefits under the plan.

(2) Number of active participants.—The number of active participants for a plan year shall be the sum of—

(A) the number of active employees who are participants in the plan and on whose behalf contributions are required to be made during the plan year;

(B) the number of active employees who are not participants in the plan but who are in an employment unit covered by a collective bargaining agreement which requires the employees' employer to contribute to the plan unless service in such employment unit was never covered under the plan or a predecessor thereof, and

(C) the total number of active employees attributed to employers who made payments to the plan for the plan year out of withdrawal liability pursuant to part 1 of subtitle E of title IV of the Employee Retirement Income Security Act of 1974, determined by dividing—

(i) the total amount of such payments, by

(ii) the amount equal to the total contributions received by the plan during the plan year divided by the average number of active employees who were participants in the plan during the plan year.

The Secretary shall by regulations provide

Code Sec. 418C (e)(2)

alternative methods of determining active participants where (by reason of irregular employment, contributions on a unit basis, or otherwise) this paragraph does not yield a representative basis for determining the credit.

(3) Average number.—The term "average number" means, with respect to pay status participants for a plan year, a number equal to one-half the sum of—

(A) the number with respect to the plan as of the beginning of the plan year, and

(B) the number with respect to the plan as of the end of the plan year.

(4) Average guaranteed benefit.—The average guaranteed benefit paid is 12 times the average monthly pension payment guaranteed under section 4022A(c)(1) of the Employee Retirement Income Security Act of 1974 determined under the provisions of the plan in effect at the beginning of the first plan year in which the plan is in reorganization and without regard to section 4022A(c)(2).

(5) First year in reorganization.—The first year in which the plan is in reorganization is the first of a period of 1 or more consecutive plan years in which the plan has been in reorganization not taking into account any plan years the plan was in reorganization prior to any period of 3 or more consecutive plan years in which the plan was not in reorganization.

(f) No Overburden Credit in Case of Certain Reductions in Contributions.—

(1) In general.—Notwithstanding any other provision of this section, a plan is not eligible for an overburden credit for a plan year if the Secretary finds that the plan's current contribution base for any plan year was reduced, without a corresponding reduction in the plan's unfunded vested benefits attributable to pay status participants, as a result of a change in an agreement providing for employer contributions under the plan.

(2) Treatment of certain withdrawals.—For purposes of paragraph (1), a complete or partial withdrawal of an employer (within the meaning of part 1 of subtitle E of title IV of the Employee Retirement Income Security Act of 1974) does not impair a plan's eligibility for an overburden credit, unless the Secretary finds that a contribution base reduction described in paragraph (1) resulted from a transfer of liabilities to another plan in connection with the withdrawal.

(g) Mergers.—Notwithstanding any other provision of this section, if 2 or more multiemployer plans merge, the amount of the overburden credit which may be applied under this section with respect to the plan resulting from the merger for any of the 3 plan years ending after the effective date of the merger shall not exceed the sum of the used overburden credit for each of the merging plans for its last plan year ending before the effective date of the merger. For purposes of the preceding sentence, the used overburden credit is that portion of the credit which does not exceed the excess of the minimum contribution requirement determined without regard to any overburden credit under this section over the employer contributions required under the plan.

SEC. 418D. ADJUSTMENTS IN ACCRUED BENEFITS.

(a) Adjustments in Accrued Benefits.—

(1) In general.—Notwithstanding section 411, a multiemployer plan in reorganization may be amended, in accordance with this section, to reduce or eliminate accrued benefits attributable to employer contributions which, under section 4022A(b) of the Employee Retirement Income Security Act of 1974, are not eligible for the Pension Benefit Guaranty Corporation's guarantee. The preceding sentence shall only apply to accrued benefits under plan amendments (or plans) adopted after March 26, 1980, or under collective bargaining agreement entered into after March 26, 1980.

(2) Adjustment of vested benefits charge.—In determining the minimum contribution requirement with respect to a plan for a plan year under section 418B(b), the vested benefits charge may be adjusted to reflect a plan amendment reducing benefits under this section or section 412(c)(8), but only if the amendment is adopted and effective no later than 2½ months after the end of the plan year, or within such extended period as the Secretary may prescribe by regulations under section 412(c)(10).

(b) Limitation on Reduction—

(1) In general.—Accrued benefits may not be reduced under this section unless—

(A) notice has been given, at least 6 months before the first day of the plan year in which the amendment reducing benefits is adopted, to—

(i) plan participants and beneficiaries,

(ii) each employer who has an obligation to contribute (within the meaning of section 4212(a) of the Employee Retirement Income Security Act of 1974) under the plan, and

(iii) each employee organization which, for purposes of collective bargaining, represents plan participants employed by such an employer,

that the plan is in reorganization and that, if contributions under the plan are not increased, accrued benefits under the plan will be reduced or an excise tax will be imposed on employers;

(B) in accordance with regulations prescribed by the Secretary—

(i) any category of accrued benefits is not reduced with respect to inactive participants to a greater extent proportionally that such category of accrued benefits is reduced with respect to active participants,

(ii) benefits attributable to employer contributions other than accrued benefits and the rate of future benefit accruals are reduced at least to an extent equal to the reduction in accrued benefits of inactive participants, and

(iii) in any case in which the accrued benefit of a participant or beneficiary is reduced by changing the benefit form or the requirements which the participant or beneficiary must satisfy to be entitled to the benefit, such reduction is not applicable to—

(I) any participant or beneficiary in pay status on the effective date of the amendment, or the beneficiary of such a participant, or

(II) any participant who has attained normal retirement age, or who is within 5 years of attaining normal retirement age, on the effective date of the amendment, or the beneficiary of any such participant; and

(C) the rate of employer contributions for the plan year in which the amendment becomes effective and for all succeeding plan years in which the plan is in reorganization equals or exceeds the greater of—

(i) the rate of employer contributions, calculated without regard to the amendment, for the plan year in which the amendment becomes effective, or

(ii) the rate of employer contributions for the plan year preceding the plan year in which the amendment becomes effective.

(2) Information required to be included in notice.—The plan sponsors shall include in any notice required to be sent to plan participants and beneficiaries under paragraph (1) information as to the rights and remedies of plan participants and beneficiaries as well as how to contact the Department of Labor for further information and assistance where appropriate.

(c) No recoupment.—A plan may not recoup a benefit payment which is in excess of the amount payable under the plan because of an amendment retroactively reducing accrued benefits under this section.

(d) Benefit Increases Under Multiemployer Plan in Reorganization.—

(1) Restoration of previously reduced benefits.—

(A) In general.—A plan which has been amended to reduce accrued benefits under this section may be amended to increase or restore accrued benefits, or the rate of future benefit accruals, only if the plan is amended to restore levels of previously reduced accrued benefits of inactive participants and of participants who are within 5 years of attaining normal retirement age to at least the same extent as any such increase in accrued benefits or in the rate of future benefit accruals.

(B) Benefit increases and benefit restorations.—For purposes of this subsection, in the case of a plan which has been amended under this section to reduce accrued benefits—

(i) an increase in a benefit, or in the rate of future benefit accruals, shall be considered a benefit increase to the extent that the benefit, or the accrual rate, is thereby increased above the highest benefit level, or accrual rate, which was in effect under the

Code Sec. 418D (d) (1)

terms of the plan before the effective date of the amendment reducing accrued benefits, and

(ii) an increase in a benefit, or in the rate of future benefit accruals, shall be considered a benefit restoration to the extent that the benefit, or the accrual rate, is not thereby increased above the highest benefit level, or accrual rate, which was in effect under the terms of the plan immediately before the effective date of the amendment reducing accrued benefits.

(2) Uniformity in benefit restoration.—If a plan is amended to partially restore previously reduced accrued benefit levels, or the rate of future benefit accruals, the benefits of inactive participants shall be restored in at least the same proportions as other accrued benefits which are restored.

(3) No benefit increases in year of benefit reduction.—No benefit increase under a plan may take effect in a plan year in which an amendment reducing accrued benefits under the plan, in accordance with this section, is adopted or first becomes effective.

(4) Retroactive payments.—A plan is not required to make retroactive benefit payments with respect to that portion of an accrued benefit which was reduced and subsequently restored under this section.

(e) Inactive Participant.—For purposes of this section, the term "inactive participant" means a person not in covered service under the plan who is in pay status under the plan or who has a nonforfeitable benefit under the plan.

(f) Regulations.—The Secretary may prescribe rules under which, notwithstanding any other provision of this section, accrued benefit reductions or benefit increases for different participant groups may be varied equitably to reflect variations in contribution rates and other relevant factors reflecting differences in negotiated levels of financial support for plan benefit obligations.

SEC. 418E. INSOLVENT PLANS.

(a) Suspension of Certain Benefit Payments.—Notwithstanding section 411, in any case in which benefit payments under an insolvent multiemployer plan exceed the resource benefit level, any such payments of benefits which are not basic benefits shall be suspended, in accordance with this section, to the extent necessary to reduce the sum of such payments and the payments of such basic benefits to the greater of the resource benefit level or the level of basic benefits, unless an alternative procedure is prescribed by the Pension Benefit Guaranty Corporation under section 4022A(g)(5) of the Employee Retirement Income Security Act of 1974.

(b) Definitions.—For purposes of this section, for plan year—

(1) Insolvency.—A multiemployer plan is insolvent if the plan's available resources are not sufficient to pay benefits under the plan when due for the plan year, or if the plan is determined to be insolvent under subsection (d).

(2) Resource benefit level.—The term "resource benefit level" means the level of monthly benefits determined under subsections (c)(1) and (3) and (d)(3) to be the highest level which can be paid out of the plan's available resources.

(3) Available resources.—The term "available resources" means the plan's cash, marketable assets, contributions, withdrawal liability payments, and earnings, less reasonable administrative expenses and amounts owed for such plan year to the Pension Benefit Guaranty Corporation under section 4261(b)(2) of the Employee Retirement Income Security Act of 1974.

(4) Insolvency year.—The term "insolvency year" means a plan year in which a plan is insolvent.

(c) Benefit Payments Under Insolvent Plans.—

(1) Determination of resource benefit level.—The plan sponsor of a plan in reorganization shall determine in writing the plan's resource benefit level for each insolvency year, based on the plan sponsor's reasonable projection of the plan's available resources and the benefits payable under the plan.

Code Sec. 418D (d) (2)

(2) Uniformity of the benefit suspension.—The suspension of benefit payments under this section shall, in accordance with regulations prescribed by the Secretary, apply in substantially uniform proportions to the benefits of all persons in pay status (within the meaning of section 418(b)(6)) under the plan, except that the Secretary may prescribe rules under which benefit suspensions for different participant groups may be varied equitably to reflect variations in contribution rates and other relevant factors including differences in negotiated levels of financial support for plan benefit obligations.

(3) Resource benefit level below level of basic benefits.—Notwithstanding paragraph (2), if a plan sponsor determines in writing a resource benefit level for a plan year which is below the level of basic benefits, the payment of all benefits other than basic benefits shall be suspended for that plan year.

(4) Excess resources.—
(A) In general.—If, by the end of an insolvency year, the plan sponsor determines in writing that the plan's available resources in that insolvency year could have supported benefit payments above the resource benefit level for that insolvency year, the plan sponsor shall distribute the excess resources to the participants and beneficiaries who received benefit payments from the plan in that insolvency year, in accordance with regulations prescribed by the Secretary.
(B) Excess resources.—For purposes of this paragraph, the term "excess resources" means available resources above the amount necessary to support the resource benefit level, but no greater than the amount necessary to pay benefits for the plan year at the benefit levels under the plan.

(5) Unpaid benefits.—If, by the end of an insolvency year, any benefit has not been paid at the resource benefit level, amounts up to the resource benefit level which were unpaid shall be distributed to the participants and beneficiaries, in accordance with regulations prescribed by the Secretary, to the extent possible taking into account the plan's total available resources in that insolvency year.

(6) Retroactive payments.—Except as provided in paragraph (4) or (5), a plan is not required to make retroactive benefit payments with respect to that portion of a benefit which was suspended under this section.

(d) Plan Sponsor Determination.—

(1) Triennial test.—As of the end of the first plan year in which a plan is in reorganization, and at least every 3 plan years thereafter (unless the plan is no longer in reorganization), the plan sponsor shall compare the value of plan assets (determined in accordance with section 418B(b)(3)(B)(ii)) for that plan year with the total amount of benefit payments made under the plan for that plan year. Unless the plan sponsor determines that the value of plan assets exceeds 3 times the total amount of benefit payments, the plan sponsor shall determine whether the plan will be insolvent in any of the next 3 plan years.

(2) Determination of insolvency.—If, at any time, the plan sponsor of a plan in reorganization reasonably determines, taking into account the plan's recent and anticipated financial experience, that the plan's available resources are not sufficient to pay benefits under the plan when due for the next plan year, the plan sponsor shall make such determination available to interested parties.

(3) Determination of resource benefit level.—The plan sponsor of a plan in reorganization shall determine in writing for each insolvency year the resource benefit level and the level of basic benefits no later than 3 months before the insolvency year.

(e) Notice Requirements.—

(1) Impending insolvency.—If the plan sponsor of a plan in reorganization determines under subsection (d)(1) or (2) that the plan may become insolvent (within the meaning of subsection (b)(1)), the plan sponsor shall—
(A) notify the Secretary, the Pension Benefit Guaranty Corporation, the parties described in section 418A(a)(2), and the plan participants and beneficiaries of that determination, and

Code Sec. 418E (e) (1)

(B) inform the parties described in section 418A(a)(2) and the plan participants and beneficiaries that if insolvency occurs certain benefit payments will be suspended, but that basic benefits will continue to be paid.

(2) Resource benefit level.—No later than 2 months before the first day of each insolvency year, the plan sponsor of a plan in reorganization shall notify the Secretary, the Pension Benefit Guaranty Corporation, the parties described in section 418A(a)(2), and the plan participants and beneficiaries of the resource benefit level determined in writing for that insolvency year.

(3) Potential need for financial assistance.—In any case in which the plan sponsor anticipates that the resource benefit level for an insolvency year may not exceed the level of basic benefits, the plan sponsor shall notify the Pension Benefit Guaranty Corporation.

(4) Regulations.—Notice required by this subsection shall be given in accordance with regulations prescribed by the Pension Benefit Guaranty Corporation, except that notice to the Secretary shall be given in accordance with regulations prescribed by the Secretary.

(5) Corporation may prescribe time.—The Pension Benefit Guaranty Corporation may prescribe a time other than the time prescribed by this section for the making of a determination or the filing of a notice under this section.

(f) Financial Assistance.—

(1) Permissive application.—If the plan sponsor of an insolvent plan for which the resource benefit level is above the level of basic benefits anticipates that, for any month in an insolvency year, the plan will not have funds sufficient to pay basic benefits, the plan sponsor may apply for financial assistance from the Pension Benefit Guaranty Corporation under section 4261 of the Employee Retirement Income Security Act of 1974.

(2) Mandatory application.—A plan sponsor who has determined a resource benefit level for an insolvency year which is below the level of basic benefits shall apply for financial assistance from the Pension Benefit Guaranty Corporation under section 4261 of the Employee Retirement Income Security Act of 1974.

(g) Financial Assistance.—Any amount of any financial assistance from the Pension Benefit Guaranty Corporation to any plan, and any repayment of such amount, shall be taken into account under this subpart in such manner as determined by the Secretary.

Part II—Certain Stock Options

Section
421. General rules.
422. Qualified stock options.
423. Employee stock purchase plans.
424. Restricted stock options.
425. Definitions and special rules.

SEC. 421. GENERAL RULES.

(a) Effect of Qualifying Transfer.—If a share of stock is transferred to an individual in a transfer in respect of which the requirements of section 422(a), 422A(a), 423(a), or 424(a) are met—

(1) except as provided in section 422(c)(1), no income shall result at the time of the transfer of such share to the individual upon his exercise of the option with respect to such share;

(2) no deduction under section 162 (relating to trade or business expenses) shall be allowable at any time to the employer corporation, a parent or subsidiary corporation of such corporation, or a corporation issuing or assuming a stock option in a transaction to which section 425(a), applies, with respect to the share so transferred; and

(3) no amount other than the price paid under the option shall be considered as received by any of such corporations for the share so transferred.

(b) Effect of Disqualifying Disposition.—If the transfer of a share of stock to an individual pursuant to his exercise of an option would otherwise meet the requirements of section 422(a), 422A(a), 423(a), or 424(a), except that there is a failure to meet any of the holding period requirements of section 422(a)(1), 422A(a)(1), 423(a)(1), or 424(a)(1), then any increase in the income

Code Sec. 418E (e) (2)

of such individual or deduction from the income of his employer corporation for the taxable year in which such exercise occurred attributable to such disposition, shall be treated as an increase in income or a deduction from income in the taxable year of such individual or of such employer corporation in which such disposition occurred.

(c) Exercise by Estate.—

(1) In general.—If an option to which this part applies is exercised after the death of the employee by the estate of the decedent, or by a person who acquired the right to exercise such option by bequest or inheritance or by reason of the death of the decedent, the provisions of subsection (a) shall apply to the same extent as if the option had been exercised by the decedent, except that—

(A) the holding period and employment requirements of sections 422(a), 422A(a), 423(a), and 424(a) shall not apply, and

(B) any transfer by the estate of stock acquired shall be considered a disposition of such stock for purposes of sections 423(c) and 424(c)(1).

(2) Deduction for estate tax.—If an amount is required to be included under section 422(c)(1), 423(c), or 424(c)(1) in gross income of the estate of the deceased employee or of a person described in paragraph (1), there shall be allowed to the estate of such person a deduction with respect to the estate tax attributable to the inclusion in the taxable estate of the deceased employee of the net value for estate tax purposes of the option. For this purpose, the deduction shall be determined under section 691(c) as if the option acquired from the deceased employee were an item of gross income in respect of the decedent under section 691 and as if the amount includible in gross income under section 422(c)(1), 423(c), or 424(c)(1) were an amount included in gross income under section 691 in respect of such item of gross income.

(3) Basis of shares acquired.—In the case of a share of stock acquired by the exercise of an option to which paragraph (1) applies—

(A) the basis of such share shall include so much of the basis of the option as is attributable to such share; except that the basis of such share shall be reduced by the excess (if any) of (i) the amount which would have been includible in gross income under section 422(c)(1), 423(c), or 424(c)(1) if the employee had exercised the option on the date of his death and had held the share acquired pursuant to such exercise at the time of his death, over (ii) the amount which is includible in gross income under such section; and

(B) the last sentence of sections 422(c)(1), 423(c), and 424(c)(1) shall apply only to the extent that the amount includible in gross income under such sections exceeds so much of the basis of the option as is attributable to such share.

SEC. 422. QUALIFIED STOCK OPTIONS.

(a) In general.—Subject to the provisions of subsection (c)(1), section 421(a) shall apply with respect to the transfer of a share of stock to an individual pursuant to his exercise of a qualified stock option if—

(1) no disposition of such share is made by such individual within the 3-year period beginning on the day after the day of the transfer of such share, and

(2) at all times during the period beginning with the date of the granting of the option and ending on the day 3 months before the date of such exercise, such individual was an employee of either the corporation granting such option, the parent or subsidiary corporation of such corporation, or a corporation of a parent or subsidiary corporation of such corporation issuing or assuming a stock option in a transaction to which section 425(a) applies.

(b) Qualified Stock Option.—For purposes of this part, the term "qualified stock option" means an option granted to an individual after December 31, 1963 (other than a restricted stock option granted pursuant to a contract described in section 424(c)(3)(A)), and before May 21, 1976 (or, if it meets the requirements of subsection (c)(7), granted to an individual after May 20, 1976), for any reason connected with his employment by a corporation, if granted by the employer corporation or its parent or subsidiary corporation, to purchase stock of any of such corporations, but only if—

(1) The option is granted pursuant to a plan which includes the aggregate number of shares which may be issued under options, and the employees (or class of employees) eligible to receive options, and which is approved by the stockholders of the granting corporation within 12 months before or after the date such plan is adopted;

(2) such option is granted within 10 years from the date such plan is adopted, or the date such plan is approved by the stockholders, whichever is earlier;

(3) such option by its terms is not exercisable after the expiration of 5 years from the date such option is granted;

(4) except as provided in subsection (c)(1), the option price is not less than the fair market value of the stock at the time such option is granted;

(5) such option by its terms is not exercisable while there is outstanding (within the meaning of subsection (c)(2)) any qualified stock option (or restricted stock option) which was granted, before the granting of such option, to such individual to purchase stock in his employer corporation or in a corporation which (at the time of the granting of such option) is a parent or subsidiary corporation of the employer corporation, or in a predecessor corporation of any of such corporations;

(6) such option by its terms is not transferable by such individual otherwise than by will or the laws of descent and distribution, and is exercisable, during his lifetime, only by him; and

(7) such individual, immediately after such option is granted, does not own stock possessing more than 5 percent of the total combined voting power or value of all classes of stock of the employer corporation or of its parent or subsidiary corporation; except that if the equity capital of such corporation or corporations (determined at the time the option is granted) is less than $2,000,000, then, for purposes of applying the limitation of this paragraph, there shall be added to such 5 percent the percentage (not higher than 5 percent) which bears the same ratio to 5 percent as the difference between such equity capital and $2,000,000 bears to $1,000,000.

(c) **Special Rules.—**

(1) **Exercise of option when price is less than value of stock.—**If a share of stock is transferred pursuant to the exercise by an individual of an option which fails to qualify as a qualified stock option under subsection (b) because there was a failure in an attempt, made in good faith, to meet the requirement of subsection (b)(4), the requirement of subsection (b)(4) shall be considered to have been met, but there shall be included as compensation (and not as gain upon the sale or exchange of a capital asset) in his gross income for the taxable year in which such option is exercised, an amount equal to the lesser of—

(A) 150 percent of the difference between the option price and the fair market value of the share at the time the option was granted, or

(B) the difference between the option price and the fair market value of the share at the time of such exercise.

The basis of the share acquired shall be increased by an amount equal to the amount included in his gross income under this paragraph in the taxable year in which the exercise occurred.

(2) **Certain options treated as outstanding.—**For purposes of subsection (b)(5)—

(A) any restricted stock option which is not terminated before January 1, 1965, and

(B) any qualified stock option granted after December 31, 1963,

shall be treated as outstanding until such option is exercised in full or expires by reason of the lapse of time. For purposes of the preceding sentence, a restricted stock option granted before January 1, 1964, shall not be treated as outstanding for any period before the first day on which (under the terms of such option) it may be exercised.

(3) **Options granted to certain shareholders.—**For purposes of subsection (b)(7)—

(A) the term "equity capital" means—

(i) in the case of one corporation, the sum of its money and other property (in an amount equal to the adjusted basis of such property for determining gain), less the amount of its indebtedness (other than indebtedness to shareholders), and

(ii) in the case of a group of corporations consisting of a parent and its subsidiary corporations, the sum of the equity capital of each of such corporations adjusted, under regulations prescribed by the Secretary, to eliminate the effect of intercorporate

Code Sec. 422 (b) (1)

IRC EXCERPTS

ownership and transactions among such corporations;

(B) the rules of section 425(d) shall apply in determining the stock ownership of the individual; and

(C) stock which the individual may purchase under outstanding options shall be treated as stock owned by such individual.

If an individual is granted an option which permits him to purchase stock in excess of the limitation of subsection (b)(7) (determined by applying the rules of this paragraph), such option shall be treated as meeting the requirement of subsection (b)(7) to the extent that such individual could, if the option were fully exercised at the time of grant, purchase stock under such option without exceeding such limitation. The portion of such option which is treated as meeting the requirement of subsection (b)(7) shall be deemed to be that portion of the option which is first exercised.

(4) Certain disqualifying dispositions where amount realized is less than value at exercise.—If—

(A) an individual who has acquired a share of stock by the exercise of a qualified stock option makes a disposition of such share within the 3-year period described in subsection (a)(1), and

(B) such disposition is a sale or exchange with respect to which a loss (if sustained) would be recognized to such individual,

then the amount which is includible in the gross income of such individual, and the amount which is deductible from the income of his employer corporation, as compensation attributable to the exercise of such option shall not exceed the excess (if any) of the amount realized on such sale or exchange over the adjusted basis of such share.

(5) Certain transfers by insolvent individuals.—If an insolvent individual holds a share of stock acquired pursuant to his exercise of a qualified stock option, and if such share is transferred to a trustee, receiver, or other similar fiduciary, in any proceeding under title 11 of the United States Code or any other similar insolvency proceeding, neither such transfer, nor any other transfer of such share for the benefit of his creditors in such proceeding, shall constitute a "disposition of such share" for purposes of subsection (a)(1).

(6) Application of subsection (b)(5) where options are for stock of same class in same corporation.—The requirement of subsection (b)(5) shall be considered to have been met in the case of any option (referred to in this paragraph as "new option") granted to an individual if—

(A) the new option and all outstanding options referred to in subsection (b)(5) are to purchase stock of the same class in the same corporation, and

(B) the new option by its terms is not exercisable while there is outstanding (within the meaning of paragraph (2)) any qualified stock option (or restricted stock option) which was granted, before the granting of the new option, to such individual to purchase stock in such corporation at a price (determined as of the date of grant of the new option) higher than the option price of the new option.

(7) Certain options granted after May 20, 1976.—For purposes of subsection (b), an option granted after May 20, 1976, meets the requirements of this paragraph—

(A) if such option is granted to an individual pursuant to a written plan adopted before May 21, 1976, or

(B) if such option is a new option substituted, in a transaction to which section 425(a) applies, for an old option which was granted before May 21, 1976, or which met the requirements of subparagraph (A). An option described in the preceding sentence shall be treated as ceasing to meet the requirements of this paragraph if it is not exercised before May 21, 1981.

SEC. 422A. INCENTIVE STOCK OPTIONS.

(a) In General.—Section 421(a) shall apply with respect to the transfer of a share of stock to an individual pursuant to his exercise of an incentive stock option if—

(1) no disposition of such share is made by him within 2 years from the date of the granting of the option nor within 1 year after the transfer of such share to him, and

(2) at all times during the period beginning on the date of the granting of the option and ending on the day 3 months before the date of such exercise, such individual was an employee of either the corporation

Code Sec. 422A (a)

granting such option, a parent or subsidiary corporation of such corporation, or a corporation or a parent or subsidiary corporation of such corporation issuing or assuming a stock option in a transaction to which section 425(a) applies.

(b) Incentive Stock Option.—For purposes of this part, the term "incentive stock option" means an option granted to an individual for any reason connected with his employment by a corporation if granted by the employer corporation or its parent or subsidiary corporation, to purchase stock of any of such corporations, but only if—

(1) the option is granted pursuant to a plan which includes the aggregate number of shares which may be issued under options and the employees (or class of employees) eligible to receive options, and which is approved by the stockholders of the granting corporation within 12 months before or after the date such plan is adopted;

(2) such option is granted within 10 years from the date such plan is adopted, or the date such plan is approved by the stockholders, whichever is earlier;

(3) such option by its terms is not exercisable after the expiration of 10 years from the date such option is granted;

(4) the option price is not less than the fair market value of the stock at the time such option is granted;

(5) such option by its terms is not transferable by such individual otherwise than by will or the laws of descent and distribution, and is exercisable, during his lifetime, only by him;

(6) such individual, at the time the option is granted, does not own stock possessing more than 10 percent of the total combined voting power of all classes of stock of the employer corporation or of its parent or subsidiary corporation;

(7) such option by its terms is not exercisable while there is outstanding (within the meaning of subsection (c)(7)) any incentive stock option which was granted, before the granting of such option, to such individual to purchase stock in his employer corporation or in a corporation which (at the time of the granting of such option) is a parent or subsidiary corporation of the employer corporation, or in a predecessor corporation of any of such corporations; and

(8) in the case of an option granted after December 31, 1980, under the terms of the plan the aggregate fair market value (determined as of the time the option is granted) of the stock for which any employee may be granted incentive stock options in any calendar year (under all such plans of his employer corporation and its parent and subsidiary corporation) shall not exceed $100,000 plus any unused limit carryover to such year.

(c) Special Rules.—

(1) Good faith efforts to value stock.—If a share of stock is transferred pursuant to the exercise by an individual of an option which would fail to qualify as an incentive stock option under subsection (b) because there was a failure in an attempt, made in good faith, to meet the requirement of subsection (b)(4), the requirement of subsection (b)(4) shall be considered to have been met. To the extent provided in regulations by the Secretary, a similar rule shall apply for purposes of paragraph (8) of subsection (b) and paragraph (4) of this subsection.

(2) Certain disqualifying dispositions where amount realized is less than value at exercise.—If—

(A) an individual who has acquired a share of stock by the exercise of an incentive stock option makes a disposition of such share within either of the periods described in subsection (a)(1), and

(B) such disposition is a sale or exchange with respect to which a loss (if sustained) would be recognized to such individual,

then the amount which is includible in the gross income of such individual, and the amount which is deductible from the income of his employer corporation, as compensation attributable to the exercise of such option shall not exceed the excess (if any) of the amount realized on such sale or exchange over the adjusted basis of such share.

(3) Certain transfers by insolvent individuals.—If an insolvent individual holds a share of stock acquired pursuant to his exercise of an incentive stock option, and if such share is transferred to a trustee, re-

Code Sec. 422A (b)

ceiver, or any other similar fiduciary in any proceeding under title 11 or any other similar insolvency proceeding, neither such transfer, nor any other transfer of such share for the benefit of his creditors in such proceeding, shall constitute a disposition of such share for purposes of subsection (a)(1).

(4) **Carryover of unused limit.**—
(A) In general.—If—
(i) $100,000 exceeds,
(ii) the aggregate fair market value (determined as of the time the option is granted) of the stock for which an employee was granted incentive stock options in any calendar year after 1980 (under all plans described in subsection (b) of his employer corporation and its parent and subsidiary corporations),
one-half of such excess shall be unused limit carryover to each of the 3 succeeding calendar years.
(B) Amount carried to each year.—The amount of the unused limit carryover from any calendar year which may be taken into account in any succeeding calendar year shall be the amount of such carryover reduced by the amount of such carryover which was used in prior calendar years.
(C) Special rules.—For purposes of subparagraph (B)—
(i) the amount of options granted during any calendar year shall be treated as first using up the $100,000 limitation of subsection (b)(8), and
(ii) then shall be treated as using up unused limit carryovers to such year in the order of the calendar years in which the carryovers arose.

(5) **Permissible provisions.**—An option which meets the requirements of subsection (b) shall be treated as an incentive stock option even if—
(A) the employee may pay for the stock with stock of the corporation granting the option,
(B) the employee has a right to receive property at the time of exercise of the option, or
(C) the option is subject to any condition not inconsistent with the provisions of subsection (b).
Subparagraph (B) shall apply to a transfer of property (other than cash) only if section 83 applies to the property so transferred.

(6) **Coordination with sections 422 and 424.**—Sections 422 and 424 shall not apply to an incentive stock option.

(7) **Options outstanding.**—For purposes of subsection (b)(7), any incentive stock option shall be treated as outstanding until such option is exercised in full or expires by reason of lapse of time.

(8) **10-percent shareholder rule.**—Subsection (b)(6) shall not apply if at the time such option is granted the option price is at least 110 percent of the fair market value of the stock subject to the option and such option by its terms is not exercisable after the expiration of 5 years from the date such option is granted.

(9) **Special rule when disabled.**—For purposes of subsection (a)(2), in the case of an employee who is disabled (within the meaning of section 105(d)(4)), the 3-month period of subsection (a)(2) shall be 1 year.

SEC. 423. EMPLOYEE STOCK PURCHASE PLANS.

(a) **General rule.**—Section 421(a) shall apply with respect to the transfer of a share of stock to an individual pursuant to his exercise of an option granted after December 31, 1963 (other than a restricted stock option granted pursuant to a plan described in section 424(c)(3)(B)), under an employee stock purchase plan (as defined in subsection (b)) if—
(1) no disposition of such share is made by him within 2 years after the date of the granting of the option nor within 6 months [9 months for taxable years beginning in 1977; 1 year for taxable years beginning after December 31, 1977] after the transfer of such share to him; and
(2) at all times during the period beginning with the date of the granting of the option and ending on the day 3 months before the date of such exercise, he is an employee of the corporation granting such option, a parent or subsidiary corporation of such corporation, or a corporation or a parent or subsidiary corporation of such corporation issuing or assuming a stock option in a transaction to which section 425(a) applies.

(b) **Employee Stock Purchase Plan.**—For purposes of this part, the term

Code Sec. 423 (b)

"employee stock purchase plan" means a plan which meets the following requirements:

(1) the plan provides that options are to be granted only to employees of the employer corporation or of its parent or subsidiary corporation to purchase stock in any such corporation;

(2) such plan is approved by the stockholders of the granting corporation within 12 months before or after the date such plan is adopted;

(3) under the terms of the plan, no employee can be granted an option if such employee, immediately after the option is granted, owns stock possessing 5 percent or more of the total combined voting power or value of all classes of stock of the employer corporation or of its parent or subsidiary corporation. For purposes of this paragraph, the rules of section 425(d) shall apply in determining the stock ownership of an individual, and stock which the employee may purchase under outstanding options shall be treated as stock owned by the employee;

(4) under the terms of the plan, options are to be granted to all employees of any corporation whose employees are granted any of such options by reason of their employment by such corporation, except that there may be excluded—

(A) employees who have been employed less than 2 years,

(B) employees whose customary employment is 20 hours or less per week,

(C) employees whose customary employment is for not more than 5 months in any calendar year, and

(D) officers, persons whose principal duties consist of supervising the work of other employees, or highly compensated employees;

(5) under the terms of the plan, all employees granted such options shall have the same rights and privileges, except that the amount of stock which may be purchased by any employee under such option may bear a uniform relationship to the total compensation, or the basic or regular rate of compensation, of employees, and the plan may provide that no employee may purchase more than a maximum amount of stock fixed under the plan;

(6) under the terms of the plan, the option price is not less than the lesser of—

(A) an amount equal to 85 percent of the fair market value of the stock at the time such option is granted, or

(B) an amount which under the terms of the option may not be less than 85 percent of the fair market value of the stock at the time such option is exercised;

(7) under the terms of the plan, such option cannot be exercised after the expiration of—

(A) 5 years from the date such option is granted, if, under the terms of such plan, the option price is to be not less than 85 percent of the fair market value of such stock at the time of the exercise of the option, or

(B) 27 months from the date such option is granted, if the option price is not determinable in the manner described in subparagraph (A);

(8) under the terms of the plan, no employee may be granted an option which permits his rights to purchase stock under all such plans of his employer corporation and its parent and subsidiary corporations to accrue at a rate which exceeds $25,000 of fair market value of such stock (determined at the time such option is granted) for each calendar year in which such option is outstanding at any time. For purposes of this paragraph—

(A) the right to purchase stock under an option accrues when the option (or any portion thereof) first becomes exercisable during the calendar year;

(B) the right to purchase stock under an option accrues at the rate provided in the option, but in no case may such rate exceed $25,000 of fair market value of such stock (determined at the time such option is granted) for any one calendar year; and

(C) a right to purchase stock which has accrued under one option granted pursuant to the plan may not be carried over to any other option; and

(9) under the terms of the plan, such option is not transferable by such individual otherwise than by will or the laws of descent and distribution, and is exercisable, during his lifetime, only by him.

For purposes of paragraphs (3) to (9), inclusive, where additional terms are contained in an offering made under a plan, such additional terms shall, with respect to options exercised under such offering, be treated as a part of the terms of such plan.

Code Sec. 423 (b) (1)

(c) **Special Rule Where Option Price Is Between 85 Percent and 100 Percent of Value of Stock.**—If the option price of a share of stock acquired by an individual pursuant to a transfer to which subsection (a) applies was less than 100 percent of the fair market value of such share at the time such option was granted, then, in the event of any disposition of such share by him which meets the holding period requirements of subsection (a), or in the event of his death (whenever occuring) while owning such share, there shall be included as compensation (and not as gain upon the sale or exchange of a capital asset) in his gross income, for the taxable year in which falls the date of such disposition or for the taxable year closing with his death, whichever applies, an amount equal to the lesser of—

(1) the excess of the fair market value of the share at the time of such disposition or death over the amount paid for the share under the option, or

(2) the excess of the fair market value of the share at the time the option was granted over the option price. If the option price is not fixed or determinable at the time the option is granted, then for purposes of this subsection, the option price shall be determined as if the option were exercised at such time. In the case of the disposition of such share by the individual, the basis of the share in his hands at the time of such disposition shall be increased by an amount equal to the amount so includible in his gross income.

SEC. 424. RESTRICTED STOCK OPTIONS.

(a) **In General.**—Section 421(a) shall apply with respect to the transfer of a share of stock to an individual pursuant to his exercise after 1949 of a restricted stock option, if—

(1) no disposition of such share is made by him within 2 years from the date of the granting of the option nor within 6 months [9 months for taxable years beginning in 1977; 1 year for taxable years beginning after December 31, 1977] after the transfer of such share to him, and

(2) at the time he exercises such option—

(A) he is an employee of either the corporation granting such option, a parent or subsidiary corporation of such corporation, or a corporation or a parent or subsidiary corporation of such corporation issuing or assuming a stock option in a transaction to which section 425(a) applies, or

(B) he ceased to be an employee of such corporations within the 3-month period preceding the time of exercise.

(b) **Restricted Stock Option.**—For purposes of this part, the term "restricted stock option" means an option granted after February 26, 1945, and before January 1, 1964 (or, if it meets the requirements of subsection (c)(3), an option granted after December 31, 1963), to an individual, for any reason connected with his employment by a corporation, if granted by the employer corporation or its parent or subsidiary corporation, to purchase stock of any such corporations, but only if—

(1) at the time such option is granted—

(A) the option price is at least 85 percent of the fair market value at such time of the stock subject to the option, or

(B) in the case of a variable price option, the option price (computed as if the option had been exercised when granted) is at least 85 percent of the fair market value of the stock at the time such option is granted;

(2) such option by its terms is not transferable by such individual otherwise than by will or the laws of descent and distribution, and is exercisable, during his lifetime, only by him;

(3) such individual, at the time the option is granted, does not own stock possessing more than 10 percent of the total combined voting power of all classes of stock of the employer corporation or of its parent or subsidiary corporation. This paragraph shall not apply if at the time such option is granted the option price is at least 110 percent of the fair market value of the stock subject to the option, and such option either by its terms is not exercisable after the expiration of 5 years from the date such option is granted or is exercised within one year after August 16, 1954. For purposes of this paragraph, the provisions of section 425(d) shall apply in determining the stock ownership of an individual; and

(4) such option by its terms is not exercisable after the expiration of 10 years from the date such option is granted, if such option has been granted on or after June 22, 1954.

Code Sec. 424 (b)

(c) **Special Rules.—**

(1) **Options under which option price is between 85 percent and 95 percent of value of stock.—**If no disposition of a share of stock acquired by an individual on his exercise after 1949 of a restricted stock option is made by him within 2 years from the date of the granting of the option nor within 6 months [9 months for taxable years beginning in 1977; 1 year for taxable years beginning after December 31, 1977] after the transfer of such share to him, but, at the time the restricted stock option was granted, the option price (computed under subsection (b)(1)) was less than 95 percent of the fair market value at such time of such share, then, in the event of any disposition of such share by him, or in the event of his death (whenever occurring) while owning such share, there shall be included as compensation (and not as gain upon the sale or exchange of a capital asset) in his gross income, for the taxable year in which falls the date of such disposition or for the taxable year closing with his death, whichever applies—

(A) in the case of a share of stock acquired under an option qualifying under subsection (b)(1)(A), an amount equal to the amount (if any) by which the option price is exceeded by the lesser of—

(i) the fair market value of the share at the time of such disposition or death, or

(ii) the fair market value of the share at the time the option was granted; or

(B) in the case of stock acquired under an option qualifying under subsection (b)(1)(B), an amount equal to the lesser of—

(i) the excess of the fair market value of the share at the time of such disposition or death over the price paid under the option, or

(i) the excess of the fair market value of the share at the time the option was granted over the option price (computed as if the option had been exercised at such time).

In the case of a disposition of such share by the individual, the basis of the share in his hands at the time of such disposition shall be increased by an amount equal to the amount so includible in his gross income.

(2) **Variable price option.—**For purposes of subsection (b)(1), the term "variable price option" means an option under which the purchase price of the stock is fixed or determinable under a formula in which the only variable is the fair market value of the stock at any time during a period of 6 months [9 months for taxable years beginning in 1977; 1 year for taxable years beginning after December 31, 1977] which includes the time the option is exercised; except that in the case of options granted after September 30, 1958, such term does not include any such option in which such formula provides for determining such price by reference to the fair market value of the stock at any time before the option is exercised if such value may be greater than the average fair market value of the stock during the calendar month in which the option is exercised.

(3) **Certain options granted after December 31, 1963.—**For purposes of subsection (b), an option granted after December 31, 1963, meets the requirements of this paragraph if granted pursuant to—

(A) a binding written contract entered into before January 1, 1964, or

(B) a written plan adopted and approved before January 1, 1964, which (as of January 1, 1964, and as of the date of the granting of the option)—

(i) met the requirements of paragraphs (4) and (5) of section 423(b), or

(ii) was being administered in a way which did not discriminate in favor of officers, persons whose principal duties consist of supervising the work of other employees, or highly compensated employees.

An option described in the preceding sentence shall be treated as ceasing to meet the requirements of this paragraph if it is not exercised before May 21, 1981.

SEC. 425. DEFINITIONS AND SPECIAL RULES.

(a) **Corporate Reorganizations, Liquidations, Etc.—**For purposes of this part, the term "issuing or assuming a stock option in a transaction to which section 425(a) applies" means a substitution of a new option for the old option, or an assumption of the old option, by an employer corporation, or a parent or subsidiary of such corporation, by reason of a corporate merger, consolidation, acquisition of property or stock, separation, reorganization, or liquidation, if—

(1) the excess of the aggregate fair market value of the shares subject to the option immediately after the substitution or assumption over the aggregate option price of such shares is not more than the excess of the aggregate fair market value of all shares subject to the option immediately before such substitution or assumption over the aggregate option price of such shares, and

(2) the new option or the assumption of the old option does not give the employee additional benefits which he did not have under the old option.

For purposes of this subsection, the parent-subsidiary relationship shall be determined at the time of any such transaction under this subsection.

(b) Acquisition of New Stock.—For purposes of this part, if stock is received by an individual in a distribution to which section 305, 354, 355, 356, or 1036 (or so much of section 1031 as relates to section 1036) applies, and such distribution was made with respect to stock transferred to him upon his exercise of the option, such stock shall be considered as having been transferred to him on his exercise of such option. A similar rule shall be applied in the case of a series of such distributions.

(c) Disposition.—

(1) In general.—Except as provided in paragraphs (2) and (3), for purposes of this part, the term "disposition" includes a sale, exchange, gift, or a transfer of legal title, but does not include—

(A) a transfer from a decedent to an estate or a transfer by bequest or inheritance;

(B) an exchange to which section 354, 355, 356, or 1036 (or so much of section 1031 as relates to section 1036) applies; or

(C) a mere pledge or hypothecation.

(2) Joint tenancy.—The acquisition of a share of stock in the name of the employee and another jointly with the right of survivorship or a subsequent transfer of a share of stock into such joint ownership shall not be deemed a disposition, but a termination of such joint tenancy (except to the extent such employee acquires ownership of such stock) shall be treated as a disposition by him occurring at the time such joint tenancy is terminated.

(3) Special rule where incentive stock is acquired through use of other statutory option stock.—

(A) Nonrecognition sections not to apply.—If—

(i) there is a transfer of statutory option stock in connection with the exercise of any incentive stock option, and

(ii) the applicable holding period requirements (under section 422(a)(1), 422A(a)(1), 423(a)(1), or 424(a)(1)) are not met before such transfer,

then no section referred to in subparagraph (B) of paragraph (1) shall apply to such transfer.

(B) Statutory option stock.—For purpose of subparagraph (A), the term 'statutory option stock' means any stock acquired through the exercise of a qualified stock option, an incentive stock option, an option granted under an employee stock purchase plan, or a restricted stock option.

(d) Attribution of Stock Ownership.—For purposes of this part, in applying the percentage limitations of sections 422(b)(7), 422A(b)(6), 423(b)(3), and 424(b)(3)—

(1) the individual with respect to whom such limitation is being determined shall be considered as owning the stock owned, directly or indirectly, by or for his brothers and sisters (whether by the whole or half blood), spouse, ancestors, and lineal descendants, and

(2) stock owned, directly or indirectly, by or for a corporation, partnership, estate, or trust, shall be considered as being owned proportionately by or for its shareholders, partners, or beneficiaries.

(e) Parent Corporation.—For purposes of this part, the term "parent corporation" means any corporation (other than the employer corporation) in an unbroken chain of corporations ending with the employer corporation if, at the time of the granting of the option, each of the corporations other than the employer corporation owns stock possessing 50 percent or more of the total combined voting power of all classes of stock in one of the other corporations in such chain.

(f) Subsidiary Corporation.—For purposes of this part, the term "subsidiary cor-

Code Sec. 425 (f)

poration" means any corporation (other than the employer corporation) in an unbroken chain of corporations beginning with the employer corporation if, at the time of the granting of the option, each of the corporations other than the last corporation in the unbroken chain owns stock possessing 50 percent or more of the total combined voting power of all classes of stock in one of the other corporations in such chain.

(g) Special Rule for Applying Subsections (e) and (f).—In applying subsections (e) and (f) for purposes of section 422(a)(2), 422A(a)(2), 423(a)(2), and 424(a)(2), there shall be substituted for the term "employer corporation" wherever it appears in subsections (e) and (f) the term "grantor corporation", or the term "corporation issuing or assuming a stock option in a transaction to which section 425(a) applies", as the case may be.

(h) Modification, Extension, or Renewal of Option.—

(1) In general.—For purposes of this part, if the terms of any option to purchase stock are modified, extended, or renewed, such modification, extension, or renewal shall be considered as the granting of a new option.

(2) Special rules for sections 423 and 424 options.—
(A) In the case of the transfer of stock pursuant to the exercise of an option to which section 423 or 424 applies and which has been so modified, extended, or renewed, then, except as provided in subparagraph (B), the fair market value of such stock at the time of the granting of such option shall be considered as whichever of the following is the highest:
(i) the fair market value of such stock on the date of the original granting of the option,
(ii) the fair market value of such stock on the date of the making of such modification, extension, or renewal, or
(iii) the fair market value of such stock at the time of the making of any intervening modification, extension, or renewal.

(B) Subparagraph (A) shall not apply with respect to a modification, extension, or renewal of a restricted stock option before January 1, 1964 (or after December 31, 1963, if made pursuant to a binding written contract entered into before January 1, 1964), if the aggregate of the monthly average fair market values of the stock subject to the option for the 12 consecutive calendar months before the date of the modification, extension, or renewal, divided by 12, is an amount less than 80 percent of the fair market value of such stock on the date of the original granting of the option or the date of the making of any intervening modification, extension, or renewal, whichever is the highest.

(3) Definition of modification.—The term "modification" means any change in the terms of the option which gives the employee additional benefits under the option, but such term shall not include a change in the terms of the option—
(A) attributable to the issuance or assumption of an option under subsection (a);
(B) to permit the option to qualify under sections 422(b)(6), 422A(b)(5), 423 (b)(9), and 424(b)(2); or
(C) in the case of an option not immediately exercisable in full, to accelerate the time at which the option may be exercised.
If a restricted stock option is exercisable after the expiration of 10 years from the date such option is granted, subparagraph (B) shall not apply unless terms of the option are also changed to make it not exercisable after the expiration of such period.

(i) Stockholder Approval.—For purposes of this part, if the grant of an option is subject to approval by stockholders, the date of grant of the option shall be determined as if the option had not been subject to such approval.

(j) Cross References.—
For provisions requiring the reporting of certain acts with respect to a qualified stock option, an incentive stock option, options granted under employer stock purchase plans, or a restricted stock option, see section 6039.

Code Sec. 425 (g)

* * *

Subchapter F—
Exempt Organizations

Part I—General Rule

Section
501. Exemption from tax on corporations, certain trusts, etc.

* * *

SEC. 501. EXEMPTION FROM TAX ON CORPORATIONS, CERTAIN TRUSTS, ETC.

(a) Exemption From Taxation.—An organization described in subsection (c) or (d) or section 401(a) shall be exempt from taxation under this subtitle unless such exemption is denied under section 502 or 503.

(b) Tax on Unrelated Business Income and Certain Other Activities.—An organization exempt from taxation under subsection (a) shall be subject to tax to the extent provided in parts II, III, and VI of this subchapter, but (notwithstanding parts II, III and VI of this subchapter) shall be considered an organization exempt from income taxes for the purpose of any law which refers to organizations exempt from income taxes.

(c) List of Exempt Organizations.—The following organizations are referred to in subsection (a):

(1) Corporations organized under Act of Congress, if such corporations are instrumentalities of the United States and if, under such Act, as amended and supplemented, such corporations are exempt from Federal income taxes.

(2) Corporations organized for the exclusive purpose of holding title to property, collecting income therefrom, and turning over the entire amount thereof, less expenses, to an organization which itself is exempt under this section.

(3) Corporations, and any community chest, fund, or foundation, organized and operated exclusively for religious, charitable, scientific, testing for public safety, literary, or educational purposes, or to foster national or international amateur sports competition (but only if no part of its activities involve the provision of athletic facilities or equipment), or for the prevention of cruelty to children or animals, no part of the net earnings of which inures to the benefit of any private shareholder or individual, no substantial part of the activities of which is carrying on propaganda, or otherwise attempting to influence legislation, (except as otherwise provided in subsection (h)), and which does not participate in, or intervene in (including the publishing or distributing of statements), any political campaign on behalf of any candidate for public office.

(4) Civic leagues or organizations not organized for profit but operated exclusively for the promotion of social welfare, or local associations of employees, the membership of which is limited to the employees of a designated person or persons in a particular municipality, and the net earnings of which are devoted exclusively to charitable, educational, or recreational purposes.

(5) Labor, agricultural, or horticultural organizations.

(6) Business leagues, chambers of commerce, real-estate boards, boards of trade, or professional football leagues (whether or not administering a pension fund for football players), not organized for profit and no part of the net earnings of which inures to the benefit of any private shareholder or individual.

(7) Clubs organized for pleasure, recreation, and other nonprofitable purposes, substantially all of the activities of which are for such purposes and no part of the net earnings of which inures to the benefit of any private shareholder.

(8) Fraternal beneficiary societies, orders, or associations—

(A) operating under the lodge system or for the exclusive benefit of the members of a fraternity itself operating under the lodge system, and

(B) providing for the payment of life, sick, accident, or other benefits to the members of such society, order, or association or their dependents.

(9) Voluntary employees' beneficiary associations providing for the payment of life, sick, accident, or other benefits to the members of such association or their dependents or designated beneficiaries, if no part

of the net earnings of such association inures (other than through such payments) to the benefit of any private shareholder or individual.

(10) Domestic fraternal societies, orders, or associations, operating under the lodge system—

(A) the net earnings of which are devoted exclusively to religious, charitable, scientific, literary, educational, and fraternal purposes, and

(B) which do not provide for the payment of life, sick, accident, or other benefits.

(11) Teachers' retirement fund associations of a purely local character, if—

(A) no part of their net earnings inures (other than through payment of retirement benefits) to the benefit of any private shareholder or individual, and

(B) the income consists solely of amounts received from public taxation, amounts received from assessments on the teaching salaries of members, and income in respect of investments.

(12)(A) Benevolent life insurance associations of a purely local character, mutual ditch or irrigation companies, mutual or cooperative telephone companies, or like organizations; but only if 85 percent or more of the income consists of amounts collected from members for the sole purpose of meeting losses and expenses.

(B) In the case of a mutual or cooperative telephone company, subparagraph (A) shall be applied without taking into account any income received or accrued—

(i) from a nonmember telephone company for the performance of communication services which involve members of the mutual or cooperative telephone company,

(ii) from qualified pole rentals, or

(iii) from the sale of display listings in a directory furnished to the members of the mutual or cooperative telephone company.

(C) In the case of a mutual or cooperative electric company, subparagraph (A) shall be applied without taking into account any income received or accrued from qualified pole rentals.

(D) For purposes of this paragraph, the term "qualified pole rental" means any rental of a pole (or other structure used to support wires) if such pole (or other structure)—

(i) is used by the telephone or electric company to support one or more wires which are used by such company in providing telephone or electric services to its members, and

(ii) is used pursuant to the rental to support one or more wires (in addition to the wires described in clause (i)) for use in connection with the transmission by wire of electricity or of telephone or other communications.

For purposes of the preceding sentence, the term "rental" includes any sale of the right to use the pole (or other structure).

(13) Cemetery companies owned and operated exclusively for the benefit of their members or which are not operated for profit; and any corporation chartered solely for the purpose of the disposal of bodies by burial or cremation which is not permitted by its charter to engage in any business not necessarily incident to that purpose, no part of the net earnings of which inures to the benefit of any private shareholder or individual.

(14)(A) Credit unions without capital stock organized and operated for mutual purposes and without profit.

(B) Corporations or associations without capital stock organized before September 1, 1957, and operated for mutual purposes and without profit for the purpose of providing reserve funds for, and insurance of, shares or deposits in—

(i) domestic building and loan associations,

(ii) cooperative banks without capital stock organized and operated for mutual purposes and without profit, or

(iii) mutual savings banks not having capital stock represented by shares.

(C) Corporations or associations organized before September 1, 1957, and operated for mutual purposes and without profit for the purpose of providing reserve funds for associations or banks described in clause (i), (ii), or (iii) of subparagraph (B); but only if 85 percent or more of the income is attributable to providing such reserve funds and to investments. This subparagraph shall not apply to any corporation or association entitled to exemption under subparagraph (B).

Code Sec. 501 (c) (10)

(15) Mutual insurance companies or associations other than life or marine (including interinsurers and reciprocal underwriters) if the gross amount received during the taxable year from the items described in section 822(b) (other than paragraph (1)(D) thereof) and premiums (including deposits and assessments) does not exceed $150,000.

(16) Corporations organized by an association subject to part IV of this subchapter or members thereof, for the purpose of financing the ordinary crop operations of such members or other producers, and operated in conjunction with such association. Exemption shall not be denied any such corporation because it has capital stock, if the dividend rate of such stock is fixed at not to exceed the legal rate of interest in the State of incorporation or 8 percent per annum, whichever is greater, on the value of the consideration for which the stock was issued, and if substantially all such stock (other than nonvoting preferred stock, the owners of which are not entitled or permitted to participate, directly or indirectly, in the profits of the corporation, on dissolution or otherwise, beyond the fixed dividends) is owned by such association, or members thereof; nor shall exemption be denied any such corporation because there is accumulated and maintained by it a reserve required by State law or a reasonable reserve for any necessary purpose.

(17)(A) A trust or trusts forming part of a plan providing for the payment of supplemental unemployment compensation benefits, if—

(i) under the plan, it is impossible, at any time prior to the satisfaction of all liabilities with respect to employees under the plan, for any part of the corpus or income to be (within the taxable year or thereafter) used for, or diverted to, any purpose other than the providing of supplemental unemployment compensation benefits.

(ii) such benefits are payable to employees under a classification which is set forth in the plan and which is found by the Secretary not to be discriminatory in favor of employees who are officers, shareholders, persons whose principal duties consist of supervising the work of other employees, or highly compensated employees, and

(iii) such benefits do not discriminate in favor of employees who are officers, shareholders, persons whose principal duties consist of supervising the work of other employees, or highly compensated employees. A plan shall not be considered discriminatory within the meaning of this clause merely because the benefits received under the plan bear a uniform relationship to the total compensation, or the basic or regular rate of compensation, of the employees covered by the plan.

(B) In determining whether a plan meets the requirements of subparagraph (A), any benefits provided under any other plan shall not be taken into consideration, except that a plan shall not be considered discriminatory—

(i) merely because the benefits under the plan which are first determined in a nondiscriminatory manner within the meaning of subparagraph (A) are then reduced by any sick, accident, or unemployment compensation benefits received under State or Federal law (or reduced by a portion of such benefits if determined in a nondiscriminatory manner), or

(ii) merely because the plan provides only for employees who are not eligible to receive sick, accident, or unemployment compensation benefits under State or Federal law the same benefits (or a portion of such benefits if determined in a nondiscriminatory manner) which such employees would receive under such laws if such employees were eligible for such benefits, or

(iii) merely because the plan provides only for employees who are not eligible under another plan (which meets the requirements of subparagraph (A)) of supplemental unemployment compensation benefits provided wholly by the employer the same benefits (or a portion of such benefits if determined in a nondiscriminatory manner) which such employees would receive under such other plan if such employees were eligible under such other plan, but only if the employees eligible under both plans would make a classification which would be nondiscriminatory within the meaning of subparagraph (A).

(C) A plan shall be considered to meet the requirements of subparagraph (A) during the whole of any year of the plan if on one day in each quarter it satisfies such requirements.

Code Sec. 501 (c) (17) (C)

(D) The term "supplemental unemployment compensation benefits" means only—

(i) benefits which are paid to an employee because of his involuntary separation from the employment of the employer (whether or not such separation is temporary) resulting directly from a reduction in force, the discontinuance of a plant or operation, or other similar conditions, and

(ii) sick and accident benefits subordinate to the benefits described in clause (i).

(E) Exemption shall not be denied under subsection (a) to any organization entitled to such exemption as an association described in paragraph (9) of this subsection merely because such organization provides for the payment of supplemental unemployment benefits (as defined in subparagraph (D)(i).

(18) A trust or trusts created before June 25, 1959, forming part of a plan providing for the payment of benefits under a pension plan funded only by contributions of employees, if—

(A) under the plan, it is impossible, at any time prior to the satisfaction of all liabilities with respect to employees under the plan, for any part of the corpus or income to be (within the taxable year or thereafter) used for, or diverted to, any purpose other than the providing of benefits under the plan,

(B) such benefits are payable to employees under a classification which is set forth in the plan and which is found by the Secretary or his delegate not to be discriminatory in favor of employees who are officers, shareholders, persons whose principal duties consist of supervising the work of other employees, or highly compensated employees, and

(C) such benefits do not discriminate in favor of employees who are officers, shareholders, persons whose principal duties consist of supervising the work of other employees, or highly compensated employees. A plan shall not be considered discriminatory within the meaning of this subparagraph merely because the benefits received under the plan bear a uniform relationship to the total compensation, or the basic or regular rate of compensation, of the employees covered by the plan.

(19) A post or organization of past or present members of the Armed Forces of the United States, or an auxiliary unit or society of, or a trust or foundation for, any such post or organization—

(A) organized in the United States or any of its possessions,

(B) at least 75 percent of the members of which are past or present members of the Armed Forces of the United States and substantially all of the other members of which are individuals who are cadets, or are spouses, widows, or widowers of past or present members of the Armed Forces of the United States or of cadets, and

(C) no part of the net earnings of which inures to the benefit of any private shareholder or individual.

(20) An organization or trust created or organized in the United States, the exclusive function of which is to form part of a qualified group legal services plan or plans, within the meaning of section 120. An organization or trust which receives contributions because of section 120(c)(5)(C) shall not be prevented from qualifying as an organization described in this paragraph merely because it provides legal services or indemnification against the cost of legal services unassociated with a qualified group legal services plan.

(21) A trust or trusts established in writing, created or organized in the United States, and contributed to by any person (except an insurance company) if—

(A) the purpose of such trust or trusts is exclusively—

(i) to satisfy, in whole or in part, the liability of such person for, or with respect to, claims for compensation for disability or death due to pneumoconiosis under Black Lung Acts;

(ii) to pay premiums for insurance exclusively covering liability; and

(iii) to pay administrative and other incidental expenses of such trust (including legal, accounting, actuarial, and trustee expenses) in connection with the operation of the trust and the processing of claims against such person under Black Lung Acts; and

(B) no part of the assets of the trust may be used for, or diverted to, any purpose other than—

(i) the purposes described in subparagraph (A), or

(ii) investment (but only to the extent that the trustee determines that a portion of the assets is not currently needed for the purposes described in subparagraph (A)) in—

(I) public debt securities of the United States,

(II) obligations of a State or local government which are not in default as to principal or interest, or

(III) time or demand deposits in a bank (as defined in section 581) or an insured credit union (within the meaning of section 101(6) of the Federal Credit Union Act, 12 U.S.C. 1752(6)) located in the United States, or

(iii) payment into the Black Lung Disability Trust Fund established under section 3 of the Black Lung Benefits Revenue Act of 1977, or into the general fund of the United States Treasury (other than in satisfaction of any tax or other civil or criminal liability of the person who established or contributed to the trust).

For purposes of this paragraph the term "Black Lung Acts" means part C of title IV of the Federal Mine Safety and Health Act of 1977, and any State law providing compensation for disability or death due to pneumoconiosis.

(22) A trust created or organized in the United States and established in writing by the plan sponsors of multiemployer plans if—

(A) the purpose of such trust is exclusively—

(i) to pay any amount described in section 4223(c) or (h) of the Employee Retirement Income Security Act of 1974, and

(ii) to pay reasonable and necessary administrative expenses in connection with the establishment and operation of the trust and the processing of claims against the trust,

(B) no part of the assets of the trust may be used for, or diverted to, any purpose other than—

(i) the purposes described in subparagraph (A), or

(ii) the investment in securities, obligations, or time or demand deposits described in clause (ii) of paragraph (21)(B),

(C) such trust meets the requirements of paragraphs (2), (3), and (4) of section 4223(b), 4223(h), or, if applicable, section 4223(c) of the Employee Retirement Income Security Act of 1974, and

(D) the trust instrument provides that, on dissolution of the trust, assets of the trust may not be paid other than to plans which have participated in the plan or, in the case of a trust established under section 4223(h) of such Act, to plans with respect to which employers have participated in the fund.

(23) Any association organized before 1880 where more than 75 percent of the members of which are present or past members of the Armed Forces and a principal purpose of which is to provide insurance and other benefits to veterans or their dependents.

(d) Religious and Apostolic Organizations.—The following organizations are referred to in subsection (a): Religious or apostolic associations or corporations, if such associations or corporations have a common treasury or community treasury, even if such associations or corporations engage in business for the common benefit of the members, but only if the members thereof include (at the time of filing their returns) in their gross income their entire pro rata shares, whether distributed or not, of the taxable income of the association or corporation for such year. Any amount so included in the gross income of a member shall be treated as a dividend received.

(e) Cooperative Hospital Service Organizations.—For purposes of this title, an organization shall be treated as an organization organized and operated exclusively for charitable purposes, if—

(1) such organization is organized and operated solely—

(A) to perform, on a centralized basis, one or more of the following services which, if performed on its own behalf by a hospital which is an organization described in subsection (c)(3) and exempt from taxation under subsection (a), would constitute activities in exercising or performing the purpose or function constituting the basis for its exemption: data processing, purchasing, warehousing, billing and collection, food, clinical, industrial engineering, laboratory, printing, communications, record center, and personnel (including selection, testing, training, and education of personnel) services; and

(B) to perform such services solely for two or more hospitals each of which is—

(i) an organization described in subsec-

Code Sec. 501 (e)

tion (c)(3) which is exempt from taxation under subsection (a),

(ii) a constituent part of an organization described in subsection (c)(3) which is exempt from taxation under subsection (a) and which, if organized and operated as a separate entity, would constitute an organization described in subsection (c)(3), or

(iii) owned and operated by the United States, a State, the District of Columbia, or a possession of the United States, or a political subdivision or an agency or instrumentality of any of the foregoing;

(2) such organization is organized and operated on a cooperative basis and allocates or pays, within 8½ months after the close of its taxable year, all net earnings to patrons on the basis of services performed for them; and

(3) if such organization has capital stock, all of such stock outstanding is owned by its patrons.

For purposes of this title, any organization which, by reason of the preceding sentence, is an organization described in subsection (c)(3) and exempt from taxation under subsection (a), shall be treated as a hospital and as an organization referred to in section 170(b)(1)(A)(iii).

(f) Cooperative Service Organizations of Operating Educational Organizations.— For purposes of this title, if an organization is—

(1) organized and operated solely to hold, commingle, and collectively invest and reinvest (including arranging for and supervising the performance by independent contractors of investment services related thereto) in stocks and securities, the moneys contributed thereto by each of the members of such organization, and to collect income therefrom and turn over the entire amount thereof, less expenses, to such members,

(2) organized and controlled by one or more such members, and

(3) comprised solely of members that are organizations described in clause (ii) or (iv) of section 170(b)(1)(A)—

(A) which are exempt from taxation under subsection (a), or

(B) the income of which is excluded from taxation under section 115(a), then such organization shall be treated as an organization organized and operated exclusively for charitable purposes.

(g) Definition of Agricultural.— For purposes of subsection (c)(5), the term "agricultural" includes the art or science of cultivating land, harvesting crops or aquatic resources, or raising livestock.

(h) Expenditures by Public Charities to Influence Legislation.—

(1) General rule.— In the case of an organization to which this subsection applies, exemption from taxation under subsection (a) shall be denied because a substantial part of the activities of such organization consists of carrying on propaganda, or otherwise attempting, to influence legislation, but only if such organization normally—

(A) makes lobbying expenditures in excess of the lobbying ceiling amount for such organization for each taxable year, or

(B) makes grass roots expenditures in excess of the grass roots ceiling amount for such organization for each taxable year.

(2) Definitions.— For purposes of this subsection—

(A) Lobbying expenditures.—The term "lobbying expenditures" means expenditures for the purpose of influencing legislation (as defined in section 4911(d)).

(B) Lobbying ceiling amount.—The lobbying ceiling amount for any organization for any taxable year is 150 percent of the lobbying nontaxable amount for such organization for such taxable year, determined under section 4911.

(C) Grass roots expenditures.—The term "grass roots expenditures" means expenditures for the purpose of influencing legislation (as defined in section 4911(d) without regard to paragraph (1)(B) thereof).

(D) Grass roots ceiling amount.—The grass roots ceiling amount for any organization for any taxable year is 150 percent of the grass roots nontaxable amount for such organization for such taxable year, determined under section 4911.

(3) Organizations to which this subsection applies.— This subsection shall apply to any organization which has elected (in such manner and at such time as the Secretary may prescribe) to have the provisions of

Code Sec. 501 (f)

this subsection apply to such organization and which, for the taxable year which includes the date the election is made, is described in subsection (c)(3) and—
 (A) is described in paragraph (4), and
 (B) is not a disqualified organization under paragraph (5).

(4) Organizations permitted to elect to have this subsection apply.—An organization is described in this paragraph if it is described in—
 (A) section 170(b)(1)(A)(ii) (relating to educational institutions),
 (B) section 170(b)(1)(A)(iii) (relating to hospitals and medical research organizations),
 (C) section 170(b)(1)(A)(iv) (relating to organizations supporting government schools),
 (D) section 170(b)(1)(A)(vi) (relating to organizations publicly supported by charitable contributions),
 (E) section 509(a)(2) (relating to organizations publicly supported by admissions, sales, etc.), or
 (F) section 509(a)(3) (relating to organizations supporting certain types of public charities) except that for purposes of this subparagraph, section 509(a)(3) shall be applied without regard to the last sentence of section 509(a).

(5) Disqualified organizations.—For purposes of paragraph (3) an organization is a disqualified organization if it is—
 (A) described in section 170(b)(1)(A)(i) (relating to churches),
 (B) an integrated auxiliary of a church or of a convention or association of churches, or
 (C) a member of an affiliated group of organizations (within the meaning of section 4911(f)(2)) if one or more members of such group is described in subparagraph (A) or (B).

(6) Years for which election is effective.—An election by an organization under this subsection shall be effective for all taxable years of such organization which—
 (A) end after the date the election is made, and
 (B) begin before the date the election is revoked by such organization (under regulations prescribed by the Secretary).

(7) No effect on certain organizations.—With respect to any organization for a taxable year for which—
 (A) such organization is a disqualified organization (within the meaning of paragraph (5)), or
 (B) an election under this subsection is not in effect for such organization,
nothing in this subsection or in section 4911 shall be construed to affect the interpretation of the phrase, "no substantial part of the activities of which is carrying on propaganda, or otherwise attempting, to influence legislation," under subsection (c)(3).

(8) Affiliated organizations.—
For rules regarding affiliated organizations, see section 4911(f).

(i) Prohibition of Discrimination by Certain Social Clubs.—Notwithstanding subsection (a), an organization which is described in subsection (c)(7) shall not be exempt from taxation under subsection (a) for any taxable year if, at any time during such taxable year, the charter, bylaws, or other governing instrument, of such organization or any written policy statement of such organization contains a provision which provides for discrimination against any person on the basis of race, color, or religion. The preceding sentence to the extent it relates to discrimination on the basis of religion shall not apply to—
 (1) an auxiliary of a fraternal beneficiary society if such society—
 (A) is described in subsection (c)(8) and exempt from tax under subsection (a), and
 (B) limits its membership to the members of a particular religion, or
 (2) a club which in good faith limits its membership to the members of a particular religion in order to further the teachings or principles of that religion, and not to exclude individuals of a particular race or color.

(j) Special Rules for Certain Amateur Sports Organizations.—

(1) In general.—In the case of a qualified amateur sports organization—
 (A) the requirement of subsection (c)(3) that no part of its activities involve the provision of athletic facilities or equipment shall not apply, and

Code Sec. 501 (j)

(B) such organization shall not fail to meet the requirements of subsection (c)(3) merely because its membership is local or regional in nature.

(2) Qualified amateur sports organization defined.—For purposes of this subsection, the term 'qualified amateur sports organization' means any organization organized and operated exclusively to foster national or international amateur sports competition if such organization is also organized and operated primarily to conduct national or international competition in sports or to support and develop amateur athletes for national or international competition in sports.

(k) Cross Reference.—
For nonexemption of Communist-controlled organizations, see section 11(b) of the Internal Security Act of 1950 (64 Stat. 997; 50 U.S.C. 790(b)).

* * *

SUBTITLE B—ESTATE AND GIFT TAXES

CHAPTER II—ESTATE TAX

Subchapter A—Estate of Citizens or Residents

Part III—Gross Estate

* * *

SEC. 2039. ANNUITIES.

(a) General.—The gross estate shall include the value of an annuity or other payment receivable by any beneficiary by reason of surviving the decedent under any form of contract or agreement entered into after March 3, 1931 (other than as insurance under policies on the life of the decedent), if, under such contract or agreement, an annuity or other payment was payable to the decedent, or the decedent possessed the right to receive such annuity or payment, either alone or in conjunction with another for his life or for any period not ascertainable without reference to his death or for any period which does not in fact end before his death.

(b) Amount Includible.—Subsection (a) shall apply to only such part of the value of the annuity or other payment receivable under such contract or agreement as is proportionate to that part of the purchase price therefor contributed by the decedent. For purposes of this section, any contribution by the decedent's employer or former employer to the purchase price of such contract or agreement (whether or not to an employee's trust or fund forming part of a pension, annuity, retirement, bonus or profit-sharing plan) shall be considered to be contributed by the decedent if made by reason of his employment.

(c) Exemption of Annuities Under Certain Trusts and Plans.—Subject to the limitation of subsection (g), notwithstanding any other provision of this section or of any provision of law, there shall be excluded from the gross estate the value of an annuity or other payment (other than an amount described in subsection (f)) receivable by any beneficiary (other than the executor) under—

(1) An employees' trust (or under a contract purchased by an employees' trust) forming part of a pension, stock bonus, or profit-sharing plan which, at the time of the decedent's separation from employment (whether by death or otherwise), or at the time of termination of the plan if earlier, met the requirements of section 401(a);

(2) A retirement annuity contract purchased by an employer (and not by an employees' trust) pursuant to a plan which, at the time of decedent's separation from employment (by death or otherwise), or at the time of termination of the plan if earlier, was a plan described in section 403(a);

(3) A retirement annuity contract purchased for an employee by an employer which is an organization referred to in section 170(b)(1)(A)(ii) or (vi), or which is a religious organization (other than a trust), and which is exempt from tax under section 501(a); or

(4) Chapter 73 of title 10 of the United States Code.

If such amounts payable after the death of the decedent under a plan described in paragraph (1) or (2), under a contract described in paragraph (3), or under chapter 73 of title 10 of the United States Code are attributable to any extent to payments or contributions made by the decedent, no exclusion shall be allowed for that part of the value of such amounts in the proportion

Code Sec. 501 (k)

that the total payments or contributions made by the decedent bears to the total payments or contributions made. For purposes of this subsection, contributions or payments made by the decedent's employer or former employer under a trust or plan described in paragraph (1) or (2) shall not be considered to be contributed by the decedent, and contributions or payments made by the decedent's employer or former employer toward the purchase of an annuity contract described in paragraph (3) shall, to the extent excludable from gross income under section 403(b), not be considered to be contributed by the decedent. The subsection shall apply to all decedents dying after December 31, 1953. For purposes of this subsection, contributions or payments on behalf of the decedent while he was an employee within the meaning of section 401(c)(1) made under a trust or plan described in paragraph (1) or (2) shall, to the extent allowable as a deduction under section 404, be considered to be made by a person other than the decedent and, to the extent not so allowable, shall be considered to be made by the decedent. For purposes of this subsection, amounts payable under chapter 73 of title 10 of the United States Code are attributable to payments or contributions made by the decedent only to the extent of amounts deposited by him pursuant to section 1438 or 1452(d) of such title 10. For purposes of this subsection, any deductible employee contributions (within the meaning of paragraph (5) of section 72(o)) shall be considered as made by a person other than the decedent.

(d) Exemption of Certain Annuity Interests Created by Community Property Laws.—In the case of an employee on whose behalf contributions or payments were made by his employer or former employer under a trust or plan described in subsection (c)(1) or (2), or toward the purchase of a contract described in subsection (c)(3), which under subsection (c) are not considered as contributed by the employee, if the spouse of such employee predeceases him, then, notwithstanding the provisions of this section or of any other provision of law, there shall be excluded from the gross estate of such spouse the value of any interest of such spouse in such trust or plan or such contract, to the extent such interest—

(1) is attributable to such contributions or payments, and
(2) arises solely by reason of such spouse's interest in community income under the community property laws of a State.

(e) Exclusion of Individual Retirement Accounts, Etc.—Subject to the limitation of subsection (g), notwithstanding any other provision of this section or of any other provision of law, there shall be excluded from the value of the gross estate the value of an annuity receivable by any beneficiary (other than the executor) under—

(1) an individual retirement account described in section 408(a),
(2) an individual retirement annuity described in section 408(b), or
(3) a retirement bond described in section 409(a).

If any payment to an account described in paragraph (1) or for an annuity described in paragraph (2) or a bond described in paragraph (3) was not allowable as a deduction under section 219 and was not a rollover contribution described in section 402(a)(5), 403(a)(4), section 403(b)(8) (but only to the extent such contribution is attributable to a distribution from a contract described in subsection (c)(3)), 405(d)(3), 408(d)(3), or 409(b)(3)(C), the preceding sentence shall not apply to that portion of the value of the amount receivable under such account, annuity, or bond (as the case may be) which bears the same ratio to the total value of the amount so receivable as the total amount which was paid to or for such account, annuity, or bond and which was not allowable as a deduction under section 219 and was not such a rollover contribution bears to the total amount paid to or for such account, annuity, or bond. For purposes of this subsection, the term "annuity" means an annuity contract or other arrangement providing for a series of substantially equal periodic payments to be made to a beneficiary (other than the executor) for his life or over a period extending for at least 36 months after the date of the decedent's death.

(f) Lump Sum Distributions.—

(1) In general.—An amount is described in this subsection if—

Code Sec. 2039 (f)

(A) it is a lump sum distribution described in section 402(e)(4) (determined without regard to the third sentence of section 402(e)(4)(A)), or

(B) it is an amount attributable to accumulated deductible employee contributions (as defined in section 72(o)(5)(B)) in any part taken into account for purposes of determining whether the distribution described in subparagraph (A) qualifies as a lump sum distribution.

(2) Exception where recipient elects not to take 10-year averaging.—An amount described in paragraph (1) shall be treated as not described in this subsection if the recipient elects irrevocably (at such time and in such manner as the Secretary may by regulations prescribe) to treat the distribution as taxable under section 402(a) (without the application of paragraph (2) thereof), except to the extent that section 402(e)(4)(J) applies to such distribution.

*****(g) $100,000 Limitation on Exclusions Under Subsections (c) and (e).**—The aggregate amount excluded from the gross estate of any decedent under subsections (c) and (e) of this section shall not exceed $100,000.

* * *

SUBTITLE C—EMPLOYMENT TAXES

CHAPTER 23— FEDERAL UNEMPLOYMENT TAX ACT

* * *

SEC. 3304. APPROVAL OF STATE LAWS.

(a) Requirements.—The Secretary of Labor shall approve any State law submitted to him, within 30 days of such submission, which he finds provides that—

(1) all compensation is to be paid through public employment offices or such other agencies as the Secretary of Labor may approve;

(2) no compensation shall be payable with respect to any day of unemployment occurring within 2 years after the first day of the first period with respect to which contributions are required;

(3) all money received in the unemployment fund shall (except for refunds of sums erroneously paid into such fund and except for refunds paid in accordance with the provisions of section 3305(b)) immediately upon such receipt be paid over to the Secretary of the Treasury to the credit of the Unemployment Trust Fund established by section 904 of the Social Security Act (42 U.S.C. 1104);

(4) all money withdrawn from the unemployment fund of the State shall be used solely in the payment of unemployment compensation, exclusive of expenses of administration, and for refunds of sums erroneously paid into such fund and refunds paid in accordance with the provisions of section 3305(b); except that—

(A) an amount equal to the amount of employee payments into the unemployment fund of a State may be used in the payment of cash benefits to individuals with respect to their disability, exclusive of expenses of administration; and

(B) the amounts specified by section 903(c)(2) of the Social Security Act may, subject to the conditions prescribed in such section, be used for expenses incurred by the State for administration of its unemployment compensation law and public employment officers;

(5) compensation shall not be denied in such State to any otherwise eligible individual for refusing to accept new work under any of the following conditions:

(A) if the position offered is vacant due directly to a strike, lockout, or other labor dispute;

(B) if the wages, hours, or other conditions of the work offered are substantially less favorable to the individual than those prevailing for similar work in the locality;

(C) if as a condition of being employed the individual would be required to join a company union or to resign from or refrain from joining any bona fide labor organization;

(6)(A) compensation is payable on the basis of service to which section 3309(a)(1) applies, in the same amount, on the same terms, and subject to the same conditions as compensation payable on the basis of other service subject to such law except that—

(i) with respect to services in an instruc-

*[*Editor's Note:* Section 2039(g) applies to the estates of decedents dying after Dec. 31, 1982.]

tional research, or principal administrative capacity for an educational institution to which section 3309(a)(1) applies, compensation shall not be payable based on such services for any week commencing during the period between two successive academic years or terms (or, when an agreement provides instead for a similar period between two regular but not successive terms, during such period) to any individual if such individual performs such services in the first of such academic years (or terms) and if there is a contract or reasonable assurance that such individual will perform services in any such capacity for any educational institution in the second of such academic years or terms.

(ii) with respect to services in any other capacity for an educational institution (other than an institution of higher education) to which section 3309(a)(1) applies, compensation payable on the basis of such services may be denied to any individual for any week which commences during a period between two successive academic years or terms if such individual performs such services in the first of such academic years or terms and there is a reasonable assurance that such individual will perform such services in the second of such academic years or terms,

(iii) with respect to any services described in clause (i) or (ii), compensation payable on the basis of such services may be denied to any individual for any week which commences during an established and customary vacation period or holiday recess if such individual performs such services in the period immediately before such vacation period or holiday recess, and there is a reasonable assurance that such individual will perform such services in the period immediately following such vacation period or holiday recess, and

(iv) with respect to any services described in clause (i) or (ii), compensation payable on the basis of services in any such capacity may be denied as specified in clauses (i), (ii), and (iii) to any individual who performed such services in an educational institution while in the employ of an educational service agency, and for this purpose the term "educational service agency" means a governmental agency or governmental entity which is established and operated exclusively for the purpose of providing such services to one or more educational institutions, and

(B) payments (in lieu of contributions) with respect to service to which section 3309(a)(1) applies may be made into the State unemployment fund on the basis set forth in section 3309(a)(2);

(7) an individual who has received compensation during his benefit year is required to have had work since the beginning of such year in order to qualify for compensation in his next benefit year;

(8) compensation shall not be denied to an individual for any week because he is in training with the approval of the State agency (or because of the application, to any such week in training, of State law provisions relating to availability for work, active search for work, or refusal to accept work);

(9)(A) compensation shall not be denied or reduced to an individual solely because he files a claim in another State (or a contiguous country with which the United States has an agreement with respect to unemployment compensation) or because he resides in another State (or such a contiguous country) at the time he files a claim for unemployment compensation;

(B) the State shall participate in any arrangements for the payment of compensation on the basis of combining an individual's wages and employment covered under the State law with his wages and employment covered under the unemployment compensation law of other States which are approved by the Secretary of Labor in consultation with the State unemployment compensation agencies as reasonably calculated to assure the prompt and full payment of compensation in such situations. Any such arrangement shall include provisions for (i) applying the base period of a single State law to a claim involving the combining of an individual's wages and employment covered under two or more State laws, and (ii) avoiding duplicate use of wages and employment by reason of such combining;

(10) compensation shall not be denied to any individual by reason of cancellation of wage credits or total reduction of his benefit rights for any cause other than discharge for misconduct connected with his work, fraud in connection with a claim for compensation, or receipt of disqualify-

Code Sec. 3304 (a) (10)

ing income;

(11) extended compensation shall be payable as provided by the Federal-State Extended Unemployment Compensation Act of 1970;

(12) no person shall be denied compensation under such State law solely on the basis of pregnancy or termination of pregnancy;

(13) compensation shall not be payable to any individual on the basis of any services, substantially all of which consist of participating in sports or athletic events or training or preparing to so participate, for any week which commences during the period between two successive sport seasons (or similar periods) if such individual performed such services in the first of such seasons (or similar periods) and there is a reasonable assurance that such individual will perform such services in the later of such seasons (or similar periods);

(14)(A) compensation shall not be payable on the basis of services performed by an alien unless such alien is an individual who was lawfully admitted for permanent residence at the time such services were performed, was lawfully present for purposes of performing such services, or was permanently residing in the United States under color of law at the time such services were performed (including an alien who was lawfully present in the United States as a result of the application of the provisions of section 203(a)(7) or section 212(d)(5) of the Immigration and Nationality Act),

(B) any data or information required of individuals applying for compensation to determine whether compensation is not payable to them because of their alien status shall be uniformly required from all applicants for compensation, and

(C) in the case of an individual whose application for compensation would otherwise be approved, no determination by the State agency that compensation to such individual is not payable because of his alien status shall be made except upon a preponderance of the evidence;

(15) the amount of compensation payable to an individual for any week which begins after March 31, 1980, and which begins in a period with respect to which such individual is receiving a governmental or other pension, retirement or retired pay, annuity, or any other similar periodic payment which is based on the previous work of such individual shall be reduced (but not below zero) by an amount equal to the amount of such pension, retirement or retired pay, annuity, or other payment, which is reasonably attributable to such week except that—

(A) the requirements of this paragraph shall apply to any pension, retirement or retired pay, annuity, or other similar periodic payment only if—

(i) such pension, retirement or retired pay, annuity, or similar payment is under a plan maintained (or contributed to) by a base period employer or chargeable employer (as determined under applicable law), and

(ii) in the case of such a payment not made under the Social Security Act or the Railroad Retirement Act of 1974 (or the corresponding provisions of prior law), services performed for such employer by the individual after the beginning of the base period (or remuneration for such services) affect eligibility for, or increase the amount of, such pension, retirement or retired pay, annuity, or similar payment, and

(B) the State law may provide for limitations on the amount of any such a reduction to take into account contributions made by the individual for the pension, retirement or retired pay, annuity, or other similar periodic payment;

(16)(A) wage information contained in the records of the agency administering the State law which is necessary (as determined by the Secretary of Health, Education, and Welfare in regulations) for purposes of determining an individual's eligibility for aid or services, or the amount of such aid or services, under a State plan for aid and services to needy families with children approved under part A of title IV of the Social Security Act, shall be made available to a State or political subdivision thereof when such information is specifically requested by such State or political subdivision for such purposes, and

(B) such safeguards are established as are necessary (as determined by the Secretary of Health, Education, and Welfare in regulations) to insure that such information is used only for the purposes authorized under subparagraph (A);

(17) all the rights, privileges, or immunities conferred by such law or by acts

Code Sec. 3304 (a) (11)

done pursuant thereto shall exist subject to the power of the legislature to amend or repeal such law at any time.

* * *

CHAPTER 24—COLLECTION OF INCOME TAX AT SOURCE ON WAGES

* * *

*SECTION 3405. SPECIAL RULES FOR PENSIONS, ANNUITIES, AND CERTAIN OTHER DEFERRED INCOME.

(a) Pensions, Annuities, Etc.—

(1) Withholding as if payment were wages.—The payor of any periodic payment (as defined in subsection (d)(2)) shall withhold from such payment the amount which would be required to be withheld from such payment if such payment were a payment of wages by an employer to an employee for the appropriate payroll period.

(2) Election of no withholding.—An individual may elect to have paragraph (1) not apply with respect to periodic payments made to such individual. Such an election shall remain in effect until revoked by such individual.

(3) When election takes effect.—Any election under this subsection (and any revocation of such an election) shall take effect as provided by subsection (f)(3) of section 3402 for withholding exemption certificates.

(4) Amount withheld where no withholding exemption certificate in effect.—In the case of any payment with respect to which a withholding exemption certificate is not in effect, the amount withheld under paragraph (1) shall be determined by treating the payee as a married individual claiming 3 withholding exemptions.

(b) Nonperiodic Distribution.—

(1) Withholding.—The payor of any nonperiodic distribution (as defined in subsection (d)(3)) shall withhold from such distribution the amount determined under paragraph (2).

(2) Amount of withholding.—

(A) Distributions which are not qualified total distributions.—In the case of any nonperiodic distribution which is not a qualified total distribution, the amount withheld under paragraph (1) shall be the amount determined by multiplying such distribution by 10 percent.

(B) Qualified total distributions.—In the case of any nonperiodic distribution which is a qualified total distribution, the amount withheld under paragraph (1) shall be determined under tables (or other computational procedures) prescribed by the Secretary which are based on the amount of tax which would be imposed on such distribution under section 402(e) if the recipient elected to treat such distribution as a lump-sum distribution (within the meaning of section 402(e)(4)(A)).

(C) Special rule for distributions by reason of death.—In the case of any distribution described in subparagraph (B) from or under any plan or contract described in section 401(a), 403(a), or 403(b) which is made by reason of a participant's death, the Secretary, in prescribing tables or procedures under paragraph (1), shall take into account the exclusion from gross income provided by section 101(b) (whether or not allowable).

(3) Election of no withholding.—

(A) In general.—An individual may elect not to have paragraph (1) apply with respect to any nonperiodic distribution.

(B) Scope of election.—An election under subparagraph (A)—

(i) except as provided in clause (ii), shall be on a distribution-by-distribution basis, or

(ii) to the extent provided in regulations, may apply to subsequent nonperiodic distributions made by the payor to the payee under the same arrangement.

(c) Liability for Withholding.—

(1) In general.—Except as provided in paragraph (2), the payor of a designated distribution (as defined in subsection (d)(1)) shall withhold, and be liable for, payment

*[*Editor's Note:* Section 3405 applies to payments and other distributions made after Dec. 31, 1982.]

Code Sec. 3405 (c) (1)

of the tax required to be withheld under this section.

(2) **Plan administrator liable in certain cases.—**

(A) In general.—In the case of any plan to which this paragraph applies, paragraph (1) shall not apply and the plan administrator shall withhold, and be liable for, payment of the tax unless the plan administrator—

(i) directs the payor to withhold such tax, and

(ii) provides the payor with such information as the Secretary may require by regulations.

(B) Plans to which paragraph applies.— This paragraph applies to any plan described in, or which at any time has been determined to be described in—

(i) section 401(a),

(ii) section 403(a), or

(iii) section 301(d) of the Tax Reduction Act of 1975.

(d) **Definitions and Special Rules.**—For purposes of this section—

(1) **Designated distribution.—**

(A) In general.—Except as provided in subparagraph (B), the term 'designated distribution' means any distribution or payment from or under—

(i) an employer deferred compensation plan,

(ii) an individual retirement plan (as defined in section 7701(a)(37)), or

(iii) a commercial annuity.

(B) Exceptions.—The term 'designated distribution' shall not include—

(i) any amount which is wages without regard to this section, and

(ii) the portion of a distribution or payment which it is reasonable to believe is not includible in gross income.

(2) **Periodic payment.**—The term 'periodic payment' means a designated distribution which is an annuity or similar periodic payment.

(3) **Nonperiodic distribution.**—The term 'nonperiodic distribution' means any designated distribution which is not a periodic payment.

(4) **Qualified total distribution.—**

(A) In general.—The term 'qualified total distribution' means any distribution which—

(i) is a designated distribution,

(ii) it is reasonable to believe is made within 1 taxable year of the recipient,

(iii) is made under a plan described in section 401(a), or 403(a), and

(iv) consists of the balance to the credit of the employee under such plan.

(B) Special rule for accumulated deductible employee contributions.—For purposes of subparagraph (A), accumulated deductible employee contributions (within the meaning of section 72(o)(5)(B)) shall be treated separately in determining if there has been a qualified total distribution.

(5) **Employer deferred compensation plan.**—The term 'employer deferred compensation plan' means any pension, annuity, profit-sharing, or stock bonus plan or other plan deferring the receipt of compensation.

(6) **Commercial annuity.**—The term 'commercial annuity' means an annuity, endowment, or life insurance contract issued by an insurance company licensed to do business under the laws of any State.

(7) **Plan administrator.**—The term 'plan administrator' has the meaning given such term by section 414(g).

(8) **Maximum amount withheld.**—The maximum amount to be withheld under this section on any designated distribution shall not exceed the sum of the amount of money and the fair market value of other property (other than employer securities of the employer corporation (within the meaning of section 402(a)(3)) received in the distribution.

(9) **Separate arrangements to be treated separately.**—If the payor has more than 1 arrangement under which designated distributions may be made to any individual, each such arrangement shall be treated separately.

(10) **Time and manner of election.—**

(A) In general.—Any election and any revocation under this section shall be made at such time and in such manner as the Secretary shall prescribe.

Code Sec. 3405 (c) (2)

(B) Payor required to notify payee of rights to elect.—

(i) Periodic payments.—The payor of any periodic payment—

(I) shall transmit to the payee notice of the right to make an election under subsection (a) not earlier than 6 months before the first of such payments and not later than when making the first of such payments,

(II) if such a notice is not transmitted under subclause (I) when making such first payment, shall transmit such a notice when making such first payment, and

(III) shall transmit to payees, not less frequently than once each calendar year, notice of their rights to make elections under subsection (a) and to revoke such elections.

(ii) Nonperiodic distributions.—The payor of any nonperiodic distribution shall transmit to the payee notice of the right to make any election provided in subsection (b) at the time of the distribution (or at such earlier time as may be provided in regulations).

(iii) Notice.—Any notice transmitted pursuant to this subparagraph shall be in such form and contain such information as the Secretary shall prescribe.

(11) Withholding includes deduction.— The terms 'withholding', 'withhold', and 'withheld' include 'deducting', 'deduct', and 'deducted'.

(e) Withholding To Be Treated as Wage Withholding Under Section 3402 for Other Purposes.—For purposes of this chapter (and so much of subtitle F as relates to this chapter)—

(1) any designated distribution (whether nor not an election under this section applies to such distribution) shall be treated as if it were wages paid by an employer to an employee with respect to which there has been withholding under section 3402, and

(2) in the case of any designated distribution not subject to withholding under this section by reason of an election under this section, the amount withheld shall be treated as zero.

* * *

SUBTITLE D—MISCELLANEOUS EXCISE TAXES

CHAPTER 43—QUALIFIED PENSION, ETC., PLANS

Section
4971. Taxes on failure to meet minimum funding standards.
4972. [Repealed effective Jan. 1, 1984].
4973. Tax on excess contributions to individual retirement accounts, certain 403(b) contracts, certain individual retirement annuities, and certain retirement bonds.
4974. Tax on certain accumulations in individual retirement accounts.
4975. Tax on prohibited transactions.

SEC. 4971. TAXES ON FAILURE TO MEET MINIMUM FUNDING STANDARDS.

(a) Initial Tax.—For each taxable year of an employer who maintains a plan to which section 412 applies, there is hereby imposed a tax of 5 percent on the amount of the accumulated funding deficiency under the plan, determined as of the end of the plan year ending with or within such taxable year. The tax imposed by this subsection shall be paid by the employer responsible for contributing to or under the plan the amount described in section 412(b)(3)(A).

(b) Additional Tax.—In any case in which an initial tax is imposed by subsection (a) on an accumulated funding deficiency and such accumulated funding deficiency is not corrected within the taxable period, there is hereby imposed a tax equal to 100 percent of such accumulated funding deficiency to the extent not corrected. The tax imposed by this subsection shall be paid by the employer described in subsection (a).

(c) Definitions.—For purposes of this section—

(1) Accumulated funding deficiency.—The term "accumulated funding deficiency" has the meaning given to such term by the last two sentences of section 412(a).

(2) Correct.—The term "correct" means, with respect to an accumulated funding deficiency, the contribution, to or under the plan, of the amount necessary to reduce such accumulated funding deficiency as of the end of a plan year in which such deficiency arose to zero.

(3) **Taxable period.**—The term "taxable period" means, with respect to an accumulated funding deficiency, the period beginning with the end of a plan year in which there is an accumulated funding deficiency and ending on the earlier of—
(A) the date of mailing of a notice of deficiency with respect to the tax imposed by subsection (a), or
(B) the date on which the tax imposed by subsection (a) is assessed.

(d) **Notification of the Secretary of Labor.**—Before issuing a notice of deficiency with respect to the tax imposed by subsection (a) or (b), the Secretary shall notify the Secretary of Labor and provide him a reasonable opportunity (but not more than 60 days)—
(1) to require the employer responsible for contributing to or under the plan to eliminate the accumulated funding deficiency, or
(2) to comment on the imposition of such tax.
In the case of a multiemployer plan which is in reorganization under section 418, the same notice and opportunity shall be provided to the Pension Benefit Guaranty Corporation.

(e) **Cross References.—**
For disallowance of deductions for taxes paid under this section, see section 275.
For liability for tax in case of an employer party to collective bargaining agreement, see section 413(b)(6).
For provisions concerning notification of Secretary of Labor of imposition of tax under this section, waiver of the tax imposed by subsection (b), and other coordination between Secretary of the Treasury and Secretary of Labor with respect to compliance with this section, see section 3002(b) of title III of the Employee Retirement Income Security Act of 1974.

*****SEC. 4972. TAX ON EXCESS CONTRIBUTIONS FOR SELF-EMPLOYED INDIVIDUALS.**
*[Editor's Note: Section 4972 was repealed by TEFRA (PL 97-248) effective Jan. 1, 1984.]

Code Sec. 4971 (c) (3)

(a) **Tax Imposed.**—In the case of a plan which provides contributions or benefits for employees some or all of whom are employees within the meaning of section 401(c)(1), there is imposed, for each taxable year of the employer who maintains such plan, a tax in an amount equal to 6 percent of the amount of the excess contributions under the plan (determined as of the close of the taxable year). The tax imposed by this subsection shall be paid by the employer who maintains the plan. This section applies only to plans which include a trust described in section 401(a), which are described in section 403(a), or which are described in section 405(a).

(b) **Excess Contributions.—**
(1) **In general.**—For purposes of this section, the term "excess contributions" means the sum of the amounts (if any) determined under paragraphs (2), (3), and (4), reduced by the sum of the correcting distributions (as defined in paragraph (5)) made in all prior taxable years beginning after December 31, 1975. For purposes of this subsection the amount of any contribution which is allocable (determined under regulations prescribed by the Secretary) to the purchase of life, accident, health, or other insurance shall not be taken into account.

(2) **Contributions by owner-employees.**—The amount determined under this paragraph, in the case of a plan which provides contributions or benefits for employees some or all of whom are owner-employees (within the meaning of section 401(c)(3)), is the sum of—
(A) the excess (if any) of—
(i) the amount contributed under the plan by each owner-employee (as an employee) for the taxable year, over
(ii) the amount permitted to be contributed by each owner-employee (as an employee) for such year, and
(B) the amount determined under this paragraph for the preceding taxable year of the employer,
reduced by the excess (if any) of the amount described in subparagraph (A)(ii) over the amount described in subparagraph (A)(i). No contribution by an owner-employee which is a deductible employee contribution (as defined in section 72(o)(5)) shall be taken into account under this paragraph.

(3) **Defined benefit plans.**—The amount determined under this paragraph, in the case of a defined benefit plan, is the amount contributed under the plan by the employer during the taxable year or any prior taxable year beginning after December 31, 1975, if—

(A) as of the close of the taxable year, the full funding limitation of the plan (determined under section 412(c)(7)) is zero, and

(B) such amount has not been deductible for the taxable year or any prior taxable year.

(4) **Defined contribution plans.**—The amount determined under this paragraph, in the case of a plan other than a defined benefit plan, is the portion of the amounts contributed under the plan by the employer during the taxable year and each prior taxable year beginning after December 31, 1975, which has not been deductible for the taxable year or any prior taxable year.

(5) **Correcting distribution.**—For purposes of this subsection the term "correcting distribution" means—

(A) in the case of a contribution made by an owner-employee as an employee, regardless of the type of plan, the amount determined under paragraph (2) distributed to the owner-employee who contributed such amount,

(B) in the case of a defined benefit plan, the amount determined under paragraph (3) which is distributed from the plan to the employer, and

(C) in the case of a defined contribution plan, the amount determined under paragraph (4) which is distributed from the plan to the employer or to the employee to the account of whom the amount described was contributed.

(6) **Excess contributions returned before due date.**—For purposes of this subsection, any contribution which is distributed in a distribution to which section 72(m)(9) applies shall be treated as an amount not contributed.

(c) **Amount Permitted to be Contributed by Owner-Employee.**—For purposes of subsection (b)(2), the amount permitted to be contributed under a plan by an owner-employee (as an employee) for any taxable year is the smallest of the following:

(1) $2,500,

(2) 10 percent of the earned income (as defined in section 401(c)(2)) for such taxable year derived by such owner-employee from the trade or business with respect to which the plan is established, or

(3) the amount of the contribution which would be contributed by the owner-employee (as an employee) if such contribution were made at the rate of contributions permitted to be made by employees other than owner-employees.

In any case in which there are no employees other than owner-employees, the amount determined under the preceding sentence shall be zero.

(d) **Cross Reference.—**

For disallowance of deduction for taxes paid under this section, see section 275.

SEC. 4973. TAX ON EXCESS CONTRIBUTIONS TO INDIVIDUAL RETIREMENT ACCOUNTS, CERTAIN SECTION 403(b) CONTRACTS, CERTAIN INDIVIDUAL RETIREMENT ANNUITIES, AND CERTAIN RETIREMENT BONDS.

(a) **Tax Imposed.**—In the case of—

(1) an individual retirement account (within the meaning of section 408(a)),

(2) an individual retirement annuity (within the meaning of section 408(b)), a custodial account treated as an annuity contract under section 403(b)(7)(A) (relating to custodial accounts for regulated investment company stock), or

(3) a retirement bond (within the meaning of section 409), established for the benefit of any individual, there is imposed for each taxable year a tax in an amount equal to 6 percent of the amount of the excess contributions to such individual's accounts, annuities, or bonds (determined as of the close of the taxable year). The amount of such tax for any taxable year shall not exceed 6 percent of the value of the account, annuity, or bond (determined as of the close of the taxable year). In the case of an endowment contract described in section 408(b), the tax imposed by this section does not apply to any amount allocable to life, health, accident, or other insurance under such contract. The tax imposed by this subsection shall be paid by such individual.

Code Sec. 4973 (a)

(b) **Excess Contributions.**—For purposes of this section, in the case of individual retirement accounts, individual retirement annuities, or bonds, the term "excess contributions" means the sum of—

(1) the excess (if any) of—

(A) the amount contributed for the taxable year to the accounts or for the annuities or bonds (other than a rollover contribution described in sections 402(a)(5), 402(a)(7), 403(a)(4), 403(b)(8), 405(d)(3), 408(d)(3), and 409(b)(3)(C)), over

(B) the amount allowable as a deduction under section 219 for such contributions, and

(2) the amount determined under this subsection for the preceding taxable year, reduced by the sum of—

(A) the distributions out of the account for the taxable year which were included in the gross income of the payee under section 408(d)(1),

(B) the distributions out of the account for the taxable year to which section 408(d)(5) applies, and

(C) the excess (if any) of the maximum amount allowable as a deduction under section 219 for the taxable year over the amount contributed (determined without regard to section 219(f)(6)) to the accounts or for the annuities or bonds for the taxable year.

For purposes of this subsection, any contribution which is distributed from the individual retirement account, individual retirement annuity, or bond in a distribution to which section 408(d)(4) applies shall be treated as an amount not contributed.

(c) **Section 403(b) Contracts.**—For purposes of this section, in the case of a custodial account referred to in subsection (a)(2), the term "excess contributions" means the sum of—

(1) the excess (if any) of the amount contributed for the taxable year to such account (other than a rollover contribution described in section 403(b)(8), 408(d)(3)(A)(iii), or 409(b)(3)(C)), over the lesser of the amount excludable from gross income under section 403(b) or the amount permitted to be contributed under the limitations contained in section 415 (or under whichever such section is applicable, if only one is applicable), and

Code Sec. 4973 (b)

(2) the amount determined under this subsection for the preceding taxable year, reduced by—

(A) the excess (if any) of the lesser of (i) the amount excludable from gross income under section 403(b) or (ii) the amount permitted to be contributed under the limitations contained in section 415 over the amount contributed to the account for the taxable year (or under whichever such section is applicable, if only one is applicable), and

(B) the sum of the distributions out of the account (for all prior taxable years) which are included in gross income under section 72(e).

SEC. 4974. EXCISE TAX ON CERTAIN ACCUMULATIONS IN INDIVIDUAL RETIREMENT ACCOUNTS OR ANNUITIES.

(a) **Imposition of Tax.**—If, in the case of an individual retirement account or individual retirement annuity, the amount distributed during the taxable year of the payee is less than the minimum amount required to be distributed under section 408(a)(6) or (7), or 408(b)(3) or (4) during such year, there is imposed a tax equal to 50 percent of the amount by which the minimum amount required to be distributed during such year exceeds the amount actually distributed during the year. The tax imposed by this section shall be paid by such payee.

(b) **Regulations.**—For purposes of this section, the minimum amount required to be distributed during a taxable year under section 408(a)(6) or (7) or 408(b)(3) or (4) shall be determined under regulations prescribed by the Secretary.

(c) **Waiver of Tax in Certain Cases.**—If the taxpayer establishes to the satisfaction of the Secretary that—

(1) the shortfall described in subsection (a) in the amount distributed during any taxable year was due to reasonable error, and

(2) reasonable steps are being taken to remedy the shortfall,

the Secretary may waive the tax imposed by subsection (a) for the taxable year.

SEC. 4975. TAX ON PROHIBITED TRANSACTIONS.

(a) Initial Taxes on Disqualified Person.—There is hereby imposed a tax on each prohibited transaction. The rate of tax shall be equal to 5 percent of the amount involved with respect to the prohibited transaction for each year (or part thereof) in the taxable period. The tax imposed by this subsection shall be paid by any disqualified person who participates in the prohibited transaction (other than a fiduciary acting only as such).

(b) Additional Taxes on Disqualified Person.—In any case in which an initial tax is imposed by subsection (a) on a prohibited transaction and the transaction is not corrected within the taxable period, there is hereby imposed a tax equal to 100 percent of the amount involved. The tax imposed by this subsection shall be paid by any disqualified person who participated in the prohibited transaction (other than a fiduciary acting only as such).

(c) Prohibited Transaction.—

(1) **General Rule.**—For purposes of this section, the term "prohibited transaction" means any direct or indirect—

(A) sale or exchange, or leasing, of any property between a plan and a disqualified person;

(B) lending of money or other extension of credit between a plan and a disqualified person;

(C) furnishing of goods, services, or facilities between a plan and a disqualified person;

(D) transfer to, or use by or for the benefit of, a disqualified person of the income or assets of a plan;

(E) act by a disqualified person who is a fiduciary whereby he deals with the income or assets of a plan in his own interest or for his own account; or

(F) receipt of any consideration for his own personal account by any disqualified person who is a fiduciary from any party dealing with the plan in connection with a transaction involving the income or assets of the plan.

(2) **Special exemption.**—The Secretary shall establish an exemption procedure for purposes of this subsection. Pursuant to such procedure, he may grant a conditional or unconditional exemption of any disqualified person or transaction or class of disqualified persons or transactions, from all or part of the restrictions imposed by paragraph (1) of this subsection. Action under this subparagraph may be taken only after consultation and coordination with the Secretary of Labor. The Secretary may not grant an exemption under this paragraph unless he finds that such exemption is—

(A) administratively feasible,

(B) in the interests of the plan and of its participants and beneficiaries, and

(C) protective of the rights of participants and beneficiaries of the plan.

Before granting an exemption under this paragraph, the Secretary shall require adequate notice to be given to interested persons and shall publish notice in the Federal Register of the pendency of such exemption and shall afford interested persons an opportunity to present views. No exemption may be granted under this paragraph with respect to a transaction described in subparagraph (E) or (F) of paragraph (1) unless the Secretary affords an opportunity for a hearing and makes a determination on the record with respect to the findings required under subparagraphs (A), (B), and (C) of this paragraph, except that in lieu of such hearing the Secretary may accept any record made by the Secretary of Labor with respect to an application for exemption under section 408(a) of title I of the Employee Retirement Income Security Act of 1974.

(3) **Special rule for individual retirement accounts.**—An individual for whose benefit an individual retirement account is established and his beneficiaries shall be exempt for [from] the tax imposed by this section with respect to any transaction concerning such account (which would otherwise be taxable under this section) if, with respect to such transaction, the account ceases to be an individual retirement account by reason of the application of section 408(e)(2)(A) or if section 408(e)(4) applies to such account.

(d) Exemptions.—The prohibitions provided in subsection (c) shall not apply to—

(1) any loan made by the plan to a disqualified person who is a participant or beneficiary of the plan if such loan—

(A) is available to all such participants or beneficiaries on a reasonably equivalent basis,

(B) is not made available to highly compensated employees, officers, or shareholders in an amount greater than the amount made available to other employees,

(C) is made in accordance with specific provisions regarding such loans set forth in the plan,

(D) bears a reasonable rate of interest, and

(E) is adequately secured;

(2) any contract, or reasonable arrangement, made with a disqualified person for office space, or legal, accounting, or other services necessary for the establishment or operation of the plan, if no more than reasonable compensation is paid therefor;

(3) any loan to a leveraged employee stock ownership plan (as defined in subsection (e)(7)), if—

(A) such loan is primarily for the benefit of participants and beneficiaries of the plan, and

(B) such loan is at a reasonable rate of interest, and any collateral which is given to a disqualified person by the plan consists only of qualifying employer securities (as defined in subsection (e)(8));

(4) the investment of all or part of a plan's assets in deposits which bear a reasonable interest rate in a bank or similar financial institution supervised by the United States or a State, if such bank or other institution is a fiduciary of such plan and if—

(A) the plan covers only employees of such bank or other institution and employees of affiliates of such bank or other institution, or

(B) such investment is expressly authorized by a provision of the plan or by a fiduciary (other than such bank or institution or affiliates thereof) who is expressly empowered by the plan to so instruct the trustee with respect to such investment;

(5) any contract for life insurance, health insurance, or annuities with one or more insurers which are qualified to do business in a State if the plan pays no more than adequate consideration, and if each such insurer or insurers is—

(A) the employer maintaining the plan, or

(B) a disqualified person which is wholly owned (directly or indirectly) by the employer establishing the plan, or by any person which is a disqualified person with respect to the plan, but only if the total premiums and annuity considerations written by such insurers for life insurance, health insurance, or annuities for all plans (and their employers) with respect to which such insurers are disqualified persons (not including premiums or annuity considerations written by the employer maintaining the plan) do not exceed 5 percent of the total premiums and annuity considerations written for all lines of insurance in that year by such insurers (not including premiums or annuity considerations written by the employer maintaining the plan);

(6) the provision of any ancillary service by a bank or similar financial institution supervised by the United States or a State, if such service is provided at not more than reasonable compensation, if such bank or other institution is a fiduciary of such plan, and if—

(A) such bank or similar financial institution has adopted adequate internal safeguards which assure that the provision of such ancillary service is consistent with sound banking and financial practice, as determined by Federal or State supervisory authority, and

(B) the extent to which such ancillary service is provided is subject to specific guidelines issued by such bank or similar financial institution (as determined by the Secretary after consultation with Federal and State supervisory authority), and under such guidelines the bank or similar financial institution does not provide such ancillary service—

(i) in an excessive or unreasonble manner, and

(ii) in a manner that would be inconsistent with the best interests of participants and beneficiaries of employee benefit plans;

(7) the exercise of a privilege to convert securities, to the extent provided in regulations of the Secretary, but only if the plan receives no less than adequate consideration pursuant to such conversion;

(8) any transaction between a plan and a common or collective trust fund or pooled investment fund maintained by a dis-

Code Sec. 4975 (d) (1)

qualified person which is a bank or trust company supervised by a State or Federal agency or between a plan and a pooled investment fund of an insurance company qualified to do business in a State if—

(A) the transaction is a sale or purchase of an interest in the fund,

(B) the bank, trust company, or insurance company receives not more than reasonable compensation, and

(C) such transaction is expressly permitted by the instrument under which the plan is maintained, or by a fiduciary (other than the bank, trust company, or insurance company, or an affiliate thereof) who has authority to manage and control the assets of the plan;

(9) receipt by a disqualified person of any benefit to which he may be entitled as a participant or beneficiary in the plan, so long as the benefit is computed and paid on a basis which is consistent with the terms of the plan as applied to all other participants and beneficiaries;

(10) receipt by a disqualified person of any reasonable compensation for services rendered, or for the reimbursement of expenses properly and actually incurred, in the performance of his duties with the plan, but no person so serving who already receives full-time pay from an employer or an association of employers, whose employees are participants in the plan, or from an employee organization whose members are participants in such plan shall receive compensation from such fund, except for reimbursement of expenses properly and actually incurred;

(11) service by a disqualified person as a fiduciary in addition to being an officer, employee, agent, or other representative of a disqualified person;

(12) the making by a fiduciary of a distribution of the assets of the trust in accordance with the terms of the plan if such assets are distributed in the same manner as provided under section 4044 of title IV of the Employee Retirement Income Security Act of 1974 (relating to allocation of assets);

(13) any transaction which is exempt from section 406 of such Act by reason of section 408(e) of such Act (or which would be so exempt if such section 406 applied to such transaction);

(14) any transaction required or permitted under part 1 of subtitle E of title IV or section 4223 of the Employee Retirement Income Security Act of 1974, but this paragraph shall not apply with respect to the application of subsection (c)(1)(E) or (F); or

(15) a merger of multiemployer plans, or the transfer of assets or liabilities between multiemployer plans, determined by the Pension Benefit Guaranty Corporation to meet the requirements of section 4231 of such Act, but this paragraph shall not apply with respect to the application of subsection (c)(1)(E) or (F).

The exemptions provided by this subsection (other than paragraphs (9) and (12)) shall not apply to any transaction with respect to a trust described in section 401(a) which is part of a plan providing contributions or benefits for employees some or all of whom are owner-employees (as defined in section 401(c)(3)) in which a plan directly or indirectly lends any part of the corpus or income of the plan to, pays any compensation for personal services rendered to the plan to, or acquires for the plan any property from or sells any property to, any such owner-employee, a member of the family (as defined in section 267(c)(4)) of any such owner-employee, or a corporation controlled by any such owner-employee through the ownership, directly or indirectly, of 50 percent or more of the total combined voting power of all classes of stock entitled to vote or 50 percent or more of the total value of shares of all classes of stock of the corporation. For purposes of the preceding sentence, a shareholder-employee (as defined in section 1379, as in effect on the day before the date of the enactment of the Subchapter Revision Act of 1982), a participant or beneficiary of an individual retirement account, individual retirement annuity, or an individual retirement bond (as defined in section 408 or 409), and an employer or association of employees which establishes such an account or annuity under section 408(c) shall be deemed to be an owner-employee.

(e) Definitions.—

(1) Plan.—For purposes of this section, the term "plan" means a trust described in section 401(a) which forms a part of a plan,

or a plan described in section 403(a) or 405(a), which trust or plan is exempt from tax under section 501(a), an individual retirement account described in section 408(a) or an individual retirement annuity described in section 408(b) or a retirement bond described in section 409 (or a trust, plan, account, annuity, or bond which, at any time, has been determined by the Secretary to be such a trust, plan, account, or bond).

(2) Disqualified person.—For purposes of this section, the term "disqualified person" means a person who is—
 (A) a fiduciary;
 (B) a person providing services to the plan;
 (C) an employer any of whose employees are covered by the plan;
 (D) an employee organization any of whose members are covered by the plan;
 (E) an owner, direct or indirect, of 50 percent or more of—
 (i) the combined voting power of all classes of stock entitled to vote or the total value of shares of all classes of stock of a corporation,
 (ii) the capital interest or the profits interest of a partnership, or
 (iii) the beneficial interest of a trust or unincorporated enterprise,
which is an employer or an employee organization described in subparagraph (C) or (D);
 (F) a member of the family (as defined in paragraph (6)) of any individual described in subparagraph (A), (B), (C), or (E);
 (G) a corporation, partnership, or trust or estate of which (or in which) 50 percent or more of—
 (i) the combined voting power of all classes of stock entitled to vote or the total value of shares of all classes of stock of such corporation,
 (ii) the capital interest or profits interest of such partnership, or
 (iii) the beneficial interest of such trust or estate, is owned directly or indirectly, or held by persons described in subparagraph (A), (B), (C), (D), or (E);
 (H) an officer, director (or an individual having powers or responsibilities similar to those of officers or directors), a 10 percent or more shareholder, or a highly compensated employee (earning 10 percent or more of the yearly wages of an employer) of a person described in subparagraph (C), (D), (E), or (G); or
 (I) a 10 percent or more (in capital or profits) partner or joint venturer of a person described in subparagraph (C), (D), (E), or (G).
The Secretary, after consultation and coordination with the Secretary of Labor or his delegate, may by regulation prescribe a percentage lower than 50 percent for subparagraphs (E) and (G) and lower than 10 percent for subparagraphs (H) and (I).

(3) Fiduciary.—For purposes of this section, the term "fiduciary" means any person who—
 (A) exercises any discretionary authority or discretionary control respecting management of such plan or exercises any authority or control respecting management or disposition of its assets,
 (B) renders investment advice for a fee or other compensation, direct or indirect, with respect to any moneys or other property of such plan, or has any authority or responsibility to do so, or
 (C) has any discretionary authority or discretionary responsibility in the administration of such plan.
Such term includes any person designated under section 405(c)(1)(B) of the Employee Retirement Income Security Act of 1974.

(4) Stockholdings.—For purposes of paragraphs (2)(E)(i), and (G)(i) there shall be taken into account indirect stockholdings which would be taken into account under section 267(c), except that, for purposes of this paragraph, section 267(c)(4) shall be treated as providing that the members of the family of an individual are the members within the meaning of paragraph (6).

(5) Partnerships; Trusts.—For purposes of paragraphs (2)(E)(ii) and (iii), (G)(ii) and (iii), and (I) the ownership of profits or beneficial interests shall be determined in accordance with the rules for constructive ownership of stock provided in section 267(c) (other than paragraph (3) thereof), except that section 267(c)(4) shall be treated as providing that the members of the family of an individual are the members within the meaning of paragraph (6).

Code Sec. 4975 (e) (2)

(6) Members of family.—For purposes of paragraph (2)(F), the family of any individual shall include his spouse, ancestor, lineal descendant, and any spouse of a lineal descendant.

(7) Employee stock ownership plan.—The term "employee stock ownership plan" means a defined contribution plan—

(A) which is a stock bonus plan which is qualified, or a stock bonus and a money purchase plan both of which are qualified under section 401(a) and which are designed to invest primarily in qualifying employer securities; and

(B) which is otherwise defined in regulations prescribed by the Secretary.

A plan shall not be treated as an employee stock ownership plan unless it meets the requirements of section 409A(h) and, if the employer has a registration-type class of securities (as defined in section 409A(e)(4)), it meets the requirements of section 409A(e).

(8) Qualifying employer security.—The term "qualifying employer security" means an employer security within the meaning of section 409A(1). If any moneys or other property of a plan are invested in shares of an investment company registered under the Investment Company Act of 1940, the investment shall not cause that investment company or that investment company's investment adviser or principal underwriter to be treated as a fiduciary or a disqualified person for purposes of this section, except when an investment company or its investment adviser or principal underwriter acts in connection with a plan covering employees of the investment company, its investment adviser, or its principal underwriter.

(9) Section made applicable to withdrawal liability payment funds.—

For purposes of this section—

(A) In general.—The term "plan" includes a trust described in section 501(c)(22).

(B) Disqualified person.—In the case of any trust to which this section applies by reason of subparagraph (A), the term "disqualified person" includes any person who is a disqualified person with respect to any plan to which such trust is permitted to make payments under section 4223 of the Employee Retirement Income Security Act of 1974.

(f) Other Definitions and Special Rules. —For purposes of this section—

(1) Joint and several liability.—If more than one person is liable under subsection (a) or (b) with respect to any one prohibited transaction, all such persons shall be jointly and severally liable under such subsection with respect to such transaction.

(2) Taxable period.—The term "taxable period" means, with respect to any prohibited transaction, the period beginning with the date on which the prohibited transaction occurs and ending on the earliest of—

(A) the date of mailing of a notice of deficiency with respect to the tax imposed by subsection (a) under section 6212,

(B) the date on which the tax imposed by subsection (a) is assessed, or

(C) the date on which correction of the prohibited transaction is completed.

(3) Sale or exchange; encumbered property.—A transfer of real or personal property by a disqualified person to a plan shall be treated as a sale or exchange if the property is subject to a mortgage or similar lien which the plan assumes or if it is subject to a mortgage or similar lien which a disqualified person placed on the property within the 10-year period ending on the date of the transfer.

(4) Amount involved.—The term "amount involved" means, with respect to a prohibited transaction, the greater of the amount of money and the fair market value of the other property given or the amount of money and the fair market value of the other property received; except that, in the case of services described in paragraphs (2) and (10) of subsection (d) the amount involved shall be only the excess compensation. For purposes of the preceding sentence, the fair market value—

(A) in the case of the tax imposed by subsection (a), shall be determined as of the date on which the prohibited transaction occurs; and

(B) in the case of the tax imposed by subsection (b), shall be the highest fair market value during the correction period.

Code Sec. 4975 (f) (4)

(5) Correction.—The terms "correction" and "correct" mean, with respect to a prohibited transaction, undoing the transaction to the extent possible, but in any case placing the plan in a financial position not worse than that in which it would be if the disqualified person were acting under the highest fiduciary standards.

(g) Application of Section.—This section shall not apply—

(1) in the case of a plan to which a guaranteed benefit policy (as defined in section 401(b)(2)(B) of the Employee Retirement Income Security Act of 1974) is issued, to any assets of the insurance company, insurance service, or insurance organization merely because of its issuance of such policy;

(2) to a governmental plan (within the meaning of section 414(d)); or

(3) to a church plan (within the meaning of section 414(e)) with respect to which the election provided by section 410(d) has not been made.

In the case of a plan which invests in any security issued by an investment company registered under the Investment Company Act of 1940, the assets of such plan shall be deemed to include such security but shall not, by reason of such investment, be deemed to include any assets of such company.

(h) Notification of Secretary of Labor.—Before sending a notice of deficiency with respect to the tax imposed by subsection (a) or (b), the Secretary shall notify the Secretary of Labor and provide him a reasonable opportunity to obtain a correction of the prohibited transaction or to comment on the imposition of such tax.

(i) Cross Reference.—

For provisions concerning coordination procedures between Secretary of Labor and Secretary of Treasury with respect to application of tax imposed by this section and for authority to waive imposition of the tax imposed by subsection (b), see section 3003 of the Employee Retirement Income Security Act of 1974.

* * *

Code Sec. 4975 (f) (5)

CHAPTER 61—INFORMATION AND RETURNS

* * *

Subpart E—Registration of and Information Concerning Pension, Etc., Plans

Section
6057. Annual registration, etc.
6058. Information required in connection with certain plans of deferred compensation.
6059. Periodic report of actuary.

SEC. 6057. ANNUAL REGISTRATION, ETC.

(a) Annual Registration.—

(1) General Rule.—Within such period after the end of a plan year as the Secretary may by regulations precribe, the plan administrator (within the meaning of section 414(g)) of each plan to which the vesting standards of section 203 of part 2 of subtitle B of title I of the Employee Retirement Income Security Act of 1974 applies for such plan year shall file a registration statement with the Secretary.

(2) Contents.—The registration statement required by paragraph (1) shall set forth—

(A) the name of the plan,

(B) the name and address of the plan administrator,

(C) the name and taxpayer identifying number of each participant in the plan—

(i) who, during such plan year, separated from the service covered by the plan,

(ii) who is entitled to a deferred vested benefit under the plan as of the end of such plan year, and

(iii) with respect to whom retirement benefits were not paid under the plan during such plan year,

(D) the nature, amount and form of the deferred vested benefit to which such participant is entitled, and

(E) such other information as the Secretary may require.

At the time he files the registration statement under this subsection, the plan administrator shall furnish evidence satisfactory to the Secretary that he has complied with the requirement contained in subsection (e).

(b) Notification of Change in Status.—Any plan administrator required to register under subsection (a) shall also notify the Secretary, at such times as may be prescribed by regulations, of—

(1) any change in the name of the plan,

(2) any change in the name or address of the plan administrator,

(3) the termination of the plan, or

(4) the merger or consolidation of the plan with any other plan or its division into two or more plans.

(c) Voluntary Reports.—To the extent provided in regulations prescribed by the Secretary, the Secretary may receive from—

(1) any plan to which subsection (a) applies, and

(2) any other plan (including any governmental plan or church plan (within the meaning of section 414)),

such information (including information relating to plan years beginning before January 1, 1974) as the plan administrator may wish to file with respect to the deferred vested benefit rights of any participant separated from the service covered by the plan during any plan year.

(d) Transmission of Information to Secretary of Health, Education, and Welfare.—The Secretary shall transmit copies of any statements, notifications, reports, or other information obtained by him under this section to the Secretary of Health, Education and Welfare.

(e) Individual Statement to Participant.—Each plan administrator required to file a registration statement under subsection (a) shall, before the expiration of the time prescribed for the filing of such registration statement, also furnish to each participant described in subsection (a)(2)(C) an individual statement setting forth the information with respect to such participant required to be contained in such registration statement.

(f) Regulations.—

(1) In General.—The Secretary, after consultation with the Secretary of Health, Education, and Welfare, may prescribe such regulations as may be necessary to carry out the provisions of this section.

(2) Plans to which more than one employer contributes.—This section shall apply to any plan to which more than one employer is required to contribute only to the extent provided in regulations prescribed under this subsection.

(g) Cross References.—

For provisions relating to penalties for failure to register or furnish statements required by this section, see section 6652(e) and section 6690.

For coordination between Department of the Treasury and the Department of Labor with regard to administration of this section see section 3004 of the Employee Retirement Income Security Act of 1974.

SEC. 6058. INFORMATION REQUIRED IN CONNECTION WITH CERTAIN PLANS OF DEFERRED COMPENSATION.

(a) In General.—Every employer who maintains a pension, annuity, stock bonus, profit-sharing or other funded plan of deferred compensation described in part I of subchapter D of chapter 1, or the plan administrator (within the meaning of section 414(g)) of the plan, shall file an annual return stating such information as the Secretary may by regulations prescribe with respect to the qualification, financial condition, and operations of the plan; except that, in the discretion of the Secretary, the employer may be relieved from stating in its return any information which is reported in other returns.

(b) Actuarial Statement in Case of Mergers, Etc.—Not less than 30 days before a merger, consolidation, or transfer of assets or liabilities of a plan described in subsection (a) to another plan, the plan administrator (within the meaning of section 414(g)) shall file an actuarial statement of valuation evidencing compliance with the requirements of section 401(a)(12).

(c) Employer.—For purposes of this section, the term "employer" includes a person described in section 401(c)(4) and an individual who establishes an individual retirement plan.

(d) Coordination With Income Tax Returns, Etc.—An individual who

establishes an individual retirement plan shall not be required to file a return under this section with respect to such plan for any taxable year for which there is—
(1) no special IRP tax, and
(2) no plan activity other than—
(A) the making of contributions (other than rollover contributions), and
(B) the making of distributions.

(e) Special IRP Tax Defined.—For purposes of this section, the term "special IRP tax" means a tax imposed by—
(1) section 408(f),
(2) section 409(c),
(3) section 4973, or
(4) section 4974.

(f) Cross References.—

For provisions relating to penalties for failure to file a return required by this section, see section 6652(f).

For coordination between the Department of the Treasury and the Department of Labor with respect to the information required under this section, see Section 3004 of title III of the Employee Retirement Income Security Act of 1974.

SEC. 6059. PERIODIC REPORT OF ACTUARY.

(a) General Rule.—The actuarial report described in subsection (b) shall be filed by the plan administrator (as defined in section 414(g)) of each defined benefit plan to which section 412 applies, for the first plan year for which section 412 applies to the plan and for each third plan year thereafter (or more frequently if the Secretary determines that more frequent reports are necessary).

(b) Actuarial Report.—The actuarial report of a plan required by subsection (a) shall be prepared and signed by an enrolled actuary (within the meaning of section 7701(a)(35)) and shall contain—
(1) a description of the funding method and actuarial assumptions used to determine costs under the plan,
(2) a certification of the contribution necessary to reduce the accumulated funding deficiency (as defined in section 412(a)) to zero,
(3) a statement—
(A) that to the best of his knowledge the report is complete and accurate, and
(B) the requirements of section 412(c) (relating to reasonable actuarial assumptions) have been complied with,
(4) such other information as may be necessary to fully and fairly disclose the actuarial position of the plan, and
(5) such other information regarding the plan as the Secretary may by regulations require.

(c) Time and Manner of Filing.—The actuarial report and statement required by this section shall be filed at the time and in the manner provided by regulations prescribed by the Secretary.

(d) Cross Reference.—

For coordination between the Department of the Treasury and the Department of Labor with respect to the report required to be filed under this section, see section 3004 of title III of the Employee Retirement Income Security Act of 1974.

Code Sec. 6059